Frommer's

1st Edition

Utah

by Don & Barbara Laine

Macmillan • USA

UTHORS

ta **Laine** have written about and traveled extensively throughout the
ns and the Southwest. In addition to *Frommer's Utah,* they author
rado and *Frommer's Denver, Boulder & Colorado Springs* and are the regional
nmer's America on Wheels: Southwest. The Laines reside in northern New
they're not out in their classic (read that old) 23-foot motor home, exploring
th their dogs, Max and Blue.

LLAN TRAVEL

x Schuster Macmillan Company
adway
k, NY 10019

online at **http://www.mgr.com/travel**
America Online at **Keyword: Frommer's**

ISBN 0-02-860478-4
ISSN 1087-3546

18046102

Editor: Cheryl Farr
Thanks to Lisa Renaud and Reid Bramblett
Production Editor: Trudy Brown
Design by Michele Laseau
Digital Cartography by Ortelius Design
Maps copyright © by Simon & Schuster, Inc.

SPECIAL SALES

Bulk purchases (10+ copies) of Frommer's travel guides are available to corporations at
special discounts. The Special Sales Department can produce custom editions to be used as
premiums and/or for sales promotion to suit individual needs. Existing editions can be
produced with custom cover imprints such as corporate logos. For more information write
to: Special Sales, Simon & Schuster, 1633 Broadway, New York, NY 10019.

Manufactured in the United States of America

Contents

List of Maps

AN INVITATION TO THE READER

In researching this book, we discovered many wonderful places—hotels, restaurants, shops, and more. We're sure you'll find others. Please tell us about them, so we can share the information with your fellow travelers in upcoming editions. If you were disappointed with a recommendation, we'd love to know that, too. Please write to:

Don & Barbara Laine
Frommer's Utah, 1st Edition
Macmillan Travel
1633 Broadway
New York, NY 10019

AN ADDITIONAL NOTE

Please be advised that travel information is subject to change at any time—and this is especially true of prices. We therefore suggest that you write or call ahead for confirmation when making your travel plans. The authors, editors, and publisher cannot be held responsible for the experiences of readers while traveling. Your safety is important to us, however, so we encourage you to stay alert and be aware of your surroundings. Keep a close eye on cameras, purses, and wallets, all favorite targets of thieves and pickpockets.

WHAT THE SYMBOLS MEAN

✪ Frommer's Favorites

Hotels, restaurants, attractions, and entertainment you should not miss.

Ⓢ Super-Special Values

Hotels and restaurants that offer great value for your money.

The following abbreviations are used for credit cards:

AE	American Express	EU	Eurocard
CB	Carte Blanche	JCB	Japan Credit Bank
DC	Diners Club	MC	MasterCard
DISC	Discover	V	Visa
ER	enRoute		

The Best of Utah

From its desolate red rock canyons to its soaring pine-covered peaks, Utah is spectacular. There aren't many places in the world where the forces of nature have come together with such dramatic results, in such a magnificent outdoor playground. It's also a land of cultural discovery; all the peoples who have settled here, from the ancient Anasazi to Brigham Young's Mormons, have left their distinctive mark, contributing to a wild, colorful history.

With so much to see and do, how to choose? It can be bewildering to plan your trip with so many options vying for your attention. We've made this task easier for you by scouring the entire state from top to bottom and choosing the very best that Utah has to offer—the places and experiences you won't want to miss.

1 The Best Travel Experiences

Of all the wonderful vacations you can have in Utah, several stand out for their uniqueness, tremendous natural beauty, and just plain fun.

- **Boating at Flaming Gorge National Recreation Area:** Flaming Gorge is a manmade creation, the result of the damming of the Green River for flood control, water storage, and electricity generation. But all that's not really important; what really matters (in our view, at least) is the by-product of the project—this huge, gorgeous, many-fingered lake. This little-known gem is a boater's paradise—floating out here, you'll feel like you're all alone in the world. It also happens to offer some of the best fishing in the West. See Chapter 10.
- **Exploring Bryce Canyon National Park:** One of Utah's—maybe the nation's—most scenic parks, Bryce Canyon is also one of the most accessible. Several trails lead down into the canyon—really walks rather than hikes—so just about everyone can get to know this beautiful jewel up close and personal; part of the Rim Trail is even wheelchair accessible. The colorful rock formations are impressive when viewed en masse from the rim, but they really become enchanting and fanciful works of art as you walk among them along the trails. See Chapter 13.
- **Enjoying Capitol Reef National Park:** This tranquil park isn't as popular as Bryce or Zion, but it has a subtle beauty all its own. And it's not too demanding, either: Wander around the orchards

of Fruita, hike to Cassidy Arch, stroll up the Grand Wash, or just sit under the stars roasting marshmallows over your campfire. See Chapter 14.

- **Houseboating on Lake Powell:** Kick back and relax while floating on the deep blue waters of Lake Powell, with towering red rocks all around and an azure sky above. This is the life—no telephone, no bosses to keep happy or meetings to attend, no deadlines to meet. Feeling warm? Slip over the side for a dip in the cool water. Want a little exercise? Anchor yourself at one of the canyons and hike a bit. See Chapter 15.

2 The Best Views

- **Boulder Mountain Viewpoints** (near Escalante): The panoramas from the roadside along the crest of Boulder Mountain are extraordinary. You can see majestic Capitol Reef, miles to the east, and any number of valleys and lakes nestled in between. It's like a tiny fairyland; we almost expected to see a little steam train chugging along, or a horse-drawn carriage passing through. See Chapter 13.
- **The Narrows, Zion National Park:** The sheer 1,000-foot-high walls are awe-inspiring, almost frightening, as they enclose you in a 20-foot-wide world of hanging gardens, waterfalls, and sculpted sandstone arches, with the Virgin River running underneath your feet. The Narrows are too narrow to allow you to walk next to the river, so you have to wade right through it—but the views are worth getting your feet wet. See Chapter 12.
- **The Queen's Garden, Bryce Canyon National Park:** Presided over by majestic Queen Victoria herself, carved in stone by Mother Nature, these thousands of colorfully striped spires present a magnificent display when viewed from the rim. From the trail below, they dazzle as the early morning sun throws them into stark relief. See Chapter 13.
- **Monument Valley Buttes at Sunset:** These stark sentinels of the desert are impressive at any time, but they take on a particularly dignified aura when the setting sun throws its deep colors over them, etching their profiles against a darkening sky. Although the park generally closes before sunset, you can arrange a sunset tour, and it's well worth it. See Chapter 17.

3 The Best Family Vacations

- **Cherry Hill Family Campground & Resort** (Ogden): This fun-packed park has something for everybody: There's a water park with slides, pools, even a pirate ship, plus miniature golf, batting cages, and aeroball (it's kind of like basketball). It's like staying in a theme park—practically a kid's dream come true. And you're not likely to find a more immaculately groomed and well-run campground. See Chapter 8.
- **Heber Valley Historic Railroad:** Take a railroad trip back in time on the "Heber Creeper," so called because of the way this historic steam train inched its way up the canyon from Provo. This once-proud passenger and freight branch line will let you experience travel the way it was in your grandparents' day. Kids of all ages, from 6 to 60, will love it. See Chapter 9.
- **Northeast Utah's Dinosaurland:** This is the real *Jurassic Park*—no special effects here. Stop first at Vernal's Utah Field House of Natural History State Park, and stroll around the Dinosaur Garden admiring the 17 life-size dinosaurs and other prehistoric creatures in a delightful garden that simulates the dinosaurs' actual habitat. Then head for Dinosaur National Monument to see and touch—yes, touch—real fossilized dinosaur bones. See Chapter 10.

- **Zion National Park:** The Junior Ranger Program, available at most national parks, is really extensive here, with both morning and afternoon activities all summer geared toward teaching kids what makes this natural wonder so special. They'll have so much fun they won't even notice that they're learning something. See Chapter 12.

4 The Best Scenic Drives

- **The Golden Spike Tour:** Heading out of Ogden on Old U.S. 89, you'll first pass through some fine fruit country (be sure to stop at a roadside stand). At the small town of Willard, turn west toward I-15; head north on I-15 to exit 368, and turn west on Utah 83, which will take you along the north side of the Great Salt Lake through picturesque farming communities until you reach the turnoff to the spot where, in 1869, the last spike was driven for the transcontinental railroad, connecting East and West for the first time. If you love trains as we do, you'll thrill to the sound of the whistle and the puffing steam as the engine chugs away and back again. See Chapter 8.
- **The National Park Tour:** From the canyons of Zion, head north along U.S. 89 through majestic forests to Red Canyon, with its walls of brilliant red rock, and then east on Utah 12 to Bryce, with its fascinating amphitheaters of multicolored stone. The route from Bryce to Capitol Reef along Utah 12 and Utah 24 takes in some of the most spectacular scenery in a state of unsurpassed landscapes. See Chapters 12, 13, and 14.
- **Moab to Monument Valley:** This may be red rock country at its finest. From Moab, U.S. 191 south takes you past huge slabs of rock—outposts of Canyonlands National Park—through one-horse towns with few services, but enough character to make up for it. At Bluff, turn southwest on U.S. 163 and drive through more ruddy desert, past the sombrero-shaped rock for which Medicine Hat was named, and finally to the solemnity of Monument Valley. See Chapters 16 and 17.

5 The Best Hiking Trails

You don't have to be able to scale Mt. Everest to enjoy these trails:

- **Indian Trail** (Ogden): Easily accessible from downtown Ogden, this 5-mile trail gets you out of town quickly, into a thick forest of spruce and fir and onto a mountainside that offers spectacular views of Ogden Canyon, including a beautiful waterfall. See Chapter 8.
- **Hidden Piñon Trail, Snow Canyon State Park** (St. George): This is a fairly easy self-guided nature trail that will reward you with breathtaking panoramic views. You'll wander among lava rock, into canyons, and over rocky flatland, along a trail lined with Mormon tea, cliffrose, prickly pear cactus, banana yucca and other wild desert plants. See Chapter 11.
- **Emerald Pools Trail, Zion National Park:** If green is your color, you'll love this trail—algae keeps the three pools glowing a deep, rich emerald green. The first part of the trail, navigable by wheelchairs with assistance, leads through a forest to the Lower Emerald Pool, with its lovely waterfall and hanging garden. The small pool just above it is so still and calm that the reflections of the towering cliffs in the water seem like a photograph lying on the ground. See Chapter 12.
- **Navajo Loop/Queen's Garden Trail, Bryce Canyon National Park:** To truly experience magical Bryce Canyon, you should climb down into it; this

not-too-difficult trail is a good way to go. Start at Sunset Point and get the hardest part out of the way first. You'll pass Thor's Hammer and wonder why it hasn't fallen, ponder the towering skyscrapers of Wall Street, and visit with some of the park's most fanciful formations, including majestic Queen Victoria herself. See Chapter 13.

- **Petrified Forest Trail, Escalante State Park** (Escalante): Along this steep nature trail, you'll find yourself walking in a stunted forest of junipers and piñons before reaching a field strewn with colorful chunks of petrified wood. As you go, you'll have panoramic views of the town of Escalante and the surrounding stair-step plateaus. See Chapter 13.

6 The Best Destinations for Fishing & Water Sports

- **Strawberry Reservoir:** The number one trout fishery in Utah for both cutthroat and rainbow is a gem of a lake, magnificently set among tall pines. You're really out in the woods here; the nearest town of any size is 30 miles away. So pick your spot, out in the middle of the reservoir or tucked away in a quiet nook, and cast your line for dinner—you can't beat fresh-caught trout cooked over an open fire. See Chapter 9.

- **Jordanelle State Park** (near Park City): This boomerang-shaped reservoir has been cut into three distinctly different recreational areas: The middle and widest part is designated for speed boats, and it's perfect for water skiing; above that, cut off by an arm of land, is the wakeless area, great for sailboating and quiet fishing; at the other end of the boomerang, low-speed motor boats are allowed. Whichever area you choose, you'll have the beautiful Wasatch Mountains on all sides. See Chapter 9.

- **The Green River through Dinosaur National Monument:** The way to see this spectacularly desolate country is from the river, the way explorer John Wesley Powell did in 1869. Do you crave excitement? Run the foaming rapids. Is peace and quiet your thing? Float mindlessly in the placid waters, leaving your troubles behind. See Chapter 10.

- **Flaming Gorge National Recreation Area:** Smaller and more intimate than Lake Powell and in a gloriously colorful setting, Lake Flaming Gorge is one of Utah's real hidden gems. You can skim the water on skis or just dose off on the deck of a houseboat. And the fishing: If you feel like the big ones always get away, this is the place for you—they're all big here. See Chapter 10.

- **Quail Creek Reservoir** (near St. George): Quail Creek has the warmest water in the state, so if you prefer being in the water to boating on top of it, this is the place to be. It's also a premier fishing spot for largemouth bass, and you can angle for rainbow trout, blue gill, and crappie as well. And there's a fish-cleaning station and barbecue grills in the picnic area, so you're free to enjoy your catch immediately. See Chapter 11.

- **Lake Powell:** This sprawling lake has what seems like zillions of finger canyons reaching off the main watercourse of the Colorado River. You could spend weeks—maybe even months—water-skiing, swimming, fishing, exploring the myriad side canyons, and just loafing about in the sun. See Chapter 15.

- **The Colorado River near Moab:** Tackle the placid stretches on your own in a canoe or kayak, or sign up with one of the many outfitters and shoot the rapids. Whatever you choose, a trip down the spectacular, scenic Colorado River is an adventure. See Chapter 16.

7   The Best Wildlife Watching

- **Rock Cliff, Jordanelle State Park** (near Park City): Over 160 species of birds either live here or pass through; this is an especially good place to spot eagles and other raptors who nest in the area. Boardwalks and trails throughout the riparian wetlands reduce the environmental impact of your visit, and give you a great chance to watch wetland life do their thing. See Chapter 9.
- **Flaming Gorge National Recreation Area:** Take a boat trip to see bighorn sheep—the biblical beasts are sometimes seen on Kingfisher Island, and near Hideout Canyon on the north side of the reservoir in spring and early summer. And keep your eyes peeled for the lovely osprey and rare peregrine falcon, occasionally seen near their nests on the high rocky spires above the lake. See Chapter 10.
- **Coral Pink Sand Dunes State Park:** If you climb the dunes early in the morning, you're sure to see the footprints of jackrabbits, kangaroo rats, even an occasional mule deer or coyote. But the real fun comes after dark, with the late-night scorpion hunt: You can follow a park ranger out onto the dunes and, using a black light, spot the luminescent creatures as they scurry across the sand. See Chapter 11.
- **Escalante State Park** (Escalante): Willows and cottonwoods line the banks of the reservoir, one of the few wetland bird viewing sites in southern Utah. It's home to a wide variety of ducks, plus coots, grebes, herons, and swallows. You also might see eagles, osprey, American kestrels, and other raptors. Small creatures of the furry variety, including cottontail and blacktail jackrabbits, ground squirrels, and even beaver, also inhabit the area. See Chapter 13.
- **Boulder Mountain** (near Escalante): As you drive through the beautiful conifers and aspens atop Boulder Mountain, you're likely to see mule deer, smaller mammals—squirrels, chipmunks, snowshoe hares, cottontails—and any number of songbirds. If you're lucky, you might even see a wild turkey. Get out of your car and onto a hiking trail, and your chances are even better. See Chapter 13.

8   The Best Downhill Skiing

- **Beaver Mountain** (The Northern Wasatch Front): Coming to this small, family-oriented ski area is like going home to see the family—it's just plain comfortable. There's no glitz, no fancy anything, just lots of personal attention, plenty of snow, and great terrain with beautifully maintained trails. See Chapter 8.
- **Snowbasin** (Ogden Valley): Families really love Snowbasin, because there's something for everyone here, no matter what their ability. It's particularly popular with intermediates, who love the long, easy, well-groomed cruising runs, but experts have plenty to keep them happy, too, including an abundance of untracked powder and the state's third highest vertical drop. See Chapter 8.
- **Alta** (Little Cottonwood Canyon): All serious skiers make a pilgrimage to Alta at one time or another. It offers the best skiing in the state—and some of the lightest powder in the world—especially for advanced skiers willing to hike a bit for perfect conditions. But if you're not up to black diamond level yet, don't worry: There's plenty of cruising ground for beginners and intermediates as well. And at $25 for an all-day adult lift ticket, it also happens to be one of the best skiing bargains anywhere. See Chapter 9.
- **Park City and Deer Valley:** Not only do these resorts offer excellent powder skiing on a wide variety of terrain, but the best shopping, nightlife, accommodations,

and dining of all Utah's ski areas—for that matter, in all of Utah. Park City is the party town; Deer Valley is its more grown-up, sophisticated sibling. They're less than five minutes apart from one another, so you can make the best of them both. Who says you can't have everything? See Chapter 9.

9 The Best Cross-Country Skiing

- **Solitude Nordic Center** (Big Cottonwood Canyon): Close to Salt Lake City, Solitude is the perfect destination for a half- or full-day cross-country excursion. At 8,700 feet, the 20 km of groomed trails pass through alpine forests, meadows, and around picturesque Silver Lake. There's also a children's trail. See Chapter 9.

- **Sundance Nordic Center:** These expertly groomed trails are in a perfect forest and meadow setting, at the base of Mt. Timpanogos. Part of the Sundance Resort complex, Sundance Nordic Center is easily accessible from downtown Provo, but light years away from civilization. See Chapter 9.

- **Bryce Canyon National Park:** Once the summer crowds go home and a blanket of snow adorns the multicolored hoodoos with a sparkling white mantle, it's time to take out the cross-country skis. Just follow the warm-weather hiking trails around the rim. Outside the park, at Ruby's Inn, are groomed trails and rental equipment. See Chapter 13.

10 The Best Four-Wheeling

Four-wheeling isn't for everyone, but for those that enjoy it, it's an exhilarating mix of muscle and machine that can take you where you could never get under the power of your own two feet.

- **Coral Pink Sand Dunes State Park** (near Kanab): Skim across the swells of smooth rose-colored sand, uphill and down, over the ever-changing dunes. It's an unending challenge, with sun and sand and wind in your face and hair—and a real thrill. See Chapter 11.

- **White Rim Road, Canyonlands National Park:** A hundred miles of winding, rocky road meanders around Canyonlands' Island in the Sky, offering ever-changing views. Sometimes, the scene is a grand panorama of monumental stone as far as the eye can see; at others, you'll have a close-up view of a stately tower of red rock or a colorful canyon wall. A high-clearance 4X4 is necessary for this one. See Chapter 16.

- **From Willow Flat to Klondike Bluffs Road, Arches National Park:** This 19-mile excursion takes you into high desert terrain, to the top tall hills and past spectacular rock formations such as stately Eye of the Needle arch, towering Elephant Butte, and the solemn Courthouse Towers. You'll have panoramic views of forested mountains, drifting sand dunes—and, at every turn, more red rock. See Chapter 16.

- **Poison Spider Mesa Trail** (near Moab): This is another of southwestern Utah's serious 4X4 roads; you'll need a short wheelbase vehicle to negotiate some of these steep hairpin turns. Before you reach the top, you'll pass through a sandy canyon and some rocky areas that really stretch the meaning of the word "road." Below—and getting ever more distant as you climb—is the Colorado River, winding its way through the Moab Valley. See Chapter 16.

11 The Best Places to Experience Native American Culture

- **The Great Gallery in Horseshoe Canyon, Canyonlands National Park:** In a remote and hard-to-reach section of Canyonlands National Park is the Great Gallery, an 80-foot-long panel of rock art that dates back several thousand years. It's one of the biggest and best prehistoric murals you'll find anywhere. See Chapter 16.
- **Hovenweep National Monument:** This deserted valley contains some of the most striking and most isolated archaeological sites in the Four Corners area—the remains of curious sandstone towers the Anasazi built more than 700 years ago. These mysterious structures are still keeping archaeologists guessing. See Chapter 17.
- **Mesa Verde National Park:** The largest archaeological preserve in the country is also home to the most impressive cliff dwellings in the Southwest. The sites run the gamut from simple pit houses to complex cliff dwellings, and they're all fascinating to explore. See Chapter 17.
- **Monument Valley Navajo Tribal Park:** For most of us, Monument Valley *is* the Old West. We've seen it dozens of times in movie theaters, on TV, and in magazine and billboard advertisements. The Old West may be gone, but many Navajos still call this home. A Navajo guide will give you the Navajo perspective on this majestic land and take you into areas not otherwise open to visitors. See Chapter 17.

12 The Best Mormon History Sites

- **Temple Square** (Salt Lake City): This is the nucleus of the Mormon religion, and its significance shows, with magnificent structures and beautiful statuary set among vibrant gardens. The egg-shaped Tabernacle may look a little peculiar, but its interior acoustics make up for it. You can take a guided tour to learn more about the Latter-day Saints (LDS) and the square itself, stroll around on your own, or just sit and meditate; this is a lovely haven in the center of a bustling city. See Chapter 7.
- **Beehive House** (Salt Lake City): Brigham Young built this house in 1894 as his family home. Restored to resemble as closely as possible the way it was when Young lived here, Beehive House offers a looking-glass into the lifestyle of the Mormon leader. Being from New England, Young designed his home in that style; it even has a widow's walk for keeping an eye on the surrounding desert. See Chapter 7.
- **Jacob Hamblin Home** (St. George): This simple home, built of pine and stone, looks as if the family just stepped out for a stroll and are expected back for dinner soon. It's cozy and comfortable, with many furnishings you'd expect to find in any pioneer home. Then you notice the two identical bedrooms—one for each of Jacob's wives—and you realize that these weren't just any pioneers. See Chapter 11.
- **St. George Tabernacle** (St. George): A magnificent example of Old World crafts-manship, from the hand-quarried red stone walls to the pine detailing so well finished that it looks like fine hardwoods and marble—a painstaking craft that clearly illustrates the strength and depth of the pioneers' religious beliefs. See Chapter 11.

13 The Best Luxury Hotels & Inns

Luxury is not a word we generally associate with Utah, but there are a few uniquely exquisite places to stay, where comfort is synonymous with elegance, and grandeur has a coziness to it.

- **The Inn at Temple Square** (Salt Lake City; ☎ 801/531-1000): The finest downtown hotel, this quietly elegant hotel has beautifully appointed rooms, a lovely dining room, and an all-around aura of old-world graciousness. Although it may look formal, it's really relaxed and homelike—come on in and set a spell. See Chapter 7.
- **Brigham Street Inn** (Salt Lake City; ☎ 801/364-4461): A showcase of understated elegance, the Brigham Street Inn is a delight to the eye. It also happens to be a great place to relax and put your feet up—there are comfortable chairs in every room and fireplaces in most. See Chapter 7.
- **Goldener Hirsch Inn** (Deer Valley; ☎ 801/649-7770): This place feels like a Bavarian Alps lodge, with roaring fireplaces, hand-painted furniture, windows looking out onto the ski slopes, feather-light down comforters, and the kind of personalized service you'd expect to find in a fine European hotel. See Chapter 9.
- **Stein Eriksen Lodge** (Deer Valley; ☎ 801/645-6451): The Stein Eriksen is both grandly elegant and warm and welcoming, with cozy niches in the dignified lobby and luxurious but comfortable suites. Attendants in the whirlpool, sauna, and fitness room are always on hand to pamper you and see to your every need, but they're so unobtrusive that you'll feel right at home—contentedly, luxuriously at home. See Chapter 9.

14 The Best Bed & Breakfasts

- **Center Street Bed & Breakfast Inn** (Logan; ☎ 801/752-3443): Welcome to fantasyland. This highly imaginative B&B is a delight for those adults who don't mind letting their inner child out now and then. The Arabian Nights Suite has sand-colored carpet, a huge round bed with a sultan's tent and stars above, and a camel and elephant surrounding the heart-shaped whirlpool tub. The Ice Fantasy has snow drifts on the mirrored walls, icicles hanging from the ceiling of a snow cave, and polar bears and penguins about. Need we say more? See Chapter 8.
- **Snowberry Inn Bed & Breakfast** (near Ogden; ☎ 801/645-2634): This new log B&B is lovingly decorated with antiques and collectibles, and each bedroom has its own personality. Although it's a wide-open design, with a broad front porch, it still manages to have a cozy, homelike atmosphere; guests gather in the kitchen to sip coffee and watch, or help, as breakfast is being prepared. See Chapter 8.
- **Seven Wives Inn Bed & Breakfast** (St. George; ☎ 801/628-3737): This was the first B&B in Utah, and it's one of the loveliest. There are no polygamists hiding in the attic anymore, but you'll still feel like you've stepped back in time when you stay here. The B&B is housed in two historic 19th-century homes outfitted with antiques, mostly Victorian and Eastlake. We loved the several decks, porches, and balconies. The innkeepers are friendly but not intrusive. See Chapter 11.
- **Sunflower Hill Bed & Breakfast** (Moab; ☎ 801/259-2974): Loaded with country charm, this delightful B&B makes you feel like you've gone back to Grandma's, where you're surrounded by family relics during the day and sleep under handmade quilts at night. What's more, this may be the quietest lodging in Moab, and the grassy, shady grounds are very inviting on a hot day. See Chapter 16.

15 The Best Lodges

This is the West, a rugged land of rugged pioneers who literally carved out a place for themselves in the forests and red rock canyons. These lodges help you feel a part of that past without requiring that you sacrifice today's modern comforts.

- **Red Canyon Lodge** (Flaming Gorge National Recreation Area; ☎ 801/889-3759): This is not really a lodge at all, but rather a group of delightful cabins dating from the 1930s, and remodeled in the 1990s. They offer a range of accommodations from rustic to luxurious, and all have freestanding wood stoves. See Chapter 10.
- **Bryce Canyon Lodge** (☎ 801/834-5361): This handsome sandstone and ponderosa-pine lodge is the perfect place to stay when you're visiting the national park. The several suites are outfitted with white wicker furniture, ceiling fans, and separate sitting rooms. But our choice would be one of the snug cabins. They're fairly small, but the tall ceilings give a feeling of spaciousness, and the gas-burning stone fireplaces, pine board walls, and log beams make them appropriately cozy. See Chapter 13.

16 The Best of the Performing Arts

- **Mormon Tabernacle Choir** (Salt Lake City): You can hear the glorious sounds of this world-renowned all-volunteer choir in their home on Temple Square. When not on tour, the choir rehearses Thursday evenings and performs their weekly radio broadcasts Sunday mornings; both events are open to the public, free of charge. See Chapter 7.
- **Utah Symphony** (Salt Lake City, Park City): Who'd expect to find one of the country's top symphony orchestras in Utah? Well, here it is, an excellent orchestra that not only tours worldwide and has produced numerous recordings, but also performs each year in schools across the state. Our favorite time to enjoy this world-class orchestra is during the symphony's summer series, when outdoor performances of Tchaikovsky's *1812 Overture* in Park City are accompanied by the booming of genuine cannons. See Chapters 7 and 9.
- **Mountain Man Rendezvous at Fort Buenaventura** (Ogden): This is the twice-yearly tribute to the mountain men who chose this site for their rendezvous, a French term given to the gatherings of the fur trappers in the early 1800s to trade their furs for supplies, instead of having to travel east to established markets. These festival-like events are fun for everyone, participants and onlookers alike. There's music, Dutch oven food, and contests that usually include a tomahawk throw, a canoe race, a shooting competition, and foot races, with all competitors in pre-1840s dress. See Chapter 8.
- **Utah Shakespearean Festival** (Cedar City): To go or not to go, that is the question. If theater's your thing, go. Four of the Bard's plays, plus two others, are presented each summer, and they're grand entertainment. See Chapter 11.

2 Land of Natural Wonders & Pioneers: Introducing Utah

Barren wasteland and scenic wonderland, an adventurer's paradise and picture-perfect Middle America—this is Utah, a land of extremes, where mountain peaks receive more than 500 inches of snow each winter and desert lowlands bake at well over 115°F in the summer. Utah is an extraordinarily beautiful place. It has a rugged beauty, with stark stone monoliths alternating with deep red canyons, tall forested mountains standing guard over a huge inland salt sea.

This relatively quiet, relatively unknown corner of America is beginning to draw nationwide, even worldwide, attention. More and more people are coming—to visit its majestic national parks, explore its pristine wilderness, bike its slickrock trails, ski the best powder in the world at its increasingly popular resorts, and discover the all-around charm of its cities and towns. To some, this is America as it should be—a wide-open country with plenty of room to roam, and some of the friendliest people on earth when you seek them out, or just happen to bump into them. Of course, it isn't quite that simple, but it comes close. But don't just take it from us; find out for yourself. Come to Utah, discover, and enjoy.

1 The Regions in Brief

Take a big knife and it's easy to cut Utah into three distinctive regions: The Colorado Plateau, in the southern half of the state, where all those fantastic rock formations are; Rocky Mountain Utah, with rugged peaks, stately pines, deep-blue lakes, and most of the state's residents; and the Great Basin Desert, the big middle-of-nowhere where you've always wanted to send that distant cousin of yours you never really liked.

Since the state is so big, we've concentrated our coverage on those areas where visitors tend to want to go, rather than on trying to catalog each of the three regions from A to Z. Truth be told, certain sections of Utah just have a whole lot of nothing. So we've organized this book by destination, based on where you'll probably want to go, or base yourself while you explore outlying areas.

We start out in the **Wasatch Front.** This Rocky Mountain region is the 175-mile-long north-central section from Logan to Provo. This is where 80% of Utah's population lives. **Salt Lake City** is the state's most populous city by far, and its most cosmopolitan. It's also the

> **❓ Did You Know?**
>
> - Utah's population is the youngest in the nation.
> - Utah boasts one of the world's largest dinosaur graveyards at Dinosaur National Monument.
> - The Mormon Tabernacle in Salt Lake City is so acoustically sensitive that a pin dropped at one end can be clearly heard at the other, 170 feet away.
> - 94% of residents age 20 and over can read and write, and 80% have graduated from high school—more than in 49 other states.
> - Utah is among the fastest growing states in the nation—while the country's population increased 1.11% from 1992 to 1993, Utah's population swelled 2.71% in the same period.
> - The waters of the Great Salt Lake cover 2,500 square miles and contain eight times more salt than any ocean.
> - Utah's state bird is the California seagull, chosen because the gull saved the Mormons' first crops from a plague of crickets in 1848.
> - Robbers Roost, an outlaw hideout for years even before Butch Cassidy found it in 1884, is located southwest of the confluence of the Green and Colorado rivers, partly within the boundaries of Canyonlands National Park.
> - Four Corners Monument, at the southeast corner of Utah, is the only place in America where you can stand—or sit, if you prefer—in four states at once: Utah, Colorado, New Mexico, and Arizona.
> - Hundreds of movies, TV shows, and commercials have been filmed in the magnificent red rock country of southern Utah—Monument Valley will look mighty familiar when you get there.

international headquarters of the Church of Jesus Christ of Latter-day Saints, more commonly known as the Mormons; Temple Square is Utah's most-visited attraction. Keep in mind, though, that Salt Lake City is still a relatively small city, and somewhat unsophisticated by 1990's standards. Maybe that's what we like best about it. One advantage Salt Lake has over all other Rocky Mountain cities its size is its location; within an hour you can be skiing some of the best downhill slopes in the West.

That brings us to the rest of the Wasatch Front. We've designated that section of the Wasatch Front that's roughly north of Salt Lake the **Northern Wasatch Front:** that mystery of nature, the **Great Salt Lake,** eight times saltier than the world's oceans; the city of **Ogden;** and **Logan,** Utah's northernmost town of any size. Historic Ogden and Logan are both worthy of visits unto themselves; they also make good bases for exploring the nearby mountains. The Great Salt Lake is really part of the Great Basin Desert (see below), but we've covered it here because of its proximity to Salt Lake City, and because it's really the only thing going on in that flat, salty desert.

Those areas basically east and south of Salt Lake City we've called the **Southern Wasatch Front:** Beautiful **Big and Little Cottonwood Canyons,** with some of the state's best skiing, and great hiking and biking in summer; **Park City,** Utah's premier ski resort town—but a great destination all year round—with a historic Main Street dominated by great shopping and restaurants; some great destinations just outside of Park City, including Heber City, Strawberry Reservoir (a real gem of a

Utah

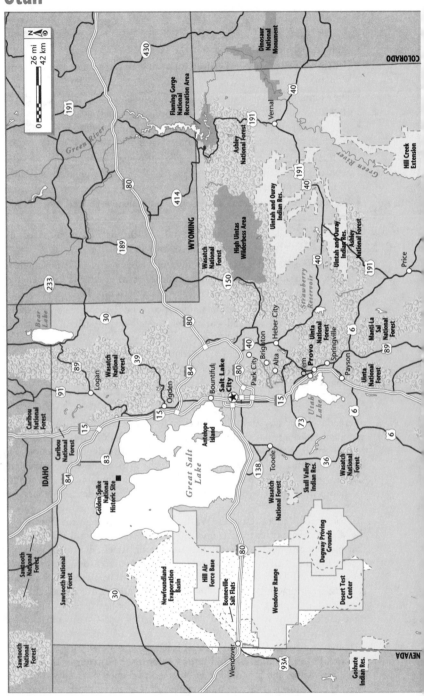

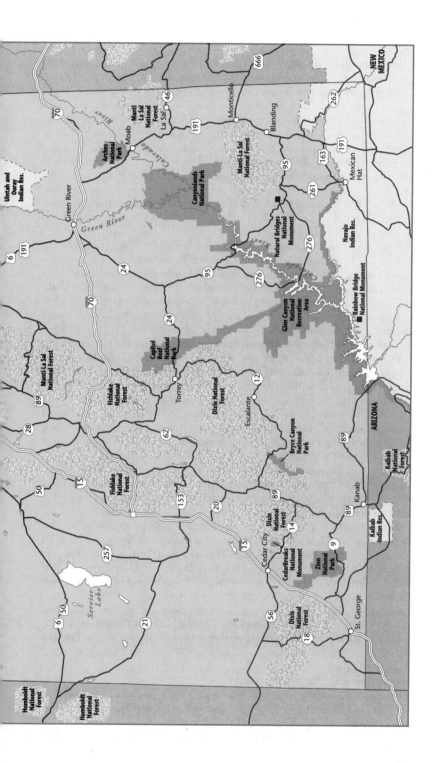

lake), and some great state parks; Robert Redford's Sundance Institute; and **Provo,** a nice enough little city whose main claim to fame is Brigham Young University. Unless you're really counting on seeing the university, you might want skip Provo.

We think we've got the Wasatch Front well covered. The western side of Utah, beginning just west of Salt Lake City, is dominated by the vast, salty nothingness of the Great Basin Desert, which includes the pristinely white Bonneville Salt Flats, so flat that you can actually *see* the curvature of the earth, and famous for the land-speed records held there. This is not the sort of place you want to go for a picnic—it's hot, the water's undrinkable, and there's really nothing there, except for **Wendover,** a little gambling town that straddles the Utah/Nevada state line (the Utah side could really use a bit of sprucing up); we've covered it as an excursion from Salt Lake City. But, having said that, it's not all bad, and you'll find quite a few Utahns driving from Salt Lake City across the desert to reach Great Basin National Park, with its beautiful caverns, just over the Nevada state line.

Next we head to **Northeastern Utah,** with two terrific recreational areas that creep into the adjoining states: **Flaming Gorge National Recreation Area,** which wanders into Wyoming; and nearby **Dinosaur National Monument,** which extends from northeastern Utah into Colorado. Both are what we consider Undiscovered Utah, because they're really off the beaten path, and not what most people think of when they think of Utah. But, as you'll notice as you peruse this book, we love this region, and consider it well worth a visit.

The **Colorado Plateau,** which extends along the state's entire southern border and halfway up the east side, is where all five of Utah's national parks are located, and with good cause—it's undeniably beautiful. Ancient geologic forces, erosion, oxidation, and other unfathomable natural forces have carved spectacular rock sculptures—delicate and intricate, bold and stately—and painted them in a riot of color. This is quite likely why you came to Utah in the first place, and we'll tell you how to spend your time wisely and enjoyably. Check out our chapter on **Zion National Park** for hints on how to avoid the crowds at this national park, the state's most popular; see if you agree with us that **Bryce Canyon National Park,** with its marvelous stone sculptures (called hoodoos), is the West's best. The chapter on **Capitol Reef National Park** explains why this little-known national park is one of Utah's hidden gems; and we'll tell you the best ways to explore eastern Utah's beautiful red rock country in the chapter on **Moab** and **Arches and Canyonlands National Parks.**

But the Colorado Plateau isn't just national parks—it's got even more to offer. Its biggest population and cultural center is in and around St. George, which you'll find in the chapter called **Utah's Dixie: The Southwest Corner.** You'll find great museums, historic Mormon sites, live theater, dance, and music here, as well as skiing (believe it or not) and the state's best golf. If you're heading into Utah from Las Vegas, Nevada, this is also the first Utah town you'll see.

Utah's best destination for water sports—maybe the best in the West—is explored in our chapter on **Lake Powell and Glen Canyon National Recreation Area.** A boating vacation here is the stuff that stressed-out big-city dreams are made of. You

TV you can make on the back lot, but for the big screen, for the real outdoor dramas, you have to do it where God put the West. . .and there is no better example of this than around Moab.

—John Wayne, while filming *The Comancheros* in 1961

may want to stay away, however, if you're not planning on bringing or renting a boat; it's not nearly as exciting if you're stuck on land.

In **The Four Corners Area,** we cover the state's southeast corner, with a few jaunts into adjacent states. Spectacular Native American sites, such as Monument Valley, really make a visit here worthwhile. But keep in mind that you'll be driving a long way through the West's vast, empty spaces to get there.

2 Utah Today

Some people really think that Utah is stuck in the '50s—quaintly or annoyingly so, depending on your perspective. This time warp is due in large part to the strong church influence and the corollary Mormon emphasis on family values, which makes Utah a real family-oriented state. People here are very friendly, the crime rate is low, and Utah is generally a very pleasant state in which to travel.

But don't expect to find the level of restaurants, nightlife, and lodging that's commonplace in Dallas, San Francisco, or even Denver and Santa Fe. With a few notable exceptions, it just doesn't exist here. And while we personally find this refreshing, those looking for five-star elegance or a happening scene will likely be disappointed.

Liquor laws and attitudes toward alcohol in Utah are, simply put, archaic. Those of us who enjoy a glass or wine or beer or a mixed drink with lunch or dinner need to choose our restaurants carefully. Outside of Salt Lake City, even some night spots are dry, like the country-and-western dance club in Provo that advertises "No cussin', no smokin', no drinkin'!" This isn't universal, of course; Park City can hold its own on nightlife with any of the top ski resorts in Colorado, and Moab is a fun, wild 'n' crazy kind of place—at least by Utah standards.

Changes are in the wind, though—along with some conflicts—as more and more outsiders move to Utah. Many escapees from California's smog, crime, crowds, and taxes have brought their mountainbikes and West Coast way of thinking to southern Utah's national park country, while others have been lured to the Wasatch Front, particularly between Salt Lake City and Provo, by computer and other high-tech industries setting up shop there. These newcomers—some 38,000 from California alone in the first three years of the decade—have brought demands for more services, better restaurants, upscale shops, and a greater range of activities; in many cases, they've opened businesses themselves that they felt were needed. They're also accused by some Utahns of bringing the very problems they sought to leave. A police chief in a small southern town was criticized when he announced in mid-1995 that many of the crimes in his community were being committed by newcomers. It may not be politically correct to say so, he admitted, but statistically it seems to be correct.

The growth of tourism is causing traffic congestion problems, mainly because there are so many of us, and we all want to visit at the same time. Zion National Park has been affected the most. Within the next few years, in an attempt to deal with the problem, the park will be instituting a mandatory shuttle bus/biking/hiking system for visitors. If you have some flexibility in your vacation schedule, avoid the busy school vacation months. You can also avoid the crowds by seeking out the lesser-visited attractions, such as Capitol Reef National Park, Flaming Gorge National Recreation Area, and Utah's many spectacular state parks.

Another current issue that will affect you—especially if you enjoy the great outdoors—is the wilderness-versus-development battle. Like in many western states, Utah has an ongoing battle between business interests, who see federal lands as prime targets for development, and environmentalists, who are intent on preserving what they consider to be one of the last unspoiled wildernesses of the American West. The wilderness preservation side sees the businesspeople as greedy land-destroyers who care nothing for the future, and understand America only as a commodity to be exploited for their personal gain; on the other hand, the ranchers, loggers, and miners see the environmentalists as selfish, well-off newcomers who don't care that other people need to earn a living, and just want the government to designate vast wilderness areas for their personal playgrounds. To some extent, they're both right. We'll just have to wait and see what happens.

Even though its feet may be planted in the 1950s, Utah is really looking toward the next century. It's trying to tackle such growing problems as population growth and air pollution, for instance, head on. But the future's not all grim: The Beehive State is looking forward to—and, in true fashion, already working hard·preparing for—the formidable but thrilling task of hosting the 2002 Winter Olympic Games.

3 History 101

Dateline

- **9000 B.C.** Desert Gatherers wander the region now called Utah
- **50 B.C.–A.D.1300** Anasazis establish thriving communities in the Four Corners Area.
- **1776** Spanish friars lead an expedition to explore the region now called Utah.
- **1801** Brigham Young is born in New England.
- **1824** Scout Jim Bridger becomes the first white man to see the Great Salt Lake.
- **1847** Brigham Young leads Mormon pioneers into the Salt Lake Valley.
- **1848** United States wins the Utah region from Mexico.
- **1849** Mormons establish the provisional state of Deseret and adopt a constitution, but their request for statehood is denied.
- **1850** U.S. congress creates the Utah territory.
- **1860–61** Pony Express route crosses Utah in its 2,000-mile, 10-day route between St. Joseph, Mo. and Sacramento, Cal.
- **1861** Telegraph lines are joined at Salt Lake City, creating transcontinental telegraph service, putting

continues

A walk through Utah is a walk through the American West. You can ponder the meaning of petroglyphs etched into canyon walls more than a thousand years ago; follow paths tread by Spanish padres hundreds of years ago; seek out the hiding place of Butch Cassidy; raft the same rapids as explorer John Wesley Powell did in 1869; and see railroads, homes, ranches, and spectacular houses of worship built by the mountain men, miners, missionaries, and all the other pioneers who built the Utah we see today.

The First Peoples   The first known inhabitants were the Desert Gatherers, who, from about 9000 B.C., wandered about the Great Basin and Colorado Plateau searching for food. Unfortunately, being nomadic, they left little evidence of their time here. The Anasazi (a Navajo word meaning "Ancient Ones") appeared in the Four Corners region at about the time of Christ; by A.D. 1200, their villages were scattered throughout present-day Utah. For some reason—possibly drought—by 1250 the villages had been abandoned, leaving the ruins we see standing today in Hovenweep National Monument and at other sites. The descendants of these early people—Shoshone, Ute, Goshute, and Paiute—were among the Native Americans inhabiting the area when the first Europeans came.

Another prehistoric Native American group, the Fremont peoples, settled in central Utah, establishing small villages of pit houses. They arrived in about A.D. 1200, but had disappeared by the time the first Europeans got to Utah.

Spanish explorer Juan Maria Antonio Rivera and his European expedition arrived at the Colorado

River near present-day Moab in 1765. Eleven years later, two Spanish Franciscan friars reached Utah Lake and mapped it, hoping to return to establish a Spanish colony. Spain did not pursue the idea, however, and the next Europeans to explore the area were fur traders in the early 1800s. Then, in July of 1847, Brigham Young lead the first Mormons (a nickname for members of the Church of Jesus Christ of Latter Day Saints) into the Salt Lake Valley, and the flood of Mormon immigrants began; these were the people who really established Utah as we know it today.

Meet the Mormons   Mormonism is a relatively young faith. It was born in the 1820s when Joseph Smith had a revelation: After much prayer asking which of the many Christian churches he should join, Smith was told by God and Jesus that he would be the one to re-establish the true Christian church. An angel named Moroni then gave Smith some ancient gold tablets that, under divine inspiration, he was able to translate into the *Book of Mormon*. In 1830, Smith and his followers published the *Book of Mormon* and founded the Church of Jesus Christ of Latter-day Saints (LDS) in upstate New York. Smith's revelations and the fervor with which his followers believed and tried to spread the word bred hostility in their more skeptical neighbors; the early Mormons were soon forced to leave New York.

Smith and his followers settled in Ohio and Missouri in the early 1830s. A few years of prosperity were succeeded by strife, and the growing Mormon community was once again forced to flee. Gathering along the Mississippi River, they established their church headquarters at Nauvoo, Ill., reclaiming a swampy area along the river. Within a few years, Nauvoo was the second largest city in Illinois, and the Mormons continued to grow and flourish, planning a university and laying the foundation for a temple. Also during these years, the practice of polygamy began slowly and quietly among church leaders. Both their nonconformism and their success bred fear and anger in their opponents, who considered Smith and his Mormons to be a real political, economic, and religious threat. In 1844, a mob stormed the jail in Carthage, Ill., where Joseph Smith and his brother Hyrum were being held on treason charges and murdered them. Brigham Young and other church leaders soon realized that the Latter-day Saints had to move West, beyond the

an end to the need for the Pony Express.

- **1869** Railroad tracks laid from the east and the west coasts are joined at Promontory Point, Utah, creating the first transcontinental railroad and connecting East and West for the first time.

- **1877** Brigham Young dies at home after a brief illness.

- **1890** Church president Wilford Woodruff issues a manifesto advising Mormons to give up their practice of polygamy.

- **1893** Mormon Temple is dedicated in Salt Lake City.

- **1896** Utah becomes the 45th state in the Union.

- **1896** Utahn Martha Hughes Cannon becomes the first female U.S. Senator.

- **1904** Polygamy is formally prohibited by the church.

- **1913** Strawberry River Reservoir, the state's first large reclamation project, is completed by the U.S. Bureau of Reclamation.

- **1919** Zion National Park is created.

- **1926** Commercial airlines start operating in Utah.

- **1928** Utah National Park, established in 1924, is renamed Bryce Canyon National Park.

- **1934** Utah ratifies prohibition repeal amendment and passes stringent state liquor laws.

- **1940** Wendover Air Force Base is established.

- **1952** Uranium is discovered near Moab.

- **1964** Glen Canyon Dam and the Flaming Gorge Dam are completed, ensuring water supply and creating scenic recreation areas. Canyonlands National Park is established.

continues

- **1971** Capitol Reef, a national monument since 1937, becomes a national park. Arches National Monument (since 1938) is expanded and made a national park.
- **1977** Gary Gilmore, convicted of the murders of two Utahns, is executed by firing squad following a media circus that garnered international attention. It's the first execution in the United States in 10 years, following the Supreme Court's reinstatement of the death penalty.
- **1978** LDS Church announces a revelation saying priesthood is now open to worthy men of any race, reversing a policy that had excluded blacks from leadership roles in the church.
- **1982** Worldwide membership in the Church of Jesus Christ of Latter-day Saints exceeds five million.
- **1995** Utah is chosen to host the 2002 Winter Olympic Games.
- **1995** More than 600 inches—that's 50 feet—of snow during the season keeps the lifts running at Snowbird, in Little Cottonwood Canyon east of Salt Lake City, through the 4th of July—the latest lift-served skiing ever in Utah.
- **1996** Utah celebrates its Centennial.

reach of the fearful communities and angry mobs.

Young, a confidant of Smith, became the second leader of the Mormon Church, displaying a genius for organization in the evacuation of Nauvoo and the subsequent migration westward in search of a new Zion. In 1846 the Mormons headed west from Illinois, establishing winter quarters on the far side of the Missouri River, near present-day Omaha, Neb. Young studied maps and journals of explorers, looking for a place that nobody else wanted, where Mormons could build their own community and practice their religion without interference.

Founding Zion   In the spring of 1847, Brigham Young started out with the first group of emigrants—two children, three women, and 143 men, hand-picked for the journey based on their abilities. Future groups were similarly organized, making this the safest and most successful migration across the American West. When the group reached the mouth of Emigration Canyon and looked out upon the empty wasteland of Salt Lake Valley, Young reportedly said "This is the right place." Within hours of their arrival, the pioneers had begun building an irrigation system and establishing fields for growing food. In the next few days, Young chose the site of the temple and laid out the new city in a grid system beginning at the southeast corner of Temple Square. Having established their new Zion, most of the company headed back to Winter Quarters to bring their families west.

That first year almost ended the settlement before it had properly begun. The flat sod roofs leaked under heavy spring snow and rain; provisions ran low, forcing the pioneers to eat whatever they could find, including the sego lily bulb (now the state flower); a late frost damaged the wheat and vegetables; and drought damaged more. Then a plague of crickets descended on the crops, consuming the little that was left. The people tried everything they could to battle the crickets—they tried beating them, drowning them, setting them on fire—but nothing worked. Suddenly, seagulls appeared from the Great Salt Lake, devouring the insects by the thousands, disgorging them, and eating more. After two weeks, the crickets were effectively eliminated, and enough of the crops were saved to feed the pioneers. The seagull is now Utah's state bird, and a monument stands in Temple Square commemorating the Saints' deliverance from famine.

By the end of 1848, almost 3,000 Latter-day Saints had arrived in the Salt Lake Valley. It was now a part of the United States, ceded to the Union by Mexico along with California, Nevada, most of New Mexico and Arizona, and parts of Wyoming and Colorado. In 1849, the Mormons petitioned to have their territory declared the State of Deseret, a name that comes from the *Book of Mormon* and means honeybee. Denied statehood, the territory of Utah—named after the Ute tribe—was created in 1850, with Brigham Young as territorial governor. Although no longer run by the LDS church, the territory was assured of the church's continued influence, since the vast majority of voters were Mormons who elected church leaders to positions of authority in the civic domain as well.

In these years, non-Mormons—or "Gentiles," as the Mormons call them—began traveling through the valley, many on their way to the gold fields of California. Salt Lake City was an ideal spot for resting and re-supplying before setting out again. Some came through on their eastbound return trip; they were giving up on the West. The Latter-day Saints often bought horses, livestock, and supplies, in turn reselling what they didn't need to other travelers. The travelers who came through to rest and trade took a collection of sometimes-confused ideas about the Mormons, including the fascinating practice of polygamy, with them when they left. Their journals gave the nation its first real knowledge—however incomplete—of Mormon faith and customs.

The Utah War   In 1857, a new governor was sent from Washington to supplant Young. Fearing he would be rejected, President Buchanan sent federal troops to escort him. The Mormons harassed the troops by driving off livestock and attacking their supply trains, forcing them to winter in western Wyoming. Although the Mormons were prepared to fight to keep the army out, neither Brigham Young nor President Buchanan wanted bloodshed. The new governor entered Salt Lake City. Families packed their belongings and awaited the order to move.

An estimated 30,000 Saints left their homes in Salt Lake City and the northern settlements, moving south over a period of two months, leaving the capital virtually deserted by mid-May. The exodus drew national and international attention and placed the U.S. government in quite an unfavorable light—the government had persecuted innocent people, steamrolling right over the fundamental right to religious freedom. An uneasy peace was finally established, the Saints returned to their homes, and the two groups lived side-by-side until the outbreak of the Civil War, when the army was called back east.

Becoming the Beehive State   After the close of the Civil War, attention was again directed toward the enforcement of antipolygamy laws, and many Saints were imprisoned. Finally, in 1890, the church leaders issued a statement: Based on a revelation from God, the church was no longer teaching plural marriage and no person would be permitted to enter into it. A major bar to statehood having been removed, Utah became the 45th state on January 4, 1896.

The Depression hit Utah hard; the unemployment rate reached 35% and per capita income was cut in half. It wasn't until World War II that industry was brought back to life in Utah. Several military bases established during the war became permanent installations, and missile plants were built along the Wasatch Front. After the

Impressions

When I was a boy on the farm in Illinois there was a great deal of timber on the farms which we had to clear away. Occasionally we would come to a log which had fallen down. It was too hard to split, too wet to burn, and too heavy to move, so we plowed around it. That's what I intend to do with the Mormons. You go back and tell Brigham Young that if he will let me alone, I will let him alone.

—President Abraham Lincoln, 1862,
when asked what his plans were for the Mormons

war, steel companies reopened, the mining industry boomed, and high-tech businesses moved in. By the mid-1960s, the economy base had shifted from an agricultural one to an industrial one.

Dams were built—Glen Canyon Dam, creating Lake Powell; Flaming Gorge Dam, creating Lake Flaming Gorge; plus several smaller ones—to further the cause of industry and to ensure water and energy supplies, but they also had an additional benefit: They provided recreational opportunities for a modern society with an increasing amount of discretionary income and more and more free time. Ski resorts began opening in the Wasatch Mountains. In the early 1980s, once outsiders started showing interest in the new playground of Utah, Salt Lake City International Airport and the city's cultural center, the Salt Palace complex, expanded. As the mining industries were winding down, tourism and service industries grew; today, they account for more of the state's economy than any other industry. The Mormons, who spent their first decades fleeing from outsiders, are now welcoming them with open arms, and they're coming in droves—my, how times have changed.

4 A Brief Look at Modern Mormonism— or Yes, You *Can* Get a Cup of Coffee in Utah

Utah is a Mormon state. Not officially, of course—strict federal laws keep church doctrine out of government—and not as much as in the past, when practically all Utahns (and definitely all the decision makers) were LDS church members. But when almost three-quarters of the state's population belong to the Church of Jesus Christ of Latter-day Saints, and given that most Mormons take their religion very seriously, it's inevitable that the teachings of the church would have a strong influence in the voting booth and echo throughout the halls of government. One recent controversy surrounding the separation of church and state—you may have seen the story on *60 Minutes*—concerned a Jewish high school chorus member, who complained that she was forced to sing almost exclusively Christian songs, and to perform in LDS churches. What was surprising was that many public school officials not only felt there was nothing wrong with the practice, but seemed baffled that anyone would complain.

While some conflict is inevitable as government and community leaders try to adapt to Utah's growing cultural diversity, this discord means little to most visitors, who come to Utah to experience its scenery, recreation, and history. What you'll discover is that Utah is much like the rest of the United States, although generally not as hip as California or as multicultural as New York. The state is inhabited in large part by actively religious people who believe it's wrong to use tobacco, addictive drugs, or drink alcoholic beverages, coffee, or tea. In accordance with church teachings, Mormons are generally hard-working and honest, with high moral standards.

WHAT MORMONS BELIEVE

Mormons are Christians, believing in Jesus Christ as the Son of God and the Bible as the Word of God, as do all the many offshoots of Christianity. But a significant difference is that they have another book they believe also to be God's Word—the *Book of Mormon*, as revealed to and translated by church founder Joseph Smith.

This book tells of three tribes of people who left Israel in Biblical times under threat of destruction by the Babylonians and made their way to North America. Mormons believe that one of these tribes was the ancestral group of the American Indians. The *Book of Mormon* teaches that after his resurrection, Christ spent about 40 days among these people, preaching, healing, and establishing his church.

The Mormons believe that Joseph Smith was commanded to restore the church as organized by Christ during his ministry on earth.

The first four principles of the Mormon faith are belief in Jesus Christ, repentance, baptism by immersion, and the laying on of hands (in which a priest places his hands on a church member for the transference of spirituality). Another important tenet of the church is respect for the supreme authority of church leaders and the belief in the revelations from God to these leaders.

The family unit is of paramount importance for Mormons, and they believe that marriage lasts literally forever, transcending death. They believe that sex outside of marriage and homosexuality—two ideas that are contrary to the sanctity of the traditional family—are sins. The church encourages the family to work, play, and study together, and young adults—most men and some women—generally spend one or two years as missionaries. Mormons also believe in the baptism and redemption of those already dead—hence their strong interest in genealogy.

It's practically impossible to discuss the Mormon Church without discussing polygamy, the infamous practice of men having more than one wife, that caused so much antagonism towards church members in the 19th century. But that's really a shame, because polygamy—or plural marriage, as the church dubbed it—has little to do with what Mormonism was and is about. Polygamy came about as a "revelation" of church founder Joseph Smith in the 1840s, was practiced by a relatively small percentage of church members, and was outlawed by church officials in 1890. Today, polygamy is prohibited both by church doctrine and state law. It reportedly continues among a small number of church rebels, who have, in some cases, left the church to practice their own brand of Mormonism, but they're few and far— very far—between.

WHAT MORMONISM MEANS FOR YOU

Mormonism has brought about some strange laws regarding alcoholic beverages, although it's definitely not true that you can't get a drink here. Cigarettes and other tobacco products are also readily available, but by state law smoking is prohibited in all restaurants—legislation that is common across America more and more these days. Although cola drinks contain caffeine, a stimulant that is generally considered to be mildly addictive, the church doesn't specifically prohibit their consumption. Some Mormons drink Coke or Pepsi, while others refrain. You'll generally have no trouble at all purchasing whatever type soft drink you want, with or without caffeine. Interestingly, there is one exception: although there are plenty of soda machines on the campus of church-owned Brigham Young University in Provo, they stock only noncaffeinated products.

What we found pleasantly surprising is that although the Mormons of Utah can be pretty tough on themselves regarding the above-mentioned "sins," virtually every Utahn we encountered in researching this book—and a great many were Mormons— were extremely tolerant of others' beliefs and lifestyles. We can't guarantee that you won't run across some holier-than-thou busybody who insists on lecturing you on the evils of Demon Rum, tobacco, promiscuity, or homosexuality; but our experience has been that Mormons generally respect each individual's right to make his or her own moral choices.

Be forewarned, though—Mormons are practically missionaries by definition, and will, with only the slightest encouragement, want to enthusiastically help you see the wisdom of their ways.

Because the church emphasizes the importance of family, you'll see lots of kids— Utah is noted for having the highest fertility rate in the nation. This makes Utah a very kid-friendly state, with lots of family-oriented activities and many attractions that are designed specifically with kids in mind. Overall, prices for kids and families are often very reasonable: For instance, state parks that charge individual admission fees charge no more than $6 per family, no matter how many kids you drag in. And since most Mormon families observe Monday evening as a time to spend together, sports facilities, amusement parks, and similar venues often offer family discounts Mondays; if you're traveling with your family, watch for them.

Although about 70% of Utah's population are LDS church members, you'll find that church membership varies greatly from community to community, so the number of Mormons you'll encounter will vary considerably. Although it's the world headquarters of the church, Salt Lake City is only about 40% Mormon, while some of the smaller towns approach 100%. Of major cities, Provo has the strongest church influence; although St. George was historically a major stronghold for church members, recent immigration from other parts of the United States is gradually diluting that influence. You'll probably find the least church influence in Park City and Moab, which in recent years have attracted large numbers of outsiders, and are generally considered to be "not really part of Utah" by long-term residents.

5 Recommended Books, Films & Recordings

To catch the mood of southern Utah, we recommend Edward Abbey's *Desert Solitaire* (New York: McGraw-Hill, 1968), a nonfiction work based on time Abbey spent in Arches National Monument. Those who like a good western story will want to grab a copy of Zane Grey's *Riders of the Purple Sage* (New York: Pocket Books, 1974).

An excellent source for additional information about the Church of Jesus Christ of Latter-day Saints is *Church History in the Fulness of Times* (Salt Lake City: Church of Jesus Christ of Latter-day Saints, 1989), a detailed history of the church. A short, easy-to-read book with simple, concise explanations of Mormon beliefs is *What do Mormons Believe?* (Salt Lake City: Deseret Book Company, 1992) by Rex E. Lee. And, of course, the *Book of Mormon* is available from the church. For an insightful look at Mormon life and Salt Lake City in the mid-19th century, you might enjoy reading *The City of the Saints and Across the Rocky Mountains to California* (New York: Alfred A. Knopf, 1963, first pub. in London, 1861) by Richard Burton.

Outdoors enthusiasts might want *The Mountain Biker's Guide to Utah* (Helena, Mont.: Falcon Press, 1994) by Greg Bromka, with detailed descriptions and maps to 80 rides; or *The Hiker's Guide to Utah* (Falcon Press, 1991) by Dave Hall and Ann Seifert. Jim Cole's *Utah Wildlife Viewing Guide* (Falcon Press, 1990) describes 92 of the best wildlife viewing sites in Utah.

If you're a budding or amateur geologist, or would just like a little more background on the rocks you're going to see, you should investigate *Pages of Stone, Geology of Western National Parks & Monuments, 4: Grand Canyon and the Plateau Country* (Seattle: The Mountaineers, 1988) by Jalka Chronic. It includes discussions of Grand Canyon, Arches, Bryce Canyon, Canyonlands, Capitol Reef, and Zion National Parks, and Cedar Breaks, Natural Bridges, and Rainbow Bridge National Monuments.

Western movie buffs will want a copy of *"Where God Put the West": Movie Making in the Desert* (Moab: Four Corners Publications, Inc., 1994) by Bette L. Stanton, which includes fascinating stories and photos from the numerous Hollywood productions shot in southern Utah. Anyone who's seen the 1969 film *Butch Cassidy and the Sundance Kid* will enjoy *The Wild Bunch at Robbers Roost* (Lincoln: University of Nebraska Press, 1989) by Pearl Baker, which tells the real story of these famous outlaws.

Speaking of movies, of the hundreds filmed in Utah, the two that say the most about the state are *Stagecoach* and *Wagon Master*, black-and-white classics by famed director John Ford that can be found in most decently stocked video rental outlets. *Stagecoach*, released in 1939, offers spectacular scenes of Monument Valley, and stars a young John Wayne on his road to stardom. Released 11 years later, *Wagon Master*, starring Ben Johnson, Joanne Dru, and Ward Bond, was filmed in the Moab area, and tells a fictionalized but highly entertaining story of a Utah-bound Mormon wagon train.

Several travel videos that let you see Utah before your trip are *Utah: Nature's Wonderland*, a splendid hour of Utah's scenic beauty; *The Iron Road*, about the completion of the first transcontinental railroad at Promontory, Utah; and *Grand Circle Tour*, a 1,400-mile tour of Grand Canyon, Zion, Bryce Canyon, Capitol Reef, Canyonlands, Arches, and Mesa Verde national parks. You can get these and other videos, many in both VHS and PAL formats, from INTERpark, P.O. Box 3590, Farmington, NM 87499 (☎ 505/325-6136).

3

Planning a Trip to Utah

Utah is an easy state to visit—you can usually expect to pay less for food and lodging than you would in other parts of the country, roads are good and generally uncrowded, and it would be hard to find friendlier people. But once you leave the Wasatch Front—the area around Salt Lake City, Ogden, and Provo—to explore the natural wonders of Utah, distances between towns are long and there are few services in between. So you'll want to plan your trip carefully and make reservations in especially popular areas, such as the national parks, or for especially popular times, like ski season, as far in advance as possible. The pages that follow will help you do that and more—we've compiled everything you need to know to handle the practical details of planning your trip in advance.

1 Visitor Information & Money

VISITOR INFORMATION

For advance information on the state as a whole, as well as an official state map, contact the **Utah Travel Council,** Council Hall, Salt Lake City, UT 84115 (☎ 801/538-1030 or 800/220-1160; fax 801/538-1399). The travel council also provides information **online** at http://www.netpub.com/utah!.

Numerous agencies can provide information on a variety of activities and destinations in Utah. For information on Utah's national forests, and to make camping reservations in them, contact the **U.S. Forest Service,** Federal Building, Room 8301, 125 S. State St., Salt Lake City, UT 84138 (☎ 801/524-5030 or 800/280-2267 for campground reservations); for forest and wilderness maps, contact the **U.S. Forest Service Intermountain Region,** 2501 Wall Ave., Ogden, UT 84401 (☎ 801/625-5306); for topographic maps, contact the **U.S. Geological Survey,** 2300 S. 2222 West, West Valley City, UT 84117 (☎ 801/975-3742); the Utah State Office of the **U.S. Bureau of Land Management** is at 324 S. State St., Suite 400, Salt Lake City, UT 84111 (☎ 801/539-4001). To make camping reservations at Utah's state parks, contact **Utah Parks and Recreation,** 1636 W. North Temple, Suite 116, Salt Lake City, UT 84116-3156 (☎ 801/538-7220, 801/322-3770 or 800/322-3770 for campground reservations); and for information on guides and outfitters throughout the state, contact **Utah Guides & Outfitters,** 153 E. 7200 South, Midvale, UT 84047 (☎ 801/566-2662).

MONEY

ATM machines are practically everywhere, including many supermarkets. For the location of the nearest ATM, dial 800/424-7787 for the Cirrus network or 800/843-7587 for the Plus system. Most ATMs will make cash advances against MasterCard and Visa, but make sure that you have your personal identification number (PIN) with you.

American Express cardholders can write a personal check, guaranteed against the card, for up to $1,000 in cash at any American Express office. The Salt Lake City branch is at 175 S. West Temple (☎ 801/328-9733). It's open Monday through Friday, from 9am to 5pm.

U.S. dollar **traveler's checks** are accepted practically everywhere in Utah, including small towns, and they can be exchanged for cash at banks and most check-issuing offices. However, be aware that smaller businesses may not be able to cash traveler's checks or even American currency in large denominations (over $50).

2 When to Go

Deciding when to visit Utah will depend on what you want to do and which sections of the state you plan to see. Generally, those traveling without children will want to avoid visiting during school vacations. In particular, stay away from ski resorts during the Christmas–New Year's holidays and from the national parks during July and August if you want to avoid the crowds. The best times to visit the parks and almost everything else in southern Utah is in spring and fall, anyway; summers are too hot, particularly in the St. George area.

Utah has four seasons, but because of the vast range in elevations—from 2,200 feet to 13,528 feet—conditions vary considerably across the state. Generally, as in the other desert states, summer days are hot but nights are cool. Winters are cold and snowy, except in southwest Utah's "Dixie" (where St. George is located)—it seldom gets very cold and snow is rare. Mountain temperatures are always pleasantly cool, and can be very cold at night, even in the summer.

Average Monthly High/Low Temperatures (°F) & Precipitation (inches)

		Jan	Feb	Mar	Apr	May	June	July	Aug	Sept	Oct	Nov	Dec
Moab	Temp. (°F)	42/19	51/25	61/33	71/42	82/50	93/58	99/65	96/63	88/53	75/41	57/30	45/21
Elev. 3,965'	Precip. "	0.6	0.5	0.7	0.9	0.7	0.4	0.5	0.8	0.7	0.9	0.7	0.7
Park City Mountains	Temp. (°F)	27/6	31/10	36/15	48/24	60/33	71/39	79/47	76/45	67/36	54/28	39/17	31/11
Elev. 8,085'	Precip. "	3.1	2.6	2.9	2.4	1.3	1.3	1.1	1.4	1.0	2.5	2.4	3.2
St. George	Temp. (°F)	54/27	61/32	67/37	76/44	86/52	96/61	102/68	99/66	93/57	81/45	65/34	55/27
Elev. 2,760'	Precip. "	1.0	0.9	1.0	0.5	0.5	0.2	0.6	0.7	0.5	0.6	0.8	0.7
Salt Lake City	Temp. (°F)	37/20	44/27	52/30	61/37	72/45	83/53	93/62	90/60	80/50	67/39	50/29	39/22
Elev. 4,222'	Precip. "	1.4	1.3	1.7	2.2	1.5	1.0	0.7	0.9	0.9	1.1	1.2	1.4

UTAH CALENDAR OF EVENTS

January

- **Utah Winter Games,** Salt Lake City, Park City, and other locations. Amateur athletes compete in downhill and Nordic skiing, figure skating, and hockey. Call 801/975-4515. Ongoing through most of the month.

- **Hof Winter Festival,** Ogden. Winter celebration honoring Ogden's sister city of Hof, Germany, with ski races on a manmade ski hill, a parade, and authentic German music and food. Call 801/629-8242. Third weekend.
- **Sundance Film Festival,** Park City. Sponsored by Robert Redford's Sundance Resort, this festival honors the best of independent films with screenings and seminars. For more information, see p. 156 or call 801/328-3456. Late January.

February
- **Bryce Canyon Winter Festival,** Bryce. A winter celebration amid the colorful rock formations of the Bryce Canyon National Park area. Call 800/468-8660. Mid-month.

March
- **Hostler Model Railroad Festival,** Ogden. Fans of model trains gather at historic Union Station, where trains of all shapes and sizes are on display, and model train collectors can locate those hard-to-find items. ☎ 801/629-8446. First week of the month.
- **Snowshine Festival,** Park City. Family ski races, snow softball, and other fun-in-the-snow events. ☎ 801/649-8111. Late March through early April.

April
- **World Conference of the LDS Church,** Salt Lake City. The church president, believed to be a prophet, speaks to Mormons from throughout the world at church headquarters on Temple Square. Those who are not members of the LDS church are also welcome. Call 801/240-2531.
- **Spring Salon,** Springville. A varied media art exhibit with an emphasis on Utah artists. Call 801/489-2727. Ongoing all month.
- ✪ **Mountain Man Rendezvous,** Ogden. A gathering of mountain men at Fort Buenaventura State Park, with black powder shooting contests and other early 19th-century activities. Call 801/621-4808. Easter weekend.
- **Arts Festival,** St. George. A celebration of the arts, with all media represented in a variety of exhibits. Call 801/634-5747. Mid-month.

May
- **Golden Spike Anniversary,** Golden Spike National Historic Site. Commemorates the moment in 1869 when rail lines from east and west coasts were joined, linking the nation. A must for historic railroad buffs. Call 801/471-2209. May 10.
- **Living Traditions Festival,** Salt Lake City. A celebration of Utah's ethnic diversity, including food, music, and traditional activities. Call 801/533-5760. Midmonth.
- **Scandinavian Festival,** Ephraim. Utahns celebrate their Scandinavian roots in one of the state's most authentic and enthusiastic folklife festivals. Call 801/283-6890 or 801/283-4535. Late May.

June
- **America's Freedom Festival,** Provo. This celebration includes fun runs and other sporting events, patriotic music concerts, art festivals, parades, and fireworks. Call 801/345-2008. Mid-June through Independence Day.
- ✪ **Utah Shakespearean Festival,** Cedar City. A highly respected professional theater production of several plays by William Shakespeare, plus a few contemporary offerings. Call 801/586-7878. Late June through August.
- **Utah Arts Festival,** Salt Lake City. Exhibits by artists and craftsmen, plus music and dance performances. Call 801/322-2428. Late June.
- **Utah!,** St. George. A highly acclaimed live outdoor drama brings Utah's early Mormon history to life, with music, comedy, drama, and spectacular special

effects, including fireworks and a flood. Call 800/746-9882. Mid-June through mid-October.

- **Music in the Mountains,** Park City. A spectacular series of concerts, including appearances by the Utah Symphony, in an equally spectacular setting. Call 801/649-6100. June through September.

July

- **Speed Trials, Bonneville Salt Flats,** Wendover. Jet-cars and other super-fast mechanical wonders try to break speed records on the incredibly smooth salt flats—they're so flat that you can see the curvature of the earth. Call 801/977-4300 or 800/426-6862. Mid-summer through early fall.
- **Dinosaur Roundup Rodeo,** Vernal. A Wild West rodeo, with bull riding, calf roping, barrel racing, steer racing, a western dance, and parade. Call 801/789-1352 or 800/421-9635. Mid-July.
- **World Folkfest,** Springville. A community celebration that includes dance and music from around the world. Call 801/489-2700. Third week.
- **Pioneer Day,** statewide. Everything comes to a stop in Utah while residents celebrate the day in 1847 when Brigham Young led the first group of Mormon pioneers to the spot that would become Salt Lake City. July 24.
- **Utah Jazz and Blues Festival,** Snowbird. Big-name musicians make this one of Utah's premier music events. Call 801/355-2200 or 801/521-6040. Late July.
- **Festival of the American West,** Logan. A multimedia historical pageant is presented nightly; there's also a fair with traditional Old West food, music, craft demonstrations, and live entertainment, including medicine man shows and square dancing. Call 800/225-FEST. Late July through early August.

August

- **Railroader's Festival,** Golden Spike National Historic Site. Reenactments of the Golden Spike ceremony, uniting the nation by rail; plus a spike-driving contest, railroad handcar races and rides, and a buffalo chip throwing contest. Call 801/471-2209. Mid-August.
- **Utah Belly Dance Festival,** Salt Lake City. Middle Eastern dancers do their thing in Liberty Park. ☎ 801/486-7780. Third week of the month.

September

- **Oktoberfest,** Snowbird. A traditional Oktoberfest celebration with German music, food, and, of course, beer. Call 801/521-6040. September and October weekends.
- **Utah State Fair,** Salt Lake City. Live entertainment, a horse show, a rodeo, livestock judging, arts and crafts exhibits, and typical state fair fun. Call 801/538-FAIR. Early September.
- ✪ **Mountain Man Rendezvous.** Ogden. A gathering of mountain men at Fort Buenaventura State Park, with black powder shooting contests and other early 19th-century activities. Call 801/621-4808. Early September.
- **Southern Utah Folklife Festival,** Springdale. Pioneer life is highlighted with craft demonstrations, music, and food. Call 801/772-3757. First week of the month.
- **Greek Festival,** Salt Lake City. The music, dance, and food of Greece are featured, along with tours of the historic Holy Trinity Greek Orthodox Cathedral. Call 801/328-9681. Early September.
- **Brian Header,** Brian Head. NORBA-sanctioned mountainbike races, a trails course, and entertainment. Call 801/677-2029. Early September.
- **Moab Music Festival,** Moab. Live classical, jazz, bluegrass, and other types of music, presented in a beautiful red rock amphitheater and other locations. Call 801/259-8431. Mid-September.

- **Hole-in-the-Rock Jeep Jamboree,** Blanding. A variety of events for four-wheel-drive vehicles, including a day on the Hole-in-the-Rock Road, a trail used by pioneers in 1879. Call 800/574-4386. Late September.

October

- **World Senior Games,** St. George. An extremely popular Olympics-style competition for seniors, with a variety of athletic events. Call 801/674-0550. Mid-October.
- **Red Rock Gem and Mineral Show,** Moab. Rockhounders show off exotic rocks, gems, and minerals. Call 801/259-5904. Mid-October.
- **Canyonlands Fat Tire Festival,** Moab. Mountainbike guided tours, hill climbs, and related events. Call 801/259-8825. Late October through early November.
- **Buffalo Roundup,** Antelope Island State Park. Stop by the park and watch the annual buffalo roundup, conducted on horseback. Take binoculars and get a close-up view of the buffalo as they get their annual medical exams. The event also includes a dance and auction. Call 801/773-2941. Late October through early November.

November

- **Christmas Parade and Lighting of the Dinosaur Gardens,** Vernal. Life-size replicas of dinosaurs are illuminated for Christmas. Call 801/789-6932. Late November.
- **America's Cup Ski Races,** Park City. Sanctioned World Cup ski races and demonstrations. Call 801/649-8111. Late November.
- **Parade of Christmas Lights,** Lake Powell. Boats decorated for Christmas, led by the *Canyon King* paddle wheeler, are reflected in the waters of Lake Powell. Both spectators and participants are welcome. Call 801/684-3046. Late November or early December.
- **Ogden Christmas Parade and Christmas Village,** Ogden. A parade begins the Christmas season, when the municipal park is transformed into a Christmas village, with thousands of lights, music, and animated decorations. Call 801/629-8214. Late November through December.
- **Temple Square Christmas Lights,** Salt Lake City. A huge, spectacular display of Christmas lights decorates Temple Square. Call 801/240-1000. From the Friday after Thanksgiving to January 1.

December

- **Railroader's Film Festival and Winter Steam Demonstration,** Golden Spike National Historic Site. Showings of classic Hollywood railroad films, plus a steam engine demonstration. Call 801/471-2209. Late December.
- **First Night New Year's Eve Celebration,** Salt Lake City. This New Year's Eve family party brings downtown Salt Lake City alive with arts and crafts, live entertainment, storytelling, and numerous other family-oriented activities, culminating in a midnight fireworks display. Call 801/359-5118. December 31.

3 Health & Insurance

STAYING HEALTHY IN UTAH

Utah's extremes of climate—from burning desert to snow-covered mountains—can produce health problems if you're not prepared. If you haven't been to the desert before, it can be difficult to comprehend the heat, dryness, and intensity of the sun. If you're prone to dry skin, moisturizing lotion is a must; even if you're not, you may end up using it. Everyone needs to use a good quality sun block and wear a hat and sunglasses with full ultra-violet protection. Hikers and others planning to be outside will also need to carry water—at least a gallon per person, per day.

The other potential problem is elevation. Utah's mountains rise to over 13,500 feet—there's less oxygen and lower humidity when you're up that high. This creates a unique set of problems for short-term visitors. If you have heart or respiratory problems, consult your doctor before planning a trip to the mountains. If you're in generally good health, you don't need to take any special precautions, but it's advisable to ease into high elevations by changing altitude gradually. Don't fly in from sea level in the morning and plan to be hiking at 10,000-foot Cedar Breaks National Monument that afternoon. Spend a day or two at 4,000 or 5,000 feet elevation to let your body adjust. Also, get plenty of rest, avoid large meals, and drink plenty of nonalcoholic fluids, especially water.

State health officials have lately been warning outdoor enthusiasts to take precautions against the Hantavirus, a rare but often fatal respiratory disease, first recognized in 1993. About half of the country's 100-plus confirmed cases have been reported in the Four Corners states of Colorado, New Mexico, Arizona, and Utah. The disease is believed to be spread by the urine and droppings of deer mice and other rodents, and health officials recommend that campers avoid areas with signs of rodent droppings. Symptoms of Hantavirus are similar to flu, and lead to breathing difficulties and shock.

INSURANCE

Before starting out, check your medical insurance policy to make certain you're covered away from home. If you're not, you can purchase a special traveler's policy from your travel agent, insurance agent, or travel club. Traveler's policies are relatively inexpensive and can usually be purchased for the exact duration of your trip. Be sure to carry a medical insurance identification card or other proof of insurance with you at all times while you're traveling.

Travel insurance can also be purchased to cover accidents, lost luggage, and trip cancellation (an especially handy thing if you've prepaid a large chunk of your vacation expenses). Again, check with your travel agent, insurance agent, or travel club. Before you buy, though, check your homeowners' or renters' policy— off-premises theft and loss of your personal property may be covered there. And most credit and charge cards offer automatic flight insurance when you purchase your airline ticket with their card.

If you're planning to drive in Utah, be sure to carry proof of automobile liability insurance, and be certain that your policy includes protection from uninsured motorists. If you're renting a car, check your credit cards to see if any of them pick up the collision-damage waiver (CDW) when you rent with their card. Also check your personal auto policy to see if it covers the CDW before you rent. The CDW can run as much as $12 a day in addition to the basic rental charge.

4 Tips for Travelers with Special Needs

FOR TRAVELERS WITH DISABILITIES

Travelers with disabilities should find Utah a generally easy place to get around. Many parks have at least one wheelchair-accessible trail. Some historic buildings, however, are not wheelchair accessible; check before going.

If you're planning to visit Utah's national parks and monuments, you can get the National Park Service's **Golden Access Passport**, available at all the parks. This lifetime pass is issued to any U.S. citizen or permanent resident who is medically certified as disabled or blind. The pass permits free entry and gives a 50% discount on park service campgrounds and activities (not on those offered by private concessionaires).

The Utah information and referral line for people with disabilities is ☎ 800/333-8824. Mobility International USA, P.O. Box 10767, Eugene, OR 97440 (☎ and TDD 503/343-1284, fax 503/343-6812), is a national nonprofit member organization that provides travel information, referrals, and other services for travelers with disabilities.

Amtrak will, with 24 hours' notice, provide porter service, special seating, and a discount (☎ 800/USA-RAIL). If you're traveling with a companion, **Greyhound** will carry you both for a single fare (☎ 800/231-2222).

FOR GAY & LESBIAN TRAVELERS

The **Utah Stonewall Center,** a community center for gays and lesbians, is located at 770 S. 300 West in Salt Lake City (☎ 801/539-8800). The **Gay Help Line** (☎ 801/533-0927) provides referral and counseling services, and can also suggest nightspots and accommodations.

FOR SENIORS

Many Utah hotels and motels offer a senior citizen's discount, and more and more restaurants, attractions, and public transportation systems are now offering discounts.

You can save sightseeing dollars if you are 62 or over by picking up a **Golden Age Passport** from any national park, recreation area, or monument. This lifetime pass has a one-time fee of $10 and provides free admission to parks, plus a 50% savings on camping and recreation fees.

The **70+ Ski Club,** 104 Eastside Dr., Ballston Lake, NY 12019, provides its members with a list of ski areas that offer free or discounted skiing to seniors.

Membership in the following senior organizations offers a wide variety of travel benefits: The **American Association of Retired Persons (AARP),** 601 E. St. NW, Washington, DC 20049 (☎ 202/434-2277 or 800/424-3410), which also puts together organized tour packages at moderate rates though the AARP Travel Service; and the **National Council of Senior Citizens,** 925 15th St. NW, Washington, DC 20005 (☎ 202/347-8800).

FOR TRAVELERS WITH PETS

Many of us wouldn't dream of going on vacation without our pets. Under the right circumstances, it can be a wonderful experience for both you and your animals. Dogs and cats are accepted at many motels around the state, but not as universally in resorts and at the more expensive hotels. Throughout this book, we've tried to consistently note those lodgings that take pets. Some properties require you to pay a fee or damage deposit in advance, and most insist they be notified at check-in that you have a pet.

Be aware, however, that national parks and monuments and other federal lands administered by the National Park Service are not pet-friendly. Dogs are prohibited on all hiking trails, must always be leashed, and in some cases cannot be taken more than 100 feet from established roads. On the other hand, U.S. Forest Service, Bureau of Land Management areas, and practically all of Utah's state parks are pro-pet, allowing dogs on trails and just about everywhere except inside buildings. State parks require that dogs be leashed; regulations in national forests and BLM lands are generally looser.

Aside from regulations, though, you need to be concerned with your pet's well-being. Just as people need extra water in Utah's hot, dry climate, so do pets. And keep in mind that, particularly in southern Utah's red rock country, trails are rough, and jagged rocks can cut the pads on your dog's feet. It's good to check their feet frequently, and also to carry tweezers to remove cactus spines. Dogs, who usually spend most of their time sleeping, aren't used to 10-hour hikes up mountainsides, and more than one exhausted pooch has had to be carried back to camp by its owner.

One final note on pets: There is no punishment too severe for the human who leaves a dog or cat inside a closed car parked in the sun. The car heats up quicker that you'd think, so don't do it, even for a minute.

FOR STUDENTS

Be sure you have your student ID in your pocket, and ask about student discounts wherever you go. Joining **Hostelling International-American Youth Hostels,** Box 37613, Washington, DC 20013-7613 (☎ 202/783-6161), will give you access to economical accommodations almost anywhere you travel; it's also a great way to meet other traveling students. For $8, they'll send you a directory of all U.S. and Canadian hostels; the directory is free with HI-AYH membership.

5 Getting There

BY PLANE

Utah's only major airport is **Salt Lake City International** (☎ 801/575-2400); you can fly directly to Salt Lake City from many cities in the U.S. and Canada. Airlines serving the airport include **America West** (☎ 800/247-5692), **American** (☎ 800/433-7300), **Continental** (☎ 801/359-9800 or 800/525-0280), **Delta** (☎ 801/532-7123 or 800/221-1212), **Northwest** (☎ 800/225-2525), **Skywest/Delta** (☎ 800/453-9417), **TWA** (☎ 801/539-1111 or 800/221-2000), and **United** (☎ 800/241-6522). In-state flights connect Salt Lake City to several other Utah cities, including Cedar City, Moab, St. George, and Vernal. See the relevant sections in this book for additional information.

An alternative for visitors planning to go to southern Utah is to fly into **McCarran International Airport** in Las Vegas, Nevada (☎ 702/261-5743), which is only 120 miles southwest of St. George, Utah. Budget-conscious travelers should check airline and vehicle rental prices at both airports to see which will provide the better deal for their particular circumstances.

BY CAR

Utah is easy to reach by car, via I-80 from the west or east, I-70 from the east, I-15 and I-84 from the north, and I-15 from the southwest. Salt Lake City is 600 miles from Albuquerque, 500 miles from Denver, 430 miles from Las Vegas, and 650 miles from Phoenix. Keep in mind that there will be long distances between services approaching Utah from any direction, as well as within the state.

Before you set out on a road trip, you might want to join the **American Automobile Association (AAA)** (☎ 800/336-4357), which has hundreds of offices nationwide. Members receive excellent maps and emergency road service; they'll even help you plan an exact itinerary.

BY TRAIN

Amtrak has several routes through Utah. The *Desert Wind* runs from Chicago to Los Angeles, with stops in Salt Lake City and a few other Utah towns; and the

California Zephyr stops in several Utah towns, including Salt Lake City, on its run from Chicago to San Francisco. Amtrak's *Pioneer* runs from Chicago through Ogden, and on to Seattle, Washington. You can get a copy of Amtrak's National Timetable from any Amtrak station or your travel agent, or by contacting Amtrak, 400 N. Capitol St. NW, Washington, DC 20001 (☎ 800/USA-RAIL). Also ask for a brochure outlining prices, and be sure to ask about special family plans, tours, and other money-saving promotions Amtrak might be offering.

6 Getting Around

BY CAR

Driving yourself is the best way to get around Utah; in fact, it's the only way to get to many destinations. However, visitors who plan to drive their own cars to and around Utah will find that steep mountain roads can put a severe strain on their vehicles, particularly on the cooling and braking systems. Tires rated for mud and snow are needed in most areas in winter, and are required on roads leading to several major ski areas from November through March. Also keep in mind that Utah is a big state; it's a 5-hour drive from Salt Lake City to St. George, and it can easily take 6 or 7 hours to get from St. George to Moab.

Car Rentals   Car rentals are available in every sizable town and city in the state, and almost always at local airports. Widely represented agencies include **Avis** (☎ 800/831-2847), **Budget** (☎ 800/527-0700), **Dollar** (☎ 800/800-4000), **Hertz** (☎ 800/654-3131), **National** (☎ 800/227-7368), **Payless** (☎ 800/729-5377), and **Thrifty** (☎ 800/367-2277).

Driving Rules   Utah law requires all drivers to carry proof of insurance, as well as a valid drivers' license. Safety belts are required for drivers and all front-seat passengers; restraints are required for all children under eight, regardless of where they are sitting. Radar detectors are permitted. Utah law allows drivers to make a right turn at a red signal after coming to a complete stop, unless otherwise posted.

Maps   You can get an official state highway map at State Welcome Centers or by mail (see "Visitor Information," above). Otherwise, you can get maps from bookstores, gas stations, or from the American Automobile Association if you're a member (see "Getting There by Car," above). **State Welcome Centers** are located along I-15 near Brigham City, I-80 near Echo Junction, I-15 near St. George, I-70 near Thompson Springs, and at the Utah Field House of Natural History in Vernal.

Roadside Assistance   In case of an accident or road emergency, contact the state police. American Automobile Association members can get free emergency road service by calling **AAA's emergency number** (☎ 800/AAA-HELP). In Utah, AAA headquarters is at 560 E. 500 South (P.O. Box 1079), Salt Lake City, UT 84110 (☎ 801/364-5615 or 800/541-9902). AAA also has offices in Ogden (☎ 801/399-1116) and Orem (☎ 801/225-4801).

PACKAGE TOURS

Most visitors to Utah design their own tours, using either their own cars or rentals. However, those who prefer looking at the scenery rather than the road have several tour companies from which to choose. **Western Leisure of Salt Lake City** offers numerous tours, which you book through your travel agent. **Gray Line Motor Tours,** 553 W. 100 South, Salt Lake City, UT 84101 (☎ 801/521-7060 or 800/309-2352; fax 801/521-7086), offers several national park packages in the summer,

Utah Driving Distances & Times

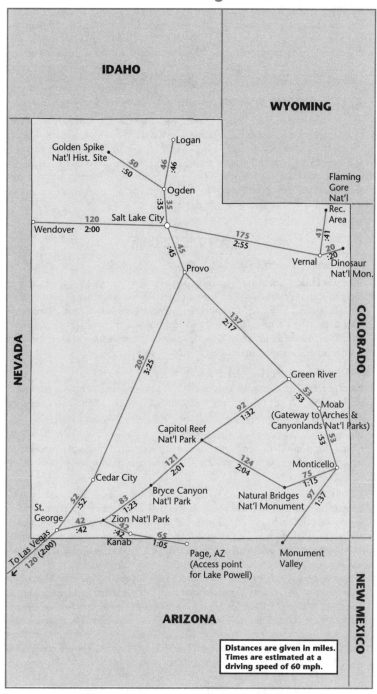

IDAHO

WYOMING

Golden Spike Nat'l Hist. Site

Logan

50
:50

46
:46

Flaming Gore Nat'l

Ogden

35
:35

Rec. Area

Wendover

120
2:00

Salt Lake City

175
2:55

41
:41

NEVADA

45
:45

Provo

Vernal

20
:20

Dinosaur Nat'l Mon.

COLORADO

137
2:17

205
3:25

Green River

53
:53

Moab
(Gateway to Arches & Canyonlands Nat'l Parks)

92
1:32

Capitol Reef Nat'l Park

124
2:04

53
:53

121
2:01

Monticello

Cedar City

75
1:15

52
:52

Bryce Canyon Nat'l Park

83
1:23

Natural Bridges Nat'l Monument

97
1:37

St. George

42
:42

Zion Nat'l Park

42
:42

Kanab

65
1:05

Monument Valley

To Las Vegas

120 (2:00)

Page, AZ
(Access point for Lake Powell)

NEW MEXICO

ARIZONA

Distances are given in miles. Times are estimated at a driving speed of 60 mph.

including a 3-day, 2-night trip to Zion and Bryce Canyon National Parks and Grand Canyon at about $450 single or $350 per person double occupancy. **Maupintour,** 1515 St. Andrews Dr., Lawrence, KS 66047 (☎ 913/843-1211 or 800/255-4266), one of the world's largest tour companies, offers tours to national parks and other destinations. A number of companies also offer specialized tours for outdoor recreation enthusiasts. See the "Active Vacation Planner," Chapter 5.

A RESERVATIONS SERVICE

An excellent compromise between doing your own thing and joining an organized tour is to work with **Utah Reservation Service,** 1173 S. 1100 East, Salt Lake City, UT 84105 (☎ 800/557-8824 or fax 719/591-7068). Tell the trip planners where you want to go, how long you want to stay, and how much you want to spend, and they will make lodging reservations for your entire trip. They can also take care of airline reservations and car rentals, and offer other trip planning assistance. The company can make immediate or advance reservations.

FAST FACTS: Utah

Area Code   The area code is **801** statewide.

Business Hours   Banks are typically open Monday through Thursday from 9am to 3pm, and on Friday from 9am to 6pm. Drive-up windows may be open later. In general, business hours are Monday through Friday from 9am to 5pm. Many stores are also open on Friday evening and Saturday; those in major shopping malls have Sunday-afternoon hours as well, and discount stores and supermarkets are often open later. Some supermarkets are open 24 hours a day.

Embassies/Consulates   See Chapter 4, "For Foreign Visitors."

Emergencies   In almost all parts of Utah, the number to dial for any emergency is 911; money is not required for emergency calls at pay phones. In a few rural areas, it will be necessary to dial "0" (zero) for an operator.

Holidays   In addition to the standard holidays, Pioneer Day, July 24, is a big holiday for many Utahns; many business and government offices close to celebrate the arrival of Brigham Young and the first wagon train of Mormon pioneers in the Salt Lake Valley.

Liquor Laws   The legal drinking age is 21. Utah's drinking laws are a bit odd, but you can buy alcoholic beverages almost everywhere in the state. Regarding package goods, you can buy 3.2% beer (see below if you're not sure what that means) and wine or malt coolers in supermarkets and convenience stores seven days a week; stronger beer, wine, and hard liquor is available only at state-owned liquor stores and package agencies, which are closed Sundays and state holidays.

Buying liquor, beer, or wine by the drink is a bit more complicated. Most of the better restaurants can serve alcoholic beverages with meals starting at noon. In most cases, you'll have to ask for a drink; they won't offer to serve you one. Some establishments are licensed as taverns, and can sell 3.2% beer only. There are also private clubs, which aren't really private: They're essentially bars, and may or may not be attached to restaurants. You have to be a member to enter, but you can go in as a guest of a member, or buy a two-week membership, usually for $5. Private clubs can serve beginning at 10am Monday through Saturday and at noon Sunday. Liquor by the drink cannot be sold after 1am Monday through Saturday or after midnight on Sunday. 3.2% beer, which is only sold in Utah, Oklahoma,

Colorado, and Kansas, does have less alcohol than beer sold elsewhere. According to the Budweiser people, 3.2% beer has about 4% alcohol by volume (which is equivalent to 3.2% alcohol by weight), while full-strength American beers have about 5% alcohol by volume.

Newspapers/Magazines   The state's two largest daily newspapers, both published in Salt Lake City, are the *Salt Lake City Tribune* and the *Deseret News*. Several other towns and regions have daily newspapers, and many smaller towns publish weeklies. You can get national newspapers such as *USA Today* and the *Wall Street Journal* on the streets of Salt Lake City and at major hotels, and you can find newspapers from other major U.S. cities at **Jeanie's Smoke Shop,** 156 S. State St., Salt Lake City (☎ 801/322-2817); and **Hayats,** 228 S. Main St., Salt Lake City (☎ 801/531-6531), which also stocks some international periodicals. The above shops also carry a wide selection of magazines, and many major bookstores also stock current magazines.

Police   Dial **911** almost everywhere, except in a few rural areas, where you should dial "0" (zero) for an operator.

Smoking   As of February 1, 1995, Utah is "smoke free." The Utah Indoor Clean Air Act prohibits smoking in any public building or office and in all enclosed places of public access. This includes restaurants but not private clubs, lounges, or taverns.

Taxes   A combination of state and local sales taxes, from 6% to 7%, is added to your bill in all areas of Utah except Indian reservations. Local lodging taxes usually add an additional 3% or 4%.

Time Zone   Utah is on mountain time, 1 hour ahead of the West Coast and 2 hours behind the East Coast. Daylight saving time is in effect from April to October.

Useful Telephone Numbers   For **road conditions** in Salt Lake City, call 801/964-6000 in Salt Lake City; for the rest of the state, call 800/492-2400. The **poison control hotline** is 800/456-7707.

Weather   For current weather information, call 801/524-5133.

4 For Foreign Visitors

American fads and fashions have spread across other parts of the world to such a degree that the United States may seem like familiar territory before your arrival. But there are still many peculiarities and uniquely American situations any foreign visitor will encounter and may find confusing or perplexing. This chapter will provide some specifics about getting to the United States as economically and effortlessly as possible, plus some helpful information about how things are done in Utah—from receiving mail to making a local or long-distance telephone call.

1 Preparing for Your Trip

ENTRY REQUIREMENTS

Document Regulations   Canadian citizens may enter the United States without visas; they need only proof of residence. Citizens of the United Kingdom, New Zealand, Japan, and most western European countries traveling on valid passports may not need a visa for fewer than 90 days of holiday or business travel to the United States, providing that they hold a round-trip or return ticket and enter the United States on an airline or cruise line that participates in the visa-waiver program. (Note that citizens of these visa-exempt countries who first enter the United States may then visit Mexico, Canada, Bermuda, and/or the Caribbean islands and then reenter the United States, by any mode of transportation, without needing a visa. Further information is available from any U.S. embassy or consulate.)

Citizens of countries other than those stipulated above must have two documents: a valid passport with an expiration date at least six months later than the scheduled end of the visit to the United States, and a tourist visa, available without charge from the nearest U.S. consulate.

To obtain a visa, you must submit a completed application form (either in person or by mail) with a $1^1/_2$-inch square photo and provide evidence of a permanent residence abroad. Usually you can obtain a visa within 24 hours, but it may take longer during the summer rush from June to August. If you cannot go in person, contact the nearest U.S. embassy or consulate for directions on applying by mail. Your travel agent or airline office may also be able to provide you with visa applications and instructions. The U.S. consulate or embassy that issues your visa will determine whether you will be issued a multiple- or single-entry visa, and any restrictions regarding the length of your stay.

Medical Requirements   No inoculations are needed to enter the United States unless you are coming from, or have stopped over in, areas known to be suffering from epidemics, particularly cholera or yellow fever.

If you have a disease requiring treatment with medications containing narcotics or drugs requiring a syringe, carry a valid signed prescription from your physician to allay any suspicions that you are smuggling drugs.

Customs Requirements   Every adult visitor may bring into the United States free of duty: 1 liter of wine or hard liquor; 200 cigarettes or 100 cigars (but no cigars from Cuba) or 3 pounds of smoking tobacco; and $100 worth of gifts. These exemptions are offered to travelers who spend at least 72 hours in the United States and who have not claimed them within the preceding six months. It is altogether forbidden to bring into the country foodstuffs (particularly cheese, fruit, cooked meats, and canned goods) and plants (vegetables, seeds, tropical plants, and so on). Foreign tourists may bring in or take out up to $10,000 in U.S. or foreign currency with no formalities; larger sums must be declared to Customs on entering or leaving.

INSURANCE

There is no national health system in the United States. Because the cost of medical care can be extremely high, it is recommended that every traveler obtain health coverage before setting out.

You may want to buy a comprehensive travel policy that covers sickness or injury costs (medical, surgical, and hospital); loss or theft of your baggage; trip-cancellation costs; guarantee of bail in case you are arrested; costs of accident, repatriation, or death. Such packages (for example, "Europe Assistance" in Europe) are sold by automobile clubs at attractive rates, as well as by insurance companies and travel agencies.

MONEY

Currency   The U.S. monetary system has a decimal base: one American dollar ($1) = 100 cents (100¢). Dollar bills commonly come in $1 ("a buck"), $5, $10, $20, $50, and $100 denominations (the last two are not welcome when paying for small purchases and are often not accepted in taxis or at subway ticket booths). There are also $2 bills (seldom encountered). There are six denominations of coins: 1¢ (1 cent or "penny"), 5¢ (five cents or "a nickel"), 10¢ (ten cents or "a dime"), 25¢ (twenty-five cents or "a quarter"), 50¢ (fifty cents or "a half dollar"), and the rare $1 piece.

Exchange   The "foreign-exchange bureaus" so common in Europe are rare even at some airports in the United States, and nonexistent outside major cities. Try to avoid having to change foreign money, or traveler's checks denominated in other than U.S. dollars, at a small-town bank, or even a branch in a big city. Although some banks will exchange currency, your best choice is Thomas Cook Currency Services, Inc., which you'll find in the major international airports on the coasts. The company has been in business since 1841 and offers a wide range of services. They sell foreign and U.S. traveler's checks, drafts, and wire transfers; they also do check collections (including Eurochecks). Their rates are competitive and their service is excellent. They maintain several offices in New York City: Fifth Avenue office (☎ 212/757-6915), JFK Airport International Arrivals Terminal (☎ 718/656-8444), and La Guardia Airport in the Delta terminal (☎ 718/533-0784).

See "Currency Exchange" under the "Fast Facts: For Foreign Visitors" section later in this chapter for exchange services in Salt Lake City and Las Vegas, Nev.

Traveler's checks   Traveler's Checks denominated in U.S. dollars are readily accepted at most hotels, motels, restaurants, and large stores; however, the best place to change traveler's checks is at a bank. Do not bring traveler's checks denominated in other currencies.

Credit cards   The method of payment most widely used is the credit card: Visa (BarclayCard in Britain), MasterCard (EuroCard in Europe, Access in Britain, Chargex in Canada), American Express, Diners Club, Discover, and Carte Blanche. You can save yourself trouble by using "plastic" rather than cash or traveler's checks in 95% of all hotels, motels, restaurants, and retail stores. A credit card can also serve as a deposit for renting a car, as proof of identity, or as a "cash card," enabling you to draw money from automatic-teller machines (ATMs) that accept them.

SAFETY

Although Utah has not seen the amount of crime against tourists that occurs in some U.S. cities, crime is on the increase, and even Utah cities tend to be less safe than those in Europe or Japan. This is particularly true in some sections of Salt Lake City. It is wise to ask local visitor information centers if you're in doubt about which neighborhoods are safe. Avoid deserted areas, including city parks, especially at night. Generally speaking, you can feel safe in areas where there are many people and open establishments.

Be especially careful in national parks and other popular public lands. Recent years have seen an increase in crime in the parks, particularly thefts from campsites and vehicles.

Remember also that hotels are open to the public, and in a large hotel, security may not be able to screen everyone entering. Always lock your room door—don't assume that once inside your hotel you are automatically safe and no longer need be aware of your surroundings.

Driving   Safety while driving is particularly important. Question your rental agency about personal safety, or ask for a brochure of traveler safety tips when you pick up your car. Obtain written directions, or a map with the route marked in red, from the agency showing how to get to your destination.

Although Utah does not have a lot of attacks against motorists, it is not unheard of. If you drive off a highway into a doubtful neighborhood, leave the area as quickly as possible. If you have an accident, even on the highway, stay in your car with the doors locked until you assess the situation or until the police arrive. If you are bumped from behind on the street or are involved in a minor accident with no injuries and the situation appears to be suspicious, motion to the other driver to follow you. Never get out of your car in such situations, but drive to the nearest police station, well-lighted service station, or all-night store.

If you see someone on the road who indicates a need for help, do not stop. Take note of the location, drive on to a well-lighted area, and telephone the police by dialing 911, or "0" (zero, not the letter "O").

Park in well-lighted well-traveled areas if possible. Always keep your car doors locked, whether attended or unattended. Look around you before you get out of your car, and never leave any packages or valuables in sight. If someone attempts to rob you or steal your car, do not try to resist the thief or carjacker, and report the incident to police immediately.

You may wish to contact the **Utah Travel Council** (☎ 800/200-1160) to discuss your plans and ask their advice.

2 Getting to the U.S.

Travelers from overseas can take advantage of the APEX (Advance Purchase Excursion) fares offered by all the major U.S. and European carriers. Aside from these, attractive values are offered by Icelandair on flights from Luxembourg to New York and by Virgin Atlantic Airways from London to New York/Newark.

Airlines offering international flights into Salt Lake City include **American** (☎ 800/433-7300; 0181/572-5555 in London), **Continental** (☎ 801/359-9800; 4412/9377-6464 in London), **TWA** (☎ 801/539-1111 or 800/221-2000; 0181/990-9900 in London). At press time, **British Airways** (☎ 081/897-4000 in London) is not yet offering direct flights from London to Salt Lake City, but Salt Lake airport officials are aggressively seeking an airline that would provide direct flights between Salt Lake City and London or other major European cities. In the meantime, travelers from the United Kingdom can take British Airways flights to such cities as Philadelphia and Chicago and make connecting flights with major U.S. airlines.

Visitors arriving by air, no matter what the port of entry, should cultivate patience and resignation before setting foot on U.S. soil. Getting through Immigration control may take as long as two hours on some days, especially summer weekends. Add the time it takes to clear Customs and you'll see that you should allow extra time for delays when planning connections between international and domestic flights— an average of two to three hours at least.

In contrast, travelers arriving by car or by rail from Canada will find border-crossing formalities streamlined to the vanishing point. And air travelers from Canada, Bermuda, and some places in the Caribbean can sometimes go through Customs and Immigration at the point of departure, which is much quicker and less painful.

3 Getting Around the U.S.

By Plane   Some large American airlines (for example TWA, American Airlines, Northwest, United, and Delta) offer travelers on their transatlantic or transpacific flights special discount tickets under the name **Visit USA,** allowing travel between various U.S. destinations at minimum rates. These tickets are not on sale in the United States, and must, therefore, be purchased before you leave your foreign point of departure. This program is the best, easiest, and fastest way to see the United States at low cost. You should obtain information well in advance from your travel agent or the office of the airline concerned, since the conditions attached to these discount tickets can be changed without advance notice.

By Rail   **Amtrak** connects Salt Lake City and Ogden to both the East and West coasts. International visitors can buy a **USA Railpass,** good for 15 or 30 days of unlimited travel on Amtrak, available through many foreign travel agents. With a foreign passport, you can also buy passes at some Amtrak offices in the United States, including those in San Francisco, Los Angeles, Chicago, New York, Miami, Boston, and Washington, D.C.

Amtrak (☎ 800/USA-RAIL) also frequently has low-cost passes available for anyone, covering certain regions of the country. Reservations are generally required for train travel and should be made for each part of your trip as early as possible.

You should be aware of the limitations of long-distance rail travel in the United States. With a few notable exceptions, service is rarely up to European standards and routes are limited. Fares (especially with the inclusion of meals) are seldom cheaper than discount airfares.

By Bus   The cheapest form of public transportation in the United States is often by bus. **Greyhound** (☎ 800/231-7222), the nationwide bus line, offers an **Ameripass** for various durations of unlimited travel; call for rates. Since bus travel in the United States can be slow and routes are limited, this option is not for everyone.

By Car   Because much of Utah is rural, with limited or nonexistent public transportation, the best way to explore the state is by car. Many car rental companies (see city listings) offer unlimited-mileage weekly specials that can be quite affordable.

FAST FACTS: For the Foreign Traveler

Automobile Organizations   Auto clubs will supply maps, suggested routes, guidebooks, accident and bail-bond insurance, and emergency road service. The major auto club in the United States is the **American Automobile Association (AAA),** with close to 1,000 offices nationwide, including offices in Salt Lake City, Ogden, and Orem. Members of some foreign auto clubs have reciprocal arrangements with the AAA and enjoy its services at no charge. If you belong to an auto club, inquire about AAA reciprocity before you leave home. The AAA can provide you with an **International Driving Permit** validating your foreign license. You may be able to join AAA even if you are not a member of a reciprocal club. To inquire, call 800/336-4357. In addition, some automobile-rental agencies now provide these services; ask about their availability when you rent your car.

Automobile Rentals   To rent a car, you need a major credit card. A valid driver's license is required, and you usually need to be at least 25 years old. Some companies do rent to younger people but add a daily surcharge. Be sure to return your car with the same amount of gas you started out with; rental companies charge excessive prices for gasoline. See "Getting Around" in Chapter 3.

Business Hours   Banks are usually open weekdays from 9am to 3 or 4pm, often until 6pm Friday, and sometimes on Saturday. There's 24-hour access to the automatic-teller machines (ATMs) at most banks, plus in shopping centers and other outlets.

Generally, business offices are open weekdays from 9am to 5pm. Stores are open six days a week, with some open on Sunday, too; department stores usually stay open until 9pm at least one day a week. Discount stores and supermarkets are often open later than other stores, and some supermarkets are open 24 hours a day.

Climate   See "When to Go" in Chapter 3.

Currency   See "Money" in "Preparing for Your Trip," above.

Currency Exchange   The **American Express Travel Service Office,** 175 S. West Temple (☎ 801/328-9733), will exchange foreign currency and handle U.S. and foreign traveler's checks, money transfers, and all American Express card member services. **First Security Bank of Utah,** International Dept., 341 E. 100 South, 1st Floor (☎ 801/246-5629), will exchange foreign currency and handle U.S. and foreign traveler's checks and money transfers. **Zions First National Bank,** 1 S. Main St. (☎ 801/974-8800) carries most major currencies, and has a branch at Salt Lake City International Airport Terminal 1.

Utah visitors flying into Las Vegas, Nev., will find a currency exchange booth operated by Travelex at McCarran International Airport.

Drinking Laws   See "Liquor Laws" in Chapter 3.

Electricity   The United States uses 110-120 volts, 60 cycles, compared to 220-240 volts, 50 cycles, as in most of Europe. In addition to a 100-volt converter, small appliances of non-American manufacture, such as hair dryers or shavers, will require a plug adapter, with two flat, parallel pins.

Embassies/Consulates   All embassies are located in the nation's capital, Washington, D.C.; some consulates are located in major cities, and most nations have a mission to the United Nations in New York City. Foreign visitors can obtain telephone numbers for their embassies and consulates by calling "Information" in Washington, D.C. (☎ 202/555-1212). The following countries have consulates in Salt Lake City: **Finland,** 79 S. Main St. (☎ 801/246-4259); **Italy,** 1784 W. 9580 South, **South Jordan** (☎ 801/254-7500); Mexico, 230 S. 500 East (☎ 801/521-8502); **France,** 175 E. 400 South (☎ 801/524-1000); and **Switzerland,** 1455 S. 1100 East (☎ 801/487-0450).

Emergencies   Call **911** or dial "0" (zero, not the letter "O") to report a fire, call police, or get an ambulance.

Gasoline (Petrol)   One U.S. gallon equals 3.75 liters, while 1.2 U.S. gallons equals 1 Imperial gallon. You'll notice there are several grades (and price levels) of gasoline available at most gas stations, and that their names change from company to company. Unleaded gasoline with the highest octane is the most expensive, but most rental cars will run fine with the least expensive "regular" unleaded.

Holidays   On the following legal U.S. national holidays, banks, government offices, post offices, and some government-run attractions are closed: January 1 (New Year's Day), third Monday in January (Martin Luther King, Jr. Day), third Monday in February (President's Day), last Monday in May (Memorial Day), July 4 (Independence Day), first Monday in September (Labor Day), second Monday in October (Columbus Day), November 11 (Veterans' Day/Armistice Day), fourth Thursday in November (Thanksgiving Day), and December 25 (Christmas). The Tuesday following the first Monday in November is Election Day and is a legal holiday in presidential-election years.

Stores and some restaurants often close only for New Year's Day, Easter, and Christmas.

Language   Major hotels sometimes have multilingual employees. You should inquire when you book as to whether they can supply a translator.

Legal Aid   The foreign tourist, unless positively identified as a member of organized crime or a drug ring, will probably never become involved with the American legal system. If you are stopped for a minor infraction, such as speeding or some other traffic violation, never attempt to pay the fine directly to a police officer; you may be arrested on the much more serious charge of attempted bribery. Pay fines by mail or directly to the clerk of the court. If you are accused of a more serious offense, it's wise to say and do nothing before consulting a lawyer. Under U.S. law, an arrested person is allowed one telephone call to a party of his or her choice; call your embassy or consulate.

Mail   If you want your mail to follow you on your vacation and you aren't sure of your address, your mail can be sent to you, in your name, c/o General Delivery at the main post office of the city or region where you expect to be. The addressee must pick it up in person and produce proof of identity (driver's license, passport, etc.).

Mailboxes   Mailboxes are blue with a red-and-white stripe and carry the inscription "U.S. Mail." If your mail is addressed to a U.S. destination, don't forget to add the five-figure postal code, or ZIP Code, after the two-letter abbreviation of the state to which the mail is addressed (CA for California, UT for Utah, FL for Florida, NY for New York, and so on).

Newspapers/Magazines   National newspapers generally available in Utah include the *New York Times, USA Today,* and the *Wall Street Journal.* National news magazines include *Newsweek, Time,* and *U.S. News & World Report.* The state's major daily newspapers are the *Salt Lake City Tribune* and the *Deseret News,* which is owned by the LDS Church.

Post   See "Mail," above.

Radio and Television   Six coast-to-coast networks—ABC, CBS, NBC, PBS (Public Broadcasting Service), Fox, and CNN (Cable Network News)—play a major part in American life. In Utah, television viewers usually have a choice of at least a dozen channels via cable or satellite, although some of the major Salt Lake City hotels offer only five or six. PBS and the cable channel Arts and Entertainment (A&E) broadcast a number of British programs. You'll also find a wide choice of local radio stations, each broadcasting particular kinds of talk shows and/or music—classical, country, jazz, pop—punctuated by news broadcasts and frequent commercials.

Safety   See "Safety" in "Preparing for Your Trip," above.

Taxes   In the United States, there is no VAT (value-added tax) or other indirect tax at a national level. Every state, as well as each city, has the right to levy its own local tax on all purchases, including hotel and restaurant checks, airline tickets, and so on. Sales taxes in Utah vary, but usually total about 6%. An exception is the tax on lodging, which often runs to 10%.

Telephone, Fax & Telegraph   The telephone system in the United States is run by private corporations, so rates, especially for long-distance service, can vary widely even on calls made from public telephones. Local calls in the United States usually cost 25¢ from pay telephones, but some of the more expensive hotels charge 50¢ to 75¢.

Most long-distance and international calls can be dialed directly from any phone. For calls to Canada and other parts of the United States, dial 1 followed by the area code and the seven-digit number. For international calls, dial 011 followed by the country code, city code, and the telephone number of the person you wish to call.

Generally, hotel fees on charged-to-your-room long-distance calls are astronomical. You can save money by calling collect, charging to a credit card, or using a public pay telephone, which you will find clearly marked in most public buildings and private establishments as well as on the street. Outside metropolitan areas, public telephones are more difficult to find; stores and gas stations are your best bet.

For **reversed-charge** or **collect calls,** and for **person-to-person** calls, dial "0" (zero, not the letter "O") followed by the area code and number you want; an operator will then come on the line, and you should specify that you are calling collect, or person-to-person, or both. If your operator-assisted call is international, ask for the overseas operator.

For local **directory assistance** ("information"), dial 1-411; for **long-distance information,** dial 1, then the appropriate area code and 555-1212.

Fax facilities are readily available in hotels, and 24-hour service is available at numerous copy centers, such as Kinko's in larger cities.

Like the telephone system, **telegraph** services are provided by private corporations such as ITT, MCI, and, above all, **Western Union.** You can bring your telegram in to the nearest Western Union office (there are hundreds across the country), or dictate it over the phone (☎ 800/325-6000). You can also telegraph money, or have it telegraphed to you, very quickly over the Western Union system.

Time   The United States is divided into four **time zones** (six, if Alaska and Hawaii are included). From east to west, these are: eastern standard time (EST), central standard time (CST), mountain standard time (MST), Pacific standard time (PST), Alaska standard time (AST), and Hawaii standard time (HST). Always keep time zones in mind if you are traveling (or even telephoning) long distances in the United States. For example, noon in New York City (EST) is 11am in Chicago (CST), 10am in Salt Lake City (MST), 9am in Los Angeles (PST), 8am in Anchorage (AST), and 7am in Honolulu (HST).

Daylight saving time (DST) is in effect in Utah and most of the country, from the first Sunday in April through the last Saturday in October (actually, the change is made at 2am on Sunday). Daylight saving time moves the clock one hour ahead of standard time. Note that Arizona (except for the Navajo nation), Hawaii, part of Indiana, and Puerto Rico do not observe DST.

Tipping   This is part of the American way of life, based on the idea that you should expect to pay for any special service you receive (service personnel are usually paid low wages and therefore depend on tips for most of their income). Here are some rules of thumb:

In **hotels,** tip bellhops 50¢ to $1 per bag. Some people (but not all) believe a tip of $1 per night is appropriate for hotel maid service if you are staying more than a night or two. Tip the doorman or concierge only if he or she has performed some specific service for you (for example, calling a cab or obtaining difficult-to-get theater tickets).

In **restaurants, bars, and nightclubs,** tip service staff 15% to 20% of the check, tip bartenders 10% to 15%, tip checkroom attendants $1 per garment, and tip valet-parking attendants $1 per vehicle. Tip the doorman only if he has served you in some special way (such as calling a cab). Tipping is not expected in cafeterias and fast-food restaurants.

As for other service personnel, tip **redcaps** at airports or railroad stations at least 50¢ per bag ($2 to $3 if you have a lot of luggage) and tip **cab drivers** 15% of the fare. **Hairdressers and barbers** usually receive a 15% to 20% tip. Tipping **gas-station attendants** and **ushers** in cinemas, movies, and theaters is not expected.

Toilets   Foreign visitors often complain that public toilets are hard to find in most U.S. cities. There are few on the streets, but you can usually find a clean one in a visitor information center, shopping mall, restaurant, hotel, museum, department or discount store, or service station (although service station facilities often leave much to be desired). Note, however, a growing practice in some restaurants of displaying a sign: TOILETS ARE FOR PATRONS ONLY. You can just ignore this sign or, better yet, avoid arguments by paying for a cup of coffee or soft drink, which will qualify you as a patron.

5

The Active Vacation Planner

Utah is one big outdoor adventure, with millions of acres of public lands where you can cast for trout or herd cattle, go rock climbing or four-wheeling, sail or ski—whatever your pleasure. Here you'll find five spectacular national parks, six national monuments, two national recreation areas, one national historic site, seven national forests, some 22 million acres administered by the federal Bureau of Land Management, and 45 state parks. But who's counting? It's enough to say that almost 80% of Utah's 85,000 square miles are yours to enjoy.

If you're a seasoned active traveler, you might want to skip section 1; but it should be a good primer for those of you who are new to this kind of travel or haven't been to Utah before. Then we've included some up-to-date information on visiting Utah's five national parks. After that, we've listed the activities you can pursue in Utah, from A to Z. Find your favorite activity, and we'll point you to the best places in the state to pursue your interest, or give you the general information you need to get started. You'll find more details in the appropriate regional chapters. Have fun!

1 Preparing for Your Active Vacation

WHAT TO PACK—AND WHAT TO RENT

Planning for a trip into the great outdoors immediately brings to mind those cartoons of vacationers loaded down with equipment, surrounded by golf clubs, skis, cameras, tents, canoes, bikes, and those wonderful Coleman lanterns and coolers that are fixtures of garages and basements across America. If this is your mode of travel, try to keep the heaviest items between the axles and as close to the floor of your vehicle as possible; this helps improve handling, especially in today's lighter cars. If you have a bike rack on the rear bumper, make sure the bike tires are far from the exhaust pipe; an owner of one bike shop told us he does a good business replacing exhaust-cooked mountainbike tires. Those with roof racks will want to measure the total height of their packed cars before leaving home. Underground parking garages often have less than seven feet of clearance.

One alternative to carrying all that stuff is to rent it. Many sporting goods shops in Utah rent camping equipment, virtually all ski areas and popular mountainbike areas offer rentals, and major boating centers such as Lake Powell and Lake Flaming Gorge rent boats. You'll find many rental sources listed throughout this book. There's a complete rental department at **Recreational Equipment Inc.,** better known as REI, 3285 E. 3300 South in Salt Lake City (☎ 801/486-2100).

In packing for your trip, you'll want to be prepared for all your favorite activities, of course, but also keep in mind that this is a land of extremes, with an often unforgiving climate and terrain. Those planning to hike or bike should take more drinking water containers than they think they'll need—experts recommend at least one gallon of water per person per day on the trail—as well as good-quality sunblock with a high SPF, hats and other protective clothing, and sunglasses with ultraviolet protection. Summer visitors will want to carry rain gear for the typical afternoon thunderstorms, and jackets or sweaters for cool evenings. Winter visitors will not only want warm parkas and hats, but lighter clothing as well—the bright sun at midday, even in the mountains, can make it feel like June.

DOING IT YOURSELF VS. USING AN OUTFITTER

Except for those instances where safety or skill is a factor, we prefer the do-it-yourself vacation route, especially in Utah, which is really a do-it-yourself kind of state. You'll have no trouble finding detailed topographic maps—essential for wilderness trips—and whatever equipment and supplies you need will likely be readily available. In addition, we found that—despite the well-publicized cuts in budgets and work force in national parks, recreation areas, and forests—every single ranger we encountered was more than willing to take the time to help visitors plan their backcountry trips. And many sporting goods shops are staffed by area residents who know their locales and activities well, and are very willing to help the would-be adventurer. In almost all cases, if you ask, there will be someone willing and able to help you make the most of your trip.

However, some activities require an outfitter or adventure travel operator, such as cattle driving. Others, such as rafting or four-wheeling, require equipment you'd have to buy or rent if you were to go on your own; besides, an outfitter might be able to take you somewhere or help you do something you couldn't do yourself. And some travelers just like the cameraderie of a group of like-minded adventurers; others don't want to deal with making all the arrangements on their own. And a professional is a must if you're attempting a dangerous sport, like rock climbing, or trying something new; then it's best to go with someone who knows the ropes.

For those who want to go with an outfitter or adventure travel operator, we've listed below some of the most respected and reliable companies operating in Utah. Most specialize in small groups and have trips for various levels of ability and physical condition. They also offer trips in a range of price categories, ranging from basic to luxurious, and of varying length.

American Wilderness Experience, P.O. Box 1486, Boulder, CO 80306 (☎ 303/444-2622 or 800/444-0099; fax 303/444-3999), offers mountain biking, hiking, horseback riding, cattle driving, and rafting excursions throughout the West, including numerous multiday trips in Utah.

Backcountry Bicycle Tours, P.O. Box 4029, Bozeman, MT 59772 (☎ 406/586-3556), provides guided multi-day mountainbike tours in the Bryce Canyon and Zion National Parks areas.

Backroads, 1516 Fifth St., Berkeley, CA 94710-1740 (☎ 800/GO-Active or 510/527-1555; fax 510/527-1444; E-mail: goactive@backroads.com), offers multiday guided hiking and/or biking (both road and mountainbike) trips to southern Utah's national parks and the Moab area, with both camping and historic inn accommodations.

Roads Less Traveled, P.O. Box 8187, Longmont, CO 80501 ☎ 303/678-8750), offers guided backcountry hiking and biking trips throughout the mountain states, including Utah.

STAYING SAFE & HEALTHY IN THE OUTDOORS

The wide-open spaces and rugged landscape that make Utah such a beautiful place to explore can also be hazardous to your health, especially if you're not used to the extreme climate; see "Health & Insurance" in Chapter 3 for details on dealing with desert climes and high altitudes. Since the isolation of many of the areas you'll seek out means there may be no one there to help in an emergency, the answer is to be prepared, like any good Boy Scout. See "What to Pack—and What to Rent," above, for tips on what to bring to protect yourself from Utah's blazing sun. Also, be sure to carry a basic first aid kit. Most importantly, check with park offices, park rangers, and other local outdoor specialists about current conditions before heading out.

OUTDOOR ETIQUETTE

Many of the wonderful outdoor areas you'll be exploring in Utah are quite isolated; although you're probably not the first human being to set foot there, you may feel like you are. Not too long ago, the rule of thumb was to "leave only footprints;" these days, we're trying to not do even that. It's relatively easy to be a good outdoor citizen—it's mostly common sense. Pack out all trash, stay on established trails, be especially careful to not pollute water, and, in general, do your best to have as little impact on the environment as possible. Some hikers even go further, carrying a small trash bag to pick up what others may have left.

2 Visiting Utah's National Parks

For many people, including us, the best part of a Utah vacation is exploring the state's five national parks. Unfortunately, these beautiful national treasures have become too popular; they're being overrun with visitors at a time when the federal government is cutting budgets, making it difficult for the parks to cope with their own success.

To get the most from your national park visit, try to go in the off-season. The parks are busiest in the summer, when most children are out of school, so try to visit at almost any other time. Fall is usually the best season. Spring is okay, but it can be windy and there may be snow in higher elevations. Winter can be delightful if you don't mind snow and cold. If you have to travel in summer, be patient. Allow extra time for traffic jams and standing in lines, and try to hike some of the longer and lesser-used trails. Rangers will be able to tell you which trails are best for getting away from the crowds.

Finally, a word about costs. National park admission fees listed in this book were current at press time; however, officials at every park told us that they expected increases, but couldn't guess as to what they would be. As we write this, American parks are one of the biggest travel bargains in the world, and we believe they still will be, even if prices double. So, if cost is a major concern for you, check before you go.

One way to save money if you'll be visiting a number of national parks and monuments within a year is to buy a **Golden Eagle Pass,** $25 at press time, which allows the bearer, plus everyone in his or her car, free admission. Camping fees are not included. The **Golden Age Passport,** for those 62 and older, has a one-time fee of $10 and provides free admission to parks plus a 50% savings on camping fees. And the **Golden Access Passport,** free for U.S. citizens who are permanently disabled under federal law, allows free access to parks and 50% off on camping fees. Passes are available at the parks.

3 Outdoor Activities A to Z

For a state that's largely desert, Utah certainly has a lot of lakes and reservoirs, from huge Lake Powell in the south to Flaming Gorge Lake in the north, and numerous reservoirs in between. We highly recommend both lakes, which are administered as national recreation areas and have complete marinas with boat rentals. Also, don't forget the lesser-known state parks, such as Jordanelle near Park City or Quail Creek—with the state's warmest water—near St. George. One of our favorite lakes is picturesque but chilly Strawberry Reservoir, southeast of Park City in the Uinta National Forest. For brochures on boating opportunities in Utah's state parks as well as information on state boating laws, contact the **Utah Division of Parks and Recreation** (☎ 801/538-7220).

CAMPING

Utah is a perfect place to camp; in fact, in some destinations, such as Canyonlands National Park, it's practically mandatory. Just about every community of any size in the state has at least one commercial campground, and several have more campgrounds than motels. Campsites are available at all the national parks and national recreation areas, but they're often crowded in the summer. However, those who can stand being without hot showers for a day or so can often find very reasonable or free campsites just outside the national parks, in national forests or Bureau of Land Management lands. Another good bet are Utah's state parks; among those with the best campgrounds are Kodachrome, just outside Bryce National Park; Coral Pink Sand Dunes, just west of Kanab; and Snow Canyon, near St. George.

CATTLE DRIVES

Opportunities abound in the western states for you to play cowboy on cattle drives that last from a day to a week or more. You actually take part in the riding and roping, just like Billy Crystal in *City Slickers.* You'll certainly get a feel for what it was like to be on a cattle drive 100 years ago, but the conditions are generally a lot more comfortable than what "real" cowboys experienced. The food will be a lot better, that's for sure. Each cattle drive is different, though, so you'll want to ask very specific questions about food, sleeping arrangements, and other conditions before plunking down your money. It's also a good idea to book your trip as early as possible. **American Wilderness Experience,** P.O. Box 1486, Boulder, CO 80306 (☎ 303/444-2622 or 800/444-0099; fax 303/444-3999) can help you plan your Utah cattle drive adventure.

FISHING

Utah has over 1,000 lakes and countless streams and rivers, with species that include rainbow, cutthroat, Mackinaw, and brown trout, plus striped bass, crappie, bluegill, walleye, and whitefish. All the lakes discussed in "Boating," above, are prime fishing spots, especially Lake Flaming Gorge. Strawberry Reservoir is Utah's premier trout fishery—in fact, it's one of the best in the West. Fly fishing is especially popular in the Park City area and in the streams of the Cache National Forest above Ogden. Contact the **Utah Division of Wildlife Resources,** 1596 W. North Temple, Salt Lake City, UT 84116 (☎ 801/538-4700) for a copy of the current *Utah Fishing Proclamation.*

Life on the Open Road:
Planning an RV or Tenting Vacation to Utah

One of the best ways to explore Utah, especially in the warm months, is in an RV—a motor home, truck camper, or camper trailer—or a tent, if you don't mind roughing it a bit more. If you own an RV, our advice is to have the mechanical systems checked out thoroughly, keeping in mind that there are some extremely steep grades in Utah; once that's done, pack up and go. If you don't have an RV or a tent, we suggest that you consider renting one for your Utah trip.

Why Camp?   One advantage to this type of travel is that many of the places you'll want to go, such as Canyonlands National Park, don't have any lodging. If you can't accommodate yourself, you'll end up sleeping 30 or 40 miles away and missing those spectacular sunrises and sunsets, and that inexplicable feeling of contentment that comes from living the experience rather than just visiting it. If you have special dietary requirements, you won't have to worry about trying to find a restaurant that can meet your needs—the options are very limited in much of the state. You'll be able to cook for yourself, either in your motor home or trailer, or on a camp stove.

There are disadvantages, of course. Tents and small trailers and campers can be cramped, even in the most luxurious motor home or trailer; facilities even in fancy commercial campgrounds are less than you'd expect in most motels; and if you cook your own meals you miss the opportunity to experience the local cuisine. But, all these pros and cons and justifications aside, camping is just plain fun—especially in a setting as spectacular as this one.

Renting an RV   Camping to save money is possible if you limit your equipment to a tent, a pop-up tent trailer, or a small pickup truck camper, but renting a motor home will probably end up costing almost as much as driving a compact car, staying in moderately priced motels, and eating in family-style restaurants and cafes. That's because the motor home will go only one-third as far on a gallon of gas as your compact car will, and they're expensive to rent, generally between $1,000 and $1,100 per week in mid-summer, when rates are highest.

Licenses are available from state wildlife offices and sporting goods stores. Keep in mind that several fishing locations, such as Lake Powell and Lake Flaming Gorge, cross state boundaries, and you'll need licenses from the adjoining state to fish those areas.

FOUR-WHEELING

The Moab area and in particular Canyonlands National Park are probably the best known four-wheeling destinations in Utah, but there are also plenty of old mining and logging roads throughout the national forests and on BLM land. Those with dune buggies like to head for Coral Pink Sand Dunes State Park, west of Kanab. Throughout this book, we've tried to let you know everywhere that four-wheeling is and is not allowed; still, you should always make sure before you start out. Brochures and other information on four-wheel driving in Utah can be obtained from the **Utah Parks and Recreation** (☎ 801/538-7220), the **U.S. Forest Service** (☎ 801/524-5030), and the **Bureau of Land Management** ☎ 801/539-4001).

If you're flying into the area and renting an RV when you arrive, choose your starting point carefully; rates vary, depending on the city you're renting in. Cruise America, one of the country's largest RV rental companies, quoted us a weekly rate of $1,077 for a 23-foot motor home in July 1996, if we started out in Salt Lake City; the rate was only $963 for the same motor home if we rented it in Las Vegas, Nevada. The rates included 1,000 free miles. Since most of Utah's national parks are closer to Las Vegas than Salt Lake City anyway, you could save by starting and ending your trip in Las Vegas. Cruise America also rents other RVs, including truck campers and lightweight trailers. For information, contact **Cruise America** (☎ 800/ RV-DEPOT or fax 602/464-7321).

Choosing a Campground   Once you've got a rig or tent, you'll need a place to put it, of course. Camping in the national parks, other federal lands, state parks, and some communities is discussed in the following sections of the book. For a brochure on the excellent campgrounds in Utah's state parks, contact the **Utah Division of Parks and Recreation** (☎ 801/538-7220, 801/322-3770 or 800/ 322-3770 for campground reservations). To find out about U.S. Forest Service facilities throughout the state, call 801/524-5030 or 800/280-2267 for campground reservations). Most of Utah's national park campgrounds are assigned on a first-come, first-served basis only. You should contact each park individually for details on camping there; see the appropriate destination chapters.

A nationwide directory of KOA franchise campgrounds (there are 15 in Utah) is available free at any KOA, or by mail for $3 from **Kampgrounds of America (KOA), Inc.,** Executive Offices, Billings, MT 59114-0558.

Members of the **American Automobile Association (AAA)** can request the club's free *Southwestern CampBook* (☎ 800/336-4357), which includes campgrounds and RV parks in Utah, Arizona, Colorado, and New Mexico. And several massive campground directories can be purchased in major bookstores, including our favorite, **Trailer Life Campground, RV Park & Services Directory,** published annually by TL Enterprises, Inc., P.O. Box 6060, Camarillo, CA 93011.

GOLF

Utah golf courses are known for their beautiful scenery and variety of challenging terrain. They range from mountain courses set among the beautiful forests of the Wasatch to desert courses with scenic views of Utah's spectacular red rock country. The warm climate of St. George, in Utah's southwest corner, makes it a perfect location for year-round golf, and it has become the premier destination for visiting golfers. *Golf Digest* recently chose St. George's Sunbrook Golf Course as Utah's best course. In the northern part of the state, the course at the Homestead Resort near Park City is well worth the trip. A free directory of the state's more than 80 courses is available from the **Utah Travel Council** (☎ 801/538-1030 or 800/220-1160).

HIKING

Hiking is the best—and sometimes the only—way to see many of Utah's most beautiful and exciting areas. The state is interlaced with hiking trails. Particularly recommended destinations for hikers are all five of Utah's national parks. You'll find splendid forest trails and more of a wilderness experience at Flaming Gorge National Recreation Area and in the Wasatch Mountains around Ogden and Logan. Those looking for spectacular panoramic views won't do better than the trails on the BLM land around Moab. State parks with especially good trails include Kodachrome, near Bryce National Park; Jordanelle, near Park City; Dead Horse Point, near Moab; and Escalante, in the town of Escalante.

When you prepare for a hike, keep in mind weather conditions, such as the brutal summer heat around St. George and the likelihood of ice and snow on high mountain trails from fall through spring. Because of loose rock and gravel on trails in the southern part of the state, good hiking boots with aggressive soles and firm ankle support are needed.

HORSEBACK RIDING

It's fun to see the Old West the way the pioneers of 100 years ago did—from the back of a horse. Although you won't find many dude ranches in Utah, there are plenty of stables and outfitters who lead rides lasting from one hour to several days. We particularly recommend the rides at Bryce and Zion National Parks, although you're likely to be surrounded by a lot of other riders and hikers. If you'd like a bit more solitude, head north to the mountains around Logan in the Wasatch Front or Flaming Gorge National Recreation Area. See the relevant regional chapters for outfitters and stables in those areas.

HOUSEBOATING

Among the best ways to experience either Lake Powell or Flaming Gorge Lake is from the comfort of a houseboat. Marinas at each of these national recreation areas have them for rent, although you'll find the best selection at Lake Powell. Essentially floating RVs, houseboats have all the comforts of home, but in somewhat tighter quarters: toilets, showers, sleeping quarters, full kitchens. Some of the larger ones have facilities for up to a dozen people. And you don't have to be an accomplished boater to drive one of these things: Houseboats are easy to maneuver, and they can't go very fast. No boating license is required, but you'll need to reserve your houseboat well in advance, especially for summer use, and send in a sizable deposit.

MOUNTAINBIKING

Although there are a few areas where road-biking is popular, Utah really belongs to mountainbikers. With some of the grades you'll find, be sure you have plenty of gears. Moab claims to be Utah's mountainbiking capital, but there's no dearth of opportunities in other parts of the state, either. Be aware that mountainbikes are prohibited from designated motor vehicle roads in most national parks, but welcome almost everywhere in areas administered by the U.S. Forest Service and Bureau of Land Management. In addition to the exciting and often challenging slickrock trails of Moab, there are excellent trail systems just outside Zion and Bryce Canyon National Parks; we also like the 30-mile Rails to Trails path at Park City and the warm-weather biking at Brian Head Ski Resort near St. George. For a free copy of the annual *Bicycle Utah Vacation Guide,* contact **Bicycle Utah,** P.O. Box 738, Park City, UT 74060 (☎ 801/649-5806).

RIVER TRIPS

The Green and Colorado Rivers are considered to be among America's top destinations for both serious white-water as well as flat-water rafting; they're also popular with kayakers and canoeists. A favorite river trip, with plenty of white water, is down the Green River through Dinosaur National Monument. Trips on the Green also start in the town of Green River, north of Moab. The Colorado River sees more boaters than the Green, though, and has a greater range of conditions, from flat, glassy waters—you just float along—to rapids so rough they can't be run at all. Most Colorado River trips originate in Moab. Several Moab companies will rent you a raft, canoe, or kayak, give you some instruction, and then wish you luck. They'll also help you decide which stretches of river are suitable for your abilities and thrillseeking level, and can arrange a pick-up at the take-out point. See the appropriate chapter for details on contacting these outfitters.

Although river trips through the Grand Canyon, which we discuss in the chapter on Utah's Dixie, are very popular, they're actually too popular for us, especially in mid-summer, when rafts are bumper-to-bumper. A worthwhile and lesser known river trip, in the Four Corners area, is along the San Juan River in Bluff. It's a relaxing excursion that will take you to relatively unknown Native American archaeological sites and striking rock formations.

A recorded report on statewide river flows and reservoir information is available from the **Colorado Basin River Forecast Center** (☎ 801/539-1311). Information on river rafting is available from the **Bureau of Land Management** (☎ 801/539-4001), and be sure to request a copy of *Raft Utah* from the **Utah Travel Council** (☎ 801/538-1030 or 800/220-1160).

ROCK CLIMBING

This dizzying sport is growing in popularity in Utah. It's growing so much, in fact, that several popular areas have imposed moratoriums on bolting, and allow climbers to use existing bolt holes only. Among the more dramatic rock climbing spots is Zion National Park, where it's as much a spectator sport as participatory activity. You'll also find some inviting walls of stone in Snow Canyon State Park near St. George, in Logan Canyon, and throughout the Wasatch Mountains in the Salt Lake City area.

For details on where you're allowed to climb and other information on climbing in Utah, contact the **Utah Travel Council** (☎ 801/538-1030 or 800/220-1160) or the government agency that controls the land you're interested in (see "Visitor Information" in Chapter 3).

SKIING & OTHER WINTER SPORTS

Utah residents like to brag that the state has "the greatest snow on earth"—and just one winter trip makes it clear to you they just might be right. Utah's ski resorts have absolutely splendid powder, runs as scary or as mellow as you'd like, and a next-door-neighbor friendliness many of us had come to believe was extinct. With a few notable exceptions—Park City and Deer Valley—you won't find all the poshness and amenities that dominate many of the ski resorts next door in Colorado, but you won't find the high prices either. What you will find are top-notch ski areas that are surprisingly easy to reach—half are within an hour's drive of Salt Lake City Airport. And they're relatively uncrowded; while Colorado chalked up more than 11 million skiers during the 1994–95 season, Utah counted just three million, a group that saw few lift lines and plenty of wide-open spaces.

Cross-country skiers who enjoy doing their own thing have plenty of national forest areas where they can break trail to their heart's content. Particularly good are the mountains above Ogden, and the old logging and mining roads southeast of Moab. Several downhill ski areas, including Sundance and Solitude, have groomed cross-country trails; and some of the hiking trails at Bryce Canyon National Park are open to cross-country skiers in winter. Snowmobilers can generally use the same national forest roads as cross-country skiers, and both cross-country skiers and snowmobilers head to Cedar Breaks National Monument in the winter, when those are the only ways to get into the monument.

Contact **Ski Utah,** 150 W. 500 South, Salt Lake City, UT 84101 (☎ 801/ 534-1779 or fax 801/521-3722; on line at http://www.skiutah.com), for a free copy of the *Ski Utah Vacation Planner,* which contains information on downhill and cross-country ski areas, as well as other winter recreation possibilities. The **Utah Travel Council** (☎ 801/538-1030 or 800/220-1160) and **Utah Parks and Recreation** (☎ 801/538-7220) will send you a free copy of *Utah Snowmobile Directory,* which describes some of the best snowmobiling spots in the state. Call 801/521-8102 for the daily ski report, and 801/364-1581 for the daily avalanche and mountain weather report.

WILDLIFE WATCHING & BIRDING

The great expanses of undeveloped land in Utah make it an ideal habitat for wildlife. In most cases, it isn't even necessary to hike very far into the backcountry to find it. There's plenty for you to see, from waterbirds at many of the lakes and reservoirs to elk and antelope in the Wasatch Mountains, lizards and snakes among the red rock country of the south, and deer and small mammals practically everywhere. All the national parks have excellent wildlife viewing possibilities, as do many state parks. Coral Pink Sand Dunes near Kanab is known for its luminescent scorpions; Escalante State Park has the best wetland bird habitat in southern Utah. Hikers on Boulder Mountain, near Escalante, are likely to see deer, elk, and wild turkey, and birders will enjoy the wide variety of songbirds to be found there.

The mountains above Ogden and Logan are especially good places to spot elk, deer, and even moose. The relatively remote Flaming Gorge National Recreation Area is one of the best areas of the state to find wildlife, so don't be surprised if a pronghorn antelope joins you at your campsite. Birders have a good chance of seeing osprey, peregrine falcons, swifts, and swallows along the cliffs; and hikers on the Little Hole National Recreation Trail just below Flaming Gorge Dam should watch for a variety of birds, including bald eagles in winter. Antelope Island State Park in the Great Salt Lake is another excellent destination for bird-watchers.

Introducing the Salt Lake Valley & the Wasatch Front

Seeking an escape from religious persecution, Brigham Young lead a group of 148 Mormon pioneers from Illinois to the Salt Lake Valley. Arriving on July 24, 1847, Young declared, "This is the place." Soon a city was born, then a state, and, as the saying goes, the rest is history.

Today, from Logan in the north to Provo in the south, the strip known as the Wasatch Front—the Wasatch Mountains and Salt Lake Valley, including Salt Lake City—holds some 80% of Utah's population and practically all its industry. But this isn't your typical urban center; in fact, one of the things we find particularly attractive about this area is its casual atmosphere. There's no urban feel here, no high-energy excitement, and residents don't see themselves as city dwellers. These Wasatch Front communities, even Salt Lake City, Ogden, and Provo—the state's largest cities—are just overgrown, unsophisticated hick towns. We like that.

Although this certainly feels like small town America, calling these cities unsophisticated is probably unfair. Attending a performance by the Utah Symphony or Mormon Tabernacle Choir, both world-class performing arts organizations, will silence any big-city naysayer. But all that really doesn't matter; the big draw, for many who come to work and live here as well as those who come to play, is what's beyond the cities' boundaries. This isn't the barren rock and desert that most likely comes to mind when you think of Utah; this is mountain Utah, with lush canyons, rushing streams, and stately pines.

Opportunities to enjoy these spectacular outdoors abound. The region's canyons all offer magnificent views from the highways that traverse them, and even more incredible experiences once you get out of the car. The lakes and reservoirs dotting the region are great for boating, fishing, and swimming; the best known are the Great Salt and Utah lakes, but we'll tell you about our favorites, two undiscovered jewels. The forests are terrific for hiking, mountainbiking, and horseback riding. And then there's the spectacular skiing: Tucked away in delightful little canyons, these resorts offer spectacular scenery year-round, usually get more than 500 inches of splendid powder each year, are reasonably priced, and probably the easiest ski areas to get to in the West.

This is a great place to relive frontier history, too. You can visit the spot where the final spike was driven to complete the first transcontinental railroad, the oldest continuously operating saloon in Utah, and the fort where 19th-century mountain men gathered to exchange news and swap furs for supplies; you can even go underground in a genuine silver mine. There's also a terrific collection of airplanes chronicling the history of flight.

1 How We've Covered This Area

Since this is such a large region—175 miles from top to bottom—you probably won't be touring the entire Wasatch Front; you're more likely to set your sights on specific destinations and explore those particular areas. To make our coverage of the region more manageable and likely to suit to your needs, we've divided it into three chapters.

Chapter 7 covers Salt Lake City, Utah's capitol and major population center, and world headquarters to the Church of Jesus Christ of Latter-day Saints, otherwise known as the Mormon Church.

Chapter 8 explores the northern section of the Wasatch Front: The Great Salt Lake, one of the country's most remarkable natural wonders, and Antelope Island State Park; Ogden, a great starting point for discovering Utah's Old West; the pretty town of Logan; and Golden Spike National Historic Site, a must-see for railroad buffs. This area is also a great base for outdoor recreation, with three of Utah's ski resorts on hand as well as lush, rugged mountains that are great for exploring in the warmer months.

Chapter 9 covers the southern half of the Wasatch Front, from Park City, home of the state's premier ski resorts, to Provo, site of Brigham Young University. This area also includes the splendid cave formations of Timpanagos Cave National Monument, and a handful of lakes and state parks—real hidden gems that make this area a terrific warm-weather playground as well. Provo makes a good base for skiing, hiking, or horseback riding at Sundance Resort and Institute in Provo Canyon.

2 Getting Outside Along the Wasatch Front

The Wasatch Front is Mountain Utah, with lofty pines, rushing streams, and, in winter, an abundance of light, powdery snow. The rugged mountains and steep canyons that surround the Great Salt Lake Valley are home to lush forests, cool lakes and reservoirs, and plenty of sunshine, just right for an hour-long nature walk, an afternoon of birding, a exciting day of downhill skiing or mountainbiking, a relaxing weekend fishing trip, or any one of a number of other adventures. There's an activity for everyone, every day of the year.

WINTER ACTIVITIES

Nowhere else in the American West are there so many excellent ski resorts in one place. Just fly into Salt Lake City in the morning, rent a car, and you can be on the slopes of your choice by early afternoon. It doesn't get any easier. Solitude and Brighton—which welcome snowboarders as well as downhill skiers—are in Big Cottonwood Canyon. At the top of Little Cottonwood Canyon is graceful, sylvan Alta, with clouds of light snow; down the canyon is the more developed Snowbird. If you crave the lap of luxury, head for the Park City resorts—Park City, Wolf Mountain, and ritzy Deer Valley—where you'll find "champagne" snow and European-style lodges. Nordic Valley, Powder Mountain, and Snowbasin, near Ogden, plus Beaver Mountain, near the Idaho border, are all at the other end of the scale, simply offering good skiing on long, uncrowded runs—no pretensions here. Rustic, comfortable Sundance is nestled in the pines on the eastern slope of Mt. Timpanogos, north of Provo.

The Wasatch Front

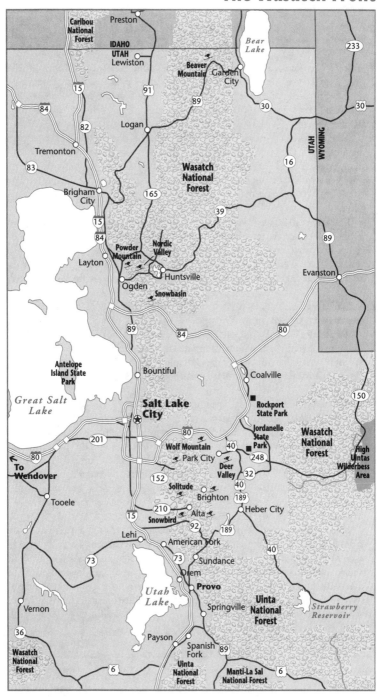

Planning for the Year 2002:
The Winter Olympic Games Come to Utah

The 21st century is a concept most of us aren't quite ready to deal with yet. The way I see it, that's fine—we've still got a few more years to go before we have to plan for the new millenium. But for Utahns in and around Salt Lake City, it's a whole different story—they're already hard at work preparing to host the 2002 Winter Olympic Games.

Never before has a city the size of Salt Lake been chosen to host the Olympic Games. But its surrounding mountains, reliable snow conditions (the Wasatch Range gets an average of about 530 inches of light, fluffy powder a year), and easy worldwide access—combined with years of serious lobbying for the honor—made the Utah capital the overwhelming choice of the International Olympic Committee.

Despite its size, Salt Lake City is remarkably well-prepared to host the games. Eight of the nine event venues are either already in place or under construction. The city's convention center, the Salt Palace, will serve as the Main Press Center. There are already more hotel rooms in and around Salt Lake than in any other city that has hosted the Winter Games, and more are being built in preparation for the Games.

And what the city doesn't yet have is already well along in the planning stages. A site has been chosen for the Olympic Village—slated to accommodate all of the 4,000 athletes, coaches, and trainers expected to attend the games—and it couldn't be more convenient: 10 minutes from downtown, on the grounds of the University of Utah campus adjacent to the Olympic Stadium. A light rail system will link the southern suburbs of the metro area (home to a number of Olympic venues) with downtown.

In reality, though, it wasn't just the city that was chosen by the Olympic Committee; the entire Wasatch Front will serve as the world's host for those two winter weeks in 2002. Events will take place as far away from Salt Lake as Snowbasin Ski Area in Ogden Canyon, 55 miles north of downtown. As you'd expect, a number of downhill ski and other nordic events will be held in and around Park City, at Park City Ski Area, Deer Valley, and the Utah Winter Sports Park, the world-class training facility that's the area's pride and joy. At the end of the day, though, it all comes back to the city: The daily medal ceremonies will be held at Olympic Plaza, in the heart of downtown.

If you're ready to make plans to see the action in 2002 (scheduled to take place from February 9th through the 24th), you'll have to be patient—a ticket program won't be in place until 1999. However, about 1.7 million tickets will be available, so if you stay on top of things, you should be able to garner some for yourself. Ticket prices are expected to range from $25 to $300, with the average price at about $55.

Visit the Salt Lake Olympic Organizing Committee on the Internet at **http://www/slc2002.org/olympics** to keep up with the preparations for 2002—it'll be here before you know it.

—Cheryl Farr

Those who prefer other forms of winter recreation also have plenty of options. The old logging and mining roads throughout the national forests are great for cross-country skiing. Sundance Nordic Center, near Provo, offers groomed trails and lots of spectacular mountain scenery. Park City also has a Nordic center, White Pine, that offers great cross-country skiing for everyone from beginner to expert. Solitude Nordic Center, Utah's oldest cross-country ski center, even has a children's trail. Snowmobilers will want to head to beautiful Strawberry Reservoir, a pristine lake near Park City that's also great for ice fishing.

WARM-WEATHER ACTIVITIES

Once the winter snows have been replaced with mountain wildflowers, you'll still find plenty to do. Hikers and mountainbikers share most of the trails here, including the well-maintained downtown riverside trails in both Provo (Chapter 9) and Ogden (Chapter 8). Other favorites of ours are the 30-mile Rails to Trails path from Park City to Echo Reservoir, and the 5-mile Indian Trail that leads through a dense forest in Ogden Canyon (Chapter 8). The national forests are popular for horseback riding; some of the best opportunities are in the rugged country outside Logan (Chapter 8), and at Park City.

There's boating at Utah Lake State Park (Chapter 9), but it gets crowded, especially on weekends. The Great Salt Lake is popular with power and sailboaters, but no rentals are available. For our money, it's well worth the drive to Strawberry Reservoir, a beautiful lake set in a quiet national forest; it's ideal for trout fishing, boating, and hiking along its shores. Or head to the lake at Jordanelle State Park, one of Utah's newest parks. Both lakes are close to Park City, have launching ramps and boat rentals, and are much less crowded than their more well-known neighbors. Ogden's Fort Buenaventura State Park (Chapter 8) is essentially an historical park, so finding several delightful ponds there, with canoe rentals, was a nice surprise.

Strawberry Reservoir also offers some of the best fishing in the state. The lakes and streams in the Cache National Forest (Chapter 8) above Ogden are good trout habitat. The streams above Park City are also a good bet for fly fishing.

The Wasatch Front is dotted with golf courses, but our favorites, for both the challenge and scenic beauty they offer, are in the Park City area: Park Meadows Golf Club, in Park City; and the courses at Wasatch Mountain State Park and The Homestead Resort, near Heber City.

WILDLIFE WATCHING

Because the Wasatch Front (like most of Utah) is largely undeveloped, you'll have plenty of opportunities for wildlife viewing and birding. Practically anywhere in the mountains you have a chance of spotting deer, elk, maybe even a moose, plus smaller animals such as badgers, chipmunks, and rabbits. Willard Bay State Park near Ogden (Chapter 8) is a good place to see deer, smaller creatures, and waterbirds; and the Great Salt Lake is home to a variety of saltwater birds. At Antelope Island State Park, you'll have an easy time seeing not antelope, but buffalo—relatively domesticated ones, not actually "wildlife," per se.

7

Salt Lake City

Lying in a valley in north central Utah, between the Wasatch Mountains on the east and the Great Salt Lake on the west, is Salt Lake City. Utah's capital and major population center is small as cities go, with a population of only 160,000. But travelers come from around the world to visit magnificent Temple Square, world headquarters of the the the Church of Jesus Christ of the Latter-day Saints (LDS), and to hear the inspired voices of the unequaled Mormon Tabernacle Choir. Salt Lake City is to Mormonism what Rome is to Catholicism—it's the center of the Mormon universe.

Although Salt Lake City may be best known for its religious prominence—and an undeserved reputation as a stodgy, uptight town where you can't get a drink—it's growing in popularity as a home base for skiers and others looking to make the most of the spectacular scenery—unlike anything you've ever seen before—and the exhilarating outdoor recreation possibilities just an hour's drive from the city, including some of the country's best ski resorts and miles of terrific mountain trails for hiking, mountainbiking, and horseback riding. With its rising prominence as an outdoor recreation center as well as its preparations to host the 2002 Winter Olympic Games—which include the addition of many new hotels, restaurants, and attractions—Salt Lake City is beginning to shed its image as "that boring Mormon town with the choir."

Incidentally, one of the first things visitors notice upon arriving is how pleasantly wide the streets are. Young laid out the city streets on a grid pattern with the Temple at the center, decreeing that the streets should be 132 feet wide, so that a team of four oxen and a covered wagon could make a U-turn. A more tantalizing tale has it that the streets were made wide enough for polygamist Young and all his wives to walk comfortably down the street arm-in-arm, with no one forced into the gutter.

1 Orientation

ARRIVING

By Plane Direct flights connect Salt Lake City to over 65 cities in the United States and Canada. **Salt Lake City International Airport** (☎ 801/575-2400) is located just north of I-80 at exit 115, on the west side of the city. Airlines serving the airport include **America West** (☎ 800/247-5692), **American** (☎ 800/433-7300),

Continental (☎ 801/359-9800), **Delta** (☎ 801/532-7123 or 800/221-1212), **Northwest** (☎ 800/225-2525), **Skywest** (☎ 800/453-9417), **TWA** (☎ 801/539-1111 or 800/221-2000), and **United** (☎ 800/241-6522).

By Car   Salt Lake City is 303 miles north of St. George, 238 miles northwest of Moab, 45 miles north of Provo, and 35 miles south of Ogden. You can reach it from the east or west via I-80, and from the north or south via I-15.

By Train   **Amtrak** has several trains arriving daily from both coasts. The passenger station is located at 320 S. Rio Grande Ave. (☎ 801/364-8562 or 800/872-7245), just west of Temple Square.

VISITOR INFORMATION

The **Salt Lake Convention & Visitors Bureau** has an information center downtown at 180 S. West Temple (☎ 801/521-2868 or 800/541-4955). It's open Monday through Friday, 8am to 5pm, and Saturday from 9am to 4pm, with extended hours in the summer. Another information center, at Salt Lake City International Airport Terminal II (☎ 801/575-2800 or 801/575-2660), is open Monday through Friday from 9am to 9pm.

The **Utah Tourism and Recreation Information Center,** in Council Hall on Capitol Hill at 300 N. State Street (☎ 801/538-1030), is staffed by members of the Utah Travel Council, Utah Division of State Parks and Recreation, National Park Service, U.S. Forest Service, Bureau of Land Management, and the Zion Natural History Association. Hours are Monday through Friday, 8am to 5pm, and Saturday, Sunday, and federal holidays, 10am to 5pm.

CITY LAYOUT

Salt Lake City is laid out in a simple grid system centered on Temple Square. The roads bounding the Square are North Temple, South Temple, West Temple, and Main Street, with ground zero at the southeast corner (the intersection of Main and South Temple), the site of the Brigham Young Monument. The road numbers increase from there by 100s in the four cardinal directions, with West Temple taking the place of 100 West, 100 North called North Temple, and 100 East known as State Street.

Addresses seem confusing at first, but are really quite clear once you get used to them. For instance, 1292 S. 400 West Street lies almost 13 blocks south of Temple Square and 4 blocks west, and 243 N. 600 East Street lies about 2 blocks north and 6 blocks east.

A good, detailed city map is produced by Gousha, and can be purchased at most bookstores. The *Salt Lake City Visitor's Guide*, available free at the visitor center, has maps showing the approximate location of many restaurants, motels, and attractions.

NEIGHBORHOODS IN BRIEF

Downtown   The Downtown area, centered on Temple Square, is both a business district and the administrative center for the LDS Church. Church offices, the

Impressions

Salt Lake City was healthy—an extremely healthy city. They declared there was only one physician in the place and he was arrested every week regularly and held to answer under the vagrant act for having "no visible means of support."
—Mark Twain, 1872

Genealogical Center, the Museum of Church History and Art, and other church buildings surround the Square. This is most likely where you'll spend the bulk of your time. Within a few blocks south, west, and east are hotels, restaurants, stores, businesses, and two major shopping centers. Not far away is the Salt Palace, home to the Utah Symphony, and the Capitol Theatre, the home of several performing companies.

Capitol Hill   The Capitol Hill district lies north of the Square and encompasses the 40 acres around the Utah State Capitol Building and Council Hall. There are some lovely old homes in the blocks surrounding the Capitol.

Marmalade District   The blocks lying west of the Capitol to Quince Street are known as the Marmalade District. The streets in this small area are named for the nut and fruit trees brought in by early settlers—hence its cognomen. The homes represent many of the city's early architectural styles; many are being renovated.

Avenues District   The Avenues District lies east of the Capitol and north of South Temple. Most of the larger homes here date from the silver boom in Little Cottonwood Canyon; they were built by either successful miners or shopkeepers of the era. Today, the tenants are college students and young professionals.

2 Getting Around

By Car   This is really the best way to get around the city. There is a public bus system (see below), but it's really geared to locals rather than visitors. The following national companies have offices in Salt Lake City: **Avis** (☎ 801/575-2847 or 800/831-2847), **Budget** (☎ 801/575-2830 or 800/527-0700 nationwide; 800/237-7251 in Park City), **Dollar** (☎ 801/575-2580 at the airport, or 800/800-4000), **Hertz** (☎ 801/575-2683 at the airport, or 800/654-3131), **National** (☎ 801/575-2277 at the airport, or 800/227-7368), **Payless** (☎ 801/596-2596 or 800/729-5377), and **Thrifty** (☎ 801/595-6677 at the airport, or 800/367-2277).

There are many public parking lots in the downtown area, costing from $1 to $4 per day. Some lots are free with validation from a particular merchant or restaurant. Parking on streets downtown is metered, costing 25¢ per half hour, and usually limited to one or two hours. For larger RVs and motorhomes, parking is limited; there's one large lot—the entire block between North and South Temple and 200 and 300 West—where you can park for $2 to $6 per hour. You might also try the lot behind the Capitol, where there are some designated large vehicle spaces; East Capitol Street is also a possibility (and it's not metered).

Public Transportation   The **Utah Transit Authority** (☎ 801/287-4636 or TDD 801/287-4657) provides bus service around the city, with a "free fare zone" in the downtown area, roughly from 400 South to North Temple, continuing up Main Street to 500 North to include the State Capitol, and between 200 East and West Temple. You can ride a bus free within the zone, getting on and off as many times as you like. You should be aware that a number of bus routes traverse Main and State streets and North and South Temple, so if you're unsure if the bus that stops for you is the one you need, ask the driver before getting on. Route schedules and maps are available at malls, libraries, visitor centers, and other places around the valley. Large-print and Braille schedules are available upon request. To find the nearest bus stop or determine the best route to your destination, ask at the front desk of your hotel or call 801/287-4636. Some buses are wheelchair accessible, and others have bicycle carriers.

The **Centennial Discovery Trolley** offers alternative transportation to historic sites and other attractions around the city. It travels from Trolley Square to Tracy

Aviary (in Liberty Park), around to Temple Square and out to the museums at the university, and to the zoo and This is the Place State Park at the mouth of Emigration Canyon. Tickets can be purchased aboard the trolley, at the ZCMI Center Mall information desk (36 S. State St., ☎ 801/359-4540), or the Salt Lake Convention and Visitors Bureau. Call 801/287-4636 for more information.

By Taxi   The three main companies are the **City Cab Co.** (☎ 801/363-5550), **Yellow Cab** (☎ 801/521-2100), and **Ute Cab** (☎ 801/359-7788), all of which are available 24 hours a day. **Handi-Van, Inc.,** provides wheelchair transportation "door through door" (☎ 801/486-8416).

FAST FACTS: Salt Lake City

American Express   The American Express Office is located at 175 S. West Temple (☎ 801/328-9733), and is a full-service travel agency. It's open Monday through Friday, from 9am to 5pm.

Business Hours   Banks are usually open weekdays from 9am to 3pm or 4pm, often until 6pm Friday; some have hours on Saturday. There's 24-hour access to the automatic-teller machines (ATMs) at most banks, as well as in shopping centers and other outlets. Generally, business offices are open weekdays from 9am to 5pm. Stores are usually open six days a week, with some also open on Sunday afternoon. Department stores usually stay open until 9pm at least one day a week. Discount stores and supermarkets are often open later than other stores, and some supermarkets are open 24 hours a day.

Camera Repair   Several camera stores offer repair services. Among the larger ones is **Forster's Camera Service, Inc.,** 40 W. 2950 South, South Salt Lake (☎ 801/487-1288), which has been in business since 1971.

Dentist   For dental referrals, contact the **Utah Dental Association,** 1151 E. 3900 South (☎ 801/261-5315), during normal business hours.

Doctor   For medical referrals, contact the **Utah Medical Association,** 1151 E. 3900 South (☎ 801/355-7477), during normal business hours. At other times, contact the nearest hospital; in an emergency, dial 911.

Emergencies   Dial **911** for police, fire, or ambulance.

Hospitals   **LDS Hospital** is the closest to downtown, at 8th Ave. and C St. (☎ 801/321-1100). Other city hospitals include **Holy Cross Health Services of Utah,** 1050 E. South Temple (☎ 801/350-4111), **Primary Children's Medical Center,** 100 N. Medical Dr. (☎ 801/588-2000), and **University Hospital & Clinics,** 50 N. Medical Dr. (☎ 801/581-2897).

Hotlines   The **Utah Poison Control Center** number is 801/581-2151 or 800/456-7707. The **Rape Crisis Center** is at 2035 S. 1300 East (☎ 801/467-7273). Call the **Crisis/Suicide Prevention Hotline** at 801/483-5444 in North Salt Lake County; at 801/566-2455 in South Salt Lake County; and at 801/773-7051 in Davis County, north of Salt Lake City.

Liquor Laws   See "Liquor Laws" in Chapter 2.

Newspapers/Magazines   The two major daily newspapers are the *Salt Lake City Tribune* and the *Deseret News,* the latter which is owned by the LDS Church. Also of interest is *Salt Lake City Magazine,* a slick publication with a section on current events.

Police   For emergencies call 911. For nonemergency police assistance, call 801/ 799-3000.

Post Office   The main post office is located at 1760 W. 2100 South (☎ 801/ 978-3005). The one closest to downtown is at 230 W. 200 South (☎ 801/978-3001).

Radio   Among AM stations, KISN (570 AM) is all sports; KFAM (700 AM) offers easy listening; KSVN (730 AM) plays Latin music; KSOS (800 AM) plays oldies; KAPN (860 AM) is all news; KANN (1120 AM) is a Christian station; KSOP (1370 AM) plays modern country music; and KCPZ (1600 AM) plays adult contemporary music.

FM stations include KCPW (simulcast on 88.3 and 105.1 FM), which broadcasts National Public Radio; KUER (90.1 FM) plays classical, jazz, and news broadcasts; KLZX (simulcast on 92.1, 96.7, and 106.9 FM) plays classic rock; KXRK (96.1 FM) offers modern music; KKAT (101.9 FM) plays young country; and KUMT (105.7 FM) plays eclectic rock.

Smoking   As of February 1, 1995, Utah is "smoke-free." The Utah Indoor Clean Air Act prohibits smoking in any publicly owned building or office, and in all enclosed indoor places of public access. This includes restaurants (but not private clubs), lounges, and taverns.

Taxes   Utah's state sales tax is just under 6%, but Salt Lake and Davis counties add a mass-transit tax, bringing the usual sales tax to just over 6%. Lodging taxes total about 10%, and restaurant taxes total just over 7%.

Television   Local stations include KUTV on channel 2 (CBS), KTVX on channel 4 (ABC), KSL on channel 5 (NBC), KUED on channel 7 (PBS), KBYU on channel 11, KJZZ on channel 3, and KSTU (FOX) on channel 13.

Transit Info   Call 801/287-4636 (TDD 801/287-4657) for **Utah Transit Authority** bus information.

Useful Telephone Numbers   For local road conditions, call 801/964-6000; for state-wide conditions, call 800/492-2400. The latter also includes information on major road construction statewide.

Weather   Call 801/575-7669 for a weather report, or 801/975-1212 for the temperature and time.

3 Accommodations

You'll have no trouble finding comfortable lodgings in Salt Lake City, usually conveniently located near to wherever you want to be, and at relatively reasonable rates compared to other western cities. One disappointment for us is the scarcity of grand old hotels of the late 19th and early 20th centuries that you find all over Colorado and other parts of the West. What would have been Salt Lake City's grandest historic lodging, the majestic 1911 Hotel Utah, was recently converted from a hotel to LDS church offices. There are, however, a number of fine hotels here, including some with at least a bit of history, as well as several bed-and-breakfasts that offer a glimpse into Salt Lake City's past.

Among major chain and franchise lodging properties, we recommend the following: the **Best Western Olympus Hotel Conference Center,** 161 W. 600 South, Salt Lake City, UT 84101 (☎ 801/521-7373 or 800/426-0722; fax 801/524-0354), has 393 units, with rates ranging from $75 to $105 for two people. The **Econo Lodge,** 715 W. North Temple, Salt Lake City, UT 84116 (☎ 801/363-0062 or

800/424-4777; fax 801/359-3926), charges $52 to $66 for two; the **Travelodge,** 144 W. North Temple, Salt Lake City, UT 84103 (☎ 801/533-8200 or 800/578-7878; fax 801/596-0332), offers rooms at rates from $48 to $74 double; and **Super 8 Motel,** 616 S. 200 West, Salt Lake City, UT 84101 (☎ 801/534-0808 or 800/800-8000; fax 801/355-7735), charges from $58.88 to $62.88 for two people. All of these are perfectly good standard properties where you'll get exactly the kind of comfort and service that you would expect from the chains.

Rates listed here are the rack rates; make a point of asking for any possible discounts. They're often given to senior citizens, members of the military, business travelers, and members of travel clubs or other organizations. The major downtown hotels that cater to businesspeople often give especially good discounts on weekends. Because the chain hotel's national reservation service may not be able to offer discounts, it's often best to call the hotel directly to get the best rate.

Hotels are organized under the following price categories: **expensive,** $100 to $175; **moderate,** $50 to $100; **inexpensive,** less than $50 per night double. Tax added to lodging bills in Salt Lake City totals about 10%. Parking is free unless otherwise noted. Pets are not accepted unless otherwise noted.

EXPENSIVE

The Armstrong Mansion Bed & Breakfast

667 E. 100 South, Salt Lake City, UT 84102. ☎ **801/531-1333** or 800/708-1333. 14 rms. A/C TV TEL. $75–$184 double. Rates include full breakfast. AE, DISC, MC, V.

This stately red brick mansion, an opulent Queen Anne–style Victorian home decorated with antiques and reproductions, has an overall feeling of splendor and luxury, from its stained-glass windows to its intricately carved oak staircase. The four-story mansion, built in 1893 and listed on the National Register of Historic Places, was renovated in 1981 and again in 1994, and has an elevator. The ornate stencils on the walls are reproductions of the mansion's original decorative patterns, discovered during renovation. A variety of rooms are available, some with double beds, many with queens, and a few with kings; most have Jacuzzis. With your room, you'll enjoy a full breakfast consisting of a hot dish, muffins, and fruit. Pets are not allowed.

✪ Brigham Street Inn

1135 E. South Temple, Salt Lake City, UT 84102. ☎ **801/364-4461** or 800/417-4461. 8 rms., 1 suite. A/C TV TEL. $85–$135 double, $185–$195 suite. Rates include continental breakfast. AE, CB, DISC, MC, V.

Located in a handsome three-story historic mansion, the elegant but relaxed Brigham Street Inn is a comfortable alternative to a luxury hotel. The inn is filled with antiques, reproductions, and original art from various periods, as well as some modern touches. Most of the individually decorated guest rooms have queen-size beds, and more than half have fireplaces. Common rooms on the main floor include a parlor, living, and dining rooms, where guests gather to relax (and sometimes conduct business). The continental breakfast is a scrumptious offering of homemade pastries or croissants, fresh fruit, juice, coffee, and tea.

Doubletree Hotel

215 W. South Temple, Salt Lake City, UT 84101. ☎ **801/531-7500** or 800/222-TREE. Fax 801/328-1289. 381 units. A/C TV TEL. Rooms $79–$149, suites $200 and up. AE, CB, DC, DISC, MC, V. Parking $6; vehicle height limit is 6′2″, but there's an outside lot for taller vehicles.

This modern high-rise hotel is an excellent choice for both the business traveler and vacationer; it's just a block from Temple Square and very close to convention and spectator sports facilities. Rooms are spacious, with either a king or two double beds and a large working desk. Some king rooms have a sofa sleeper, or an easy chair and ottoman. The upper floors have terrific views of the mountains, Temple Square, and the Capitol. There's a restaurant and private club (bar) on site, a full-service business center, a small indoor heated pool, an exercise room (plus access to two nearby health clubs), and all the other amenities and services you'd expect at a top-notch hotel.

✪ Inn at Temple Square

71 W. South Temple, Salt Lake City, UT 84101. ☎ **801/531-1000** or 800/843-4668. Fax 801/536-7272. 95 units, including 10 suites. A/C TV TEL. $113–$132 double; $155–$220 suite. Rates include full breakfast. AE, DC, DISC, MC, V.

A beautiful hotel brimming with 18th-century European elegance and style, the Inn at Temple Square is an exquisite little gem, offering wonderful service, food, and facilities. Actually built in 1930, the inn has been restored and then some—it offers an experience reminiscent of the grand hotels of old, but with a warm, homey touch. The lobby is like a living room, with fine artwork, couches, and chairs you can sink into. On the mezzanine level is a baby grand piano, a library with inviting reading areas, and a fireplace. Rooms are spacious, with a comfortable, Old World feel and at least one upholstered chair.

The Inn's Carriage Court Restaurant serves three meals daily in a quietly elegant setting. Guest services include a free pass to a nearby health club, valet parking, airport shuttle, room service, and same-day valet service.

The inn is centrally located, just across from Temple Square, and within easy walking distance of downtown theaters, restaurants, spectator sports, historic sites, and shopping. The entire facility is smoke-free, and pets are not allowed.

Radisson Hotel Salt Lake City Airport

2177 W. North Temple, Salt Lake City, UT 84116. ☎ **801/364-5800** or 800/333-3333. Fax 801/364-5823. 128 units, including 29 suites. A/C TV TEL. $129–$139 double; weekend rates $84–$114. AE, CB, DC, DISC, ER, JCB, MC, V.

You might think you just arrived in the Swiss Alps when you first see this rugged gray-stone building. It could be a Swiss chalet or hunting lodge; actually, it's a well-appointed contemporary hotel. The spacious and elegant lobby has a gracefully curving stairway to the second floor, with richly stained carved-and-turned woodwork and a pastoral mural. The "signature," or basic, rooms all feature a gas fireplace and handsome country French decor, and top-floor rooms have cathedral ceilings. Loft suites have an upstairs sleeping area and a kitchen with a balcony overlooking the living room. French provincial furnishings are homelike and plush.

The gracious services include concierge, room service, airport transportation, and morning coffee and newspaper. A whirlpool, a large outdoor pool, and an executive exercise room are available for guests' use. Pets are not allowed.

Salt Lake City Marriott

75 S. West Temple, Salt Lake City, UT 84101. ☎ **801/531-0800** or 800/228-9290. Fax 801/532-4127. 515 units, 6 suites. A/C TV TEL. $145–$165 double, $275–$600 suite; weekend rate $105 double. AE, CB, DC, DISC, EU, JCB, MC, V. Parking $5 per day, or $1 per hour up to 8 hours; vehicle height limit is 6'2".

Just a block south of Temple Square and adjoining the Crossroads Plaza, this Marriott is a good choice for those visiting downtown Salt Lake. Geared to business travelers, the standard rooms are attractively decorated, with solid cherry furniture, plush chairs, large work desks, and two telephones with a computer data-port. The spacious, skylit lobby has a cozy fireplace and lots of plants. There are several restaurants, a bar, and an espresso kiosk on the premises.

Salt Lake City Accommodations

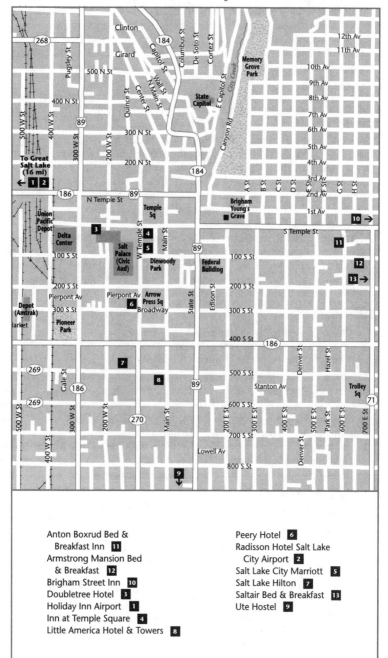

Anton Boxrud Bed & Breakfast Inn **11**

Armstrong Mansion Bed & Breakfast **12**

Brigham Street Inn **10**

Doubletree Hotel **3**

Holiday Inn Airport **1**

Inn at Temple Square **4**

Little America Hotel & Towers **8**

Peery Hotel **6**

Radisson Hotel Salt Lake City Airport **2**

Salt Lake City Marriott **5**

Salt Lake Hilton **7**

Saltair Bed & Breakfast **13**

Ute Hostel **9**

Services include a concierge, room service, dry cleaning and laundry service, newspaper delivery, massage, express checkout, airport shuttle, courtesy car, and valet parking. Facilities include VCR, a large indoor/outdoor heated pool, health club, whirlpool, sauna, sundeck, business center, conference rooms for up to 1,500 people, laundromat, car-rental desk, and gift shop. Pets are accepted, with a deposit.

Salt Lake Hilton

150 W. 500 South, Salt Lake City, UT 84101. ☎ **801/532-3344** or 800/HILTONS. Fax 801/531-0705. 351 rms., including 33 suites. A/C TV TEL. $120–$175 double; $150–$350 suite. AE, CB, DC, DISC, ER, MC, V.

Many of the rooms in this modern hotel offer incredible views of the surrounding city and mountains. All are spacious, comfortably designed and decorated, and perfect for relaxing after a busy day of sightseeing, skiing, or whatever. Some of the more sumptuous suites have large sunken baths, and the attractive courtyard king rooms, overlooking a courtyard of lawn and trees, provide an especially quiet and peaceful atmosphere. The concierge level offers on-floor check-in and -out, a private lounge, and other exclusive amenities.

Restaurants on the premises serve three meals a day, and the hotel has its own bar. Services include an airport shuttle, room service, and secretarial service; a masseuse is available. Guests can use the on-site fitness center, hot tub, outdoor pool, sundeck, and video-game room. There's also a business center offering laptop computer rental and complete conference facilities. Pets are accepted, with a deposit.

MODERATE

Anton Boxrud Bed & Breakfast Inn

57 S. 600 East, Salt Lake City, UT 84102. ☎ **801/363-8035** or 800/524-5511. 6 rms. A/C. $55–$119 double. Rates include full breakfast. AE, DISC, MC, V.

This beautiful three-story red brick structure, built in 1901, is listed on the Salt Lake City Historical Register as "Victorian Eclectic." A boarding house between 1938 and 1968, it's now a lovely, comfortable bed-and-breakfast. Each room is individually decorated with a mix of antiques and reproductions; all have queen beds with down comforters. Pocket doors and stained-glass windows grace the sitting room, where guests can gather to enjoy refreshments in the evening. An outside Jacuzzi is available year-round. The full breakfast always includes a hot dish, but never meat; a continental breakfast is available for early risers. Pets are not allowed.

❾ Holiday Inn Airport

1659 W. North Temple, Salt Lake City, UT 84116. ☎ **801/533-9000** or 800/HOLIDAY. Fax 801/364-0614. 191 units. A/C TV TEL. $77–$79 double. Rates include continental breakfast. AE, CB, DC, DISC, JCB, MC, V.

This modern, comfortable hotel adjacent to the airport isn't too far from the many things to see and do in Salt Lake City; in fact, the lobby and other public areas are decorated with art showing the city's many attractions. Rooms surrounding the central courtyard offer views of an attractively landscaped pool; outside rooms have parking at the door, but may be a bit noisier. All have one king or two queen beds, a comfortable easy chair with ottoman, and a desk. The Holiday Inn offers complimentary 24-hour airport transportation and in-room movies, and has a fitness center, outdoor hot tub, and volleyball court.

✪ Little America Hotel & Towers

500 S. Main St., Salt Lake City, UT 84101. ☎ **801/596-5785** or 800/453-9450. Fax 801/322-1610. 850 units, including 17 suites. A/C TV TEL. $65–$99 double; $104–$114 suite. AE, DC, DISC, MC, V.

👪 Family-Friendly Hotels

Salt Lake Hilton *(see p. 66)*   The video-game room is perfect for teens, everyone loves the pool, and kids can bring their pets.

Holiday Inn Airport *(see p. 66)*   The central courtyard is a safe haven from city traffic, and the pool and volleyball court keep everyone in shape.

The Little America is among Salt Lake City's finest hotels. It offers a wide variety of rooms, all individually decorated. Choices range from standard courtside rooms in the two-story motel-like buildings to extra large deluxe tower suites in the 17-story high-rise. All are gracefully appointed in French provincial style, yet they're homey and comfortable, with 31-inch color televisions. The locally popular coffee shop opens at 5am; there's also an elegant dining room and a lounge for afternoons and evenings.

The hotel offers concierge and room service. Facilities include a health club with exercise equipment, a second-floor sundeck with an indoor/outdoor pool plus a beautifully landscaped outdoor pool, conference rooms, a beauty salon, boutiques, and shops. Pets are not allowed.

Peery Hotel

110 W. 300 South (Broadway), Salt Lake City, UT 84101. ☎ **801/521-4300** or 800/331-0073. Fax 801/575-5014. 77 rms. A/C TV TEL. $59–$109 double. Rates include continental breakfast. AE, DC, DISC, MC, V.

The Peery is one of the few truly historic hotels left in Salt Lake City. Built in 1910, it has been restored to its former understated elegance, offering comfortable, tastefully decorated accommodations. The lobby is delightful, with the old-style pigeonholes for letters, room keys behind the front desk, and a broad central staircase to the upper floors. Each unique room is a bit small, but most have a large closet, double bed, vanity outside the bath, and a desk and chair. Facilities include a whirlpool and exercise room, conference rooms, gift shop, bar, and restaurant serving three meals daily. Among the services offered are daily newspapers, airport shuttle, room service, concierge, and fax service. Pets are not accepted.

Saltair Bed & Breakfast

164 S. 900 East, Salt Lake City, UT 84102. ☎ **801/533-8184.** 8 units (3 with shared bath), including 3 suites. A/C. $65–$145 double. Rates include full breakfast. AE, CB, DC, DISC, MC, V.

Opened in 1980, the Saltair is one of the oldest continuously operating B&Bs in Utah, although the building itself is a bit older. Now listed on the National Historic Register, it was constructed in 1903 and housed Salt Lake City's Italian Consulate in the early part of the century. Named for the resort built on the Great Salt Lake in the late 1800s (see "Great Salt Lake State Park" in Chapter 8), this inn boasts an enormous collection of Saltair memorabilia, from funny postcards to knickknacks of all kinds. Rooms vary in size and specifics, but all are comfortably furnished with an eclectic variety of antiques, and goose-down comforters grace each bed. Bathrooms have showers only except in the suites, which have whirlpool tubs for two. There's also an outdoor hot tub. Fax, photocopy, and secretarial services are available, plus modem hookup. Although there's no covered parking available, the staff will happily brush snow off your vehicle when needed. Pets are not allowed.

INEXPENSIVE

The Ute Hostel

21 E. Kelsey Ave., Salt Lake City, UT 84111. ☎ **801/595-1645.** 2 private rms, 14 beds in 3 dorm rms. A/C. $13–$15 dorm bed, $30–$35 private rm. No credit cards.

Located in a safe residential neighborhood, this hostel offers bunk beds in three dorm rooms, plus two private rooms—one with a queen-sized bed and the other with a king. As you would expect, everyone shares bathrooms and showers. There's a fully equipped kitchen with free beverages, both smoking and nonsmoking lounges with cable TV and video games, and a public telephone. The hostel is unusually clean and free linen is provided. Complimentary pick-up and drop-off at the airport, train and bus depots, and information center are available; there's free off-street parking; and inexpensive bike, ski, skate, and golf rentals can be arranged. Plans call for the addition of a hot tub and sundeck in 1996. Pets are accepted.

CAMPGROUNDS

Camp VIP

1400 W. North Temple, Salt Lake City, UT 84116. ☎ **801/328-0224** or 800/226-7752. 530 sites. $20–$27; camping cabins $30–$34. MC, V.

This huge place is the closest camping and RV facility to Salt Lake City. It's got two pools, a hot tub, a playground, two coin-operated laundries, several bathhouses, a convenience store with RV supplies, a car wash, and large, well-established shade trees. Bus route 50 heads east on North Temple to downtown, providing easy access to the sites there. Advance reservations are recommended from May through September. Those with RVs who plan to hook up to the campground's water supply should take or plan to buy regulators to control the erratic water pressure.

4 Dining

Salt Lake City restaurants are more casual than those in most major American cities, but the service is generally excellent and very friendly. Alcoholic drinks are not offered when diners are seated; you'll have to ask for a drink, except in private clubs. Diners should also be aware that since many Utahns do not drink coffee or tea, you may have to request your morning beverage—servers do not typically wander the dining room carrying a coffee pot.

Restaurants have been organized into the following price categories: **expensive,** most main courses priced over $18; **moderate,** most main courses priced between $10 and $18; and **inexpensive,** most main courses priced under $10.

EXPENSIVE

Market Street Broiler

54 Market St. ☎ **801/583-8808.** Reservations not accepted. Main courses $6.99–$29.99 at dinner, $4.99–$15.99 at lunch. AE, DISC, MC, V. Mon–Thurs 11am–10pm, Fri–Sat 11am–10:30pm, Sun 4–9pm. Bus: 19, 20, or 23 along Main Street; at the east end of Market Street. SEAFOOD.

Market Street Broiler has combined the atmosphere of the San Francisco wharf with the Southwest's famed mesquite wood to produce—drum roll, please—mesquite-grilled fresh seafood. The Broiler's lobby is actually a fresh-fish market; you could take some fish home to prepare yourself, but it's a lot more fun to sit at the counter around the glass-enclosed kitchen and watch the chef-artisans do their thing with some mesquite, a match, and fish that's flown in fresh daily. Those not interested in a show can eat in the upstairs dining room.

Our favorites from the mesquite broiler include the scallops, shrimp, and halibut plate, prepared on a skewer with bell peppers and onion, and the fresh Pacific red snapper. If you're not in the mood for mesquite, there's always the fryer—try the halibut fish-and-chips or the fresh catfish. If you're not interested in seafood at all, you still won't go away hungry—there are hickory-smoked barbecued baby-back ribs, several varieties of barbecued chicken, and steaks. Full liquor service is available.

Market Street Grill

48 Market St. ☎ **801/322-4668.** Reservations not accepted. Main courses $2.69–$7 at breakfast, $4.99–$12.99 at lunch, $11.99–$39.99 at dinner; Sun brunch $5.99. AE, DISC, MC, V. Mon–Thurs 6:30am–3pm, 5–10:30pm; Sat 7am–3pm, 5–11:30pm; Sun 9:30am–3pm, 4–9:30pm. Bus: 19, 20, or 23 along Main Street; at the east end of Market Street. SEAFOOD/ STEAK.

A fancier version of Market Street Broiler (it's owned by the same company), the Market Street Grill is quite possibly Utah's best seafood restaurant. Expect a wait before you're led into the noisy, somewhat cramped dining room. There's a good reason the place is packed—fresh fish is flown in daily from around the world, and the Grill knows how to do it up right.

Favorites include the Pacific red snapper Monterey, served with fresh tomato sauce, sliced mushrooms, garlic, parsley, white wine, and gulf shrimp; and the cioppino, a seafood stew of lobster, shrimp, crab, clams, snapper, and mussels; or choose one of almost two dozen other seafood offerings. You'll also find a good choice of steaks— including an excellent slow-roasted prime rib if you arrive early enough—pastas, and dinner salads. Look for all the standard choices during the day, plus a seafood omelet, of course, at breakfast. Full liquor service is available.

☺ The New Yorker

60 Market St. ☎ **801/363-0166.** Reservations accepted. Dining room main courses $6.95– $15.95 at lunch, $12.95–$49.95 at dinner; cafe main courses $7.95–$21.95. AE, DISC, MC, V. Mon–Fri 11:30am–2:30pm; Mon–Thurs 5:30–10pm, Fri–Sat 5:30–11pm. Bus: 19, 20, or 23 along Main Street; at the east end of Market Street. AMERICAN.

This is Salt Lake's finest restaurant. With rich woods, understated elegance, quiet sophistication, excellent food, and impeccable service, The New Yorker feels more like a London club than a Utah one. Technically a "private" club, you'll have to buy a membership ($5 for two weeks) to enter, but trust us, it's worth it. You sit either in the dining room or in the less formal cafe, where you dine under the original stained-glass ceiling from the old Hotel Utah.

From the dining room dinner menu, you might choose the sautéed sweetbreads and fresh foie gras with port wine and orange sauce; Dungeness crab cakes, which aficionados say are as good as—or better—than those you'll find anywhere; or the rack of lamb with roasted garlic cream sauce. The lunch menu offers dishes such as sautéed chicken breast with tomato, artichokes, olives, thyme, and garlic; and an excellent tenderloin of beef with cabernet sauce as well as sandwiches and salads. The cafe menu, served from 2:30pm weekdays and 5:30pm Saturdays, offers similar but somewhat lighter fare at slightly lower prices. As a private club, The New Yorker offers complete liquor service. Unlike many restaurants, you can buy a drink here without ordering any food.

MODERATE

Baci Trattoria

134 W. Pierpont Ave. ☎ **801/328-1500.** Main courses $8.99–$12.99. AE, DISC, MC, V. Mon– Fri 11:30am–4pm; Mon–Thur 5–10pm, Fri–Sat 5–11pm. Bus: 81 along 200 South, about 1¹/₂ blocks north of Pierpont Avenue; or 19, 20, or 23 along Main Street, about 2 blocks east. NORTHERN ITALIAN.

It may be a bit noisy here, but the food's good and there's plenty of it. The long bar has three large, art deco–style decorated glass panels; behind them is a long, narrow dining room hung with the flags of Italian provinces, which give it the feel of a Roman outdoor cafe. You can also eat outside underroof, next to the parking lot. The traditional northern Italian menu includes a wide selection of pizzas and pastas, plus chicken, beef, veal, and seafood dishes. Try the lasagna, prepared with spicy Italian sausage and baked in a wood-burning oven; or the *Pappardelle con Pollo*, wide pasta ribbons with grilled chicken, sundried tomatoes, snow peas, and a roasted garlic cream sauce. Service is well-timed, friendly, and efficient. Full liquor service is available.

Diamond Lil's

1528 W. North Temple (15¼ blocks west of Temple Square). ☎ **801/533-0547.** Reservations for large parties only. Main courses $3.95–$8.25 at lunch, $8.95–$16 at dinner. AE, CB, DC, DISC, MC, V. Mon–Thur 11am–10pm, Fri 11am–11pm, Sat 4–11pm. Bus: 49 or 50. STEAK/SEAFOOD.

Head on down to Diamond Lil's for a visit to the Old West—and to chow down on some of the best prime rib and steaks you'll find in Utah. The stuffed-shirt crowd might find the western saloon motif here a bit hokey, with the log walls, wanted posters, and cowboy mannequins, but lighten up—this is a fun place. The house specialty, prime rib, lives up to its billing as "succulent, seasoned, and cooked to perfection." The steaks are good, too, especially the 12-ounce New York strip, served charbroiled and smothered in mushrooms. Other choices include Alaskan king crab, boneless chicken breast, and lots of steak-and-seafood combos. Complete liquor service is available.

Ferrantelli

Trolley Square. ☎ **801/531-8228.** Reservations required for 6 or more. Main courses $4.95–$10.95 at lunch, $7.95–$16.95 at dinner; pizza $6.95–$7.95. AE, DC, DISC, MC, V. Mon–Thur 11:30am–10pm, Fri–Sat 11am–11pm, Sun 1–10pm. Bus: 33 or 45. NORTHERN ITALIAN.

A busy shopping mall restaurant with an atrium greenhouse setting, Ferrantelli is known for its reliable northern Italian dishes—made fresh from scratch—as well as for being a super late-evening dessert stop. For dinner, we suggest either of the lasagna choices: The vegetarian lasagna has roasted eggplant, grilled zucchini, caramelized onions, spinach, and a light sauce; meat-eaters will love the beef and sausage version, with ricotta, grilled mushrooms, and a béchamel sauce. If seafood's your thing, try the *Pescatore:* prawns, mussels, and clams lightly sautéed with garlic, shallots, and fresh herbs, and served with a saffron tomato sauce. The Italian-style desserts are fresh-baked daily. Full liquor service is available.

✪ Lamb's Restaurant

169 S. Main St. ☎ **801/364-7166.** Main courses $3.65–$16.95. AE, DC, DISC, MC, V. Mon–Sat 7am–9pm. Bus: 19, 20, or 23. AMERICAN/CONTINENTAL.

Opened in 1919 in the northern Utah town of Logan by Greek immigrant George Lamb, the restaurant was moved to Salt Lake City's Herald Building in 1939 and has been serving the Who's Who of Utah in this location ever since. But this isn't one of those fancy places you go to be seen; Lamb's is so successful simply because it consistently serves very good food at reasonable prices, with friendly, efficient service.

Decorated with antiques and many furnishings from the 1920s and '30s, Lamb's is comfortable and unpretentious, from the long counter and softly padded booths in front to the more formal dining rooms with white-linen tablecloths in back. The extensive menu offers mostly basic American and continental fare, although the restaurant's Greek origins are also evident. In a tip of the hat to the restaurant's moniker, several lamb dishes appear on the menu, including broiled French-style lamb chops and barbecued lamb shanks.

Salt Lake City Dining

Baci Trattoria ❹	Lamb's Restaurant ❷
Café Trang ❽	Marianne's Delicatessen ❸
Crown Burgers ❿	Market Street Broiler ❼
Diamond Lil's ❶	New Yorker ❻
Ferrantelli ❾	Pierpont Cantina ❺

Other popular dinner selections—all available after 11:30am and cooked to order, of course—are broiled New York steak with sautéed mushrooms, grilled calf's liver with sautéons, steamed finnan haddie, Greek-style broiled half chicken with oregano, and grilled fresh rainbow trout. There's also a good selection of sandwiches and salads, a soup of the day, and a variety of desserts, including an extra special rice pudding and a Burgundy wine Jell-O(!). Full liquor service is available.

Pierpont Cantina

122 W. Pierpont Ave. ☎ **801/364-1222.** Reservations not accepted. Main courses $6.49–$11.99. AE, DISC, MC, V. Lunch Mon–Thur 11:30am–10pm, Fri 11:30am–11pm, Sat 4–11pm, Sun 4–9:30pm. Bus: 81 along 200 South, walk south about 1¹/₂ blocks to Pierpont Avenue; or 19, 20, or 23 along Main Street, walk about 2 blocks west. MEXICAN.

A lively Americanized version of a Mexican cantina, the Pierpont is decorated with red, green, and white streamers (the colors of the Mexican flag) and other festive touches that give the restaurant an everyday-is-a-fiesta atmosphere. Portions are generous, to say the least, and the quality is excellent, although those used to the fiery chile of New Mexico may find some of the dishes here a bit tame. Of course, you can get all the standard combination plates plus a variety of tacos, enchiladas, burritos, and chile rellenos. But the real reason to come here is for the fajitas. You choose among chicken, steak, or shrimp; they're mesquite-grilled and delivered to your table sizzling hot, with onions, guacamole, black beans, and hot tortillas. Also highly recommended is the crunchy almond shrimp, an appetizer of Mexican gulf shrimp that are dipped in almonds and coconut, deep fried, and served with jalapeño jelly. For dessert try the flan, a traditional Mexican custard covered with caramel sauce. Complete liquor service is available.

INEXPENSIVE

⑤ Café Trang

818 S. Main St. ☎ **801/539-1638.** Reservations recommended in the winter. Main courses $5–$10. AE, MC, V. Sun–Thur 11:30am–9:30pm, Fri–Sat 11:30am–10pm. Bus: 47. VIETNAMESE/CHINESE.

Known for having the best Vietnamese food in the state practically since it opened in 1987, this family-owned and -operated restaurant now also serves Chinese dishes, mostly Cantonese with some Vietnamese influences. The dining room is unpretentious—plain would probably be a better word—but the consistently good food makes up for the lack of ambiance. Menu items are listed by number—from 1 to 197—with brief English descriptions of each one; little hearts indicate dishes that are completely vegetarian, and stars indicate spiciness. Among popular vegetarian specialties is the fried bean curd with grilled onions and crushed peanuts, served with rice papers, a vegetable platter, and peanut sauce. Meat eaters will likely enjoy the spicy *Bun Ga Xao*, rice vermicelli noodles with sautéed chicken and lemongrass, served with vegetables, grilled onions, and peanuts. Beer is available with meals.

Crown Burgers

3190 S. Highland Dr. ☎ **801/467-6633.** Main courses 99¢–$5.50. DISC, MC, V. Mon–Sat 10am–10pm. From downtown, follow State Street south to 2100 South and turn left (east); go about 1¹/₂ miles and turn right (south) onto Highland Drive; Crown is about 2 miles down on your right. FAST FOOD.

In-the-know locals say this place serves the best fast-food burger in Salt Lake City. All you need to do is drive into the parking lot to know this isn't your average hamburger joint. Decorated like a European hunting lodge, with wall sconces, chandeliers, and a stone fireplace, Crown is something of an upscale fast foodery—but you

🎪 Family-Friendly Restaurants

Market Street Broiler *(see p. 68)*   The kitchen-view counter here provides a show that's almost as good as your kids' favorite TV show.

Diamond Lil's *(see p. 70)*   A visit to this Wild West–style steakhouse brings out the kid in all of us.

Pierpont Cantina *(see p. 72)*   Kids love the fiesta-like atmosphere and the yummy Mexican finger foods served up at this noisy cantina.

Crown Burgers *(see p. 72)*   All kids like fast-food joints; this is one even parents will like. The burgers are fresh and good, and the hunting lodge–like setting is much more pleasant than your average Burger King.

still order at the counter, wait for your number to be called, and pick up your paper-wrapped food yourself. The minichain's signature burger is a cheeseburger covered with pastrami; the menu also offers plain old burgers, beef burritos, hot pastrami sandwiches, steak sandwiches, gyros, fishburgers, fries, onion rings, and more. The food is good, hot, and fast—just like you want it. No alcohol is served.

Additional Salt Lake City locations include 377 E. 200 South (☎ 801/532-1155) and 118 N. 300 West (☎ 801/532-5300).

✪ Marianne's Delicatessen

149 W. 200 South. ☎ **801/364-0513.** Main courses $3.50–$7.95. AE, MC, V. Restaurant Mon–Sat 11am–3pm; delicatessen Mon–Fri 9am–6pm, Sat 9am–4pm. Bus: 81. GERMAN.

At this cafe-style combination delicatessen-restaurant, you can peruse a German newspaper or magazine over a bratwurst or liverwurst sandwich, a variety of sausage platters, or a bowl of the goulash soup that locals love (it's served Tuesdays and Fridays only). As you would expect in a German restaurant, portions are generous, and all the sausage is homemade in Marianne's own kitchen. Try the sausage sampler platter, with a small bratwurst, a knackwurst, and a weisswurst, served with buttered rye bread and your choice of potato salad, sauerkraut, fried potatoes, or red cabbage. The sausages and other menu items are available to go from the deli. Domestic and imported beer is served.

5 Exploring Temple Square

This is Mecca for the members of the Church of Jesus Christ of Latter-day Saints, also known as Mormons. The four-block square is enclosed by 15-foot walls, with a gate in the center of each. In addition to the church buildings, the square is home to the North and South Visitor Centers as well as lovely gardens and statuary. Even if you start at the South Visitor Center, you may want to stop into the North Visitor Center for a look at its murals and 11-foot replica of Thorvaldsen's *Cristus.*

The **Temple** is used only for the Mormons' most sacred ordinances and is not open to the public. Brigham Young, within four days of entering the valley, chose the sight, and work was begun on the six-spired granite structure in 1853; it took 40 years to complete.

The oval **Tabernacle** seats 6,500 people and has one of the West's largest unsupported domed roofs. The Tabernacle served as the cultural center for the city for over a century. The acoustics are unbelievable. The Utah Symphony performed here for years before moving to the new Symphony Hall in 1979.

On Thursday evenings, you can listen to the ✪ **Mormon Tabernacle Choir** rehearse (except when they're on tour; call 801/240-3221 to check), and on Sunday mornings you can attend their broadcast from 9:30 to 10am (you must be seated by 9:15am). The choir was formed shortly after the first pioneers arrived, and is entirely volunteer, with many husband-and-wife members and families sometimes partici- pating for generations. The Tabernacle organ has been rebuilt several times over the years, and has grown from the original 1,600 pipes and two manuals to 10,857 pipes and five manuals. It has been said that the organ has a signature sound, instantly rec- ognizable and with individual character. Half-hour organ recitals take place Monday through Saturday at noon, and on Sunday at 2pm.

Assembly Hall was constructed in Gothic style from leftover granite from the Temple in 1880, and is often the site of concerts and lectures. Inquire at one of the visitor centers for schedules. In front of the Assembly Hall are two monuments: one depicting a pioneer family arriving with a handcart filled with their belongings, the second commemorating the salvaging of the first crops from a plague of crickets (seagulls swooped down and ate the insects).

Guided tours of the Square, lasting approximately 45 minutes, leave every 10 or 15 minutes from in front of the Tabernacle; personnel in the visitor center can direct you. Tour guides give you a general history of the church (touching upon the Mormon doctrine), and take you around the Square, briefly explaining what you are seeing. Our favorite part of the tour is in the Tabernacle: To demonstrate the incred- ible acoustics, the group is ushered to the back of the seats and someone stands at the podium and drops three pins—the sound is clear as a bell! The tour ends at the North Visitor Center with a short movie about Mormon beliefs. You are then asked to fill out a card with your name and address, and indicate whether you would like to receive a visit from Mormon missionaries.

The square is bounded by Main Street on the east, and North, South, and West Temple streets. The enclosed square is open daily from 6:30am to 10:30pm. Tours are given continuously from 8am to 9pm. Open hours are shorter on Christmas Day. Call 801/240-2534 for more information. Buses 3, 4, 5, 23, and 50 will get you there.

6 More to See & Do

Genealogy Research Center

35 N. West Temple. ☎ **801/240-2331.** Free admission. Mon 7:30am–6pm, Tues–Fri 7:30am–10pm, Sat 7:30am–5pm. Closed major holidays and July 24. Bus: 3, 4, 5, 23, or 50 to Temple Square.

This is an incredible facility, with probably the world's largest collection of genea- logical records under one roof. Most of the records date from about 1550 to 1910, and are from governments, many different church denominations, other organiza- tions, and individuals. There is a substantial collection of records from around the United States, fairly comprehensive data from Scotland and England, and records from many other countries, and the collection is growing all the time.

Why did the LDS create such a huge genealogical library? Mormons believe that families are united for eternity when all members are baptized in their sacred temples. Baptism can be done on behalf of ancestors—hence the Mormon interest in tracing all deceased family members.

When you enter the library, you'll find people ready and willing to help with your research. They have forms you can fill out with any and all data you already know (so come prepared with copies of whatever you have), and they can direct you from there. In addition, you can watch a 15-minute video that explains procedures;

Downtown Salt Lake City Attractions

Beehive House **8**
Capitol Building **1**
Council Hall **2**
Genealogy Research Center **6**
Governor's Mansion **10**
Hansen Planetarium **9**
John W. Gallivan Utah Center **12**

Joseph Smith Memorial Building **7**
Museum of Church History and Art **5**
Pioneer Memorial Museum **3**
Salt Lake Art Center **11**
Temple Square **4**
Utah State Historical Society Museum **13**

a 25¢ booklet that will help you focus your search and a map of the library are other helpful orientation tools. Volunteers are also stationed in the various areas to help you when the volumes overwhelm you.

Many of the records are in books, and many have been converted to microfilm or microfiche. Don't be afraid of the technology; the volunteers will help you learn to use any unfamiliar machines. One of the easiest places to start is the place where your ancestor lived, since records are organized first by the geographical origin of the data. From there, you can lose hours immersed in finding out more about the whos, whats, wheres, and whys of your family history—we know, we did it!

HISTORIC BUILDINGS & MONUMENTS

✪ Beehive House

67 E. South Temple. ☎ **801/240-2672.** Free admission. Mon–Sat 9:30am–4:30pm; Sun 10am–1pm; closes at 1pm on all holidays. Bus: 3, 4, 5, 23, or 50 to Temple Square, and walk a half block east.

Brigham Young built this house in 1894 as his family home, but he also kept an office and entertained church and government leaders here. Young, who loved New England architecture, utilized much of that style, even including a widow's walk for keeping an eye on the surrounding desert. The house, which gives visitors a glimpse into the lifestyle of this famous Mormon leader, has been restored and furnished with period furniture to resemble as closely as possible the way it was when Young lived here, as described in a journal by his daughter Clarissa. Many pieces are original to the home. Young's bedroom is to the left of the inviting entrance hall (handy when late callers arrived to confer with him). The Long Hall, where formal entertaining took place, is on the second floor; when necessary, it was used as a dormitory to house visitors. The sewing room was a gathering place for the children, where they helped with chores, bathed by the cozy stove, and were taught Christian principles. Of Brigham Young's 27 wives, only one at a time lived in the Beehive House; the rest, with some of the children, would live next door, in the **Lion House** (not open for tours). Built of stuccoed adobe in 1855–56, the house was named for the stone lion guarding its entrance.

Before you leave, be sure to catch a glimpse of **Eagle Gate,** a 76-foot gateway that marked the entrance to the Brigham Young 1859 homestead, located at the corner of State Street and South Temple. It's been altered several times over the years, and the original wooden eagle has now been replaced with a 6,000-pound metal one with a 20-foot wing span.

Brigham Young Monument and Meridian Marker

At Main and South Temple streets.

The marker, at the southeast corner of Temple Square, is the beginning point for the numbering system in the city. The monument was placed here to honor Young and the fur trappers and original 148 Mormon pioneers who accompanied him here in 1847.

✪ Capitol Building

Capitol Hill, at the north end of State Street. ☎ **801/538-3000.** Free admission. Memorial Day–Labor Day Mon–Sat 6am–8pm; Labor Day–Memorial Day Mon–Sat 6am–6pm. Closed major holidays. Bus: 23 up Main Street.

Built between 1912 and 1915 of unpolished Utah granite and Georgia marble, the capitol rests on a hill in a 40-acre park that's beautifully landscaped with trees, flowers, and shrubs. The state symbol, the beehive (representing industry and cooperation), is a recurring motif both inside and out. You can take a guided tour of the building (call Council Hall at 801/538-1030 for schedules), or walk through on your own.

The **Rotunda,** which stretches upward 165 feet, is decorated with murals painted during the WPA years (the four largest depict important scenes in the state's early history) and houses several busts of prominent historical figures, including Brigham Young and Philo T. Farnsworth, the man we can all thank for bringing us television. The chandelier is astounding—it weighs 6,000 pounds and hangs from a 7,000-pound chain.

Other rooms worth seeing are the State Reception Room, known as the Gold Room because the walls are made from locally mined gold-traverse marble; to the west, the offices of the governor and lieutenant governor; the Hall of Governors, a portrait gallery that honors all those who have served as governor of Utah since statehood in 1896; and at the east end, the offices of Utah's attorney general. Downstairs are a small souvenir shop and some exhibits, including a large topographical map of Utah.

The third floor houses the Senate, House of Representatives, and Supreme Court of Utah. You can either climb one of the two marble staircases or take the elevator. The state legislature meets for 45 days in January and February; visitors are welcome to sit in the galleries on the fourth floor, which overlook the chambers. In front of the House of Representatives is a replica of the Liberty Bell, one of 53 bronzed and cast in France in 1950.

Council Hall

Capitol Hill, 300 N. State St. ☎ **801/538-1467.** Free admission. Mon–Fri 8am–5pm, Sat–Sun and federal holidays 10am–5pm. Bus: 23 to the Capitol.

Completed in 1866, the Hall is a fine example of Federal-Greek Revival architecture. Originally located downtown, it first served as City Hall and the meeting place for the Territorial Legislature; it was dismantled, coded, and reassembled in its present location. Today it houses the Utah Travel Council upstairs, and the Utah Tourism and Recreation Information Center and a gift shop on the ground floor.

Governor's Mansion

603 E. South Temple. ☎ **801/538-1005.** Tours by reservation, May–early Dec, Tues and Thurs 2–4pm. Bus: 4.

Silver magnate Thomas Kearns built this palatial home around the turn of the century, sparing no expense to make it as lavish as possible; exotic woods from around the world and African and Italian marble were used extensively throughout. Kearns' widow deeded it to the state in 1937, and the 36-room mansion is now the governor's residence.

Joseph Smith Memorial Building

15 E. South Temple. ☎ **801/536-7277.** Free admission. Mon–Sat 9am–10pm. Bus: 3, 4, 5, or 50 to Temple Square.

Formerly the historic Hotel Utah, this magnificent building has been renovated and converted to offices, meeting space, and reception areas (it's very popular for wedding receptions). Between 1911 and 1987, this was a world-renowned hotel; the lobby retains its art-glass ceiling and massive marble pillars, and the architectural details have been lovingly restored throughout. It's worth a stop for a peek inside.

The theater offers free showings of "Legacy," the story of the early days of Mormonism in Nauvoo, Ill., and the trek west. It's just under an hour long, with about 10 showings a day. Although it's free, you do need to reserve a seat and get a ticket; call 801/240-4383.

MUSEUMS
Hansen Planetarium
15 S. State St. ☎ **801/538-2098.** Free admission to museum, $3–$6 for shows. Mon–Thurs 9am–9pm, Fri–Sat 9am–midnight, Sun noon–5pm. Bus: 1, 2, or 49.

Housed in the former city library, this planetarium presents star and laser shows, plus exhibits ranging from the naming of the planets to a Foucault pendulum; the planetarium's original Spitz star projector is also on display.

Museum of Church History and Art
45 N. West Temple. ☎ **801/240-3310.** Free admission. Apr–Dec Mon–Fri 9am–9pm, Sat–Sun and holidays 10am–7pm; Jan–Mar Mon and Wed 10am–9pm, Tues and Thurs–Sun 10am–7pm. Bus: 3, 4, 5, or 50 to Temple Square.

This collection of church artifacts, begun in 1869, includes the plow that cut the first furrows in the valley. The history of the LDS Church is described in the exhibits on each of the church presidents, from Joseph Smith to the present, and a theater presentation describes the museum's work and related topics.

Pioneer Memorial Museum
300 N. Main St. ☎ **801/538-1050.** Free admission, but contributions are welcome. Mon–Sat 9am–5pm, plus June–Aug Sun 1–5pm. Closed major holidays. Bus: 23.

Operated by the Daughters of Utah Pioneers, this Grecian-style building houses an immense collection of pioneer portraits and memorabilia. Built in 1950, it's a replica of the old Salt Lake Theatre, which was torn down in 1928. The main floor includes theatrical exhibits, paintings, photos, and the personal effects of church leaders Brigham Young and Heber C. Kimball. There's also a manuscript room, household displays, and exhibits on spinning, weaving, railroading, mining, and guns. All four stories are crammed with relics of Utah's history. You can go through on your own or with the aid of a guide sheet; guided tours are also available. A 12-minute film is shown at 30-minute intervals, or on request.

Salt Lake Art Center
In the Salt Palace complex, 20 S. West Temple. ☎ **801/328-4201.** Free admission, but donations are welcome. Mon–Sat 10am–5pm, Sun 1–5pm. Bus 23 along South Temple.

The changing exhibits here, featuring local, regional, and national artists, aren't exactly world class, but they're still worth a visit. There are generally several simultaneous exhibitions in a variety of media, including paintings, photographs, sculptures, and ceramics. Check the schedule for lectures, poetry readings, concerts, and workshops.

✪ University of Utah Museums
At the University of Utah, University and 200 South streets. ☎ **801/581-6773.** Bus: 1, 2, 5, 7, or 29.

The Mormons opened the University of Deseret in 1850, just 2¹/₂ years after they arrived in the Salt Lake Valley. It closed two years later, due to lack of funds and the greater need for primary education, but reopened in 1867 as a business academy. The name changed in 1892, and the growing school moved to its present location in 1900. The University now sprawls over 1,500 acres on the east side of the city, almost at the mouth of Emigration Canyon.

The university's ✪ **Red Butte Garden and Arboretum** (☎ 801/581-4747 for a recording, 801/585-5322 for the Visitor Center) has 20 acres of display gardens and another 200 acres in their natural state, with 4 miles of nature trails. Located in the foothills of the Wasatch Mountains, this is a terrific spot to take a break from hectic city sightseeing. The gardens are open Tuesday through Sunday from April until October, and Wednesday through Sunday from November until March. Hours are 8am to sunset Memorial Day to Labor Day, and 10am to sunset the rest of the year. Admission is $3 for adults, $2 for students with ID, children ages 4 to 15, and seniors over 60; children under 4 get in free. From downtown, drive east on 400 South, past the University entrance, continuing until 400 South becomes Foothill Drive; turn east on Wakara Way and continue to the entry drive for the gardens. The bus to take is no. 4; ask for the Red Butte Garden stop.

The ✪ **Utah Museum of Fine Arts,** 1530 E. South Campus Dr. (☎ 801/581-7332), is probably the best art museum in the state, with small, select exhibits of the museum's permanent collection, plus changing exhibits. The displays cover 4,000 years of human artistic endeavors, from ancient Egypt to the Italian Renaissance, European and American art from the 17th century to the present, and art objects from Southeast Asia, China, Japan, and African and pre-Columbian cultures. Admission is free. The museum is open Monday to Friday, 10am to 5pm, and weekends from 2 to 5pm.

Utah Museum of Natural History, University Street at President's Circle (☎ 801/581-4303), located in the old university library building, has over 200 exhibits. The collection takes you on a journey through time, describing the geologic and natural creation of Utah right up to the present. It's open Monday to Saturday 9:30am to 5:30pm, and on Sundays and holidays from noon till 5pm. Admission is $3 for adults, and $1.50 for seniors and children ages 3 to 14; children under 3 are free.

Utah State Historical Society Museum

300 S. Rio Grande St. ☎ **801/533-5755.** Free admission. Mon–Fri 8am–5pm, Sat 10am–2pm. Bus: 81 along 200 South; walk a block south on Rio Grande.

This museum, housed in the waiting room of the 1910 Denver and Rio Grande Depot, exhibits pioneer regalia and historic photos and paintings. There are full-sized replicas of a Conestoga wagon and a Mormon handcart as well as one of the artificial hearts developed in 1976 by the University of Utah's Dr. Jarvic. The large gift shop has a nice variety of early Americana gifts and toys, plus one of the widest selections of books on Utah—travel and otherwise—found anywhere in the state.

The John W. Gallivan Utah Center

36 E. 200 South (the entire block between Main and State streets, and 200 and 300 South). ☎ **801/532-0459.** Free admission. Daily 7am–10pm. Bus: 23 along Main Street.

Some call this Salt Lake City's outdoor living room. You'll find intimate spaces, performances, food, all kinds of characters and activities, and good vantage points for watching the goings-on. There's a gigantic outdoor chess board with waist-high pieces, a large art exhibit you can wander through, an ice rink and pond, an amphitheater, and an aviary.

PARKS & GARDENS

International Peace Gardens

Jordan Park, 1000 S. 900 West. Free admission. May–Sept dawn to dusk. Bus: 16 or 17.

Begun in 1939 by the Salt Lake Council of Women, the Peace Gardens have grown and expanded over the years, and now belong to the city. It's soothing to stroll along the Jordan River, through many gardens and past statuary and displays representing different countries; benches are scattered about for moments of rest and contemplation.

This Is the Place State Park

2601 Sunnyside Ave. ☎ **801/584-8391.** Admission $1.50 adults, $1 children 6–12, $6 family. Daily 8am–5pm. Bus: 4.

Greater Salt Lake Valley Attractions

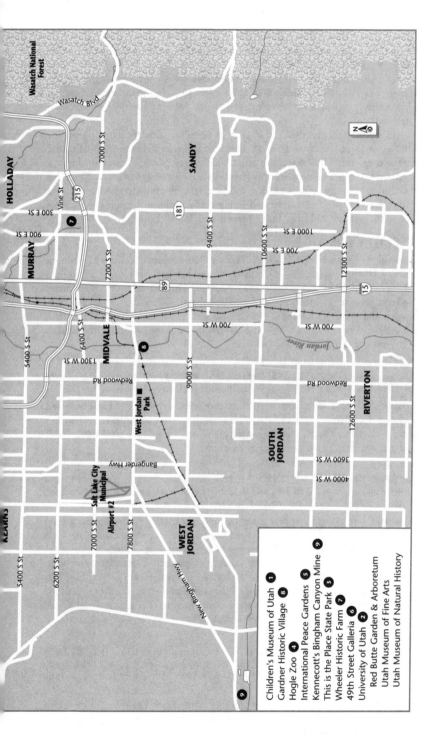

Children's Museum of Utah ❶
Gardner Historic Village ❽
Hogle Zoo ❹
International Peace Gardens ❺
Kennecott's Bingham Canyon Mine ❾
This is the Place State Park ❸
Wheeler Historic Farm ❼
49th Street Galleria ❻
University of Utah ❷
Red Butte Garden & Arboretum
Utah Museum of Fine Arts
Utah Museum of Natural History

This newly refurbished historic park, formerly called Pioneer Trail State Park, is where Brigham Young and the first group of pioneers got their first glimpse of the Salt Lake Valley. A tall granite and bronze sculpture was erected in 1947 to commemorate the centennial of their arrival. **Old Deseret** is a pioneer village made up of many original pioneer buildings from across the state. In the summer, it becomes a living history museum, with people in period garb, living and working the way their forefathers did.

A new visitor center, scheduled to open in 1996, contains exhibits depicting the Mormon pioneers' trek from Illinois to the Great Salt Lake Valley in 1847. The park, which covers over 1,600 acres, also offers hiking along part of the trail used by the Mormon pioneers, and there are opportunities for cross-country skiing in winter. It's also a good place for wildlife viewing and birding, with mule deer and a variety of birds often spotted in the winter and spring, and additional songbirds and raptors seen in the summer and fall. There's a picnic area, but no camping.

ESPECIALLY FOR KIDS

In addition to what's listed below, the **Hansen Planetarium** and **Utah Museum of Natural History** (see pp. 78–79), offer shows and exhibits that kids love. And once they tire of more educational diversions, you might want to head for the **49th Street Galleria,** an entertainment mall with bowling alleys, roller skating, miniature golf, arcades, and more. It's located at 4998 S. 360 West in Murray (☎ 801/265-3866). To get there, take I-15 exit 303 for 5300 South, head west to the traffic light at 700 West and turn north to the Galleria.

The Children's Museum of Utah

840 N. 300 West. ☎ **801/328-3383.** Admission $3 adults, $2.50 children 2–12, children under 2 free. Mon 9:30am–9pm, Tues–Sat 9:30am–5pm, Sun noon–5pm. Bus: 70.

Activities and hands-on exhibits are the attraction here. Kids can try face painting and make-up, folk-dancing and art, or operate a telephone switchboard, uncover an animal skeleton on an archaeological dig, or pilot a jet. Target ages are 2 through 12, and children must be accompanied by an adult.

Hogle Zoo

2600 E. Sunnyside Ave. ☎ **801/582-1631.** Admission $5 adults, $3 seniors over 65 and children 14 and under. Nov–Feb daily 9am–4:30pm; Mar–May and Sept–Oct daily 9am–5pm; June–Aug 9am–6pm. Closed Christmas and New Year's Day. Bus: 4.

This small but modern zoo near the entrance to Emigration Canyon offers a good selection of creatures for kids of all ages to ogle. There's a petting zoo for the little ones, and a small replica of an 1869 steam train they can ride in the summer for the bargain-basement price of 70¢. There's also a solarium with exotic plants and birds, and a giraffe house with a balcony so you can see eye-to-eye with one of those tall-necked creatures. Emigration Creek meanders through the tree-shaded grounds. As with any zoo, it's best to visit in one of the cooler seasons, or at least the coolest part of the day, when more animals are out and about.

Wheeler Historic Farm

In the Cottonwood Regional Park, 6351 S. 900 East (just north of I-15 exit 9). ☎ **801/ 264-2241.** Admission $1.25 adults, 75¢ children under 12 and seniors 65 and older. Spring and fall daily 9:30am–5:30pm; summer daily 9:30am–8pm; winter daily 1–5pm. Bus: 9 or 27.

Kids especially enjoy a visit to this working farm during the summer ice cream social in late June. There are special events throughout the year, including things like a brass band festival in August, a teddy bear Victorian tea in September, and breakfast with Santa in December. You can take a hay ride in the summer and a sleigh ride in the winter; historic farming demonstrations also take place regularly during the summer season. Call for a schedule of events. And be sure to check out the facilities while you're there: The restored Victorian farmhouse boasts the first indoor bathroom in the county.

NEARBY ATTRACTIONS

Gardner Historic Village

1095 W. 7800 South, West Jordan. ☎ **801/566-8903.** Free admission. Shops open Mon–Sat 10am–6pm, Sun noon–5pm. Take I-15 south to exit 301 for Midvale; head west on 7200 South and follow the brown "Gardner Historic Mill" signs: go south on 700 West, then right (west) on 7800 South or Center Street; it's about a half mile to the village.

This quaint village is a cluster of historic homes restored and converted into stores and dining places. The village museum tells the story of pioneer and polygamist Archibald Gardner, who first built a sawmill, then replaced it with a larger flour mill. As the area grew, he added a woolen mill, and mattress, broom, and button factories. Be sure to check out the furniture store in the restored 1877 mill.

Kennecott's Bingham Canyon Mine

Utah 48 (7200 South), about 25 miles southwest of Salt Lake City outside of Copperton. ☎ **801/322-7300.** Admission $2 per car, $1 per motorcycle. Daily Apr–Oct 8am–8pm. Closed Nov–Mar. Take I-15 south to exit 301 for Midvale, and head west on Utah 48 to the mine.

The world's largest open-pit copper mine is a sight to see. The visitor center is inside the mine, with exhibits and video presentation that tell the history and geology and describe the operations of the mine. No guided tours are offered, but you'll get a spectacular view of the open-pit mine from an observation area; you might even see an explosion, as rock is blasted away to expose additional copper ore.

7 Organized Tours

Gray Line Tours, 553 W. 100 South (☎ 801/521-7060 or 800/309-2352), offers several tours of the city and surrounding areas, including the Bingham Copper Mine and Great Salt Lake beaches. The 2$^1/_2$-hour tour of the city and Mormon trail costs $16 for adults, and $9 for children ages 5 through 12; kids 4 and under are free. The 4-hour tour to the mine and lake is $26 for adults and $13 for children. You can get an all-day combination tour for $40 and $20, respectively. The line also offers several national park package tours.

Innsbrook Tours, 57 W. South Temple, No. 400 (☎ 801/534-1001), offers city tours, with pickups at several locations around town, including some campgrounds and motels. Cost is $15, and you can add the Great Salt Lake for $5. Pickups are between 10 and 11am, and the city tour ends at 3pm (the one including the lake ends at 4pm). You should call before 10am to reserve a seat.

Old Salty, a replica trolley, gives 1$^1/_2$-hour historical tours of the city from Memorial Day weekend through the first week in October. Departures are from Temple Square South Gate at 11am, 1pm, and 3pm, and from the Trolley Square Water Tower at 12:15pm and 2:15pm daily. Cost for the tour is $7.50 adults, $6.50 seniors, $3.25 children ages 5 to 12, children 4 and under free. A family pass, for parents and up to eight children under age 18, runs $24. Tickets can be purchased at Rainbows at Trolley Square and from the conductor, or you can make reservations by calling 801/359-8677 and using a credit card.

Back Country Tours, Inc., 582 Isgreen Circle, Tooele, UT 84074 (☎ 800/882-0630), conducts all-day tours to Antelope Island or into the Great Basin in May and June, and up into the Wasatch and Uintah Mountains July through September. Each van's guide explains the route and history of the area. Round-trip van transportation plus a Dutch oven barbecue is $49 per person. Reservations must be made 24 hours in advance, and each tour requires a minimum 6 persons. Three-day trips for 8 people, and specialty trips can be arranged.

8 Outdoor Activities & Spectator Sports

OUTDOOR ACTIVITIES

Gart Sports outlets, open Monday to Friday 9am to 9pm, Saturday 9am to 7pm, and Sunday 10am to 6pm, can meet most of your recreational equipment needs. There are several locations in the Salt Lake City area, including 1176 E. 2100 South (☎ 801/487-7726); 5550 S. 900 East, Murray (☎ 801/263-3633); 838 E. 9400 South, Sandy (☎ 801/571-8812); and in the ZCMI Center Mall at 36 S. State St., downtown (☎ 801/359-4540). **Recreational Equipment, Inc. (R.E.I.),** offers a wide range of sporting goods, both sales and rentals. They're located at 3285 E. 3300 South (☎ 801/486-2100).

Biking   There are a number of bikeways along city streets, some separate but paralleling a road, some a defined part of a road with a line designating the bike lane, and others sharing the driving lane with motor vehicles. You can pick up a map of these bikeways at one of the visitor information centers. Bicycle rentals and repairs are available from **Bike Board Blade,** downtown at 703 E. 1700 South (☎ 801/467-0992), and in Sandy at 8801 S. 700 East (☎ 801/561-2626); and **Guthrie Bicycle,** downtown at 156 E. 200 South (☎ 801/363-3727) and at the University of Utah at 1330 E. 200 South (☎ 801/581-9977).

Boating   The Great Salt Lake, at the city's front door, has a marina on the south shore and on Antelope Island. See Chapter 8, "The Northern Wasatch Front," for details.

Fishing   Trout can be found in the rivers feeding into the Great Salt Lake, although no fish can live in the lake itself. Popular fishing choices are Big and Little Cottonwood Creeks and Mill Creek. Fishing licenses are required; you can get one, along with maps and suggestions, at most sporting goods stores. A good source for supplies is **Anglers Inn,** 2292 S. Highland Dr. (☎ 801/466-3921); they also offer guided trips.

Golf   There are seven city courses with one central telephone number for general information and reservations (☎ 801/972-7888). All require seven days notice for reservations: the 18-hole, par-72 **Bonneville,** at 954 Connor St. (☎ 801/596-5041), with hills, a large ravine and creek; the 9-hole, par-36 **Forest Dale,** 2375 S. 900 East (☎ 804/483-5420), a re-designed historic course with huge trees; the 18-hole, par-72 **Glendale,** 1560 W. 2100 South (☎ 801/974-2403), one of the most popular of Salt Lake City's courses; the 36-hole, par-72 **Mountain Dell** in Parley's Canyon east on I-80 (☎ 801/582-3812), a challenging mountain course; the 9-hole, par-34 **Nibley Park,** 2780 S. 700 East (☎ 801/483-5418), a good beginner course; the flat but challenging 18-hole, par-72 **Rose Park,** 1386 N. Redwood Rd. (☎ 801/596-5030); and the city's top course, the 18-hole, par-72 **Wingpointe,** 3602 W. 100 North, near the airport (☎ 801/575-2345), a links-style course designed by Arthur Hills.

From Monday to Thursday, greens fees for city courses are $7 to $8 for nine holes and $14 to $15 for 18 holes. Add $1 to $2 on weekends and holidays. Local players often head to nearby Park City and the highly rated Park Meadows course (see Chapter 9).

Hiking There are innumerable hiking opportunities in the Salt Lake Valley. You can pick up a pamphlet with descriptions of some easy trails, suitable for just about all family members, at any of the visitor centers. It describes a few trails handy to downtown, plus some in Millcreek Canyon and Big and Little Cottonwood Canyons.

If you prefer more strenuous trails, you might explore the Stansbury Mountains, southwest of the city. For maps and more detailed information, contact the **Wasatch Cache National Forest,** Supervisor's Office, 125 S. State St. (☎ 801/524-5030).

Those of you traveling with pets should note that they're not welcome on trails in watershed areas.

Ice-Skating The **John W. Gallivan Utah Center** has an ice rink; see p. 79 for details.

In-line Skating Stop at **Canyon Sports, Ltd.,** 517 S. 200 West (☎ 801/322-4220), for rentals and tips on where to skate.

Jogging Memory Grove Park and City Creek Canyon are both terrific places for walking and jogging. The park is on the east side of the Capitol, and the canyon follows City Creek to the northeast. In town, stop at one of the city parks, such as Liberty Park (entrance at 600 E. 900 South, between 900 and 1300 South streets and 500 and 700 East streets; ☎ 801/596-5036).

Rock Climbing The Wasatch Mountains are a climber's paradise. Contact **Exum Mountain Adventures,** 1427 E. Ironwood Ave., 84121 (☎ 801/273-1850), for courses and guided tours in rock, ice, and alpine climbing. Private instruction can be arranged also ($90 to $180 per person for 8 hours and $54 to $108 for 4 hours, depending on number of persons). They will be happy to custom design a trip for your group, supplying all technical equipment, and can help if you need to rent gear.

Skiing For all the details on the nearby ski resorts, see Chapters 8 and 9, "The Northern Wasatch Front" and "The Southern Wasatch Front."

Tennis There are numerous public courts in the city if your hotel doesn't have one. Check with the front desk for the one closest to you, or call the city parks department at 801/972-7800. There is a pro shop at Liberty Park, entrance at 600 E. 900 South (☎ 801/596-5036), between 900 and 1300 South streets and 500 and 700 East streets.

SPECTATOR SPORTS

Collegiate Sports The **University of Utah's Runnin' Utes** and **Lady Utes** compete in the NCAA and Western Athletic Conference. The football team plays at Rice Stadium (☎ 801/581-UTIX or 581-8849), and the gymnastics and highly rated basketball teams compete at Jon M. Huntsman Center (☎ 801/581-UTIX or 581-8849). The women's gymnastic team has been national champion 9 out of the last 15 years. Tickets are usually available on fairly short notice, although it's best to call as far in advance as possible for football games.

Minor League Baseball The city's newest sports team, the Triple-A **Salt Lake Buzz** (☎ 801/485-3800) of the Pacific Coast League, plays at Franklin Quest Field, at the intersection of 1300 South and West Temple. Tickets are usually available on short notice.

Pro Basketball The NBA's **Utah Jazz** (☎ 801/355-3865) plays basketball—not music—at Delta Center, 301 W. South Temple. Star players John Stockton and

Karl Malone are both veterans of the U.S. Olympic "Dream Team." This winning team usually packs the house, so get your tickets early.

Pro Hockey   The **Utah Grizzlies** (☎ 801/325-7328) of the International Hockey League currently play in Delta Center, although a new arena is expected to be completed by fall 1997. As the team's popularity is growing, it's best to call early for tickets.

Volleyball   The **Utah Predators** (☎ 801/485-9799) are members of the National Volleyball Association. Call for game locations and other details.

9 Shopping

Salt Lake City is not a major shopping destination. Certainly, there are plenty of stores, but with a few exceptions they're the same as the ones you have at home.

Many stores are closed Sundays—the influence of the Mormon Church—and typical store hours are Monday through Saturday from 9am to 6pm. Shopping malls are the exception; they're often open Sunday afternoons from noon until 5 or 6pm, and also stay open a few hours later weeknight evenings.

The Temple Square Area   This is the city's top shopping area. The best place to start is **Crossroads Plaza,** 50 S. Main St. (☎ 801/531-1799), right across the street from the Square. This enclosed mall houses close to 150 stores, and can supply almost all your wants and needs, from books and clothing to music boxes and original art.

Nearby, **ZCMI Center Mall,** 36 S. State St. (☎ 801/321-8745), is the home of the original **Zion's Cooperative Mercantile Institution,** which claims to be America's first department store, opened by the Mormon church in 1868. Also here is **Deseret Books,** where you'll find an abundance of books on the Mormon church and recordings of the Mormon Tabernacle Choir; plus Gart Sports, a branch post office, and several dozen food and specialty shops.

Also close by is **Mormon Handicraft,** at 105 N. Main St. (☎ 801/355-2141), which was begun during the Depression to encourage home industry and preserve pioneer arts. The shop carries a large inventory of quilting fabrics and supplies, as well as handmade quilts, a wide variety of other crafts, and religious books and videos. ZCMI Center Mall and Mormon Handicraft are both closed on Sundays.

Trolley Square   Another popular shopping spot for visitors is **Trolley Square,** 602 E. 500 South (☎ 801/521-9877), where you'll find modern shops, galleries, and restaurants in an old-fashioned setting. You'll also see two of the city's original trolley cars on their original tracks, a historic water tower, and two of the city's first street lamps.

Western Wear   If you think you can't go home without a genuine Stetson or your very own pair of Tony Lama cowboy boots, head to **Sheplers,** 5584 S. Redwood Rd. (☎ 801/966-4200), a chain and catalog store that claims to be the largest western-wear retailer in the world.

Outlet Shopping   Shoppers looking for bargains—or who need to replace that shirt they just spilled their dinner on—should head to the **VF Factory Outlet,** 12101 S. Factory Outlet Dr., in Draper (☎ 801/572-6440 or 800/772-8336). Located just south of Salt Lake City, off I-15 at exit 294, this complex houses more than two dozen outlets, including Danskin, Welcome Home, Van Heusen, Bugle Boy, and Bass Shoes.

10 Salt Lake City After Dark

PERFORMING ARTS

The theater season in Salt Lake City runs mainly from September through May, but many companies make presentations year-round, and music festivals help fill up the summer months. Get the Friday morning issue of the *Salt Lake Tribune* and Friday evening's *Deseret News* for listings of upcoming events. For additional entertainment news and event listings, you can pick up one or both of the free papers: *The Event* and *Private Eye,* which also offers alternative news articles. What's more, the Salt Lake City Convention and Visitors Bureau publishes an annual calendar of events, along with monthly updates; inquire at the visitor center.

The historic **Capitol Theatre,** 50 W. 200 South (☎ 801/355-2787 box office), is home to several local performing arts companies, and you can attend dance, theater, and musical productions there (see below), including Broadway musicals. Call to see what's on.

CLASSICAL MUSIC

The highly acclaimed ✪ **Utah Symphony,** considered one of the country's top symphony orchestras, performs year-round in Abravanel Hall, 123 W. South Temple (☎ 801/533-6683), an elegant 2,800-seat hall known for its excellent acoustics. Favorite annual performing arts events include the November "Messiah Sing-in," with the Utah Chorus and soloists, and "New Year's Eve at Symphony Hall." But the summer series in July is probably the best time to see the orchestra, when it performs Tchaikovsky's *1812 Overture,* using real cannons at outdoor concerts at Snowbird and Park City.

The ✪ **Utah Music Festival** offers fine chamber music during July and most of August in Salt Lake City, Snowbird, Logan, and Deer Valley. In Salt Lake, performances take place at the Utah Museum of Fine Arts at the University, and at Temple Square. Contact the Festival at P.O. Box 3381, Logan, UT 84323-3381 (☎ 800/ 816-UTAH).

DANCE

The nationally acclaimed **Ballet West** (☎ 801/363-9318) performs at Capitol Theatre (see above). There are usually four productions between September and March, ranging from classical to contemporary.

For modern dance lovers, there are two companies to check out, both also at Capitol Theatre. The **Repertory Dance Theatre** (☎ 801/534-6345) mostly produces American works, both classic and contemporary; and the **Ririe-Woodbury Dance Company** (☎ 801/328-1062), one of the ten most active national touring companies, performs locally several times each year.

OPERA

Also at the Capitol Theatre (see above) is the **Utah Opera Company** (☎ 801/ 534-0842), featuring international artists. Operas are sung in their original language, with English translations.

THEATER

The **Pioneer Theatre Company,** 300 S. 1340 East (☎ 801/581-6961), is Utah's resident professional theater. Located on the University campus, its repertoire includes a wide variety, from classical to contemporary plays and musicals. Call to see what's on.

THE CLUB SCENE
Live Music

Country The **Dead Goat Saloon,** 156 S. West Temple, in Arrow Press Square (☎ 801/328-4628) is a fun, funky beer bar with live acoustic and blues every night, plus satellite TV, darts, pool, and grill food. **Sandy's Station,** 8925 S. 255 West, Sandy (☎ 801/255-2078) is a popular country-western swing bar.

Jazz, Blues & Folk For jazz and blues, try the **Zephyr Club,** 301 S. West Temple (☎ 801/355-2582). **D.B. Coopers,** 19 E. 200 South (☎ 801/532-2948), has been around for 25 years, featuring folk and rhythm and blues, including occasional big-name entertainers.

Sports Bars

Club Baci, 140 W. Pierpont Ave. (☎ 801/328-1333), has big screen TVs that are terrific for watching sports events.

After-Theater

Club Baci (see "Sports Bars," above) is also a good spot for after the theater, since the Capitol is about a half block northeast. Two other good before- or after-theater choices are **The New Yorker,** 60 Market St. (☎ 801/363-0166), and the **Oyster Bar** (☎ 801/531-6044), located above The New Yorker. They're just a block and a half south of the Capitol Theatre, close to several parking areas.

11 Rolling the Dice on the Nevada State Line: An Easy Side Trip to Wendover

The little community of Wendover sits along I-80 at the edge of the Bonneville Salt Flats, half in Utah and half in Nevada. It isn't really close to anything. One of Wendover's claims to fame is that the terrain here is so flat that you can actually see the curvature of the earth. Remarkable geography aside, Wendover is a popular gambling destination for Salt Lake City residents, who park their cars at the casinos on the Nevada side of town.

ESSENTIALS

Getting There Wendover is 120 miles west of Salt Lake City on I-80, at the Utah/Nevada border.

Visitor Information The **Wendover Welcome Center** is on Wendover Boulevard, just off I-80 at exit 1 in Nevada. They'll give you exact directions to the best vantage point—about a mile west on Wendover Boulevard—to see the earth's curvature. For additional information on Wendover, contact the **Wendover USA Visitor and Convention Bureau,** P.O. Box 2468, Wendover, NV 89883 (☎ 702/664-3414 or 800/426-6862).

THE CASINOS

Casinos offering lodging, food, live big-name entertainment, seemingly endless rows of slot machines and gambling tables, and all the other Vegas-style trappings include **The State Line,** straddling said state line at 295 E. Wendover Boulevard (☎ 800/848-7300); **The Red Garter Hotel and Casino,** west of the Welcome Center at the corner of Wendover Boulevard and Camper Drive (☎ 702/664-2111 or 800/982-2111); and **Peppermill Inn and Casino,** just across Wendover Boulevard from the Welcome Center (☎ 702/664-2255 or 800/648-9660).

THE NEARBY SALT FLATS

Even those without the urge to roll the dice or wrestle one-armed bandits enjoy watching the famous land speed trials at the salt flats, about 10 miles east of Wendover off I-80, or just staring out across this unbelievable white expanse. The adventurous might even want to do a few time trials of their own, although it's unlikely that many Sunday drivers would want to even approach the 622.4 mph record that Gary Gabolich set in his rocket car, "Blue Flame," in 1970. There are displays and information on the salt flats at viewpoints along I-80, and a short access road leads out onto them. For information, contact the **Bureau of Land Management,** Salt Lake District, 2370 S. 2300 West, Salt Lake City, UT 84119 (☎ 801/977-4300).

8

The Northern Wasatch Front: The Great Salt Lake & Utah's Old West

Just northwest of Salt Lake City is the Great Salt Lake, one of the most extraordinary natural features in North America and one of the city's favorite playgrounds. The lake's largest island, Antelope Island, is also Utah's largest state park. North of Salt Lake City on I-84 is Ogden, which owes its prosperity to the transcontinental railroad; it's a good starting point for discovering northern Utah's Old West. It's also a great home base for outdoor recreation; there's skiing at three nearby resorts in the winter, and hiking and horseback riding in the rugged mountains in the summer. Considered mandatory for all railroad buffs is a visit to Golden Spike National Historic Site, the point where the East and West coasts of America were joined by rail in 1869. I-84 also leads to U.S. 89/91 and the pretty little town of Logan, which offers good hiking, horseback riding, and biking opportunities.

1 The Great Salt Lake & Antelope Island State Park

You wouldn't expect to come across what is essentially a small ocean in the middle of the desert, but here it is: the Great Salt Lake. The lake is all that's left of ancient Lake Bonneville, which once covered most of western Utah and parts of Idaho and Nevada. Unlike its mother lake, though, the Great Salt Lake has no outlet, so everything that flows into it—some two million tons of minerals annually—stays there until someone or something—usually brine flies, brine shrimp, birds, and man—removes it. So when you see swarms of flies, don't wonder why the powers that be haven't eliminated them. Besides, they don't bite, and rarely even light on people. Minerals, including salt, potassium, and magnesium, are mined here; don't be surprised to see front-end loaders moving huge piles of salt to the Morton Company along I-80, on the lake's south shore.

This natural wonder might be worth checking out, but don't expect much. Although Salt Lake City residents enjoy spending weekends at the lake, it really isn't a major tourist destination, and facilities are limited. Boaters should bring their own boats, as no rentals are available. Despite its salinity, it's a relatively flat lake—kind of like a big puddle—so don't pack your surfboard. Campers will find an acceptable but uninspiring campground at Great Salt

Lake State Park, and some pleasant primitive camping—plus the lakes best beaches, with the cleanest sand—at Antelope Island State Park.

ANTELOPE ISLAND STATE PARK

The largest of 10 islands in the Great Salt Lake, measuring about 5 miles wide and 15 miles long, Antelope Island was named by Kit Carson and John Frémont in 1843 for the many pronghorns they found here. Hunting wiped out the herd by the 1870s, but buffalo were introduced in 1893, and have been joined by elk, deer, and other wildlife.

The beaches of Antelope Island don't have the fine-grained sand and shells of an ocean beach; rather, they're a mixture of dirt and gravel. But the water is a great place to relax; because of its high salinity, you don't have to work very hard to stay afloat—the water buoys you up effortlessly.

ESSENTIALS

Getting There   Antelope Island is about 30 miles northwest of downtown Salt Lake City, and about 16 miles southeast of downtown Ogden. Take I-15 to exit 335, go 6¹/₂ miles west to the park entrance, and cross the the 7-mile causeway to the island.

Information   For information, contact **Antelope State Park,** 4528 W. 1700 South, Syracuse, UT 84075-6861 (☎ 801/538-7326). The Visitor Center (☎ 801/773-2941), open daily from 9am to 5pm, has exhibits and information on the Great Salt Lake and the island's wildlife and migratory birds. It's on your right as you enter the island from the causeway.

Fees   Day-use fees are $5 per vehicle and $2 for walk-ins, bicycles, and in-line skates. The marina offers dock rental overnight for $6 ($9 if you camp on the boat) or monthly.

Pets   Pets are welcome in the park, but should be leashed at all times.

SPORTS & OUTDOOR ACTIVITIES

Biking, Hiking & Horseback Riding   Most of the island is closed to vehicular traffic, but there are over 30 miles of hiking trails and bike and horse paths. Although generally unmarked, trails follow old ranch roads. Check at the visitor center or talk with a ranger before heading out; they can fill you in on current conditions and tell you where you're most likely to spot wildlife.

At this writing, there are no concessions for rentals on the island, so you'll have to bring your own bikes (and horses, if you'd like to ride). For information on bike-rental shops in Salt Lake City, see p. 84.

The 3-mile **Lake Side Trail** leaves the Bridger Bay Campground and follows the beach around the northwestern tip of the island to the group camping area on White Rock Bay. The walk is magnificent at sunset. Other trails take you away from the crowds, where you might catch a glimpse of buffalo or some of the other wildlife that make the island their home.

Swimming   The largest beach is at Bridger Bay, where you'll find picnic tables and modern restrooms with outdoor showers to wash off the salt.

Wildlife Watching   You can drive to the buffalo corral and see these great shaggy creatures fairly close up. If you head into the less-traveled areas, you might see deer, buffalo, bobcats, elk, or coyote.

The annual bison roundup takes place in late November and early December. You can usually see wranglers herding the bison into corrals in the last weekend of

November (binoculars might be helpful), and get a close-up view the next weekend as the bison get their annual checkups. Call to find out exactly when the roundup will be on.

CAMPING

There are two camping areas in the park: **Bridger Bay Campground** offers primitive camping at $9 per night; you can also use the parking area at **Bridger Bay Beach** for $11 a night (extra vehicles are $7). Although there are no hookups at either area, there are modern restrooms with showers, and picnic tables at Bridger Bay Beach. Camping reservations can be made with a major credit card by calling 801/773-2941 or 800/322-3770.

MORE TO SEE & DO

Ten miles south of the visitor center, down a washboard-like gravel road, is the **Fielding Garr Ranch House.** The original three-room adobe house, built in 1848, was lived in until the state acquired it in 1981. In addition to the ranch house, there's the small building that was a schoolroom by day and sleeping quarters for the farmhands at night, plus a spring house, the only freshwater source.

In 1995, the ranch was open several weekends in the warmer months, but plans are underway to improve the road and have the house open year-round. Volunteers are usually available to answer questions and talk about the ranch. Inquire at the visitor center.

There's a small food concession at the ranch (open only when the ranch is open), as well as a large shady picnic area. Half-hour wagon rides are available at a cost of $5 for adults, $4 for children ages 6 to 12, and $20 for a family of up to six. Check with the visitor center for schedule.

GREAT SALT LAKE STATE PARK

A less-than-exciting stretch of muddy-sandy beach greets you as you step out of your car at the beach end of this park. But the expanse of water and distant islands can be lovely, especially at dusk or early in the morning. Prickly-pear cactus blooms along the shore of the Great Salt Lake in the late spring. And for those susceptible to the lure of the sea, this huge inland ocean is mysteriously irresistible any time of year.

One thing you need to be prepared for: The air can be heavy with the stench of rotting algae at times, making even a brief stroll on the beach here quite unpleasant. At other times, when the wind is right or the lake high enough, trekking out to the water's edge is downright enjoyable.

ESSENTIALS

Getting There   Great Salt Lake State Park is 16 miles west of Salt Lake City. Take I-80 west out of Salt Lake City to exit 104; head east on the frontage road about 2 miles to the park entrance.

Information   For information, contact **Great Salt Lake State Park,** P.O. Box 323, Magna, UT 84044-0323 (☎ 801/250-1898). Park headquarters are located at the marina, two miles west of the I-80, exit 104 interchange.

Fees & Regulations   Day use from 8am to sunset is free. Alcoholic beverages are forbidden.

Pets   Pets are not allowed in this park, though they are allowed at most of Utah's state parks.

OUTDOOR ACTIVITIES

Sailing and water sports are the main attractions here, plus lazing on the beach. There are picnic tables, open showers for washing off salt and sand after a float in the lake, and modern restrooms. The marina, two miles west of the I-80 exit 104 interchange, is open year-round. Boat slips and a launching ramp are available, but no boat rentals.

CAMPING

Camping is allowed along the beach, where there are a few picnic shelters, flush toilets, and outdoor showers for washing off sand and salt. Camping fees, collected by a ranger, are $7 Sunday through Thursday, and $8 on Fridays, Saturdays, and holidays.

MORE TO SEE & DO

The Moorish **Saltair Resort & Pavilion** (☎ 801/250-4400) is a striking sight, set on the south side of the Great Salt Lake. The first resort, even more lavishly Moorish, was built in 1893 on 2,500 10-inch wooden pillars and went out over the water. The resort, burned to the pilings in 1925, was rebuilt, abandoned in the late 1950s after the receding lake left it high and dry, and finally burned again in 1970. After several attempts to revive it succumbed to flooding and fire, the present building was built south of the original site, back on the sand.

Dances and concerts take place in the huge domed ballroom, and there are a variety of food concessions here. It's open daily in the summer from 10am to 8pm, to 5pm daily in winter; there are extended hours on concert nights. Admission fees vary depending on the event; inquire at the information desk or check the daily newspaper entertainment section for schedules and prices.

2 Ogden: Utah's West at its Wildest

Located in the deltas of the Ogden and Weber rivers, Ogden has always been a bit different, a city apart from the rest of Utah. Although founded by Mormon pioneers, laid out by church leader Brigham Young, and called home by a sizeable Mormon population, Ogden really began life as a popular rendezvous site for mountain men and fur trappers in the 1820s, and became —much to the chagrin of the church—a seriously rowdy railroad town in the 1870s. It retains some of that devil-may-care attitude today.

But Ogden's current popularity has little to do with such sinful beginnings. Like other Wasatch Front communities, the bustling city of more than 60,000 has fine little museums and historic sites, good restaurants and hotels, and, most importantly, is a great base for enjoying the surrounding mountains, whatever your preference: skiing, snowmobiling, hiking, mountainbiking, horseback riding, or boating. Mt. Ben Lomond Peak, which lies to the east of the city, may look familiar—it inspired the famous Paramount Pictures logo.

ESSENTIALS
GETTING THERE

By Car   Ogden is 35 miles north of Salt Lake City. It's easily accessible from the north and south via I-15, and from the east and northwest from I-84.

By Airport Shuttle   Shuttle service is available to and from Salt Lake International Airport from **Rocky Mountain Transportation** (☎ 801/627-5555 in Ogden, 801/

576-0772 in Salt Lake). The one-way, per-person cost is $20 to $22. For best service, call at least 24 hours in advance. **Classic Limousine & Airport Shuttle** (☎ 801/393-4055) offers shared and private vehicle service. Shared service for the Ogden area costs $16 to $18 per person, one way. Private rates are $64 for one to four persons one way, $10 each additional person.

By Train Amtrak (☎ 800/872-7245) provides service to Union Station, 2501 Wall Ave., on several runs weekly from Portland, Seattle, Spokane, San Francisco, and Chicago. There's no local service from Salt Lake City.

INFORMATION

The **Ogden/Weber Chamber of Commerce & Convention & Visitor's Bureau** maintains an information center in Union Station, 2501 Wall Ave., Ogden, UT 84401 (☎ 801/627-8290 or 800/255-8824). From I-15 north, take exit 342, follow Riverdale Road to Wall Avenue and turn north (left) to the station. From I-84 west, take exit 81 for Riverdale Road to Wall Avenue and turn north (left). From I-15 south/I-84 east, take exit 345, follow 24th Street east to Wall Avenue, and turn south (right) to the station.

For information regarding the national forests in the area, contact the **Ogden Ranger District,** National Forest, 507 25th St., Suite 103, Ogden, UT 84401 (☎ 801/625-5112). National forest information is also available at the visitor information center at Union Station.

GETTING AROUND

As in most of Utah, driving is the easiest way to get around Ogden. The streets are laid out in typically neat Mormon pioneer fashion, but with a slightly different nomenclature. Those running east–west are numbered from 1st Street in the north to 47th in the south, and north–south streets are named for U.S. presidents and other historical figures. The city center is usually considered to be at the intersection of historic 25th Street and Washington Boulevard.

Car-rental agencies with offices in Ogden include **Avis** (☎ 801/394-5984 or 800/831-2847), **Budget** (☎ 800/237-7251 or 800/527-0700), **Hertz** (☎ 801/621-6500 or 800/654-3131), **National** (☎ 801/393-8800 or 800/227-7368), **Sears** (☎ 800/237-7251) and **Thrifty** (☎ 801/627-3069 or 800/367-2277).

The **Utah Transit Authority,** 135 W. 17th St. (☎ 801/627-3500), provides regular bus transportation throughout the greater Ogden area, Monday through Saturday. Schedules are available at the information center in Union Station.

For taxi service, call **Yellow Cab Co.** (☎ 801/394-9411). Limousine service is available from **Classic Limo** (☎ 801/393-4055).

FAST FACTS: OGDEN

There are two fairly large hospitals in Ogden: The **McKay-Dee Hospital Center,** 3939 Harrison Blvd. (☎ 801/627-2800, in emergencies 801/625-2020), and the **Ogden Regional Medical Center,** 5475 S. 500 East (☎ 801/479-2111, in emergencies 801/479-2376). The **main post office** is at 3680 Pacific Ave. (☎ 801/627-4184). The local **newspaper** is the *Standard Examiner* (☎ 801/625-4200). **Sales tax** in Ogden is just over 6%.

WHAT TO SEE & DO

Eccles Community Art Center

2580 Jefferson Ave. ☎ **801/392-6935.** Free admission. Mon–Fri 9am–5pm, Sat 10am–4pm. From I-15, take exit 345 and head east on 24th Street to Jefferson Avenue, and turn right (south); the Art Center is two blocks ahead.

This 2½-story turreted, castle-like mansion was built in 1893 and purchased three years later by David and Bertha Eccles. Throughout her life, Bertha welcomed community groups into her home and made it known to her family that she wished the house always to be used for education and cultural enrichment. Since 1948 her wish has been fulfilled, and in 1959 the Ogden Community Arts Council moved in.

Changing art exhibits are displayed in the Main House and Carriage House galleries, featuring works by local, regional, and national artists in a variety of media. Works from the Art Center's permanent collection are on display in the offices and the third-floor hall. Included are works by past Utah painters, but the focus is on contemporary Utah artists; at least two works are added to the collection each year.

Classes in the visual arts and dance are offered, as well as occasional piano recitals; call for schedules and details.

Fort Buenaventura State Park

2450 South "A" Ave. ☎ **801/621-4808.** Admission $1.50 for adults, $1 for children ages 6–15, $6 maximum per family. Daily 8am–dark. Take 24th Street west across the railroad tracks and turn south onto "A" Avenue to the park.

With a replica of an 1846 fort and trading post, and exhibits depicting the mountain men and fur trade of the area back to the 1820s, this historical park shows what life was like in this rugged land before "civilization" arrived. Built in 1846 by fur trapper and horse trader Miles Goodyear, Fort Buenaventura was the first permanent Anglo settlement in the Great Basin. The Mormons bought the fort when they arrived in 1849, and the city of Ogden grew up around it.

Today, the reconstructed fort represents the area's transition from the territory of nomadic Native American tribes and trappers to permanent settlements in the American West. The ranger who guides your tour will be able to answer any questions you have about the mountain man era. A visitor center has exhibits of Native American artifacts typical of the area; there's also a huge buffalo head on the wall.

Fort Buenaventura hosts several traditional mountain man rendezvous each year, with music, Dutch oven food, and a variety of contests that usually include a tomahawk throw, a canoe race, a shooting competition, and foot races, with all competitors in pre-1840s dress. The rendezvous are usually scheduled on Easter (with a nondenominational sunrise service and Easter egg hunt) and Labor Day weekends. There's also a Pioneer Skills Festival on July 24th.

Mountain man supplies are available in a shop in the fort every Saturday year-round. The park also has ponds, canoes for rent ($5 per hour, $10 for 3 hours), and a picnic area. A 2-mile hiking trail meanders around the park, and fishing is permitted with a current license. There is group camping only (be sure to make a reservation) at all times except Rendezvous.

George S. Eccles Dinosaur Park

1544 E. Park Blvd., Ogden River Parkway. ☎ **801/393-3466.** Admission $3.50 adults, $1.50 children 3–17, $2.50 seniors. Mon–Sat 10am–6pm, Sun noon–6pm. Follow 12th Street, which becomes Canyon Road, east to the mouth of Ogden Canyon; turn right and then right again onto Park Boulevard.

Wander among life-size reproductions of over 40 prehistoric monsters from the Cretaceous, Jurassic, and Triassic periods. There are interactive displays and activities, as well.

✪ Hill Aerospace Museum

7961 Wardleigh Rd., Hill Air Force Base. ☎ **801/777-6818.** Free admission. Tues–Fri 9am–4:30pm, Sat–Sun 9am–5:30pm. From I-15, take exit 341 to the museum.

You'll get a close-up view of more than 50 planes, plus missiles and bombs, on your self-guided walking tour through this museum. Among the most prized displays are the SR-71 "Blackbird" spy plane and the B-17 "Flying Fortress." You'll also see a World War II chapel, a fire truck, a Gatling gun, and a Norden bombsight. Displays show visitors the history of the Air Force, how aircraft fly, and what the Air Force does today.

Ogden Nature Center

966 W. 12th St. ☎ **801/621-7595.** Admission $1 ages 4 and older, under 4 free. Mon–Sat 10am–4pm. From I-15, take exit 347 and head east on 12th Street.

A place to get away from the hustle and bustle of the city, this wildlife sanctuary is also an animal hospital where injured wild animals are treated, released back to the wild when possible, and kept when not. There are trails for warm-weather strolling, and snowshoeing or cross-country skiing when snow blankets the ground. A new Learning and Visitors Center houses wildlife exhibits, a library, educational programs, and a museum shop.

Treehouse Children's Museum

Ogden City Mall. ☎ **801/394-9663.** Admission $1 adults, $2 children 3–13. Mon 4–9pm (10am–9pm in summer and on Mon holidays), Tues–Thurs 10am–6pm, Fri 10am–9pm, Sat 10am–7pm. Take exit 246 off I-15 and head east on 21st Street to Washington Blvd.; turn right for one block, then right at 22nd Street and enter the north Mall parking lot.

This is a hands-on entertaining and learning experience for kids and grown-ups, where you can climb into the giant treehouse or walk around the state of Utah in a matter of minutes. In the Pen and Ink Studio, you can make books, bookmarks, cards, or stationery. There are scheduled events, including a theater program and group craft activities based on children's books; call for schedule. And, just like the children who come here, Treehouse keeps growing and changing—so who knows what you might find on your visit?

✪ Union Station

2501 Wall Ave. ☎ **801/629-8535.** Admission to museums $2 adults, $2.50 seniors over 65, $1 children 3–12, free under 3. Mon–Sat 10am–5pm. Take exit 344 off I-15 and follow 31st Street east to Wall Avenue; go north six blocks to the station.

This stately depot faces historic 25th Street, with lovely flowers and a fountain gracing the cobbled courtyard in front. Built in 1924 to replace the original depot (destroyed by fire), the station now houses several museums, an art gallery, a gift shop, a theater, the Union Grill (see "Where to Dine," below), a visitor information center, the Amtrak ticket office, and the Ogden/Weber Convention and Visitors Bureau.

The **Utah State Railroad Museum** displays gas turbine locomotive designs and has an extensive HO-gauge layout that depicts the construction and geography of the 1,776-mile transcontinental route. You can either wander around on your own or be guided through by a railroad buff who can describe the whys and wherefores of what you'll be seeing.

The **Browning Firearms Museum** displays Browning guns from 1878 to modern times. There's also a replica of an 1880s gun shop and a film describing the Browning legacy.

The **Browning-Kimball Car Collection** displays beautiful examples of classic cars, mostly luxury models. You can see about a dozen vehicles from the early 1900s, including a 1901 curved-dash Oldsmobile, Pierce-Arrows from 1909 and 1931, a 1910 Simplex Runabout, a 1931 Lincoln, and a 1932 Lincoln 12-cylinder Berline. There's also a display of historical license plates and early gas pumps.

The station's restored **waiting room,** now stripped of the long wooden benches of yesteryear, is used for large functions. The immense room boasts a mural at either end commemorating the building of the railroad and the linking of east and west (which you can learn more about on a visit to Golden Spike National Historic Site; see p. 106). Both 12-by-50–foot murals were done in the late 1970s by Edward Laning, and based on murals he painted in 1935 for New York's Ellis Island Immigration Building.

The **Myra Powell Gallery** exhibits a variety of art through invitational and competitive shows.

Outside the depot is a pavilion containing historic railroad rolling stock. Displays include the Union Pacific turbine X26 and tender, 6916 Centennial locomotive, GP-9 Southern Pacific diesel, and several cabooses.

A WALKING TOUR
Historic Downtown Ogden

A walk through Ogden's past is a walk through the history of the American West. Allow between 1 and 2 hours, and begin your tour at the:

1. **Miles Goodyear Cabin & The Weber Stake Relief Society Building,** 2148 Grant Ave., on Tabernacle Square. The cabin was built in 1845 of cottonwood logs on the Weber River at Fort Buenaventura, now a state park (see above), and was probably the first permanent pioneer home in Utah. The 1902 Gothic-style brick Relief Society Building now houses the Daughters of Utah Pioneers Museum (☎ 801/393-4460), containing pioneer photographs, artifacts, and memorabilia, and is open Monday to Saturday in the summer.

   Now head south on Grant Avenue for three blocks to:

2. **Ogden Post Office,** 298 24th St. This is one of two fine examples of Classical Revival Federal architecture in Utah (the other is the Salt Lake City Post Office). This building, built between 1905 and 1909, was a post office, a courthouse, and offices until 1974. The courtroom, on the second floor, the lobby, elevator, and much of the beautiful woodwork has been lovingly renovated; the building now houses a bank and other offices.

   Next turn east on 24th Street; a block down the street, you'll reach the:

3. **Eccles Building,** 385 24th St. This steel-framed, brick-faced, box-like 1913 building with "Chicago-style" windows combines elements of the Prairie style with classical details, evident in the terra-cotta figurines and geometric motifs along the second and eighth floor cornices.

   Turn south onto Washington Boulevard, and continue to the:

4. **Egyptian Theatre,** 439 Washington Blvd. Built as a movie theater in the Egyptian Revival style in 1924, the theater was under renovation during our visit, and the work should be completed by fall 1996. The facade has four fluted columns, with two sculpted Pharaohs between each, and two sculptures of deities perched on the roof. The exotic interior is equally unusual for this area, with the proscenium decorated with paintings of Egyptian figures and colorful columns.

   Cross the street now to the:

5. **Radisson Hotel,** 2510 Washington Blvd., located in the Italian Renaissance Revival Bigelow Hotel, built in 1927 around the remains of the 1890 Reed Hotel. The lobby is fascinating with its rococo trim, elaborate ceilings, and crystal chandeliers.

   Finally, cross again to the:

6. **Municipal Building,** 2539 Washington Blvd. One of the finest representations of the art deco style of architecture in Ogden, and probably all of Utah. It's also

an excellent example of a WPA project from the 1930s. Built in 1939, the Municipal Building is brick with glazed terra-cotta trim. It's a series of rectangular blocks, symmetrically tapered to the tall central mass—grand and awe-inspiring.

WINDING DOWN   Take a few minutes to walk along **Historic 25th Street.** The collection of early 20th-century buildings has been undergoing a much-needed renovation in the last few years. Many of the old businesses have moved to suburban shopping centers, but antique shops, restaurants, and pubs are taking over. A few empty lots, though, are silent reminders that some of the past has been lost forever.

NEARBY SIGHTS & ATTRACTIONS
HUNTSVILLE: THE "SIN & SALVATION TOUR"

Locals jokingly refer to visiting Huntsville as taking the "Sin and Salvation Tour." The town is about 15 miles east of Ogden on Utah 39; it'll take you 20 or 25 minutes to get there, but it's well worth the drive.

Your first stop is the ✪ **Shooting Star Saloon,** 7350 E. 200 South (☎ 801/745-2002), for a draft beer and one of the best hamburgers in the state. Opened in the last years of the 19th century, it's said to be the oldest continuously operating saloon in Utah. The decor is eclectic, to say the least—dollar bills are pinned to the ceiling, and the walls are decorated with animal trophies, steer skulls, and cowboy art; a pool table and a jukebox round out the fun. Don't forget to pat the St. Bernard's head that's hanging above one of the booths. The Shooting Star is open Monday through Saturday from noon to 1am, and Sunday from 2pm to midnight.

Now that you've done a bit of sinning, head to the **Abbey of Our Lady of the Holy Trinity Trappist Monastery,** 1250 S. 9500 East (☎ 801/745-3784), for a bit of saving. To get there, take Utah 39, turn southeast (right) at the Huntsville American Legion Hall, and follow the signs to the monastery. This community of more than 30 monks established themselves here in 1947 to live "an austere and simple life of prayer and manual labor." They raise Herefords, tend colonies of bees, farm, and make and sell flavored and straight honeys in liquid and cream form, baked goods (their whole-wheat and raisin breads are a real treat), and whole-grain cereals. The reception room and chapel are open to the public, and visitors are welcome to attend any of the scheduled services. Hours for the reception room are Monday through Saturday, 8am to noon and 1 to 5pm.

A HISTORIC FAMILY FUN CENTER IN FARMINGTON

Lagoon, 375 N. Lagoon Lane, Farmington (☎ 801/451-8000), is a delightful combination of an amusement park, water park, and entertaining historical park. In the beginning, swimming was the attraction; then, in 1906, an early version of a roller coaster opened. Next came a carousel of 45 hand-carved animals (still in operation today), and so on; now there are more than 125 rides, games, shops, and food courts, plus all sorts of family entertainment, from stage shows to marching bands.

Lagoon's Pioneer Village represents Utah as it was a hundred years ago. You can see one of America's finest collections of horse-drawn carriages, a gun collection, and exhibits of pioneer and Indian artifacts. But it's not just a museum; there are 19th-century shops to browse through, a stage coach and train to ride, musical entertainment, and gunslingers, outlaws and desperadoes throwing their weight around.

If it's water you enjoy, visit the **Lagoon A Beach,** with a 65-foot twisting, turning enclosed tube ride, three serpentine slides, white-water rapids you shoot in a river tube, and more. For the less intrepid, there's a lazy river with crystal-clear waterfalls, exotic tunnels, steamy hot tubs, and sultry lagoons.

Admission to Lagoon and Pioneer Village is $19.80, $15 children under 51-inches tall, $9.50 seniors over 60 and children under age 3. It's open Memorial Day to Labor Day Sunday and Monday from 11am to 10:30pm, Tuesday to Thursday till 11pm, and Friday and Saturday till midnight; from mid-April to May and the month of September, Saturday and Sunday from 11am to 8pm. Closed in the winter. To get there, take exit 326 from I-15.

There's an RV park and campground with over 200 shady sites, both pull-through with hookups and grassy tent sites. The campground has a mini-store, and campers receive discounts on Lagoon All-Day Passports. Call 800/748-5246, ext. 3100, for reservations.

SPORTS & OUTDOOR ACTIVITIES

There are plenty of opportunities for outdoor recreation in the nearby Wasatch National Forest. For all your sporting goods needs, visit **Gart Sports** (☎ 801/ 399-2310) in the Ogden City Mall, 24th St. and Washington Blvd.

Biking The ✪ **Ogden River Parkway** is a 3-mile handicapped-accessible paved path along the Ogden River, extending from the mouth of Ogden Canyon west to Washington Boulevard. It's excellent for walking, jogging, and bicycling; it also leads to Big D Sports Park, Lorin Farr Park, (see "Parks & Recreation Centers," below) and George S. Eccles Dinosaur Park (see "What to See & Do," above).

There are two strenuous road rides east of Ogden. The **Trappers Loop Road** winds 9 miles along Utah 167 from Mountain Green (exit 92 off I-84) north to Huntsville. This route alternates between wide-open meadows backed by high mountain peaks and tall evergreens and aspens that seem to envelope you.

The second, along **Snowbasin Road,** climbs over 2,000 feet from Pineview Reservoir to the base of Snowbasin Ski Resort. Your effort is rewarded at the end with stunning views of the ski runs and towering peaks all around.

You can get additional trail information at the visitor information center in Union Station. For bicycle repairs and accessories, stop at **Bingham Cyclery,** 3259 Washington Blvd. (☎ 801/399-4981), or Canyon Sports Outlet, 705 W. Riverdale Rd. (☎ 801/621-4662).

Fishing Brown, rainbow, cutthroat, brook, and lake trout are abundant in the lakes, reservoirs, and streams of the Cache National Forest around Ogden. You might also find perch, bass, catfish, whitefish and crappie. For your fishing needs, try **Anglers' Inn,** 927 W. Riverdale Rd. (☎ 801/621-6481), or **The Fly Line,** 2943 Washington Blvd. (☎ 801/394-1812).

Golf There are several public courses in the Ogden area. The challenging **Mount Ogden Golf Course,** 3000 Taylor Ave. (☎ 801/629-8700), is an 18-hole, par-71 championship course located on the east side of the city against the mountains. Another 18-hole, par-71 course is **Schneiter's Riverside Golf Course,** 5460 S. Weber Dr., Riverdale, near exit 81 off I-84 (☎ 801/399-4636), with a clubhouse and driving range. The **Ben Lomond Golf Course,** 1600 N. 500 West, Harrisville, north of Ogden off U.S. 89 (☎ 801/782-7754), is an 18-hole, par-72 course.

El Monte Golf Course, 1300 Valley Dr. (☎ 801/629-8333), is a scenic 9-hole, par-35 course of rolling hills and old-style greens. The **Golf City Golf Course,** 1400 E. 5600 South (☎ 801/479-3410), offers something for the entire family. There's a night-lighted driving range, a baseball and softball batting cage, miniature golf, and a 9-hole, par 27 course. For one of the finest practice areas around, try **Mulligan's Golf & Games,** 1690 W. 400 North, at exit 349 off I-15 (☎ 801/

392-4653); there's a 9-hole, par 27 course, two 18-hole miniature golf courses, and a night-lighted driving range.

Hiking   In addition to the ✪ **Ogden River Parkway** (see "Biking," above) there are several hiking trails accessible from the east side of downtown Ogden. **Indian Trail** takes off from the parking area at 22nd Street and Buchanan Avenue and winds 5 miles along a narrow path through thick stands of oak, spruce, and fir trees. The trail offers some of the finest views of the canyon from above—particularly of the waterfall at the mouth of Ogden Canyon—before dropping down to the parking area on Utah 39. The trail is moderately difficult, and takes about 4 hours one way.

A little over a half mile along Indian Trail, **Hidden Valley** trail cuts off sharply to the south. The route is difficult, climbing steadily through the old Lake Bonneville terraces, with dense stands of oak, maple, and aspen. After 2 miles, you reach a turnaround; from here, you have a clear view of the rugged face of Mt. Ogden to the southeast. The hike takes about 2 hours one way.

An easy 1-hour hike is the **Mt. Ogden Exercise Trail,** linking the parking lots at 29th and 36th streets. It's mostly flat, surfaced with bark chips, and follows the east edge of a golf course most of the way, encountering splashing streams and even occasional small wildlife. The views are inspiring at sunrise and sunset.

Additional trail information is available at the visitor information center in Union Station.

Horseback Riding   There are numerous opportunities for horseback riding in the national forest around Ogden. For guided trail rides, contact **Red Rock Outfitters,** 13554 E. Utah 39, Huntsville, UT 84401 (☎ 801/745-6393). They offer children's rides for 1/2 to 8 hours ($10–$84) and adult rides for 1 to 8 hours ($15–$95), plus a 2-hour Dutch oven dinner ride ($42 adult, $37 child). Pack trips are also available (limited space; call for dates), as well as sunset, sunrise, covered wagon, and moonlight sleigh rides.

Ice-Skating   **The Ice Sheet,** 4390 Harrison Blvd., in the southeast part of the city (☎ 801/399-8750), offers ice skating year-round.

In-line Skating   The **Classic Skating Center,** 4181 Riverdale Rd., at exit 342 off I-15 or exit 81 off I-84 (☎ 801/394-0822), is open for afternoon skating Monday, Wednesday, and Friday from 3 to 6pm for $3.50, and Saturday from 11am to 5pm for $4. Skate on Monday evening from 6 to 9pm for $3.50; Tuesday is Dollar Night—skate from 6 to 8pm or 8 to 10pm for just $1; and Friday and Saturday nights you can skate from 7pm to midnight for $4.

Water Sports   Willard Bay State Park (see "Parks & Recreation Centers," below) is your destination for boating, waterskiing, and swimming.

RECREATION CENTERS

Big D Sports Park
Ogden River Parkway. ☎ **801/629-8284.** Free admission.

You'll find a playground here, along with soccer, baseball, and volleyball fields, a basketball court, plus pavilions, shelters, and picnic grounds.

Lorin Farr Park
Canyon Rd. and Gramercy Ave., Ogden River Parkway. ☎ **801/629-8691.**

This is a great place to come to cool off. There are water slides and a swimming pool, plus a playground and a picnic area with grills.

Swenson Gymnasium
Weber State University, south end of the campus. ☎ **801/626-6466.** Admission $3 per visit.

Swenson Gym has swimming, racquetball, tennis, basketball, indoor track, and weight-room facilities open to the public. Hours and availability of the various facilities vary according to school and class schedules; call ahead.

Willard Bay State Park
650 North 900 West A, Willard, UT 87340-9999. ☎ **801/734-9494.** Take I-15 exit 354 to South Marina, or exit 360 for North Marina.

For boating and waterskiing, head 10 miles north to Willard Bay State Park. Popular with locals and tourists alike, Willard Reservoir offers birding, wildlife viewing, and wetland plant observation in addition to water recreation. **South Marina** is open April through October, and has a 30-site campground and modern restrooms. Larger **North Marina,** open year-round, has 62 campsites, modern restrooms with showers, and a sewage disposal station. A trail leads from the Willow Creek Campground at North Marina (between sites 45 and 48) to a wide sandy beach for swimming and sunbathing. Other footpaths branch off towards the ponds to the east where ducks and geese often paddle. The Willow Creek Campground has some open waterfront sites, but most are along a meandering access road among the cottonwoods and willows that grow profusely along Willard Creek. Day-use fee is $3, and camping fees are $9 to $10.

SPECTATOR SPORTS

Weber State University, southeast of downtown, belongs to the Big Sky Athletic Conference for men's sports and the Mountain West Athletic Conference for women. Basketball and football games take place in **Dee Events Center,** 4450 Harrison Blvd.; call 801/626-8500 to find out what's on.

WHERE TO STAY

In addition to what's listed below, there are several chain and franchise motels in the Ogden area, including the **Best Western High Country Inn,** at 1335 W. 12th St., Ogden, UT 84404 (☎ 801/394-9474 or 800/528-1234); the **Sleep Inn,** 1155 S. 1700 West, Ogden, UT 84404 (☎ 801/731-6500 or 800/221-2222); **Travelodge,** 2110 Washington Blvd, Ogden, UT 84401 (☎ 801/394-4563 or 800/578-7878; fax 801/394-4568); **Super 8 Motel,** 1508 W. 2100 S., Ogden, UT 84401 (☎ 801/731-7100 or 800/800-8000; fax 801/731-2627); and **Motel 6,** 1455 Washington Blvd, Ogden, UT 84404 (☎ 801/627-4560 or fax 801/392-1878).

Room tax added to lodging bills totals just over 9%. Pets are not allowed unless otherwise noted.

Best Western Ogden Park Hotel
247 24th Street, Ogden, UT 84401. ☎ **801/627-1190** or 800/421-7599. Fax 801/394-6312. 287 units, including 18 suites. A/C TV TEL. $89–$109 double. Rates include full breakfast buffet. AE, CB, DC, MC, V. From northbound I-15, take exit 345; from southbound I-15, take exit 346.

This modern, full-service hotel and convention center has a guest-first attitude that results in quick, friendly, and responsive service. And the location, in downtown Ogden, is great: a few blocks east of I-15, just a block north of historic 25th Street, and a few blocks from the Union Station. The recently renovated public areas are comfortably and casually decorated, with areas for meeting with friends, a gift shop, and liquor store, and a restaurant for family-style dining. Rooms are spacious and traditionally decorated; suites include wet bars, and many have large sunken tubs.

The hotel van provides transportation around town with advance notice. Services include room service, dry cleaning, laundry, secretarial service, and express checkout; facilities include a large indoor pool, fitness center, Jacuzzi, sundeck, game room, business center, conference rooms, beauty salon, boutiques, private club and sports bar, and access to a nearby health club. Pets are accepted with a damage deposit.

Ⓢ Big Z Motel

1123 W. 2100 South, Ogden, UT 84401. ☎ **801/394-6632.** 32 units, including 4 family units. A/C TV TEL. $35–$45 double. AE, DISC, MC, V.

The Big Z is a good choice as your basic motels go; it's more homey and comfortable than most. Rudy and Edith Zuech built the motel in 1978 on part of their family farm, and have been running it ever since. Rooms are generally furnished with either two double beds or one queen, and there are four family units that sleep up to six comfortably, with a separate bedroom and complete kitchen. The restaurant serves three meals daily. Small pets are accepted with prior approval.

Comfort Suites of Ogden

1150 W. 2150 South, Ogden, UT 84401. ☎ **801/621-2545** or 800/462-9925. Fax 801/627-4782. 142 suites. A/C TV TEL. $60–$90 double, regular suite; $125–$175 presidential suite. Rates include continental breakfast. AE, DC, DISC, JCB, MC, V. Take exit 346 off I-15, head east on Utah 24 about a block, turn south.

Completed in 1995, this property is modern, comfortable, and reasonably priced. Standard suites are loaded: They have two queen-sized beds or one king, a sleeper sofa, a large closet, a large-screen TV, a small refrigerator, and a microwave. There are two presidential suites, each with king bed and three rooms; one has a view of the indoor pool, and the other, on the top floor, has a vaulted ceiling and a beautiful view of the Wasatch Mountains to the east.

Services include room service, laundry, dry cleaning, turndown on request, secretarial service, express checkout, and free refreshments in the lobby. Facilities include kitchenettes, movie channel, indoor heated pool, exercise room, Jacuzzi, sundeck, one lighted tennis court, a business center, conference rooms to accommodate 450, car-rental desk, and laundromat. Cactus Red's Restaurant serves three meals daily (see "Where to Dine," below), and plans are in the works to add 150 new units by 1997. Pets are allowed, with a deposit.

Radisson Suite Hotel

2510 Washington Blvd., Ogden, UT 84401. ☎ **801/627-1900** or 800/333-3333. Fax 801/394-5342. 146 units. A/C TV TEL. $79–$199 double. Rates include full buffet breakfast. AE, CB, DC, DISC, MC, V.

This may be Utah's only hotel listed in the National Register of Historic Places. Located on the corner of historic 25th Street and Washington Boulevard, the Radisson is a stately building, with hand-painted ceilings and graceful chandeliers. Each of the luxury suites are attractively outfitted with reproductions in solid wood, a large bath, a cozy sitting area, two TVs, wet bar, refrigerator, and microwave. Standard suites are somewhat simpler, but still come with wet bars and refrigerators. There are also about twenty standard motel rooms available.

In Huntsville

Jackson Fork Inn

7345 E. 900 South (Utah Highway 39), Huntsville, UT 84317. ☎ **801/745-0051** or 800/255-0672. 8 units. $50–$90 double. Rates include breakfast. AE, DISC, MC, V.

This is a unique little inn. The building is an old family barn, believed to have been built in the 1920s, and now in its third location. Each unit has two stories, with a spiral staircase leading to an upstairs bedroom loft. Rooms are brightly painted and cheery, with one or two queen-size beds and full bath; four rooms have whirlpool tubs. Although there's no air-conditioning, each unit has a ceiling fan. A restaurant (see "Where to Dine," below) serves continental dinners. No smoking is allowed in the rooms. Pets are accepted for an additional fee. A "Jackson fork," incidentally, is a type of hay fork used to load hay into the loft area of the barn.

IN NEARBY EDEN

☉ Snowberry Inn Bed & Breakfast

1315 N. Utah Highway 158, Eden, UT 84310. ☎ **801/645-2634.** 5 units. $85–$95 double. Rates include breakfast. DISC, MC, V. From Ogden, follow Utah 39 east about eight miles and turn north on Utah 159; the inn is about four miles up on the west side of the road.

The Snowberry, built in 1992, is a large log cabin–style inn within 15 minutes of three ski areas, and accessible to all the outdoor activities of the surrounding national forest. Each room is individually decorated with antiques and collectibles according to its name: The Indian and Pioneer (handicapped-accessible) rooms are downstairs, the Alaskan, Mountain Man, and Mexican rooms are upstairs. Each room has its own bath, some with showers only; the Alaskan has no shower, only a claw-foot tub. The inn has an open, friendly atmosphere; the dining room is right off the living room, and guests are welcome to gather around the tall kitchen counter for morning coffee while the morning meal is being cooked. Breakfast is always made from scratch, and might include scones, homemade jams, and oatmeal with nuts and raisins—and always freshly ground coffee. Pets are accepted with prior approval.

CAMPING

Century Park Mobile Home & RV Park

1399 W. 2100 South, UT 84401 . ☎ **801/731-3800.** 142 sites. $14.50–$18.75. MC, V. Take exit 346 off I-15, head west on Utah 24 about a block, turn south at sign.

This campground, conveniently located just off the interstate and not far from downtown, has shade trees, pull-through and back-in gravel sites, and grass. Amenities include hot showers, a dump station, RV supplies, and a convenience store.

☉ Cherry Hill Family Campground

1325 S. Main St., Kaysville, UT 84037. ☎ **801/451-5379.** 240 sites. $16–$22.

Every inch of this campground is utilized, but the entire park is immaculately maintained, with manicured lawns, shade trees, and paved interior roads. There's plenty to do here, with a water park, miniature golf, batting cages, and aeroball (kind of like basketball). It also offers RV hookups, a dump station, RV supplies, and a convenience store.

WHERE TO DINE

The tax added to dining bills totals just over 7%.

ABC Mandarin

5260 S. 1900 West, Roy, UT 84067. ☎ **801/776-6361.** Reservations accepted. Main courses $3.25–$5.75 lunch, $4.25–$9.95 dinner. DISC, MC, V. Daily 11am–9:45pm. From I-15, take exit 342 for Riverdale Road west, follow it to 1900 West, and turn right. Bus: 10. SCHEZUAN/MANDARIN/CHINESE.

This looks like an American cafe or coffee shop with just a few Asian accents: There are large windows, booths along three walls, about a half-dozen faux marble-top tables, Chinese dragons on one wall, and a large tank of tropical fish. But the food is thoroughly Chinese—the menu is even written in both Chinese and English. All the standards are here for lunch, from chicken chow mein and several kinds of fried rice to Mongolian beef and sweet and sour shrimp. The dinner menu is expanded to include three-course family dinners and a variety of other dishes. Imported and domestic beer is available.

Berconi's Pasta House

4850 Harrison Blvd. ☎ **801/479-4414.** Reservations for 6 or more only. Main courses $5.95–$15.95. AE, DC, DISC, MC, V. Mon–Thurs 4–10pm, Fri–Sat 4–11pm, Sun 4:30–9:30pm. From downtown Ogden, follow 24th or 25th Street east to Harrison Boulevard and turn right (south); it's about 3¹/₂ miles to the restaurant. ITALIAN.

The red, white, and green table coverings, hanging plants, and high ceiling create an open yet cozy atmosphere. The indoor greenhouse area and outdoor patio are reminiscent of cafes that line the streets of Italy. The menu includes Sicilian-style pizza, Italian sandwiches, salads, and innumerable pasta dishes. Specialties include Chicken Parmesan, Scampi alla Venezia (shrimp sautéed in garlic butter), and Bistecca alla Berconi, New York strip steak smothered with sautéed onions, bell peppers, and mushrooms. Full liquor service is available.

Cactus Red's Restaurant

In Comfort Suites, 1150 W. 2150 South. ☎ **801/621-1560.** Main courses $4.95–$12.95. AE, DC, DISC, JCB, MC, V. Mon–Sat 6am–10pm, Sun 6am–9pm. From I-15, take exit 346 and head east on 20th Street; it's about a half block to the access road for Comfort Suites. SOUTHWESTERN.

This is a light and airy restaurant serving tasty southwestern cuisine that can be very tangy at times—everything's made from scratch though, so ask for mild chile if you aren't used to it. Breakfast includes the usual egg dishes, lighter fare like fruit and yogurt, and a wide range of southwestern specialties such as the Fajita Scramble: grilled, marinated chicken strips, bell peppers, onions, and fajita spices sautéed with whipped eggs and served with flour tortillas, guacamole, salsa, and sour cream. The lunch and dinner menu includes a number of salads, pasta platters, prime rib, hamburgers, and sandwiches. Two popular items are the Aztec Chicken Salad, a grilled chicken breast on a bed of mixed greens with tomato wedges, cucumber slices, bell pepper rings, and cheddar cheese; and Pollo Casa Grande, which consists of chunks of grilled chicken sautéed with zucchini, mushrooms, and black olives, simmered in Alfredo sauce, and tossed with a mushroom pasta. For dessert, try a slice of Painted Desert Pie, a house specialty that includes chocolate and mocha ice creams in a macaroon cookie crust, topped with crushed butter toffee crunch, mocha sauce, and whipped cream. Full liquor service is available.

✪ Delights of Ogden

258 Historic 25th St. ☎ **801/394-1111.** Main courses $4.50–$5 lunch, $9.95–$19.95 dinner. AE, MC, V. Lunch Mon–Sat 11am–4pm, dinner Wed–Sat 5:30–10pm. From I-15, take exit 345, head east on 24th Street, then south on Wall Avenue to Union Station, and turn left (east) on 25th Street. AMERICAN.

True to its name, this is a delightful little restaurant in one of the oldest buildings in this part of Ogden, built in 1888 and restored in 1984. There's a narrow front dining room and a magnificent old wooden bar complete with mirrors behind the glassware, a large atrium dining room in back, and an outdoor patio. The menu includes homemade soups, breads, and desserts, freshly made sandwiches, and daily specials. Popular appetizers include seared crab cakes with Dijon sauce and corn relish. Favorite dinner courses include marinated game hen with roasted garlic, mashed potatoes, and Tuscan bean sauce; salmon strudel, filo-wrapped salmon with spinach, mascarpone, and fresh dill; and saffron-seasoned Bouillabaisse. Each month a different cuisine is featured on the specials menu. This is also a great place for after-theater coffee and dessert: Sweet specialties include carrot cake, cream with fresh berries in a puff pastry, and tiramisu. There's full liquor service, and one of the best selections of fine wines in Utah.

Farr Better Ice Cream

286 21st St. ☎ **801/393-8629.** Cones start at 89¢. Daily 9am–11pm in summer, 9am–10pm in winter. ICE CREAM.

Farr Better Ice Cream has been making great ice cream since 1920. There are 75 flavors to choose from, and a wide range of malts, shakes, and sundaes, plus frozen yogurt and sherbets. You can "dine in" or take your tasty treat with you—and you can purchase your favorite flavor by the pint, quart, and gallon, of course.

Prairie Schooner Steak House

445 Park Blvd. ☎ **801/621-5511.** Main courses $10.95–$25.95. AE, DC, DISC, MC, V. Mon–Thurs 5–10pm, Fri–Sat until 11pm, Sun 4–9pm. Head north on Washington Boulevard past 20th Street; turn right (east) on Park Boulevard. STEAK/SEAFOOD.

Diners are served in their own private "Conestoga wagon" circled around a fire at this theme restaurant. As you would expect, the main menu item is steak. It comes in all shapes and sizes, cooked the way you like it—T-bone, filet mignon, New York strip, porterhouse, prime rib. On Mondays and Wednesdays you can get Prairie Bones, which are baked, marinated spareribs. The restaurant also offers Prairie Chicken (marinated boneless breast served with a light Dijon sauce), and several shrimp and lobster dishes. There's a children's menu and full liquor service.

Roosters 25th Street Brewing Co.

253 Historic 25th St. ☎ **801/627-6171.** Reservations not accepted. Main courses $5.95–$16.95, sandwiches $4.95–$6.95, pizza from $2.25 per slice. AE, DISC, MC, V. Mon–Thurs 11am–11pm, Fri–Sat 11am–midnight, Sun 10am–9pm. From I-15, take exit 345, head east on 24th Street, then south on Wall Avenue to Union Station and turn left (east) on 25th Street. INTERNATIONAL.

This two-story red brick brew pub, with the brewing vats prominently displayed and tables that are an intriguing juxtaposition of metal and wood, offers indoor and patio seating. For an appetizer, try the crunchy Onion Loops, hand-dipped in a homemade beer batter. Soup lovers will likely enjoy the restaurant's special version of French onion soup—Baked Cheese and Ale. There are four kinds of pizzas, including a vegetarian one with mushrooms, tri-colored peppers, onions, mozzarella, roasted garlic, sun-dried tomatoes, and parsley. The pub standard, beer-battered fish-and-chips, is light and crisp. Also on the menu are several other fish plates, some barbecue platters, and about a half-dozen sandwiches. Freshly brewed beer is served, as you might expect.

Timbermine

1701 Park Blvd. ☎ **801/393-2155.** Reservations for 10 or more only. Main courses $10.95–$23.95. AE, DC, MC, V. Mon–Thurs 5–10pm, Fri–Sat until 11pm, Sun until 9pm. Follow 12th Street (which becomes Canyon Road) east to the mouth of Ogden Canyon, turn right and then right again onto Park Boulevard. STEAK/SEAFOOD.

Utah's mining days are the theme here—the rough timbered rooms resemble mine shafts, and collectibles and antiques from the mining era are scattered about. The menu offers steaks, prime rib, fish, and seafood. Barbecue is featured on Monday, Tuesday, and Wednesday nights. There's a children's and senior citizens' menu, plus full liquor service.

Union Grill

In Union Station, 2501 Wall Ave. ☎ **801/621-2830.** Reservations not accepted. Main courses $4.95–$11.99. AE, DC, DISC, MC, V. Mon–Thurs 11:30am–10pm, Fri–Sat till 10:30pm. From I-15, take exit 345, head east on 24th Street, then south on Wall Avenue to Union Station. AMERICAN.

This cafe-style room in Ogden's historic train depot offers diners a view of the trains rumbling by, and historic railroad photos and memorabilia decorating the walls. Daily specials are written on a blackboard, and the menu includes fresh fish, pasta, homemade soups, and sandwiches. A special vegetarian pasta sauce changes weekly. There's full liquor service.

IN HUNTSVILLE

Jackson Fork Inn

7345 E. 900 South (Utah Highway 39), Huntsville. ☎ **801/745-0051.** Reservations recommended. Main courses $9.75–$34.40. AE, DISC, MC, V. Mon–Sat 5–9:30pm; plus brunch in the summer Sat–Sun 9am–2pm, in the winter Sun 10am–2pm. CONTINENTAL.

A charming country atmosphere pervades the Jackson Fork Inn, an old bar that has been converted to an inn (see "Where to Stay," above) and restaurant. The menu includes items such as filet mignon or T-bone steak, slow-roasted prime rib, chicken teriyaki, and fish selections such as salmon, mahi-mahi, and lobster. Full liquor service is available.

OGDEN AFTER DARK

Weber State University's Department of Performing Arts presents live entertainment at **Dee Events Center,** 4450 Harrison Blvd. (☎ 801/626-8500); call to see what's on.

For classical offerings, call for the schedule of the **Ogden Symphony and Ballet,** 2580 Jefferson Ave. (☎ 801/399-9214).

The **Utah Musical Theater** (ticket office at 3750 Harrison Blvd; ☎ 801/626-8500), offers presentations in the summer only, and will continue to be hosted by Weber State until the Egyptian Theater re-opens in the fall of 1996 (see "A Walking Tour: Historic Downtown Ogden," above).

For after-hours entertainment, there's the **City Club,** 264 25th St. (☎ 801/392-4447) with good food and nonstop Beatles. If you want to relax with background piano music, stop at the **Skyline Club** in the historic Radisson, 2510 Washington Blvd. (☎ 801/627-1900). **Señor Frogs,** 455 25th St. (☎ 801/394-2323), has a private dance club downstairs, with temporary memberships available. The **Gray Moose Pub,** 2327 Grant Ave. (☎ 801/399-0553), provides jazz on Friday and Saturday nights. The **Tamarack Private Club** at the Flying J, 1254 W. 2100 South (☎ 801/394-4741), has '50s music and dancing during the week and western music on weekends.

3 Where East Met West: Golden Spike National Historic Site

On May 10, 1869—after the laying of thousands of miles of track over desert, rivers, and mountains—the Central Pacific met the Union Pacific at Promontory Summit, and America's East and West coasts were finally joined by rail. The nation's second transcontinental telegraph had been strung along the track as it was laid, and as the final spike was driven home, the signal flashed across the country, "Done"— and jubilation erupted coast to coast. A ragged town of tents quickly sprang up along the track at Promontory Summit, but in six months the railroads moved their terminal operations to Ogden. In 1904, the Lucin Cutoff bypassed Promontory altogether, and in 1942 the rails were torn up for scrap needed for the war effort.

Today, there are only about 1.7 miles of track here, re-layed on the original roadbed, where you can see exact replicas of the two engines, the Central Pacific's "Jupiter" and Union Pacific's "119," that met here in 1869. From the end of April into early October, the magnificent machines are on display and make short runs (inquire at visitor center for schedule). Presentations are given track-side, sometimes in period dress.

JUST THE FACTS

The park is open daily from 8am to 6pm from Memorial Day to Labor Day, and 8am to 4:30pm the remainder of year. Admission is $3 per vehicle or $1 per adult, whichever is less. There are no camping facilities.

Getting There   From Ogden, head north on I-15 to exit 368, and turn west on Utah 83 for 29 miles to a sign for Golden Spike, then turn south for 7^1/$_2$ miles.

Information & Visitor Centers   Contact Golden Spike National Historic Site at P.O. Box 897, Brigham City, UT 84302 (☎ 801/471-2209). Restrooms, picnic areas, and vending machines with soft drinks and snacks are located at the visitor center, which also has a bookstore and slide programs, films, and museum exhibits detailing the linking of the nation.

Special Events   The park schedules several special events throughout the year, with free admission. On May 10, there's usually a reenactment of the original **Golden Spike Ceremony,** with hot food, souvenirs, and handicrafts. In mid-August is the **Annual Railroader's Festival,** with reenactments of the ceremony, a spike-driving contest, and handcar races and rides. Hot food, handicraft booths, and live music add to the festivities. The **Annual Railroader's Film Festival and Winter Steam Demonstration,** held during the Christmas season, includes classic Hollywood railroad films and a special winter appearance by one of the two resident steam locomotives.

EXPLORING THE HISTORIC SITE

Diehard railroad buffs can drive the self-guiding **Promontory Trail** along 9 miles of the historic railroad grades. A booklet explaining the markers along the tour is available at the visitor center. You'll see the two parallel grades laid by the competing companies, clearings for sidings, original rock culverts, and many cuts and fills. Allow about 1^1/$_4$ hours for the drive.

HIKING AT THE HISTORIC SITE

The **Big Fill Trail** is a 1^1/$_2$-mile loop hike along part of the original rail beds to the Big Trestle and the Big Fill. The Big Fill was created when some 250 dumpcart teams and over 500 workers dumped load after load of fill into a ravine to create the 170-foot-deep, 500-foot span of fill required to lay the Central Pacific's track. The Union Pacific built their trestle just 150 feet away. It was never intended as a permanent structure; speed was the goal, rather than strength. Constructed by hand by Irish and Chinese crews in 1869, the last spike went into the 85-foot-high, 400-foot-long trestle on May 5, just 36 days after it was begun.

The hike can be done on either the Central or Union Pacific rail bed, although the Central rail bed is an easier walk. There are markers along both grades pointing out cuts and fills, quarries, vistas, and caves.

This is the desert so take water, wear a hat, and be prepared for mosquitoes and ticks. Remember that rattlesnakes, though rare on the trail, have the right-of-way. And be glad that you weren't one of the workers in that back-breaking labor effort of 1869.

4   Skiing Ogden Valley & the Northern Wasatch Front

Those looking for good powder skiing, low prices, few lift lines, and friendly people will find all this in abundance at the relatively undeveloped, uncommercial ski areas of northern Utah. Don't expect fancy lodges (at least not yet); but be prepared for breathtaking scenery, a wide variety of fine terrain, and a relaxed family atmosphere.

THE OGDEN VALLEY RESORTS

These resorts are just northwest of Ogden; to reach any of them, exit I-15 at 12th Street in Ogden (exit 347) and follow Utah 39 east. **Nordic Valley** and **Powder Mountain** are just off Utah 158, and **Snowbasin** is just off Utah 226.

NORDIC VALLEY SKI MOUNTAIN

This family-oriented ski area, Utah's smallest and least expensive, has the best night-lighting system in the state. Refreshingly informal and casual, Nordic Valley is a favorite of Ogden-area families because it's a good place to learn, with enough variety in its terrain to keep everyone happy. Recently added snowmaking equipment has improved conditions, and several runs have been designed especially for snowboarders.

Just the Facts

Nordic Valley Ski Mountain, P.O. Box 478, Eden, UT 84310 (☎ 801/745-3511 or 801/476-8027), has two double chairlifts serving 18 runs on 85 acres, and snowmaking on 50 acres. The vertical drop is 1,200 feet from the top elevation of 6,400 feet to the base of 5,200 feet. The ski season is generally mid-November to mid-March, with the lifts operating 9am to 4pm Friday to Sunday and holidays; there's night skiing Monday to Saturday from 5:30 to 10pm. Annual snowfall averages 300 inches. The terrain is rated as 30% beginner, 50% intermediate, and 20% advanced.

The ski shop, in Nordic Valley Lodge, has both ski and snowboard equipment for sale and rent, and accessories for sale. Sorry, there are no child-care facilities.

Getting There   From I-15, follow Utah 39 east about 11 miles, turn north (left) onto Utah 158 for about 3 miles, and turn west (left) onto North Fork Road to the ski area.

Lift Tickets   An all-day adult lift ticket is $16; a half-day adult ticket and child's all-day is $13; seniors over 65 pay $5. Night skiing costs $10.

Lessons & Programs   The **ski school** offers private lessons beginning at $30 for 1 1/2 hours, and 2-hour group classes for $15 per person, with a minimum of four people.

Cross-Country Skiing   You can cross-country ski at the nearby **Nordic Valley Golf Course.** Passes, available at Nordic Valley Lodge, are $5 per day, and cross-country ski rental packages are available for $8.

Where to Stay & Dine

There's no overnight lodging on the mountain; see "Where to Stay" in the Ogden section of this chapter for nearby accommodations.

Nordic Valley Lodge serves hot sandwiches, homemade soups and chile, pizza, and hot and cold beverages. You can relax around the fireplace or pot-bellied stove on a cold day, or outside on the deck when it's sunny and warm.

POWDER MOUNTAIN RESORT

This is a family ski area in two ways: It was begun in 1972 by the Cobabe family, who still own and run it; and it's aimed at providing a variety of skiing to suit everyone in the family—not just theirs, but yours, too. There are plenty of beginner runs, which appropriately seem to grade upwards in difficulty as you move from the Sundown to the Timberline to the Hidden Lake areas, so by the time you're skiing Three Miles, you can consider yourself an intermediate and try cruising over the big, swooping blue fields. There's no dearth of expert and powder skiing in the wilds, either. Powder Mountain is very aptly named, and uses snow cats and shuttle buses to get skiers to the more than 2,400 acres of spectacular powder that are not served by its three lifts—it's an out-of-bounds, backcountry skiier's dream come true. A bonus is the view: On a clear day, you can see across the Great Salt Lake or south to Park City.

Powder Mountain is also a favorite among snowboarders; boarding is allowed everywhere on the mountain.

Just the Facts

Powder Mountain Resort, P.O. Box 450, Eden, UT 84310 (☎ 801/745-3772; 801/745-3771 for snow conditions), has one triple and two double chairs, two surface lifts and one platter lift, servicing 1,600 acres of packed runs and powder skiing. There's an additional 1,200 acres of backcountry powder skiing accessible by snow cat, and another 1,200 acres on the back side of the mountain, with return to the lift via shuttle bus. The terrain is rated as 10% beginner, 60% intermediate, and 30% advanced. With over 500 inches of snowfall annually, Powder Mountain doesn't have—or need—any snowmaking. The elevation at the summit is 8,900 feet, the vertical drop is 1,300 feet, and the base elevation is 7,600 feet. The season is generally mid-November through April, with day skiing from 9:30am to 4:30pm, and night skiing until 10pm.

Powder Mountain Lodge and Sundown Lodge both have ski shops. Skis and snowboards are available for rent, and accessories are for sale. There are no child-care facilities.

Getting There   From I-15, follow Utah 39 east about 11 miles, turn north (left) onto Utah 158 and drive about 8 miles to the ski area.

Lift Tickets   An all-day adult lift ticket is $24, a half-day ticket is $19, and a children's all-day ticket is $14; night skiing passes are $12. Seniors age 65 and over pay just $18.

Lessons & Programs   The **ski school** offers a full range of ski and snowboarding lessons and other activities, both group and private, from half- to multi-day, including children's lessons, a program designed especially for and taught by women, and guided alpine tours. Private lessons start at $28. Call for other rates.

Where to Stay & Dine

Most skiers stay in Ogden (see "Where to Stay," in the Ogden section of this chapter), but for those who want to sleep slope-side, the **Columbine Inn,** P.O. Box 450, Eden, UT 84130 (☎ 801/745-1414), has five rooms and two suites, all nonsmoking, with a pleasant ski chalet atmosphere. It's located at the main parking lot next to the lodge. Rates are in the $80 to $90 range for double rooms, and $130 to $140 for suites. Room tax of a little over 9% is added to your bill.

Powder Mountain Lodge serves homemade soups and sandwiches. **Hidden Lake** provides food at the summit. The **Powder Keg** serves sandwiches and draft beer around a cozy fireplace.

SNOWBASIN

Begun in 1939, Snowbasin is among America's oldest ski areas, although the first real chair lift wasn't installed until 1946. Still, it has remained mostly a locals' secret, particularly popular for its intermediate runs, with plenty of untracked powder and long, wide, well-groomed trails, plus Utah's third largest vertical drop. Beginners have plenty of terrain to find their ski-legs on, and there are some great transitional runs off the Wildcat lift to help them move from novice to intermediate status and start cruising.

Expert skiing at Snowbasin has been growing by leaps and bounds recently, beyond even its traditionally popular powder bowls and racing pistes. It has always been a powder paradise of Alta status, and with the gearing up for the 2002 Olympics, many new black diamond and racing runs are being laid out and making their debuts for the speediest slalom racers to test themselves on. A new quad lift was installed in 1994 to access a new run, expected to be the site of some of the Olympic downhill races in 2002.

Snowboarders are welcome at Snowbasin and all lifts are open to them, with retaining devices required.

Just the Facts

Snowbasin Resort, P.O. Box 460, Huntsville, UT 84317 (☎ 801/399-1135 or 801/399-0198 for snow conditions; fax 801/399-1138), has 39 runs, rated 20% beginner, 50% intermediate, and 30% advanced. Included in its 1,800 acres are beautiful powder bowls, tree, and glade skiing. There are one double and four triple chairlifts, with a vertical drop of 2,400 feet from a top elevation of 8,800 to the base of 6,400 feet. With over 400 inches of annual snowfall, Snowbasin has no snowmaking facilities, although some are planned. The season is generally Thanksgiving to April, with lifts operating weekdays from 9:30am to 4pm and weekends and holidays from 9am to 4pm.

The base lodge offers ski and snowboard equipment rental and repairs, plus accessories for sale. There are no nursery or child-care facilities at Snowbasin. There's usually live entertainment and outdoor barbecues on ski-season weekends.

Getting There　From I-15, follow Utah 39 east about 15 miles, turn south (right) onto Utah 226; it's about 10 miles to the ski area.

From I-84, take exit 92 for Mountain Green and Huntsville, head east about 1¹/₂ miles and turn north (left) on Utah 167, go about 12 miles to Utah 39, turn west (left) and go about 2 miles to Utah 226, then turn south (left) to the ski area.

Lift Tickets　All-day adult lift tickets cost $26, half-day tickets are $22, a children's all-day ticket is $19, and seniors over 65 pay $18.

Lessons & Programs　The **ski school** (☎ 801/399-4611) offers both private and group skiing and snowboarding lessons seven days a week for all ages and abilities. Learn-to-ski packages and half- or full-day children's programs—the Littlecat Kittens for ages four to six, and Wildcat Kids for ages seven to 11—are also available.

Where to Stay & Dine

There is no lodging at the ski area itself. **Snowbasin Day Lodge** serves both snacks and full meals, and prepares outdoor barbecues on weekends.

The **Hillhaus Mountain Lodge** (☎ 801/621-2202, fax 801/394-1416), about a mile back down the road (or only a quarter mile on a ski trail through the forest), has four suites, three rooms, and a loft wing (which can sleep up to seven) with a total sleeping space for 29 people. Rooms are in the $50 to $60 range for two, and suites start at $65. The **Hillhaus Mountain Lodge Restaurant** serves three meals daily, offering standard American fare with prices from $2 to $4 for breakfast or sandwiches, and $6 to $11 for complete dinners.

Area lodgings add room tax of a little over 9% to your bill.

NEAR THE IDAHO BORDER: BEAVER MOUNTAIN SKI AREA

Skiing at Beaver Mountain is like going home to see the family. Located at the top of beautiful Logan Canyon in the Wasatch-Cache National Forest, this small resort has been operated by the Seeholzer family since 1939. The emphasis is on friendliness, personal attention, and, as Ted Seeholzer puts it, "helping skiers find the right runs for them." There's plenty of snow, a good mix of terrain, extremely well-maintained slopes, and a northeast exposure that helps make morning runs a warm, sunny experience. Snowboarders and bump skiers like the steep Lue's Run, named for Ted's mother Luella; and hotdoggers are directed to Harry's Hollow (named for Ted's father), with plenty of bumps—and located right under a lift so everyone can see them showing off.

Snowboarders are welcome at Beaver Mountain, but are restricted from Little Beaver, Ridge, and Stump runs.

JUST THE FACTS

Beaver Mountain Ski Area, 1045½ N. Main, Suite 4, P.O. Box 3455, Logan, UT 84323 (☎ 801/753-0921 or 801/753-4822 for ski reports; fax 801/753-0975), receives an average of 400 inches of snow annually, has a top elevation of 8,800 feet, a vertical drop of 1,600 feet, and a base elevation of 7,200 feet. There are 16 runs on 464 acres, serviced by three double chairlifts. The terrain is rated as 35% beginner, 40% intermediate, and 25% advanced. The season runs from early December through early April, with the lifts operating daily from 9am to 4pm. The mountain is closed on Christmas Day.

A ski shop in the day lodge has about 425 pairs of skis for rent, rental lockers, plus a small retail shop that sells hats, gloves, and other accessories. Sorry, no child-care facilities are available.

Getting There   Take I-15 to exit 364, then go east on U.S. 89 about 50 miles, through Logan and beautiful Logan Canyon, to the turn-off (left) to the ski area.

Lift Tickets   All-day adult tickets are $20; half-day, children's all-day, and tickets for seniors ages 65 to 69 are $15; those 70 and over ski free.

Lessons & Programs   The **ski school** offers group and private lessons. Private lessons start at $23 for 1 hour; group classes start at $9.50 for a half day.

WHERE TO STAY & DINE

Most lodging and restaurants can be found 27 miles west in Logan (see section on Logan, below). A cafeteria at the day lodge sells hamburgers, sandwiches, and soft drinks.

Nearby places to stay include **Beaver Creek Lodge,** P.O. Box 3621, Logan, UT 84323 (☎ 801/753-1076), located a half mile east of the ski area along U.S. 89. Open all year, this 10-room log lodge, which is completely nonsmoking, offers all the modern conveniences and then some, in a spectacular mountain setting surrounded by the national forest. Rooms have log furnishings and whirlpool tubs with showers, a large common room has a big-screen TV with a VCR and a stone fireplace, and decks offer panoramic views. There's hiking, mountainbiking, horseback riding, and snowmobiling on the property and in the surrounding national forest. Rooms are $60 to $90, and breakfast and dinner are available at an additional charge. Room tax of nearly 10% is added to your bill.

WARM-WEATHER CAMPING

A small RV park, with 15 sites, is open in the summer. The charge is $12 for a site with hookups and $6 without hookups.

5 Logan

At an elevation of 4,525 feet, Logan is nestled in the fertile Cache Valley, flanked by the Wasatch and Bear River mountains. Once part of the prehistoric Lake Bonneville, then home to the Blackfoot, Paiute, Shoshone, and Ute Indians, the valley is now a rich farming area famous for its cheeses. Mountain men first came here in the 1820s to trap beaver in the Logan River, caching (hence the valley's and county's name) the pelts in holes they dug throughout the area. Brigham Young sent Mormons to the valley in 1855, and several villages sprang up.

Today, with a population of a little over 30,000, Logan is a small city, but with many of the attractions of its larger neighbors to the west. Particularly worthwhile are visits to the Mormon Church's Tabernacle and Temple, both handsome 19th-century structures; and it's fun to drive out to the Ronald V. Jensen Living Historical Farm for a trip back to 1917.

Thanks in large part to Utah State University, there's no lack of art exhibits, live music, and theater to choose from. Summer visitors can enjoy the chamber music performances that are part of the Utah Music Festival.

But nobody who comes to Logan really wants to spend much time indoors. Beautiful Logan Canyon is a delightful escape for hikers, mountainbikers, fishers, and rock climbers—but our favorite activity is a horseback ride into the high mountains.

ESSENTIALS

GETTING THERE

By Car   Logan is 81 miles northeast of Salt Lake City. From Salt Lake City and Ogden, take I-15 north to exit 364, then follow U.S. 89/91 northeast about 24 miles to downtown Logan.

By Airport Shuttle   The **Cache Valley Limo Airport Shuttle,** 550 N. Main St., Logan (☎ 801/752-2900) provides direct shuttle service to and from Salt Lake International Airport. Two-day notice is recommended. One-way fare is about $35; a round-trip costs about $60.

VISITOR INFORMATION

The **Cache Chamber of Commerce** maintains a visitor information center at 160 N. Main St., Logan, UT 84321-4541 (☎ 801/752-2161).

GETTING AROUND

As with most Mormon cities, Logan is laid out on a grid, with ground zero at the intersection of Main (north–south) and Center (east–west). Tabernacle Square is the block to the northeast of the intersection. U.S. 89/91 enters town on a diagonal from the southwest, along the golf course at the south end of town. Utah State University is located on the northeast side of town, north of U.S. 89 between 700 and 1400 East.

The **Logan Transit District Transportation System,** or LTD, is a free city-wide bus service. A route map is available at the information center on Main Street, but one of the easiest ways to get information about the bus is to call 801/752-2877 Monday through Friday between 6am and 6:30pm, and Saturday from 9am to 6:30pm. If you tell them where you are (street address or intersection) and where you want to go, the staff can tell you where and when to catch your bus, and what its route number, letter, and destination sign are. Hearing-impaired people should call 801/750-7118 for bus information, Monday through Friday from 8:30am to 5pm. LTD also offers service for people with disabilities; call 801/753-2255 for information.

Car-rental agencies with offices in Logan include **Dale's Car Rental,** 625 N. Main (☎ 801/752-8257), **Enterprise,** 1155 N. Main (☎ 801/755-6111 or 800/325-8007), **Palmers Freedom Car Rental,** 1220 N. Main (☎ 801/752-2075), and **Hertz,** 447 N. Main (☎ 801/752-9141 or 800/654-3131).

FAST FACTS: LOGAN

The **Logan Regional Hospital** is located at 1400 N. 500 East (☎ 801/752-2050). The **main post office** is at 151 N. 100 West (☎ 801/752-7246). The **state liquor store** is at 75 W. 400 North (☎ 801/752-4145).

WHAT TO SEE & DO

Cache Valley Historical Museum
(Daughters of the Utah Pioneers Museum)

160 N. Main St., Logan, UT 84321. ☎ **801/752-1055** or 801/753-1635. Free admission. Memorial Day–Labor Day Tues–Sat 10am–4pm, otherwise by appointment.

Housed in the same building as the information center, this small museum displays pioneer artifacts from 1859 to 1899—basically the first forty years of Mormon settlement in the area. You can see guns, musical instruments (including the first organ used in the LDS Tabernacle), handmade pioneer furniture, clothing, and kitchen items. There are several pieces of furniture made by Brigham Young for his daughter Luna Young Thatcher, who lived in Logan. Also on display are dresses made by Mary Ann Weston Maugham, the area's first white woman settler, who arrived in 1859.

LDS Tabernacle

50 N. Main St., Logan, UT 84321. ☎ **801/755-5598.** Daily 9am–5pm.

The Tabernacle was built with locally quarried stone in a style that's an amalgam of Greek, Roman, Gothic, and Byzantine architectural styles. The main stone, quartzite, is from Green Canyon, 8 miles northeast of Logan, and the white limestone used for the corners and trimmings came from 20 miles north, in Idaho. The foundation was started in 1864, but the building took 27 years to complete. The stained-glass windows were installed in the early 1900s, and the organ in 1908. The main hall and balcony can accommodate about 1,800 people. The ceiling decoration was originally painted on oil cloth and then attached, but when renovated in 1989, the paintings were traced directly onto the ceiling. The pillars are wood, expertly painted to simulate marble, a technique widely used throughout pioneer Utah.

LDS Temple

175 N. 300 East, Logan, UT 84321. ☎ **801/752-3611.** Not open to the public.

The site of the Temple was known to the Shoshone as "a most sacred place," where they held their healing ceremonies. It's on a slight rise, and can be seen from just about anywhere in the valley. Octagonal towers give the four-story limestone temple the appearance of a medieval castle. The site was chosen on May 17, 1877, by church president Brigham Young, and the completed Temple dedicated May 17, 1884, by his successor. The building was extensively renovated in the late 1970s.

Ronald V. Jensen Living Historical Farm

4025 South U.S. 89/91 (6 miles southwest of Logan), Wellsville, UT 84339. ☎ **801/245-4064.** Admission $4 adults, $1 children, $3 seniors and students. June–Aug, Tues–Sat 10am–4pm. Closed Sept–May except special events.

This authentic 1917 dairy farm is a 120-acre interpretive center operated by Utah State University graduate students. Guides in period costume will take you around, discussing life on the farm and explaining the farm equipment and implements. Although not open on a regular basis from September through May, there are usually two special events planned each month. These might include a turn-of-the-century wedding, sheep shearing, quilting bees, hay threshing, or an old-fashioned Christmas celebration, complete with a horse-drawn sleigh and caroling; call for schedule.

Utah State University

102 Old Main, Logan, UT 84322-1440. ☎ **801/797-1710.** The 400-acre campus lies north of U.S. 89 and mostly east of 800 East.

Founded in 1888, Utah State University (USU) is situated on a bench that was once the shore of the great lake Bonneville. Established through the Federal Land-Grant Program as the Agricultural College of Utah, USU has an international reputation for research and teaching.

Old Main was the first USU building, begun just one year after the college was established; it's the oldest building in continuous use on any Utah college campus. At various times it has housed nearly every office and department of the school. Its tall bell tower is a campus landmark.

The **Nora Eccles Harrison Museum of Art,** 650 N. 1100 East (☎ 801/797-0163), has a fine collection of ceramics on display, and offers changing exhibits of a variety of media. It's open Tuesday through Friday from 10:30am to 4:30pm, and Saturday and Sunday from 2 to 5pm. Admission is free.

If you'd like to grab a snack—like some of the famous Aggie's ice cream—stop at the **Taggart Student Center,** just a block north of Old Main (☎ 801/797-1710). It also houses the bookstore, a ticket office, a post office, a movie theater, and a full restaurant on the fourth floor serving lunch during the week and dinner on weekends.

Willow Park Zoo

419 W. 700 South. ☎ **801/750-9893.** Admission free, 25¢ donation suggested. Daily 9am–dusk. From Main Street, head west on 600 South for three blocks, turn south (left) onto 300 West for one block, then west (right) onto 700 South.

This small but intriguing zoo is home to cute capuchin monkeys, noisy macaws, ugly condors, a fun turtle pond, waddling raccoons, elegant swans, slinking coyote, brightly colored Amazon parrots, and more. The grounds are quite attractive, with a lovely, grassy play and picnic area shaded by tall trees. Many of the animal enclosures are on the small side, and not as animal-friendly as many modern big-city zoos, but the personnel are making improvements when and where they can, money and space permitting.

NINETEENTH-CENTURY LOGAN COMES TO LIFE
A Walking Tour of Historic Main Street

This tour will give you a glimpse into the city's colorful past, and a taste of life in late 19th-century Logan. Allow 45 minutes to an hour to browse the Victorian-lined street, plus additional time for browsing and window-shopping.

Start your walking tour at:

1. **The Chamber of Commerce,** at 160 N. Main St. in what was originally the **Federal Building,** built as a post office and to house other government functions—hence the naming of the adjacent east–west street as Federal Avenue. Inside, in the old courtroom, is the Daughters of Utah Pioneers Museum, with displays depicting the life of early settlers in the Cache Valley.

   Head south on Main Street to:

2. **First Interstate Bank,** located on the corner of Tithing Square. Each Mormon settlement in the valley had a tithing house that constituted the economic center of the community. Residents were expected to contribute 10% of their income to the church. The tithing house or square was also the location for gathering and disbursing produce, livestock, and even, on occasion, cash. Above the door of the present bank is a sculptural depiction of the trappers and Indians that were typical of the early inhabitants of Cache Valley.

   Turn east on 100 North and walk a block to:

3. **St. John's Episcopal Church.** The founders of St. John's were the first non-Mormon Christians to establish a congregation in Logan. They also set up a school in 1873. After that, Methodists, Congregationalists, and Presbyterians sent missionaries and school teachers.

   Cross the street and head over to the:

4. **Tabernacle,** in the center of Tabernacle Square facing Main Street. This imposing brick structure was begun before the Temple (three blocks east), but finished after, taking over 25 years to complete. Although the Temple is open only to Mormons, the Tabernacle is accessible to the general public, and has been used over the years for both church and community meetings.

   Walk south to the corner of Main and Center, and cross over to the:

5. **First Security Bank,** on the site of the 1890 Thatcher Brothers Bank and Opera House. On April 17, 1912, the building was destroyed by fire; it was an event that overshadowed the sinking of the *Titanic* in the local paper. The opera house was on the second floor and could house an audience of about 800. Theater and opera productions by both local amateur and professional groups took place here, as well as political and civic gatherings.

   Continue south along Main to the:

6. **Capitol Theatre.** Eleven years after the Thatcher Brothers Bank and Opera House fire, one of the brothers and some associates built a new theater, one of the finest of

its day, with the only full-size stage and fly loft in the area. Since the 1950s, it's seen more movies than live productions, but it's being restored to its original splendor and has recently staged full productions of *Carousel, South Pacific,* and *The Mikado.*

Continue to the corner of Main and turn west onto 100 South, looking across the street to the remains of the:

7. **Thatcher Milling and Elevator Co.** In 1888, this now-crumbling mill had the capacity to mill 1,100 bushels of grain each day. After a half block, turn north on the drive into the mid-block parking lot; you'll walk past the back of the Capitol Theatre and through the drive-in for First Security Bank. At Center Street you'll reach the:

8. **Lyric Theatre,** also built by the Thatchers. Constructed in 1913, the theater was refurbished in 1962 and is operated by Utah State University, and used by the Old Lyric Repertory Company during the summer months. It's reportedly the home of a friendly ghost, who appears on the edge of the balcony in Elizabethan costume wearing a fool's cap, and has been heard laughing during rehearsals of *Hamlet.*

To the west of the theater, near the Bluebird Candy Company, is the location of the original stagecoach and livery stable for downtown Logan.

Now walk out to Main and turn north across Central to:

9. **Larsen's Hallmark,** in the old J.R. Edwards Saloon building; note the name still carved in stone above the second-floor windows. This was Logan's finest saloon and billiard hall in the late 1800s. The president of the Agricultural College was incensed that his students were frequenting Edwards' establishment; when letters got him nowhere, President Paul strode into the saloon and was promptly struck on the back of the head by Edwards. After paying his $5 fine, Edwards finally posted notices excluding minors from his saloon, and Paul returned to his duties on College Hill. Next door to the Hallmark is the:

10. **Bluebird Restaurant,** in business since 1914, on this site since 1923. This has been a gathering place for generations of Loganites, and is a place of nostalgia today, with its imported marble soda fountain and historic photos. It's a good place to stop for a snack from the soda fountain or a more substantial meal.

Continue north along Main to the corner of 100 North to:

11. **Zion's Bank,** once the Cache Valley branch of Zion's Cooperative Mercantile Institution. ZCMI was begun by Brigham Young in the late 1860s to protect the local economy from the outside influences brought in by the newly completed transcontinental railroad. The plan included the establishment of a large whole-sale store in Salt Lake City, with retail cooperatives in all outlying settlements. Mormons were to buy only from their local ZCMI, which in turn would deal only with the central Salt Lake wholesale store. This form of merchandising declined toward the end of the 1800s, and the Logan store was disbanded.

Cross the street and continue north on Main one block to the:

12. **Cache County Courthouse,** the oldest county building in Utah still in use as a county building. Before this structure was built in 1883, the old county office was on the site; in 1873, a lynching took place here: Vigilantes, angered by the shooting of the sheriff's nephew, broke into the jail, took the prisoner out, and hung him from the courthouse signpost.

SPORTS & OUTDOOR ACTIVITIES

Biking   Cache Valley's patchwork of farms, wetlands, and migratory-bird habitats offer excellent biking through the countryside on well-maintained country roads. A booklet describing several bike trails in and around Logan is prepared jointly by the

Bridgerland Travel Region (☎ 801/752-2161 or 800/882-4433) and the national forest's **Logan Ranger District** (☎ 801/755-3620). You can pick up a copy at the visitor center at 160 N. Main Street.

If you'd like to rent either a mountain or road bike, stop at **Guido's Cycle & Sport,** 565 N. Main St., Logan (☎ 801/752-2770), open Monday through Saturday. Guido's also repairs bicycles and has a wide selection of clothing and accessories. Another rental shop is **Adventure Sports,** 51 S. Main St. (☎ 801/753-4044), open Monday through Saturday; Adventure Sports also offers guided bicycle tours.

Fishing   Logan Canyon is popular for rainbow and albino trout in impoundments. The Upper Canyon is great for natural cutthroat and brook trout. First, Second, and Third dams are good for stocked fish, and Second Dam is handicapped accessible. For guide services and a full-service fly shop, stop at the **Riverside Angler,** 590¹/₂ S. Main St. (☎ 801/753-3646).

Golf   The **Logan River Golf Course,** 550 W. 1000 South (☎ 801/750-0123), is an 18-hole, par-17 public course winding along the river among the trees. Greens fees are $8.50 for 9 holes and $15 for 18, with carts costing $10 and $17 respectively. About 12 miles southwest of Logan, on U.S. 89/91 on the way to Brigham City, is **Sherwood Hills** (☎ 801/245-6055), a 9-hole, par-36 public mountain course. The greens fee is $8.50, and carts rent for $9.

Hiking   For a brochure describing several hiking trails in the Cache National Forest east of Logan, stop at the visitor center on Main Street, or at one of the sponsoring sporting goods stores: **Al's Sporting Goods,** 99 W. Center (☎ 801/752-5151); **Trailhead Sports,** 117 N. Main (☎ 801/753-1541); or **Adventure Sports,** 51 S. Main (☎ 801/753-4044).

Horseback Riding   About 12 miles southwest of Logan, on U.S. 89/91 on the way to Brigham City, is **The Stables at Sherwood Hills** (☎ 801/245-5054), offering 1- and 2-hour rides, supper rides (with a minimum of 18 persons), and group hay rides. You'll ride into the surrounding forests, where the scenery is breathtaking and there is a good possibility of spotting wildlife.

Beaver Creek Inc., in Logan Canyon (☎ 801/753-1076) is about 25 miles northeast of Logan on U.S. 89 just east of Beaver Mountain Ski Resort. One, 1¹/₂- and 3-hour guided rides are available, for beginner and expert riders. Prices range from $15 to $35. Trails include a wide range of terrain, from rolling hills covered with aspens, pine trees, and wildflowers along a mountain stream, to more challenging rides to the top of a mountain for panoramic views of the forest. Reservations are recommended; kids have to be at least seven, although the little ones are often led around the stable area free of charge.

Rock Climbing   With the increased use of bolt climbing in America, new climbs have been developed in Logan Canyon. For detailed information, stop in at the visitor center.

SPECTATOR SPORTS

A member of the Big West Athletic Conference, **Utah State University** takes part in intercollegiate athletics, plus a program of intramural sports. Call the school's ticket office (☎ 801/797-0305) for information.

WHERE TO STAY

The sales and lodging taxes in Logan total just over 9%. Pets are not allowed unless otherwise noted.

Alta Manor Suites

45 E. 500 North, Logan, UT 84321. ☎ **801/752-0808.** Fax 801/752-2445. 8 suites. A/C TV TEL. $75–$85 double. Rates include continental breakfast. AE, CB, DC, MC, V.

This is a modern lodging, built in 1994 in the old English Tudor style, with spacious suites elegantly furnished with Queen Anne reproductions. All units have whirlpool baths and a separate shower, natural gas fireplaces, TVs with several premium-movie channels, full kitchens, and one or two queen beds plus a sofa sleeper. It is entirely smoke-free, and there's one wheelchair-accessible room.

Best Western Baugh Motel

153 S. Main, Logan, UT 84321. ☎ **801/752-5220** or 800/462-4154. Fax 801/752-3251. 77 rms, 5 suites. A/C TV TEL. $48–$66 double, $84–$88 suites. AE, CB, DC, DISC, MC, V.

This attractively landscaped property is great for those who would rather not be stuck inside whenever they're at their motel: It has large shade and evergreen trees, a large outdoor swimming pool, a smaller children's pool, and a nice picnic area out back along a stream. The standard rooms are spacious, with two extra long double beds (or a king or queen bed), and comfortable lounge chairs. Some rooms have a swivel rocker or recliner, and all have a desk area and plenty of storage. Suites are really just oversized rooms, but with a very nice sitting area, and either a king or two queen beds. One suite has a whirlpool tub, the others have fireplaces, and some have a microwave and refrigerator.

Room service, dry cleaning, laundry service, local limousine, and free refreshments in the lobby are offered. Videos can be rented for $6.99 including a VCR, and free passes (two per room) to a nearby recreation center are available. The Cottage Restaurant, featuring American cuisine, serves three meals daily.

✪ Center Street Bed & Breakfast Inn

169 E. Center St., Logan, UT 84321. ☎ **801/752-3443.** 18 units. A/C TV. $55–$180 double (including breakfast) with private bath, $25–$30 for two small rooms that share bath. AE, MC, V.

This three-story Victorian mansion, built in 1879, is Utah's own little Madonna Inn, for those of you familiar with that California coast landmark. Nothing is as you would expect it to be here, but everything is fun and comfortable. The living room has a Michaelangelo-style fresco on the ceiling, and everything is done in bright colors. The themed rooms are named in keeping with their decor. The Jesse James' Hide-Out and Waterhole Saloon for instance, is huge, with a 60-inch TV, pool table, knotty pine walls, kitchenette, and gas fireplace. The decor is, of course, western, and includes wanted posters, a stuffed rattlesnake, and a pressed-brass ceiling; there's a private 900-gallon Jacuzzi just 20 yards away in the corner of the backyard. The Castle of the Purple Dragon feels like—you guessed it—a stone castle, and comes complete with a mounted purple dragon's head. The entire suite is medieval—except for the 45-inch TV, gas fireplace, and Jacuzzi—slightly decadent, and totally different. Other rooms include the Egyptian Suite, Amazon Rainforest, Arabian Nights Suite, Caribbean Sea Cave, Aphrodite's Court, and Space Odyssey. Smoking is strictly prohibited inside.

The Logan House Inn

168 N. 100 East, Logan, UT 84321. ☎ **801/752-7727.** 6 rms, 3 suites. A/C TV TEL. $78–$150 double. Rates include breakfast. AE, CB, DC, DISC, MC, V.

This 100-year-old Georgian manor house has a traditional American feel, relaxed and quiet, with solid wood furnishings. Each room has its own whirlpool tub, phones have computer modem hook-ups, and all suites have fireplaces. Smoking is permitted only on the verandah.

WHERE TO DINE

⑤ Angie's Restaurant
690 N. Main. ☎ **801/752-9252.** Main courses breakfast $1.65–$9.95. AE, DISC, MC, V. Sun–Thurs 5:30am–10pm, Fri–Sat 5:30am–11pm. From Center Street, head north about seven blocks. AMERICAN.

This local favorite is a busy family restaurant, noisy and casual. It's particularly popular for breakfast, which is served all day. Scones and cinnamon rolls are baked fresh each day, and the omelets—all 11 varieties—are gigantic. In fact, all Angie's portions are generous. The menu has a wide selection of breakfast goodies, from pancakes and waffles to skillet breakfasts, standard egg dishes, and southwestern offerings. If it's after 11am and you're not in the mood for breakfast, the lunch menu offers about four dozen sandwiches and burgers, plus several salads and southwestern platters. The dinner menu includes pasta, chicken, steak, and seafood. Seniors' and children's menus are available.

The Bluebird
19 N. Main St. ☎ **801/752-3155.** Main courses $3.50–$12.95. AE, DISC, MC, V. Mon–Thurs 11am–9pm, Fri–Sat 11am–10pm, Sun noon–8pm, slightly shorter hours in the winter. Just north of Center Street. AMERICAN.

The Bluebird opened in 1914 as a candy shop and soda fountain, and soon expanded to include a few lunch items, such as chile and sandwiches, on its menu. In 1921, it moved to its present location, expanding its menu again to include dinner. Today, the Bluebird continues to offer good food along with fountain treats. The decor is reminiscent of the 1920s, with the original marble behind the soda fountain and a mural depicting Logan from 1856 to modern times.

The menu offers the old-fashioned luncheon fare you'd expect, including a Monte Cristo and a minced ham sandwich. English-style chips can be ordered with any sandwich. There are several full meal offerings for lunch also, including a 6-ounce sirloin steak, chicken teriyaki, and a 5-ounce halibut steak. In addition to a few sandwiches, the dinner menu includes full dinners like vegetarian pasta primavera, chicken-fried steak (not everything's like it was in the '20s—it's now grilled, not deep fried), and the popular slow-roasted prime rib. A children's menu and senior discounts are available. No alcohol is served.

Copper Mill Restaurant
55 N. Main St., in the Emporium Building. ☎ **801/752-0647.** Main courses lunch $4.25–$6.95, dinner $7.95–$27.95. AE, CB, DC, DISC, MC, V. Mon–Thurs 11am–9:30pm, Fri–Sat 11am–10:30pm. A half block north of Center Street. STEAK/SEAFOOD.

You'll feel right at home in this upscale family restaurant, with wooden booths and tables, lots of plants, and copper-milling artifacts all around. Known for its unique beef seasonings, the restaurant's most popular items include a 6-ounce tenderloin steak, and prime rib on Friday and Saturday nights. There are also several chicken offerings, including a Louie and a Cordon Bleu version. The seafood offerings include halibut, scallops, and shrimp. There's a children's menu, and beer and wine are served.

Grapevine
129 N. 100 East. ☎ **801/752-1977.** Reservations recommended. Main courses $11.95–$17.95. AE, DISC, MC, V. Wed–Sat 5:30–10pm. From Center and Main, head east on Center one block, turn left (north) onto 100 East; it's a little more than a block to the restaurant. CONTINENTAL.

The Grapevine offers informal elegance in a contemporary but comfortable dining room, with fresh flowers and white linen on the tables. There's also patio dining in summer. The menu changes about three times a year, as owner-chef Bill Oblock experiments with innovative cooking techniques and sauces from different countries. Dishes range from game to fish, poultry to beef. The Grapevine has a full liquor license, with good quality wines (mostly from California), and Utah beers.

❸ Kate's Kitchen

71¹/₂ 1200 South. ☎ **801/753-5733** or 801/753-1223 for take-out. Reservations accepted for parties of 8 or more. Main courses $8.95–$10.95. MC, V. Tues–Sat 4–10pm. Follow Main Street south and take Utah 165 towards Hyrum (the left fork when U.S. 89/91 head right to Wellsville); turn east (left) onto 1200 South; Kate's is on the left. AMERICAN.

Kate was born in 1992, so her Dad is presently running the establishment. You'll find home cookin' served family-style in the large, informal dining room; everything is homemade, even the ice cream. Menu choices include Kate's pot roast, country-fried steak, country-style BBQ ribs, or home-roasted chicken. Dinners come with plenty of homemade muffins and honey butter, fresh garden salad with house dressing, mashed potatoes and gravy or seasoned rice, and corn-on-the-cob or the veggie of the day. If you need more, just flag down a server; you can't miss them—they're the ones wearing hats. Once a month, Kate's offers an all-you-can-eat prime rib dinner, by reservation only; call to see when it's on. An early bird supper for $7.95 is available Tuesday through Thursday from 4 to 6pm. No alcohol is served.

Old Grist Mill Bread Co.

78 E. 400 North. ☎ **801/753-6463.** Sandwiches $3–$4, bagels 3/$1, with cream cheese $1. No credit cards. Bakery Mon 7:30am–7pm, Tues–Sat 7am–7pm, sandwiches Mon–Sat 10:30am–7pm. From Center, head north on Main four blocks and turn right (east) on 400 North. BAKERY/DELI.

You can just about fill up by breathing the bread-scented air here. On any day, you can choose from five or six breads for your sandwich—standards like honey whole wheat, multigrain, sourdough, and whole-wheat sourdough—and more unique breads such as sunflower whole wheat, sourdough tomato herb, onion-dill rye, cinnamon-raisin-walnut wheat, and apple almond cinnamon. There are also a selection of bagels available. Breads and bagels can be topped with a variety of cream cheese spreads and top-quality meats and cheeses. All orders are take out; you're welcome to call in your order. This is a great place to pick up a sandwich to take on a hike, a bike ride, or a picnic.

LOGAN AFTER DARK

The ❖ **Utah Music Festival** offers fine chamber music at three locations on USU campus and at the Tabernacle in Logan. Recent performances have included Bach's "Brandenburg Concerto No. 4," "Oboe Concerto" by Vaughn-Williams, and "Japanese Songs" by Garwood for soprano, flute, cello, and piano. Performances take place during July and most of August. Contact the Festival at P.O. Box 3381, Logan, UT 84323-3381 (☎ 800/816-UTAH).

Dramas, concerts, and musical theater are presented at the historic **Capitol Theatre,** also known as the Ellen Eccles Theatre, at 43 S. Main (☎ 801/752-0026). The box office is open Monday through Saturday from noon to 6pm.

Plays, concerts, and exhibitions featuring both students and faculty, plus a performing arts series showcasing national and international artists, take place at **Utah State University.** Contact the University Relations Department (☎ 801/797-1158) for information on upcoming events.

The Southern Wasatch Front: World-Class Skiing & More

9

Now we'll head to the area of the Wasatch Front south and east of Salt Lake City. This chapter is arranged geographically from north to south, from the Cottonwood Canyon and Park City resorts to Provo and nearby Timpanogos Cave National Monument, with a few stops in between, including pristine Strawberry Reservoir and Robert Redford's Sundance Resort and Institute.

1 The Cottonwood Canyon Resorts: Brighton, Solitude, Alta & Snowbird

You say you want snow? Here it is, some 500 inches of it every year, just piling up, waiting for you powder-hungry skiers to make that short drive from Salt Lake City. You'll find Brighton and Solitude ski resorts in Big Cottonwood Canyon, and Alta and Snowbird in its sister canyon, known as Little Cottonwood.

If you're skiing on a budget, you might want to stay in Salt Lake City, where lodging is much cheaper, rather than at the resorts themselves. The resorts are so close—less than an hour's drive from Salt Lake—that city dwellers sometimes hit the slopes after a hard day at the office!

But this area is more than just a winter playground. Big Cottonwood Canyon, cut by ancient rivers over more centuries than we can imagine, is a spectacular setting for warm-weather picnicking, camping, mountainbiking, and hiking. Rugged, glacier-carved Little Cottonwood Canyon, where you'll find Alta and Snowbird ski resorts, is filled with lush fields of wildflowers in the summer; that rainbow of color later takes a back seat to the brilliant hues of autumn.

GETTING THERE

By Car   From Salt Lake City, take I-215 to exit 7; follow Utah 210 south. Turn east onto Utah 190 to reach Solitude and Brighton in Big Cottonwood Canyon; continue on Utah 210 south and east to Snowbird and Alta in Little Cottonwood Canyon. It'll take about an hour to reach any of the four ski areas from Salt Lake City International Airport.

By Bus   The **Utah Transit Authority** (☎ 801/287-4636 or TDD 801/287-4657) provides bus service from downtown Salt Lake City hotels and various park-and-ride lots throughout the city into Big and Little Cottonwood Canyons during ski season.

By Shuttle   Lewis Bros. Stages (☎ 801/359-8677 or 800/366-0288; fax 801/975-0289) offers shuttles from the airport and downtown Salt Lake City, and between the ski resorts. **Park City Transportation Services** (☎ 801/649-8567 or 800/637-3803; fax 801/649-3549) offers airport service to all major Utah ski areas.

BIG COTTONWOOD CANYON

Utah 190 is the road that takes you through Big Cottonwood Canyon to Brighton and Solitude. Each turn along your drive to the summit of this 15-mile-long canyon will bring you to another grand, dizzying vista. Rock climbers love these steep, rugged canyon walls—look for them along your drive.

BRIGHTON SKI RESORT

Brighton has been hosting skiers since 1936. Located 25 miles from downtown Salt Lake City at the top of Big Cottonwood Canyon, this low-key, family-friendly resort is where many Utahns learn to ski: The ski school is highly regarded, children 10 and under stay and ski free with their parents, and teens particularly enjoy the bumps of Lost Maid Trail as it winds through the woods. But don't let its reputation as a beginner's mountain fool you; Brighton's slopes are graced with a full range of terrain, all the powder you can ski, and virtually no crowds. You'll find more Utahns than out-of-staters on the slopes here—visitors tend to stay away because of the paucity of lodgings in the area. So there's always plenty of elbow room on the intermediate and advanced slopes, even on weekends; you'll probably have them all to yourself on weekdays. Due to the relatively small number of skis crossing the mountain, the powder never gets skied out—you can ski all week without ever seeming to run out of deep virgin snow. And you can explore the slopes until late: Brighton lights up 18 of its runs for night skiing until 9pm.

Brighton is also one of the best snowboarding destinations in the state; snowboarding is permitted anywhere on the mountain.

Just the Facts

Brighton Ski Resort, Star Route, Brighton, UT 84121 (☎ 801/532-4731 or 800/873-5512; 801/943-8309 for ski report), has two high-speed quad lifts, two triples, and three double chairs servicing over 850 acres in the Wasatch-Cache National Forest. The vertical drop is 1,745 feet, with a base elevation of 8,755 feet and summit of 10,500 feet. There are 64 runs, 21% of which are rated beginner, 40% intermediate, and 39% advanced. Elk Park Ridge is the longest run, at 3 miles.

Lifts are open daily from 9am to 4pm, mid-November to late April, with night skiing (18 runs on 200 acres) from mid-December through late March, Monday through Saturday, 4pm to 9pm.

The resort can make snow on 170 acres, but with 430 inches average snowfall per year, the manmade stuff isn't usually necessary.

Brighton recently built a beautiful new 20,000-square-foot day lodge, the Brighton Resort Center, which provides ticket windows, restrooms, a common area, and a convenient depot for those using the bus. **Brighton Mountain Sports** (☎ 801/649-7909) is here too, providing retail, rental, and repair of ski equipment.

Lift Tickets   There are several options for purchasing lift tickets at Brighton. An all-day ticket is $29, half-day is $25, and a single ride is $6. Children 10 and under ski free with an adult (limit two children per adult); without an adult, children pay half price. Seniors 70 and over ski free.

Lessons & Programs   Brighton Ski School, located in the Alpine Rose building, offers lessons for all levels both privately and in 2-hour group sessions. Group lessons range from $30 to $45 including equipment and lift ticket, or $20 for the lesson only (you'll get a discount on your lift ticket). The size of the class is limited to 10 people, and participants must be at least seven years of age. Private lessons start at $45. Night ski lessons are available Thursday evenings from mid-December through late March, and cost $20.

The Ski School also offers a variety of workshops and clinics, including a telemark series as well as adult parallel, senior, and women's workshops. Inquire at the school for details. Snowboarding lessons are $38, including equipment rental and lift ticket.

Kinderski, for ages four to seven in classes no larger than six children, is $24; a lesson plus lunch is $37 to $57; equipment rental is $8 with class.

Where to Stay & Dine

Brighton Lodge, at the ski resort (☎ 801/532-4731 or 800/873-5512) is your only option. It has 20 rooms, with nightly rates of $57 to $105, plus special multinight packages. There's both an outdoor heated pool and whirlpool to help loosen those muscles for the next day's skiing. Room tax of about $9^1/2$% is added to your bill.

Cafeteria-style dining is available daily 8am to 8:30pm at the **Alpine Rose** restaurant. **Molly Green's Pub** opens for lunch and stays open through après ski and dinner.

Warm-Weather Activities

Mountainbiking and hiking are popular summer activities. Although not available at this writing, mountainbike rentals are a possibility in the future; check at the resort for information. Sorry, mountainbikers—lifts aren't open in the summer.

SOLITUDE SKI RESORT

Solitude is a friendly, family-oriented ski area that hasn't been "discovered" yet, so lift lines are virtually nonexistent. The snow is terrific, and it's easy to reach, just 28 miles from downtown Salt Lake City in Big Cottonwood Canyon.

Like its next-door neighbor Brighton—which is connected to Solitude via the Solbright Trail—Solitude enjoys excellent powder and no big crowds. It has over 1,200 acres of skiable terrain, from well-groomed, sunny beginner and intermediate trails to gently pitched bowls and glades; there's plenty to keep advanced skiers who would rather avoid Alta at peak times very happy. The mountain is well-designed, with runs laid out so beginners won't suddenly find themselves in more difficult terrain. You can start at the bottom and work your way up the mountain through intermediate to expert runs. Intermediates have wide-open bowls to cruise on and practice their powder skiing, several excellent forest runs, and some great bumpy stretches to hone their mogul skills. Advanced skiiers have many long fall lines, open powder areas, and steeply graded chutes to choose from, and will often find themselves exploring the terrain surrounded only by the solitude of the mountain.

Solitude is the state's only downhill ski area with a world-class Nordic center out its back door: The University of Utah and U.S. Olympic teams train here.

Snowboarders are welcome on the slopes on weekdays.

Just the Facts

Solitude, P.O. Box 21350, Salt Lake City, UT 84121-0350 (☎ 801/534-1400 or 800/748-4754; fax 801/649-5276), operates one high-speed quad lift, two triples, and four doubles to service 63 runs and three bowls. Runs are rated as 20% beginner, 50% intermediate, and 30% advanced/expert. The resort is open from early November through late April, 9am to 4:30pm daily. With a summit elevation of 10,035 feet and a vertical drop of 2,047 feet, Solitude receives an average snowfall of 430 inches.

For the winter of 1995–96, Solitude added snowmaking to over 18 trails. The ticket office, rental shop, and ski shops are all located in the Main Lodge.

Lift Tickets   All-day lift tickets cost $32 for adults and $23 for skiers between the ages 11 to 13 and 60 to 69; those 10 and under or 70 and over ski free. Half-day lift tickets are $27 for adults.

Lessons & Programs   Solitude's **ski school** has something for everyone. Adult classes are $40 for a half day and $50 for all day; customized private lessons are available. The **Moonbeam Learning Center** is set up for kids age 4 through 12; the children's all-day ski instruction program, including lunch, is $55, and the afternoon-only program is $35.

Cross-Country Skiing   Solitude Nordic Center is Utah's oldest cross-country ski center. It has 20km of groomed trails, including a children's trail. The center is located between Solitude and Brighton at 8,700 feet, and connects the two downhill areas. Trails pass through alpine forests, meadows, and around the frozen Silver Lake. The **Silver Lake Day Lodge** offers rentals, retail, lessons, and light snacks. An all-day trail pass for ages 11 to 69 costs $8, half-day is $6. Those 10 and under or 70 and over ski free.

Where to Stay & Dine

Creekside at Solitude, a 36-unit condominium property, offers 1- to 3-bedroom units priced from $169 to $529. Mediterranean and Italian cuisine is available at the restaurant; pizzas start at $7, and main courses are in the $9 to $15 range. It's centrally located in the resort village, close to three of the lifts, and not far from the day lodge. Room tax of about $9^{1}/2$% is added to your bill.

The **Main Lodge** houses a cafe and bakery offering pastries, soups, and sandwiches. Adjacent to the Apex Chairlift and with terrific views of the mountain, the day lodge, **Last Chance Mining Camp,** offers heartier fare, breakfasts and lunches, plus après ski refreshments.

The **Roundhouse Restaurant** and **Sunshine Grill** are part way up the mountain, at 9,000 feet elevation. The Roundhouse offers fine dining at lunch—you can ski in—and a special "one-cat open sleigh" five-course gourmet dinner—accessible by snowcat, of course. Reservations are required (☎ 800/748-4754, ext. 5709). The Sunshine Grill, with an outside deck and terrific views of the slopes, serves lunch and snacks daily.

For an unusual experience, make reservations at the **Yurt** (☎ 800/748-4754, ext. 5709), in the forest above the main lodge. You can either cross-country ski or snowshoe through the evergreens to get to your elegant five-course gourmet meal, served at a table set with linen, silver and crystal. Dress is casual, but the meal isn't.

Warm-Weather Activities

Solitude remains open on a limited basis in the summer, offering chairlift rides, mountainbike rentals, and a place to hike or just kick back and watch the wildflowers grow. Call for exact open days and times.

LITTLE COTTONWOOD CANYON

Utah 210 takes you on a lovely scenic drive through the canyon; the towering peaks rise 11,000 feet above the road on both sides. At the mouth of the canyon, at the junction of Utah 209 and Utah 210, is the site where the first Mormons quarried the granite used to build the Salt Lake Temple.

ALTA SKI AREA

Alta is not only famous for its snow—over 500 inches annually of some of the lightest powder in the world—but at just $25 for an all-day adult lift ticket, it's one of the best skiing bargains anywhere.

About an hour's drive southeast of Salt Lake City at the end of Little Cottonwood Canyon, Alta is an excellent choice for serious skiers of all levels. Beginners have their share of runs; there's even a bit of easy-going tree skiing through the woods for the more adventurous novices. First-timers and slower skiiers might want to steer clear of Sunnyside, though. The traffic can get heavy, and you'll often have to deal with the more advanced skiiers who come swooshing through from off the higher runs.

Intermediates will find plenty of open cruising ground, long, arcing chutes, and forested areas to glide through, plus opportunities to work on their bumps technique (try Challenger for a moderately pitched set) or practice their turns in the powder. Experts will find an abundance of the Cottonwood Canyons' famous powder and spectacular runs, like steep and long Alf's High Rustler. Alta offers much for the expert and the extreme skier—far too much to cover here—but hardcore skiers should know that you'll have to step out of the bindings and do a bit of hiking to get to some of the longest drops and best powder-laden runs.

Alta's fans are many, and boy, are they loyal. That's because the emphasis here is on quality skiing. The lifts and other facilities here aren't state-of-the-art and the slopes tend to be ungroomed, but don't be put off—this is the way it's meant to be. This is a classic ski resort, with both European-style terrain *and* sensibilities. This means that people are turned away on those occasions when the ski gods determine there are already enough skiers on the mountain. An announcement is made on 530 AM radio about a half hour before the closure. The slopes themelves are opened and closed throughout the day on a staggered schedule dictated by conditions, but they tend to follow a rough order. You may want to ferret out and follow some locals who know their way around the mountain and its timetable.

Snowboarders aren't allowed on the slopes here, so the crowd tends to be a more sedate one than you'll find at the more lenient resorts.

Just the Facts

Although famous for its expert runs, **Alta,** P.O. Box 8007, Alta, UT 84092-8007 (☎ 801/742-3333; snow report 801/572-3939), also has fine beginner and intermediate trails. The breakdown is 25% beginner, 40% intermediate, and 35% advanced, with a base elevation of 8,550 feet rising to 10,650 feet at the top, yielding a vertical drop of 2,100 feet. Alta is generally open by mid-November and remains open until mid-April, with lifts operating daily from 9:15am to 4:30pm. There are six double and two triple lifts servicing 39 runs on 2,200 skiable acres, with snowmaking on 25 acres.

Alta Ski Lifts Company owns and operates the ski area only, and all other businesses and services are privately run. At the base of Albion and Sunnyside lifts are a day lodge with a cafeteria, lift ticket sales, day care, the ski school, and rentals. There are two more cafeterias on the mountain.

A transfer tow connects the Albion and Wildcat lift areas; in this base area, there are four lodges with dining facilities, ski rentals, and kid's programs. See "Where to Stay," below, for contact information.

Lift Tickets   An all-day, all-lifts ticket costs $25—a real bargain in today's world—with half-day tickets costing $19. Beginner lifts only are $18 for all day and $13 for half. In addition to the office at the day lodge, you can buy lift tickets at the base of the Wildcat and Collins lifts.

Lessons & Programs   Founded in 1948 by Alf Engen, the highly regarded **ski school** (☎ 801/742-2600) is recognized for its contribution to the development of professional ski instruction. Morning and afternoon class lessons are available for adults and teens, costing from $23 to $35; private instruction starts at $55.

The **day care program** (☎ 801/742-3042) offers packages, including lessons for the kids, with prices ranging from $58 to $90, including lift and lunch. Day care alone is $35 to $50 for all day and $30 to $44 for a half day, and is open to children from 6 weeks to 11 years old. Reservations are encouraged.

Where to Stay & Dine

You can check out the lodging possibilities in Alta by calling the **Alta Reservation Service** (☎ 801/942-0404), which represents lodges and condominiums at Alta, and also books rooms in Snowbird or Salt Lake City, and arranges airline reservations and car rentals. Room tax of about 11% plus restaurant tax of about 9% are added to bills.

Our favorite places to stay in Alta are slope-side. Both add a 15% service charge to your bill in lieu of tipping; neither accepts credit cards:

Alta Lodge (☎ 801/742-3500 or 800/707-2582) is perhaps the quintessential mountain ski lodge, simple and rustic, where you'll often find snow drifts halfway up your windows as you look out toward the mountain. Rooms vary from small and basic to large and almost luxurious, with fireplace and private balcony. Rates, including an excellent breakfast and dinner, range from $200 to $320 for two people; or $90 to $100 per person for a dorm room with two bunk beds.

Rustler Lodge (☎ 801/742-2200 or 800/451-5233; fax 801/742-3832) is similar to Alta Lodge, with a great mountain lodge ambiance and rooms that range from basic to deluxe; there are also several two-room suites. Rates, including full breakfast and dinner, range from $180 to $450 for two; a bed for one in a dorm room, with breakfast and dinner, is $80 to $90.

SNOWBIRD SKI & SUMMER RESORT

A combination of super skiing and super facilities lure both hardcore skiers seeking out spectacular powder as well as those who enjoy the pampering that comes at a full-service resort to Snowbird. Consistently rated among America's top-ten ski resorts, Snowbird has been called classic Alta's "younger, slicker sister." You'll find the same wonderful snow here as you will there, but with a wider range of amenities with which to supplement your stay, including Snowbird's extremely popular spa and salon—worth the trip even if you don't ski. Some, however, find its dense, modern village and resort atmosphere cold compared to Alta's historic, European-style lodges and classic, ruggedly western attitude.

Snowbird gives over almost half of its skiable terrain to the expert skier, including plunging cliff runs like Great Scott, one of the steepest in the country. Mogul-meisters will want to take the Peruvian or Gad II lifts to find their happiness, popping off the bumps as they pick from among a great variety of fall lines on the steep and sinuous bump runs.

There's not a lot for beginners and intermediates, but enough to keep them happy; what's here is top notch. There are even some "family-only" ski zones. Novices might want to head over to explore West Second South in its woodsy glade setting. Intermediates will enjoy the excellent runs coming off the Gad II lift, but if you decide to take the tram, wait around a bit at the top while your fellow riders take off; you'll then have these blue runs all to yourself—the next tramload won't get dumped off for another five minutes. It also has a particularly good program for skiers with disabilities.

Except for the Gad II chair, the entire mountain is open to snowboarders.

Just the Facts

Snowbird, P.O. Box 929000, Snowbird, UT 84092-9000 (☎ 801/521-6040 or 800/453-3000; fax 801/742-3300; 801/742-2222, ext. 4285 for snow conditions) has 66 runs on 2,000 acres, 25% designated as beginner, 30% intermediate, and 45% advanced. The ski season is generally from mid-November to early May, although the record-breaking 600 inches—that's 50 feet—of snow received in 1994–95 allowed Snowbird to keep the lifts running through the 4th of July—the latest lift-served skiing ever in Utah. The vertical rise from a base elevation of 7,900 feet is 3,100, to Hidden Peak at 11,000 feet. About 70% of the mountain is groomed nightly, leaving the rest untouched for those who love to ski deep powder. With 2,000 skiable acres, there's plenty of quality skiing. The resort has snowmaking on about 25 acres.

An aerial tram transports 125 skiers at a time 2,900 vertical feet to Hidden Peak in about eight minutes; it's quick, but can feel like you're taking a crowded New York City subway to the mountaintop. With eight double chairlifts as well, Snowbird has a total uphill capacity of 9,200 skiers per hour. The tram and lifts operate between 9am and 4:30pm daily.

The **Cliff Spa and Salon** offers a lap pool and huge whirlpool, aerobic and weight training rooms, plus individual treatment rooms for massages, body wraps, mud baths, and hydrotherapy. The **Snowbird Canyon Racquet Club,** 15 minutes from the slopes, has 23 tennis courts (10 indoor), racquetball, aerobic and cardiovascular facilities, and an indoor climbing wall. Snowbird offers a variety of facilities for children, including a state-licensed day care center and a youth camp; call to inquire.

Lift Tickets   Adult lift tickets are $34 for a full day and $28 for a half day; for both lifts and tram the cost is $44 and $36, respectively. Children 12 and under ski free with parents (two kids per paying parent). Seniors between the ages of 62 to 69 are charged $29 for a full day and $22 per half day; those 70 and older ski free.

Lessons & Programs   The **ski and snowboarding school** has about 200 instructors to provide lessons in either private or group format. There's an all-day class (which includes lunch), a package for first-timers, plus specialized workshops for racers, women, and seniors. Adult rates for a full-day ski or snowboarding class start at about $60, while a 1-hour private ski lesson for one costs from $60 to $80.

Established in 1977, Snowbird's **Disabled Skier Program** is considered among the best in the country. Using state-of-the-art adaptive ski devices and a team of specially trained ski instructors, the program is available to both children and adults. Sit-skis, mono-skis, and outriggers are available at no cost.

Heli-Skiing   Between December 15 and May 15, helicopter skiing is available on more than 80,000 acres within the Wasatch Mountains; contact **Wasatch Powderbird Guides** (☎ 801/742-2800). Cost for the first six runs starts at $325 per person; custom and scenic tours are available.

Where to Stay & Dine

There are about 900 rooms at Snowbird, from standard lodge rooms to luxurious condominium units with kitchens and fireplaces. **Snowbird Central Reservations** (☎ 800/453-3000) books all lodging for the resort; they can also book air and ground transportation. Room tax adds about 11%.

The Cliff Lodge, Spa, and Conference Center is in a ski-in, ski-out pedestrian mall. Practically every one of the 532 rooms, done in modern Southwest style, has splendid views of the mountain or canyon. Standard-size and extra large rooms are available, as well as one- and two-bedroom suites and dorm rooms. There's a splendid spa, restaurants, shops, and practically anything else you could ask for. Dorm beds are in the $40 to $60 range; rooms for two people cost from $120 to $325; and suites range from $280 to $850 for two.

The Lodge at Snowbird, **The Inn**, and **Iron Blosam Lodge** are condominium properties, offering individually decorated rooms, efficiencies, studios, and one-bedroom and one-bedroom-with-loft units. All have kitchens and fireplaces. Many are done in Southwest or western decor and have Murphy beds and/or sofa beds. Rates range from $80 to $550.

Dining facilities at the resort include the luxurious **Aerie Restaurant** in the Cliff Lodge (see above), serving regional cuisine in a Far Eastern–style setting, with spectacular views of the ski slopes and live dinner music. Main courses range from $10 to $25. The **Summit Restaurant,** also at Cliff Lodge, offers a lighter menu and lower prices. To reserve a table at either restaurant, call 801/521-6040.

Warm-Weather Activities

After the skiers go home, Snowbird is still active with hiking and mountainbiking. Two lifts, the Aerial Tram and Peruvian, haul mountainbikers up the slopes. There's also a July music program that includes performances by the Utah Symphony; call for details.

2 Park City, Utah's Premier Resort Town

The cry of "Silver!" brought thousands to Park City in the 1870s, but today it's the thrill of skiing, biking, and other outdoor adventures that keeps the town bustling. Utah's most sophisticated resort community, Park City reminds us of Aspen, Colorado and Taos, New Mexico, other historic western towns that have made the most of excellent ski terrain while evolving into popular year-round vacation destinations offering a casual western atmosphere—plus a touch of elegance for those willing to pay for it.

Park City's 19th-century silver boom lasted for about 30 years, and saw a population of 10,000 at its height, with over 30 saloons along Main Street and a flourishing red light district. Once the minerals dwindled, Park City spent a half century dozing in the summer sun and under a blanket of winter snow. Then, in the late 1960s, the area's first ski lift was built (rates were $2.50 for a weekend of sledding and skiing), and Park City was on the road to becoming one of the West's most popular ski towns.

Today's visitors find three separate ski areas, lodgings that range from basic to luxurious, some of the state's most innovative restaurants and best shopping opportunities, an abundance of fine performing arts events, many of the state's liveliest nightspots, and plenty of hiking, mountainbiking, fishing, and other outdoor recreation possibilities.

Like many tourist towns, prices here can be a bit steep, so if you're watching your wallet, comparison shopping might be in order, and you may want to avoid visiting during the Christmas season and other peak periods. Those who are really pinching pennies might want to stay in Salt Lake City and drive to Park City in the morning for a day of skiing, exploring, or adventuring.

ESSENTIALS
GETTING THERE

Most visitors fly into Salt Lake International Airport and drive or take a shuttle to Park City.

By Car   Park City is 31 miles east of Salt Lake City via I-80. At exit 145 take Utah 224 into Park City. Driving time from the airport is about 35 minutes.

By Shuttle   Several companies offer shuttle service to and from Salt Lake International Airport. **Lewis Bros. Stages** (☎ 801/649-2256 or 800/826-5844), has been serving the Park City area since 1948.

Other companies offering shuttle service between Salt Lake City and Park City include **Park City Transportation Services, Inc.** (☎ 801/649-8567); **All Resort Express** (☎ 801/649-3999 or 800/457-9457); **Le Bus Motorcoaches** (☎ 801/975-0202 or 800/366-0288, fax 801/975-0289); and **Super Express Airport Shuttle** (☎ 801/566-6400 or 800/321-5554).

INFORMATION

The **Park City Chamber of Commerce/Convention & Visitors Bureau,** 1910 Prospector Ave. (P.O. Box 1630), Park City, UT 84060 (☎ 801/649-6100 or 800/453-1360), maintains an information center at 528 Main St., in the Park City Museum. Be sure to pick up a copy of the *Park City Main Street Historic Walking Tour* brochure, which will lead you to 45 buildings and historic sites that have somehow managed to survive fires, hard times, and progress through the decades. The historic walk, complete with engaging features and anecdotes, really brings the town's lively past to life.

GETTING AROUND

Parking in Park City is very limited especially in the historic Main Street area; if you're driving a motorhome or pulling a trailer, the situation is chronic. If you've arrived in a car, the best plan is to park it and ride the free city bus.

Park City's transit system is very efficient and handy, with regular service connecting Deer Valley, Main Street, and the Park City Ski Area. The **Main Street Trolley** traverses Main Street daily from 1 to 5pm in the summer and 10am to 11pm in the winter, connecting to the bus loops at the bottom of Main. In the winter, **public buses** run between 7:40am and 1am, every 10 minutes until 11pm, every 30 minutes thereafter. In the summer, buses start around 7:45am and run every 20 minutes until about 10:30pm. Routes are interconnecting, so you can get just about anywhere fairly easily. A good route map is printed in the weekly booklet *This Week Park City,* available at the visitor center and most lodgings; it also contains several fine area maps, including one of Main Street.

If, however, you want to rent a car and brave the parking problem, there are several rental agencies in Park City to serve your needs: **All Resort,** 1821 Sidewinder Dr. (☎ 801/649-4909), **Budget,** at Shadow Ridge Condominiums (☎ 800/237-7251), and **Mountain,** 740 E. Kearns Blvd. (☎ 801/649-7626); in ski season, you can also call **Avis** (☎ 801/649-7419 or 800/831-2847).

FAST FACTS: Park City

For medical services, call the **Park City Family Health & Emergency Center,** 1665 Bonanza Dr. (☎ 801/649-7640), or the **Park City Chiropractic & Sports Medicine Clinic,** 1678 Bonanza Dr. (☎ 801/649-1017).

The **post office** is at 450 Main Street (☎ 801/649-9191). The **local newspaper** is *The Park Record*, 1670 Bonanza Dr. (☎ 801/649-9014), published every Thursday.

There are two **state liquor stores** in Park City. The outlet at 1901 Sidewinder Drive offers a wide selection of liquor plus a good choice of wines; the one downstairs at 524 Main Street has a fine selection of wines, but a more limited liquor selection.

SKIING THE PARK CITY AREA RESORTS

The three area ski resorts, all within a few minutes' drive of Park City, are vastly different. There's something for everyone here: **Deer Valley** is Utah's Aspen; **Park City** is the party resort, big and lively; and **Wolf Mountain** is small, casual, and friendly. Many skiers make a point of trying all three. Snowboarders are welcome only at Wolf Mountain.

DEER VALLEY RESORT

Unquestionably Utah's most elegant and sophisticated resort, Deer Valley offers perfectly manicured slopes, ski valet service, heated sidewalks, and some of the state's finest dining and lodging. Along with all this, you get great skiing—especially if you crave long, smooth, perfectly groomed cruising runs that let you enjoy the spectacular mountain scenery around you. Although half of the terrain is rated intermediate, beginners love Success, a long run that gives them the feeling they're actually getting somewhere; and much of the intermediate terrain is fit for advancing novices, as the entire mountain is kept very skiable. There are some steep, scary-enough trails on top, through majestic aspen and evergreen glades, for the experts, plus plenty of woodsy terrain to weave through. More advanced runs with a new chairlift are planned for the 1996–97 season. But Deer Valley is not meant for extreme skiing; it's primarily a pampering resort experience, meant for cruising the wide lanes of impeccably groomed snow all day, then hobnobbing with the rich—and often famous—in the evenings over gourmet meals and by the heated indoor pools in the plush lodges.

Just the Facts

Deer Valley, P.O. Box 3149, Park City, UT 84060 (☎ 801/649-1000 or 800/424-3337; 801/649-2000 for snow conditions), offers 67 runs and three bowls spread over Flagstaff, Bald, and Bald Eagle mountains. There are two high-speed quad lifts, nine triple, and two double chairs for a total of 13 chairlifts. The base is at 7,200 feet and the summit at 9,400 feet, yielding a 2,200-foot vertical drop. The ski season is generally from early December to early April, with the lifts running between 9am and 4:15pm daily. With 1,100 skiable acres, the terrain is rated as 15% beginner, 50% intermediate, and 35% advanced. Deer Valley has snowmaking over 290 acres.

Lift Tickets   All-day adult lift tickets cost $49 ($52 during holidays); a half-day ticket is $35. Child all-day lift tickets are $27. Seniors 65 and older can buy an all-day lift ticket for $34.

Lessons & Programs   There are several **ski school** options at Deer Valley, including private or group lessons, workshops, and clinics. Group lessons start at $57 for 4 hours for adults and $62 for 5 hours for children; private lessons start at $62 an hour.

The licensed **child care center,** open 8:30am to 4:30pm daily, costs $46 per day for kids 2 to 12, $62 for children 2 to 24 months; half-day rates are lower. During holiday and peak periods, the child care center offers evening supervision from 6 to 10pm for $26, open to children 5 to 12.

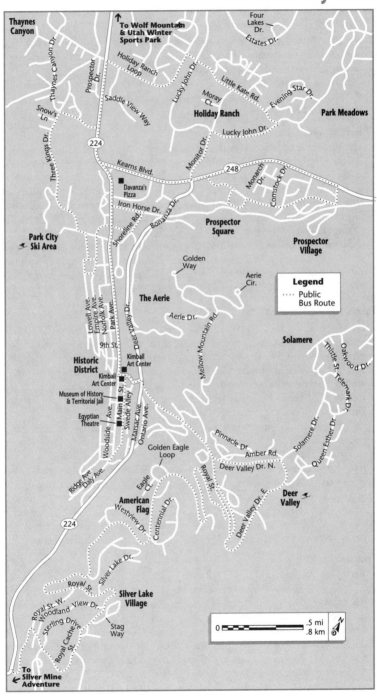

The Park City Area

Thaynes Canyon

To Wolf Mountain & Utah Winter Sports Park

Four Lakes Dr.

Estates Dr.

Holiday Ranch Loop

Thaynes Canyon Dr.

Prospector Dr.

Saddle View Way

Lucky John Dr.

Moray Ct.

Little Kate Rd.

Evening Star Dr.

Holiday Ranch

Park Meadows

Snow's Ln.

Three Kings Dr.

224

Lucky John Dr.

Monitor Dr.

Kearns Blvd.

248

Monarch Dr.

Comstock Dr.

Davanza's Pizza

Iron Horse Dr.

Shoreline Rd.

Bonanza Dr.

Prospector Square

Prospector Village

Park City Ski Area

Golden Way

Aerie Cir.

The Aerie

Aerie Dr.

Legend

···· Public Bus Route

Mellow Mountain Rd.

Solamere

Oakwood Dr.

Thistle St.

Telemark Dr.

Lowell Ave.
Empire Ave.
Norfolk Ave.
Park Ave.

9th St.

Deer Valley Dr.

Historic District

Kimball Art Center

Kimball Art Center

Museum of History & Territorial Jail

Egyptian Theatre

Main St.

Swede Alley

Marsac Ave.

Ontario Ave.

Woodside Ave.

Golden Eagle Loop

Pinnacle Dr.

Amber Rd.

Deer Valley Dr. N.

Royal St.

Solamere Dr.

Queen Esther Dr.

Ridge Ave.
Daly Ave.

Eagle Ct.

American Flag

Westview Dr.

Centennial Dr.

Deer Valley Dr. E.

Deer Valley

224

Silver Lake Dr.

Royal St.

Royal St. W.

Woodland View Dr.

Silver Lake Village

Sterling Drive

Royal Cache St.

Stag Way

0   .5 mi   .8 km

To Silver Mine Adventure

131

Where to Stay

Deer Valley Resort operates a **Central Reservation Service** (☎ 800/424-3337) that can reserve lodging for you at a nearby condo, at the **Goldener Hirsch Inn** (see p. 140), or at the **Stein Erikson Lodge** (see p. 140). The service can also make airline, car-rental, and lift ticket reservations for you.

Deer Valley Lodging (☎ 801/649-4040 or 800/453-3833) offers a fine selection of upscale condos, each with daily housekeeping, bell, and concierge service; see p. 139 for details.

Where to Dine on the Mountain

There's a variety of on-mountain dining facilities:

Snow Park Lodge (☎ 801/645-6603), at the base, houses a bakery, a gourmet market, two restaurants, and a lounge. **Snow Park Restaurant,** serving breakfast and lunch daily, features a natural foods buffet as well as the standard soup-and-sandwich fare. The **Seafood Buffet,** open Monday through Saturday evenings only, offers hearty hot dishes, a salad and seafood buffet, and fancy desserts. The **Snow Park Lounge** has hors d'oeuvres available after 3:30pm.

Silver Lake Lodge (☎ 801/645-6724), midway up the mountain, has a variety of quick-and-easy food available all day, including continental breakfast with fresh-baked pastries, salads, grilled fare, and pizzas. There's also a fine continental dining room, **The Mariposa** (☎ 801/645-6715), open evenings only.

PARK CITY SKI AREA

Park City Ski Area, Utah's largest and liveliest ski resort, is where the U.S. Olympic team comes to train. If it's good enough for them, it's good enough for us. What brings them here? Plenty of good, dependable, powdery snow and a variety of terrain and runs that offer something for everyone. Surveys continually rank Park City among the country's top resorts for both its terrain and challenging runs. And, located right in the heart of Park City, what more could you ask for in terms of amenities?

Beginners have plenty of great training ground that's blessedly free from that frequent mountain problem—hordes of advanced skiers whizzing their way right through the green runs on their way down to the resort at the bottom. Once they have a good handle on the sport, beginners and novices can head up the lift to Summit House and then glide to the bottom of the hill on their own, scenic 3¹/₂-mile green run. Intermediates will find some good cruising ground and powder runs, and there's some 650 acres of expert fun in the wide-open bowls and hair-raising narrow chutes up on top. After a good storm, the locals know to race up early to the top of the Mayflower Bowl and carve their way back down through the fresh powder.

Just the Facts

Park City Ski Area, P.O. Box 39, Park City, UT 84060 (☎ 801/649-8111 or 800/ 222-7275, 801/647-5335 for snow reports; fax 801/647-5374), has a four-passenger gondola, plus three quad, six triple, and four double chairs servicing 89 runs on 2,200 skiable acres; there's even a triple-chair access lift directly from the Old Town onto the mountain, and two runs (Quit'n' Time and Creole) that you can ski back into town on, so those staying in Park City proper don't have to ride back and forth to the to the base resort every day. Trails are rated 16% beginner, 45% intermediate, and 39% expert. With a base elevation of 6,900 feet and summit of 10,000 feet, the vertical drop is 3,100 feet. Park City's ski season generally runs mid-November to mid-April, with lifts operating between 9am and 4pm daily. Night skiing is usually available from Christmas through March from 4 to 9pm, on First Time (easier) and PayDay (more difficult) runs. Park City has snowmaking capabilities on 420 acres.

The **Resort Center,** at the base of the mountain, houses the ski school, equipment sales and rentals, a restaurant and bar, lockers, and ticket office.

Lift Tickets   An all-day adult lift ticket costs $47; a half-day ticket is $34. Seniors between 65 and 69 pay half price; those over 70 ski free. A child's all-day ticket is $21.

Lessons & Programs   The **Park City Ski School** (☎ 800/227-2754) offers a wide variety of choices for every level of skier. There are group and private lessons for adults and kids ages 7 to 13, plus a **kinderschule** for kids ages 3 to 6 that includes snack, lunch, and lessons. Group lessons start at $35 for 2 hours; kinderschule starts at $65. Customized packages are also available. Reservations are highly recommended, and are required for kinderschule during peak periods.

In keeping with the philosophy that skiing is a sport that can be learned at any age, Park City has developed a program for older beginners, **It's Never Too Late.** The director of senior services says that you just need to be "in reasonably good condition, at least able to walk briskly," and you can learn to ski. Call for details.

Cross-Country Skiing   **White Pine** (☎ 801/649-8701 or 801/645-5158) is Park City's cross-country ski center, with 20km of groomed trails on the golf course on Utah 224. The center offers rentals, instruction (including telemark lessons), guided tours, and sales and service. The terrain is rated 60% beginner, 20% intermediate, and 20% advanced. Trail passes cost $6 for a full day and $3 for a half day. Seniors over 65 ski free. White Pine is open daily from 9am to 6pm.

Ice-Skating   The ski area's Resort Center has an outdoor ice rink (☎ 801/649-8111). Skate rentals are available.

Ski Jumping   The **Utah Winter Sports Park,** 3000 Bear Hollow Drive, P.O. Box 682382, Park City, UT 84068-2328 (☎ 801/649-5447; fax 801/647-9650), already built for the 2002 Olympics, has four state-of-the-art ski jumps. The U.S. Ski Team regularly uses the facility. It's open for self-guided tours and public ski jumping, even for amateurs. A 2-hour ski-jumping session, with an introductory lesson, is $20 for adults, $12 for kids between the ages of 13 and 17, and $8 for kids under 13. Call for days and times.

Where to Stay

The town of Park City offers almost any kind of lodging you could want. See "Where to Stay" on p. 139 for details on what's available. Park City Ski Area operates a **Reservation Service** (☎ 800/222-7275) that books lodging in Park City, as well as airline reservations, ground transportation, and lift tickets.

Where to Dine on the Mountain

In addition to the wide variety of options in Park City (see "Where to Dine," p. 143), there are the following slope-side facilities. None require reservations.

Steeps Restaurant and Private Club, in the gondola building, has homemade soups and stews, sandwiches, a salad and baked potato bar, and fresh roasted meats. A bar on the second floor also serves lunch, and has live entertainment for après ski from 4 to 6:30pm.

Mid-Mountain Lodge is at the base of Pioneer Lift on the Webster Ski Run, at 8,700 feet. Built about 1898, the lodge may be the oldest original mine building in Park City. Completely renovated in recent years, it's open daily, serving vegetarian dishes, homemade soups and stews, salads, burgers, sandwiches, and pizza.

Summit House Restaurant, at the top of the gondola, offers sandwiches, ribs, and salads. The outdoor deck has magnificent panoramic views, and inside is a cozy fireplace.

The **Snow Hut,** at the bottom of the Prospector high-speed quad lift, serves breakfast and lunch daily.

WOLF MOUNTAIN RESORT

Wolf Mountain (formerly ParkWest Ski Area) is a small, friendly ski area with personalized service, lots of powdery snow, and plenty of on-trail and off-trail skiing. The terrain is somewhat awkward and the top elevation is just 9,000 feet, but the resort has made terrific do with what they have. There are outstanding beginner areas and great kids' programs; experts will find some good hike-to runs to the top. In general, an enthusiatic spirit and sense of fun energizes the whole place.

Beginners are in for a treat—the green slopes here are much more interesting and offer a more varied terrain on which to learn than most mountains do. There are even several green routes down from higher up the mountain so that novices can get a feel for real skiing on long trails without having to move on to rough terrain before they're ready.

The intermediate runs at Wolf tend to lean a bit more towards the expert end of things than at many mountains, so intermediates don't have too many options unless they feel ready to start tackling more challenging runs. The expert runs at Wolf are hair-raising and steep, but tend to be short, single fall-line runs straight off the ridges. Their steepness means that when snow conditions aren't too good, neither are the options for runs with adequate ground coverage. After a good snowfall, however, Wolf's best skiing can be found in the natural bowls near the end of each ridge.

This is the one area resort that welcomes snowboarders, and it does so with open arms. You can even try night snowboarding at the new lighted snowboard park. Lessons are available.

Just the Facts

Wolf Mountain Resort, 4000 Parkwest Dr., Park City, UT 84060 (☎ 801/649-5400 or 800/754-1636; fax 801/649-7374) has 62 runs on 1,400 skiable acres, serviced by seven double chairlifts. It receives over 300 inches of snow a year, and has 20 acres of snowmaking capabilities. The vertical drop is 2,200 feet, with a summit elevation of 9,000 feet and base of 6,800 feet. Runs are rated 22% beginner, 30% intermediate, and 48% advanced. The scheduled season is mid-December through early April, with lifts operating from 9am to 4pm daily. Night skiing is available from 4 to 9pm.

The day lodge has a ski and snowboard rental shop and a fully-licensed day care center. The resort was purchased by new owners in 1994, who have begun work on adding more snowmaking equipment and new chairlifts, and improving the other facilities.

Lift Tickets   An all-day adult lift ticket is $28; a half-day is $20. A child's all-day ticket is $16. Seniors over 70 ski free.

Lessons & Programs   The **ski school** offers personalized service, with instructors who tailor lessons to the needs of individual skiers. Both private and group lessons are available, plus snowboard instruction. Adult group rates start at $25 for a half day, $40 for a full day; private lessons start at $60 an hour.

There's also a top-notch children's school, **Kids Central,** for ages 4 to 12. Kids Central offers several packages, starting at $35 for an afternoon.

Day care is available for $40 all day, and $25 half day.

Tours   **The Sports Desk** (☎ 801/649-5400) can arrange 1- and 2-hour tours of Wolf Mountain that wrap up with dinner. Tours are via snowmobile, snow cat, cross-country skis, or snowshoes. Call for information and prices.

Where to Stay

The owners have announced plans for a ski-in/ski-out hotel but, for the time being, you'll have to stay in Park City, Deer Valley, or Salt Lake City.

Where to Dine on the Mountain

There are four restaurants at the ski area: At the top of Golden Eagle Lift is the **Rockin' Mountain Grill**, with great munchies; **Buffalo Bob's**, at mid-mountain, has everything from soup and salad to pasta and burgers; at the base, you'll find **Avalanche at Trail's End**, which often has live entertainment, and **Saddle and Spur**, featuring fresh seafood, steak, and pasta, complete with live entertainment and dancing. Reservations are recommended at the Saddle and Spur (☎ 801/649-2086).

WARM-WEATHER ACTIVITIES IN & AROUND PARK CITY

FLY-FISHING

Several professional guide services in Park City offer a variety of fishing trips. **Jans Mountain Outfitters,** 1600 Park Ave. (☎ 801/649-4949 or 800/745-1020), offers half-day to three-day trips, ranging from $180 to $935 for one or two people. The rates include casting and fishing instruction as needed, plus meals (lunch only with half- and full-day trips) and lodging. Equipment rentals are available as well.

The Fly Shop, 2065 Sidewinder Dr., Prospector Square (☎ 801/645-8382 or 800/324-6778), has some of the most experienced guides in the area. In addition to guided trips, they offer equipment sales and rentals, clinics, and general all-around information for the angler.

G.G.S. Guide Service, 748 E. Richmond Dr. (☎ 801/649-6857) has access permits to four private ranches for fly-fishing access. You can arrange for one-, two- and three-day trips, costing from $250 to $950 for up to two people, in areas generally off-limits to the public.

GOLF

Park City Municipal Golf Course, with a pro shop at 1541 Thaynes Canyon Dr. (☎ 801/649-8701), is an 18-hole, par-72 course near the bottom of the ski resort area. Greens fees are $26 for 18 holes, $13 for 9. The other public course is **Park Meadows Golf Club,** 2000 Meadows Dr. (☎ 801/649-2460), an 18-hole, par-72 Jack Nicklaus course, with 105 sand bunkers and water on 12 holes. Greens fees are $59 for 18 holes, including cart and range balls; after 4pm fees drop to $35.

HIKING

Deer Valley Ski Area has two great trails, a 5-mile loop and an 8-mile one, with ski lift access Wednesday to Sunday in the summer. As you might expect, the terrain is steep but beautiful.

For a short hike with a variety of terrain and good views of the mountains and town, try the 1.5-mile **Sweeny Switchbacks Trail,** on the west side of town above the Wasatch Brew Pub.

The 30-mile **Rails to Trails** path (see "Mountainbiking," below) is also popular with hikers.

For a good description of several other trails in the area, pick up a copy of the *Park City Hiking & Biking Trail Guide* at the visitor center, or call 800/453-1360.

HORSEBACK RIDING

Guided trail rides are available from several outfitters in the area. You can choose from a 1- or 2-hour ride, or a ride with a meal.

Park City Stables, P.O. Box 680846, Park City, UT 84068 (☎ 801/645-7256), has a stable at Park City Ski Area and another at Deer Valley Resort. They operate daily between the end of May and the latter part of October. Rates range from $22 to $69 for adults, slightly less for children ages 6 to 12 and seniors over 65. Reservations are required for all meal rides, and are recommended for others. For information about a special getaway at their U Bar Wilderness Guest Ranch, call 800/303-7256.

Big Springs Riding Stable at Wolf Mountain (☎ 801/649-9023 or 800/554-8094) is open daily from mid-April to the end of October. One-, two- and 3-hour rides run from $24 to $52; meal rides range from $45 to $75 for adults, less for children ages 7 to 10. Reservations are required for all meal rides, and are recommended for others.

IN-LINE SKATING

You can rent in-line skates at **Cole Sport,** 1615 Park Ave. (☎ 801/649-4806); **Gart Brothers,** Park City Resort Center (☎ 801/649-2002); **Jans Mountain Outfitters,** 1600 Park Ave. (☎ 801/649-4949); and **Rennstall,** at the Resort Center, Park City Ski Area (☎ 801/649-1833).

The **Wolf Mountain roller hockey rink** (☎ 801/649-5400), indoors at the base of the resort, has organized hockey games, lessons, and open skating.

MOUNTAINBIKING

Guided mountainbike tours are available from **Park City Mountain Bike Tours** (☎ 801/647-3058), **Sport Touring Ventures,** 4719 Silver Meadows Dr. (☎ 801/649-1551), and **White Pine Touring,** 201 Heber Ave., at the bottom of Main Street (☎ 801/649-8710); White Pine also offers rentals. Other rental agencies include **Cole Sport,** 1615 Park Ave. (☎ 801/649-4806), **Gart Brothers, Park City Resort Center** (☎ 801/649-2002), and **Jans Mountain Outfitters,** 1600 Park Ave. (☎ 801/649-4949).

The 30-mile ✪ **Rails to Trails** bike path follows the old Union Pacific railroad bed from Park City to Echo Reservoir. The 135-foot-wide trail offers great views of meadows, the volcanic crags of Silver Creek Canyon, the Weber River, Echo Reservoir, and the steep walls of Echo Canyon. There's always the possibility of spotting deer, elk, moose, and bald eagles along the trail, too. An end-of-the-trail pick-up service is available from **Daytrips** (☎ 801/649-8294).

For a good description of several other area trails, pick up a copy of the *Park City Hiking & Biking Trail Guide* at the visitor center, or call 800/453-1360.

For information on ski lift–accessible trails, contact **Cole Sport** (☎ 801/649-4601), **Deer Valley Resort** (☎ 801/649-100), or **Wolf Mountain** (☎ 801/649-5400).

TENNIS

Athletic clubs with tennis courts available to the public include **Park City Racquet Club,** 1200 E. Little Kate Rd. (☎ 801/645-5100), with four indoor and seven outdoor courts; and **Prospector Athletic Club,** in the Inn at Prospector Square, 2080 Gold Dust Lane (☎ 801/649-6670), with two outdoor courts.

MORE TO SEE & DO IN PARK CITY

Kimball Art Center

638 Park Ave., at the bottom of Main Street. ☎ **801/649-8882**. Free admission. All bus loops will stop here.

This highly respected center for visual arts has two galleries, with changing exhibits that include regional and national traveling shows, as well as exhibits by local artists that are often surprisingly good. Art classes, workshops, and seminars are offered throughout the year, and the gift shop sells local and regional art.

Park City Museum of History & Territorial Jail

528 Main St. ☎ **801/649-6100**. Free admission. Nov–Mar and May–Sept Mon–Sat 10am–7pm, Sun noon–6pm; April and Oct daily noon–5pm. Bus: Main Street Trolley.

The original Territorial Jail downstairs is a must-see—the tiny cells were state-of-the-art in 1886! Upstairs is a bit more civilized, with an assay office, 19th-century mining equipment, historic photographs, early ski gear, and several beautifully tooled doorknobs and locks. There are also a variety of personal items that immigrants to Park City brought with them, ranging from a Dutch hymnal to a tin lunch bucket.

Park City Silver Mine Adventure

1.5 miles south of Park City on Utah 224. ☎ **801/649-8011**. Admission to exhibits and mine tour $12.95 adults, $9.95 seniors and children under 12; exhibits only $6.95 adults, $5.50 seniors and children under 12. Jan–Mar and July–Aug daily 10am–8pm; Apr–June and Sept–Dec daily 10am–6pm.

Scheduled to open by early 1996, this mine offers not only interactive displays and exhibits demonstrating mining, but also a trip down into the Ontario, Park City's greatest silver mine. In operation from the 1870s to the 1980s, the Ontario produced about $400 million in silver, helping 23 miners become millionaires.

Planned displays include a Geological Wall and Mineral Exhibit, where you can see actual core samples and mining equipment; a Mine Mythology display describing legendary characters like the man in the yellow slicker and the lady in white; and Digging for Gemstones, where you can search for deposits of pyrite and silver ore.

After wandering through the displays, don a hard hat and yellow slicker, and get ready to descend 1,500 feet into the No. 3 shaft of the Ontario Mine. You'll board a train for a little more than a half-mile ride through tunnels into the heart of the mountain, and see for yourself the workings of a real silver mine. Once you emerge from the shaft, you can refresh yourself at a turn-of-the-century-style soda fountain.

SHOPPING

Historic Main Street is lined with galleries, boutiques, and a wide variety of shops. Although you won't find many bargains here, prices aren't too far out of line for a tourist and ski town, especially when compared to places like Aspen and Santa Fe. Bargain hunters will want to head for the Factory Stores (see "Malls," below).

ART GALLERIES

Images of Nature

556 Main St. ☎ **801/649-7579**. Bus: Main Street Trolley.

Animal lovers will enjoy browsing through the selection of photographs of animals in their natural habitats. There's everything from the playful to the serene, in a variety of sizes, framed or unframed.

The Queen of Arts Gallery
515 Main St. ☎ **801/649-9370.** Bus: Main Street Trolley.

This handsome shop features unusual hand-painted dishes and glassware, handmade jewelry, and original oils.

The Saguaro Gallery
314 Main St. ☎ **801/645-7667.** Bus: Main Street Trolley.

This gallery offers a wide range of fine artwork—oils, watercolors, and numerous sculptures by internationally recognized artists.

BOOKS

A Woman's Place Bookstore
Park City Plaza, at Bonanza Drive and Prospector Avenue. ☎ **801/649-2722.** Bus: Prospector Square.

This bookstore specializes in books by, for, and about women.

CLOTHING & ACCESSORIES

Pleasures
513 Main St. ☎ **801/649-5733.** Bus: Main Street Trolley.

If you're looking for Southwest-style clothing and accessories, this is the shop to explore. Native American jewelry is also available.

CRAFTS & COLLECTIBLES

The Silver Junction Mercantile
558 Main St. ☎ **801/645-8654.** Bus: Main Street Trolley.

This grand place, stuffed with all manner of collectibles and antiques, brings back memories of the old general store.

"Z" Treasure Trove
427 Main St. ☎ **801/645-7193.** Bus: Main Street Trolley.

Do you have fond memories of old-style church bazaars? Then you won't want to miss this place, a large room with lots of small booths offering a wide variety of small, handcrafted items.

FOR NEW AGERS

The Expanding Heart
505 N. Main St. ☎ **801/645-1255.** Bus: Main Street Trolley.

Burning incense and new-age music greets you as you enter this shop, where you'll find sculpture, wind chimes, small fountains, music tapes, lotions, candles, crystals, and books to enlighten and entertain.

HOUSEWARES

No Place Like Home
Park City Plaza, at Bonanza Drive and Prospector Avenue. ☎ **801/649-9700.** Bus: Prospector Square.

If you're looking for kitchen and home accessories, you'll find just the thing you want here. Choose from a wide variety of glassware, gadgets, cookbooks, gourmet coffee beans, and lots more.

MALLS

The Factory Stores at Park City

6699 N. Landmark Dr. ☎ **801/645-7078.** Take I-80 to exit 145, then go west on the south frontage road.

This center houses about 50 manufacturer's outlets, including American Tourister, Bass, Brooks Brothers, Bugle Boy, Cape Isle Knitters, Carter's Childrenswear, Hanes, Danskin, Eddie Bauer, Leather Loft, Levi's, Maidenform, and Nike. There's plenty of parking, including room for RVs.

Main St. Marketplace

333 Main St. ☎ **801/645-2321.** Bus: Main Street Trolley.

This mini-mall has about a dozen shops. If you're in need of a snack, the Pretzel Gourmet offers a variety of soft pretzels to choose from: plain for purists, or cinnamon, garlic, parmesan, and other flavors for the more adventuresome.

WHERE TO STAY

The Park City area offers a wide variety of places to stay, and it's probably home to the largest portion of the state's deluxe accommodations. Even some of the most luxurious properties, however, don't have air-conditioning; at this elevation—6,900 feet in Park City and higher in the mountains—it's seldom needed.

Sales and lodging taxes in Park City total just over 10%. Pets are not allowed, unless otherwise noted.

PROPERTY MANAGEMENT COMPANIES

Although it's possible to book your reservations directly with individual lodges, many people find it's more convenient to go the one-stop shopping route, calling one of Park City's major property management and reservation services, which can provide information and reservations for a variety of accommodations.

Deer Valley Lodging (☎ 801/649-4040 or 800/453-3833; fax 801/645-8419) offers a fine selection of upscale condos—from one- to four-bedroom condos, plus eight houses—each with air-conditioning, TV, and telephone plus daily housekeeping, bell, and concierge service. Units come with a range of amenities, from vaulted ceilings and stone fireplaces to full kitchens and outdoor Jacuzzis with mountain views. Winter rates range from $235 to $2,170, with a 4- to 7-night minimum; off-season rates range from $150 to $650, with a 2-night minimum. A complimentary skier shuttle is available between the Snow Park area condos and the Snow Park base Lodge at the Deer Valley Resort daily from 8:30am to 5pm. Evening transportation, also complimentary, is available within Park City or Deer Valley. Both smoking and nonsmoking units are available.

Park City Reservations (☎ 801/649-9598 or 800/453-5789; fax 801/649-8063) is the largest reservations company in the area, representing 400 units, including dorm rooms, one- to five-bedroom condos, and private homes. Each property is individually decorated by the owner; all come with air-conditioning, TV, and telephone; and most have ski storage of some kind. Some units come with fireplaces, full kitchens with microwaves, and/or balconies. Those at the Park Meadows Racquet Club are near the golf course/cross-country ski center and have access to a year-round outdoor pool; units at Park City Village are slope-side, so you can ski in and out. Dorm rooms are very clean and modern, with two sets of bunk beds and two desks, much like a college dorm; ensuite baths are common, but there are separate locked ski storage units. Winter rates range from $70 to $1,500 double; off-season rates start at $40 double. There may be a 2- to 7-night minimum. Both smoking and nonsmoking units are available.

ACCOMMODATIONS IN DEER VALLEY

✪ Goldener Hirsch Inn

7570 Royal St. East, Silver Lake Village, Deer Valley (P.O. Box 859), Park City, UT 84060. ☎ **801/649-7770** or 800/252-3373. Fax 801/649-7901. 20 rms and suites. MINIBAR TV TEL. Winter (including continental breakfast) $195–$660 double; summer $95–$220 double. AE, MC, V.

This chateau-style inn combines warm hospitality with European charm. Austrian antiques dot the common areas and decorate the walls, reminiscent of the inn's sister hotel in Salzburg, the Hotel Goldener Hirsch. Rooms are elegantly furnished with hand-painted and -carved furniture from Austria, king-size beds with down comforters, and minibars stocked with snacks and non-alcoholic beverages. Suites have wood-burning fireplaces and small private balconies. Some rooms face the ski slopes on Bald Mountain, giving a fascinating view of the "night monsters" grooming the runs. The restaurant, done in Austrian decor, features continental cuisine; the menu features Austrian specialties, wild game, and fresh fish, plus lighter dishes.

✪ Stein Eriksen Lodge

Deer Valley Resort (P.O. Box 3177), Park City, UT 84060. ☎ 801/645-6451 or 800/453-1302. Fax 801/649-5825. 120 rms, including 50 suites. TV TEL. Winter (including breakfast buffet) $365–$550 double, suites starting at $630; holidays $420–$630 double, suites starting at $875; mid-Apr to early Dec $140–$175 double, suites starting at $225. AE, CB, DC, DISC, MC, V.

The Stein Eriksen is a luxurious, full-service lodge with a warm and friendly atmosphere. It opened in 1982 under the direction of Stein Eriksen, the Norwegian 1952 Olympic Gold Medalist, and retains the Scandinavian decor and charm of his original plan. The lobby is most impressive, with a magnificent three-story stone fronted by an elegant seating area.

There are 13 rooms in the main lodge, with the remaining units in nearby buildings. The connecting sidewalks are heated, and the grounds are beautifully landscaped with aspen trees, manicured lawns, and flowers cascading over rock gardens and retaining walls. The spacious deluxe rooms, each individually decorated, have one king or two queen beds, lots of closet space, whirlpool tubs, vaulted ceilings, and tasteful, solid wood furniture. The one- to four-bedroom suites come with all the amenities, and three large mountain chalet-style townhouse suites each have a stone fireplace, full kitchen with service for eight, and deck off the living room.

Dining: The lodge has several dining venues, but only two are open year-round. **The Glitretind** (see "Where to Dine," below) serves three meals daily; **Troll Hallen Lounge** is open from 11:30am to midnight in the winter and from 4pm to midnight in the summer for beer and light meals; hors d'oeuvres or fresh shellfish from the oyster bar are available for après ski. In the winter, **The Forest Room** offers intimate evening dining from a menu that includes wild game, seafood, and spit-roasted meats; there's also a casual and cozy breakfast or luncheon spot, and a deck bar overlooking the ski slopes that offers daytime dining in fine weather.

Services: Concierge, room service, dry cleaning, newspaper delivered to room, turndown, in-room massage, twice-daily maid service in the winter, baby-sitting, secretarial service, valet parking, free refreshments in lobby.

Facilities: Video rental, year-round outdoor heated pool, exercise room, Jacuzzi, sauna, sundeck, two tennis courts, nature trails, conference rooms, laundromat, boutiques.

ACCOMMODATIONS IN PARK CITY

✪ Best Western Landmark Inn

6560 N. Landmark Dr., Park City, UT 84060. ☎ **801/649-7300** or 800/548-8824. Fax 801/ 649-1760. 104 rms and 2 kitchen suites. A/C TV TEL. $69–$169 double; lowest in late fall. AE, CB, DC, DISC, MC, V.

Located just off I-80 at exit 145, this motel looks deceptively simple from the out-side, but the lobby is attractively furnished with sitting areas and a brick fireplace. The western-style rooms have either two queen-sized beds or a king; the king rooms come with a separate sitting area. Most rooms have a small refrigerator, and some have small balconies. Four family rooms have two queens and two twins. The honeymoon suite has a large whirlpool tub in a solarium room, a gas fireplace, a refrigerator, wet bar, and two TVs (what honeymooners need two TVs?). There's also a large family suite with two bedrooms, two baths, a living room, and kitchen—great for two fami-lies traveling together.

Free refreshments are offered in the lobby, dry-cleaning service is available, and there's a Denny's restaurant on the premises. Facilities include an indoor heated pool, health club, Jacuzzi, sundeck, laundromat, and a gift shop in the winter. Fax and photocopy service and personal computers are available. Pets are allowed.

⊗ Chateau Apres Ski

1299 Norfolk Ave., Park City, UT 84060. ☎ **801/649-9372.** 32 rms. TV TEL. Winter (includ-ing breakfast) $65 double; summer $35 double; dorm rooms $22–$24 per bed. AE, DISC, MC, V.

This looks like a Swiss Alps–style lodge from the outside—simple but attractive. Rooms are basic and clean, with a queen bed or a double and a single, and private baths with showers only. There are separate men's and women's dorms, and each dorm has a shared bath. This is a good budget place to stay close to the ski area.

The Old Miner's Lodge—A Bed & Breakfast Inn

615 Woodside Ave (P.O. Box 2639), Park City, UT 84060. ☎ **801/645-8068** or 800/648-8068. Fax 801/645-7420. 7 rms, 3 suites. Winter (including breakfast) $105–$190 double; summer (including breakfast) $60–$105 double. AE, DISC, MC, V.

Established in 1889 as a boarding house for local miners, the lodge still exudes the spirited warmth and hospitality of that time. Rooms are comfortably decorated with antiques and country pieces, often of light knotty pine, and some historic photos. Each is named for an historic figure of the Old West and outfitted with touches suit-ing the individual's persona. Suites are spacious and come with minirefrigerators; two have a queen hide-a-bed plus a king bed. Some rooms have terrific views of the val-ley and surrounding mountains.

The lodge is within easy walking distance of the triple-chair Town Lift—the only lift in historic downtown Park City— and historic Main Street. Evening refreshments are available in the large living room, where guests sometimes gather around the fire-place. There's no TV, but plenty of reading material and games, and you're welcome to play the electronic organ. Breakfast is a hearty meal that often includes such items as homemade omelets, waffles, French toast, or pancakes, plus cereal and granola.

Old Town Guest House

1011 Empire Ave (P.O. Box 162), Park City, UT 84060. ☎ **801/649-2642.** 4 units. Winter (including breakfast) $70–$200 double; off-season $50–$70 double. MC, V.

This cozy little B&B, within easy walking distance of both the Park City Ski Area and Main Street, has a delightfully homey living room, where you can relax in front of the original 1910 fireplace. The decor is country, with lodge-pole pine furniture and hardwood floors throughout; but, as with most bed-and-breakfasts, each guest room is unique. Treasure Hollow has its own entrance, a queen-size bed, its own TV and phone, lots of storage, and a private bath with shower. Two small rooms in back have private toilets and sinks, but share a shower. Each has a queen bed and a small table with chairs. McConky's Suite, upstairs, has a queen bed and two twins, a whirlpool tub and shower, TV, VCR, and phone.

There's an outdoor deck and hot tub for guests' use. You'll also have kitchen and laundry privileges, and can order a "fanny-pack lunch" to take to the slopes or wherever. You'll start your day off right with a hearty breakfast, to sustain your energy throughout a day of hiking, biking, or skiing.

Silver King Hotel

1485 Empire Ave (P.O. Box 2818), Park City, UT 84060. ☎ **801/649-5500** or 800/331-8652. Fax 801/649-6647. 64 suites. A/C TV TEL. Winter (including breakfast) $140–$535 double, higher on holidays; mid-Apr to mid-Nov $80–$330 double. AE, DISC, MC, V.

This five-story condominium hotel, located only about a hundred yards from the lifts, offers a variety of accommodations: studio suites, one- and two-bedroom suites, some spa suites, even a penthouse. Each unit is individually owned and decorated, and comes with a fully equipped kitchen, a wood-burning fireplace (free firewood provided), a jetted whirlpool tub, and washer and dryer. All but the studio suites have pull-out hide-a-bed sofas. Some units have a Southwest look, some are done in country style, and others are furnished with antiques. There's a large locker area for your skis.

Washington School Inn

543 Park Ave (P.O. Box 536), Park City, UT 84060. ☎ **801/649-3808** or 800/824-1672. Fax 801/649-3802. 12 rms and 3 suites. TEL. Winter (including breakfast) $135–$235 double, $225–$350 suite; summer $85–$100 double, $130–$165 suite. AE, DISC, MC, V.

Housed in an 1889 limestone schoolhouse nestled against the Wasatch Mountains, this lovely country inn has managed to retain its original charm even though it's been completely modernized. The exterior has been faithfully restored to its turn-of-the-century appearance, while the interior has been reorganized to better meet the requirements of an inn—yet it remains true to its historical roots. Rooms are individually decorated, many in country style, with antiques and reproductions of different periods. Two suites have wood-burning fireplaces. Most rooms have a king or queen bed; one has two twins. Although there's no air-conditioning, each room has a fan. All have private baths with shower/tub combos.

Downstairs is a whirlpool spa and lounge area, sauna, shower rooms, and a bicycle storage area and ski lockers with outside access. The inn provides a full breakfast buffet each morning, afternoon tea in the summer, and some hearty après ski refreshments in the winter.

The Yarrow Resort Hotel & Conference Center

1800 Park Ave (P.O. Box 1840), Park City, UT 84060. ☎ **801/649-7000.** Fax 801/649-4819. 181 units. A/C TV TEL. Winter (including breakfast) $149–$199 double, $169–$219 efficiency, $209–$379 suite; off-season $99 double, $119 efficiency, $179–$259 suite. AE, CB, DC, DISC, MC, V.

This first-class mountain resort hotel has several types of rooms to choose from, ranging from a standard room with two double beds to a deluxe suite with a king bed, two sofa sleepers, and kitchenette. Decor is modern, with dark-stained solid wood furniture. The entire second floor is nonsmoking, and all the rooms on that floor have small balconies. Rooms that face south look out over the parking lot to the ski runs and mountains. Five rooms meet ADA specifications; two have roll-in showers.

The Yarrow is located adjacent to the Holiday Village Mall, with several shops and restaurants, and is on two of the free Park City bus routes.

Dining: The cafe serves American cuisine from 6:30am to 11pm daily. Room service is available between 7am and 10:30pm. A skiers' buffet is offered from 7:30pm in the winter.

Services: Concierge, room service, dry cleaning, laundry service, newspaper delivery in winter, massage, and baby-sitting.

Facilities: Kitchenettes, outdoor year-round pool, well-equipped health club, Jacuzzi, sundeck, nearby golf course, conference room for up to 500, coin-operated laundry, and a ski shop with rentals (in the winter).

WHERE TO DINE

Barking Frog Grill
368 Main St. ☎ **801/649-6222.** Main courses $12.50–$21.50. AE, MC, V. Daily 5:30–11pm. Bus: Main Street Trolley. SOUTHWESTERN.

On a nice day, it's great to relax on the Barking Frog's outdoor patio, where the linen-covered tables are surrounded by planters filled with flowers. The red brick dining room is a bit more eclectic, with a guitar-wielding skeleton holding court. The Southwest-style menu includes such main courses as barbecued baby-back ribs, blue corn–crusted Utah red trout, Southwest seafood pasta, and venison. Full liquor service is available.

Burgie's
570 Main St. ☎ **801/649-0011.** Reservations required only for parties of 6 or more. Main courses $3.95–$7.45. AE, DISC, MC, V. Daily 11am–11pm. Bus: Main Street Trolley. AMERICAN.

This is a cafe with a down-home, country feel; you can sit at the wooden counter around the grill and watch your food being cooked. The menu includes—surprise—a wide selection of burgers (even a vegetarian one), plus homemade soups, several chicken sandwiches, and killer Olympic onion rings, a local favorite. Beer and wine are served.

✪ Cafe Terigo
424 Main St. ☎ **801/645-9555.** Main courses $6.95–$10.95 at lunch, $10.95–$18.95 at dinner; pizzas $8.95–$10.95. AE, MC, V. Daily 11:30am–2:30pm, 5:30–10pm. Bus: Main Street Trolley. EUROPEAN/CONTINENTAL.

In fine weather, you can dine outdoors under a large umbrella; otherwise, it's in the simple yet elegant white-walled dining room, cheerfully decorated with fresh flowers. Lunches include burgers, roast turkey sandwich, grilled pesto chicken breast, and our favorite: a grilled vegetable sandwich with sweet onions, zucchini, mushrooms, roasted red peppers, and provolone cheese on homemade foccacia. The dinner menu features such main courses as pan-seared duck breast, grilled flank steak, and fresh Atlantic salmon; plus unusual pizzas with such toppings as shrimp and artichoke hearts, and a variety of pastas. They serve a mean lemonade, too, plus espresso and full liquor service.

The Claimjumper Steak House
573 Main St. ☎ **801/649-8051.** Main courses $9.95–$18.95. AE, MC, V. Daily 5:30–10pm. Bus: Main Street Trolley. STEAK/RIBS/SEAFOOD.

This three-story brick-and-masonry building opened in 1913 as the New Park Hotel; all meals, including Sunday dinner, were 50¢. Prices are a bit higher now, but a meal at this renowned western-style restaurant is well worth what you'll pay. The Claimjumper is known for its steaks—especially its thick buffalo steaks—as well as prime rib, seafood, and desserts. Full liquor service is available.

○ Glitretind Restaurant

Stein Eriksen Lodge, Deer Valley. ☎ **801/645-6451.** Reservations requested. Skier's buffet lunch $21.95 adults, $14.95 children under 12; dinner main courses $18–$35, four-course prix fixe $49. AE, DISC, MC, V. Daily 7–10am, 11:30am–2:30pm, 6–9pm. Bus: Deer Valley Loop. CONTEMPORARY INTERNATIONAL.

Located in the elegant Stein Eriksen Lodge (see "Where to Stay," above), this is an equally elegant restaurant, serving innovative, impeccably prepared cuisine. The modern, airy dining room looks out on the spectacular Wasatch Mountains. The top-notch buffet breakfast offers such delights as muffins, breads, granola, oatmeal, and seasonal fruits, as well as hot dishes like southwestern eggs Benedict with crisp tortilla; chorizo hash and Hollandaise sauce; and an egg-white omelet with spinach, mushrooms, and tomatoes. Lunch in the winter features an all-you-can-eat skier's buffet, with hearty choices such as smoked salmon, wild game chile, grilled breast of duck, baked halibut, and carved roasts. The rest of the year, the lunch menu features salads and sandwiches, usually including Oriental chicken salad, an Ahi tuna sandwich, and seafood Caesar salad.

For an evening appetizer, you might try the dill-cured salmon, crisp potato lasagna with wild mushrooms and lemon-parsley sauce, or smoked duck tamale with spicy pepper coulis. For your main course, you might want to go for the peppered Ahi tuna with Asian vegetables; rack of lamb with warm barley salad and roasted garlic rosemary jus; grilled Muscovy duck with potato purée, foie gras, and blackberry-cassis sauce; or grilled beef tenderloin with gorgonzola potato purée and a three-peppercorn sauce.

Grappa Italian Restaurant

151 Main St. ☎ **801/645-0636.** Reservations required. Main courses $6–$25. AE, DISC, MC, V. Wed–Sun 5:30–10pm. Bus: Main Street Trolley. ITALIAN.

The chefs make everything from scratch at this elegant restaurant, using the freshest herbs and vegetables available; preparing the tomato sauce alone requires cases of Roma tomatoes each day. Located in a century-old building at the top of Main Street, Grappa is decorated to feel like a Tuscan farmhouse. There are three floors, with a small patio on the ground floor and a larger second-floor deck with a delightful view of historic Main Street and the surrounding mountains. Baskets of fresh fruits and vegetables decorate the dining areas.

Popular dishes include grilled chicken and spinach lasagna, pan-seared lamb chops stuffed with sausage and spinach, and open-spit–roasted guinea fowl. The meats and fowl are seasoned in the style of southern French and Italian cooking, then grilled or rotisseried over a wood-burning flame.

Main Street Deli

525 Main St. ☎ **801/649-1110.** Reservations not accepted. Breakfast (till 11:30am) $1.35–$4.75, sandwiches $3.59–$5.99. No credit cards. Daily 7:30am–9pm. Bus: Main Street Trolley. DELI/CAFE.

This is a busy, noisy little deli/cafe that's a good place to make yourself at home for awhile—there are plenty of newspapers scattered around to read. Breakfast offers omelets and other egg dishes, plus French toast, oatmeal, and the like. There's a wide range of sandwiches—two dozen in all—including bratwurst, pastrami, and egg salad. Bagels are made fresh and the gourmet coffee is freshly ground. Homemade cakes, cookies, and pies are available for dessert, as well as ice cream and frozen yogurt.

Morning Ray

268 Main St. ☎ **801/649-5686.** Reservations not accepted. Main courses $3.25–$6.95. AE, DISC, MC, V. Daily 7am–3pm. Bus: Main Street Trolley. AMERICAN.

This bakery and cafe, with its solid wood furniture and lacy cafe curtains, is a locals' favorite breakfast stop (breakfast is served until noon). There are five kinds of omelets, including the "Sweetheart," made with marinated artichoke hearts, scallions, and Havarti cheese; and the "Morning Ray," a large serving of house fries topped with sautéed vegetables, melted jack cheese, sour cream, and guacamole. Other eccentric breakfast dishes include organic buckwheat-cornmeal-buttermilk cakes (did they leave anything out?) and sourdough French toast. There's also lots to choose from at lunch, from a standard Greek salad or Reuben to the Morning Ray's very own bean burger, a blend of black beans, lentils, and brown rice. The "Mandy Bagel"—a toasted open-face bagel with sautéed mushrooms, peppers, tomatoes and scallions, topped with melted cheddar and sprouts—is either breakfast or lunch—you decide.

✪ Texas Red's Pit Barbecue & Chili Parlor

440 Main St. ☎ **801/649-7337.** Reservations not accepted. Main courses $6.95–$15.95. AE, DISC, MC, V. Daily 11:30am–10pm. Bus: Main Street Trolley. BARBECUE/CHILE.

This is about as Texan as you can get in Utah—and you can get pretty Texan here. The walls are decorated with moose, deer, and buffalo heads, and there's a picture of—who else?—John Wayne; Western music fills the air, and plenty of authentic Texas-style barbecue fills the paper plates. Barbecued beef is the specialty, but the barbecued pork ribs and homemade chile—from a secret family recipe—are also popular. Beer, wine, and tequila drinks are offered.

Wasatch Brew Pub

250 Main St. ☎ **801/649-9500.** Reservations. Main courses $7.25–$15.95. AE, MC, V. Daily 11am–10pm (bar open until midnight). Bus: Main Street Trolley. AMERICAN.

The bar overlooks the brewing area in this popular, noisy brew pub. You can get the usual pub foods, including fish-and-chips, beer-battered shrimp, and cheese steaks. Dinner is a bit more adventuresome, with dishes such as fresh Utah trout with roasted garlic herb butter, rack of New Zealand lamb with fresh mint sauce, and an Oriental stir-fry of fresh vegetables cooked in seasoned sesame oil. There's a sports bar upstairs, and an outside patio for warm-weather dining.

MUSIC & MORE IN THE MOUNTAINS: THE PERFORMING ARTS

Summer in Park City resounds with music. The annual **Music in the Mountains** series hosts different kinds of music in several locales from mid-June through August. Free concerts take place every Wednesday evening from 6 to 8pm at the Jack Green Bandstand at City Park (☎ 801/649-6100). One week you might hear bluegrass, the next, classical, and yet another it might be rock or jazz.

The **Saturday Afternoon Performing Arts Series** schedules free live entertainment Saturday afternoons in the summer on Main Street and at the Resort Center. The music simply wafts around the storefronts of the areas. Enjoy as you shop, eat, or rest.

The annual **Folk and Bluegrass Festival** (☎ 801/649-6100) is probably one of the most popular entertainments in the valley. National bluegrass artists perform at the Deer Valley Resort outdoor amphitheater for a full day in mid-August. Tickets cost $18 to $22 single, $35 to $40 family.

The ✪ **Utah Symphony Summer Series** takes place during most of July at the outdoor amphitheater at Snow Park Lodge in Deer Valley. The music includes classical masterpieces such as Tchaikovsky's *1812 Overture,* plus popular works by composers such as Rogers and Hammerstein and John Philip Sousa. The stage faces the mountainside; listeners bring chairs or blankets and relax under the stars. Call the symphony box office (☎ 801/533-6683) or Deer Valley Resort (☎ 801/649-1000) for schedule and ticket information.

The **Wolf Mountain Concert Series** hosts nationally known rock, country, and jazz performers. Having recently added an indoor 3,000-seat arena, Wolf Mountain now showcases popular music all year long. For information, contact their events office (☎ 801/649-5400), or the concert hotline (☎ 801/536-1234).

The **Park City International Music Festival** (☎ 801/649-5309) has been presenting classical performances at locations throughout Park City since 1984. Classical musicians from around the world attend, and programs include soloists, small-ensemble and chamber music, and full orchestra. The festival runs from mid-July to mid-August.

The **Historic Egyptian Theatre,** 328 Main Street (☎ 801/649-9371), is the place to go for live theater. Built in 1926 in the popular Egyptian Revival style, the theater was originally used for vaudeville and silent films, and was the first theater in Park City to offer the "new talking pictures." Today it's the home of the Park City Performers, offering theatrical presentations throughout the year, including a children's play each spring. The 1995–96 season included the comedy *The Best Christmas Pageant Ever*, the musical comedy *Forever Plaid*, and Neil Simon's comedy *Rumors*. Tickets are $12 to $18 (subscription tickets are less).

PARK CITY AFTER DARK: THE CLUB SCENE

Park City is known as Utah's Party Town; it's got probably the best nightlife scene in the state.

If you're looking for drinking and dancing, join a private club. This isn't as difficult as you might think. Memberships are available on a short-term basis for a nominal fee, usually $5, and membership entitles you to bring several guests.

Adolph's (Park City Golf Course; ☎ 801/649-7177) is mainly a social bar with piano music on some nights. **The Alamo Saloon** (447 Main St.; ☎ 801/649-2380) offers live music and dancing most evenings, plus pool, darts, and pinball. **Cisero's** (downstairs at 306 Main St.; ☎ 801/649-5044), with a recently expanded dance floor, hosts good bands, including a jam band Wednesday nights; there's also a big-screen TV for sports events. You'll find two bars at **The Club** (449 Main St.; ☎ 801/649-6693); the downstairs one has food and drinks, and there's dancing to a DJ upstairs. **Cooters** (on the second floor of the Radisson Hotel, 2121 Park Ave.; ☎ 801/649-5000) has terrific views of the surrounding mountains, plus a big-screen TV and a variety of live entertainment, from fashion shows to bands. **The Cozy** (438 Main St.; ☎ 801/649-6038) has a spacious dance area, live entertainment on weekends, a game room, and a number of TV monitors for sports enthusiasts. **Mileti's** (412 Main St.; ☎ 801/649-8230), a cozy, friendly, sociable place, is the oldest private club on Main Street.

3 Side Trips from Park City: Heber City, Strawberry Reservoir & Some Great State Parks

This region of the Wasatch Front isn't just about skiing. The great lakes and parks near Park City are some of Utah's best-kept secrets. To the northeast is Rockport State Park, a manmade lake that attracts water sports enthusiasts year-round, from swimmers to ice fishers. Right nearby Park City is Jordanelle State Park, Utah's newest state park and a great boating destination; and Wasatch Mountain State Park, Utah's second-largest state park and one of its major golf destinations. Heading southeast from Park City, you'll reach Heber City, whose main claim to fame is its historic steam train; it's also where you pick up U.S. 40 to northeastern Utah

(See Chapter 10). A bit farther afield along U.S. 40 is pristine Strawberry Reservoir, one of our favorite water playgrounds in Utah.

ROCKPORT STATE PARK

One of the Utah State Park System's manmade lakes, Rockport is a great place to play. A full range of outdoor activities, from windsurfing to wildlife watching, all take place in, on, or around the lake in the summer. In the winter, add ice fishing and cross-country skiing.

JUST THE FACTS

Rockport Lake has a marina, a concessionaire for rentals, a boat ramp and courtesy docks, a picnic area, and camping in a variety of settings. At press time, a concessionaire was slated to offer a limited number of small boats for rent in summer; call the park office for details.

The Wanship Dam, at the north end of the lake, is an important water storage and flood control dam on the Weber River, with headwaters high in the Uinta Mountains.

Getting There   From Park City, head east on I-80 for about 10^1/$_2$ miles to exit 156, then go 4^1/$_2$ miles south on Utah 32 along the western bank of Rockport Lake to the access road. The park entrance is at the lake's southern tip. Turn east to the park entrance, and then follow the road around to the north along the eastern bank.

Information, Fees & Regulations   Address inquiries to **Rockport State Park**, 9040 N. Utah 302, Peoa, UT 84061-9702 (☎ 801/336-2241). The half-mile-wide, 3-mile-long lake is open year-round. The day use fee is $3 per vehicle. Pets are allowed, but must be confined or leashed. Unless otherwise posted, speed limit within the park is 15 mph. Off-highway vehicles are not permitted.

WARM-WEATHER SPORTS & ACTIVITIES

Water Activities   The day-use area, located about 3^1/$_2$ miles north of the park entrance, offers the lake's best swimming. The lake is also popular for boating, windsurfing, waterskiing, sailing, kayaking, and fishing. Both the lake and river are home to rainbow and brown trout, yellow perch, and smallmouth bass.

Hiking & Wildlife Watching   A 4-mile round-trip hike takes off from Juniper Campground. This easy, relatively flat walk among juniper and sagebrush is a good one for spotting mule deer, yellow-belly marmots, badgers, raccoons, weasels, skunks, and ground squirrels. Less visible are elk, moose, coyote, bobcat, and cougar. Birds also abound, and Western grebes, Canada geese, whistling swans, great blue herons, and golden and bald eagles can sometimes be spotted. More frequently seen are ducks, redtail hawks, magpies, scrub jays, and hummingbirds.

CROSS-COUNTRY SKIING

There are groomed cross-country ski trails in the open sagebrush areas, which offer a better chance of seeing wildlife than the more forested areas in the surrounding national forest. Ice fishing is popular on the lake in the winter.

CAMPING

There are 86 campsites in six areas around the lake. The first campground is to the right of the access road, along the Weber River rather than the lake. Sites are shady, and give easy access to a trail along the river that's handy for fishermen. The remainder of the sites lie between the road and the lake, along its eastern bank, and most have vault toilets only. One campground, Juniper, has 34 sites with water and electric hookups, a dump station, and modern restrooms. Primitive sites cost $9 Sunday through Thursday nights and $10 Friday, Saturday, and holidays; developed sites are $3 more. Reservations are available (☎ 800/322-3770), but not generally necessary for individual sites. Visa and MasterCard are accepted, and there is a $5 non-refundable reservation fee.

JORDANELLE STATE PARK

Utah's newest state park, completed in the spring of 1995, offers two recreation areas on Jordanelle Reservoir in the beautiful Wasatch Mountains. Both sites are great for boating, fishing, picnicking, and camping.

JUST THE FACTS

The reservoir is shaped rather like a boomerang, with the dam at the elbow. The Perimeter Trail connects the highly developed **Hailstone Recreation Site** to the more primitive **Rock Cliff Recreation Site.** Hailstone is on the terraced peninsula poking into the upper arm just above the dam; Rock Cliff is at the southeastern tip of the lower arm of the reservoir. Hailstone's camping and picnicking areas face the widest part of the reservoir, which is perfect for speedboats, water skiing, and jet skiing. Above Hailstone is a wakeless water area, excellent for sailboats and quiet fishing. The narrow arm reaching down to Rock Cliff is designated for low-speed water use. The 27 miles of trails that encircle the reservoir and connect to other trails in the region are open to hikers, mountainbikers, horseback riders, and cross-country skiers.

Getting There   From Park City, head east on Kearns Boulevard (Utah 248) for about $3^3/_4$ miles; at U.S. 40, go southeast 4 miles to exit 8 and follow the entrance road east into Hailstone. From Heber City, take U.S. 40 northwest about 6 miles. For Rock Cliff, follow U.S. 40 northwest from Heber City for about 4 miles, then head east onto Utah 32 for about 6 miles to the entrance.

Information, Fees & Regulations   Address inquiries to **Jordanelle State Park,** P.O. Box 309, Heber City, UT 84032-0309 (☎ 801/645-8036). Stop at the **visitor center** at Hailstone or the **Nature Center,** a nature-oriented visitor center, at Rock Cliff for information and trail maps. The exhibit room in the visitor center at Hailstone presents an overview of human history in the area, from the early natives through the trappers, the Mormon settlers, and up to the present.

The park is open year-round at Hailstone, and from April through September at Rock Cliff. Day-use hours in the summer are 6am to 10pm; from October through March, 8am to 5pm. The visitor centers are open from 9am to 6pm in the summer; the Hailstone visitor center is open to 5pm in the winter. The day-use fee is $3 per vehicle.

In order to protect the abundance of wildlife, particularly birds, pets are not allowed at Rock Cliff. They're welcome at Hailstone, but must be confined or leashed. Bicycling is permitted on established public roads, in parking areas, and on the Perimeter Trail; off-highway vehicles are prohibited.

HAILSTONE RECREATION SITE

Hailstone has three camping areas and a group pavilion; a swimming beach and a picnic area are available for day use. There's a 76-slip marina with camping and picnicking supplies and rentals, a small restaurant, an amphitheater, boat ramps, a jet-ski ramp, a wheelchair-accessible fishing deck, and a fish cleaning station.

Warm-Weather Sports & Activities

Powerboats are available for rent at $139 per day for a two-seater, $159 per day for a three-seater; for 6 hours the cost is $99 and $119, respectively, from 8am to 2pm; $119 and $139 from 2 to 8pm; or $40 and $50 per hour. Gas is not included. Fishing boats can be rented for $75 per day for a 14-footer, $85 per day for a 16-footer. Both have 15 hp motors, and rates include gas. Water-skiing accessories are available. Eighteen-speed mountainbikes can be rented at $16 for a half day and $24 full day.

Camping

Hailstone's three camping areas have a total of 100 sites, including walk-in tent sites, RV/tent sites without hookups, and RV sites with water and electric hookups. Facilities include modern restrooms, showers, a small laundromat, and a playground. Cost is $9 to $11 Sunday to Thursday, and $10 to $12 Friday, Saturday, and holidays.

ROCK CLIFF RECREATION SITE

Rock Cliff has three walk-in camping areas; three picnic tables; group pavilions; the **Nature Center,** offering maps, environmental programs, and exhibits on the various habitats of the area and how man's activities impact on them; and the **Jordanelle Discovery Trail,** a boardwalk interpretive trail that winds through the Provo River riparian terrain.

Wildlife Watching

Rock Cliff is a great place for bird-watching, with more than 160 species of birds either living here or passing through, and eagles and other raptors nesting in the area.

Situated as it is among numerous riparian wetlands, Rock Cliff is designed to protect these sensitive habitats. Trails and boardwalks traverse the area, and bridges cross the waterways at four points, enabling you to really get close to a variety of wetland life without inadvertently doing any harm to the habitats.

Camping

There are three walk-in campgrounds with 50 sites and two modern restrooms with showers. These sites are more nature-oriented than those at Hailstone, and are scattered over 100 acres, providing great privacy. Cost is $9 Sunday to Thursday and $10 Friday, Saturday, and holidays.

WASATCH MOUNTAIN STATE PARK

The second largest of Utah's State Parks (after Antelope Island) is also its most developed—and may be its most popular. This year-round destination is a well-maintained, well-serviced park that's easy to enjoy, and it just keeps getting better. It's a terrific golf and camping destination, and trails are being continually expanded to meet the demands of hikers and mountainbikers. In the winter, a network of groomed cross-country skiing and snowmobiling trails leads from the park into the surrounding forest, and cross-country ski and snowmobile rentals are available. Wasatch Mountain is also a learning park—its rangers offer a variety of instructive and interpretive programs. For the photographer, fall is the time to visit; the incomparable juxtaposition of rich reds and ochres and deep evergreens defy the imagination.

JUST THE FACTS

A major draw here is the scenic 27-hole golf course; plans are afoot to add another nine holes to the golf course by 1997. The course becomes a cross-country ski track in the winter. There is both tent camping, and RV sites with hookups.

Getting There   It's about 5¹/₂ miles from Heber City to the park: From downtown, turn west on Utah 113 (100 South) to Midway; following signs for the state park, jog north on 200 West, then west on 200 North, and finally north again on Homestead Drive. The visitor center is located on Homestead Drive (where it becomes Snake Creek Road), in the park.

Information & Visitor Centers   Address inquiries to **Wasatch Mountain State Park,** P.O. Box 10, Midway, UT 84049-0010 (☎ 801/654-1791). The day-use fee is $3 per vehicle.

The visitor center, which also serves as a lounge for golfers, is open daily from 8am to 5pm, and includes a large mountain lodge–style room with comfortable seating. You can talk with rangers about park activities and get trail maps and other park information here.

Fees & Regulations   The day-use fee is $3 per vehicle. Off-highway vehicles are permitted on designated roadways only. Pets are welcome in the park, but must be confined or on a leash at all times.

Ranger Programs   Interpretive programs take place most Friday and Saturday summer nights at the amphitheater, and a junior ranger program is offered Saturday mornings. The stocked pond adjacent to the visitor center provides fishing fun for children under 16 in the summer. Call for details.

WINTER SPORTS & ACTIVITIES

Cross-Country Skiing   A 12-kilometer Nordic ski track, with both diagonal stride and skating lanes, is laid out on the golf course. Neither dogs nor snowmobiles are allowed on the track, which is open from 8am to 5pm.

Snowmobiling   Snowmobiling is very popular, as the park has about 90 miles of groomed trails, some of which take you into Pine Creek, Snake Creek, and American Fork canyons. Warming stations are located at the clubhouse and visitor center.

WARM-WEATHER SPORTS & ACTIVITIES

Golf   With a USGA-sanctioned 27-hole, par-72 course, golfing is the most popular pastime at the park. There are 10 lakes scattered throughout the tree-lined fairways, and the views of the lovely Heber Valley are grand. There's a full-service pro shop, a driving range, practice greens, and a cafe. The course is open daily during daylight hours.

Greens fees for adults are $7.50 for 9 holes, $15 for 18, and $120 for a 20-round pass, which is useable by any member of the holder's immediate family. On weekdays (except holidays), greens fees for seniors (age 62 and older) and juniors (age 17 and under) are $6.50 for 9 holes and $13 for 18. Pull carts for 9 holes cost $2.25; riding carts are $8.50 for 9 holes and $17 for 18.

Tee times should be reserved the preceding Monday for weekends, and the preceding Saturday for Tuesday to Friday play. Reservations can be made by calling 801/654-1901 or 801/654-0532.

Hiking & Wildlife Watching   The **Pine Creek Nature Trail** is just over a mile in length, and encompasses three smaller loops. Many songbirds make their homes in the trees along the trail, so you might catch a glimpse of Steller jays, chickadees, wrens, robins, and Western tanagers. You might also see the tracks of mule deer along the creek, where they come to forage. From the large parking area in Pine Creek campground, follow the half-mile trail to the Pine Creek trailhead, which lies just north of the Oak Hollow loop. The trail begins at an elevation of 6,100 feet and climbs 220 feet, crossing Pine Creek four times and traversing several boulder ridges. A trail guide is available for 25¢, and describes some of the plants you will see. Don't attempt this trail after a rain, as it becomes quite muddy and slick. No bikes or motorized vehicles are allowed. And be sure to take water, a sun hat, and binoculars.

Literature describing the plant and animal life of the park is available at the camp manager's office near the entrance to the campground, and at the visitor center.

Mountainbiking & ATV Trails There's an 18-mile loop that's great for mountainbiking and all-terrain vehicles. The road leaves the visitor center and heads west, winding through magnificent wooded country, and offering occasional breathtaking views of the valley.

CAMPING

There are three camping loops, with a total of 122 sites, in the **Pine Creek Campground,** two of which do not allow tents. All three loops have modern restrooms with showers. Some sites are nestled among trees and are quite shady, others are more open. All have a paved parking pad, water, electricity, a picnic table, and a barbecue grill; 66 sites have sewer hookups. Call for information about the group-use area. There's a dump station near the entrance to the campground. Camping fees, Monday through Thursday, are $11 to $13 for hookups, $7 for no hookups; Friday through Sunday, the cost is $12 to $15 with hookups, $10 for none. Reservations are advised and can be made by calling 800/322-3770. Visa and MasterCard are accepted, and there is a $5 nonrefundable reservation fee.

HEBER CITY

Nestled in the lovely Heber Valley, Heber City has managed to retain its small-town atmosphere, despite its proximity to Salt Lake City and Park City. It's the point where you pick up U.S. 40 if you're heading into the Northeast Corner, to Flaming Gorge Recreation Area or to Dinosaur National Monument.

ESSENTIALS

Getting There From Salt Lake City, head east on I-80 for 25 miles to exit 148, and follow U.S. 40 south about 25 miles. From Park City, Utah 248 east and U.S. 40 south take you to the 20 miles to Heber City.

Visitor Information There's a visitor center at 475 N. Main St. (☎ 801/ 654-3666), in a delightful Bavarian chalet–style building with a split cedar roof.

WHAT TO SEE & DO

✪ Heber Valley Historic Railroad

450 S. 600 West. ☎ **801/654-5601;** 801/581-9980 from Salt Lake City. Round-trip $14–$16 adults, $8–$10 children 3–12, $12–$14 seniors 65 and older. One way $9–$10 adults, $5–$6 children 3–12, $8–$9 seniors 65 and older; the railroad does not provide transportation back for one-way trips. Jun–Sept one or two runs daily, reduced schedule remainder of year. Ticket office is open 8:30am–4pm on two-run days, 12:30–4pm single-run days.

"The Heber Creeper," as the train is affectionately known, is all that's left of the once busy branch connecting Heber City to Provo. For 70 years the train carried people, livestock, and general freight up and down Provo Canyon. Sheep were frequent travelers as they were shipped to market from Heber City, one of the largest sheep shipping centers in the nation. But in the late 1960s, the train stopped running; the automobile and truck had usurped its function.

Now it's an excursion train. The diversity of the landscape on this short trip is unparalleled. On its 1¹/₂-hour run, the train passes through a lush valley, along the shore of a fair-sized lake, and between towering canyon walls before reaching Vivian Park. During the half-hour stay there, the engine moves to the other end of the train via a passing track, and then starts the slow haul back up the 2% grade out of the canyon.

Fall is one of the prettiest times to ride the train, as the mountainsides are gradually decorated with the rich hues of changing leaves—the reds of oak and maple, golds of cottonwood and aspen, and the ever-present greens of piñon, juniper, spruce, and pine.

The train is usually powered by a turn-of-the-century steam engine, but is occasionally replaced by a diesel. If steam power is critical to your enjoyment, call ahead to confirm locomotion. Special excursions are scheduled periodically throughout the year, such as the Santa Claus Express, so you might want to ask about them when planning your trip.

A NEARBY RESORT HOTEL & GOLF COURSE

The Homestead

700 N. Homestead Dr. (P.O. Box 99), Midway, UT 84049. ☎ **801/654-1102** or 800/ 327-7220. Fax 801/654-5087. 117 rms, 9 suites. TV TEL. $79–$139 double, $150–$305 suite. AE, CB, DC, DISC, MC, V.

The historic Homestead is a small resort hotel with the atmosphere of a country inn. Swiss-born Simon Schneitter came here in 1886 to farm, but soon realized the warm mineral springs, a bane to farming, offered a better opportunity for success. He built a board-enclosed pool, and soon added his wife's chicken dinners to the attractions. The Schneitter family home (called the Virginia House) is now only one part of the Homestead, where you can enjoy all the old-fashioned charm, but with all the modern amenities.

The Homestead has both indoor and outdoor pools, a mineral bath, a whirlpool, a sauna, two lighted tennis courts, and lawn games. In the summer you can enjoy hay rides ($6) or a horse-drawn buggy ride ($15), and in the winter there are sleigh rides ($8 to $15 per person). They offer horseback riding (cost ranges from $5 for a half hour around the barnyard to $45 for a picnic ride), mountainbike rentals ($5 to $18), snowmobiling ($35 to $125), and cross-country skiing, with 19 kilometers of groomed trails (equipment rentals $7 to $12, lessons available).

The 18-hole, par-72 championship golf course meanders through the beautiful Snake Creek Valley, providing magnificent views of the surrounding mountains. Greens fees are $11 to $32, and cart fees are $37 to $47 for 18 holes. Private lessons cost $25 for a half hour and $40 for 1 hour. An hour miniclinic is $5 per person, with a minimum of six persons.

In addition to lodge rooms and suites, the Homestead offers some condos and private homes with two to four bedrooms, for $205 to $550. A variety of packages are also available, which might include meals, golf, skiing, or other entertainment.

You can have a romantic dinner at **Simon's Fine Dining** (open 5:30 to 9:30pm daily), where the menu choices include grilled salmon, turkey scallopine, rack of lamb, or vegetable manicotti. **Simon's Pub** offers soups, salads, and finger food from 5:30 to 10pm daily. And the **Grill Room** serves hearty breakfasts and lunches daily, and dinner in the summer.

STRAWBERRY RESERVOIR

Located along U.S. 40 in the eastern portion of the Uinta National Forest, the jewel-like Strawberry Reservoir is a terrific water playground offering terrific fishing—this is Utah's premier trout fishery—plus boating, hiking, and mountainbiking opportunities. It's also great for cross-country skiing, ice fishing, and snowmobiling in the winter.

JUST THE FACTS

Strawberry Reservoir has four marinas, with the largest at **Strawberry Bay** (☎ 801/ 548-2261). This is the only one that provides year-round services; the other three have limited services, but all marinas have restrooms, convenience stores, boat and slip rentals, gas, and guide service. Strawberry Bay Marina also offers lodging, a cafe, dry boat storage, deep-moorage rental, public pay telephones, snowmobile rentals in the winter, propane and lantern fuel, firewood, charcoal, and ice. Strawberry Bay offers **lodging,** too (☎ 801/548-2500), with prices for two in the $50 to $100 range.

The other marina on the main part of the reservoir is located at Renegade Point, and there are two in the Soldier Creek area at Aspen Grove and Soldier Creek.

Getting There From Heber City, drive 21¹/₂ miles southeast on U.S. 40 and turn south onto the access road. After about a half mile, you'll come to the USFS visitor center for Strawberry Reservoir.

Information & Fees Address inquiries to **Heber Ranger District,** P.O. Box 190, Heber, UT 84032 (☎ 801/654-0470), or **Strawberry Visitor Center,** open daily May through October (☎ 801/548-2321). Day-use is free, except for a $2 fee for boat-ramp parking.

WARM-WEATHER SPORTS & ACTIVITIES

Fishing & Boating Strawberry Reservoir is Utah's premier trout fishery—indeed, one of the premier trout fisheries in the West—with both huge cutthroat and rainbow, so it's no surprise that fishing is the number-one draw. Fishing boats with outboard motors are available at Strawberry Bay Marina for $50 to $75 per day; large pontoons start at $125 a day.

Powerboats are allowed everywhere on the main reservoir, with sailboats staying mostly in the smaller area below Haws Point; the Soldier Creek area to the east is best for canoes and kayaks. The water in Strawberry Reservoir is quite cold, so only the extremely hardy try swimming.

Hiking There are a number of hiking trails around the reservoir. The easiest is **Telephone Hollow,** a 2¹/₂-mile loop hike for beginner to intermediate hikers that takes off from the north side of U.S. 40 about 5 miles west of the entrance road to the reservoir.

For the advanced hiker, there's the **25-mile loop** that follows forest roads 299 and 134 along Clyde Creek up to Strawberry Ridge, overlooking the reservoir from the west. Forest Road 135 heads south along the ridge to Squaw Creek; you'll follow it back to the main road around the reservoir, and finally back to your starting point.

Just outside the visitor center is a self-guided **nature trail** where you can learn about stream ecology and view fish, wildflowers, and a variety of birds.

WINTER SPORTS & ACTIVITIES

Explore the canyons, mountains, and meadows of the Strawberry Bay area on cross-country skis, snowmobiles, or dogsleds. And chop through the ice on the reservoir for some chilled trout. **Strawberry Bay Marina** (☎ 801/548-2261), open year-round, offers guide services, supplies, and snowmobile rentals.

CAMPING

Campgrounds are located at each of the four marinas on the reservoir. Sites in the Strawberry Bay and Soldier Creek campgrounds have hookups; Aspen Grove and Renegade do not. The camping fee is $11, $17 with hookups; the dump station fee is $2. Boat ramps and fish-cleaning facilities are located adjacent to each campground. Reservations can be made for a limited number of designated campsites at Strawberry Bay and Soldier Creek by contacting the **National Reservation System** at 800/280-2267. The remainder of the sites are on a first-come, first-served basis.

4 Sundance Resort & Institute

Situated in beautiful Provo Canyon at the base of 12,000-foot Mt. Timpanogos, Sundance is a year-round resort that emphasizes its arts programs as much as its skiing and other outdoor activities. That should come as no surprise, though—it's owned by actor/director Robert Redford, who bought the property in 1969 and named it after his character in the classic film *Butch Cassidy and the Sundance Kid.* You might recognize the area; Redford and director Sydney Pollack set their 1972 film *Jeremiah Johnson* here.

The goal for Sundance was to create a place where the outdoors and the arts could come together in a really unique mountain community, and it seems to be a success. We tend to think it's a bit overrated, but there's no arguing about the setting—it's really majestic. The rustic-yet-elegant (for these prices, it better be elegant), environmentally friendly retreat is a full-service ski resort in the winter; in the summer, you'll find great hiking trails and other outdoor activities, as well as the Sundance Institute, which Redford founded in 1980 to support and encourage independent American filmmaking and playwriting.

ESSENTIALS

Getting There   Sundance is less than an hour's drive from Salt Lake City via I-15. From Park City, take U.S. 189 south to Sundance. From Provo, take I-15 to exit 275, go east on Utah 52 for 5¹/₂ miles, then north on U.S. 189 up Provo Canyon for 7 miles, then turn north on Utah 92 for about 2 miles to Sundance, which is on the left. The road beyond Sundance is often closed in the winter.

A van shuttle service connects Sundance with both Salt Lake International Airport and Provo Airport. The charge is $40 per person, one way; call the **Sundance Resort and Institute** at 801/225-4107 or 800/892-1600 to arrange for pick-up.

Visitor Information   For information, contact **Sundance Resort and Institute,** R.R. 3 Box A-1, Sundance, UT 84604 (☎ 801/225-4107 or 800/892-1600; fax 801/226-1937; 801/225-4100 for snow reports). The nearest hospital is in Provo, about 20 minutes away.

SKIING SUNDANCE

With a limit of 1,500 skiers per day, Sundance is known for its quiet, intimate setting and lack of lift lines. It has runs for all levels—some quite challenging—including several delightfully long cruising trails for novices. The area is gaining a reputation as a good place to learn to ski, epecially as the two levels of skiing are pretty well separated from one another: The beginner and some of the intermediate terrain is on the front mountain, while the prime blue runs and all of the expert slopes are on the back mountain.

Lessons for beginners and novices are well done and fruitful. For those of you who have moved far beyond lessons, the blue cruising ground on the back mountain is good—but it's the blue runs, if any, that get crowded. The expert crowd will be pleased with the steep glades, precipitous bump runs (due to the general lack of traffic, the mountain never really bumps up too high, though), and untracked snow on the back mountain (where you'll have to work at it to run into another skiier).

Sorry, snowboarders—you're not welcome on the mountain here.

JUST THE FACTS

Sundance offers 20% beginner, 40% intermediate, and 40% advanced terrain, with a total of 41 runs over 450 acres. There are seven double chair lifts with a vertical drop of 2,150 feet, from a base elevation of 6,100 feet to the top at 8,250 feet. Sundance is usually open from mid-December through April, although its relatively low elevation makes it susceptible to early closures due to fickle weather. Lifts operate daily 9am to 4:30pm.

Bearclaw Cabin, the only mountaintop day lodge in Utah, offers snacks and hot drinks daily from 10am to 4pm, as well as stupendous views while sipping or munching. **Creekside,** at the base of the ski area, serves lunch during ski season.

Equipment rental and sales are available.

Lift Tickets   The cost of an adult all-day lift ticket is $32; half day is $26; all day for children is $22; and seniors over 65 ski free. If you're staying at the resort, the lift ticket is built into the price of your room.

Lessons & Programs   The **ski school** (☎ 801/225-4107, ext. 4130) at Sundance offers private and group lessons daily, as well as specialized ski workshops. One-hour private lessons start at $45, group lessons start at $25 for a half day.

Sundance Kids ski school offers several programs, including group sessions for kids ages six and older and all-day programs that include supervision, lunch, and instructions. You can enroll the younger kids in private lessons; however, there is no actual day-care facility.

CROSS-COUNTRY SKIING

Sundance's excellent **Nordic Center** is 1 1/2 miles north of the main Sundance entrance. It has 14km of Nordic trails in the Elk Meadows Preserve, groomed for both classic and skate skiing. Classic, skating, and telemark rentals and lessons are available. Trails are rated as 20% beginner, 40% intermediate, and 40% advanced. Trail passes for adults cost $5 for full day and $3 for half day. Children 12 and under and seniors over 65 ski free. There's night skiing on Monday, Wednesday, and Friday from 5 to 9pm.

WARM-WEATHER SPORTS & ACTIVITIES

An abundance of warm-weather activities and spectacular scenery make Sundance just as popular a destination in the summer.

Hiking   Sundance is home to a terrific network of about 10 hiking trails, some of which connect to trails farther afield in the Uinta National Forest. The resort's trails range from hour-long nature walks to all-day affairs, and include three summit trails to the top of Mount Timpanogos.

So You Wanna Be in Pictures . . .

Forget Cannes; forget Hollywood. If you want to be (or at least be up on) the next art-house cinema sensation, go to Utah.

Tired of waiting for the next Great American Novel, many across the nation—maybe even yourself—have traded their reading glasses for tubs of popcorn. They're packing the moviehouses to watch the latest work of the new creative hero: the American independent filmmaker. These next Tarentinos have to start somewhere—and that somewhere is, more often than not, the Sundance Film Festival.

For more than a decade now, the hottest independent films have been discovered at this week-long January event, hosted by Robert Redford's Sundance Institute. (The festival doesn't actually take place at Sundance, however; it's held 30 miles away, in Utah's premier resort town, Park City, covered earlier in this chapter.) The festival has seen the rise to glory of many pictures, from *sex, lies, and videotape* to *The Brothers McMullen*, with *Slacker, Gas Food Lodging, Paris Is Burning, Like Water for Chocolate, Hoop Dreams, Clerks,* and *Crumb* in between—and that's just the short list.

And hosting the nation's premier annual film festival is only part of the Sundance Institute's role in the world of American cinema. Think you might have what it takes to be the next Tarantino? Then it might be a good idea to take a summer trip to Sundance to take part in the Institute's Filmmakers Lab. Quentin did; afterwards, he released a little flick called *Reservoir Dogs*.

Since Robert Redford founded the Institute in 1981, it has brought some of the finest and most well-respected directors, actors, and producers to Utah for three weeks every June to serve as advisors while students rehearse, shoot, and edit scenes from their works. Denzel Washington and Glenn Close have lent their services; so have directors Terry Gilliam and Sydney Pollack, producer James L. Brooks, and actor Morgan Freeman. Redford himself even stops by occasionally to lend a hand. The Institute's success can be measured by the films it has helped develop: *El Norte, Impromptu, Reservoir Dogs, I Like It Like That, Mi Vida Loca,* and many others. Sundance also runs workshops to help writers polish their scripts, directors polish their actors, and producers polish their negotiating skills for when all the big-time studio distributors descend on them at the Festival, eager for the rights to the next *Devil in a Blue Dress* (another notable developed through the Sundance Labs).

Unlike most staid film-industry institutions, Sundance—the Institute and the Festival—has grown and changed with the times. Since its inception, Sundance has supported American independent feature films and documentaries, and has

The **Sundance Nature Trail** is a 1- to 1½-hour hike that winds through groves of spruce, oak, and maple and across alpine meadows before reaching a cascading waterfall. The **Great Western Trail,** one of the Wasatch Front's most spectacular trails, climbs nearly 4,000 feet to some amazing scenic vistas. It starts at the base of Aspen Grove, winds to the crest of North Fork and American Fork canyons, and ends at the top of Alta ski area. This is, as you might expect, an 8- to 10-hour hike.

And there's more to choose from: Contact the resort for a comprehensive trail guide. Guided hikes are available for all trails.

Horseback Riding The **Sundance Stables** offer guided mountain rides. Standard rides are an hour, but longer rides can be arranged. Rates are about $40 for an slowly added workshops and scholarship programs for young, promising Latin American, French, and Japanese filmmakers, as well as development programs for children's plays and family entertainment. The festival itself also screens foreign films and film shorts; for the first time this year, it's home to a special new-media center devoted to cutting-edge interactive CD-ROM films and games.

Although greater numbers of big names—from stars to studio executives—are showing up in little ol' Park City every year, Redford and the Institute's directors have made every effort to keep the festival uncompromised by Hollywood and a haven for American independent film. Redford asked for grittier films in 1996, and he got them—no slick, Big Studio–ready productions on these screens. The pieces that produced the most buzz included *Shine,* an Australian drama about a stammering pianist with an overbearing father (which was being fought over by distributors within a few days of its screening), and the offbeat *I Shot Andy Warhol,* based on the life of radical feminist Valerie Solanis, who, well, who shot Andy Warhol.

But there were two films in particular that really seemed to earmark the festival as "safe"—at least for the time being—from encroaching Hollywood consumerism. *Hype!,* a documentary detailing the corruption and co-option of the Seattle grunge music scene was a clear message to keep the independent, nonconformist spirit alive. And the mere entry, and success, of the drama, *Drunks,* whose world revolves around an Alcoholics Anonymous group, served as a piece of poetic justice—and as proof that the Festival's directors won't timidly kowtow to capitalist concerns. (*Drunks* was shown as part of Sundance's new American Spectrum series. The American Spectrum series is sponsored by Absolut Vodka—how's that for irony?)

Admission to the festival—as a filmmaker or as an audience member—is nonexclusive; that means you and I can rub shoulders with the rich and famous and the up-and-coming next January. Contact the **Sundance Institute,** P.O. Box 16450, Salt Lake City, Utah 84116 (☎ 801/328-3456) for a free guide, and to reserve tickets. (If you show up at the last minute, there's always the chance you'll be able to pick some up at the box office.)

And get your Great American Movie ready. The Sundance workshops still have room for this year, and entries for the Festival are due in mid-October. Call the Sundance Institute for details.

—Reid Bramblett

hour-long ride, about $50 for a two-hour ride; call 801/225-4107 or 800/892-1600 for information and reservations.

Fishing   Deer Creek Reservoir offers great fishing just ten minutes away. Sundance offers guided fishing trips that include equipment rentals and license. Rates range from $110 to $150 for a 4-hour fly-fishing trip; call 801/225-4107 or 800/892-1600 for information and reservations.

SHOPPING

The pricey **General Store** at Sundance was the inspiration for the *Sundance* Catalog; it may have come to you in the mail at some time or another. If so, you'll recognize the Native American art and jewelry, local crafts, and high-end Southwest-style clothing and outdoor wear that lines the shelves. Sundance's eco-sensitive complete bath product line, Sundance Farms, is available here, as well. There's also hiking and fishing apparel and gear in the warm weather, ski accessories in the winter, and fresh-baked goodies year-round. The store is open daily from 8am to 10pm.

ACCOMMODATIONS

Sundance offers one-, two-, and three-bedroom cottage suites that range from $150 to $595 per night, as well as several luxury mountain homes. The 20 "River Run" cottages are streamside, near the base area; the other 62, the "Mandan" cottages, are nestled in the mountains and offer fabulous views. Each suite is outfitted with well-crafted handmade furnishings that suit the rustic luxury of the entire resort, as well as Native American crafts, stone fireplaces, and outdoor decks; most have fully equipped kitchens. All accommodations come complete with Sundance's own natural bath products—such as eco-sensitive oatmeal soap—and wildflower bouquets throughout. A complete range of ski packages are available; call 801/225-4107 for reservations.

DINING

Sundance's restaurants have a unique culinary style that stresses the use of natural, seasonal ingredients prepared in a New American style that draws on Native American and other culinary traditions, such as southwestern cooking and California cuisine. Chickens are naturally raised, meats are hormone-free, and the vegetables come from Sundance's own organic garden. Just to give you an idea of how all this adds up, signature dishes include Navajo tacos with smoked salmon and marinated snowcap beans; roast prairie chicken with corn-mashed potatoes and cider cranberry sauce; Hopi vegetable stew with blue-corn dumplings; and lighter, Sundance-style twists on more standard fare, like California-style pizzas, for lunch.

Where do you enjoy all this? The resort has two main dining rooms: The **Tree Room,** the resort's elegant dining room, lined with Native American art and western memorabilia; and the **Grill Room,** a more informal eatery with a bistro-style menu. Be sure to reserve ahead of time, particularly in peak seasons.

There's also the **Zoom Roadhouse Grill,** a casual western-style eatery housed in a Victorian building that was once Park City's Union Pacific Railway Depot. Barbecues and cookouts are held throughout the warmer months.

SUNDANCE AFTER SUNDOWN

The excellent **Sundance Institute screening room** shows foreign films, movie classics, American independent films (see the box on the Sundance Institute), and documentaries year-round. Screenings are free to Sundance guests.

For 25 years the **Sundance Summer Theatre** has been showcasing innovative productions in a beautiful outdoor setting, a natural amphitheater backed by firs. There are generally four productions staged each season; call to find out what's on.

5 Provo & Environs

Provo is the second largest city in Utah, with a population of more than 90,000. Its largest draw is Brigham Young University, with its attendant museums, cultural events, and spectator sports. The Ute Indian tribe reigned here until Mormon leader Brigham Young sent 30 families south from Salt Lake City in March of 1849 to colonize the area. Today, the city remains primarily Mormon; most restaurants plus the museums on the BYU campus are closed on Sunday.

South of Provo lies **Springville,** a town of about 14,000 that likes to refer to itself as "Utah's Art City." Although not primarily a tourist destination, it boasts one of Utah's finest art museums.

Orem, which abuts Provo on the northwest, is the home of various computer-related businesses. Utah Lake State Park, just west of downtown, is great for boating, and the surrounding Wasatch Mountains abound with natural beauty and recreational opportunities.

ESSENTIALS
GETTING THERE

By Car   Provo is 45 miles south of Salt Lake City and 258 miles northeast of St. George. Provo and Orem are easily accessible from the north or south by I-15. If you're driving in from the east on I-70, take exit 156 at Green River and follow U.S. 6 northwest to I-15 north.

By Train   Amtrak (☎ 800/872-7245) offers intercity passenger service. The train station is located at 600 South and 300 West.

VISITOR INFORMATION

The **Utah County Travel Council** has its offices and an information center in the magnificent Historic County Courthouse, 51 S. University Ave. (☎ 801/370-8393 or 800/222-8824). Take I-15 to exit 268, follow Center Street east to University, turn south past the Courthouse, then turn east, where you'll find a visitors' parking lot behind the courthouse. Drivers of motorhomes and vehicles with trailers should try to park along the street.

A *Parks and Recreation Map and Facilities Guide* is available at the information center. There's also a **parks and recreation information hotline;** call 801/379-6629.

For information about the surrounding national forest, contact the **Uinta National Forest**, Supervisor's Office, 88 W. 100 North, Provo, UT 84601 (☎ 801/ 377-5780).

GETTING AROUND

The easiest way to get around is by car. The streets are organized in a numbered grid pattern, beginning at the intersection of Center St. (exit 268 off the I-15) and University Ave. (exit 266) in Provo. The numbers increase by 100 from there in all four directions, such as 100 South, 200 West, 700 North, and so forth. University Parkway cuts diagonally northwest across the grid from Brigham Young University to connect with 1300 South (I-15, exit 272) in Orem. "Ground zero" in Orem is at the intersection of Center Street (I-15, exit 274) and State Street (U.S. 89).

Car rental agencies with offices in Provo include **Avis** (☎ 801/359-2177 or 800/ 831-2847), **Budget** (☎ 800/237-7251 or 800/527-0700), **Hertz** (☎ 801/377-7495 or 800/654-3131), **National** (☎ 801/373-2114 or 800/227-7368), and **Payless** (☎ 801/374-9000 or 800/729-5377).

The **Utah Transit Authority** has about a dozen routes in and around the Provo area, with connections to Salt Lake City, Lehi, and Springville. Call 801/375-4636 for schedules, between 6am and 7pm, Monday to Saturday. Route maps and schedules are also available at the visitor information center in the County Courthouse.

FAST FACTS: PROVO

The main hospital is **Utah Valley Regional Medical Center,** 1034 N. 500 West (☎ 801/373-7850 or 801/371-7001 for emergencies). The main **post office** is at

95 W. 100 South (☎ 801/374-2000). The local **newspaper** is *The Daily Herald,* 1555 N. 20 West (☎ 801/373-6450). The sales tax in Provo and Orem is just over 6%. Outside the city limits, the county sales tax is just under 6%.

EXPLORING BRIGHAM YOUNG UNIVERSITY

Founded in 1875 by Brigham Young, Brigham Young University (University Hill, Provo; ☎ 801/378-4636) is one of the nation's largest church-affiliated universities, with over 30,000 students. The 646-acre campus is located on the east side of Provo at the base of the Wasatch Mountains. Free tours are offered through the **Hosting Center** (☎ 801/378-4678), Monday through Friday at 11am and 2pm, or by appointment. Cost is $2 for adults and $1 for children. Admission to campus museums is free unless otherwise noted.

The 112-foot-tall **Centennial Carillon Tower,** a campus landmark, houses 52 bells that toll at intervals throughout the day.

The **Monte L. Bean Life Science Museum,** 1430 North, just east of the Marriott Center (☎ 801/378-5051), houses extensive collections of insects, plants, reptiles, fish, shells, mammals, and birds from around the world, with an emphasis on Utah's wildlife. It's open Monday from 1 to 9pm, and Tuesday to Saturday from 10am to 9pm.

The **Earth Science Museum,** 1683 N. Provo Canyon Rd., west of Cougar Stadium (☎ 801/378-3680), offers one of Utah's largest collections of dinosaur bones from the Jurassic period. Hours are Monday 9am to 9pm, Tuesday to Friday 9am to 5pm, and Saturday noon to 4pm.

The **Harris Fine Arts Center,** Campus Dr. (☎ 801/378-2881), houses galleries featuring American and European artists, and shows student and faculty artwork. The center also has a collection of unique musical instruments on display. Hours are Monday through Saturday 8am to 11pm at the **B.F. Larsen Gallery;** Monday and Tuesday 10am to 5pm and Wednesday and Thursday 10am to 8pm at **Gallery 303.** The center also hosts theatrical and musical performances in its five theaters; call for schedule and cost.

The state-of-the-art **Museum of Art,** located north of the Fine Arts Center at 492 E. Campus Dr. (☎ 801/378-2787), is one of the largest museums in the West. Its 14,000-piece collection includes something for everyone, from ceramics to sculptures, paintings to pottery; there are etchings by Rembrandt and Monet, and jade and ivory from Asia. There's also a bookstore and gift shop. The museum cafe is open for lunch from 11am to 2pm. Admission is charged for special exhibitions.

The **Museum of Peoples and Cultures,** in Allen Hall, 700 N. 100 East (☎ 801/378-6112), focuses on the cultures of the western hemisphere, but also looks at Colombian, Egyptian, Israeli, Polynesian, and Syrian societies. It's open Monday through Friday, 9am to 5pm.

To get to the university: From I-15 north, take exit 266, University Avenue, then U.S. 189 north to the campus; from I-15 south, take exit 272, 12th St. South (which becomes University Parkway), then Utah 265 east to the campus.

A WALKING TOUR
Historic Downtown Provo

Here in Provo, home of Brigham Young University, it should be no surprise that you'll see a number of stately homes that once belonged to well-to-do church officials.

Walking Tour—Historic Downtown Provo

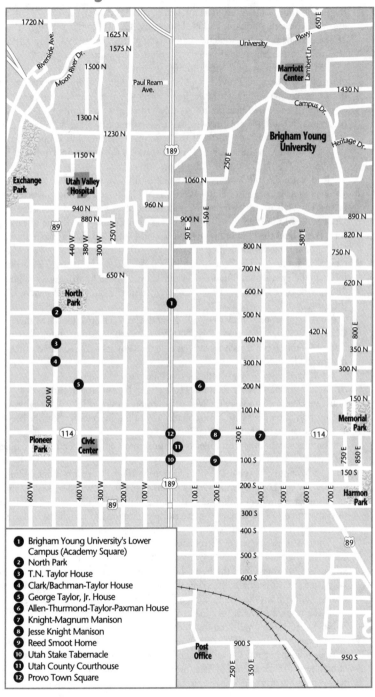

1. Brigham Young University's Lower Campus (Academy Square)
2. North Park
3. T.N. Taylor House
4. Clark/Bachman-Taylor House
5. George Taylor, Jr. House
6. Allen-Thurmond-Taylor-Paxman House
7. Knight-Magnum Manison
8. Jesse Knight Manison
9. Reed Smoot Home
10. Utah Stake Tabernacle
11. Utah County Courthouse
12. Provo Town Square

1. Begin the tour at **Brigham Young University's "Lower Campus,"** officially known as Academy Square, 550 N. University Ave. The university started life in 1875 as Brigham Young Academy, and moved to this site in 1892, almost 10 years after the first meeting place burned. It's still used by students.

Next, head west on 500 North to 500 West to:

2. **North Park,** where the Provo Daughters of Utah Pioneers Museum is located (for details, see below). Here's where the first Mormon settlers moved when the original Fort Utah (see below) became too swampy to support a community. The move began in 1850, and took about two years to complete. Several of the original cabins from this second fort are north of the museum. The museum is open Monday through Saturday in the summer, 1 to 5pm, and in the winter on Thursdays from 1 to 5pm (☎ 801/379-6609). Admission is free.

Head south on 500 West a couple blocks to the:

3. **T.N. Taylor House,** 344 N. 500 West. "T.N.T.," as he was known, was manager of the Taylor Brothers Store and served as mayor of Provo and President of the Utah Stake of the LDS. Church. His home, built in the first decade of this century, exemplifies the kind of house most second-generation Utahns aspired to have. Continue south a few buildings to the:

4. **Clark/Bachman-Taylor House,** 310 N 500 West, thought to be the oldest home in Utah Valley still standing on its original site. The adobe structure was built in 1854, with later additions of the two-story front, trim around the windows, and the gables.

Now turn east one block to 400 West and head south two blocks to the:

5. **George Taylor Jr. House,** 187 N. 400 West. This blue-painted house is reminiscent of Gothic Revival architecture, as evidenced by its lace-decorated porch and high-arched windows.

Next, head east on 200 North for five blocks to the:

6. **Allen-Thurmond-Taylor-Paxman House,** 135 E. 200 North. Built in 1893, the house was later occupied by the wife of Mormon President John W. Taylor. During antipolygamy raids by U.S. marshalls, Taylor hid in a cranny near the fireplace in the master bedroom.

Continue east another three blocks and turn south onto 400 East for two blocks, then west on Center Street to the:

7. **Knight-Mangum Mansion,** 381 E. Center St. This three-story English Tudor–style home was completed in 1908 and cost $40,000. It was designed by one of Utah's most prominent architects of the time, Walter E. Ward, and is now divided into apartments. The color of the exterior was designed to match the bark on the sycamore trees on the grounds.

Continue west on Center Street about two blocks to the:

8. **Jesse Knight Mansion,** 185 E. Center St. Built in 1905 by Knight, the financier and mining businessman, the home began a major trend in building, with similar designs and materials appearing throughout the county. The design is neoclassic, copied from the 1893 Chicago World's Fair, utilizing white pressed brick. Only the front sections are original.

Now head south on 200 East a block to the:

9. **Reed Smoot Home,** 183 E. 100 South. Reed Smoot was a U.S. senator, advisor to five presidents, and an apostle in the Mormon Church. Presidents, senators, and church leaders alike assembled here for confidential conferences. Both political and religious arguments were waged here, sometimes both at once—this place is a great candidate for the "Oh, if the walls could talk" award.

Now head west on 100 South to the:

10. Utah Stake Tabernacle, 100 S. University Ave. This two-story brick edifice seats 2,000 and is still used for LDS Stake Conferences. Built in 1883, it was partly condemned when the roof started sagging under the weight of the central tower. Around 1916, the stained-glass windows were installed, the tower was removed, and the structure was again declared sound.

Turn north on University a short distance to the:

11. Utah County Courthouse, 51 S. University Ave. This magnificent structure was built of Manti limestone in the 1920s. The interior, with marble floors and detailing, a fine collection of artwork displayed on the walls, and the overall feeling of grandeur emanating from the classical balance of the design, is well worth a visit.

Continue along University north to the:

12. Provo Town Square, at the intersection of University Avenue and Center Street. Most of the commercial buildings date from the 1890s, when the core of the business community developed here. The **Knight Block,** a big red building with a large clock, was built in 1900. The **Gates & Snow Furniture Co.**, to the east of the Knight Block, has one of Utah's best pressed tin fronts. The **Zion Bank,** at the northwest corner, is situated in what was originally the Bank of Commerce building. West along Center Street is a row of period store fronts, with the newer businesses of today capitalizing on the original details still apparent on their second stories.

MORE TO SEE & DO IN & AROUND PROVO

✪ Bridal Veil Falls Skytram

Provo Canyon, about 4 miles east of Provo. ☎ **801/225-4461.** Admission $5.95 adults, $4.95 seniors, $2.75 children. Mid-May–mid-Oct 9am–9pm. From downtown Provo follow U.S. 189 north and east into Provo Canyon to the falls.

This steep tram climbs 1,228 vertical feet from the edge of the river to above the cataract, and provides magnificent views not only of the falls, but also of Provo Canyon, Mt. Timpanogos, and Utah Valley to the west.

Note: At press time, the tram had just been severely damaged by an avalanche, and repair plans were uncertain. Call before going.

Daughters of Utah Pioneers Museum

175 S. Main St., Springville. ☎ **801/489-7525.** Free admission, donations accepted. Tues and Sat 2–5pm, Wed 1–5pm.

From I-15, take exit 263 east to Springville; turn left, then north on Main Street; it's about six blocks to the museum. This small museum houses memorabilia from the early settlers of Springville. You'll see clothing, furnishings (including an entire bedroom), musical instruments, children's furniture, weapons and tools, plus many photographs. You can research pioneers of the area here, too.

Fort Utah Park

200 N. 2050 West (Geneva Rd.). Take I-15 to exit 268; follow Center Street west to Geneva Road and turn right.

In the early spring of 1849, Mormon pioneers built a fort here to protect themselves, their young crops, and their livestock from the Utes, who didn't want to share their land with the newcomers. When church leader Brigham Young visited later in the year, however, he realized the site was not as desirable as he'd originally thought; the flooding Provo River made the area quite marshy. He ordered the settlement to move east, and by 1852 the fort was virtually deserted. This historic site is now a civic park, with a fort replica, a rugby field, a baseball diamond, playgrounds, and picnic tables.

John Hutchings Museum of Natural History

55 N. Center St., Lehi. ☎ **801/768-7180**. Admission $2 adults, $1.50 seniors, $1 children. Mon–Sat 9:30am–5:30pm. Bus: 10 from Provo. From I-15, take exit 282, follow Main Street west to Center Street, and turn right; it's a half block to the museum.

Born in 1889, John Hutchings had an insatiable curiosity about the world around him. Every facet was intriguing—the geological, historical, anthropological, and philosophical. He collected things to study, discussing his observations with friends and family. In 1955, as his collections overflowed his home, he donated them to be held in trust for the people of the town of Lehi, and this museum was born.

Today, it houses mineral displays, describing their links to mining districts of the region, plus rare specimens of varacite and crystal aluminum; fossils such as flamingo tracks from Spanish Fork Canyon, dinosaur bones, and a piece of tusk from a woolly mammoth; tools and pottery from early man; and artifacts from Mormon and other Utah pioneers.

McCurdy Historical Doll Museum

246 N. 100 East. ☎ **801/377-9935**. Admission $2 adults, $1 children. Winter, Tues–Sat 1–5pm; summer, Tues–Sat noon–6pm. From I-15, take exit 268 and head east on Center Street to 100 East and turn left (north); it's 2^1/$_2$ blocks to the museum.

Laura McCurdy Clark began collecting dolls from around the world in 1910; in 1979 the museum was founded to exhibit her collection and others. Today, over 4,000 dolls are on display in this restored carriage house, including antique dolls crafted in Germany, France, and England; lovely wax dolls representing the work of such famous artists as Lewis Sorensen of Utah and California, and Tussaud's Eden Musee of London; rare dolls of yesteryear from the Laura Galbraith collection; 40 first ladies of America copied from their likenesses in the Smithsonian Institute; priceless antique dolls representing historical figures; and many dolls depicting fashions from the caveman to the present, plus dolls in national folk dress from around the world. In addition, the museum offers storytelling, lectures, craft classes, and a doll "hospital," which provides repair services. An Academy Award–winning documentary about dolls and toys is shown as part of the tour.

Peppermint Place

155 E. 200 North, Alpine. Free admission. Mon–Sat 10am–6pm (optimum factory observation Mon–Fri 10am–2pm). Take I-15 to exit 287, head east on Utah 92, then north on Utah 74 to Alpine.

If you like candy, you'll love Peppermint Place. There's hand-dipped chocolates, crunchy nut brittles, 24 stick flavors, chocolate-covered potato chips(!), 15 kinds of licorice, and even sugar-free candies (there oughta be a law against such abominations). Non-candy gift items are also available, such as music boxes, porcelain dolls, and Bavarian cuckoo clocks. If you can't make the optimum observation time, there's always a videotape available.

❂ Springville Museum of Art

126 E. 400 South (corner of 400 South and 100 East), Springville. ☎ **801/489-2727**. Free admission, donations accepted. Tues–Sat 10am–5pm, Wed 5–9pm, Sun 3–6pm. Closed legal holidays. From I-15, take exit 263 east to Springville, entering town on 400 South.

The art of Utah is the cornerstone of this fine museum. The present Spanish colonial revival–style building was completed in 1937, with a two-story addition made in 1964. Today you can browse through nine galleries and see one of the finest displays of Utahn art available, arranged in chronological order to illustrate the development of art in the state. Four galleries are reserved for changing exhibits, drawing from around the world. The museum offers lectures, concerts, and guided tours on weekdays; there's also a research library and videos.

Utah Lake State Park

4400 W. Center St. ☎ **801/375-0731.** $3 per vehicle day-use; $9–$10 camping. Take I-15 exit 268B, Center St. West; it's about 3 miles to the park.

Utah's largest freshwater lake, a favorite of local residents, is great for fishing, boating, and swimming. The 96,000-acre lake is particularly popular for those with speedboats, personal water crafts, and sail boats, although you'll occasionally see a canoe or kayak. The skyline is dominated by mountains in all directions, with the lights of the city in the foreground to the east at night. There are four boat-launching ramps and 78 boat slips available, but no boat rentals. There's also an Olympic-size ice rink that's usually open from December through March. Although there are no hiking or biking trails in the park itself, the **Provo River Parkway Trail** leads from the edge of the park into Provo Canyon (see "Sports & Outdoor Activities," below). The 71-site campground—mostly just paved parking areas, although there are some grassy spots for tents—has no RV hookups, but there is a dump station and modern restrooms with showers in one bath-house.

SPORTS & OUTDOOR ACTIVITIES

Biking & Hiking   The 9-mile **Provo River Parkway Trail** winds through the city from Utah Lake to Provo Canyon, following the Provo River some of the way. A slag trail (slag is what's left over from mining out the metal desired), it's also open to both bicyclists and hikers.

Hundreds of miles of trails wind through the **Uinta National Forest** (☎ 801/377-5780) in the mountains around Provo. The *Utah County Hiking and Bicycling Guide* describes over a dozen rides, including the one mentioned above. Bicyclists can pick up the guide at the visitor center (see "Visitor Information," above).

Pedersen's Ski & Sports, University Mall, Orem (☎ 801/225-3000), is a full-service bike shop, staffed by bikers who can direct you to some terrific area rides. **Gourmet Bicycles,** 1155 N. Canyon Rd., Provo (☎ 801/377-3969), rents and repairs mountainbikes. **The Bike Peddler,** 187 W. Center St., Provo (☎ 801/374-5322), and in Orem at 736 S. State St. (☎ 801/222-9577), is another full-service bicycle store.

Boating   See Utah Lake State Park, above.

Fishing   Check with **Great Basin Fly & Outfitters,** 120 W. Center St. (☎ 801/375-2424), for all your supplies, and tips on where they're biting.

Golf   There are three public golf courses in the Provo/Orem area. **Cascade Fairways Golf Course,** 1313 E. 800 North, Orem (☎ 801/225-6677), has a driving range and 9 holes, par-35. Reservations are required, and greens fees are about $7. The **East Bay Golf Course,** 1860 S. East Bay Blvd. (☎ 801/379-6612), on the south side of the city, also requires reservations for its 18-hole, par-71 course; there's also a driving range, lodging, and RV facilities. Greens fees are about $7 weekdays, $8 weekends. The **Seven Peaks Resort** (☎ 801/375-5155), has a challenging mountainside 18-hole, par-58 course with spectacular views of the city to the west; there's also a driving range, lodging, and RV facilities. Reservations are required. The private **Riverside Country Club,** 2701 N. University Ave. (☎ 801/373-8262), is the site of the Nike Utah Classic and Brigham Young University's Cougar Classic. Reservations are required for the 18-hole, par-72 course.

Horseback Riding The **Big Springs Riding Stable,** at Southfork Provo Canyon, Orem (☎ 801/225-8589), offers guided mountain trail rides, overnight pack trips, horse rentals, and wagon and sleigh rides. Tours range from 1 hour to three days; call for current rates and schedules.

Ice-Skating In the winter, **Utah Lake State Park** (see p. 165) opens its outdoor rink Monday through Saturday 1 to 3pm and 4 to 6pm, and 7 to 9pm Tuesday through Saturday; 10pm to midnight Friday and Saturday, and on Sundays from 1 to 4pm. Cost is $3 for adults, $2 for kids ages 6 to 11. Skate rentals are $1.

  Seven Peaks (see below) has an ice-skating rink that opens for the season around Thanksgiving. It's open Monday to Thursday 6 to 9pm, Friday 6 to 11pm, and Saturday from 1 to 5pm and 6 to 11pm. Admission is $3 for adults, $2 for kids ages 4 to 11; skate rentals are $1.

Rock Climbing The **Rock Garden Indoor Climbing Center,** 22 S. Freedom Blvd. (☎ 801/375-2388), offers classes for everyone from novice to advanced, and a place to practice your skills out of the elements. Beginner classes include an introduction to body, balance, and hand positions. Call for class schedules and costs. Equipment is available for rent, and a day pass is $7. Open Monday to Thursday noon to 10pm; Friday noon to midnight; and Saturday 10am to midnight.

WATER PARKS & RECREATION CENTERS

Orem Recreation Center

165 S. 580 West, Orem. ☎ **801/224-7155.** Mon–Sat; call for rates and hours.

Facilities include an Olympic-sized swimming pool, indoor track, racquetball, basketball, and indoor rifle range.

Provo Recreation Center & Pool

1155 N. University Ave. ☎ **801/379-6610.** Mon–Sat; call for current rates and hours.

The center has a large indoor swimming pool, 10 racquetball courts, 10 wallyball courts, two weight rooms, and one basketball court.

Seven Peaks Water Park

1330 E. 300 North. ☎ **801/373-8777.** All-day admission is $13 adults, $10 children 3–11; half-day (after 4pm) $7.50; seniors (60 and older) and toddlers (2 and under) are free. Late May–mid-Sept, Mon–Sat 11am–8pm, Sun noon–5pm. From I-15, take exit 268 and head east on Center Street. Bus: 3.

This is the place to come for a wide variety of water fun—you'll find some 45 heated water attractions on 26 acres butting against the mountains. There's a wave pool, winding slides, three children's pools, a 95-foot-high breaker, a lazy river, and a 550-foot-long, totally dark tube ride through foggers, lasers, and sound effects. For relaxing or picnicking, there are large pavilions, shaded cabanas, and plenty of lawn.

✪ Trafalga Family Fun Center

168 S. 1200 West, Orem. ☎ **801/224-6000.** Admission to grounds free; miniature golf $4.25 adults, $2.25 children 7 and under, $16 family; basketball $2.75; arcade tokens 4 for $1, 25 for $5. Mon–Fri 10am–midnight, Sat from 9am, Sun 1–9pm (hours may be shorter in the winter). From I-15 take exit 274, go east on Center Street and almost immediately turn right (south) onto 1200 West to the park.

This all-around family fun center has three 18-hole miniature golf courses, a huge arcade with more than 100 games, "shoot-a-round" basketball with 17 baskets that move and talk, and a terrific 400-foot winding water slide, all open year-round. If weather permits, the slick-track raceway and batting cages are open. You say you like water fights? Try the bumper boats (open May through October). There's a pavilion and picnic tables, hamburgers and hot-dogs with all the trimmings, barbe-cue beef, fried chicken, corn-on-the-cob, pizza, and ice cream.

Veterans Memorial Pool & Waterslide Park

450 W. 500 North. ☎ **801/379-6610.** Pool only admission $1.50 adults, $1 seniors (65 and older) and children 13 and under. Pool and water slide passes $2.50–$5.50, depending on num-ber of rides. Memorial Day–Labor Day, Mon–Thurs 1–8pm, Fri–Sat 1–6pm.

Facilities include a large heated outdoor swimming pool, two enclosed 100-yard-long water slides, and sunbathing decks.

SPECTATOR SPORTS

Brigham Young University is part of the Western Athletic Conference. The **Cougars football** team plays at the 65,000-seat Cougar Stadium; tickets are hard to come by, so call as far ahead in advance as you can. The **basketball** team plays in the 23,000-seat Marriot Center; tickets are relatively easy to come by. For ticket information call 801/378-2981; for other sports information call 801/378-8326.

WHERE TO STAY

In addition to what's listed below, there are several chain and franchise motels in the Provo area, including three Best Westerns: **Best Western Columbian,** 70 E. 300 South, Provo, UT 84606 (☎ 801/373-8973 or 800/321-0055), with rates of $42–$68 double; **Best Western Cotton Tree Inn,** 2230 N. University Parkway, Provo, UT 84604 (☎ 801/373-7044 or 800/662-6886), with rates of $65–$87 double; and **Best Western Rome Inn,** 1200 S. University Ave., Provo, UT 84601 (☎ 801/375-7500 or 800/528-1234), with rates of $49–$59 double. **Motel 6** is located at 1600 S. University Ave. (I-15, exit 266), Provo, UT 84601 (☎ 801/375-5064), with rates of $36–$40 double. **Super 8 Motel** is at 1288 S. University Ave. (I-15, exit 266), Provo, UT 84601 (☎ 801/375-7569), with rates of $40–$50 double. The **Provo–Days Inn** is located at 1675 N. 200 West (I-15, exit 272 then east 3 miles), Provo, UT 84604 (☎ 801/375-8600 or 800/DAYS-INN), with rates of $55–$65 double.

Rates may be higher during Brigham Young University special events, and rooms can be very scarce at graduation time. Tax added to lodging bills totals is just over 9%. Pets are not allowed unless otherwise noted.

Fairfield Inn Provo

East Bay Business Park, 1515 S. University Ave. (exit 266 off I-15), Provo, UT 84601. ☎ **801/377-9500** or 800/228-2800. Fax 801/377-9591. 72 rms, 6 suites. A/C TV TEL. Summer $55–$75 double, $99–$115 suite; higher for special events, but generally lower in the winter. Rates include continental breakfast. AE, DC, DISC, MC, V.

Even in the smallest room at the Fairfield Inn, you'll find rich wood furnishings and comfortable upholstered chairs. Regular rooms have a queen, king, or two double beds; extended king rooms offer a king bed plus a couch that pulls out into a bed. The suites have one king or two doubles plus a hide-a-bed couch; they're more elegantly appointed than the standard rooms, with a wet bar with sink and refresh-ments, two TVs, and attractive black-and-white photos on the walls.

Provo Park Hotel

101 W, 100 North, Provo, UT 84601. ☎ **801/377-4700** or 800/777-7144. Fax 801/377-4708. 232 units. A/C TV TEL. $85–$95 double. AE, CB, DC, DISC, MC, V.

This highly rated high-rise hotel in downtown Provo provides comfortable—even luxurious—accommodations, with splendid views (especially from the upper floors), and all the amenities you might want. Both public areas and rooms are handsomely appointed, decorated primarily in light earth tones, with attractively upholstered seating. Some in-room refrigerators are available. There's an outdoor heated pool, whirlpool, sauna, and fitness center. The restaurant serves three meals daily, including room service; there's also a bar, a state liquor store, a gift shop; free covered parking, with a height limit of 6'9"; and a courtesy shuttle to the bus depot and train station.

Travelodge

124 S. University Ave. (I-15 exit 266), Provo, UT 84601. ☎ **801/373-1974** or 800/578-7878. 60 rms. A/C TV TEL. $35–$65 double. AE, DISC, MC, V.

This basic, two-story motel offers rooms with queen or king beds, some with two doubles. Rooms may be a bit cramped, but are well-appointed, with in-room coffee, walk-in closet, and a lighted dressing table. Some rooms have a tub/shower combination, some shower only. There are five spacious three-bed family units that sleep up to six persons.

IN SPRINGVILLE

✪ Victorian Inn Bed & Breakfast

94 W. 200 South, Springville, UT 84663. ☎ **801/489-0737.** Fax 801/489-8875. 8 units, including 2 suites. A/C TV TEL. $65–$115 double. Rates include breakfast. AE, DISC, MC, V.

Located in the historic Kearns Hotel, this lovely B&B is a favorite of honeymooners and anniversary celebrants, but retirees and business travelers are also drawn by the mix of Victorian ambiance and modern amenities. One room boasts a double bed from the original hotel, built in 1910; the rest have queen beds. Suites have a TV in both the living room and bedroom; four rooms have Jacuzzis; and all are decorated in grand Victorian style with a mixture of antiques and reproductions, such as marble-topped dressers and hand-carved beds. Breakfast is served in what used to be the parlor, which still has the original stained-glass windows.

WHERE TO DINE

Provo is a very conservative, family-oriented city, and many restaurants do not serve alcohol. The tax added to dining bills totals just over 7%.

La Dolce Vita

61 N. 100 East. ☎ **801/373-8482.** Reservations taken for large parties on weekends only. Main courses lunch $2.75–$11.50, dinner $6.50–$11.50. AE, CB, DC, DISC, MC, V. Mon–Thurs 11am–10pm, Fri–Sat till 10:30pm. From I-15, take exit 268 and follow Center Street east to 100 East; turn left (north) to the restaurant. NEAPOLITAN/ITALIAN.

Giovanni Della Corte was born in Naples, where he began his restaurant career at the age of 12. In 1984 he moved his family to Utah and opened La Dolce Vita, where he continues to serve fine Italian dinners complete with salad and warm homemade breads. The outside is unprepossessing, but once you cross the threshold you'll feel like you've just stepped into an Italian cafe.

You can choose from a variety of pastas, plus pizzas and calzones. The homemade sauces are thick and subtly seasoned. Portions are large, but try to save room for one of the special desserts: spumoni, Amaretto or chocolate mousse cake, or homemade Italian pastries. Soft drinks, beer, cappuccino, and espresso are served.

Magelby's

1675 N. 200 West, Village Green (behind Days Inn). ☎ **801/374-6249.** Reservations for 6 or more. Main courses lunch $6.95–$10.95, dinner $8.95–$21.95. AE, DISC, MC, V. Mon–Thurs 11am–10pm, Fri till 11pm (dinner starts serving at 4pm), Sat 4–11pm. From I-15, take exit 272 and follow Utah 265 for 5 miles. STEAK/SEAFOOD.

This quietly elegant dining room has lace curtains at the windows, upholstered chairs at the tables, quiet booths, and is decorated with antiques, collectibles, and original artwork. The house specialty is Black Angus rib eye smothered with sautéed mushrooms and onions. Also popular are Magleby's lightly breaded gourmet shrimp, blackened chicken, fresh fish, and prime rib. The most popular of the homemade desserts is Lenora's Famous Deep Dish Apple Pie. The locally popular all-you-can-eat buffet on Friday and Saturday evenings from 5:15 to 9:15pm features roast beef, roast ham, baked seafood Newburg, and all kinds of side dishes; the cost is $18.95. No alcohol is served.

Sensuous Sandwich

163 W. Center St. ☎ **801/377-9244.** Sandwiches "by the inch," $1.99 (4")–$8.29 (24"). No credit cards. Mon–Sat 10:30am–8pm. From I-15, take exit 268 and follow Center Street east. SANDWICHES.

You can eat at one of the few tables at this speedy sandwich shop, or take your choice with you. All sandwiches come with the usual condiments, including a spicy brown mustard and horseradish, as well as extras like olives, avocados, and cheese. Top-of-the-line is, of course, the Sensuous Sandwich, with ham, turkey, roast beef and jack cheese. They also have pastrami, crab, chicken breast, and tuna. No alcohol is served.

PROVO AFTER DARK
PERFORMING ARTS

Brigham Young University Theatre, on the BYU campus, offers a variety of performances year round (☎ 801/378-7447 for information, 801/378-4322 for tickets).

For Broadway musicals and concerts under the stars, contact the **Shell Outdoor Theatre,** 699 S. State St., Orem (☎ 801/225-2560). The season runs through the summer and early fall.

NIGHTLIFE

Provo is not a drinkers' town; virtually the entire nightlife scene is geared to families. None of the following serves alcohol.

The Station, 117 N. University Ave. (☎ 801/377-5454), has musical entertainment on weekends. Thursday is jazz night, beginning at 8pm; on Friday and Saturday the music varies, starting at 9:30pm. There's a cover charge on Friday and Saturday only.

Johnny B's Comedy Club, 177 W. 300 South (☎ 801/377-6910), is a popular place for stand-up comedy. The show starts at 9pm Thursday, and 8pm and 10pm on Friday and Saturday. Cover charge is $5.50.

For local musical entertainment, try **Mama's Cafe**, 840 N. 700 East (☎ 801/373-1525 or 801/371-8452 for the Hot Line). The entertainment starts around 9pm and goes to about 11:30pm.

For dancing, try **The Edge,** 143 W. Center (☎ 801/375-0011), open Monday, and Wednesday to Saturday from 9pm to 1am. Wednesday is ladies' night and Thursday is country night. Cover is $5.

The **Palace Dance Club,** 501 N. 900 East (☎ 801/373-2623), has something for practically everybody. Country rules on Tuesday and Thursday, a variety of live bands play on Wednesday, Friday is Latino night, and Saturday is for high-school students. The Palace is open 9pm to 1am. Cover is $4.

The **Western Dance Club of Utah** has country and western swing, two-step, waltz, and line dancing every Saturday night at the Utah National Guard Armory,

222 W. 500 North (☎ 801/226-3040). Cost is $3 and proceeds go to the Primary Children's Medical Center. From 8:30 to 9:30pm the club offers lessons, with dancing until midnight.

6 Timpanogos Cave National Monument

This national monument is actually comprised of three caves—Hansen, Middle, and Timpanogos—linked together by manmade tunnels. Martin Hansen discovered the first cavern in 1887 while tracking a mountain lion. The other two were reported in the early 1920s, and the connecting tunnels were constructed in the 1930s. The caves are filled with every kind of cave formation, from stalactites and stalagmites to draperies and helictites. They're not easy to reach, but the beauty and variety of the caves make them worth the climb.

JUST THE FACTS

The monument is open from Memorial Day to Labor Day, daily from 7am to 5:30pm. The caves close in the winter because snow and ice make the access trail too hazardous.

Getting There/Access Points   Timpanogos Cave National Monument is 20 miles from Provo, and 35 miles from Salt Lake City. From Salt Lake City, head south on I-15 to exit 287, and east on Utah 92 to the visitor center parking lots. From Provo, follow U.S. 89 north to Utah 146 north, and then east onto Utah 92 to the visitor center, which is on the south side of the road. The road through American Fork Canyon is narrow and winding, but quite lovely, so take your time.

Information & Visitor Centers   For information, contact Timpanogos Cave National Monument at R.R. 3, Box 200, American Fork, UT 84003-9800 (☎ 801/756-5239, 801/756-1679 for reservations).

Parking at the visitor center is limited for large vehicles, such as motorhomes over 20 feet. Although small, the visitor center offers a short film about the caves, plus a few explanatory displays, booklets, and postcards. You'll find a snack bar and gift shop next to the visitor center, and two picnic areas located along the shady banks of the American Fork Creek. One is across from the visitor center; a larger one, with fire grills and restrooms, is about a quarter mile west.

Fees & Regulations   Cave tours are $5 for ages 16 to 61, $4 for ages 6 to 15, $2.50 for seniors over 61, and free for those 5 and under. Pets are not allowed on the trail or in the cave.

EXPLORING THE MONUMENT

The only way to see the cave is on a ranger-guided tour. You'll need to allow about 3 hours total: It's a 1 1/2-hour hike up to the cave, you'll spend an hour in the cave, and it's about a 1/2- to 3/4-hour hike back down. The tours are limited to 20 persons and often fill up early in the morning, so it's best to call ahead and reserve your space with a credit card. The temperature inside the caves is around 45° (about the same as a refrigerator), so bring a jacket or sweatshirt.

THE HIKE TO THE CAVES

The change in elevation between the visitor center and the cave entrance is 1,065 feet, and the steep trail is 1 1/2 miles long; it's a physically demanding walk, but quite rewarding. The trail is not navigable by either wheelchairs or strollers, and anyone with breathing, heart, or walking difficulties should not attempt it. You'll need good walking shoes, and it's wise to carry water and maybe even a snack.

This is a self-guided hike, so you can travel at your own pace, stopping at the benches along the way to rest and enjoy the views of the canyon, the Wasatch Range, and Utah Valley. A trail guide is available at the visitor center to help you identify the wildflowers growing amid the Douglas fir, white fir, maple, and oak trees. You'll also spot chipmunks, ground squirrels, lizards, and a myriad of birds along the way. When you reach the cave entrance, restrooms and drinking water are available, so you can refresh before your cave tour begins.

TOURING THE CAVES

The ranger-guided tour of the caves is along a surfaced, well-lit, and fairly level route. You'll enter at the natural entrance to Hansen Cave, and continue through Hansen, Middle, and Timpanogos Caves. Nature decorated the limestone chambers with delicately colored stalactites, stalagmites, draperies, graceful flowstone, and the helictites for which the caves are famous, all in soft greens, reds, yellows, and white. The huge cave formation of linked stalactites in the Great Heart of Timpanogos is impressive, and the profusion of bizarre, brilliant white helictites in the Chimes Chamber of Timpanogos is stunning. Mirrorlike cave pools reflect the formations.

High-speed film or a flash is necessary for photos, and tripods are not allowed. Remember that the formations are fragile and easily damaged by merely the touch of your hand; the oils from your skin will change their chemical makeup immediately. There are two stalagmites that the park has designated as "touchable"; your ranger guide will point these out to you.

10

Land of the Lost: Dinosaurs & Natural Wonders in Utah's Undiscovered Northeast Corner

Utah has more than its share of natural treasures, with Zion and Bryce Canyon national parks springing to mind first—and drawing ever-increasing crowds. But tucked away in the state's far northeastern corner, more rugged and less accessible, is a playground of great scenic beauty, filled with fascinating historic (and prehistoric) sites. And there aren't any tourist crowds here: this land where the dinosaurs once roamed is still relatively undiscovered and unspoiled.

1 The Mirror Lake Highway & the Uinta Mountains

Just east of Park City lies the tiny town of Kamas. It's not much of a destination in itself, but here begins one of the loveliest drives in Utah, a route filled with gorgeous alpine scenery.

Utah 150 (the **Mirror Lake Highway**) begins here and ascends up into the pine-covered Uinta Mountains before heading into Wyoming. The road is open only from mid-June to mid-October, and it's a popular family camping destination for Utahns. This route is perhaps the best-known scenic drive in the region, offering splendid views of towering peaks, virgin pine and spruce forests, and lush meadows carpeted with wildflowers as it climbs up Bald Mountain Pass (at 10,678 feet). Trailheads branch off from the road and head into the backcountry.

Along the way you'll pass a seemingly infinite string of blue-ribbon trout streams and crystal-clear alpine lakes. Just bring a good supply of flies and try your luck; cutthroat and brook trout are fairly jumping out of thewater.

Much of the route follows the Provo River, and 24 miles from Kamas, you might want to stop to view the beautiful terraced cascades of **Upper Provo River Falls.**

The highway also passes a good number of developed campsites; since these tend to fill up on summer weekends, try making reservations in advance by calling **Mistix** at 800/246-CAMP. The largest of these is the **Mirror Lake Campground,** with 91 sites in a lovely pine forest setting on the lake. It's located about 31 miles into the drive, and offers trout fishing, hiking trails, and picnicking. The campgrounds further along the drive tend to be less crowded.

Before starting out, check with the **Kamas Ranger District** office, 50 E. Center St. (☎ 801/783-4338), which has detailed maps and information on hiking, camping, road conditions, and more.

East of the Mirror Lake Highway, the Uinta Mountains, the only major range in the continental United States that runs east-to-west, are the major feature of northeastern Utah's landscape. The **High Uintas Wilderness Area** remains wild and unspoiled, a refuge for bighorn sheep, elk, moose, mule deer, eagles, osprey, owls, mink, and beaver. Tiny towns and lonely highways surround the preserve, making it accessible for the hikers, campers, and anglers who come to enjoy this region's summer beauty. The wilderness area itself is closed to vehicles (though horses are allowed on many trails); you do not need a permit to hike and explore the backcountry, but for safety's sake it's a good idea to register at the trailheads. A good guide for backpackers is *The Hiker's Guide to Utah* (Falcon Press), which describes several outings in greater detail than space can allow us to include here. You can also contact the **Utah Wilderness Association,** 455 E. 400 South, Salt Lake City, UT 84111 (☎ 801/359-1337).

2 Vernal: Gateway to the Region's Top Recreational Areas

A perfect base for exploring Dinosaur National Monument (which is only 20 miles from town) and Ashley National Forest, Vernal is the largest town in the region. You'll find all the outfitters and services you could need here, and a few attractions in town serve as a good introduction to the compelling geologic and natural history of the surrounding region.

ESSENTIALS

Getting There   From Heber City, Highway 40 leads east, past Strawberry Reservoir (there's world-class fishing here if you have time to stop—see Chapter 9), Duchnesne, and Roosevelt before leading to Vernal. Roosevelt has a few motels, restaurants, and services. From here, you could also take Route 20 east to get to Vernal.

Skywest/Delta (☎ 801/789-7263 or 800/453-9417) has several flights daily from Salt Lake City to the Vernal airport (☎ 801/789-4636).

Visitor Information   Information on area lodging, dining, and recreational facilities can be obtained from the **Dinosaurland Travel Board,** 25 E. Main St., Vernal, UT 84078 (☎ 801/789-6932 or 800/477-5558).

Getting Around   Car rentals are available at the airport from **Avis** (☎ 801/789-7264 or 800/331-1212); and in downtown Vernal from **Showalter Motors** (☎ 801/789-3818) and **Utah Motors** (☎ 801/789-0455 or after hours 801/790-5028). Travel trailers can be rented from **B&D RV Sales & Service** (☎ 801/789-1970).

Local transportation is also available around the clock from **T-Rex Taxi** (☎ 801/790-7433); and **Wilkins Bus Lines** (☎ 801/789-2476) provides shuttle services and tours.

Special Events   In May there's a **Square Dance Jamboree.** The **Outlaw Trail Festival** runs from mid-June through July, featuring a historical outdoor musical, storytelling, trail rides, a western art show, and a parade. Call 800/477-5558) for details. Cowboys test their mettle in July at the **Dinosaur Roundup Rodeo;** call 800/421-9635 for details. August sees the **Uintah County Fair,** and in September there's the **Dina Soar Hot Air Balloon Fest.**

GETTING OUTSIDE

Don Hatch River Expeditions, 55 E. Main St. (☎ 801/789-4316 or 800/342-8243), offers guided fishing trips plus one- to five-day rafting trips on the Green and Yampa Rivers in nearby Dinosaur National Monument. **Dinosaur River Expeditions,** 540 E. Main St. (☎ 801/649-8092 or 800/247-6197), also offers rafting trips, plus jeep and mountainbike tours; from the spring through fall, **Old Moe Guide Service** also operates from this office, offering scenic guided fly-fishing floats.

Boat and raft rentals are available from **Blue Mountain Motor & Marine,** 2217 N. Vernal Ave. (☎ 801/789-5661), and **River Runners' Transport & Rentals,** 126 South 1500 West (☎ 801/781-1180). Fishing equipment is available from **Basin Sports,** 511 W. Main St. (☎ 801/789-2409).

Just north of town, **Steinaker State Park** offers a sandy swimming beach, good fishing for trout and bass, and a campground. Slightly further north, **Red Fleet State Park** offers another good fishing spot, plus boating, short hikes, and camping.

ASHLEY NATIONAL FOREST

This vast forest encompasses more than a million acres of the beautiful mountain country near Vernal; in fact, Flaming Gorge National Recreation Area (see later this chapter) and the High Uintas Wilderness (see above) actually lie within the forest. But there's much more to this wilderness area, too: backpacking, trout fishing, campgrounds, cross-country ski trails, and more. **Kings Peak,** at over 13,000 feet, lies in the forest and is Utah's tallest mountain. The staff at the **Vernal Ranger District** office of the Ashley National Forest, in town at 355 N. Vernal Ave. (☎ 801/789-1181; open weekdays), can provide information on hiking and camping.

OURAY NATIONAL WILDLIFE REFUGE

Hundreds of species of migratory birds and waterfowl make their home in this wetlands refuge, which lies south of Vernal, along the Green River. A driving loop begins at the information center; there are also hiking trails and an observation tower. Call 801/545-2522 or 801/789-0351 for further information.

SEEING THE SIGHTS IN TOWN

The **Utah Field House of Natural History State Park,** at 235 E. Main St. (☎ 801/789-3799), gives visitors a close-up look at a huge dinosaur skeleton, plus exhibits on paleontology, geology, and Fremont and Ute culture. Your kids will love its **Dinosaur Garden,** with 17 life-size models of dinosaurs and other prehistoric creatures in a delightful garden that simulates the dinosaurs' actual habitat. An attached gift shop sells dinosaur-related souvenirs and books; and there's a picnic area but no camping. The museum is open daily except Thanksgiving, Christmas, and New Year's Day. Admission is $1.50 for those 16 and older, $1 for kids from 6 to 15, free for children under six, and there's a maximum $6 charge for families.

"THE DRIVE THROUGH THE AGES"

One of the most scenic drives in the state is the Flaming Gorge–Uintas Scenic Byway—Highway 191 from Vernal up to Manila and Flaming Gorge (see later this chapter); it was one of America's first designated national scenic byways. The 67-mile

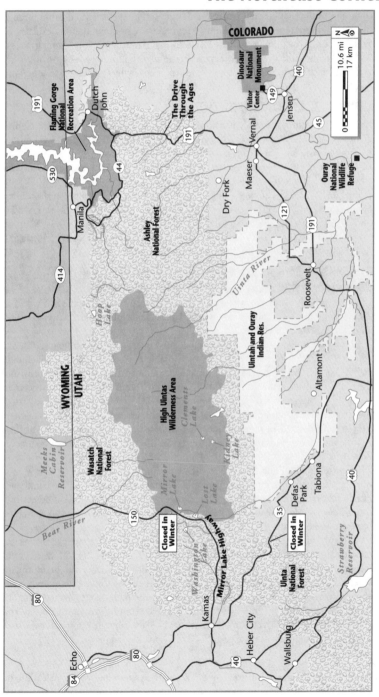

route climbs through foothills covered with pine and juniper trees and passes through the national forest and into the Uinta Mountains; signs along the way explain the evolution of the intriguing geologic formations you're seeing. Near Flaming Gorge, you'll pass the billion-year-old exposed core of the Uintas. Many turnouts are available for scenic views, short walks, and wildlife viewing (you might spot bighorn sheep, elk, mule deer, and moose, especially in the spring).

CAMPING & ACCOMMODATIONS

Among area campgrounds with full RV hookups and hot showers are **Camp-ground Dina & RV Park,** 930 N. Vernal Ave. (☎ 801/789-2148), with 95 sites, including grassy tent sites, with rates in the $12 to $18 range.

There are about a dozen motels in town, including the **Best Western Dinosaur Inn,** 251 E. Main St. (☎ 801/789-2660 or 800/528-1234; fax 801/789-2467), with rates from $65 to $80 double in the summer and $48 to $65 double in the winter; **Days Inn,** 260 W. Main St. (☎ 801/789-1011 or 800/DAYS-INN; fax 801/789-0172), charging $48 to $58 double; and the **Econo Lodge,** 311 E. Main St. (☎ 801/789-2000 or 800/424-4777; fax 801/789-0947), charging $44 to $58 double. Room tax adds about 9%.

3 Dinosaur National Monument

In some ways this preserve is two separate experiences: a look at the lost world of dinosaurs on one side, and a scenic wonderland of colorful rock, deep river canyons, and Douglas firs on the other.

About 145 million years ago this region was wetter, with an abundance of ferns, conifers, and other plants. This made it a suitable habitat for dinosaurs, including vegetarians that grazed here, such as diplodocus, brontosaurus, and stegosaurus; and the sharp-toothed carnivores, such as allosaurus, that hunted down their vegetarian cousins. When these creatures died, most of their skeletons decayed and disappeared, but in at least one spot floodwaters washed dinosaur carcasses onto a sandbar, where they were preserved in sand and covered with sediment, creating a sort of time capsule for today's visitor—the largest quarry of Jurassic-period dinosaur bones ever discovered.

But visitors who limit their trip to the Dinosaur Quarry, fascinating as it is, miss quite a bit. Encompassing 325 square miles of stark canyonlands at the confluence of two rivers, the monument also offers hiking trails to explore, a pioneer homestead, thousand-year-old rock art, spectacular panoramic vistas, great wildlife-watching opportunities, and the thrill of white-water rafting.

The Yampa, Green, and other smaller rivers bring life-giving water into the area, creating micro-climates that support hanging gardens of mosses and ferns, cotton-woods, and even an occasional Douglas fir—all just yards from the predominant sagebrush, cactus, and dwarfed piñon and juniper trees. Wildlife here tends to be species that can survive the the harsh extremes of the high desert climate: bighorn sheep, coyote, rabbits, and snakes; but you'll also find mule deer, beaver, and porcupine along the river banks. Birds that are occasionally spotted in the area include the peregrine falcon, sage grouse, and Canadian goose.

JUST THE FACTS

Getting There/Access Points   Situated partly in Utah and partly in Colorado, Dinosaur National Monument is accessed by two main roads—one from each state—and these don't meet inside the monument.

The main **visitor center** and the Dinosaur Quarry are in Utah, 34 miles northwest of monument headquarters and the entrance to the Colorado side of the park. The visitor center and quarry are 20 miles east of Vernal (195 miles east of Salt Lake City). To get there, take U.S. 40 from either the east or west to Jensen, Utah (where you can gas up your car or pick up something to eat), and drive 7 miles north on Utah 149 into the park.

To get to the Colorado entrance to the park, take U.S. 40 to the visitor center and monument headquarters, 2 miles east of the community of Dinosaur.

Other monument entrances (all without visitor centers) are located at the far eastern edge of the monument off U.S. 40 to Deerlodge Park (open in the summer only); at the northern tip, off Colo. 318, to the Gates of Ledore; just inside the Utah border at Jones Hole Fish Hatchery via the Jones Hole Road from Vernal; and at the Rainbow Park section, off Island Park Road (impassable when wet) from the monument's western edge.

Information & Visitor Centers To get a copy of the national monument's color brochure and other information, contact Dinosaur National Monument, 4545 U.S. 40, Dinosaur, CO 81610 (☎ 970/374-3000). In addition, the nonprofit **Dinosaur Nature Association,** 1291 E. U.S. 40, Vernal, UT 84078 (☎ 800/845-3466; fax 801/781-1304), offers numerous publications, maps, posters, and videos on the park, its geology, wildlife, history, and especially its dinosaurs. Information on area lodging, dining, and recreational facilities can be obtained from the **Dinosaurland Travel Board,** 25 E. Main St., Vernal, UT 84078 (☎ 801/789-6932 or 800/477-5558).

As we noted above, there's a visitor center at the quarry (☎ 801/789-2115), with exhibits and a short slide program. Attached is a shop where you can buy books, hiking and driving guides, maps, and of course, model dinosaurs. Administrative offices and a small visitors' center (☎ 970/374-2216) are located about 2 miles east of the town of Dinosaur, Colo., at the intersection of U.S. 40 and Harpers Corner Drive.

The visitor centers are open daily year-round, except Thanksgiving, Christmas, and New Year's Day.

Fees, Backcountry Permits, Regulations & Safety The admission fee, charged only at the Utah entrance as of this writing, is $5 per vehicle, and $3 per person for those on foot, motorcycles, bicycles, or in buses. If you want to camp in the backcountry, you must obtain a permit, available free from park rangers.

Regulations here forbid damaging or taking anything, particularly fossils and other natural, historical, or archaeological items. Off-road driving is not permitted. Dogs must be leashed at all times; Fido is not allowed in buildings, on trails, more than 100 feet from developed roads, or on river trips.

Rangers warn that rivers are not safe for swimming or wading; water is cold and the current is stronger than it may first appear.

Seasons & Avoiding the Crowds Summers are both the busiest and hottest time of the year at Dinosaur National Monument, with daytime temperatures that often soar into the upper 90s. Winters are a lot quieter, but can be cold, with fog, snow, and temperatures below zero. The best times to visit are spring (although you should be prepared for rain showers) and fall (this is perhaps the very best time, when the cottonwood trees turn a brilliant gold).

Ranger Programs Rangers present a variety of activities in the summer, including evening campfire programs; check the schedules posted at either visitor center.

SEEING THE HIGHLIGHTS

Those with only a short amount of time should make their first stop the **Dinosaur Quarry.** It's accessible only from the Utah side, and this is the only place in the monument where you can see honest-to-god dinosaur bones. It contains the remains of many long-vanished species, including fossils of sea creatures two to three times older than any land dinosaurs. This is believed to be one of the world's most concentrated and accessible deposits of the petrified remains of dinosaurs, crocodiles, turtles, and clams. The quarry—which looks like a long slab of frozen pudding with bones sticking out of it—is enclosed in the visitor center, along with exhibits that help us make sense of this prehistoric zoo. There's one section of bones you can actually reach out and touch, and models to show what paleontologists believe these dinosaurs looked like when they still had their skin. Sometimes visitors can see workers carefully chiseling away the hard rock to expose more bones, and park naturalists are on hand to explain the process.

After spending about an hour in the quarry, drive the scenic **Tour of the Tilted Rocks,** which will take an hour or two. Then, if time remains, or if you're heading east into Colorado anyway, take another few hours to drive the very beautiful **Harpers Corner Drive.** See below for details.

EXPLORING DINOSAUR NATIONAL MONUMENT BY CAR

Scenic drives in both the Utah and Colorado sections of the park allow motorists to see spectacular scenery in relative solitude. Brochures for each of the following drives are available (50¢ each) at the visitor centers.

From the Quarry Visitor Center on the Utah side of the park, the **Tour of the Tilted Rocks** along Cub Creek Road is a 24-mile round-trip drive that's suitable for most passenger cars. This route takes you to 1,000-year-old rock art left by the Fremont people, a pioneer homestead, and views of nearby mountains and the Green River. Watch for prairie dogs both alongside and on the road. Although mostly paved, the last 2 miles of the road are dirt, narrow, and may be dusty or muddy. Allow 1 to 2 hours.

For the best scenic views you'll have to drive to Colorado and take the ✪ **Harpers Corner Drive**. This paved 62-mile round-trip drive has several overlooks offering panoramic views into the gorges carved by the Yampa and Green Rivers, a look at the derby-shaped Plug Hat Butte, and close-ups of a variety of other colorful rock formations. The drive also offers access to the easy half-mile round-trip Plug Hat Nature Trail, and the moderately-difficult 2-mile round-trip Harpers Corner Trail (see "Hiking," below), at the end of the road. Allow about 2 hours for the drive, more if you also plan to do some hiking.

SPORTS & ACTIVITIES
BOATING

To many, the best way to see this beautiful, rugged country is on the river, crashing through thrilling white water and floating over smooth, silent stretches admiring the scenery. About a dozen outfitters are authorized to run the Yampa and Green Rivers through the monument, offering trips ranging from one to five days, usually from mid-May through mid-September. Among companies providing river trips are **Hatch River Expeditions** in Vernal (☎ 801/789-4316 or 800/342-8243), with prices starting at $60 to $70 for a one-day trip. Reservations are recommended. A complete list of authorized river-running companies is available from monument headquarters (see "Information & Visitor Centers" above).

FISHING

Catfish are most often caught in the Green and Yampa Rivers, although there are also some trout. Several endangered species of fish—including the Colorado squawfish and humpback chub—must be returned unharmed to the water if caught. You'll need either Utah or Colorado fishing licenses (or both), depending on which side of the state line you're fishing.

HIKING

Because most visitors spend their time at the quarry and along the scenic drives, hikers willing to exert a bit of effort can discover spectacular and dramatic views of the colorful canyons, and enjoy an isolated and unusually quiet wilderness experience. The best times for hiking are spring and fall, and even then, hikers should carry at least a gallon of water per person, per day.

In addition to several developed trails, experienced hikers with the appropriate maps can explore miles of unspoiled canyons and rock benches. Check with rangers on the numerous possibilities.

In the Utah section of the park, you'll find solitude and colorful uplifted rocks along the **Sound of Silence Trail,** a difficult 2-mile hike that leaves Cub Creek Road about 2 miles east of the Dinosaur Quarry. Sweeping panoramic views can be had along the moderately difficult **Desert Voices Nature Trail,** a 2-mile round-trip trail in the Split Mountain area off Cub Creek Road.

Visitors to the Colorado side of the park enjoy the ✪ **Harpers Corner Trail,** which begins at the end of the Harpers Corner Scenic Drive. This 2-mile round-trip hike is moderately difficult and highly recommended for a magnificent view of the deep river canyons.

HORSEBACK RIDING

Half-hour guided trail rides are offered by **Cassidy Trail Rides,** based just outside the park's Utah entrance (☎ 801/789-9334). Cost is $8 per person. Wagon rides, at $5 per person, are also scheduled.

CAMPING

The **Green River Campground,** 5 miles east of the Dinosaur Quarry within park boundaries, has 88 sites, modern restrooms, drinking water, tables, and fireplaces, but no showers or RV hookups. Cost is $8 per night in the summer, and free in the winter when water is turned off and only pit toilets are available. Several smaller campgrounds with limited facilities are also available in the park; check with the visitor centers or superintendent's office.

Flaming Gorge National Recreation Area

Tucked away in the far northeast corner of Utah and stretching up into Wyoming, Flaming Gorge National Recreation Area was created by man. A dam was built on the Green River—for flood control, water storage, and the generation of electricity. But the wonderful by-product was the creation of a huge and gorgeous lake—some 91 miles long, with more than 350 miles of coastline—that has become one of the prime fishing and boating destinations of the region.

Here you'll find some of the best fishing in the West, well over 100 miles of hiking and mountainbiking trails, and hundreds of camp and picnic sites. It's a boaters' paradise: Out on the water you'll see everything from kayaks and canoes to

"The river enters the range by a flaring, brilliant red gorge, that may be seen from the north a score of miles away . . . We name it Flaming Gorge."
—Explorer Major John Wesley Powell, May 26, 1869

personal watercraft, ski and fishing boats, pontoons, and gigantic houseboats complete with everything (including the kitchen sink).

Named by Major John Wesley Powell during his exploration of the Green and Colorado Rivers in 1869, Flaming Gorge has a rugged, wild beauty that comes alive when the rising or setting sun paints the red rocks around the lake with a fiery, brilliant palette. It's a land of clear blue water, colorful rocks, tall cliffs, and dark forests, where the summer sun is hot and the winter wind is cold. It'll take more than a dam to tame Flaming Gorge.

JUST THE FACTS

Flaming Gorge National Recreation Area lies in the northeast corner of Utah, crossing into the southwest corner of Wyoming. The dam and main visitor center, in the southeast section of the national recreation area, are 41 miles north of Vernal (210 miles east of Salt Lake City via U.S. 40).

Getting There   From Vernal and other points to the south, take U.S. 191 north to its intersection with Utah 44 at the southern edge of the reservoir. U.S. 191 goes up the east side of the reservoir, leading to the dam and the community of Dutch John; and Utah 44 goes around the reservoir on the west side, eventually ending at the village of Manila. Both of these towns have services, accommodations, and outfitters.

From I-80 in Wyoming, follow U.S. 191 south along the reservoir's east side to the dam; or Wyo. 530 and Utah 44 to Manila and the west and south sides of the reservoir.

Information & Visitor Centers   The recreation area is administered as part of the Ashley National Forest. For information, contact the **District Ranger,** Flaming Gorge National Recreation Area, USDA Forest Service, Box 279, Manila, UT 84046 (☎ 801/784-3445). The **Flaming Gorge Natural History Association,** P.O. Box 188, Dutch John, UT 84023 (☎ 801/885-3305), sells maps, books, and other publications.

The **Flaming Gorge Dam Visitor Center** (☎ 801/885-3135), along U.S. 191 on the east side of the recreation area, is open daily year-round except Thanksgiving, Christmas, and New Year's Day. Here you'll find information on the geology, history, plants, and wildlife of the area; construction of the dam; and facilities and recreation possibilities. You can talk with rangers about where to camp, hike, boat, and fish; and take a guided or self-guided tour of the dam and generating plant.

Fees & Regulations   Admission to the recreation area is free. Administered by the U.S. Forest Service, regulations here are mostly common sense, aimed at preserving water quality and protecting the forest and historic sites. In addition, Utah and Wyoming fishing and boating regulations apply in those states' sections of the recreation area. Dogs are not permitted in buildings and should be leashed at all times, but are permitted on hiking trails.

Seasons & Avoiding the Crowds   As one would expect, summer is the busy season at this major boating destination, when both the air and water are their warmest. This is the best time to come for any water sports, and with elevations from 5,600 feet to over 8,000 feet, it never gets as hot here as in many other parts of Utah. Although the summer is the busiest time of year, this remains a relatively undiscovered destination, and you will likely not have any trouble finding campsites, lodging, or boat rentals. Hikers will enjoy the area in fall, of course, and during the cold, snowy winter, it's popular with cross-country skiers and ice fishermen.

EXPLORING FLAMING GORGE NATIONAL RECREATION AREA BY CAR

There are numerous viewpoints along U.S. 191 and Utah 44 in the Utah section of Flaming Gorge; especially dramatic is the ✪ **Red Canyon Overlook** on the southern edge, where a rainbow of colors adorns 1,000-foot-tall cliffs. In Wyoming, highways are further from the rim, offering few opportunities to see the river and its canyons.

Sheep Creek Canyon, south of Manila on the western side, has been designated a special geological area by the forest service because of its dramatically twisted and upturned rocks. A mostly paved 11-mile loop road cuts off from Utah 44, offering a half-hour tour of this beautiful, narrow canyon, with its lavish display of rocks that have been eroded into intricate patterns, a process that began with the uplifting of the Uinta Mountains millions of years ago. This loop may be closed in the winter; check at the visitor center before heading out.

SPORTS & ACTIVITIES
BIKING

A number of mountainbiking trails provide splendid views of the recreation area's scenery, especially in the Utah section. Bikes are permitted in most of Flaming Gorge and adjacent Ashley National Forest, except in the High Uintas Wilderness, where all wheeled vehicles are prohibited. Bikes are also outlawed on the Little Hole National Recreation Trail, along the Green River below the dam, because of its very heavy use from fishermen and hikers. Keep in mind that mountainbikers here often share trails with hikers and four-wheelers. A free mountainbiking brochure is available at visitor centers.

Among recommended trails are the scenic **Green River Trail,** a relatively easy 7-mile round-trip ride along the north side of the Green River, starting at the northeast side of the dam. For an easy 3-mile round-trip ride to a scenic overlook offering a terrific view of the lake, try the **Bear Canyon–Bootleg Trail,** which starts just off U.S. 191 opposite Firefighters Memorial Campground, 3 miles south of the dam. **Death Valley Trail** is a moderately difficult 15-mile round-trip ride that offers good views of the Uinta Mountains, and ends with a fine view of the lake from the top of Sheep Creek Hill. The trailhead is located along Utah 44, south of Manila, at milepost 16.5.

BOATING & HOUSEBOATING

Boaters get to enjoy a unique perspective on some memorable scenery, with magnificent fiery red canyons surrounding the lake in the Utah section, and the wide open Wyoming badlands further north.

Three marinas on Lake Flaming Gorge provide boat rentals, fuel, launching ramps, and boating and fishing supplies. **Cedar Springs Marina** (☎ 801/889-3795) is located 2 miles south of Flaming Gorge Dam; **Lucerne Valley Marina** (☎ 801/784-3483) is on the west side of the lake, 7 miles east of Manila; and

Buckboard Marina (☎ 307/875-6927) is also on the west side of the lake, off Wyo. 530, 25 miles south of the town of Green River, Wyoming.

There are nine boat ramps for those who brought their own craft, and boat and water ski rentals are available at the three marinas. Although types of boats and costs vary somewhat, a 14-foot fishing boat with a small outboard motor will cost from $60 to $70 per day, a 19-foot ski boat with a powerful outboard motor will cost about $160 to $180 per day; and a 24-foot pontoon boat with a 50-horsepower outboard motor will cost from $120 to $150 per day. Hourly rentals are also available. Three-person personal watercraft, available at Lucerne Valley Marina, cost about $160 per day; and a 36-foot houseboat, also from Lucerne Valley Marina, costs about $600 for three nights during the summer, with discounts in spring and fall. Fuel is extra and damage deposits are required.

FISHING

You might want to bring a friend with lots of muscles if you plan to fish Lake Flaming Gorge, which is becoming famous as the place to catch record-breaking trout, such as the 51-pound, 8-ounce lake (Mackinaw) trout caught in 1988, the 26-pound, 2-ounce rainbow caught in 1979, or the 33-pound, 10-ounce brown caught in 1977. You'll also catch other cold-water species such as smallmouth bass and kokanee salmon. Fishing is popular year-round, although ice fishermen are warned to make sure ice is strong enough to hold them. Utah and/or Wyoming fishing licenses are required, and can be purchased at the three marinas (see "Boating & Houseboating," above) and local sporting goods stores.

Cedar Springs and Lucerne Valley Marinas (see above) offer fishing guide services. Call for current rates. Also providing guide service is Bruce Parker of **Conquest Expeditions,** 196 N. 200 East, Bountiful, UT (☎ 801/295-2748 or 801/784-3370). The rate for 4 hours of fishing for one or two people, aboard a 28-foot boat, with all equipment, is about $250. Advance reservations are recommended.

Trout fishing on the Green River below the dam is also outstanding. **Flaming Gorge Recreation Services,** based in Dutch John (☎ 801/885-3191), offers guided fishing trips for one or two people, including a full-day float trip that costs about $300. Rafts are also available for rent, starting at about $50 per day, and there's a full line of camping gear and fishing supplies.

HIKING

There are plenty of trails here, many offering spectacular, scenic views of the reservoir and its colorful canyons. Remember, though, that in most cases you'll be sharing the trail with mountainbikers, and in some cases horses and four-wheel-drive vehicles. Dogs are permitted on the trails, but must be leashed.

The ✪ **Canyon Rim Trail** runs 5 miles (one-way) from the Red Canyon Visitor Center to the Greendale Rest Area, which is located along Utah 44 one mile northwest of the highway's intersection with U.S. 191. You can access the trail at either of those points, or Green Lake or Canyon Rim Campgrounds. The trail wanders through a forest of Douglas fir and pine, with stops along the canyon rim providing outstanding views of the lake far below.

One trail hikers won't be sharing with mountainbikers is the popular **Little Hole National Recreation Trail,** which runs from the dam spillway downstream to Little Hole, a distance of about 7 miles, where you'll find fishing platforms and picnic areas. The trail is easy to moderate, and offers splendid vistas of the Green River, which appears to be a mere ribbon of emerald when seen from the cliffs above. It's also a good trail for bird-watchers, who may spot osprey in the summer and bald eagles in the winter.

Hikers also use mountainbiking trails listed above. A free hiking trails brochure is available at the visitor centers.

HORSEBACK RIDING

Many of the more than 100 miles of trails in Flaming Gorge are open to riders. Guided rides are available from **Red Canyon Stables** at Red Canyon Lodge (just north of Utah 44 via Red Canyon Road; ☎ 801/889-3759), with prices starting at $12 for a 1-hour ride and $75 for a full day. Rates for children under 12 and seniors over 65 are slightly less.

SWIMMING

Sometimes you've just got to dive right in, even though the water is pretty cold. Lake Flaming Gorge has two designated swimming beaches: Sunny Cove, just north of the dam, and Lucerne Beach, a mile west of Lucerne Campground. Neither has a lifeguard.

WILDLIFE VIEWING

This is one of the best places in Utah for seeing a wide variety of wildlife. Boaters out on the lake should watch for osprey, peregrine falcons, swifts, and swallows along the cliffs. Bighorn sheep are sometimes spotted clambering on the rocky cliffs on the north side of the lake in the spring and early summer. On land, watch for pronghorn antelope year-round along the west side of the lake, particularly in Lucerne Valley, and even in the campground there. Hikers on the Little Hole National Recreation Trail should watch for a variety of birds, including bald eagles in the winter.

WINTER SPORTS

Ice fishing is popular, but check with rangers first on the ice conditions. Also popular from mid-January until the snow melts are cross-country skiing and snowmobiling. At Red Canyon Lodge (☎ 801/889-3759) you can rent snowmobiles starting at $50 per hour.

MANMADE ATTRACTIONS
FLAMING GORGE DAM AND POWER PLANT

Completed in 1963 at a cost of $50 million for the dam and another $65 million for the power plant, Flaming Gorge is part of the Colorado River Storage Project, which also includes Glen Canyon Dam on the Colorado River along the Arizona-Utah border, Navajo Dam on the San Juan River in New Mexico, and a series of three dams on the Gunnison River in Colorado. At full capacity the lake is 91 miles long and holds almost 4-million acre-feet of water. The dam, constructed in an arch shape for strength, is 1,285 feet long and stands some 450 feet tall; and its three turbine generators can produce 152,000 kilowatts of electricity, enough to take care of the needs of 210,000 people.

The dam and power plant are open for free guided and self-guided tours daily year-round, except Thanksgiving, Christmas, and New Year's Day. Allow about 20 minutes; total round-trip walking distance is just under half a mile. Check at the visitor center for hours and times of guided tours. You'll walk along the crest of the dam, then take an elevator ride to the power plant below, where you'll see the inner workings of the hydroelectric plant, with its huge transformers, generators, and turbines.

SWETT RANCH HISTORIC SITE

This homestead, listed on the National Register of Historic Sites, was constructed by Oscar Swett starting in 1909, and contains two cabins, a five-room house, a meat house, a root cellar, sheds, a granary, and a barn, built and improved over the next 58 years. Swett and his wife Emma raised nine children here, running the ranch equipment using only horse and human muscle power, before selling the property in 1968. To get to the ranch, from Utah 44 take U.S. 191 north for a half mile and turn west (left) onto Forest Road 158, which you follow 1.5 miles to the ranch. The Forest Road is not paved, is muddy when wet, and not recommended for large RVs and trailers at any time. The ranch is open weekends from Memorial Day to Labor Day only.

UTE MOUNTAIN FIRE LOOKOUT TOWER

Built by the Civilian Conservation Corps in the mid-1930s, this was the first fire lookout tower in Utah, and the last one to operate in the state before being replaced by aircraft reconnaissance in the late 1960s. It offers a panoramic view of the Flaming Gorge area and Uinta Mountains.

The lookout tower is located off Utah 44 on the western side of the lake. Take the Sheep Creek Geologic Loop to Forest Road 221 (signs say Browne and Spirit Lakes), and go west 1 mile to Forest Road 5, which you follow south 1.5 miles to the tower. Forest Road 5 is not recommended for low-clearance vehicles. The historic tower is open weekends from Memorial Day to Labor Day only.

CAMPING

U.S. Forest Service campgrounds are located throughout Flaming Gorge Recreation Area, and they range from primitive boat-in-only sites to modern facilities with showers and flush toilets, but no RV hookups. Some are open year-round, and others in the summer only, and rates range from free for some of the primitive sites to $10 for more developed campgrounds with showers. Improvements were being made as of this writing; check with the district ranger's office or visitor centers for current information.

Commercial campgrounds with full RV hookups are located in Vernal (see earlier this chapter). In Manila there's a KOA campground (☎ 801/784-3184), open from mid-April through October, that charges from $17 to $22 per night.

ACCOMMODATIONS

Flaming Gorge Lodge

155 Greendale, U.S. 191 (4 miles south of Flaming Gorge Dam), Dutch John, UT 84023. ☎ **801/889-3773.** Fax 801/889-3788. 45 units. A/C TV TEL. Mar–Oct $55–$95 double; Nov–Feb $40–$80 double. AE, DISC, MC, V.

Units here are either standard modern motel rooms or one-bedroom condominiums. Motel rooms have two double beds and an optional roll-away. Condominium units have one queen-sized bed, a single, and a hide-a-bed, plus a fully equipped kitchen. There's a restaurant serving three meals daily, a gas station, raft rentals, a liquor and convenience store, and a fly and tackle shop.

✪ Red Canyon Lodge

Just north of Utah 44 via Red Canyon Road within Flaming Gorge National Recreation Area (mailing address: P.O. Box 211145, Salt Lake City, UT 84121-8145). ☎ **801/889-3759.** 16 units. $35–$100 double. AE, DISC, MC, V. Closed Nov–Mar, except luxury cabins, which are available Sun–Thurs mid-Jan through Mar at reduced rates.

A variety of delightful cabins dating from the 1930s, but remodeled in the 1990s, offer a range of possibilities from rustic to luxurious, and all have free-standing wood stoves. The most basic have one queen-sized bed and share a central bath house, while simple cabins with private bath are also available. The top-of-the-line luxury units are beautifully appointed cabins with two queen beds in a separate bedroom, a hide-a-bed in the living room, full bath, vaulted ceilings, kitchenettes, and a covered porch. A restaurant serves three meals daily (see below). There are two private lakes plus a free kids' fishing pond, tackle shop and fly fishing instruction, snowmobile rentals, horseback rides, hiking and mountainbiking trails, and a convenience store. Pets are not permitted in the luxury units, but are allowed in the rustic cabins.

DINING

Red Canyon Lodge Dining Room

In Red Canyon Lodge, just north of Utah 44 via Red Canyon Road within Flaming Gorge National Recreation Area. ☎ **801/889-3759.** Reservations not accepted. Breakfast and lunch items $2.95–$8.95; main dinner courses $8.95–$18.95. AE, DISC, MC, V. Apr–Oct daily 6am–10pm; mid-Jan–Mar Fri–Sat 4:30–9pm. Closed Nov–mid-Jan. AMERICAN.

You'll find a classic mountain lodge atmosphere here, along with views of tall pines and a small lake. Popular among locals as well as visitors, the menu features basic fish, steaks, chicken, and prime rib, as well as more exotic selections such as Cajun-style shrimp and a daily special. You'll also find standard American breakfasts, and burgers and sandwiches at lunch. Full liquor service is available.

11

Utah's Dixie: The Southwest Corner

Small towns and big rocks—that's what you'll find in Utah's southwest corner, known as "Utah's Dixie" for its climate as well as its Civil War–era cotton growing. Those days are long gone, but the stiflingly hot summers and delightfully mild winters remain, making this region a terrific winter playground. Snow-weary Salt Lake City residents come here every year, seeking an escape from frigid temperatures and the cold-and-flu season. There's no need to ever put away the golf clubs or swimsuits in this neighborhood.

There's lots to see and do in this colorful corner of Utah. You can step back more than a hundred years in history at Brigham Young's winter home at St. George, the region's largest town, or go back in time a thousand years at Anasazi Indian Village State Park. Our favorite stops are outdoors: the rugged red rock cliffs at Snow Canyon State Park; the ruddy sands of Coral Pink Sand Dunes State Park; the panoramic views from atop Boulder Mountain.

Utah's Dixie isn't only a warm-weather destination, though. Its extremes of elevation can often mean that you can lounge around the pool in the morning and build a snowman that same afternoon. From the scorching desert at St. George, it's only 74 miles—and 7,500 feet up—to the cool mountain forest at Cedar Breaks National Monument. Home to a variety of scenic and recreation areas (you'll even find a ski resort here), a surprising number of historic attractions, and some excellent performing arts events (such as the Utah Shakespearean Festival), this region also serves as the gateway to most of Utah's spectacular national parks—probably the main reason you're here.

Despite the number of attractions in and around Utah's Dixie, don't expect much in terms of amenities. Many of the lodging and dining establishments here are somewhat basic—perfectly adequate, but not overly exciting. Keep in mind that distances are long— "nearby" can mean 100 miles away—and services may be far apart. But this is a starkly beautiful part of the American West—still very much like it was more than 100 years ago, and well worth a visit.

1 Getting Outside in Utah's Dixie

This is Utah's playground, a year-round mecca for hikers, mountainbikers, golfers, boaters, anglers, and anybody else who just wants to get outdoors. Among the top spots for experiencing nature at its best are Boulder Mountain, with its alpine forests and pristine lakes and streams; Cedar Breaks National Monument, a high-mountain oasis of towering pines and firs, and wild-flowers galore; and state parks such as Snow Canyon, Coral Pink Sand Dunes, and Quail Creek.

The best seasons for outdoor activities here are based on elevation: In St. George and other lowlands, spring and fall are best, the winter's okay, and the summer is awful, with temperatures soaring well over 100°. But not everyone says no to St. George in the summer: Its desert climate makes it the golfing capital of Utah. The Sunbrook is considered the state's best course, with a challenging layout and spec-tacular views of the White Hills, but you can stay a week in St. George and play a different course each day. On the other side of the seasonal coin, don't try to drive to Cedar Breaks until June at the earliest; the roads will be closed by snow.

Our favorite way to see this part of Utah is on foot. Hiking trails abound at Boul-der Mountain and throughout the Dixie National Forest north of St. George. But several of the best trails are in state parks, particularly Snow Canyon State Park near St. George and Escalante State Park in Escalante.

Biking here generally means mountainbiking. This is true even for those who confine most of their riding to city streets, because you never know when you're going to discover that great little trail turning off into the red rock desert or through alpine meadows. Also, some of the roads—especially secondary roads—can be a bit rough, with only minimal shoulders; a sturdy mountainbike will survive better. The best mountainbiking is at Brian Head Ski Resort near Cedar Breaks National Monument. Both road and mountainbikes can take you to beautiful areas in and around Snow Canyon State Park near St. George.

For an area with so much desert, there's certainly a lot of boating here: Utahns have had to create reservoirs to provide the desert and its residents drinking and irrigation water. The best boating is at Quail Creek State Park near St. George, but those who would like a bit more solitude might prefer the relatively undeveloped Gunlock State Park nearby. The top fishing hole in these parts is at Quail Creek State Park, but there are also plenty of smaller lakes and hidden streams in the forests on Boulder Mountain, and in the Dixie National Forest north of St. George.

Off-road vehicles can simply be a means to get to an isolated fishing stream or hiking trail, or part of the adventure itself. The old mining and logging roads in the Dixie National Forest or at Boulder Mountain are great for four-wheel exploring. Among the best is the Hole-in-the-Rock Scenic Backway near Escalante, which leads to a particularly scenic view of Lake Powell. Visitors with their own dune buggies will want to challenge the shifting dunes at Coral Pink Sand Dunes State Park, just outside Kanab.

There's an abundance of wildlife in this part of the state. Sure, you'll see deer, squirrels, chipmunks, and other furry creatures at Boulder Mountain and Cedar Breaks National Monument, but there's also animal life in the desert, including our favorites: the luminescent scorpions at Coral Pink Sand Dunes State Park, and the Gila monster at Snow Canyon State Park. Boulder Mountain and Snow Canyon are home to numerous songbirds, and Escalante State Park has the best wetland bird habitat in southern Utah.

It may be hot down in the desert, but there's plenty of snow up on those mountaintops. Your best bet here for downhill skiing is Brian Head Ski Resort. Cross-country skiers and snowmobilers will want to head to nearby Cedar Breaks National Monument after the winter snows have closed the roads to cars.

The Southwest Corner

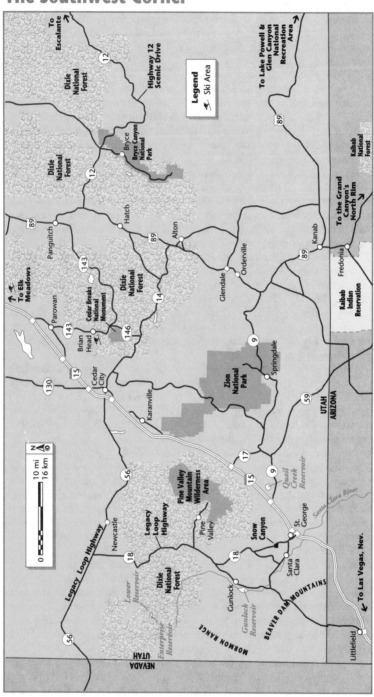

Legend
≮ Ski Area

2 St. George, Gateway to Southern Utah's Natural Wonders

In the fall of 1861, Brigham Young sent 309 families to establish a cotton-growing community in the semi-arid Virgin River Valley; today, St. George has almost 40,000 inhabitants. Known as one of Utah's more conservative communities, life in St. George is still strongly influenced by the Mormon Church; it is also a winter home to many snowbirds and retirees, who love the hot, dry summers and mild winters. Despite the climate, this desert city appears quite green, with tree-lined streets and lovely grassy areas. There are eight golf courses, with more in the planning stages, and recreational and cultural facilities to suit every taste.

St. George is also the gateway to some of the most spectacular scenery in the West. Zion, Bryce, Grand Canyon, and Great Basin National Parks are within relatively easy driving distance, as are Cedar Breaks and Pipe Springs National Monuments and Snow Canyon, Gunlock, and Quail Creek State Parks. Depending on your itinerary, St. George may be your biggest stopping point en route to Lake Powell and Glen Canyon National Recreation Area, Capitol Reef National Park, and southeastern Utah's attractions.

ESSENTIALS
GETTING THERE

By Plane   The closest major airport is **McCarran International Airport** in Las Vegas (☎ 702/261-5743). Most major airlines fly into McCarran, where you can rent a car and drive the 120 miles northeast on I-15 to St. George. The **St. George Shuttle** (☎ 801/628-8320) provides daily service to and from the Las Vegas airport.

Delta/Skywest Airlines (☎ 801/673-3451 or 800/453-9417) and **Pacific Air West Airlines** (☎ 801/674-0096 or 800/729-7229) fly into **St. George Airport** (☎ 801/628-0481), located on a bluff on the west side of the city.

For car rentals in St. George, see "Getting Around," below.

By Car   St. George is on I-15, 120 miles northeast of Las Vegas and 305 miles south of Salt Lake City. Take exit 6 (Bluff Street) or 8 (St. George Boulevard) for St. George.

INFORMATION

The **St. George Area Chamber of Commerce** is in the historic Pioneer Courthouse at 97 E. St. George Blvd., St. George, UT 84770 (☎ 801/628-1658; fax 801/673-1587).

For information on the state and national parks in the area, as well as the Dixie National Forest and land administered by the Bureau of Land Management, call the numbers above or visit the **Interagency Offices and Visitor Center** at 345 E. Riverside Drive. Open seven days a week, the office has a variety of free brochures, plus maps, books, posters, and videos for sale. Rangers can answer questions and recommend trails, and supply backcountry permits. To get there, take exit 6 off I-15, and turn east. Or call the **Bureau of Land Management** at 801/628-4491 or the **United States Forest Service** at 801/652-3100.

You can also contact the **Dixie National Forest's Pine Valley Ranger District** office, 345 E. Riverside Dr., St. George, UT 84770 (☎ 801/652-3100); or the **BLM's Dixie Resource Area office,** 225 N. Bluff St., St. George, UT 84770 (☎ 801/673-4654).

GETTING AROUND

The street grid system is centered on the point where Tabernacle Street (running east–west) crosses Main Street (running north–south), with numbered streets increasing in each direction by hundreds. St. George Boulevard takes the place of 100 North, Bluff Street runs along a bluff at the western edge of the city, I-15 cuts through in a northeast direction (from exit 6 at the south end of Bluff Street to exit 8 at the east end of St. George Boulevard), and River Road lies at the eastern edge, becoming Red Cliffs Road north of St. George Boulevard. Other than that, the system stays true to the grid.

Car rental agencies with St. George offices include **ABC Rent-A-Car,** 219 W. St. George Blvd. (☎ 801/628-7355); **A-1 Car Rental,** 568 E. St. George Blvd. (☎ 801/ 673-8811); **Avis,** St. George Municipal Airport (☎ 801/673-3451 or 800/ 331-1212); **Budget Rent-A-Car,** 116 W. St. George Blvd. (☎ 801/673-6825 or 800/527-0700); **Dollar Rent-A-Car,** 1175 S. 150 East (☎ 801/628-6549); and **National Car Rental,** St. George Municipal Airport (☎ 801/673-5098 or 800/ CAR-RENT).

For a taxi, call **Dixie Taxi Cab** (☎ 801/673-4068), or **Zion Limo** (☎ 801/ 628-9224).

There's free on-street parking in much of the city, and many of the streets are tree-lined and shady.

FAST FACTS: ST. GEORGE

One of the larger hospitals in this part of the state is **Dixie Regional Medical Center,** 544 S. 400 East (☎ 801/634-4000). The **post office** is located at 180 N. Main St. (☎ 801/673-3312). The regional **newspaper** is the *Daily Spectrum* (☎ 801/673-3511).

DISCOVERING MORMON HISTORY IN & AROUND ST. GEORGE

Because the Church of Jesus Christ of Latter-day Saints was the primary driving force in the settlement of St. George, it should come as no surprise that most of the sightseeing in town is church related. At the town's historic buildings, staffed by knowledgeable church members, you'll learn about all about the church as well as the specific site; expect a little sales pitch on the benefits of Christianity, and the Mormon faith in particular.

Brigham Young Winter Home Historical Site

67 W. 200 North. ☎ **801/673-2517.** Free guided tours. Memorial Day–Labor Day daily 8:30am–8:30pm; Labor Day–Memorial Day daily 9am–6pm. From I-15, take exit 8, head west on St. George Boulevard to Main Street, turn right (north) for one block, then left (west) onto 200 North.

Church leader Brigham Young was one of St. George's first snowbirds. He escaped the Salt Lake City cold during the last few winters of his life by coming south to this house. In addition to its obvious religious importance to the Church of Jesus Christ of Latter-day Saints, it's a handsome example of how the well-to-do of the late 19th century lived. Allow about a half hour for the guided tour.

Daughters of Utah Pioneer Museum

133 N. 100 East. ☎ **801/628-7274.** Free admission, donations accepted. Mon–Sat 10am–5pm. Closed last 2 weeks Dec. From I-15 take exit 8, head west on St. George Boulevard to 100 East and turn right (north).

This "Grandma's attic" contains an eclectic collection of items belonging to the pioneers who settled this area more than one hundred years ago. There's some

St. George & Environs

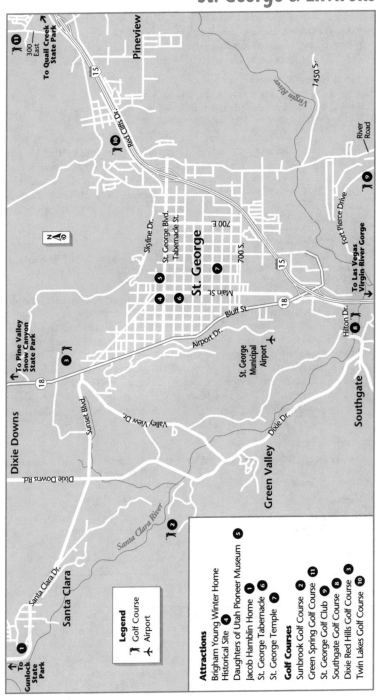

furniture—including a bed used by Brigham Young—spinning wheels, an 1894 loom, guns, tools, musical instruments, and other relics from bygone days. Historic photos, mostly of pioneer families, are on display; you can purchase copies if you like. Guided tours are given by volunteers from the Daughters of Utah Pioneers.

✪ Jacob Hamblin Home

Main St., Santa Clara. ☎ 801/673-2161. Free guided tours. Memorial Day–Labor Day daily 8:30am–8pm; Labor Day–Memorial Day daily 9am–5pm. From St. George, go 3 miles west on U.S. 91 to the community of Santa Clara, then watch for sign.

This stone and pine house, built in the 1860s, is typical of pioneer homes throughout the West—and more of what you'd think of as a pioneer home than the refined houses of St. George—except for one aspect that is definitively Mormon: It has two identical bedrooms, one for each of Hamblin's wives. You'll also notice that the dining table is set in the typical Mormon fashion, with plates upside down and chairs facing away from the table to facilitate kneeling for before-meal prayers. The guided tour lasts about a half hour.

✪ St. George Tabernacle

Main and Tabernacle streets. ☎ 801/628-4072. Free guided tours. Daily 9am–6pm. From I-15 take exit 8, head west on St. George Boulevard to Main Street, turn left (south) for a block to the Tabernacle.

This is the most beautiful building in St. George. It's an excellent example of fine Old World craftsmanship, from the hand-quarried red stone walls to the intricate interior woodwork; craftsmen finished pine, which was all they had, to look like exotic hardwoods and even marble. Completed in 1876 after 13 years of work, the Tabernacle served as a house of worship and town meeting hall. During the 1880s, when a nearby silver strike brought many Catholics to the area, the Tabernacle was used for a Roman Catholic high mass led by a Roman Catholic priest, but with music from the liturgy sung by the local Mormon choir—in Latin. Today, the Tabernacle is a community center that presents free weekly concerts and other cultural events. The guided tour takes about a half hour.

St. George Temple

440 S. 300 East. ☎ 801/673-5181. Temple not open to the public; free guided tours of visitor center exhibits. Daily 9am–9pm. From I-15 take exit 8, head west on St. George Boulevard to 200 East, turn left and go about six blocks to the large parking lot on your left.

Completed in 1877, the St. George Temple was the first LDS temple in Utah, and remains the oldest still in use in the world today. The majestic white temple is not open to the general public, but you can walk among the beautiful gardens, and stop at the visitor center south of the Temple for a multimedia program on the beliefs of the Church of Jesus Christ of Latter-day Saints. At the conclusion of the tour/program, which takes just under an hour, you'll be asked if you would like a member of the Church to call on you to discuss the church's beliefs further.

EXPLORING SNOW CANYON STATE PARK

✪ **Snow Canyon** is among Utah's most scenic state parks, offering great opportunities for photography, hiking, and horseback riding. You'll see rock cliffs and walls of Navajo sandstone in every shade of red imaginable, layered with white and black from ancient lava flows. Wander just a few feet from your campsite, and you're likely to discover ancient petroglyphs. Or hike the trails and discover shifting sand dunes, mysterious lava caves, colorful desert plants, and a variety of rock formations.

Because the summers here are hot—well over 100°F hot—the best time to visit is any other time. Winters are mild, but nights can be chilly. Spring and fall are probably the most popular, and therefore the busiest, times to visit. By the way, don't come looking for snow—Snow Canyon was named for the pioneers Lorenzo and Erastus Snow, who found it.

Just the Facts

Be aware that rattlesnakes are common in this part of Utah, so watch where you put your hands and feet. If you do encounter a rattler, give it a wide berth.

Getting There   The park is located 11 miles northwest of St. George, off Utah 18.

Information, Fees & Regulations   For a copy of the park's full-color brochure, contact **Snow Canyon State Park Headquarters,** P.O. Box 140, Santa Clara, UT 84765-0140 (☎ 801/628-2255). Day-use fee is $3 per vehicle, or $1 per person on foot, bike, or motorcycle. Like most state parks, dogs are welcome, including on the trails, but must be leashed.

Sports & Activities

Hiking   The best way to see Snow Canyon is on foot or horseback (see below). Several short trails make for easy full- or half-day hikes. The **Hidden Piñon Trail** is a 1¹/₂-mile round-trip self-guided nature trail that wanders among lava rocks, through several canyons, and onto rocky flatlands, offering panoramic views of the surrounding mountains. The trail begins across the highway from the campground; you can pick up a brochure at the park office/entrance station. The walk is fairly easy, but allow at least an hour, especially if you're planning to keep an eye out for Mormon tea, cliffrose, prickly pear cactus, and banana yucca.

An easy three-quarters-mile one-way trail leads to **Johnson Arch.** It begins just south of the campground, passes by the popular rock-climbing wall (see below), some low sand dunes, and then a small canyon with a view of Johnson Arch (named after pioneer wife Maude Johnson) high above.

Also popular is the **Lava Caves Trail,** a 1¹/₂-mile round-trip that starts just north of the campground. The caves are about a half mile along the trail, but watch carefully—it's easy to miss them. The caves were formed from liquid lava, and the large rooms have at times been occupied by Native American tribes. Another quarter mile past the caves is the West Canyon Overlook, with a breathtaking view into West Canyon.

Several longer and steeper trails lead to spectacular views of the canyons and distant vistas; check with park rangers.

Horseback Riding   Snow Canyon Stables, P.O. Box 577, Santa Clara, UT 84765 (☎ 801/628-6677), offers horseback rides of various lengths into some of the more inaccessible and beautiful parts of the park, year-round. Prices start at $15 for a 1-hour ride; an overnight camping trip, including dinner and breakfast, is $125.

Rock Climbing   Climbers love the tall wall of rock on the east side of the road just south of the campground, but it has become so popular that the park has issued a moratorium on bolting. Check with the park office for information.

Wildlife Watching   You're likely to see cottontail rabbits, ground squirrels, and songbirds; luckier visitors may also spot desert mule deer, bobcats, coyote, kit foxes, eagles, and owls. Although it's unlikely you'll see one, desert tortoises (a federally listed threatened species) and Gila monsters also live in the park. There are also some rattlesnakes, which you'll want to avoid.

CAMPING

The 36-site campground is one of the best in the state. One section has electric hookups, and sites there are a bit close; those not needing electricity can set up camp in delightful little side canyons, surrounded by colorful red rocks and Utah juniper. The views are spectacular no matter where you choose to set up. There are hot showers, modern restrooms, and an RV sewage dump station. Campsites with electricity are $11 Sunday through Thursday, and $12 on Friday, Saturday, and holidays. Sites without electric hookups are $9 and $10, respectively. Reservations are recommended from February to May and September to November; call 800/322-3770. There's a $5 nonrefundable reservation fee.

MORE OUTDOOR ACTIVITIES IN THE ST. GEORGE AREA

In addition to what's available in Snow Canyon State Park, there's great hiking, biking, and fishing in the Dixie National Forest and on nearby lands administered by the Bureau of Land Management. For contact information, see "Information" under "Essentials," above.

Road Biking & Mountainbiking   For bike repairs and accessories, stop at **Bicycles Unlimited,** 90 S. 100 East (☎ 801/673-4492). You can get repairs or rentals at **Swen's Cyclery,** 1060 E. Tabernacle (☎ 801/673-0878), where mountainbike rental prices run from $5 per hour to $25 per day.

A popular road trip is the scenic **24-mile loop** from St. George through Santa Clara, Ivins, and Snow Canyon State Park. The trip is on paved roads with narrow shoulders but generally little traffic. Allow 2- to 3- hours. Head north out of St. George on Bluff Street (Utah 18), and follow it to its intersection with U.S. 91. Turn west (left) and go about 6 miles to the village of Santa Clara, where you can visit the Jacob Hamblin Home (see "Discovering Mormon History In & Around St. George," above). From Santa Clara, continue west about a mile before turning north (right); follow the signs to Ivins and the Tuacahn Amphitheater. At Ivins, turn east (right) onto the Snow Canyon Road, following signs for Snow Canyon State Park, where you can easily spend several hours or several days exploring the red rock formations, lava pools, and sand dunes. From the park, continue east to Utah 18, turn south (right), and pedal back into St. George.

Mountainbiking opportunities abound on land administered by the **U.S. Forest Service** (☎ 801/652-3100) and the **Bureau of Land Management** (☎ 801/628-4491); call for details.

Fishing   Quail Creek and Gunlock State Parks (see below) are the local fishing holes. For equipment, licenses, and tips on where they're biting, visit **Hurst Sports Center,** 160 N. 500 West (☎ 801/673-6141).

Golf   Utah's golf capital, St. George attracts golfers from around the country to more than a half-dozen public courses (and more on the way), known for their challenging designs, well-maintained fairways and greens, and spectacularly scenic settings. The best is the 18-hole, par-72 **Sunbrook Golf Course,** 2240 W. Sunbrook Dr. (☎ 801/634-5866), rated tops in the state for 1994–95 by *Golf Digest,* both for its design and spectacular scenery. Greens fees in the winter are $16 for 9 holes and $26 for 18 holes; in the summer they're $9 and $17, respectively. Also highly rated by *Golf Digest*—and considered by many to be the state's second-best course—is **Green Spring Golf Course,** 588 N. Green Spring Dr., Washington (☎ 801/673-7888), several miles northeast of St. George. Challenging Green Spring is an 18-hole, par-71 course, with winter greens fees of $14 for 9 holes and $24 for 18 holes ($10 and $16, respectively, in the summer).

Other 18-hole courses include the par-73 **St. George Golf Club,** 2190 S. 1400 East (☎ 801/634-5854); and the par-70 **Southgate Golf Course,** 1975 S. Tonaquint Dr. (☎ 801/628-0000). Green fees at both of these city-owned courses are $8 for 9 holes and $15 for 18 holes in the winter, and $7 for 9 holes and $9 for 18 holes in the summer. The Southgate also has a **Family Golf Center** (☎ 801/674-7728), with an outdoor driving range and putting and chipping greens, plus state-of-the-art indoor facilities that include computerized golf swing analysis.

Nine-hole courses in St. George include the par-34 **Dixie Red Hills Golf Course,** 100 N. 700 West (☎ 801/634-5852), with winter green fees of $8 for 9 holes and $15 for 18 holes (and summer fees of $7 and $9, respectively); and the par-27 **Twin Lakes Golf Course,** 660 N. Twin Lakes Dr. (☎ 801/673-4441), with year-round fees of $4.50 for 9 holes.

Golfers can often save money by checking with local motels on various lodging/golf packages; see "Where to Stay," below.

Hiking   Some of the best hiking in the area is at Snow Canyon State Park (see above). The Dixie National Forest to the north also offers vast opportunities, with some 200 miles of trails. Check with forest rangers on current trail conditions, and be sure to carry detailed maps on any long hikes, especially if you're venturing into the Pine Valley Wilderness Area. Stop in at the **Interagency Offices and Visitor Center** at 345 E. Riverside Drive for maps and details.

TWO STATE PARKS FOR WATER SPORTS ENTHUSIASTS

Year-round warm weather makes Utah's Dixie, home to several large reservoirs, a mecca for water sports enthusiasts. **Quail Creek State Park** (P.O. Box 1943, St. George, UT 84770-1943; ☎ 801/879-2378), 14 miles northeast of St. George off I-15 and Utah 9, has the warmest water in the state in the summer, making it extremely popular with boaters, water-skiers, wind surfers, scuba divers, and swimmers. The two boat ramps accommodate practically all types of watercraft; there are also docks and sandy beaches. Quail Creek Reservoir is considered one of the state's best fishing holes for largemouth bass; anglers also catch rainbow trout, blue gill, and crappie. Facilities include a fish-cleaning station, modern restrooms, a campground with 23 sites (but no showers or RV hookups), and a picnic area with barbecue grills. The park is open year-round; day-use costs are $3 per vehicle or $1 per individual on foot, bike, or motorcycle; camping is $7 Sunday to Thursday and $8 on Friday, Saturday, and holidays.

Gunlock State Park (P.O. Box 140, Santa Clara, UT 84765-0140; ☎ 801/628-2255), 15 miles northwest of St. George via U.S. 91, is also a great place to enjoy water sports year-round, in a less developed setting than Quail Creek. Activities at the 240-acre Gunlock Reservoir include boating (there's a boat ramp), water-skiing, swimming, and excellent fishing for bass and catfish. There's no day-use fee. The park offers free primitive camping, although with pit toilets and no security; you'll probably be happier camping (and paying) at Snow Canyon State Park (see above), about 20 miles away.

Neither Quail Creek nor Gunlock State Parks offer on-site boat rentals, but rentals are available from several dealers in St. George: **RV Rental Express,** 875 E. St. George Blvd. (☎ 801/680-7447), has 14-foot aluminum fishing boats with 10-horsepower outboard motors starting at about $50 per day, and ski boats from about $150 per day; both include trailers and life jackets. **Funtime Rentals,** 770 E. 700 South (☎ 801/628-6511), rents 2- and 3-passenger personal watercraft, including trailers and life jackets, for $100 to $135 per day. Fuel is extra.

SPECTATOR SPORTS

Team Sports   **The Dixie College Rebels** are the ones to root for in St. George. The football, women's volleyball, men's and women's basketball, men's baseball, and women's softball teams at this two-year community college are often nationally ranked. You're not likely to have any trouble getting tickets to join the school's 3,000 students in the 5,000-seat Hansen Stadium or Burns Arena. Tickets cost from $3 to $7, and are available at the Athletic Department offices (☎ 801/652-7525).

Drag Racing   Drag racing fans head to **St. George Raceway Park** (☎ 801/635-2447) during its March through November season for two to three racing days per month. Special races take place on Memorial Day, Labor Day, and Thanksgiving. Admission is $8; kids under 12 get in free. To get to the raceway, take I-15 to exit 8 on the north side of St. George, head south on River Road for about 4 1/2 miles, then watch for signs to the track.

SHOPPING

You probably wouldn't travel across the country to shop in St. George; the stores are similar to what you'd find almost anywhere in Middle America. Some of the town's more interesting shops (and one of our favorite local restaurants—see "Where to Dine," below) are located at **Ancestor Square,** at the corner of St. George Boulevard and Main Street. Among the shops are **Cassidy's Casuals,** 2 W. St. George Blvd. (☎ 801/628-6665), specializing in all-cotton fashions; and **Artists' Gallery,** 5 W. St. George Blvd. (☎ 801/628-9293), showing the works of regional and local artists.

You'll find WalMart, ZCMI department store, and the standard mall fare at **Red Cliffs Mall,** 1770 E. Red Cliffs Dr. (☎ 801/673-0099). It's located on the east side of I-15, between exits 8 (St. George Boulevard) and 10 (Green Springs Drive), and is open Monday to Saturday 10am to 9pm, and Sunday noon to 5pm.

If you can't resist a bargain, head for **Zion Factory Stores,** 250 N. Red Cliffs Dr. (☎ 801/674-9800), where you'll find more than three dozen outlet shops, including Corning-Revere, London Fog, Book Warehouse, Toy Liquidators, Bass, Etienne Aigner, Carter's, J. Crew, Cape Isle Knitters, Clothestime, and Van Heusen. Located on the east side of I-15 just north of exit 8, the mall is open Monday to Saturday from 10am to 8pm, and Sunday 11am to 5pm.

Those in the market for alcoholic beverages will find them at the **Utah State Liquor Store,** 929 W. Sunset Blvd. (☎ 801/673-9454).

WHERE TO STAY

You'll find a good selection of lodgings in St. George, with a range of facilities and prices. Most are on St. George Boulevard and Bluff Street, within easy walking distance of restaurants and attractions. Summer is the slow season here—people tend to head to the mountains when the temperature hits 115°F—so prices are lowest then. High seasons are spring and fall, and it's almost impossible to find a room during the World Senior Games in mid- to late October. Golfers will want to ask about special golf packages offered by many hotels and motels in St. George.

In addition to the accommodations described below, you'll find branches of the following reliable chain motels: **Motel 6,** 205 N. 1000 East St. (exit 8 off I-15), St. George, UT 84770 (☎ 801/628-7979 or 505/891-6161), with rates for two of $35.99–$39.99; **Super 8 Motel,** 915 S. Bluff St., St. George, UT 84770 (☎ 801/628-4251 or 800/800/8000, fax 801/628-6534), charging $46.88–$49.88 for two people; and **Comfort Inn,** 999 E. Skyline Dr., St. George, UT 84770 (☎ 801/628-4271 or 800/221-2222), with rates for two of $48–$64.

Room tax adds about 9% to your lodging bill. Pets are not accepted unless otherwise noted.

Best Western Coral Hills

125 E. St. George Blvd., St. George, UT 84770. ☎ **801/673-4844** or 800/542-7733. Fax 801/673-5352. 98 rms, including 5 suites. A/C TV TEL. $49–$65 double. Rates include continental breakfast. AE, CB, DC, DISC, MC, V.

A bit more homey than your average Best Western, the Coral Hills has floral bedspreads and lace curtains, along with king- or queen-sized beds and polished-wood furnishings that include an armoire/dresser combo that hides the TV. Swimmers can choose between good-sized indoor and outdoor heated pools, both with whirlpools, plus a kiddie pool. There's also a game room with a pool table, an exercise room, and a putting green. If you're here to work, fax and photocopy services are available.

Dixie Palms Motel

185 E. St. George Blvd., St. George, UT 84770. ☎ **801/673-3531.** 15 rms. A/C TV TEL. $26–$30 double. MC, V.

Travelers on tight budgets should head to the Dixie Palms—basic lodging at bargain-basement rates. Located right in the center of town, within walking distance of several restaurants and attractions, this older, redbrick property doesn't have a swimming pool and some rooms have showers only, but rooms are clean and well-maintained, and the price is right.

Claridge Inn

1187 S. Bluff St., St. George, UT 84770. ☎ **801/673-7222** or 800/367-3790. Fax 801/634-0773. 50 rms. A/C TV TEL. Sun–Thurs $31–$33 double; Fri–Sat $43–$49 double; higher for special events. Rates include continental breakfast at a nearby restaurant. AE, DISC, MC, V.

This recently built motel is popular with families because of its outdoor heated pool and low rates. The rooms—most with two queen-sized beds—are well-kept but rather plain, with stucco walls and no artwork. All have a small dining table with two comfortable chairs. The Claridge Inn is entirely nonsmoking.

Ⓢ Econo Lodge

460 E. St. George Blvd., St. George, UT 84770. ☎ **801/673-4861** or 800/424-4777. 54 rms, including 4 suites. A/C TV TEL. Feb–early Sept $42–$72 double; early Sept–Jan $40–$68 double. AE, DISC, JCB, MC, V.

This attractive and well-kept Econo Lodge boasts a large, well-landscaped outdoor heated swimming pool, making the poolside rooms the best choice. Rooms come in a variety of sizes and bed choices, with standard motel furnishings. The four king suites, however, are extra special, with a king bed, wet bar with refrigerator, a couch, tables and chairs, and plenty of room—perfect for families. Also above average is the motel's one wheelchair-accessible room, with its very spacious and easy-to-use bath facilities. Pets are welcome.

Greene Gate Village Bed & Breakfast

76 W. Tabernacle St., St. George, UT 84770. ☎ **801/628-6999** or 800/350-6999. Fax 801/628-5068. 15 rms, 1 large family unit. A/C TV TEL. $50–$115 double. Rates include full breakfast. AE, DISC, MC, V.

One of the most delightful places to stay in southwest Utah, this bed-and-breakfast inn is actually nine separate buildings, all restored pioneer homes from the late 1800s, sitting in their own flower-filled little "village" in downtown St. George. There are lots of genuine antiques—mostly Victorian—plus modern "necessities" such as TVs; some rooms also have VCRs. Most rooms have shower/tub combos, but some have showers only. Breakfasts are full and generous, and Bentley's Fine Dining (see

"Where to Dine," below) serves dinner Thursday, Friday, and Saturday evenings, by reservation only. There's a small outdoor heated pool and hot tub. Unlike at many B&Bs, children, even babies, are welcome; pets generally are not. Tobacco use of any kind is prohibited inside.

Hilton Inn of St. George

1450 S. Hilton Dr., St. George, UT 84770. ☎ 801/628-0463 or 800/662-2525 in Utah. Fax 801/628-1501. 100 rms, including 2 suites. A/C TV TEL. $70–$105 double (rates are highest in spring and fall; lowest in the summer). AE, CB, DC, DISC, EU, JCB, MC, V.

One of the few full-service hotels in southwest Utah, this Hilton is everything you'd expect from such a respected chain. What makes the hotel particularly interesting is that all the rooms are different: Some have two sinks, some one; some are decorated with dark wood, others light; and a variety of color themes and wallpaper designs are used. All rooms are done in a subdued Southwest decor and have computer dataports and voice mail; some have desks. A full range of services are provided, and facilities include two large pools (one indoor, one out), a sundeck, three lighted tennis courts, a gift shop, and conference rooms for up to 200. A restaurant serves three meals daily and has complete liquor service. A complete renovation was underway in late 1995. Pets are accepted with a $25 nonrefundable fee.

Holiday Inn Resort Hotel & Convention Center

850 S. Bluff St., St. George, UT 84770. ☎ **801/628-4235** or 800/457-9800. Fax 801/628-8157. 164 rms, including 7 suites. A/C TV TEL. Winter, $69–$89 double; summer, $110–$140 double. AE, CB, DC, DISC, JCB, MC, V.

With its Holidome recreation center, this is an excellent choice for travelers with kids or anyone who wants easy access to a large indoor-outdoor heated pool, whirlpool, lighted tennis court, putting green, weight room, pool table, Ping-Pong table, video arcade, and a separate children's play area. That should keep you busy, but if you find time to get to your room, you'll find it attractively decorated, with floral bedspreads on king- or queen-sized beds and solid wood furniture. Family rooms are slightly larger and come with hide-a-beds; king rooms have hair dryers and hot beverage makers in addition to the standard furnishings; and the luxury suites have individual whirlpool spas. The hotel offers a full range of services, and just off the beautiful cathedral-ceilinged lobby is a gift shop selling local crafts in addition to the standard magazines, T-shirts, and souvenirs. A formal dining room and coffee shop serve three meals daily, and full liquor service is available. Small pets may be accepted with management approval.

✪ Seven Wives Inn Bed & Breakfast

217 N. 100 West, St. George, UT 84770. ☎ **801/628-3737** or 800/600-3737. 12 units, including 1 suite. A/C TV TEL. $55–$125. Rates include full breakfast. AE, CB, DC, DISC, JCB, MC, V.

There are no polygamists hiding in the attic of Seven Wives Inn anymore—as they did in the 1880s after polygamy was outlawed—but it's still fun to imagine what things were like in those days. Innkeepers Jon and Alison Bowcutt will be happy to chat with you about the property's history. This bed-and-breakfast consists of two historic homes: the main house, built in 1873, is where polygamists hid; next door is the President's house, a four-square Victorian built 10 years later that played host to many of the Mormon church's early presidents. All of the dozen rooms have private baths, two with shower only. The honeymoon suite has a whirlpool tub for two. Many rooms have functioning fireplaces or wood-burning stoves, and the entire inn is decorated with antiques, mostly Victorian and Eastlake. Many of the rooms have decks or balconies. The inn is completely nonsmoking.

Singletree Inn

260 E. St. George Blvd., St. George, UT 84770. ☎ **801/673-6161** or 800/528-8890. Fax 801/673-7453. 48 units, including 2 family suites. A/C TV TEL. $50–$55 double; $60–$70 family suite. All rates include continental breakfast. AE, CB, DC, DISC, MC, V.

A few personal touches, such as dried-flower wall decorations, give this family-owned and -operated motel a homey feel; it's not institutional like many motels in this price category. Light-colored wallpaper is accented by the dark wood furnishings, and prints depicting area attractions hang on the walls. Rooms have either one king- or two queen-sized beds, there's an outdoor heated pool and whirlpool, and the motel's golf packages are better than most in the area. Small pets are accepted.

AN RV PARK

Settler's RV Park

1333 E. 100 South, St. George, UT 84770. ☎ **801/628-1624.** 155 sites. $16.90 with full hook-ups. MC, V. From I-15, take exit 8 (St. George Boulevard), go east one block, turn right onto River Road, then left onto 100 South.

Situated below a bluff just off I-15, this RV park is convenient for those seeing the area's attractions. The paved sites are fairly well-spaced, and once the trees grow a bit, they'll be at least partly shaded. The bath house is large and well-kept, there's a coin-operated laundry, and in addition to a heated pool and spa there are barbecues, a playground, a game room, shuffleboard, and horseshoes.

WHERE TO DINE

Andelin's Gable House Restaurant

290 E. St. George Blvd. ☎ **801/673-6796.** Reservations required spring and fall for prix fixe only. Main courses $4.50–$15.95; lunch $4.50–$9.95. Prix fixe dinner $25.95 for five courses, $21.95 for three courses. AE, DISC, MC, V. Mon–Sat 11:30am–10pm. From I-15, take exit 8 and head west on St. George Boulevard for about eight blocks. AMERICAN.

The Old English–garden decor, with lots of plants, flowered wallpaper, an eclectic display of antiques and collectibles, and a somewhat casually elegant atmosphere make the Gable House a popular special-occasion spot. At lunch you'll find croissant sandwiches, a good selection of salads, and chicken pot pie. Dinners include the very popular chicken pot pie again, with an especially flaky crust; slow-cooked beef brisket; and pink mountain trout, which is lightly floured and sautéed in butter. Among dinner entree salads, particularly recommended is the Oriental salad, with grilled chicken breast, Chinese noodles, Mandarin oranges, and almonds. The prix fixe dinners give you a choice of prime rib, roast rack of pork, or the fish of the day. No alcohol is served.

✪ Basila's Greek & Italian Cafe

Ancestor Square No. 38, 2 W. St. George Blvd. ☎ **801/673-7671.** Reservations for 6 or more only. Main courses $7.95–$16.95; lunch $3.75–$6.95. AE, DISC, MC, V. Tues–Sat 11:30am–2:30pm and 5–9pm. From I-15, take exit 8, head west on St. George Boulevard to Main Street; Ancestor Square is on the northwest corner. GREEK/ITALIAN.

Tucked away toward the back of Ancestor Square, Basila's is worth finding. You start off with crusty homemade bread and "Greek butter," a delightfully light mixture of olive oil and Balsamic vinegar. For lunch we had the four-cheese (ricotta, parmesan, romano, and feta) ravioli in marinara sauce, and a gyro with layers of seasoned lamb and beef on a bed of parsley and tomato with Tzatziki cucumber yogurt sauce; we highly recommend both. The spanakopeta, baked on the premises with thin layers of filo dough rolled with fresh spinach, ricotta, and parmesan cheese, and served with a lemon sauce, is a favorite at both lunch and dinner. For dessert, try the house favorite: Greek custard bread pudding. The tables are closely spaced in the fairly narrow, L-shaped dining room. There are plants in the windows, an eclectic collection of Mediterranean artwork arranged on high shelves around the exposed adobe walls, and slow-moving fans hanging from the open-beamed ceiling. There's also a small outdoor patio. Complete liquor service is available.

Bentley's Fine Dining

Greene Gate Village Bed & Breakfast, 76 W. Tabernacle St. ☎ **801/628-6999.** Reservations required. Five-course prix fixe $18. AE, DISC, MC, V. Thurs–Sat 6–9pm. Closed major holidays. From I-15, take exit 8, head west on St. George Boulevard to Main Street, turn left (south) on Main for one block to Tabernacle Street, then right (west) to the restaurant. AMERICAN.

Come to this handsome Victorian home for a quiet, romantic, elegant evening. A pianist plays quietly in the background as you dine, surrounded by antiques from the 1870s. Although the menu varies, you might have broiled filet mignon with sautéed mushrooms, chicken Cordon Bleu, or salmon poached in white wine. Desserts are always homemade, and include a variety of pies and cheesecakes. No alcoholic beverages are served.

Dick's Cafe

14 E. St. George Blvd. ☎ **801/673-3841.** Reservations required for groups and on holidays. Main courses $4.50–$10.95; breakfast $2.50–$7; lunch $3.25–$5.95. AE, DISC, MC, V. Daily 6am–9:30pm. From I-15 take exit 8, head west on St. George Boulevard for about 11 blocks and the cafe will be on your left. SOUTHWESTERN/AMERICAN.

Dick's, which claims to be the oldest eating establishment in St. George, opened in 1935. It's the sort of place you would expect to find in the Old West: a funky hometown cafe, with a long counter plus booths and tables, and regulars who specialize in drinking pots of coffee and swapping lies. You can get breakfast all day; all the American standards are available, plus a few spicy Mexican dishes that will really open your eyes. Lunches include sandwiches and burgers, salads and some other healthy stuff, and luncheon plates such as fresh roast turkey or liver and onions. At dinner, you can get more of the roast turkey and liver and onions, plus steaks, roast beef, grilled halibut, and fish-and-chips. Fans of chicken fried steak say Dick's is about the best around. Pies are fresh-baked on the premises. Children's and seniors' menus are available. No alcohol is served.

✪ Sullivan's Roccoco Steakhouse

511 S. Airport Rd. ☎ **801/673-3305.** Reservations accepted. Main courses $6.95–$25.95; lunch $3.50–$7.95. AE, DISC, MC, V. Mon–Fri 11am–10pm, Sat–Sun 5–10pm. From I-15, take exit 8, head west on St. George Boulevard to Bluff Street, cross over onto Airport Road, which immediately turns to the left and climbs the bluff; follow Airport Road to the restaurant. STEAK/SEAFOOD.

Excellent beef and the best views from any St. George restaurant make Sullivan's a great spot for special occasions. Sitting on a bluff overlooking the city, large glass windows take full advantage of a spectacular panorama of the city and surrounding red rock formations, especially as the sun begins to set and the city lights begin to twinkle below. Generous portions of prime rib and a variety of steaks are king here; the Roccoco is also considered the best spot in southwest Utah for lobster. All baking is done in-house, so try to save some room for a piece of pie—the shredded apple with caramel sauce and ice cream is spectacular. Those dropping by for lunch can choose from several sandwiches, including an extra special prime rib sandwich, burgers, and salads. The restaurant has full liquor service.

Tom's Delicatessen

175 West 900 S. Bluff. ☎ **801/628-1822.** Sandwiches $3.69–$6.19. MC, V. Tues–Sat 11am–6pm. From I-15, take exit 8, head west on St. George Boulevard to Bluff Street and turn left (south) for about two blocks. DELI.

Hidden in a narrow storefront in a small shopping center next to the Holiday Inn, Tom's quietly goes about its business of creating tasty, filling sandwiches. A St. George institution since 1978, Tom's offers 16 hot and 21 cold selections—just about all the basics: roast beef, turkey, pastrami. You can eat yours at one of the Formica tables along the wall, or carry it out for a picnic. No alcohol is served.

ST. GEORGE AFTER DARK

St. George, with its large non-drinking Mormon population, isn't one of the West's hot spots as far as the bar scene is concerned. Locals going out on the town will often attend a performing arts event (see below), and then stop in for a nightcap at one of the local restaurants that serves alcohol, such as Sullivan's Roccoco Steakhouse or Basila's Greek & Italian Cafe (see "Where to Dine," above). Keep in mind that these are not private clubs, so you'll need to buy something to eat in order to purchase a drink.

The Dixie Center, 425 S. 700 East (☎ 801/628-7003), is St. George's primary performing arts venue. The four-building complex hosts a wide range of events, from country and rock music to symphony, ballet, opera, and even sports.

Dixie College, 225 S. 700 East (☎ 801/673-4811), offers a variety of events throughout the school year. The Celebrity Concert Series, each October through April, has developed a strong following for programs such as *The Nutcracker* by the Nevada Dance Theatre, Ballet Hispanico, the BYU Folk Dance Ensemble, Joe Muscolino Little Big Band, the Utah Symphony Orchestra, and other solo and ensemble performers. Not to be outdone, the college's drama department offers its own series of five productions each year. There's usually a major musical in February; other productions will likely include dramas, comedies, a children's production, maybe even a Greek tragedy. Admission to college productions usually costs between $5 and $12 per person, and performances are presented at one of two theaters at the **College's Graff Fine Arts Center.** Call the box office (☎ 801/652-7800) to find out what's scheduled during your visit.

Music lovers will enjoy St. George's own **Southwest Symphonic Chorale and Southwest Symphony** (☎ 801/673-0700), the only full symphony orchestra between Provo and Las Vegas. Their repertoire includes classical, opera, and popular music. You'll want to get tickets early for the annual Christmas performance of Handel's *Messiah,* performed with the Dixie College Concert Choir, which usually sells out. Concerts are scheduled from October through early June, and tickets are in the $5 to $7 range.

The **St. George Tabernacle** (☎ 801/628-4072) presents free weekly concerts in a beautiful setting; see "Discovering Mormon History In & Around St. George," above, for further details.

For a spectacular outdoor musical drama that blends history, songs, drama, and dynamite special effects, take the short trip from St. George to the **Tuacahn Amphitheater & Center for the Arts,** 1100 Tuacahn Dr., Ivins (☎ 801/674-0012 or 800/746-9882 box office; fax 801/652-3227). Presented Monday through Saturday evenings at 8:30pm from mid-June through early October, ✪ *Utah!* depicts the settling of southern Utah by Mormon pioneers, particularly the life of Jacob Hamblin, known for his peacekeeping efforts with the Native Americans of the area. The musical, with live vocals but recorded instrumental accompaniment, comes to life with its state-of-the-art sound system and special effects, including lightning, a gigantic flood, and dazzling fireworks for the finale. Reservations are recommended. Tickets cost $14.50–$24.50 for adults, $9–$16 for children under 12. Free pre-show entertainment and backstage tours are offered, and Dutch oven dinners are served at $9 for adults and $7 for children under 12; call for details.

3 Enjoying the Outdoors Around Cedar City: Cedar Breaks National Monument & the Southern Ski Resorts

This is a great little area, home to some unheralded—and uncrowded—natural gems. Cedar Breaks National Monument is like a mini Bryce Canyon, a stunning multi-colored amphitheater of stone, with great hiking trails, camping, and a plateau ablaze with wildflowers in the summer. Brian Head is Utah's southernmost ski resort, but because it has the highest base elevation of any of the state's ski areas, it gets about 400 inches of powder each winter. Where else but southern Utah can you be on the links in the morning and on the slopes in the afternoon? And because Brian Head— and Elk Meadows Ski Resort, a bit farther afield—are off the average skier's beaten track, lift lines are usually nonexistent.

But this area is more than an outdoor playland—with Iron Mission State Park and the nationally renowned Shakespearean Festival, Cedar City happens to be a great place to step back in time. Even if the past isn't your thing, you'll probably end up in Cedar City anyway—it's where almost all the area's accommodations and restaurants are.

BASING YOURSELF IN CEDAR CITY

Since there are no lodging or dining facilities at Cedar Breaks National Monument, you'll have to stay here. If you're here to ski and you'd like to save money on accommodations, skip Brian Head's relatively pricey condos and stay in town. You can head to the slopes in the morning—it's only 28 miles to Brian Head (but beware: it can be a mean 28 miles when the weather's bad). Even if you choose to stay at one of Brian Head's relatively pricey condos, you'll be heading into town to eat. In addition to what we've mentioned below, you'll find a good selection of motels, restaurants, campgrounds, gas stations, grocery stores, and other services on I-15 at exits 57, 59, and 62.

ESSENTIALS

Getting There   Cedar City is just off I-15, 53 miles northeast of St. George and 251 miles southwest of Salt Lake City.

Delta/Skywest Airlines (☎ 800/453-9417) and **Pacific Air West Airlines** (☎ 801/674-0096 or 800/729-7229) fly into Cedar City Airport (☎ 801/586-3033).

Information   Contact the **Iron County Tourism and Convention Bureau,** 286 N. Main St. (P.O. Box 1007), Cedar City, UT 84720 (☎ 801/586-5124 or 800/354-4849).

Car Rentals   Car-rental agencies at the Cedar City Airport include **Alamo** (☎ 800/327-9633), **Avis** (☎ 800/831-2847) and **National** (☎ 801/586-7059 or 800/227-7368).

Fast Facts   The hospital serving this area is Cedar City's **Valley View Medical Center,** 595 S. 75 East, Cedar City (☎ 801/586-6587).

WHERE TO STAY & DINE

Popular chain and franchise motels in Cedar City include the **Best Western El Rey Inn,** 80 S. Main St., Cedar City, UT 84720 (☎ 801/586-6518 or 800/528-1234), with rates of $48–$70 for two in the winter and $60–$78 in the summer; and **Quality Inn,** 18 S. Main St., Cedar City, UT 84720 (☎ 801/586-2433 or 800/228-5151), charging $43–$68 in the winter and $68–$78 in the summer for two. Room tax adds about 9% to lodging bills.

The **Cedar City KOA Campground,** 1121 N. Main St., Cedar City, UT (☎ 801/586-9872), is open year-round, and charges $15–$20 per site.

Cedar City eateries include **Brad's Food Hut,** 546 N. Main St. (☎ 801/586-6358), an attractive, independent fast-food restaurant offering sandwiches, burgers, and ice cream in the $1–$4 range for lunch and dinner; and the locally recommended **Milt's Stage Stop,** 5 miles east of Cedar City on Utah 14 (☎ 801/586-9344), serving steak and seafood for dinner only, from $12–$32, with complete liquor service.

A BRIEF LOOK AT CEDAR CITY'S PIONEER PAST: IRON MISSION STATE PARK

If you're into the horse-drawn wagons of the past, this is the place for you. Essentially a local museum, Iron Mission has several dozen wagons and horse-drawn sleighs on display. In addition to all the usual buckboards, a bullet-scarred Old West stagecoach, and elaborate, for-the-very-very-rich-only coaches, you'll see an original Studebaker White Top Wagon (predecessor of the present-day station wagon), and several hearses. (You might be interested to learn—we were—that black hearses drawn by black horses were used only for deceased adults—white hearses pulled by white horses were reserved for children.) In addition to the wagon collection, there are Native American and pioneer artifacts from the region, and a diorama depicting the 1850s iron furnace and equipment for which the park is named. Periodically, demonstrations of pioneer crafts, such as weaving, spinning, candlemaking, cooking, and toy-making, are held.

Iron Mission State Park (☎ 801/586-6290) is located in downtown Cedar City at 585 N. Main Street. Admission is $1.50 adults, $1 for kids 6 to 16, and free for children under 6; the whole family can get in for $6. It's open daily from 9am to 7pm from Memorial Day to Labor Day, to 5pm at other times of the year; the park is closed Thanksgiving, Christmas, and New Year's Day.

CEDAR BREAKS NATIONAL MONUMENT

This is a great little park. It's a wonderful place to spend a few hours, or even several days gazing down from the rim into the spectacular natural amphitheater, hiking the trails, and camping among the spruce, firs, and the wildflowers that blanket the plateau in the summer.

This natural coliseum, which reminds us of Bryce Canyon, is more than 2,000 feet deep and over 3 miles across; it's filled with stone spires, arches, and columns shaped by the forces of erosion and painted in everchanging reds, purples, oranges, and ochres. But why "Cedar Breaks?" Well, the pioneers who came here called such badlands "breaks," and they mistook the juniper trees along the cliff bases for cedars.

JUST THE FACTS

At over 10,000 feet elevation, it's always pleasantly cool at Cedar Breaks. It actually gets downright cold at night, so take a jacket or sweater, even if the temperature is scorching just down the road in St. George. The monument opens for its short

Renaissance Pleasures on the Colorado Plateau: The Utah Shakespearean Festival

As you would expect, Southern Utah is no hotbed of cultural activity—most of the year, that is. But when the summer rolls around, all that changes: Humble Cedar City becomes home to Utah's premier theater event, the **Utah Shakespearean Festival.** The Bard's plays have been professionally staged in this unlikely setting since 1962, and the festival has been going strong and getting better ever since.

If you're going to be anywhere near Cedar City between mid-June and early September, it's well worth working one of the season's productions—four plays by Shakespeare, plus two others are staged every year—into your travel plans. They're presented with top actors in true Elizabethan style, in an open-air replica of the original Globe Theatre, with musicians trained in the music of the Renaissance. (If it rains, productions are moved into the adjacent enclosed theater.) At press time, productions scheduled for the 1996 season were *Henry IV, Macbeth, The Comedy of Errors,* and *The Winter's Tale,* plus *The Mikado* by Gilbert and Sullivan and Alexandre Dumas' *The Three Musketeers.*

The festival is held on the Southern Utah University campus at 351 W. Center St., Cedar City, UT 84720. At this writing, ticket prices for the 1996 season range from $19 to $27 for evening performances, $10 to $27 for matinees. For tickets and information, call **801/586-7878** or 800/PLAYTIX.

And the plays are only part of the fun. "Royal Feastes," complete with medieval entertainment and winsome serving wenches, are held several evenings each week in festival season; the Elizabethan-style prix fixe is $27 per person. Backstage tours are offered Tuesdays through Saturdays for $6 per person. A variety of other programs, such as literary seminars, special workshops, and other entertainments are held during the season; call for further details.

summer season only after the snow melts, usually in late May, and closes in October—unless you happen to have a pair of cross-country skis or a snowmobile, in which case you can visit year-round.

Getting There   Cedar Breaks National Monument is 21 miles east of Cedar City, 56 miles west of Bryce Canyon National Park, and 247 miles south of Salt Lake City.

From I-15, drive east of Cedar City on Utah 14 to Utah 148, turn north (left), and follow Utah 148 into the monument. If you're coming from Bryce Canyon or other points east, the park is accessible from the town of Panguitch via Utah 143. If you're coming from the north, take the Parowan exit off I-15 and head south on Utah 143. It's a steep climb from whichever direction you choose, and vehicles prone to vapor lock or loss of power on hills (such as motorhomes) may have some problems.

Information & Visitor Centers   One mile from the south entrance gate is the visitor center, open daily June to Labor Day, with exhibits on the geology, flora, and fauna of Cedar Breaks. You can purchase books and maps there, and rangers can help plan your visit. For advance information, contact the Superintendent, **Cedar Breaks National Monument,** P.O. Box 749, Cedar Breaks, UT 84720 (☎ 801/586-9451).

Fees & Regulations   Admission is $4 per vehicle or $2 per person on foot, bike, or motorcycle; there is no charge for those passing through the park on Utah 143.

Regulations are similar to most national parks: Leave everything pretty much as you found it. Mountainbikes are not allowed on hiking trails. Dogs, which must be leashed at all times, are prohibited on all trails, in the backcountry, and in public buildings.

Health & Safety Concerns   The high elevation—10,350 feet at the visitor center—is likely to cause shortness of breath and tiredness, and those with heart or respiratory conditions should probably consult their doctors before making the trip to Cedar Breaks. You should avoid overlooks and other high, exposed areas during thunderstorms; they're often targets for lightning.

Ranger Programs   During the monument's short summer season, rangers offer nightly campfire talks at the campground; talks on the area's geology at Point Supreme, a viewpoint near the visitor center, on weekday mornings at 10am; and guided hikes on Saturday and Sunday mornings. A complete schedule is posted at the visitor center and the campground.

EXPLORING CEDAR BREAKS BY CAR

The 5-mile road through Cedar Breaks National Monument offers easy access to the monument's scenic overlooks and trailheads. Allow 30 to 45 minutes to make the drive. Start at the visitor center and nearby **Point Supreme** for a panoramic view of the amphitheater. Then drive north, past the campground and picnic ground turn-off, to **Sunset View** for a closer view of the amphitheater and its colorful canyons. From each of these overlooks you'll be able to see out across Cedar Valley, over the Antelope and Black Mountains, into the Escalante Desert.

Continue north to **Chessman Ridge Overlook,** so named because the hoodoos directly below the overlook look like massive stone chess pieces. Watch for swallows and swifts soaring among the rock formations. Get back into the car and head north to **Alpine Pond,** a trailhead for a self-guided nature trail (see "Hiking," below) with an abundance of wildflowers. Finally, you'll reach **North View,** which offers you perhaps your best look into the amphitheater. The view here is reminiscent of Bryce Canyon's Queen's Garden, with its stately statues frozen in time.

A LATE SUMMER BONANZA: THE WILDFLOWERS OF CEDAR BREAKS

During its brief summer season, Cedar Breaks makes the most of the warmth and moisture in the air with a spectacular wildflower show. The rim comes alive in a blaze of color, and it's truly a sight to behold. The dazzling display begins practically as soon as the snow melts, and reaches its peak during late July and August. It's as though the flowers were trying to outshine the colorful rocks below. Watch for mountain bluebells, spring beauty, beardtongue, and fleabane early in the season; those beauties then make way for columbine, larkspur, Indian paintbrush, wild roses, and other varieties.

WARM-WEATHER SPORTS & ACTIVITIES

Hiking   There are no trails from the rim to the bottom of the amphitheater, but the monument has two high country trails. The fairly easy 2-mile **Alpine Pond Trail** loop leads to a picturesque forest glade and pond surrounded by wildflowers and through a woodlands of bristlecone pines, offering panoramic views of the amphitheater along the way. A trail guide is available at the trailhead.

A somewhat more challenging hike, the 4-mile **Spectra Point Trail** (also called the Rampart Trail) follows the rim more closely than the Alpine Pond Trail, offering changing views of the colorful rock formations. It also takes you through fields of wildflowers and by bristlecone pines more than 1,500 years old. You'll need to be especially careful of your footing along the exposed cliff edges, and allow yourself some time to rest—there are lots of ups and downs along the way.

Wildlife Watching   Because of its relative remoteness, Cedar Breaks is a good place for spotting wildlife. You're likely to see mule deer, the monument's largest animals, grazing in the meadows along the road early and late in the day. Marmots make their dens near the rim, and are often seen along the Spectra Point Trail. You'll spot ground squirrels, red squirrels, and chipmunks everywhere; pikas, which are related to rabbits, are here too, but it's unlikely you'll see one. They're small, with short ears and stubby tails, and prefer the high, rocky slopes.

Birders should have no trouble spotting the Clark's nutcracker in the campground, with its gray torso and black-and-white wings and tail. The monument is also home to swallows, swifts, blue grouse, and both golden and bald eagles.

CAMPING

The ✪ **30-site campground,** just north of the visitor center, is open from June to mid-September, with sites available on a first-come, first-served basis. It's a beautiful high-mountain setting, among tall ponderosa pines and firs. There are restrooms, drinking water, picnic tables, grills, and an amphitheater for the ranger's evening campfire programs. There are no showers or RV hookups. Keep in mind that, even in mid-summer, temperatures can drop into the 30s at night at this elevation, so bring cool-weather gear.

WINTER SPORTS & ACTIVITIES

The monument is essentially shut down from late October through mid-May because of the blanket of deep snow that covers it. The snow-blocked roads will keep cars out, but they're perfect for snowmobilers and cross-country skiers, who usually come over from nearby Brian Head ski area (see below). Keep in mind, though, that all facilities are closed and the only people you're likely to see will be an occasional park ranger, patrolling on a snowmobile.

HITTING THE SLOPES IN UTAH'S DIXIE

Like the ski areas in the Ogden and Logan areas, Southwest Utah's ski resorts, Brian Head and Elk Meadows, keep their energies focused on terrain and snow; they don't have the amenities you'll find in Park City, Deer Valley, and Snowbird. In the summer, mountainbikers converge on Brian Head to make the most of the slopes.

BRIAN HEAD RESORT

Brian Head has the distinction of being Utah's southernmost ski resort, just a short drive from the year-round shirt-sleeve warmth of St. George. But with the highest base elevation of any of the state's ski areas, it gets an average of 400 inches of powdery snow each winter. Its location makes it particularly popular with skiers from the Las Vegas area and Southern California.

Brian Head is known for its variety of terrain, especially since snow-cat service to the top of Brian Head Peak (elevation 11,307 feet) started in the 1995–96 season, offering spectacular advanced terrain for the adventurous. Intermediates have fine cruising runs a little further down the mountain. There's also a good learning hill, Navajo Peak, for beginners. Another plus of Brian Head is the scenery: The only ski resort in Utah's famed red rock country, it offers stunning views, especially from the tops of the lifts.

Snowboarders are welcome at Brian Head; there are two snowboarding parks just for them.

Just the Facts

Brian Head Resort (Brian Head, UT 84719; ☎ 801/677-2035, 800/272-7426 for lodging and snow conditions) has one double and five triple chairlifts servicing 53 trails on 500 acres. The vertical drop is 1,707 feet, from a top elevation of 11,307 feet to a base of 9,600 feet. The highest elevations are serviced by snowcat. Terrain is rated as 30% beginner, 40% intermediate, and 30% advanced. Brian Head has snowmaking capabilities on 150 acres. The ski season generally runs from early November to late spring, with lifts operating daily from 9am to 4:30pm. On weekends and holidays, night skiing is available from 4:30 to 10pm.

Giant Steps Lodge, at the base of Brian Head Peak, and **Navajo Lodge,** at the base of Navajo Peak, offer ski shops with sales and rentals, ski school, and information services. Navajo Lodge also has arcade games. The closest hospital is in Cedar City (see "Basing Yourself in Cedar City," above).

Getting There   From Cedar City, it's 28 miles to Brian Head; take I-15 to exit 75 and head south on the very steep Utah 143 about 12 miles.

Lift Tickets   An adult all-day lift ticket is $32; a half-day ticket is $24. An all-day child's or senior's (those between 65 to 69) ticket is $20; seniors 70 and up ski free. Night skiing is $10.

Lessons & Programs   The **ski school** at Brian Head offers private and group lessons, plus clinics, snowboard classes, and children's ski instruction. Adult group ski and snowboard lessons start at $20 for a half day. Private lessons start at $46 for an hour; lessons for children ages five and up start at $23. The adult learn-to-ski program, for ages 11 and up, has several options, with prices starting at $30.

Day care is available for an hourly rate of $5 for kids 2^1/$_2$ and older, $6.50 for infants and toddlers. There are also packages available combining day care and ski lessons.

Cross-Country Skiing   Brian Head has 42km of trails—10km of them groomed—rated 50% beginner, 30% intermediate, and 20% advanced. Lessons and rentals are available, and there's no charge for trail use.

Ice-Skating   From mid-December to early March, weather permitting, ice-skating is available at no charge at Navajo Lodge. Rentals are available.

Where to Dine

There are several places to get a quick breakfast or lunch at Brian Head, including the Navajo and Giant Steps Base Lodge Grilles, with meals in the $5 range. The Summit Dining Room at Brian Head Hotel offers fine dining nightly from 5pm to 10pm, with steaks, seafood, and pasta dishes in the $12 to $22 price range.

Where to Stay

The Brian Head area offers a variety of lodging possibilities, mostly condos, with rates ranging from just less than $100 to about $400 per night. Contact **Brian Head Resort Central Reservations** (☎ 801/677-3000 or 800/272-7426). Room tax here is about 10%. You can also stay in Cedar City, 28 miles away (see "Basing Yourself in Cedar City," above).

Warm-Weather Activities

Once the snow melts, mountainbikers, hikers, and horseback riders claim the mountain. With elevations ranging from 9,700 feet to 11,307 feet, Brian Head is always cool, crisp, and just perfect for working up a sweat. Evenings are busy too, with live musical entertainment ranging from jazz and country to bluegrass and classical; there's even an occasional bagpipe.

Mountainbiking   This ski resort isn't just for skiers anymore. It's fast becoming a major destination for serious—and we do mean serious—mountainbikers. This a wonderful place for mountainbiking, with endless trails, superb scenery, and about the freshest air you're going to find. What's more, they make it oh-so-very easy: A mountainbike chairlift hauls you and your bike up the mountain; it's about $12 for a full-day pass. Or, for about $10, you can take a shuttle to and from several locations. That way, you can pedal the fun parts, and travel under someone else's power for the steeper sections.

If you didn't bring your own, mountainbike rentals are available for about $25 per day for adults, $20 for kids 12 and younger. Contact **Bike Brian Head** at 801/ 677-2035.

Horseback Riding   If those newfangled bikes with all those gears are too much for you, make your saddle the western kind, and do your traveling on the back of a sure-footed horse. High Adventure Trail Rides (☎ 801/559-2362) offers guided trail rides starting at $15 for an hour, $70 for all day.

ELK MEADOWS RESORT

This is an excellent ski area for families. Elk Meadows has a well-respected program for beginners; they even get their own mountain. Of course, they won't stay beginners long, which is good—Elk Meadows rates over 60% of its terrain as intermediate, the most of any Utah ski area. Its high base elevation, second only to Brian Head, helps guarantee plenty of powder snow; and its location—somewhat off the beaten track—means that lift lines are practically nonexistent. In addition to its designated runs, there's off-trail skiing. Snowboarders are allowed on the hill.

Just the Facts

Elk Meadows Resort (P.O. Box 511, Beaver, UT 84713; ☎ 801/438-5433 or 800/ 248-7669) has a vertical drop of 1,300 feet from a top elevation of 10,400 feet to a base of 9,100 feet. There are five lifts—two doubles, one triple, a T-bar, and a poma—servicing 30 runs on 200 acres. The terrain is rated as 14% beginner, 62% intermediate, and 24% advanced. Elk Meadows receives about 400 inches of snow each year and has no snowmaking capabilities. The season generally runs from early December to mid-April, with lifts operating from 9am to 4pm daily.

A day lodge has a ski shop with rental equipment and a general store. The closest hospital is **Beaver Valley Hospital,** at 85 North 400 East, in Beaver (☎ 801/ 438-2531).

Getting There   From Cedar City, it's about 70 miles to Elk Meadows. From I-15, take exit 109 or 112 to Beaver, and head east on Utah 153 about 20 miles.

Lift Tickets   An all-day adult lift ticket is $25; a half-day ticket costs $18; an all-day child's ticket is $15; seniors 65 and older ski free.

Lessons & Programs   The **ski school** has what is considered to be one of the best learn-to-ski programs in the state, and offers downhill, Nordic, and snowboarding lessons. Private lessons start at $30 per hour, and group lessons start at $18 for 2 hours.

Cross-Country Skiing   There are some fine Nordic trails at the resort and heading off into the national forest. Cross-country skiers who use the lifts buy a regular pass; those who don't use the lifts ski free.

Where to Stay & Dine

Condominiums of one, two, and three bedrooms are available, all with full kitchen and either a fireplace or wood-burning stove. Rates vary: a one-bedroom one-bath unit runs from $105 to $130, although rates are considerably lower mid-week and considerably higher during the Christmas holiday period. Call 801/438-5433 or 800/248-7669 for particulars. The resort also has a restaurant, a cafeteria, and a lounge. Room tax of about 9% is added to your bill.

4 The *Real* Dodge City: Kanab

Another southern Utah town founded by Mormon pioneers sent here by Brigham Young in the 1870s, Kanab is best known for its starring role in the movies and TV. This is the Wild West many of us grew up with, on shows like *Gunsmoke, The Lone Ranger, Death Valley Days,* and *F Troop*; and in *She Wore a Yellow Ribbon, Sergeants Three, Bandolero,* and *The Outlaw Josie Wales* on the big screen. You can see some of the buildings and most of the scenery from these films and shows, including the Johnson Canyon movie set where *Gunsmoke* was shot for some 20 years.

But Kanab does more than live on Old West memories; it serves as a stopping point for travelers on their way to southern Utah's major sights. Travelers coming from Arizona are likely to pass through on their way to Zion and Bryce Canyon. If you're starting your Lake Powell trip in Page, Arizona, you'll probably come through Kanab. And the Grand Canyon is directly to the south, so if you're heading to the north rim, you'll come right through. None of these natural wonders are all that close to Kanab, but in Utah terms, they're "just around the corner."

ESSENTIALS
GETTING THERE
Kanab is 82 miles east of St. George, 80 miles south of Bryce Canyon National Park, 42 miles east of Zion National Park, 68 miles west of Lake Powell and Glen Canyon Recreation Area, 79 miles north of the Grand Canyon, and 303 miles south of Salt Lake City.

By Car   Kanab is located on U.S. 89 at the junction of U.S. 89A, which crosses into Arizona just 7 miles south of town.

VISITOR INFORMATION
Contact the **Kane County Visitors Center,** 78 S. 100 East, Kanab, UT 84741 (☎ 801/644-5033 or 800/SEE-KANE).

Getting Around   If you don't drive to Kanab, you'll need to rent a car when you get here. Car rentals, including four-wheel-drives, minivans, and RVs, are available from Hunt's Rentals (☎ 801/644-2370).

Kanab is pretty easy to get a handle on. Ground zero is where Center and Main streets intersect. U.S. 89 comes in from the north on 300 West Street, turns east onto Center Street, south again on 100 East Street, and finally east again on 300 South. U.S. 89A follows 100 East Street south to the airport and, after about 7 miles, Arizona.

Fast Facts   The **Kane County Hospital & Skilled Nursing Facility** is at 220 W. 300 North St. (☎ 801/644-5811). The **post office** is at 39 S. Main St. (☎ 801/644-2760). In an **emergency,** call 801/644-2667 if you're outside of town; otherwise use 911.

CORAL PINK SAND DUNES STATE PARK
Long a favorite for dune buggy enthusiasts (off-road vehicle users lobbied hard to have this designated a state park), Coral Pink Sand Dunes has recently been attracting an

increasing number of campers, hikers, photographers, and all-around nature-lovers as well. While Big Boys—and occasionally Big Girls—play with their expensive motorized toys, others hike, hunt for wildflowers, scorpions, and lizards, or just sit and wiggle their toes in the smooth, cool sand. The colors are especially rich at sunrise and sunset. Early-morning visitors to the dunes will find the tracks of yesterday's dune buggies gone, replaced by the tracks of lizards, kangaroo rats, snakes, and the rest of the park's animal kingdom, which ventures out in the coolness of night once all the people have gone home.

JUST THE FACTS

Getting There   From downtown Kanab, go about 8 miles north on U.S. 89, then southwest (left) on Hancock Road for about 12 miles to the park.

Information & Visitor Centers   For copies of the park brochure and off-highway vehicle regulations, contact the **park office** at P.O. Box 95, Kanab, UT 84741-0095 (☎ 801/874-2408). At the **park entry station** there's a small display area with sand from around the world, fossils of the area, and live scorpions, lizards, and tadpoles.

Fees & Regulations   The day-use fee is $3 per vehicle for up to eight people. The standard state park regulations apply here, plus a few extra because of the park's popularity with off-road vehicle users: Quiet hours last from 10pm to 9am, a bit later in the morning than in most parks. The dunes are open to hikers anytime, but to motor vehicles only between 9am and 10pm. Vehicles going onto the dunes must have safety flags, available at the entry station; and vehicles on the dunes must stay at least 10 feet from vegetation and at least 100 feet from hikers. Dogs are permitted on the dunes but must be leashed.

Ranger Programs   Regularly scheduled ranger talks explain the geology, plants, and animals of the dunes. For a real thrill, take a guided evening **Scorpion Walk,** using a black light to find luminescent scorpions that make the park their home. You'll definitely want to wear shoes for this activity! Call to find out if there's one scheduled at the time you'll be in Kanab.

SPORTS & ACTIVITIES

Four-Wheeling   This giant 1,000-acre sandbox offers plenty of space for off-road–vehicle enthusiasts, who can race up and down the dunes, stopping to perch on a crest to watch the setting sun. Because the sand here is quite fine, extra wide flotation tires are needed, and lightweight dune buggies are usually the vehicle of choice. Adjacent to the park, there are hundreds of miles of trails and roads for off-highway–vehicles on Bureau of Land Management property.

Hiking   The best time for ✪ **hiking the dunes** is early morning, for several reasons: It's cooler, the lighting at and just after sunrise produces beautiful shadows and colors, and there are no noisy dune buggies until after 9am. Sunset is also very pretty, but you'll be sharing the dunes with off-road vehicles. Keep in mind that hiking through fine sand can be very tiring, especially for those of us who insist on hiking barefoot. A self-guided half-mile loop nature trail has numbered signs through some of the dunes; allow a half hour for it.

Several other good hikes of various lengths are possible within and just outside the park, but because there are few signs, and landmarks change with the shifting sands, it's best to check with park rangers before setting out. Those spending more than a few hours in the dunes will discover that even their own tracks disappear in the wind, leaving few clues to the route back to park headquarters.

CAMPING

The spacious and mostly shady 22-site campground, open all year, has hot showers, modern restrooms, and an RV dump station, but no hookups. Camping costs $9 Sunday through Thursday nights, and $10 on Fridays, Saturdays, and holidays. Call 800/322-3770 for reservations, for an additional $5 reservation fee per site.

MORE TO SEE & DO IN & AROUND KANAB

✪ Heritage House

At 100 South and Main streets, Kanab. ☎ **801/644-2381.** Adults 50¢, children 12 and under free. May–Sept Mon–Fri 9:30am–5pm, or call for an appointment. From the intersection of Center and Main streets, head south one block.

Although there are 16 historic houses in the downtown area of Kanab, this is the only one open to the public. Built in 1894, this Victorian was purchased by Thomas H. Chamberlain in 1896. (Chamberlain's sixth wife, Mary, was elected mayor of Kanab in 1912.) Purchased by the city in 1974, the house has been restored to its original appearance. The guided tour of the property can take anywhere from a half hour to 2 hours, depending on your available time and level of interest.

A booklet describing all of Kanab's historic houses, and a map showing their locations, is for sale for $4.

Johnson Canyon Movie Set

☎ **801/644-3187.** Guided tours $3 adults, children under 18 free. Daily dawn–dusk. From Kanab, go 9 miles east on U.S. 89, turn north into Johnson Canyon and go about 5¹/₂ miles; watch for sign.

It's not hard to imagine Marshall Dillon in a shoot-out in the dusty street, Miss Kitty serving up a stiff shot of whisky in the Long Branch Saloon, and Doc tending to the wounded wherever they fell. As the set for the television show *Gunsmoke* for some 20 years, many of us feel like we grew up on these streets. Although a bit worse for wear and neglect, the town is being restored by Max Bertola and his family, who offer lively tours year-round. You'll see the weathered saloon, Doc's office, the livery stable, and the blacksmith shop from *Gunsmoke;* and other buildings constructed for the numerous full-length films shot here, including the 1952 Robert Taylor hit *Westward the Women,* and the 1979 epic *How the West Was Won,* which brought *Gunsmoke's* James Arness back home to co-star with Eva-Marie Saint.

Mock gunfights and genuine Dutch oven dinners were planned for 1996; call to see what's going on when.

Moqui Cave

On the north side of U.S. 89, about 5.5 miles north of Kanab. ☎ **801/644-2987.** Admission $3.50 adults, $3 seniors, $2.50 youths 13–17, $1.50 children 6–12. Memorial Day–Labor Day Mon–Sat 9am–7pm, spring and fall Mon–Sat 9am–6pm. Closed mid-Oct to Apr.

Native Americans known as the Moqui are believed to have spent time in this cave 800 to 900 years ago. Times have changed since then, and so has the cave; the Moqui would be amazed at what they would find here today. The Chamberlain family, descendants of Thomas and Mary Chamberlain (see Heritage House, above), bought the cave in 1951, and the following year opened a tavern and dance hall in it. Although you can't order a drink today, the unique bar is still there, along with a huge collection that ranges from authentic dinosaur tracks more than 140 million years old to a beautiful fluorescent mineral display. You'll also see Native American pottery, spear points, and other art and artifacts. There's a large gift shop, too, that specializes in Native American arts and crafts.

Can't Make it to the Grand Canyon?
Get a Bird's-Eye View

You're so close to the Grand Canyon. There it is, beckoning you over the state line into Arizona. You'd love to see it, but you've got other plans—maybe you're on your way to Zion National Park or Lake Powell and Glen Canyon National Recreation Area. And there's already so much to see and do! Well, you're in luck. Several companies offer tours of the canyon by air. **Cowboy Aviation** (☎ 801/644-2299) has flights from Kanab Airport starting from about $80 per person.

If you're heading to Lake Powell and you don't have time to stop and take a flight from Kanab, don't despair—you can get a bird's-eye view of the canyon from Page, Arizona, the lake's major access point. **Scenic Airlines** (☎ 702/739-1900 or 800/634-6801) offers combination air tours over the Grand Canyon's north rim, as well as Bryce Canyon and Zion National Parks. Tours, which leave from Page and other cities, are given year-round, with prices starting at $275 for adults and $225 for children.

WHERE TO STAY

Kanab offers a nice range of lodging choices. In addition to the properties described below, Kanab has a **Super 8 Motel,** 70 S. 200 West, Kanab, UT 84741 (☎ 801/644-5500 or 800/800/8000, fax 801/644-5576), with rates for two of $60.88–$64.88 in the summer and $40.88–$52.88 the rest of the year.

Room tax adds about 10% to lodging bills. Pets are not accepted unless otherwise noted.

Best Western Red Hills

125 W. Center St., Kanab, UT 84741. ☎ **801/644-2625** or 800/830-2675. Fax 801/644-5915. 72 rms. A/C TV TEL. Mid-Apr–mid-May $64 double; mid-May–Oct $76 double; Nov–mid-Apr $49 double. AE, CB, DC, DISC, MC, V.

Spacious rooms and baths at this well-kept Best Western are made to feel even bigger because of their beige walls and light wood-grained furnishings. Rooms have two queen- or one king-sized bed, and all king rooms have refrigerators. Framed photos highlight the area's scenery. VCRs are available, and there's an outdoor heated swimming pool, whirlpool, and sundeck. Free coffee and tea are available in the lobby.

Holiday Inn Express

815 East U.S. 89, Kanab, UT 84741. ☎ **801/644-8888** or 800/HOLIDAY. Fax 801/644-8880. 68 rms. A/C TV TEL. May–mid-Nov $69–$84 double, mid-Nov–Apr $49–$64 double (including breakfast bar). AE, DISC, MC, V.

This is the place for golfers. Adjacent to the 9-hole Coral Cliffs Golf Course, this comfortable three-story motel, built in mid-1994, has a relaxed western atmosphere. One golf pass per day is included in the price of the rooms, all of which have good views. Most have two queen-sized beds, although there are a few with a king and a comfortable recliner. The rooms and lobby are decorated with photos of southern Utah attractions. There's a heated outdoor pool, a whirlpool, self-service laundry, and a gift shop.

Nine Gables Inn Bed & Breakfast

106 W. 100 North, Kanab, UT 84741.☎ **801/644-5079.** 4 rms. A/C. $70–$80. Rates include full breakfast. Closed mid-Oct–mid-May. MC, V.

This stately white brick home, built in 1872, is considered to be Kanab's first permanent residence. Today, its four guest rooms offer not only an attractive alternative to the standard motel but also a glimpse into southern Utah's past. All rooms have private baths with showers only, not tubs (which is somewhat ironic, since this house was the first in town to have a bath tub). The house is furnished with owners Frank and Jeanne Bantlin's family antiques, an eclectic collection from the late 1800s and early 1900s. There's one room on the first floor, with two twin beds. On the second floor, there's one room with one double and one twin-sized bed and a private balcony; one room with a queen-sized bed; and a third room with one queen-sized bed, a marvelous horsehair rocking chair, and private balcony.

The full breakfasts are homemade and include such innovative selections as fresh asparagus quiche. The Bantlins grow many of their own vegetables, and serve whatever fresh fruits are in season. Guests share a parlor with TV and VCR, and parking is off-street. If by chance you get a creative urge here, you won't be alone: Western writer Zane Grey reportedly stayed here while researching his novel *Riders of the Purple Sage*.

○ Parry Lodge

89 E. Center St. (U.S. 89), Kanab, UT 84741. ☎ **801/644-2601** or 800/748-4104. Fax 801/644-2605. 89 units. A/C TV TEL. Summer $46–$65 double, $73 family unit; winter $30–$46 double, $54 family unit. AE, DISC, MC, V.

This is the place where the stars stayed—Frank Sinatra, Dean Martin, John Wayne, Roddy McDowell, James Garner, and Ronald Reagan, to name just a few—when they were filming in Kanab. In 1931, Chauncey Parry decided to open a motel for the film people who were coming to town regularly. The lodge has a colonial atmosphere, with two chandeliers from Paris in the lobby, and photos of movie stars scattered about the public areas. The original rooms, which make up about one-third of the total number, each have the name of a movie star who stayed there above the door. The newer rooms date from the 1970s, and are smaller than the original ones (though none are huge). A few of the units come with shower only, no tub. There's HBO, an outdoor heated pool, a laundromat, one unit with a kitchenette, and a gift shop open in the summer. Room service is available when the restaurant is open (see "Where to Dine," below). Both smoking and nonsmoking rooms are available, and pets are accepted for a $5 fee.

Shilo Inn

296 W. 100 North, Kanab, UT, 84741-3228. ☎ **801/644-2562** or 800/222-2244. Fax 801/644-5333. 68 units. A/C TV TEL. Summer $60–$72, winter $45–$55. Rates include continental breakfast. AE, DC, DISC, JCB, MC, V.

This attractive modern motel, with a southwestern flair, offers all mini-suites, with three phones in each, built-in hair dryers, microwave ovens, small refrigerators, and an above-average amount of storage space. The king rooms have a king-sized bed and a small hide-a-bed; rooms with two queen-sized beds seem a bit more crowded. The single queen-sized bedrooms seem plenty roomy. Rooms adjacent to the small outdoor pool can be a bit noisy, but the rest are very quiet. The motel also has a whirlpool, sundeck, gift shop, and conference rooms for up to 130. VCRs are available for rent ($7.95 per night), and movies are free. Pets are permitted with a $7 fee.

A CAMPGROUND & RV PARK

Kanab RV Corral

483 S. 100 East, U.S. 89A, Kanab, UT 84741. ☎ **801/644-5330.** 40 sites with hookups; 10–15 tent sites. $18 hookups; $13.50 tent. MC, V.

Open all year, this campground and RV park makes a good base camp for exploring this part of Utah. The sites are a bit close and you do get some highway noise; but the bath houses are exceptionally nice (with extra large shower stalls), the coin-operated laundry is kept spotless, and the small kidney-shaped pool is a lot of fun.

WHERE TO DINE

Houston's Trail's End Restaurant & Mobile Catering

32 E. Center St. ☎ **801/644-2488.** Main courses $7.90–$16.75; breakfast $3.25–$6.50; lunch $4.90–$7.25. AE, DISC, MC, V. Memorial Day–Labor Day daily 6am–10:30pm; Labor Day–Christmas and mid-Feb–Memorial Day daily 6am–9:30pm. Closed Christmas–mid-Feb. From the intersection of Center and Main Streets, head east on Center a short distance; the restaurant will be on your right. STEAK/SEAFOOD/MEXICAN.

Houston's offers a true western atmosphere, with historic photos and memorabilia displayed on wood-plank walls, and waitresses with "guns on their hips and smiles on their lips." Family-owned since 1975, the Houstons age their own beef and make their famous gravy fresh daily. For breakfast, you can choose among all the usual egg dishes, plus biscuits and gravy, and an especially hearty western omelet. Lunch is sandwiches and burgers, plus pork spare ribs, fish-and-chips, roast beef, and salads. For dinner, the rather darker steakhouse in the back is opened. Its computerized player piano adds to the Old West atmosphere created by flocked red wallpaper and neon designs of cowboy hats, boots, and brands. Houston's is best known for chicken-fried steak, but the rib eye is also popular. A children's menu is available. No alcohol is served.

Parry Lodge

89 E. Center St. ☎ **801/644-2601.** Reservations recommended for dinner. Main courses $7.50–$17.75; breakfast and lunch $2.95–$6.95. AE, DISC, MC, V. Summer daily 7am–10pm; early and late season daily 7am–noon, 6–10pm. Closed Nov–Easter. From the intersection of Center and Main streets, head east about a block; the lodge will be on your left. AMERICAN.

The restaurant at the Parry Lodge (see "Where to Stay," above) is Victorian in style, with photos of the many movie stars who have stayed and dined here covering the walls. The small but elegant main restaurant has only 14 tables, and these are a bit close, but there's plenty more seating and the same menu in the coffee shop. Most of the American standards are offered for breakfast, and lunches (served only in the summer) include burgers, sandwiches, and salads; plus chicken-fried steak and the house specialty, chicken and dumplings, for those looking for something more substantial.

For dinner, we highly recommend the boneless chicken with gravy, cranberry sauce, and the fresh, homemade, soft dumplings. Beef eaters should thoroughly enjoy the slow-cooked roast prime rib. Other dinner selections include poached salmon, grilled baby beef liver, deep-fried chicken, and several broiled steaks. Portions are large, and half portions of some dinner items are available at 20% off the menu price. All desserts are made daily in-house. Full liquor service is available.

⑤ Rose's Country Inn

625 E. 300 South, U.S. 89. ☎ **801/644-8144.** Reservations not accepted. Lunch and dinner $2.25–$8.95; breakfast $1.95–$6.95. MC, V. Daily 7am–10pm; closed Sun in the winter. From Center (U.S. 89) and Main streets, follow U.S. 89 as it turns right (south) onto 100 East for three blocks, and then turn left (east) onto 300 South; go about three blocks.

This is where locals come for real home cooking. The atmosphere is typical American cafe: red-and-white checked plastic tablecloths, paper placemats, and plastic "glasses." The room is small, with about a dozen tables. Breakfast selections include all the basics, including the "Trucker Special": an 8-ounce ham steak, eggs, home fries, and toast or biscuit, all for less than $4. The rest of the day, you can choose from about two dozen hot or cold sandwiches, homemade soup, several salads, and dinners such as roast sirloin, filet of sole, pork chops with apple sauce, or jumbo shrimp. The broiled 12-ounce New York steak for about $9 is especially good. No alcohol is served.

The Wok Inn

86 S. 200 West. ☎ **801/644-5400.** Main courses $5.95–$15.95, combo lunch plate special $3.95. AE, DISC, MC, V. April–Oct Mon–Fri 11:30am–10pm, Sat–Sun 3–10pm; call for winter hours. From the intersection of Center and Main Streets, head west on Center for two blocks and go left (south) onto 200 West for about a block. HUNAN/SZECHUAN/CHINESE.

The decor here is western steakhouse overlaid with Chinese lanterns, parasols, screens, and artwork. But there's no western influence in the food: It's strictly Chinese, prepared by Chinese chefs. The Moo Goo Gai Pan and Szechuan Pork (the special during our visit) were both good; the pork was spicy, but not too hot. Several items on the menu are marked hot, and reliable locals informed us they are to be believed! The chicken curry could have been spicier, but was tasty nonetheless. Full liquor service and children's portions are available.

12 Zion National Park

So named by Mormon pioneers because it seemed to be a bit of heaven on earth, Zion National Park casts a spell over you as you gaze upon its sheer multicolored walls of sandstone, explore its narrow canyons, hunt for hanging gardens of wildflowers, or listen to the roar of the churning, tumbling Virgin River.

It's easy to conjure up a single defining image of the Grand Canyon or the delicately sculpted rock hoodoos of Bryce, but Zion is more difficult to pin down, a collage of images and secrets. It's not simply the towering Great White Throne, deep Narrows Canyon, or cascading waterfalls and emerald green pools. There's an entire smorgasbord of experiences, sights, and even smells here, from massive stone sculptures and monuments to lush forests and rushing rivers. Take time to walk its trails, visit viewpoints at different times of the day to see the changing light, and let the park work its magic on you.

Because of its extremes of elevation (from 3,800 feet to almost 9,000 feet) and climate (with temperatures soaring over 100°F in the summer and a landscape carpeted with snow in the winter), Zion harbors a vast array of plants and animals. About 800 native species of plants have been found: cactus, yucca, and mesquite in the hot, dry desert areas; ponderosa pine trees on the high plateaus; and cottonwoods and box elders along the rivers and streams. Of the 14 varieties of cactus that grow in the park, watch for the red claret cup, which has spectacular blooms in the spring. Wildflowers common in the park include the manzanita, with its tiny pink blossoms; buttercups; and the bright red hummingbird trumpet. Dubbed the "Zion Lily" because of its abundance in the park, the sacred datura has large funnel-shaped white flowers that open in the cool of night and are often closed by noon.

While exploring Zion, be sure to watch for "spring lines" and their hanging gardens, which you'll see clinging to the sides of cliffs. Because sandstone is porous, water can percolate down through it until it is stopped by a layer of harder rock. Then the water simply changes direction, moving horizontally to the rock face, where it oozes out, forming the "spring line" that provides life-giving nutrients to whatever seeds the wind delivers.

Speaking of living things, Zion National Park is a veritable zoo, with mammals ranging from pocket gophers to mountain lions, hundreds of birds (including golden eagles), lizards of all shapes and

How Nature Painted Zion's Landscape

Zion National Park is many things to many people: a day-hike down a narrow canyon, a rugged climb up the face of a massive stone monument, or the quiet appreciation of the red glow of sunset over majestic peaks. But at least to some degree, each of these experiences is possible because of rocks—their formation, uplifting, shifting, breaking, and eroding. The most important of Zion's nine rock layers in creating its colorful formations is Navajo sandstone, the thickest rock layer in the park, at up to 2,200 feet. This formation was created some 200 million years ago, during the Jurassic period, when North America was hot and dry. Movements in the earth's crust caused a shallow sea to cover windblown sand dunes, and minerals, including lime from the shells of sea creatures, glued sand particles together to form sandstone. Later crust movements caused the land to uplift, draining away the sea but leaving rivers that gradually carved the relatively soft sandstone into the spectacular shapes we see today.

So where do the colors come from? Essentially, from plain old rust. Most of the rocks at Zion are colored by iron, or hematite (iron oxide), either contained in the original stone or carried into the rocks by groundwater. Although iron often creates red and pink hues, seen in much of Zion's sandstone faces, it can also result in blacks, browns, yellows, and even greens. Sometimes the iron seeps into the rock, coloring it through, but it can also stain just the surface, often in vertical streaks. White streaks are frequently caused by deposits of salt left when water evaporates. Rocks can also be colored by bacteria that live on rock surfaces, ingest dust, and expel iron, manganese, and other minerals that stick to the rock and produce a shiny black, brown or reddish surface called desert varnish.

sizes, and a dozen species of snakes (only the western rattlesnake is poisonous, and they usually slither away from you faster than you can run from them). Mule deer are common, and although they're seldom seen, there are a few shy elk and bighorn sheep, plus foxes, coyote, ringtail cats, beaver, porcupines, skunks, and plenty of squirrels and bats. Practically every summer visitor sees lizards of some sort, often the colorful collared and whiptail lizards; and it's easy to hear the song of the canyon wren and the call of the piñon jay.

1 Just the Facts

Located in southwest Utah, at elevations ranging from 3,700 feet to 8,726 feet, Zion National Park has several sections: **Zion Canyon,** the main part of the park, where everyone goes, and the less-visited **Kolob Canyons.** The main east–west road through Zion Canyon is Utah 9, from which you can reach a 14-mile round-trip scenic drive/tram route that provides access to most scenic overlooks and trailheads.

Getting There/Access Points   St. George and Cedar City are the closest towns to Zion National Park with airport service. From either airport, it's easy to rent a car and drive to Zion (see Chapter 11 for complete details). The park is located 42 miles northeast of St. George, and 56 miles south of Cedar City. From I-15 on the park's western side, the drive into Zion Canyon, the main part of the park—following Utah 9, or Utah 17 and Utah 9 to the south entrance—is easier but less scenic than the approach on the eastern side. Though the western approach is less scenic, it's the best route into the park; it's more direct, avoids possible delays at the Zion–Mt. Carmel

Zion National Park

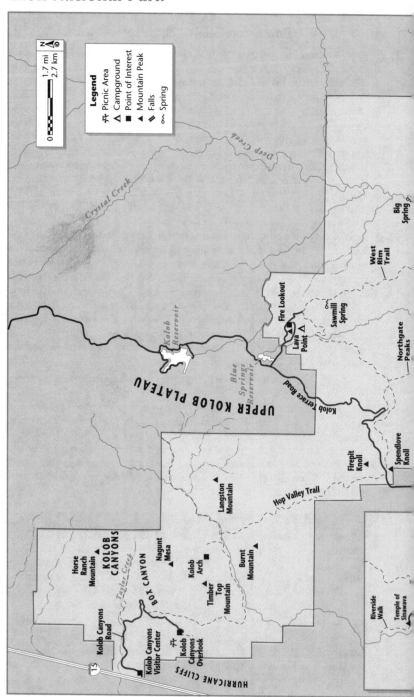

Legend
- ⊼ Picnic Area
- △ Campground
- ■ Point of Interest
- ▲ Mountain Peak
- ◈ Falls
- ∿ Spring

0 ___ 1.7 mi
0 ___ 2.7 km

Deep Creek

Crystal Creek

Kolob Reservoir

UPPER KOLOB PLATEAU

Blue Springs Reservoir

Fire Lookout

Lava Point △

Sawmill Spring

West Rim Trail

Big Spring

Northgate Peaks

Kolob Terrace Road

Firepit Knoll ▲

Spendlove Knoll ▲

Langston Mountain ▲

Hop Valley Trail

Horse Ranch Mountain ▲

KOLOB CANYONS

Nagunt Mesa ▲

Kolob Arch ■

Burnt Mountain ▲

Timber Top Mountain ▲

BOX CANYON

Taylor Creek

Kolob Canyons Road

Kolob Canyons Visitor Center ■

Kolob Canyons Overlook ■

⊼ Kolob Canyons

HURRICANE CLIFFS

Riverside Walk

Temple of Sinawava

15

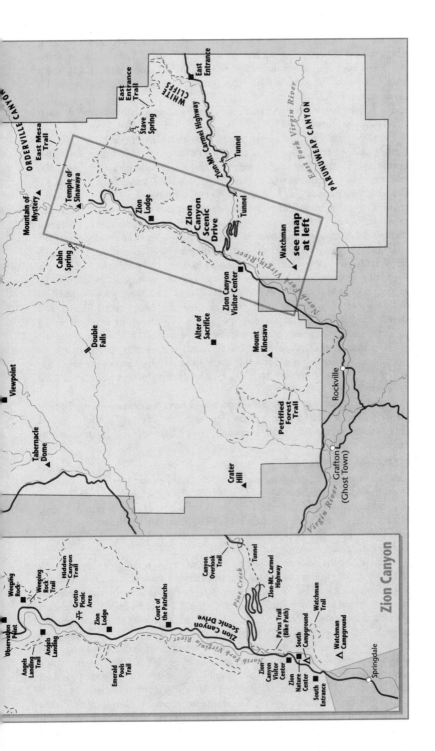

Zion Canyon

Tunnel, and delivers you to Springdale, just outside the park's southern entrance, where most of the area's lodging and restaurants are located. Outside Zion Canyon you'll find additional viewpoints and trailheads along Kolob Terrace Road, which starts just east of the park's southern entrance at the village of Virgin. This road is closed in the winter.

The Kolob Canyons section, in the park's northwest corner, is reached on the short Kolob Canyons Road off I-15.

From the east it's a spectacularly scenic 24-mile drive from Mt. Carmel on Utah 9, reached from either the north or south via U.S. 89. The park is 41 miles northwest of Kanab. However, be aware that this route into the park drops over 2,500 feet in elevation, passes through the mile-long Zion–Mt. Carmel Tunnel, and winds down six steep switchbacks. The tunnel is too small for two-way traffic that includes vehicles larger than standard passenger cars and pickup trucks. Buses, trucks, and most recreational vehicles must be driven down the center of the tunnel, and therefore all oncoming traffic must be stopped. This applies to all vehicles over 7'10" wide (including mirrors) or 11'4" tall (including luggage racks, etc.). From March through October, large vehicles are permitted in the tunnel only from 8am to 8pm daily; during other months arrangements can be made at park entrances or by calling park headquarters (☎ 801/772-3256). There is a $10 fee, good for two trips during a seven-day period, for affected vehicles. All vehicles over 13'1" tall and certain other particularly large vehicles are prohibited from driving anywhere on the park road between the east entrance and Zion Canyon.

From March to October, all vehicles over 21 feet long are prohibited from stopping at two parking areas: Weeping Rock (these vehicles may not enter the area) and the Temple of Sinawava (vehicles may be driven through but cannot park between 9am and 5pm).

You may also need to know that the park is 83 miles southwest of Bryce Canyon National Park, and 120 miles northwest of the north rim of Grand Canyon National Park in northern Arizona. It's 309 miles south of Salt Lake City and 158 miles northeast of Las Vegas, Nevada.

Information & Visitor Centers   For advance information on what to see in the park, hiking trails, camping, and lodging, contact Superintendent, **Zion National Park,** Springdale, UT 84767-1099 (☎ 801/772-3256). It's best to write at least a month before your planned visit, and specify what type of information you need. Officials request that those seeking trip-planning information write rather than call, leaving the phone lines open for those needing current and changeable information such as hiking trail conditions and closures.

If you want even more details to help plan your trip, you can order books, maps, and videos from the nonprofit **Zion Natural History Association, Zion National Park**, Springdale, UT 84767 (☎ 801/772-3264 or 800/635-3959). The association publishes several excellent books, including the colorful and informative 55-page *Zion National Park, Towers of Stone*, by J. L. Crawford, which sells for $9.50; and the easy-to-understand 22-page booklet *An Introduction to the Geology of Zion National Park*, by Al Warneke, which sells for $2.95. Some publications are available in foreign languages, and several videos can be purchased in either VHS or PAL formats. Major credit cards are accepted. Those wanting to help the nonprofit association can join ($15 single or $25 family annually) and get a 20% discount on purchases.

The park has two visitor centers. The more comprehensive **Zion Canyon Visitor Center** (☎ 801/772-3256), near the south entrance to the park, has a museum with exhibits on the geology and history of the area and presents an introductory slide show on the park. Rangers can answer questions and provide backcountry permits, several free brochures are available, and books, maps, videos, postcards, and posters are sold. The smaller **Kolob Canyons Visitor Center** (☎ 801/586-9548), in the northwest corner of the park off I-15, can provide information, permits, books, and maps.

The Sentinel, a small free newspaper available at both visitor centers, is packed with extremely helpful information about the park.

Fees, Backcountry Permits & Regulations Entry into the park (for up to seven days) costs $5 per private vehicle or $3 per motorcycle, bicycle, or pedestrian. A $15 annual pass is also available.

Oversized vehicles (see "Getting There/Access Points," above) are charged $10 for use of the Zion–Mt. Carmel Tunnel on the east side of the park.

Free permits, available at either visitor center, are required for all overnight trips into the backcountry.

Backcountry hikers should practice minimum impact techniques, are prohibited from building fires, and cannot travel in groups of 12 or more. A free booklet on backcountry travel, available at the visitor centers, lists all regulations plus descriptions of close to 20 backcountry trails.

Bicycles are prohibited in the Zion–Mt. Carmel Tunnel, the backcountry, and on trails, except the Pa'rus Trail. Feeding or molesting wildlife, vandalism, and disturbing any natural feature of the park is forbidden. Dogs, which must be leashed at all times, are prohibited on all trails, in the backcountry, and in public buildings.

Seasons & Avoiding the Crowds The park is open year-round (visitor centers are closed Christmas Day), 24 hours a day, although weather conditions may limit some activities at certain times. For instance, you'll want to avoid long hikes in midsummer, when the park bakes under temperatures that can exceed an unbearable 110°F, or during and immediately after winter storms, when ice and snow at higher elevations can make trails dangerous.

If possible, try to avoid the peak summer months of June, July, and August, when Zion receives almost half its annual visitors. The quietest months are December, January, and February, but of course it's cold then, and you may have to contend with snow and ice.

A good compromise, if your schedule permits, is to visit in April, May, September, or October, when the weather is usually good but the park is less crowded than in the summer.

The best way to avoid crowds is simply to walk away from them, either on the longer and more strenuous hiking trails or into the backcountry. It's sad but true—most visitors never bother to venture far from their cars, and their loss can be your gain. You can have a wonderful solitary experience if you're just willing to expend a little energy to get it. You can also avoid hordes of tourists by spending time in Kolob Canyons, in the far northwest section of the park; it's spectacular and receives surprisingly little use, at least in comparison to Zion Canyon.

Ranger Programs A variety of free programs and activities are presented by park rangers. Evening amphitheater programs, which sometimes include a slide show, take place most evenings at campground amphitheaters. Topics vary, but could include the animals or plants of the park, geology, man's role in the park, or perhaps some unique aspect such as Zion's slot canyons. Rangers also give short talks on similar subjects several times daily at the Zion Canyon Visitor Center and other locations. Ranger-guided hikes and walks, which may require reservations, might take you to little-visited areas of the park, on a trek to see wildflowers, or out at night for a hike under a full moon. Schedules of the various activities are posted on bulletin boards at the visitor centers, campgrounds, and other locations.

Kids from 6 to 12 years old can join the **Junior Rangers,** participate in a variety of programs, and earn certificates, badges, and patches. Morning and afternoon sessions, each lasting 2^1/$_2$ hours, are scheduled Tuesdays through Saturdays from Memorial Day through Labor Day, with children meeting at the Nature Center in the South Campground. There's a one-time fee of $1 per child, and the age range is strictly enforced.

Getting a Bird's-Eye View of the Park   Scenic Airlines (☎ 800/634-6801) offers combination air tours over Bryce Canyon and Zion national parks, plus the north rim of Grand Canyon National Park. Tours are given year-round, with prices starting at $275 for adults and $225 for children.

2 Seeing the Highlights

The best way to see Zion is to spend a week there, starting with the visitor center displays and programs, then a driving or guided tram tour, and gradually working from short hikes and walks to full-day and overnight treks into the backcountry. That's the ideal, but for most visitors, time and finances dictate a shorter visit.

If you have only a day or two at the park, we recommend starting at Zion Canyon Visitor Center for the slide show and exhibits, and then talking with a ranger about the amount of time you have, your abilities, and interests. Because Zion has such a variety of landscape and activities, each visitor can easily create a personalized itinerary. If your goal is to see as much of the park as possible in one full day we suggest the following:

After a quick stop at the visitor center, drive to **Zion Lodge** and take a ✪ **tram tour,** which hits the major roadside viewpoints and leaves the driving to someone else so that you can enjoy what you're seeing. It's a 1-hour ride that goes from the lodge to the Temple of Sinawava and back, with an informative and entertaining commentary by the tram driver, who points out prominent formations, historic sites, and things you might have missed on your own, such as daring climbers scaling the rock walls. There are several stops where passengers can get off for better views, or connect with trailheads, and then return to the lodge on a later tram. Cost is $2.95 for adults; $1.95 for children under 12, with tickets available at a window inside Zion Lodge. The tram operates daily from April to October, on the hour from 10am to 4pm.

Instead of staying on the tram all the way back to the lodge, we suggest you get off at the **Temple of Sinawava** and take the easy 2-mile round-trip **Riverside Walk,** which follows the Virgin River through a narrow canyon past hanging gardens. Then take the next tram back to the lodge (total time: 2- to 4-hours), where you might stop at the gift shop and possibly have lunch in the lodge restaurant. Near the lodge you'll find the trailhead for the **Emerald Pools.** Especially pleasant on hot days, this easy walk through a forest of oak, maple, fir, and cottonwood trees leads to a waterfall, hanging garden, and the shimmering lower pool. This part of the walk should take about an hour, round-trip, but those with a bit more ambition may want to add another hour and another mile to the loop by taking the moderately strenuous hike on a rocky, steeper trail to the upper pool. If time and energy remain, drive back toward the south park entrance and stop at **Watchman** (east of Watchman Campground), for the 2-mile, 2-hour round-trip moderately strenuous hike to a plateau with beautiful views of several rock formations and the town of Springdale. That evening, try to take in the campground amphitheater program.

3 Exploring Zion by Car

If you enter the park from the east, along the steep **Zion–Mt. Carmel Highway,** you'll travel 13 miles to the **Zion Canyon Visitor Center,** passing Checkerboard Mesa, a massive sandstone rock formation covered with horizontal and vertical lines that make it look like a huge fishing net. Continuing, you'll view a fairyland of fantastically shaped rocks of red, orange, tan, and white, as well as the Great Arch of Zion, carved high in a stone cliff.

Historically, almost all Zion National Park visitors have aimed their cars toward the 14-mile round-trip **Zion Canyon Scenic Drive,** which starts at the Zion Canyon Visitor Center. At this writing, visitors have the option of driving their own vehicles into the canyon, stopping at viewpoints and trailheads, and setting their own pace.

But that's expected to change. Traffic congestion, damage to roadside vegetation, noise, pollution, and a lack of parking are making the experience less and less pleasant, especially during the busy summer months, and park officials expect to have a mandatory shuttle bus service operating in Zion Canyon by 1998. In the meantime, motorists can still drive themselves, but be forewarned: especially in the summer, traffic is awful. Parking is hard to find, and you'll feel more like a Los Angeles or New York commuter than a national park visitor. We strongly recommend that you leave your car at the Zion Lodge parking lot and take the open-air tram.

You can take a much less crowded scenic drive in the northwest corner of the park. The ✪ **Kolob Canyons Road** (about 45 minutes from Zion Canyon Visitor Center at I-15 Exit 40) runs 5 miles among spectacular red and orange rocks, ending at a high vista. Allow about 45 minutes round-trip, stopping at numbered viewpoints. Here's what you'll pass along the way:

Leaving **Kolob Canyons Visitor Center,** you'll drive along the Hurricane Fault to **Hurricane Cliffs,** a series of tall, gray cliffs composed of limestone, and onward to **Taylor Creek,** where a piñon-juniper forest clings to life on the rocky hillside, providing a home to the bright blue scrub jay. Your next stop is **Horse Ranch Mountain,** which, at 8,726 feet, is the national park's highest point. Passing a series of colorful rock layers, where you might be lucky enough to spot a golden eagle, your next stop is **Box Canyon,** along the south fork of Taylor Creek, with sheer rock walls soaring over 1,500 feet high. Next you'll see a multicolored layer of rock, pushed upward by tremendous forces from within the earth. Continue to a canyon, exposing a rock wall that likely began as a sand dune before being covered by an early sea and cemented into stone. Next stop is a side canyon, with large, arched alcoves boasting delicate curved ceilings. Head on to a view of **Timber Top Mountain,** which is a sagebrush-covered desert at its base, but is covered with stately fir and ponderosa pine at its peak. Watch for mule deer on the brushy hillsides, especially between October and March, when they might be spotted just after sunrise or before sunset. From here

Impressions

Nothing can exceed the wondrous beauty of Zion . . . in the nobility and beauty of the sculptures there is no comparison.

—Geologist Clarence Dutton, 1880

continue to **Rockfall Overlook;** a large scar on the mountainside marks the spot where a 1,000-foot chunk of stone crashed to the earth in July, 1983, the victim of erosion. And finally, stop to see the canyon walls themselves, colored orange-red by iron oxide and striped black by mineral-laden water running down the cliff faces.

More detail is provided in a road guide, which can be purchased for $1 at the Kolob Canyons Visitor Center.

4 Sports & Activities

For information as well as just about any piece of recreational equipment you might need, stop at **Bike Zion,** 445 Zion Park Blvd., Springdale (☎ 801/772-3929 or 800/4SLIKROK), and **Forest, Camping, and Hiking World,** at the same address and phone numbers.

BIKING & MOUNTAINBIKING

With one notable exception, bikes are prohibited on all trails, as well as forbidden to travel cross-country within the national park boundaries. This leaves only the park's established roads (except for the Zion–Mt. Carmel tunnel, where bikes are also prohibited), which are often clogged with motor vehicles.

But there's hope. The **Pa'rus Trail,** opened in late 1994, is the first phase of a new transportation plan for Zion National Park. It runs 2 miles along the Virgin River from the entrance to Watchman Campground to the beginning of the Zion Canyon Scenic Drive, crossing the river and several creeks, and providing good views of Watchman, West Temple, the Sentinel, and other lower canyon formations. The trail is paved, and open to bicyclists, pedestrians, and those with strollers or wheelchairs, but closed to cars. Plans call for allowing only shuttle buses, bicyclists, and hikers on the scenic drive, making the park truly bike-friendly.

Although mountainbikers will find they are generally not welcome in Zion National Park, outside the park, mostly on Bureau of Land Management property, they'll find numerous rugged jeep trails that are great for mountainbiking, plus slickrock cross-country trails and about 10 miles of single-track trails. Many are above the town of Springdale on Wire, Grafton, and Gooseberry Mesas, offering incredible high-country views across the national park. Talk with the knowledgeable staff at Bike Zion (see address above) about the best places for mountainbiking in the area. This full-service bike shop also offers maps, a full range of bikes and accessories, repairs, and rentals ($21 per day for a 21-speed mountainbike).

HIKING

Zion offers a wide variety of hiking trails, ranging from easy half-hour walks on paved paths, to grueling overnight hikes over rocky terrain along steep drop-offs. Following are our hiking suggestions; several free brochures on hiking trails are available at the visitor centers, and the **Zion Natural History Association** publishes a good 48-page booklet ($3.95) describing 18 trails (see "Information & Visitor Centers" earlier in this chapter). Hikers with a fear of heights should be especially careful when choosing trails; many include steep, dizzying drop-offs.

The **Weeping Rock Trail,** among the park's shortest and easiest rambles, is a half-mile round-trip walk from the Zion Canyon Scenic Drive to a rock alcove with a spring and hanging gardens of ferns and wildflowers. Although paved, the trail is not suitable for wheelchairs.

Another short hike is the ✪ **Emerald Pools Trail,** which can be an easy 1-hour walk or a moderately strenuous 2-hour hike, depending on how much of the loop you choose to do. A 0.6-mile paved path from the Emerald Pools Parking Area, through a forest of oak, maple, fir, and cottonwood, leads to a waterfall, hanging garden, and the Lower Emerald Pool, and is suitable for those in wheelchairs, with assistance. From here, a steeper, rocky trail (not appropriate for wheelchairs) continues past cactus, yucca, and juniper another half mile to Upper Emerald Pool, with another waterfall. A third pool, just above Lower Emerald Pool, offers impressive reflections of the cliffs. The pools are named for the green color of the water, which is caused by algae.

A particularly scenic hike is the **Hidden Canyon Trail,** a 2-mile moderately strenuous hike that takes about 3 hours. Starting at the Weeping Rock parking area, the trail climbs 1,000 feet through a narrow water-carved canyon, ending at the canyon's mouth. Those wanting to extend the hike can go another 0.6 mile to a small natural arch. Hidden Canyon Trail includes long drop-offs, and is not recommended for anyone with a fear of heights.

Another moderately strenuous but relatively short hike is the **Watchman Trail,** which starts by the service road east of Watchman Campground. This 2-mile round-trip hike, which takes about 2 hours, gets surprisingly light use, possibly because it can be very hot in the middle of the day. Climbing to a plateau near the base of the formation called The Watchman, it offers splendid views of lower Zion Canyon, the Towers of the Virgin, and West Temple formations.

For a strenuous, 4-hour, 5-mile hike—one that is most certainly not for anyone with even a mild fear of heights—take the **Angel's Landing Trail** to a summit that offers spectacular views into Zion Canyon. But be prepared: the final half mile follows a narrow, knife-edge trail along a steep ridge, where footing can be slippery even under the best of circumstances. Support chains have been set along parts of the trail.

✪ **Hiking the Narrows** is not hiking a trail at all, but walking or wading along the bottom of the Virgin River, through a spectacular 1,000-foot-deep chasm that, at 20 feet wide, definitely lives up to its name. Passing fancifully sculptured sandstone arches, hanging gardens, and waterfalls, this moderately strenuous hike can be completed in less than a day or in several days, depending on how much you want to do. However, the Narrows are subject to flash flooding, and may be closed. Signs indicating the Narrows' danger level are posted, and permits are required for full-day and overnight hikes (check with park rangers for details). Permits are not required for easy, short day hikes, with access just beyond the end of the Riverside Walk, a 2-mile trail that starts at the Temple of Sinawava parking area.

HORSEBACK RIDING

Guided rides in the park are available March through October from **Canyon Trail Rides,** P.O. Box 128, Tropic, UT 84776 (☎ 801/772-3967), with ticket sales and information at Zion Lodge. A 1-hour ride along the Virgin River costs $12.75 and a half-day ride on the Sand Beach Trail costs $37.10. Riders must weigh no more than 220 pounds, and children must be at least five years old for the 1-hour ride and eight years old for the half-day ride. Reservations are advised.

ROCK CLIMBING

Technical rock climbers like the sandstone cliffs in Zion Canyon, although rangers warn that much of the rock is loose, or "rotten," and climbing equipment and techniques suitable for granite are often less effective on sandstone. Free permits are required for overnight climbs, and because some routes may be closed at times, climbers should check at the visitor center before setting out.

WILDLIFE WATCHING

It's a rare visitor to Zion who doesn't spot a critter of some sort, from mule deer—often seen along roadways and in campgrounds—to the numerous varieties of lizards, including the park's largest, the chuckwalla, which can grow to 20 inches. The ringtail cat, a relative of the raccoon, prowls Zion Canyon at night, and is not above helping itself to your camping supplies. Along the Virgin River you'll see bank beaver, so named because they live in burrows instead of building dams. The park is also home to several types of squirrels, gophers, and pack rats. And if you're interested in spotting birds, you're in luck at Zion. The rare peregrine falcon, among the world's fastest birds, sometimes nests in the Weeping Rock area, where you're likely to see the dipper, winter wren, and white-throated swift. Also in the park you might see golden eagles, plus several species of hummingbirds, ravens, piñon jays, and possibly a roadrunner or two.

Snakes include the poisonous western rattler, found below 8,000 feet elevation, and there are also nonpoisonous kingsnakes and gopher snakes. Tarantulas, those large, usually slow-moving hairy spiders, are often seen in the late summer and fall. Contrary to popular belief, the tarantula's bite is not deadly, although it may be somewhat painful.

Remember, it's illegal to feed the wildlife; no matter how much you may want to befriend an animal by offering food, please remember that it's not healthy for the wildlife to eat human food or to get used to being fed this way.

5 Camping

The absolutely best places to camp are at one of the ✪ **national park campgrounds,** if you can find a site. Reservations are not accepted, and the campgrounds often fill by noon in the summer, so get there early in the day to claim a site. Some campers stay at nearby commercial campgrounds their first night in the area, then hurry into the park the next morning, circling like vultures until a site becomes available.

Both of Zion's main campgrounds, just inside the park's south entrance, have paved roads, well-spaced sites, lots of trees, and that national park atmosphere you came here to enjoy. There are restrooms with flush toilets but no showers, and no RV hookups. There is a dump station and public telephone, and sites for those with disabilities are available. The fee is $8 per night. **South Campground** has 141 sites, and is usually open from mid-March through mid-October only; **Watchman Campground** has 228 sites and is open year-round.

Lava Point, with only six sites, is located in Kolob Canyons. It has fire grates, tables, and toilets, but no water, and there is no fee. It is usually open from May through October.

If you can't get a site in the park, or if you prefer hot showers or complete RV hookups, there are several campgrounds in the surrounding area. The closest, **Zion Canyon Campground,** on Zion Park Boulevard a half mile south of the park entrance (P.O. Box 99), Springdale, UT 84767 (☎ 801/772-3237; fax 801/772-3844), has 180 sites, many shaded, and is open year-round. Although it's quite crowded in the summer, the campground is clean and well-maintained, and in addition to the usual showers and RV hookups, there's a self-service laundry, dump station, a store with groceries, souvenirs, and RV supplies, and a restaurant. Tenters are welcome; rates are from $13 to $20 for two people.

6 Accommodations

The only lodging actually in Zion National Park is at Zion Lodge (see below). The other properties listed here are all in Springdale, a village of some 350 people at the park's south entrance that has literally become the park's bedroom. Room tax is about 10% in Springdale; 9% in the park. Pets are not accepted unless otherwise noted.

You can also base yourself in St. George, which is 42 miles away; Kanab, which is 40 miles away; or Cedar City, 56 miles away. See Chapter 11 for listings.

Best Western Driftwood Lodge

1515 Zion Park Blvd., Springdale, UT 84767. ☎ **801/772-3262** or 800/528-1234. 47 units, including 2 family suites. A/C TV TEL. Apr–Oct $64–$76 double, $94–$102 family unit; Nov–Mar $54–$66 double, $84–$92 family unit. All rates include continental breakfast. AE, DC, DISC, MC, V.

This attractive, well-kept motel (extensively renovated in 1994) has beautiful lawns and gardens, offering a quiet, lush setting for sitting back and admiring the spectacular rock formations that practically surround the town. Spacious rooms have white walls and light wood-grain furnishings, and many have patios or balconies. Your room will have one queen, one king, or two king beds, and the two family suites each have one king-size and two queen beds. There's an outdoor heated pool with a sundeck, a Jacuzzi, and an art gallery and gift shop, but no restaurant on the premises. Pets are accepted at management discretion.

Bumbleberry Inn

897 Zion Park Blvd., Springdale, UT 84767. ☎ **801/772-3224** or 800/828-1534. Fax 801/772-3947. 23 rms. A/C TV TEL. Apr–Oct $54–$59 double; Nov–Mar $49–$54 double. DISC, MC, V.

Set back from the main highway, the Bumbleberry offers large, quiet rooms at a good price. Built in 1972, the motel was last renovated in 1991. Furnishings are simple but more than adequate, with a desk in addition to a table and two chairs, and decorated with art prints depicting the area's scenery. Most rooms have two queen-size beds and tub/shower combinations, although five rooms have one queen bed and shower only. There's a heated outdoor pool, picnic area, and an adjacent restaurant that serves three meals daily. Pets are accepted at the discretion of the management.

⑤ Canyon Ranch Motel

668 Zion Park Blvd. (P.O. Box 175), Springdale, UT 84767. ☎ **801/772-3357.** 21 units. A/C TV. Mar–Oct $48–$68 double; Nov–Feb $38–$54 double. AE, DISC, MC, V.

Consisting of a series of two- and four-unit cottages set back from the highway, this place has the look of an old-fashioned auto camp on the outside while providing modern motel rooms inside. Rooms are either new or newly remodeled, and options include one queen- or king-size bed, two queens, or one queen and one double. Some rooms have showers only, while some have shower/tub combos, and there are no in-room telephones. Kitchen units are also available. Room 13, with two queen-size beds, offers spectacular views of the Zion National Park rock formations with several large picture windows, and views from most other rooms are almost as good. The units surround a lawn with trees and picnic tables, and there is an outdoor heated swimming pool and Jacuzzi. Pets are accepted at the discretion of the management.

Cliffrose Lodge & Gardens

281 Zion Park Blvd. (P.O. Box 510), Springdale, UT 84767. ☎ **801/772-3234** or 800/243-UTAH. Fax 801/772-3900. 36 units, including 6 suites. A/C TV TEL. Summer $109–$145 double. Lower rates in the winter. AE, DISC, MC, V.

With river frontage and 5 acres of lawns, shade trees, and flower gardens, the Cliffrose offers a beautiful setting just outside the entrance to Zion National Park. The modern well-kept rooms have all the standard motel appointments, with wood furnishings, floral-print bedspreads, and unusually large bathrooms with shower/tub combinations. On the lawns you'll find comfortable seating, including a lawn swing, plus there's a playground and large outdoor heated pool. Guests have use of a self-service laundry, and pets are accepted for a $10 fee.

✪ Flanigan's Inn

428 Zion Park Blvd. (P.O. Box 100), Springdale, UT 84767. ☎ **801/772-3244** or 800/765-RSVP. Fax 801/772-3396. 40 units. A/C TV TEL. Mid-Mar–Nov $69–$89 double; Dec–mid-Mar $49–$69 double. All rates include continental breakfast buffet. AE, DISC, MC, V.

A mountain lodge atmosphere pervades this very attractive complex of natural wood and rock, set among trees, lawns, and flowers just outside the entrance to Zion National Park. Parts of the inn date to 1947, but all rooms were completely renovated in the early 1990s, and have Southwest decor with wood furnishings and local art. Some units have whirlpool tubs and bidets, kitchenettes are available, and there is one room with a fireplace. This is a place where you might actually want to spend some time, unlike the other area options, which are just good places to sleep at the end of a long day spent exploring Zion. Flanigan's has its own nature trail leading to a hilltop vista, a heated outdoor swimming pool, a volleyball court, and a weight room. An on-site restaurant serves dinner, in addition to a continental breakfast for guests only (see "Dining," below). Summer reservations are often booked three to four months in advance.

Harvest House Bed & Breakfast at Zion

29 Canyonview Dr. (P.O. Box 125), Springdale, UT 84767. ☎ **801/772-3880.** Fax 801/772-3327. 4 rms. A/C. $75–$90 double. Rates include full breakfast. DISC, MC, V.

Even the smallest, least expensive room here is quite charming, with one queen-size bed, wicker furniture, and original paper art. Comfortable and quiet, this Utah territorial–style house was built in 1989; there's a cactus garden out front and a garden sitting area in back with a koi (Japanese carp) pond and spectacular views of the national park rock formations. We agree with owners Steven and Barbara Cooper, who call their decor "urban eclectic," with a smattering of collectibles, antiques of various periods, modern furnishings, original art, and photography. Two rooms have shower/tub combos, one has a tiled shower plus separate tub, and one has a shower only. Two rooms have decks, and all come with homemade cookies.

The homey living room—open to all—has a television and VCR with a collection of both new and classic movies, but the Coopers like to see their guests enjoying the great outdoors, and are anxious to share their knowledge of hiking and biking trails. Breakfasts are elegant and not at all run-of-the-mill, and might include selections such as homemade bagels with smoked salmon, frittatas, scrambled eggs with cheddar cheese, homemade granola, fruit, and yogurt. Facilities include an outdoor whirlpool. Children over six are welcome.

Zion Lodge

In Zion National Park. ☎ **801/586-7686.** Fax 801/586-3157. 120 units. A/C TEL. Motel rooms $75–$80 double; suites $113–$120 double; cabins $79–$85 double. AE, DISC, MC, V.

The motel units and cabins are nice enough, but then again, you don't come to Zion National Park to be indoors—you come for the scenery, and there's a pretty incredible view from the lobby's large picture windows. Sitting in a forest with spectacular views of the park's rock cliffs, the charming cabins each have a private porch, stone (gas-burning) fireplace, two double beds, pine board walls, and log beams. The comfortable motel units are basically just that—motel units—with two queen-sized beds and all the usual amenities except televisions. Motel suites each have one king-sized bed, a separate sitting room, and refrigerator. A gift shop offers everything from postcards to expensive silver-and-turquoise Native American jewelry.

Zion Park Inn

1215 Zion Park Blvd., Springdale, UT 84767. ☎ **801/772-3200** or 800/932-PARK. 120 rms. A/C TV TEL. $60–$80 double. AE, DC, DISC, JCB, MC, V.

Under construction when we went to press and scheduled to open in March 1996, this full-service hotel will be tied with Zion Lodge as the largest in the immediate Zion National Park area. There's a heated outdoor swimming pool, a restaurant serving American cuisine for three meals daily, and conference rooms with seating for up to 100. Pets are accepted with a deposit.

7 Dining

With the exception of Zion Lodge, which is in the park, these restaurants are all located on the main road through Springdale to the park.

Bit & Spur Saloon

1212 Zion Park Blvd., Springdale. ☎ **801/772-3498.** Reservations recommended. Main courses $8.50–$18. MC, V. Daily 5–10pm (beer bar open until 1am); brunch served mid-Mar–Oct Sat–Sun 8:30am–noon. Closed Dec–Jan. MEXICAN/SOUTHWESTERN.

This may look like an Old West–saloon, with its rough wood-and-stone walls and exposed beam ceiling, but it's an unusually clean saloon that also has a family dining room and patio dining. The food here is also a notch or two above what we expected, a bit closer to what you'd find in a good Santa Fe restaurant. The menu includes Mexican standards such as burritos, flautas, chile rellenos, and a traditional chile stew with pork; but you'll also find more creative dishes, including the pollo relleno—a grilled breast of chicken stuffed with cilantro pesto and goat cheese, and served with smoked pineapple chutney. Also good are the smokey chicken—a smoked, charbroiled game hen with sourdough stuffing and chipotle sauce—and the deep-dish chicken enchilada, with scallions, green chiles, and cheese. The Bit & Spur has a full liquor license and extensive wine list.

✪ Flanigan's Inn

428 Zion Park Blvd., Springdale. ☎ **801/772-3244.** Reservations recommended. Main courses $8.95–$19.95; pastas and salads $7.95–$11.95. AE, DISC, MC, V. Mon–Thurs 5–9:30pm; Fri–Sun until 10pm. Shorter hours in the winter. REGIONAL/WILD GAME.

With a greenhouse/garden atmosphere, this restaurant makes the most of the area's spectacular scenery with large windows for inside diners plus an outdoor patio. Specializing in southern Utah–style cooking, Flanigan's uses fresh local ingredients and herbs from the inn's garden whenever possible. The broiled salmon, served with a butter sauce and wild and brown rice, is always fresh; and the breast of chicken, served charbroiled, is free-range and chemical-free. Also popular are the Utah lamb chops, charbroiled and served with mint pear chutney and rice; the wild game plate with grilled elk, quail, and buffalo sausage, covered with a rich sauce and sprinkled with local pine nuts; and rabbit with mushrooms and sage—a commercially raised rabbit that is broiled and smothered in a traditional southern Utah sauce. Selections might also include a chicken curry salad or shrimp salad, and several pastas. Entrees are served with French country bread, the vegetable du jour, and a salad. A lighter menu, served until 6:30pm, is priced from $6.95. Microbrewery draft beers are available.

Zion Lodge

Zion National Park. ☎ **801/772-3213.** Dinner reservations required in the summer. Breakfast items $3.50–$5.95; lunch items $4.25–$6.95; main dinner courses $9.95–$15.95. AE, DC, DISC, MC, V. Daily 6:30–9:30am, noon–2:30pm, and 5:30–9pm. AMERICAN.

A mountain lodge atmosphere prevails here, complete with large windows that look out toward the park's magnificent rock formations from this spacious dining room above the Zion Lodge lobby. House specialties at dinner include an excellent slow-roasted prime rib au jus, and the very popular Utah red mountain trout. The menu also includes several chicken dishes, such as a skinless chicken breast basted with a spicy Caribbean sauce and served with a red onion relish. There are several vegetarian items on the menu, such as spinach linguini with roasted tomato sauce. Ask about the lodge's specialty ice creams and other exotic desserts. At lunch you'll find the trout and barbecued pork, plus burgers, sandwiches, and salads; and breakfasts offer all the usual American selections. The restaurant will pack lunches to go for hikers, and offers a children's menu and full liquor service.

Zion Pizza & Noodle

868 Zion Park Blvd., Springdale. ☎ **801/772-3815.** Reservations not accepted. Pizza $7.95–$10.95; pasta, calzone, and stromboli $6.95–$7.95; bagels 75¢–$3.95. No credit cards. President's Day–Thanksgiving noon–10pm; shorter hours in the winter. Bagels and espresso served 8am–3pm in the summer. Closed Jan–Feb. PIZZA/PASTA.

Located in a former LDS church with a turquoise steeple, this cafe has small, closely spaced tables and is decorated with black-and-white photos. Patrons order at the counter and help themselves at the beverage bar while waiting for their food to be delivered. The 12-inch pizzas are baked in a slate stone oven, and have lots of chewy crust. They're good, but New York–style pizza purists might be put off by oddly topped specialty pies, such as the southwestern burrito pizza or barbecue chicken pizza. But have no fear—you can get a basic cheese pizza, or add any of some 15 extra toppings from pepperoni to green chiles to pineapple. The noodle side of the menu offers a variety of pastas, such as fettuccini with roma tomatoes, fresh mushrooms, pesto sauce, cream, and grated parmesan; stromboli; and very often a locally popular nightly special of manicotti marinara. In the summer, bagel lovers will find plain or cream cheese–topped bagels plus several bagel sandwiches to munch with their espresso, latte, or cappuccino. The restaurant serves no alcohol. Take out and delivery are available.

8 Virtual Nature at Two Nearby Theaters

Just outside the south entrance to Zion National Park, in Springdale, are two worthwhile attractions.

"The Grand Circle: A National Park Odyssey," a multimedia production presented on a 24-by-40–foot screen in the outdoor Obert C. Tanner Amphitheater, is an excellent introduction to the national parks and monuments of southern Utah and northern Arizona. Using a state-of-the-art sound and projection system, and with the cliffs of Zion National Park in the background, the 1-hour program gives a brief look at the geology of the area, but devotes most of its time, sounds, and sights to the awe-inspiring scenery. Showings are scheduled at dusk nightly from late May through early September. Tickets cost $4 for adults, $3 for students and children under 12, or $10 per family.

The amphitheater, located just off Zion Park Boulevard, is also the venue for about a dozen **concerts** each summer, ranging from the annual Utah Symphony pops concert in late June or early July, to bluegrass, country, and acoustic. Tickets cost $5 to $9, depending on the performer. For information on the multimedia production or concert series contact **Dixie College in St. George** (☎ 801/652-7994).

You'll find an even bigger screen—some six stories high by 80 feet wide—at **Zion Canyon Theatre,** just outside the south entrance to Zion National Park at 145 Zion Park Blvd. (☎ 801/772-2400), where the 37-minute film "Treasure of the Gods" is presented year-round. There are thrilling scenes of the Zion National Park area, including a hair-raising flash flood through Zion Canyon's Narrows and some dizzying bird's-eye views, but don't take the history that's presented too literally—it's confusing at best. Admission costs $7 for adults; $4.50 for children 3 to 11. Shows begin hourly, 365 days a year; March through October from 9am to 9pm, and November through February from 11am to 7pm. The theater complex also includes a tourist information center, picnic area, gift and souvenir shops, a food emporium, a 30-minute photo processor, bookstore, and art gallery.

13 | Bryce Canyon National Park

If you could visit only one national park in your lifetime, we'd send you to Bryce Canyon. Here you'll find magic, inspiration, and spectacular beauty among thousands of intricately shaped hoodoos: Those silent sentinels and congregations gathered in these colorful cathedrals, in formations that let your imagination run wild.

Hoodoos, geologists tell us, are simply pinnacles of rock, often oddly shaped, left standing by the forces of millions of years of water and wind erosion. But perhaps the truth really lies in a Paiute legend. These Native Americans, who lived in the area for several hundred years before being forced out by Mormon pioneers, told of a "Legend People" who lived here in the old days; for their evil ways they were turned to stone by the powerful Coyote, and even today they remain frozen in time.

Whatever the cause, Bryce Canyon is unique. Its intricate and often whimsical formations are smaller and on a more human scale than the impressive rocks seen at Zion, Capitol Reef, and Canyonlands national parks. And it's far easier to explore than the huge and sometimes intimidating Grand Canyon: Bryce is comfortable and inviting in its beauty. We feel we know it simply by gazing over the rim, and we were on intimate terms after just our first morning on the trail.

Although the colorful hoodoos are the first things that grab your attention, it isn't long before you notice the deep amphitheaters that are their homes, with their cliffs, windows, and arches—all colored in shades of red, brown, orange, yellow, and white—that change and glow with the rising and setting sun. Beyond the rocks and light are the other faces of the park: Three separate life zones, each with its own unique vegetation, changing with elevation; and a kingdom of animals, from the busy chipmunks and ground squirrels to delicate mule deer and their archenemy, the mountain lion.

Human exploration of the Bryce area likely began with the Paiutes, and it's possible that trappers, prospectors, and early Mormon scouts may have visited here in the early to mid-1800s, before Major John Wesley Powell conducted the first thorough survey of the region in the early 1870s. Shortly after Powell's exploration, Mormon pioneer Ebenezer Bryce and his wife Mary moved to the area and tried raising cattle. Although they stayed only a few years before moving to Arizona, Bryce left his name and his oft-quoted description of the canyon as "a helluva place to lose a cow."

1 Just the Facts

Getting There/Access Points   **Bryce Canyon Airport** (☎ 801/834-5239), several miles from the park entrance on Utah 12, expanded in mid-1995 with a new terminal in anticipation of more scenic, charter, and commuter flights. Direct flights from Las Vegas, Nevada are provided by **Scenic Airlines** (☎ 702/739-1900) and Air Vegas (☎ 702/795-7144). A local company, **Bryce Canyon Airlines** (ask for the flight desk at Ruby's Inn; ☎ 801/834-5341), was expected to begin a commuter service by the spring of 1996. Car rentals at **Bryce Canyon Airport** are available from **Bryce Canyon Car Rental** (☎ 801/834-5200 or 800/432-5383).

You could also fly into St. George (126 miles southwest of the park on I-15) or Cedar City (also on I-15) and rent a car at either of these airports. See Chapter 11 for details on airlines and rental companies. From St. George, travel north on I-15 10 miles to exit 16, then head east on Utah 9 for 63 miles to U.S. 89, north 43 miles to Utah 12, and east 17 miles to the park entrance road. The Entrance Station and Visitor Center are just 3 miles south of Utah 12.

Situated in the mountains of southern Utah, the park is crossed east–west by Utah 12, with the bulk of the park, including the visitor center, accessed by Utah 63, which branches off from Utah 12 and goes south into the main portions of the park. Utah 89 runs north–south along the western side of the park, and Utah 12 branches off to the east from here, south of the town of Panguitch, which is 24 miles from the park.

From Salt Lake City, it's 260 miles to the park. Take I-15 south about 200 miles to exit 95, head east 13 miles on Utah 20, south on U.S. 89 for 17 miles to Utah 12, and east 17 miles to the park entrance road.

From Capitol Reef National Park, take Utah 24 west 10 miles to Torrey, turn southwest onto Scenic Highway Utah 12 (through Boulder and Escalante) for about 110 miles to the park entrance road.

A couple of other handy driving distances: Bryce is 83 miles east of Zion National Park, and 245 miles northwest of Las Vegas, Nevada.

Getting Around   Although most visitors to Bryce have cars or RVs, this is one of the few national parks where a vehicle isn't absolutely necessary, at least in the summer. **Bryce Canyon Scenic Tours & Shuttles** (☎ 801/834-5200 or 800/432-5383) operates a shuttle bus during July and August with stops at all major trailheads, viewpoints, the visitor center, and campgrounds. Cost is $5 for an all-day pass, and reservations are requested. The company can also arrange car rentals.

Information & Visitor Centers   For advance information on what to see in the park, hiking trails, camping, and lodging, write: Superintendent, **Bryce Canyon National Park**, Bryce Canyon, UT 84717, or call weekdays between 8am and 4:30pm mountain time (☎ 801/834-5322). It's best to write at least a month before your planned visit, and ask for a copy of the national park newspaper *Hoodoo*, which contains a map of the park, plus information on hiking trails, services, weather, ranger-conducted activities, and current issues such as road construction in the park.

If you want even more details to help plan your trip, you can order books, maps, posters, and videos from the nonprofit **Bryce Canyon Natural History Association,** Bryce Canyon, UT 84717 (☎ 801/834-5322). The association publishes a number of excellent books, and offers a special trip-planning packet that includes a driving and hiking guide, natural history guide, and a descriptive and photographic guide to both Bryce and Zion National Parks, for a package price of $8.75. A 48-page book, *Bryce Canyon: The Continuing Story,* is available in English ($6.95) or German,

French, Japanese, or Chinese ($7.95); and several videos are available, both in VHS and PAL formats. Shipping charges are extra. Major credit cards are accepted.

The **visitor center**, at the north end as you enter the park, has exhibits on the geology and history of the area and presents a short introductory slide show on the park. Rangers can answer questions and provide backcountry permits, several free brochures are available, and books, maps, videos, postcards, and posters are sold. The visitor center is open daily year-round except Thanksgiving, Christmas, and New Year's days.

Fees, Backcountry Permits & Regulations   Entry into the park (for up to seven days) is $5 per private vehicle or $3 per motorcycle, bicycle, or pedestrian. A $15 annual pass is also available.

Free permits, available at the visitor center daily until 5pm, are required for all overnight trips into the backcountry, and backcountry camping is permitted on only two trails, with details at the visitor center.

Backcountry hikers should practice minimum-impact techniques, are prohibited from building fires, and must carry their own water. Bicycles are prohibited in the backcountry and on all trails. Feeding or molesting wildlife, vandalism, and disturbing any natural feature of the park are all prohibited. Dogs, which must be leashed at all times, are prohibited on all trails, in the backcountry, and in public buildings.

Seasons & Avoiding the Crowds   Although Bryce Canyon National Park receives only two-thirds the number of annual visitors that pour into Zion, the park can still be crowded, especially during its peak season from mid-June to mid-September, when the campgrounds are often full by 2pm. If you have to visit then, try to hike some of the lesser-used trails (ask rangers for recommendations), and get out onto the trails as soon after sunrise as possible.

A better time to visit, if your schedule allows, is spring or fall. If you don't mind a bit of cold and snow, the park is practically deserted in the winter—a typical January sees some 22,000 to 25,000 visitors, while in August there are well over 10 times that number—and the sight of bright red hoodoos capped with fresh white snow is something you won't soon forget.

Safety Concerns   While most visitors to Bryce Canyon enjoy an exciting vacation without mishap, accidents can occur, and here—possibly because of the nature of the trails—the most common injuries by far are sprained, twisted, and broken ankles. Park rangers strongly recommend that hikers—even those just out for short day hikes—wear sturdy hiking boots with good traction and ankle support.

Another concern in the park in recent years has been bubonic plague, which, contrary to popular belief, is treatable with antibiotics if caught early. The bacteria that causes bubonic plague has been found on fleas in prairie dog colonies in the park, so you should avoid contact with wild animals, especially prairie dogs, chipmunks, ground squirrels, and other rodents. Those taking pets into the park should dust them with flea powder. Avoiding contact with infected animals will greatly minimize the chances of contracting the plague, but caution is still necessary. Symptoms, which generally occur from two to six days after exposure, may include high fever, headache, vomiting, diarrhea, and swollen glands. Anyone with these symptoms following a park visit should get medical attention immediately, because the plague can be fatal if not treated promptly.

Ranger Programs   Park rangers present a variety of free programs and activities. Evening programs, which may include a slide show, take place most evenings at campground amphitheaters. Topics vary, but could include such subjects as the animals and plants of the park, geology, and man's role in the park's early days.

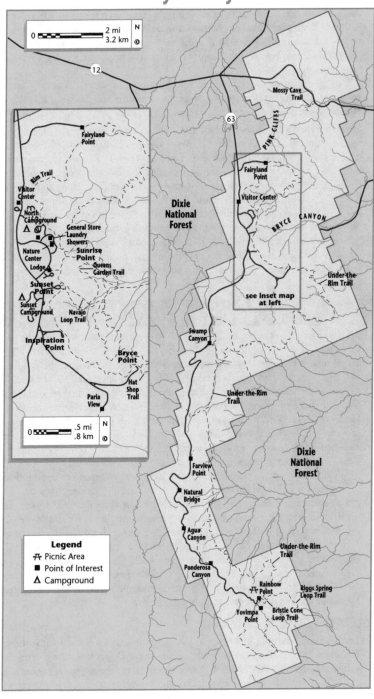

Legend
🏕 Picnic Area
■ Point of Interest
△ Campground

Rangers also give half-hour talks on similar subjects several times daily at various locations in the park, and lead hikes and walks, including a moonlight hike (reservations required) and a wheelchair-accessible 1-hour canyon rim walk. Schedules are posted on bulletin boards at the visitor center, general store, campgrounds, and Bryce Canyon Lodge.

During the summer, children 12 and younger can join the **Junior Rangers**, participate in a variety of programs, and earn certificates and patches. Junior Ranger booklets are available at the visitor center.

Getting a Bird's-Eye View of the Park   For an unforgettable view of the canyon and its numerous formations, contact **Bryce Canyon Helicopters** (ask for the flight desk at Ruby's Inn, ☎ 801/834-5341). Tours last from 15 minutes to more than an hour, and the longer trips include the entire park plus surrounding attractions of Kodachrome Basin State Park and a nearby ghost town. Air is clearest and lighting is best in the morning, and reservations should be made a day ahead, if possible. Prices start at $55 for a 15-minute flight over the northern section of the park, and range up to $200. Anyone weighing less than 100 pounds is charged half.

Scenic Airlines (☎ 800/634-6801) offers combination air tours over Bryce Canyon and Zion National Parks plus the north rim of Grand Canyon National Park. Tours are given year-round, with prices starting at $275 for adults and $225 for children.

2 Seeing the Highlights

Because Bryce Canyon is our absolutely favorite national park, we would be happy to spend our entire vacation here. But, if you insist on being unreasonable and saving time and energy for the many other fascinating and extremely beautiful parts of Utah, there are ways to see a good deal of Bryce in a short amount of time.

Start at the **visitor center**, of course, and watch the short slide show that explains some of the area geology—the why of Bryce. Then either drive the 18-mile (each-way) dead end **park road**, stopping at viewpoints to gaze down into the canyon (see, "Exploring Bryce Canyon by Car," below), or hop on the **Bryce Tours van** for a 1^1/$_2$-hour guided tour, complete with lively commentary (see "Guided Tours," below).

Whichever way you choose to get around, make sure you spend at least a little time at **Inspiration Point**, which offers a splendid (and yes, inspirational) view into **Bryce Amphitheater** and its hundreds of statuesque pink, red, orange, and brown hoodoo stone sculptures. After seeing the canyon from the top down, it's time to get some exercise, so walk at least partway down the Queen's Garden Trail. If you can spare 3 hours, hike down the Navajo Loop and return to the rim via Queen's Garden Trail (see "Sports & Activities," below). Those not willling or physically able to hike into the canyon can enjoy a leisurely walk along the **Rim Trail**, which provides spectacular views down into the canyon, especially about an hour before sunset. That evening, try to take in the campground amphitheater program.

GUIDED TOURS

For a personalized tour of Bryce Canyon viewpoints that lets you look at the scenery instead of the road, consider one of two tours. ✪ **Bryce Tours** departs Bryce Canyon Lodge (☎ 801/834-5361) several times daily during the summer months and takes you to the major viewpoints, including Bryce and Inspiration Points and Paria View, as well as providing insights into the history and geology of the canyon.

Cost for the van tour is $4.95 for adults and $2 for children 4 to 12; younger children not occupying seats ride free.

Bryce Canyon Scenic Tours & Shuttles (☎ 801/834-5200 or 800/432-5383) offers 2-hour tours year-round, leaving from Ruby's Inn just outside the park entrance several times daily. Cost is $18 for adults and $9 for youths 15 and younger. Specialized sunrise, sunset, and wildlife tours are also offered; call for details.

3 Exploring Bryce Canyon by Car

The park's **17-mile scenic drive** (one way) follows the rim of Bryce Canyon, offering easy access to a variety of views into the fanciful fairyland of stone sculptures below. Trailers are not permitted on the road, but can be left at several parking lots. Also, because all overlooks are on your left as you begin your drive, it's best to avoid crossing traffic by driving all the way to the end of the road and stopping at the overlooks on your return. Allow from 1 to 2 hours.

After leaving the visitor center, drive 17 miles to **Yovimpa and Rainbow Point overlooks**, which offer expansive views of southern Utah, Arizona, and sometimes even New Mexico. From these pink cliffs you can look down on a colorful platoon of stone soldiers, standing at eternal attention. A short loop trail from Rainbow Point leads to an **1,800-year-old bristlecone pine**, believed to be the oldest living thing at Bryce Canyon.

From here, drive back north to **Ponderosa Canyon Overlook**, where you can gaze down from a dense forest of spruce and fir at multicolored hoodoos, before continuing to **Agua Canyon Overlook**, with some of the best color contrasts you'll find in the park. Looking almost straight down, watch for a hoodoo known as **The Hunter**, with a hat of green trees.

Now continue on to **Natural Bridge**, actually an arch carved by rain and wind and spanning 85 feet. From here, continue to **Fairview Point**, where there's a panoramic view to the distant horizon and the Kaibab Plateau at the Grand Canyon's north rim. Passing through **Swamp Canyon**, you'll turn right off the main road to three viewpoints, the first of which is **Paria View**, with views to the south of the White Cliffs, carved into light-colored sandstone by the Paria River. To the north of Paria View, you'll find **Bryce Point**, a splendid stop for seeing the awesome **Bryce Amphitheater**, the largest natural amphitheater in the park, as well as distant views of the Black Mountains to the northeast and Navajo Mountain to the south. From here it's just a short drive to **Inspiration Point**, offering views similar to those at Bryce Point plus the best view in the park of the **Silent City**, a sleeping city cast in stone.

Now return to the main road and head north to **Sunset Point**, where you can see practically all of Bryce Amphitheater, including the aptly named **Thor's Hammer** and the 200-foot-tall cliffs of **Wall Street**.

Continue north to a turn-off for your final stop at **Sunrise Point**, where there's an inspiring view into Bryce Amphitheater. This is the beginning of the **Queen's Garden Trail**, an excellent choice for even a quick walk below the canyon's rim.

4 Sports & Activities

BIKING & MOUNTAINBIKING

Bikes are prohibited on all trails, as well as forbidden for traveling cross-country within the national park boundaries. This leaves the park's established scenic drive, which is open to cyclists, although you need to be aware that the 17-mile road through the park is narrow and winding, and can be crowded with motor vehicles during the summer.

Because mountainbikers are not welcome on national park hiking trails, you'll have to leave Bryce in search of trails. Fortunately, you won't have to go far. The **Dave's Hollow Trail** starts at the Bryce Canyon National Park boundary sign on Utah 63, the park entrance road, about a mile south of Ruby's Inn. The double-track trail goes west for about a half mile before connecting with Forest Road 090, where you turn south and ride for about three-quarters of a mile before turning right onto an easy ride through Dave's Hollow to the Dave's Hollow Forest Service Station on Forest Road 087. From here you can retrace your route for an 8-mile round-trip ride; for a longer 12-mile trip, turn right on Forest Road 087 to Utah 12 and then right back to Utah 63 and the starting point. A third option is to turn left on Forest Road 087 and follow it to Tropic Reservoir (see "Fishing" below). For further information, contact the **Dixie National Forest**, P.O. Box 580, 82 North 100 East, Cedar City, UT 84720 (☎ 801/865-3700).

FISHING

The closest fishing hole to the park is at **Tropic Reservoir**, a large lake in a ponderosa pine forest. From the intersection of Utah 63 (the park entrance road) and Utah 12, drive west about 3 miles to a gravel road, and then drive about 7 miles south. There is a forest service campground open in the summer, a boat ramp, and fishing for rainbow, brook, and cutthroat trout. Locals say fishing is sometimes better in streams above the lake than in the reservoir itself. For further information, contact the Dixie National Forest, P.O. Box 580, 82 North 100 East, Cedar City, UT 84720 (☎ 801/865-3700).

HIKING

One of the things we like best about Bryce Canyon is that you don't have to be an advanced backpacker to really get into the park.

The park's twice-yearly free newspaper, *Hoodoo*, contains short information and a map on nine day-hikes, and *The Bryce Canyon Auto and Hiking Guide* ($2.95), published by the Bryce Canyon Natural History Association, describes them in more detail (see "Information & Visitor Centers," earlier this chapter).

All trails below the rim have at least some steep grades, so you should wear hiking boots with a traction tread and good ankle support to avoid ankle injuries, the most common accidents in the park. During the hot summer months you'll want to hike either early or late in the day, and keep in mind that it gets hotter the deeper you go into the canyon.

The ✪ **Rim Trail**, which does not drop into the canyon but offers splendid views from above, meanders along the rim for over 5 miles. An easy to moderate walk, it offers a section between two overlooks—Sunrise and Sunset—that is suitable for wheelchairs. Overlooking Bryce Amphitheater, the trail offers excellent views almost everywhere, and is a good choice for an after-dinner walk, when you can watch the changing evening light on the rosy rocks below.

An easy, often-overlooked trail located outside the main part of the park offers a picturesque 45-minute walk. The **Mossy Cave Trailhead** is located on Utah 12, about 3.5 miles east of the highway's intersection with Utah 63. Only 0.8 mile round-trip, the trail follows an old irrigation ditch up a short hill to a cave, where seeping water nurtures the cave's namesake moss. Just off the trail you'll also see a small waterfall.

Your best choice for getting down into the canyon and seeing the most with the least amount of sweat is to combine two popular trails—✪ **Navajo Loop and**

Queen's Garden. The total distance is just under 3 miles, with a 521-foot elevation change, and most hikers take from 2 to 3 hours. It's best to start at the Navajo Loop trailhead at Sunset Point and leave the canyon on the less-steep Queen's Garden Trail, returning to the rim at Sunrise Point, one-half mile to the north. The Navajo Loop section is considered fairly strenuous, while Queen's Garden is rated moderate. Along the Navajo Loop section you'll pass Thor's Hammer, wonder why it hasn't fallen, and ponder the towering skyscrapers of Wall Street. Turning onto the Queen's Garden Trail you'll see some of the park's most fanciful formations, including majestic Queen Victoria herself, for whom the trail was named, plus the Queen's Castle and Gulliver's Castle.

Those looking for more of a challenge might consider the **Hat Shop Trail**, a strenuous 3.8-mile hike (round-trip) with a 900-foot elevation change. Leaving from the Bryce Point Overlook, you'll drop quickly to the Hat Shop, so-named because it consists of hard gray "hats" perched on narrow reddish brown pedestals. Allow 4 hours.

For diehard hikers who don't mind rough terrain, Bryce has two backcountry trails, usually open in the summer only. The **Under-the-Rim Trail** runs for some 22.6 miles, providing an excellent opportunity to see the park's spectacular scenery on its own terms. **Riggs Spring Loop Trail** is 8.8 miles long, and offers splendid views of the pink cliffs in the southern part of the park. The really ambitious can combine the two trails for a week-long excursion. Free permits, available at the visitor center, are required for all overnight trips into the backcountry.

HORSEBACK RIDING

To see Bryce Canyon the way early pioneers did, you need to look down from a horse. **Canyon Trail Rides** (☎ 801/834-5219 or 801/679-8665 in the off-season), with a desk inside Bryce Lodge, offers a close-up view of Bryce's spectacular rock formations from the relative comfort of a saddle, and welcomes first-time riders. A 2-hour ride to the canyon floor and back costs $25 per person (no one under five years old), and a half-day trip further into the canyon costs $35 per person (no one under eight years old). Riders for both trips must weigh 220 pounds or less, and rides are offered, weather permitting, from April through October.

Guided rides are also provided by **Ruby's Outlaw Trail Rides** (☎ 801/679-8761 or 800/679-5859), at Ruby's Inn, at similar rates, and Ruby's also offers a full-day ride with lunch for $75. Reservations are recommended for both companies.

WILDLIFE WATCHING

The park has a variety of wildlife, ranging from mule deer—which really seem to get around—to the commonly seen mountain short-horned lizard, often spotted while hiking down into the canyon. Occasionally you'll catch a glimpse of a mountain lion, most likely on the prowl in search of a mule deer dinner; and elk and pronghorn antelope may also be seen at higher elevations.

The Utah prairie dog, listed as a threatened species, is actually a rodent. It inhabits park meadows, but should be avoided, as its fleas may carry disease (see "Safety Concerns" earlier this chapter).

Of the many birds in the park, you're bound to hear the rather obnoxious call of the piñon blue jay. Watch for swifts and swallows as they perform their exotic acrobatics along cliff faces; binoculars will come in handy.

The Great Basin rattlesnake, although pretty, should be given a wide berth. Sometimes growing to more than 5 feet long, this rattler is the park's only poisonous reptile. However, like most rattlesnakes, it is just as anxious as you are to avoid a confrontation.

WINTER ACTIVITIES

Bryce is beautiful in the winter, with the white snow creating a perfect frosting for the red, pink, orange, and brown statues standing proudly against the cold winds. A limited number of **snowshoes** are loaned free of charge at the visitor center, and may be used anywhere in the park except on cross-country ski tracks. **Cross-country skiers**, meanwhile, will find several marked, ungroomed trails (all above the rim), including The Fairyland Trail, which leads 1 mile through a pine and juniper forest to the Fairyland Point Overlook. From here you can take the 1-mile Forest Trail back to the road, or continue north along the rim for another 1.2 miles to the park boundary. Although the entire park is open to cross-country skiers, rangers warn that it's extremely dangerous to try to ski on the steep trails leading down into the canyon. Stop at the visitor center for additional trail information, and stop at Best Western Ruby's Inn, just north of the park entrance (☎ 801/834-5341), for information on cross-country ski trails and **snowmobiling** opportunities outside the park. Ruby's grooms over 30 kilometers of ski trails, and also rents cross-country ski equipment starting at $7 for a half day.

5 Camping

IN THE PARK

Typical of the West's national park campgrounds, the two facilities at Bryce offer plenty of trees with a genuine "forest camping" experience, easy access to trails, but very limited facilities. ○ **North Campground** has 105 sites and **Sunset Campground** has 111 sites. A section of North Campground is open year-round, but Sunset Campground is open May through September only. We prefer North Campground because it's closer to the Rim Trail, making it easier to rush over to catch those amazing sunrise and sunset colors. But we would gladly take any site in either campground. Neither has RV hookups or showers, but there are modern restrooms with running water. Reservations are not accepted, so get to the park early to claim a site (usually by 2pm in the summer). Cost is $7 per night, and there is a 14-day limit. Private showers (25¢ coin-feed for 10-minute intervals) are located at a general store in the park, although it's a healthy walk from either campground. The park service also operates an RV dump station ($2 fee) in the summer.

NEARBY

Bryce Pioneer Village

80 S. Main St. (Utah 12) (P.O. Box 119), Tropic, UT 84776. ☎ **801/679-8546** or 800/222-0381. Fax 801/679-8607. 10–15 sites. $15 hookups, $5 tent. $3 dump station. $2 showers for noncampers. DISC, MC, V.

This small motel/cabins/campground combination in nearby Tropic offers an adequate campground at a reasonable price, with RV hookups and hot showers, and easy access to several restaurants. It's usually open mid-April through October.

King's Creek Campground

82 North 100 East (P.O. Box 580), Dixie National Forest, Cedar City, UT 84720. ☎ **801/865-3700**. 34 sites, no hookups. $7. No credit cards.

Located above Tropic Reservoir, this primitive forest service campground is open from Memorial Day to Labor Day, with graded gravel roads and sites nestled among tall ponderosa pines. There are flush toilets and an RV dump station, but no showers. The reservoir has two boat ramps; see "Fishing," earlier in this chapter. To get to the campground from the Bryce Canyon National Park entrance, go north 3 miles on Utah 63 to Utah 12, turn west (left), and go 2.5 miles to the King's Creek Campground Road, turn south (left) and follow signs to Tropic Reservoir for about 8 miles to the campground.

Red Canyon Campground

82 North 100 East (P.O. Box 580), Dixie National Forest, Cedar City, UT 84720. ☎ 801/865-3700. 36 sites, no hookups. $8. No credit cards.

This forest service campground is set among the trees along the south side of Utah 12, offering easy access and good views of the red rock formations across the highway, but some highway noise. From the Bryce Canyon National Park entrance, go north 3 miles on Utah 63 to Utah 12, turn west (left), and go 9.5 miles to the campground.

Ruby's Inn RV Park & Campground

Utah 63 (P.O. Box 22), Bryce, UT 84764. ☎ 801/834-5301 or 801/834-5341. 227 total sites: 127 with RV hookups, 100 tent. Full hookups $20, electric/water only $18.50, tent space $12. AE, DC, DISC, MC, V.

The closest campground to Bryce Canyon National Park that offers complete RV hookups, Ruby's even has shuttle bus service into the park during July and August. Many sites are shaded, including an attractive tent area, and a lake and horse pasture are adjacent to the campground. Campers have free use of the swimming pools at Ruby's Best Western motel next door, and the campground offers two coin-operated laundries, a game room, horseshoes, barbecue grills, and a store with groceries and RV supplies. It's open April through October.

6 Accommodations

IN THE PARK

✪ Bryce Canyon Lodge

Bryce Canyon National Park, UT. ☎ 801/834-5361. Information and reservations: TW Recreational Services, Inc., P.O. Box 400, Cedar City, UT 84721. ☎ 801/586-7686. Fax 801/586-3157. 114 units in motel rooms and cabins; 3 suites and 1 studio in lodge. TV TEL. $75–$80 motel double; $87–$95 cabin; $112–$115 lodge unit. Room tax is about 9%. AE, DISC, MC, V. Closed Nov–mid-Apr.

Location is what you're buying here, and there's no denying that this is the perfect place to stay while seeing Bryce Canyon National Park, allowing you to see the play of changing light on the rock formations at various times of the day. The handsome sandstone and ponderosa pine lodge, which opened in 1924, contains a busy lobby, with desks for horseback riding, tram tours, and other activities; and a gift shop that offers everything from postcards and cheap souvenirs to top-quality silver-and-turquoise Native American jewelry. The luxurious lodge suites are wonderful, with white wicker furniture, ceiling fans, and separate sitting rooms. The motel rooms are just that. Although the outside looks like a hunting lodge, the guest units are pleasant, modern motel rooms, quite spacious, with two queen-sized beds and either a balcony or patio. There's nothing at all wrong with them, except that the surroundings and exterior lead you to expect something more interesting. Our choice would be a cabin, with a decor we'd describe as "rustic luxury." They're fairly small, although the tall ceilings give a feeling of spaciousness, with stone (gas-burning) fireplaces, two queen-sized beds, pine board walls, and log beams. It just seems like the right place to stay in a national park setting such as Bryce Canyon. Reserve four to six months in advance.

NEARBY

Room taxes add about 9% to the total cost. Pets are not accepted unless otherwise noted.

Best Western Ruby's Inn

Utah 63 at the entrance to Bryce Canyon (P.O. Box 1), Bryce, UT 84764. ☎ **801/834-5341** or 800/528-1234. Fax 801/834-5265. 369 units including 6 family suites, 49 whirlpool jet tub suites, and 6 suites with free-standing whirlpool tubs. A/C TV TEL. June–Sept $80–$100 double, $115–$125 family suite, $95–$125 whirlpool suite; Apr–May and Oct $55–$81 double, $90–$110 family suite, $70–$110 whirlpool suite; Nov–Mar $42–$49 double, $80–$85 family suite, $65–$95 whirlpool suite. AE, CB, DC, DISC, EU, JCB, MC, V.

This large Best Western provides most of the beds for tired hikers and canyon rim gazers visiting Bryce Canyon National Park. The lobby, with a stone fireplace and a western motif of animal head trophies and Indian blankets, is among the busiest places in the area, with an ATM, a small liquor store, car rentals, a beauty salon, a 1-hour film processor, and tour desks where you can arrange excursions of all sorts, from horseback and all-terrain–vehicle rides to helicopter tours. Just off the lobby is a restaurant; a western art gallery; a huge general store that offers souvenirs, western clothing including cowboy hats, camping supplies, and groceries; and a U.S. post office. Outside there's a gas station.

Spread among nine separate buildings, the modern motel rooms have light-colored walls decorated with art depicting scenes of the area, wood furnishings, and shower/ tub combos. Some have whirlpool tubs, including a few with two-person whirlpool tubs. Rooms at the back of the complex will be a bit quieter, but you'll have to walk further to all the lobby activities. Services include a concierge and courtesy transportation from the Bryce Airport; and facilities include two indoor pools, one indoor and one outdoor Jacuzzi, a sundeck, bicycle rental, nature and cross-country ski trails, a game room, a business center, conference rooms for up to 300, and a coin-operated laundry. Also see the "Nearby Attractions: Kodachrome Basin State Park & More" section below. The motel accepts pets.

Bryce Pioneer Village

80 S. Main St. (Utah 12; P.O. Box 119), Tropic, UT 84776. ☎ **801/679-8546** or 800/ 222-0381. Fax 801/679-8607. 28 motel rms, 20 cabins. A/C TV TEL. Cabins $39–$79; rooms $60–$65 double. MC, V.

The small, no-frills motel rooms in a modular building have showers only (no tubs) but they're clean, have fairly large walk-in closets, and are completely adequate for those seeking a night's rest at a reasonable rate. Cabins, which were relocated from inside the national park, are more interesting and each is unique. Most are small but cute, with one queen-size bed plus a twin bed, one chair, and a small bathroom with a corner shower but no tub. Several others, which have been renovated within the past few years, are much larger, with two queen-size beds, attractive floral-print wallpaper, and average-size bathrooms with shower/tub combinations. There are also two rooms with three queen-size beds. The motel has no pool, but there is a picnic area and a small curio shop. Just outside the motel office you can see the cabin where Ebenezer and Mary Bryce, for whom the national park is named, lived in the late 1870's. The motel accepts pets. Check on possible winter closure.

Bryce Point Bed & Breakfast

61 N. 400 West (P.O. Box 96), Tropic, UT 84776-0096. ☎ **801/679-8629**. 5 rms. TV. $70 double. Rates include full breakfast. MC, V.

Each room in Lamar and Ethel LeFevre's bed-and-breakfast is named for and decorated in the style of one of the couple's children. For instance, son Les is a firefighter, so the Les and Dela room contains firefighting memorabilia and photos; and because son Lynn is in the airline industry you'll find mementos centering on airplanes in Lynn and Karen's room. The decor is tasteful and not overdone, and most rooms offer beautiful views of Bryce Point through large picture windows. All rooms have queen-size beds and private baths (showers only); and all have TV/VCR combos, with free use of the LeFevre's video collection. Breakfasts are full, satisfying, and homemade, with selections such as bacon and eggs with pancakes and apple cider syrup. A honeymoon cottage was under construction and expected to be completed sometime in 1996; call for rates and specifics. The B&B is entirely nonsmoking.

Foster's
Utah 12 (Star Route, Panguitch, UT 84759), Bryce, Utah. ☎ **801/834-5227** or 800/475-4318. Fax 801/834-5304. 52 units. A/C TV TEL. Winter $39.95 double; summer $49.95 double. AE, DISC, MC, V.

You'll find clean, quiet, and economical lodging at Foster's, located 1½ miles west of the Bryce Canyon National Park access road turn-off. Also on the grounds is a restaurant (see "Dining," below), a grocery store, and AAA towing service. A modular unit contains small rooms, each with either one queen-size or two double beds decorated with posters showing scenery of the area; bathrooms have showers only. A plus is the excellent bakery in the adjacent grocery store.

World Host Bryce Valley Inn
2nd North and Main streets, Tropic, UT 84776. ☎ **801/679-8811** or 800/442-1890. Fax 801/679-8846. 65 rms. A/C TV TEL. Apr–Oct $60–$75 double; Nov–Mar $30–$45 double. AE, MC, V.

These simply decorated, basic motel rooms offer a clean, economical choice for park visitors. Rooms, all of which have shower/tub combos and light-colored walls, are furnished with either one or two queen-size beds. There's one suite with two queen beds and a hideabed, and one handicapped-accessible room. The motel has an outdoor whirlpool tub (but no pool), and a 24-hour coin-operated laundry. The Hungry Coyote Restaurant & Saloon (see "Dining," below) serves three meals daily featuring American and Mexican cuisine, and there's a separate ice cream parlor. A gift shop on the premises offers a large selection of Native American arts and crafts, handmade gifts, rocks, and fossils. Pets are accepted with a $5 fee.

7 Dining
IN THE PARK

Bryce Canyon Lodge
Bryce Canyon National Park. ☎ **801/834-5361**. Reservations required for dinner. Breakfast $3.50–$5.95; lunch $4.25–$6.95; dinner $10.50–$15.95. AE, DC, DISC, MC, V. Daily 6:30–10am, 11:30am–2:30pm, and 5:30–9:30pm. Closed Nov–mid-Apr. AMERICAN.

It's worth coming here just for the mountain lodge atmosphere, with two large stone fireplaces, Native American weavings and baskets, a huge 45-star 1897 American flag, and large windows looking out on the park. But the food's pretty good, too—and reasonably priced considering that this is the only real restaurant actually in the park. House specialties at dinner include an excellent slow-roasted prime rib au jus, and several barbecue selections, including slow-roasted pork ribs and broiled chicken breast. We also recommend the fresh mountain trout. There are several vegetarian items on the menu, such as spinach and cheese tortellini, served with white sauce; and ask about the lodge's specialty ice creams, such as the exotic and very tasty wild berry crunch. At lunch you'll find the trout and barbecued pork plus burgers, sandwiches, and salads; and breakfasts offer all the usual American selections. Service is attentive and friendly, but a bit too speedy at dinner. The restaurant will pack lunches to go for hikers, and offers a children's menu and full liquor service.

NEARBY

Canyon Diner
Just north of the park entrance on Utah 63, in the Ruby's Inn complex, Bryce Canyon. ☎ **801/ 834-5341.** Most items $2–$6. No credit cards. Daily 6:30am–10pm. AMERICAN.

This fast-food restaurant adjacent to the Best Western Ruby's Inn is a great place to fill up the kids without going broke. Breakfasts include several egg croissants; for lunch and dinner you can get hoagies, burgers, hot dogs, stuffed potatoes, pizza, fried chicken, and lots of salads, including a good crab salad. On a hot day, try a basic salad complemented by a filling malt or milkshake. No alcohol is served.

✪ Foster's Family Steak House
Utah 12 about 1.5 miles west of the park entrance road. ☎ **801/834-5227** or 800/475-4318. Reservations not accepted. Breakfast and lunch items $1.75–$5.99; main dinner courses $8.99–$18.99. AE, DISC, MC, V. Mar–Nov daily 7am–10pm; Dec–Feb daily 5–10pm. STEAK/SEAFOOD.

The simple western decor here provides the appropriate atmosphere for a family steakhouse, popular among locals for its slow-roasted prime rib and steamed Utah trout. Foster's also offers several steaks, including a 14-ounce T-bone, sandwiches, a soup of the day, and homemade western-style chile with beans. All the pastries, pies, and breads are baked on the premises, and a children's menu is available. Bottled beer is available with meals, and all menu items can be ordered to go.

Hungry Coyote Restaurant & Saloon
200 N. Main St. (Utah 12; 8 miles east of the park entrance road), at the World Host Bryce Valley Inn, Tropic. ☎ **801/679-8822.** Main courses $3.95–$6.95 at lunch; $4.95–$20.75 at dinner. AE, MC, V. Daily 7am–10pm; slightly shorter hours in the winter. AMERICAN/MEXICAN.

The Old West is king here, with rough wood walls, old ranch tools, kerosene lanterns, and warnings that patrons must "check your gun with the waitress." Beef eaters will savor the thick 20-ounce T-bone, the most expensive item on the menu, while fans of Mexican food go for the Supreme Burrito, a flour tortilla stuffed with either beef or chicken strips and covered with salsa and cheese. You can also get crisp deep-fried fish-and-chips, a variety of sandwiches and burgers, or the ever-popular all-you-can-eat barbecued beef ribs. The restaurant has a full liquor license.

Ruby's Inn Cowboy's Buffet and Steak Room
Just north of the park entrance on Utah 63, in the Ruby's Inn complex, Bryce. ☎ **801/ 834-5341.** Breakfast buffet $6.75 adults, $5.75 children 3–12; lunch buffet $8.75 adults, $6.75 children 3–12; main courses breakfast and lunch $3–$12.75; dinner buffet $13.95; main dinner courses $5.25–$18.50. AE, CB, DC, DISC, EU, JCB, MC, V. Summer daily 6:30am–9:30pm; winter daily 6:30am–8:30pm. STEAK/SEAFOOD.

The busiest restaurant in the Bryce Canyon area, Ruby's moves 'em through with buffets at every meal plus a well-rounded menu and friendly service. The breakfast buffet offers the usual family-restaurant buffet staples of scrambled eggs, fresh fruit, several breakfast meats, potatoes, and cereals; you can also get omelets and eggs cooked to order. At the lunch buffet you'll find country-style ribs, fresh fruit, salads, soups, vegetables, and breads; and the dinner buffet features slow-roasted beef and other meats, pastas, potatoes, and salads. Regular menu dinner entrées include prime rib, huge ribs, breaded-and-grilled southern Utah rainbow trout, broiled chicken breast, burgers, and salads. Especially good is the filet and shrimp combo, which includes an extremely tender 8-ounce filet with your choice of grilled or broiled shrimp, plus fresh sourdough bread, potato or rice, and soup or salad. Full liquor service is available.

8 Nearby Attractions: Kodachrome Basin State Park & More

SHOPPING & OTHER DIVERSIONS JUST OUTSIDE BRYCE CANYON

The **Best Western Ruby's Inn** (☎ 801/834-5341), on Utah 63 just north of the Bryce Canyon National Park entrance (see "Accommodations," above), is practically a one-stop entertainment center for those looking for a bit of variety in their Bryce Canyon vacation.

Directly across Utah 63 from the motel are **Old Bryce Town Shops,** open from mid-May through September, where you'll find a rock shop, souvenir shops, a Christmas store, and an opportunity to buy that genuine cowboy hat you've been wanting. Next to the shops is a children's petting farm (free admission), with performing horses and a cowboy poet; you can also try your hand at gold-panning ($4 pan rental).

Nearby, **Bryce Canyon Country Rodeo** has bucking broncos, bull riding, calf roping, and all sorts of rodeo fun in a 1-hour program from Memorial Day through August, Monday through Saturday evenings at 7:30pm. Admission is $6 for adults and $3 for children under 12.

KODACHROME BASIN STATE PARK

This park is one of the most scenic in Utah's fine state park system. Kodachrome Basin lives up to its name, begging to be captured on film (regardless of brand). Named by the National Geographic Society in 1949, the park is filled with tall stone towers—called chimneys—and pink-and-white sandstone cliffs, all set among the contrasting greens of sagebrush, and piñon and juniper trees.

JUST THE FACTS

Because it gets a bit warm here during the summer—the park is at 5,800 feet elevation—the best times to visit, especially for hikers, are the months of May, September, and October, when there are also fewer people.

Getting There   From Bryce Canyon National Park, go 3 miles north to the junction of Utah 63 and Utah 12, go east (right) on Utah 12 for about 12 miles to Cannonville, turn south onto the park's access road (there's a sign), and go about 7 miles to the park entrance.

Information, Fees & Regulations   Contact the **park office** at P.O. Box 238, Cannonville, UT 84718 (☎ 801/679-8562) for a color brochure and answers to questions about park facilities and services.

The day-use fee is $3 per vehicle, or $1 each for those entering the park by foot, bicycle, or motorcycle.

Dogs are permitted in the park and on trails, but must be kept on leashes no more than 6 feet long.

SPORTS & ACTIVITIES

Hiking   Kodachrome Basin offers several hiking possibilities. Starting just south of the campground, the **Panorama Trail** is only moderately difficult, with no steep climbs. At first it follows an old relatively flat wagon route, then climbs to offer views of the park's rock formations before reaching the well-named Panorama Point. Along the way are several possible side-trips, including a short walk to the **Hat Shop,** so named because the formations resemble broad-brimmed hats; and **White Buffalo Loop,** where you'll try to find a formation that looks like—guess what?—a white buffalo. The optional **Big Bear Geyser Trail** is a bit more difficult, winding past Big Bear and Mama Bear before returning to Panorama Trail. Allow 2 to 3 hours for the Panorama Trail, and an extra hour for Big Bear Geyser Trail.

Fans of arches will want to drive the dirt road to the trailhead for the half-mile round-trip hike to **Shakespeare Arch,** discovered by park manager Tom Shakespeare. This trail also has views of a large chimney rock formation.

Horseback Riding & Stagecoach Rides   Located in the park, Trail Head Station (☎ 801/679-8536) offers guided horseback or horse-drawn stagecoach rides. Call for rates and seasons.

Wildlife Watching   Jackrabbits and chukar partridges are probably the most commonly seen wildlife in the park, although you'll also hear the piñon jay, and might see an occasional coyote and rattlesnake.

CAMPING

The park's attractive 24-site **campground** has flush toilets, showers, drinking water, picnic tables, barbecue grills, and an RV dump station, but no RV hookups. Camping costs $9 Sunday through Thursday nights; $10 Fridays, Saturdays, and holidays. Contact the park office (see "Information, Fees & Regulations," above) for more information and reservations.

NATURAL WONDERS BEYOND KODACHROME BASIN STATE PARK
✪ GROSVENOR ARCH

Ten miles east of Kodachrome Basin stands a magnificent stone arch, with an opening 99 feet wide, named for National Geographic Society founder and editor Gilbert H. Grosvenor. The rather rough dirt road to the arch is passable by most motor vehicles in dry weather, but if you value your car at all, you'll drive slowly. Don't attempt the trip in wet weather or under the threat of rain. To get there, leave Kodachrome State Park and turn left; follow the dirt road 10 miles to the Arch. Allow 1¹/₂ to 2 hours to make the round-trip. The trip is a bit of a pain, but it's worth it.

RED CANYON

About 9 miles west of Bryce Canyon National Park in the Dixie National Forest is **Red Canyon**, named for its vermilion-colored rock formations, accented by stands of rich green ponderosa pine. The canyon is a favorite of hikers and mountainbikers in the summer and cross-country skiers and snowshoers in the winter.

Among Red Canyon's various trails, the **Casto Canyon Trail** is an especially scenic 17-mile one-way mountainbiking trail that's also used by all-terrain vehicles. Watch for elk in the winter, and pronghorn antelope and raptors any time. The trail starts at Tom Best Road (Forest Road 117), about 8 miles east of the junction of U.S. 89 and Utah 12. After following Tom Best Road northeast for about 3 miles, turn west (left) onto Berry Spring Creek Road (Forest Road 120), which goes about 3 miles to Cabin Hollow Road in Red Canyon, where you turn north (right), and go about 3 miles more to Casto Canyon. Here you'll turn west (left) onto a single-track trail, which you'll follow downhill some 5 miles through a beautiful red rock canyon, sprinkled with hoodoos and other bizarre, colorful rock formations. At the bottom of the canyon is a parking area, where you turn left onto a graded road that leads after 3 miles to Utah 12. It's about 6 miles east back to your starting point at Tom Best Road.

For information, contact **Dixie National Forest,** P.O. Box 580, 82 North 100 East, Cedar City, UT 84720 (☎ 801/865-3700). There's also a visitor center (open Memorial Day to Labor Day) about 10½ miles west of the intersection of Utah 12 and Utah 63 (the Bryce Canyon National Park entrance road).

9   From Bryce Canyon to Capitol Reef: Escalante & the Highway 12 Scenic Drive

Even if it didn't have a beautiful national park at each end—Bryce Canyon and Capitol Reef—the Highway 12 Scenic Byway would be well worth the drive, with its richly varied scenery and sightseeing along the way: red rock spires and canyons, evergreen forests, pastoral meadows, colorful slickrock, plunging waterfalls. There are terrific scenic viewpoints at which to stop along the way, and some wonderful natural areas and Native American and pioneer historic sites that deserve a little more of your attention. With the pleasant village of Escalante at its heart, the drive is a destination unto itself.

STARTING OUT

The Highway 12 Scenic Byway begins just outside Bryce Canyon National Park, (off U.S. 89) south of the town of Panguitch, and heads east through Red Canyon (see "Natural Wonders Beyond Kodachrome Basin State Park," above). Rising in elevation as it heads roughly east, the drive climbs out of red rock country and into Dixie National Forest toward Bryce Canyon National Park. If you're coming from Bryce, this is where your scenic drive will begin, at the junction of Utah 12 and Utah 63.

EN ROUTE TO ESCALANTE: ESCALANTE STATE PARK

Large chunks of colorful petrified wood decorate this unique park, which offers hiking, fishing, boating, camping, and panoramic vistas of the surrounding countryside. There's wildlife to watch, trails to hike, and a 30-acre reservoir for boating, fishing, and somewhat chilly swimming. It's open all year, but spring through fall are the best times to visit. Hikers should be prepared for hot summer temperatures and carry plenty of water, though.

JUST THE FACTS

Getting There   The park is 47 miles from Bryce Canyon. It's located about 2 miles before Escalante on Utah 12 at Wide Hollow Road.

Information & Visitor Centers   For a copy of the park brochure, contact **Escalante State Park,** P.O. Box 350, Escalante, UT 84726-0350 (☎ 801/826-4466). The **visitor center** has displays of petrified wood, dinosaur bones, and fossils, plus an exhibit explaining how petrified wood is formed.

Fees & Regulations   Admission costs $3 per vehicle for day-use. Like they are at most state parks, regulations are generally common sense and courtesy: Don't damage anything, drive slowly on park roads, and observe quiet hours between 10pm and 7am. In addition, you're asked to resist the temptation to carry off samples of petrified wood. Pets are welcome, even on trails, but must be restrained on leashes no more than 6 feet long.

Rock or Wood—What Is this Stuff?

It looks like a weathered, multicolored tree limb, shining and sparkling in the light—but it's heavy, hard, and solid as a rock. Just what is this stuff? Why, it's petrified wood.

Back in the old days—some 135 to 155 million years ago—southern Utah was not at all like we see it today. It was closer to the equator than it is now, which made it a wet and hot land, with lots of ferns, palm trees, and conifers providing lunch for the neighborhood dinosaurs.

Occasionally, floods would uproot the trees, dumping them in flood plains and along sandbars, then burying them with mud and silt. If this happened quickly, the layers of mud and silt would cut off the oxygen supply, halting the process of decomposition—and effectively preserving the tree trunks intact.

Later, volcanic ash covered the area, and groundwater rich in silicon dioxide and other chemicals and minerals made its way down to the ancient trees. With the silicon dioxide acting as a glue, the cells of the wood mineralized. Other waterborne minerals produced the colors: Iron painted the tree trunks in reds, browns, and yellows; manganese produced purples and blues in the preserved wood.

Later, uplifts from within the earth, along with various forms of erosion, brought the now-petrified wood to the surface in places like Utah's Escalante State Park, breaking it into the shapes we see today in the process—one that's taken only a hundred million years or so to complete.

SPORTS & ACTIVITIES

Fishing & Boating   Wide Hollow Reservoir, located partially inside the park, has a boat ramp (sorry, no rentals are available) and is a popular fishing hole for rainbow trout and bluegill. There's ice fishing in the winter.

Hiking   The 1-mile self-guided ✪ **Petrified Forest Trail** is a moderately strenuous hike among colorful rocks, through a forest of stunted juniper and piñon pine, past a painted desert, to a field of colorful petrified wood. The hike also offers panoramic vistas of the town of Escalante and surrounding stair-step plateaus. A free brochure is available at the visitor center. Allow about 45 minutes for the walk.

An optional three-quarter-mile loop off the main trail leads through lots more petrified wood, but is considerably steeper than the main trail.

Wildlife Watching   This is one of the best spots in this part of the state to see waterbirds: The reservoir is home to ducks, geese, and coots. Chukar partridges wander throughout the park, and you're also likely to see eagles, hawks, lizards, ground squirrels, and both cottontails and jackrabbits. Binoculars are helpful.

CAMPING

The 22-unit **campground**, within easy walking distance of the park's hiking trails and reservoir, is open all year. It has hot showers, modern restrooms, and drinking water, but no RV hookups. Camping is $9 Sunday through Thursday nights and $10 Fridays, Saturdays, and holidays. Camping reservations (☎ 800/322-3770) are available for a $5 nonrefundable fee using MasterCard or Visa.

BASING YOURSELF IN ESCALANTE

Originally called Potato Valley, this community's name was changed in the 19th century to honor Spanish explorer and missionary Father Silvestre Velez de Escalante (although it's believed Escalante never visited this particular part of southern Utah on his trek from Santa Fe, New Mexico, to California a hundred years earlier). It's now home to nearly 100 historic buildings, and Escalante is your best bet for lodging, food, and supplies as you travel Utah 12. It's also a good home base for exploring the nearby mountains, or for finally taking a hot shower after a week of backpacking. Be aware that services in this town of 800 are somewhat limited in the winter, though.

ESSENTIALS

Getting There   Escalante is 50 miles east of Bryce Canyon National Park and 63 miles south of Capitol Reef National Park on the Highway 12 Scenic Byway. Utah 12 becomes Main Street as it goes through Escalante.

Information   An information booth is open during the summer months on Main Street (Utah 12), just east of Center Street. Information is also available from the **Escalante Chamber of Commerce**, P.O. Box 326, Escalante, UT 84726 (☎ 801/826-4810).

The **National Park Service, Dixie National Forest**, and the **Bureau of Land Management** operate an interagency office that provides recreation information year-round. It's located on the west side of town at 755 W. Main St. (Utah 12), P.O. Box 246, Escalante, UT 84726 (☎ 801/826-5499). From April to October, the office is open daily from 7am to 6pm; the rest of the year, it's open Monday through Friday from 8am to 5pm.

Fast Facts   The **Ivan Kazan Memorial Clinic** is at 65 N. Center St. (☎ 801/826-4374). The **post office** is at 230 W. Main St. (☎ 801/826-4314).

WHERE TO STAY

A room tax of about 9% is added to all bills. Pets are not accepted unless otherwise noted.

⑤ Circle D Motel

475 W. Main St. (Utah 12; P.O. Box 305), Escalante, UT 84726. ☎ **801/826-4297.** Fax 801/826-4402. 29 units. A/C $25–$45 double; $50–$75 family units. AE, MC, V.

You'll find clean, well-maintained basic lodging at this family-owned and -operated motel, one of the few in Escalante that's open year-round. Rooms are simple, and you have a choice of two double beds, one queen-size bed, or a king. Family units sleep from five to eight, and some units have small refrigerators. There's no swimming pool, but at these rates, who can complain? Pets are accepted for a $5 fee.

Escalante Outfitters, Inc.

310 W. Main St. (Utah 12; P.O. Box 158), Escalante, UT 84726. ☎ **801/826-4266.** Fax 801/826-4388. 7 cabins. $24.95 double. DISC, MC, V. Check on possible closure Nov–Feb.

These cute little log cabins are a favorite of backpackers who want a break from sleeping on the ground. Think of this place as a cross between a motel and a campground; actually, it's closer to the auto camps of the 1930s. Built in 1994–95, the cabins have either one double bed or a pair of bunk beds, a chair, a small table with a lamp, and two small windows. There's heat in cool weather and fans for warm weather. That's it. There are no private baths; guests share a simple but adequate and well-maintained bathhouse. On the grounds are a duck pond, barbecue pits, picnic tables, horseshoe pits, and a volleyball court. A pay phone is nearby.

Prospector Inn

380 W. Main St. (Utah 12; P.O. Box 296), Escalante, UT 84726. ☎ **801/826-GOLD.** Fax 801/826-4285. 51 rms. A/C TV TEL. $50–$60 double. AE, MC, V. Check on possible winter closure.

You can't miss this distinctive two-story motel (built in 1994), with its vertically set red brick-and-metal roof. Rooms are particularly quiet and spacious, with two double beds, and decorated with framed photos of the area's scenery. There's a small gift shop, but no swimming pool. Free morning coffee is available in the lobby. A restaurant and lounge was under construction in late 1995; it's scheduled to serve three meals daily and specialize in steak.

WHERE TO DINE

Circle D Restaurant

475 W. Main St. (Utah 12), Escalante. ☎ **801/826-4297.** Main courses $5–$13.75; breakfast $3.50–$5.50; sandwiches $3.25–$6.95. AE, MC, V. Daily 7am–9pm. MEXICAN/AMERICAN.

This southwestern cafe-style restaurant, with four separate dining rooms, offers a good variety of food, from burgers and sandwiches to the popular rib eye steak, liver and onions, and breaded veal cutlet. Particularly good are the Navajo tacos, which consist of traditional Navajo fry bread stuffed with taco ingredients; and Mexican items such as the huge burritos smothered in red chile sauce and served with rice, beans, chips, and salsa. Breakfasts include all the usual selections, plus eye-openers such as the Moqui omelet, with mushrooms, sausage, two cheeses, and a spicy marinara sauce. No alcohol is served.

Cowboy Blues Diner

530 W. Main St. (Utah 12), Escalante. ☎ **801/826-4251.** Main courses $4.75–$13.95; breakfast $2.25–$8.75; sandwiches $3.50–$5.75. DISC, MC, V. Daily 7am–10pm, shorter hours in the winter. SOUTHWESTERN/AMERICAN.

This western diner—the wood plank walls are even decorated with steer skulls—offers lots of steak, hot and cold sandwiches, and its specialty southwestern dishes such as chicken quesadillas, Navajo tacos, and the combo: a beef enchilada, a cheese enchilada, soft taco, rice, beans, chips, and salsa. The tasty, but not overly spicy, chile is served on the side to let you add just the right amount. Breakfasts include all the usual selections. Alcohol is not served.

SIDE TRIPS FROM ESCALANTE
POSEY LAKE

This picturesque mountain lake, under the jurisdiction of the **U.S. Forest Service** (☎ 801/826-5499), is located 13 miles northwest of Escalante via Utah 12 and the Posey Lake Scenic Backway (Forest Road 153).

The trout fishing's good, there's a boat ramp, and powerboats are allowed. The numerous dirt roads are popular with mountainbikers and hikers in the summer, with cross-country skiers and snowmobilers in the winter. The primitive **Posey Lake Campground,** open in the summer only, has 19 sites; call the Forest Service for details.

HOLE-IN-THE-ROCK SCENIC BACKWAY

Starting about 5 miles east of Escalante off Utah 12, this clearly marked dirt road travels 57 miles (one way) to the **Hole-in-the-Rock,** where Mormon settlers, in 1880, cut a passage through solid rock and used ropes to lower their wagons down a 1,200-foot cliff to the canyon floor and Colorado River below. Administered by the **Bureau of Land Management** (☎ 801/826-5499), the road passes through **Devil's Rock Garden,** an area of unique rock formations and arches, and offers other views of southern Utah's scenery—including, at the end, a scenic overlook of Lake Powell.

The last 5 miles of the road require a high clearance vehicle, and you'll want to avoid the byway in wet weather. Allow about 6 hours round-trip, and make sure you have plenty of fuel and water.

FARTHER ALONG UTAH 12
CALF CREEK RECREATION AREA

Located about 15 miles northeast of Escalante via Utah 12, this recreation area is operated by the federal **Bureau of Land Management** (☎ 801/826-5499), and has a primitive campground with about a dozen sites, a picnic area, and trout fishing stream. The best part of the recreation area, though, is the fairly easy 5.5-mile round-trip hike to **Lower Calf Creek Falls**; you can pick up an interpretive brochure at the trailhead. A sandy trail leads along **Calf Creek,** past beaver ponds and wetlands, to a beautiful waterfall, cascading 126 feet down a rock wall into a tree-shaded pool.

ANASAZI INDIAN VILLAGE STATE PARK

Visitors to this state park, in the village of Boulder (about 27 miles northeast of Escalante along Utah 12), step back to the 12th century A.D. when the Kayenta Anasazi lived here, in one of the largest Anasazi communities west of the Colorado River. The 6-acre park includes the ruins of the village, a full-size six-room replica of an Anasazi home, a gift shop, a picnic area, a 30-seat auditorium, and a museum. From mid-May through mid-September, the park is open daily from 8am to 6pm; the rest of the year it's open daily from 9am to 5pm. Admission is $1.50 for those 16 and older, $1 for those ages 6 to 15, and free for children under six; there's a family rate of $6. The park has no campground. For further information, contact **Anasazi Indian Village State Park**, P.O. Box 1329, Boulder, UT 84716-1329 (☎ 801/335-7308).

BOULDER MOUNTAIN

Among the most dramatic views along Utah 12 are at an elevation of 9,670 feet, from the pullouts atop ✪ **Boulder Mountain**, some 45 miles northeast of Escalante. From viewpoints such as **Point Lookout**, you'll gaze out over the colorful sandstone rock cliffs of Capitol Reef National Park to the imposing Henry Mountains, Navajo Mountain, and sights more than 100 miles away.

Those venturing into the backcountry by foot, four-wheel-drive, mountainbike, or horse will discover rugged, remote beauty; the area is also a trout fisherman's paradise, with dozens of secluded mountain lakes and streams hidden among the tall pines and firs. Don't be surprised to see mule deer, elk, and wild turkey in the open meadows.

Several primitive campgrounds are operated by the **U.S. Forest Service** (☎ 801/826-5499), with both RV and tent sites. The **Wildcat Ranger Station** of the Dixie National Forest has an information center along the highway.

ON THE ROAD TO CAPITOL REEF

After Boulder, it's not too much farther to Capitol Reef National Park. The next community you'll reach is Torrey, where Utah 12 intersects with Utah 24. Turn right and proceed to the park. See Chapter 14 for complete coverage of Capitol Reef.

14 Capitol Reef National Park

We don't want to write this chapter. Capitol Reef National Park is one of those little-known gems, drawing far fewer visitors than its more famous neighbors, Bryce Canyon and Zion. To be honest, we'd like to be selfish, and keep this jewel of a park to ourselves.

Alas, we can't. For one thing, Capitol Reef is a place you really should know about. In the summer of 1995, *Outside* magazine sang the praises of Capitol Reef as one of America's eight undervisited national parks—"parks as they were meant to be." So the secret's getting out.

Capitol Reef offers more of that spectacular southern Utah scenery, but with a unique twist and a personality of its own. The area's geologic formations are downright peculiar. This is a place to let your imagination run wild. You'll see appropriately named Hamburger Rocks, sitting atop a white sandstone table; the tall, bright red Chimney Rock; the silent and eerie Temple of the Moon; and the commanding Castle. The colors of Capitol Reef's canyon walls draw from a spectacular palette, which is why the Navajos called the area "The Land of the Sleeping Rainbow."

But unlike some of southern Utah's other parks, Capitol Reef is more than just brilliant rocks and barren desert. Here the Fremont River has helped create a lush oasis in an otherwise unforgiving land, with cottonwood, willow, ash, and other trees along its banks. In fact, 19th-century pioneers found the land so inviting and the soil so fertile that they established the community of Fruita, planting orchards that have been preserved by the Park Service.

Because of differences in elevation and the lack of water in different sections of the park, you'll find a variety of terrain and possible activities. There are hiking, mountainbiking, and four-wheeling trails; the lush fruit orchard; rich, green forests and desert wildflowers; an abundance of songbirds; and a surprising amount of wildlife—from lizards and snakes to the bashful ring-tailed cat (which isn't a cat at all, but a member of the raccoon family). You'll find thousand-year-old petroglyphs, left behind by the ancient Fremont and Anasazi peoples, and other traces of history left by relatively modern Southern Paiutes, Wild West outlaws, and industrious Mormon pioneers (in the Fruita Schoolhouse, their children learned the three Rs and studied the Bible and Book of Mormon).

The name Capitol Reef, which conjures up an image of a tropical shoreline, seems odd for a park composed of cliffs and canyons and situated in landlocked Utah. But many of the pioneers who settled the West were former seafaring men, and they extended the traditional meaning of the word "reef" to include these seemingly impassable rock barriers. The huge round white domes of sandstone reminded them of the domes of capitol buildings, and so this area become known as Capitol Reef.

Actually, to be accurate, the park should probably be called The Big Fold. When the earth's crust uplifted some 65 million years ago, creating the Rocky Mountains and Colorado Plateau, most of this uplifting was relatively even. But here, through one of those fascinating quirks of nature, the crust wrinkled into a huge fold. Running for 100 miles, almost all within the national park, it's known as the Waterpocket Fold.

1 Just the Facts

Getting There   Capitol Reef National Park is 121 miles northeast of Bryce Canyon National Park, 204 miles northeast of Zion National Park, 224 miles south of Salt Lake City, and 366 miles northwest of Las Vegas, Nev. The park straddles Utah 24, which connects with I-70 both to the northeast and northwest. Those coming from Bryce Canyon National Park can follow Utah 12 northeast (see "From Bryce Canyon to Capitol Reef: Escalante and the Highway 12 Scenic Drive" in Chapter 13) to its intersection with Utah 24, and follow that east into Capitol Reef. If you're approaching the park from Glen Canyon National Recreation Area and the Four Corners region, follow Utah 276 and/or Utah 95 north to the intersection with Utah 24, where you'll then go west into the park.

Information & Visitor Centers   For advance information on what to see in the park, hiking trails, and camping, write: Superintendent, **Capitol Reef National Park,** Torrey, UT 84775 (☎ 801/425-3791).

The **visitor center** is located on the park access road at its intersection with Utah 24. There's a path along the access road that connects the visitor center and campground, passing the historic blacksmith shop of Fruita, orchards, and a lovely shaded picnic ground. The visitor center has exhibits on the geology and history of the area and presents a short introductory slide show on the park. Rangers can answer questions and provide backcountry permits, several free brochures are available, and books, maps, videos, postcards, and posters are sold. The visitor center is open daily year-round.

Fees, Regulations & Backcountry Permits   Entry into the park (for up to seven days) costs $4 per vehicle or $2 per motorcycle, bicycle, or pedestrian.

Free permits, available at the visitor center, are required for all overnight trips into the backcountry.

As for regulations, bicycles are prohibited in the backcountry and on all hiking trails. Feeding or molesting wildlife, vandalism, and disturbing any natural feature of the park are all prohibited. Because skunks refuse to follow park rules regarding wildlife diet, campers should be especially careful of where they store food, and dispose of garbage promptly. Dogs, which must be leashed at all times, are prohibited on all trails, more than 100 feet from any road, and in public buildings.

Seasons & Avoiding the Crowds   Although Capitol Reef National Park receives only a half-million visitors annually—making it among the least-visited national parks in the West—it can still be busy, especially during its peak summer season. For this reason, the best time to visit is fall; particularly in October and November, when

Butch Cassidy, Utah's Most Infamous Son

Robert LeRoy Parker wasn't a bad kid. He was born into a hard-working Mormon family in a little southwestern Utah town called Beaver on April 13, 1866. Robert was the oldest of 13 children; he was a great help to his mother, working on the small ranch his parents bought near Circleville.

Circleville was where the problems began. Teenaged Robert fell in with some rather unsavory characters, including one Mike Cassidy, the ne'er-do-well role model who gave the youth his first gun. The boy made his way to Telluride, Colorado, worked for one of the mines there for a while, and then wandered up to Wyoming. A little more wandering took him back to Telluride—and, strangely enough, the Telluride bank was robbed. Butch Cassidy had officially begun his life of crime.

In the following years, Butch—who gained the nickname after a short stint working in a butcher shop—became an expert at rustling cattle, robbing banks, and, his ultimate glory, robbing trains. Butch wanted to call his gang the Train Robbers Syndicate, but they raised such hell in celebration of their economic successes that saloon keepers in Vernal and other Utah towns began calling them "that wild bunch," and the name stuck. The Wild Bunch would travel through Utah, hiding out in the desolate badlands that were to become Bryce Canyon, Capitol Reef, and Canyonlands National Parks. Capitol Reef's Cassidy Arch was named after Butch; it was supposedly one of his favorite hiding places.

If you've seen the 1969 movie *Butch Cassidy and the Sundance Kid,* with Paul Newman as Butch and Robert Redford as his partner-in-crime Sundance, you can't forget that spectacular scene where Butch and his cohorts blow the door off a railroad car; they then use too much dynamite to open the safe, sending bills flying into the air. Apparently, it's basically true, having taken place on June 2, 1899 near Wilcox, Wyoming. According to reports of the day, they got away with $30,000.

The Union Pacific Railroad took exception to Butch's antics. When the posses started getting a bit too close, Butch, Sundance, and Sundance's lady friend, Etta Place (Katharine Ross in the film), took off for South America, where it's said they continued a life of crime for a half dozen or so years. There are also some stories—unconfirmed—that it was in South America that Butch first killed anyone, that up until that time he had avoided bloodshed whenever possible.

According to some historians (as well as the movie version of Butch's life), Butch and Sundance were shot dead in a gun battle with army troops in Bolivia. But others say it's not so, that Butch returned to the United States, visited friends and family in Utah and Wyoming, and eventually settled in Spokane, Washington, where he lived a peaceful and respectable life under the name William T. Phillips, until he died of natural causes in 1937.

temperatures remain warm enough for comfortable hiking and camping, but not so hot as to send you constantly in search of shade. You also don't have to be as worried about flash floods through narrow canyons as you do during the July-through-September thunderstorm season.

Safety Concerns   While most visitors to the park enjoy a wonderful vacation without mishap, problems can occur. Hikers need to carry plenty of water, especially in midsummer, and watch out for rattlesnakes. The midget rattlesnake is only 12 to 18 inches long, while its larger cousin, the Great Basin rattlesnake, can grow to 2 feet in length. Both will try to avoid you, but will strike if cornered.

Capitol Reef National Park

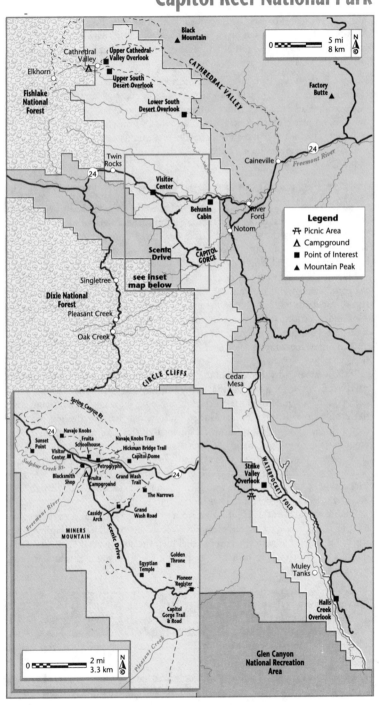

Black Mountain ▲

0 ___ 5 mi
0 ___ 8 km
N

Cathedral Valley ○
Elkhorn ○
△

Upper Cathedral Valley Overlook ■
Upper South Desert Overlook ■
Lower South Desert Overlook ■

CATHREDRAL VALLEY

Factory Butte ▲

Fishlake National Forest

24

Caineville ○

Freemont River

Twin Rocks ○

24

Visitor Center ■

Behunin Cabin ■

River Ford ○
Notom ○

Legend
⅄ Picnic Area
△ Campground
■ Point of Interest
▲ Mountain Peak

Scenic Drive

CAPITOL GORGE

see inset map below

Singletree ○

Dixie National Forest

Pleasant Creek ○

Oak Creek ○

CIRCLE CLIFFS

Cedar Mesa △ ○

Strike Valley Overlook ■
⅄

WATERPOCKET FOLD

Inset map

Spring Canyon Rt.

24
Navajo Knobs
Sunset Point ■
Fruita Schoolhouse
Navajo Knobs Trail
Hickman Bridge Trail
Visitor Center ■
Petroglyphs
Capitol Dome
Sulphur Creek Rv.
Blacksmith Shop
Fruita Campground △
Grand Wash Trail
24
The Narrows
Freemont River
Cassidy Arch
Grand Wash Road

MINERS MOUNTAIN

Scenic Drive

Egyptian Temple
Golden Throne
Pioneer Register

Capitol Gorge Trail & Road

Pleasant Creek

0 ___ 2 mi
0 ___ 3.3 km
N

Muley Tanks ○

Halls Creek Overlook ■

Glen Canyon National Recreation Area

The other major concern is the weather: Afternoon thunderstorms during July, August, and September can bring flash floods, which fill narrow canyons without warning. Steep-walled Grand Wash can be particularly hazardous, and should be avoided whenever storms are threatening.

Ranger Programs   Park rangers present a variety of free programs and activities from the spring through fall. Campfire programs take place most evenings at the outdoor amphitheater near Fruita Campground. Topics vary, but could include the animals and plants of the park, geology, and man's history in the area. Rangers also give short talks at the pioneer Fruita Schoolhouse on its history, and lead hikes and walks. Schedules are posted on bulletin boards at the visitor center and Fruita Campground.

2 Exploring the Highlights by Car

As with most national parks, it would be easy to spend a week or more here, hiking the trails, admiring the views, and loafing about the campground. However, those with a limited amount of time, or who prefer the comfort of a car to the demands of the hiking trail, will find that Capitol Reef is relatively easy to see.

Start at the **visitor center,** of course, and watch the short slide show explaining the park's geology and early history. From the visitor center, a paved 25-mile round-trip **scenic drive** leads south into the park, offering good views of the dramatic canyons and rock formations that comprise Capitol Reef. Pick up a copy of the free scenic drive brochure at the visitor center, then set out, stopping at viewpoints to gaze up and out at the array of colorful cliffs, monoliths, and commanding rock formations.

If the weather is dry, drive down the gravel **Capitol Gorge Road** at the end of the paved scenic drive for a look at what many consider the best backcountry scenery in the park. It's a 5-mile round-trip drive. If you're up for a short walk, the relatively flat 2-mile (round-trip) **Capitol Gorge Trail,** which starts at the end of Capitol Gorge Road, takes you to the historic **Pioneer Register,** a rock wall where traveling pioneers "signed in" (see "Sports & Activities," below).

Another dry-weather option is the **Grand Wash Road,** a maintained dirt road that is subject to flash floods, but in good weather offers an easy route into spectacular backcountry. Along the 2-mile round-trip you'll see **Cassidy Arch,** where famed outlaw Butch Cassidy is said to have hidden out.

Utah 24, which crosses Capitol Reef from east to west, also has several viewpoints offering a good look at the park's features, such as the monumental **Capitol Dome,** which resembles the dome of a capitol building; the aptly named Castle formation; the historic **Fruita Schoolhouse;** and some roadside **petroglyphs** left by the prehistoric Fremont people (see below).

3 From Petroglyphs to a Pioneer Schoolhouse: Capitol Reef's Historic Sites

Throughout the park you'll find evidence of man's presence here through the centuries.

The Fremont People   The Fremont people lived along the river as early as A.D. 700, staying until about A.D. 1250. Primarily hunters and gatherers, the Fremont also grew corn, beans, and squash to supplement their diet, and when they abandoned the area they left little behind. They lived in pit houses, which were dug into the ground

Impressions

The colors are such as no pigments can portray. They are deep, rich, and variegated; and so luminous are they, that light seems to flow or shine out of the rock.

—Geologist C.E. Dutton, 1880

and surrounded with boulders that supported the roof. The remains of one can be seen from the **Hickman Bridge Trail**. Many of the Fremont's petroglyphs (images carved into rock) and some pictographs (images painted on rock) are still visible on the canyon walls. If we could read them, they might even tell us why these early Americans left the area, a puzzle that continues to baffle historians and archaeologists.

Nineteenth-Century Pioneers   Prospectors and other travelers passed through the **Capitol Gorge** section of the park in the late 1800s, leaving their names on the Pioneer Register. You can reach the **Pioneer Register** via a 2-mile loop; see "Hiking," below.

Mormon pioneers established the aptly named community of **Fruita** when it was discovered that this was a good locale for growing fruit. The tiny Fruita Schoolhouse, built in 1896, was a church, social hall, and community meeting hall in addition to a one-room schoolhouse. The school closed in 1941, but was carefully restored by the National Park Service in 1984, and is authentically furnished with old wood and wrought-iron desks, a wood stove, chalk board, and textbooks. The handbell used to call students to class still rests on the corner of the teacher's desk. The orchards those Mormon settlers planted continue to flourish, tended by park workers who invite you to sample the "fruits" of their labors.

4 Sports & Activities

Among the last areas in the continental United States to be explored, many parts of Capitol Reef National Park are still practically unknown, perfect for those who want to see this rugged country in its natural state.

FOUR-WHEELING & MOUNTAINBIKING

As in most national parks, bikes and four-wheel-drive vehicles are restricted to established roads, but Capitol Reef has several so-called roads—that are actually little more than dirt trails—that provide exciting opportunities for those using 4X4's or pedal-power.

The only route appropriate for road bikes is the 25-mile round-trip scenic drive, described above, but both the Grand Wash and Capitol Gorge roads (see "Exploring the Highlights," above), plus three much longer dirt roads, are open to mountainbikes as well as four-wheel-drive vehicles. Be aware that rain can make the roads impassable, so it's best to check on current conditions with park rangers before setting out.

Our recommended trip is the **Cathedral Valley Loop**. It covers more than 60 miles on a variety of road surfaces, including dirt, sand, and rock, and requires the fording of the Fremont River, where water is usually 1- to 1 1/2-feet deep. But your rewards are beautiful, unspoiled scenery, including bizarre sandstone monoliths and majestic cliffs, in one of the park's most remote areas. There's a small primitive campground in Cathedral Valley (see "Camping," below). Access to this loop is from Utah 24, just outside the park, 11.7 miles east of the visitor center via the River Ford

Road, or 18.6 miles east of the visitor center on the Caineville Wash Road. A road guide can be purchased (50¢) at the visitor center.

Mountainbike tours into the national park and surrounding areas are provided by **Pedal Pusher Bikes & Tours** in Torrey (☎ 801/425-3378 or 800/896-5773). Prices start at about $20 for a short evening trip; full-day trips cost about $60, and three-day trips are about $400. Pedal Pusher also operates a full-service bike shop, including parts, accessories, and repairs.

Four-wheel-drive jeep tours are available from **Hondoo Rivers & Trails** in Torrey (☎ 801/425-3519 or 800/332-2696), starting at about $60 per person with a three-person minimum.

HIKING

Trails through Capitol Reef National Park offer sweeping panoramas of colorful cliffs and soaring spires, eerie journeys through desolate, steep-walled canyons, and cool oases along the tree-shaded Fremont River. Watch carefully for petroglyphs and other reminders of this area's first inhabitants. This is also the real Wild West, little changed from the way cowboys, bank robbers, settlers, and gold miners found it in the late 1800s, and one of the best things about hiking here is the combination of scenic beauty, Native American art, and western history you'll discover.

Park rangers can help you choose trails best suited to the time of year, weather conditions, and your personal physical condition; and those planning serious backpacking will want to buy topographic maps, available at the visitor center. The summer sun is intense, so hats and sunscreen are mandatory, and a gallon of water per person is recommended. Also see the "Safety Concerns" section above.

Among our favorite short hikes at Capitol Reef is the 2-mile round-trip ✪ **Capitol Gorge Trail**. It's easy, mostly level walking along the bottom of a narrow canyon, but looking up at the tall, smooth walls of rock conveys a good sense of what the pioneers must have seen and felt 100 years ago when they moved rocks and debris to haul their wagons up this canyon. Starting at the end of the dirt Capitol Gorge Road, the hiking trail leads past the **Pioneer Register,** where prospectors and other early travelers carved their names. The earliest legible signatures were made in 1871 by J.A. Call and "Wal." Bateman.

Another short hike, but quite a bit more strenuous, is the 3.5-mile round-trip **Cassidy Arch Trail**. This offers spectacular views as it climbs steeply from the floor of Grand Wash to high cliffs overlooking the park. From the trail you'll also get several perspectives of Cassidy Arch, a natural stone arch named for outlaw Butch Cassidy, who is believed to have occasionally used the Grand Wash as a hideout. The trail is off the Grand Wash dirt road, which branches off the east side of the highway about halfway down the park's scenic drive.

Those seeking a longer outing might enjoy the strenuous **Navajo Knobs** hike, a 9-mile round-trip hike that starts with a look at **Hickman Natural Bridge,** then climbs up 1,000-foot cliffs for a view of the **Fruita Orchard and campground.** It then continues several miles to Navajo Knobs for a spectacular 360° panoramic view of the park. The trail starts at Utah 24 at the Hickman Bridge trailhead, east of the visitor center, and follows that trail until it branches off to the north.

HORSEBACK RIDING

Horses are welcome on some park trails but prohibited on others; check at the visitor center. **Pleasant Creek Trail Rides**, P.O. Box 102, Bicknell, UT 84715 (☎ 801/425-3315 or 800/892-5497; fax 801/425-3806), offers a variety of rides in the area, ranging from 1 hour to six days. A full-day ride through Capitol Reef National Park, including lunch, costs about $85.

WILDLIFE VIEWING

Although summer temperatures are hot and there's always the threat of a thunderstorm, it's a good season for wildlife viewing. There are many species of lizards in the park, and you will probably catch a glimpse of one warming itself on a rock. The western whiptail, eastern fence, and side-blotched lizards are the most common, but the loveliest is the collared lizard, dark in color but with light speckles that allow it to blend easily with lava rocks and become almost invisible to its foes. Watch for deer throughout the park, especially along the path between the visitor center and Fruita Campground. This area is also where you're likely to see chipmunks and antelope ground squirrels. If you keep your eyes to the sky you may see a golden eagle, and numerous songbirds pass through each year. Although they're somewhat shy and only emerge from their dens at night, the ring-tailed cat, a member of the raccoon family, also makes the park his home; as do the seldom-seen bobcat, cougar, fox, marmot, and coyote.

5 Camping

IN THE PARK

The 71-site **Fruita Campground**, open year-round, has modern restrooms, drinking water, picnic tables, fire grills, and an RV dump station, but no showers or RV hookups. It's located along the main park road, 1 mile south of the visitor center. Reservations are not accepted. Camping costs $7 year-round, and water may be turned off in the winter, leaving only pit toilets.

The park also has two primitive campgrounds, free and open year-round on a first-come, first-served basis. **Cedar Mesa Campground** is located in the southern part of the park, about 8 miles down unpaved Notom-Bullfrog Road, which heads south off Utah 24 just outside the eastern entrance to the park. It has five sites, tables, fire grills, and pit toilets, but no water. Check road conditions before going, as it may be impassable in wet weather. **Cathedral Valley Campground** is located in the northern part of the park. From Utah 24 (about 5 miles east of the park), turn north on unpaved Cathedral Valley Road and go about 30 miles. It has five sites, tables, fire grills, and pit toilets, but no water. A high-clearance or four-wheel-drive vehicle is necessary, and the road may be impassable in wet weather.

Backcountry camping is permitted in much of the park with a free permit, available at the visitor center.

NEARBY

The **Rim Rock Rustic Inn**, 2523 E. Utah 24, in Torrey (☎ 801/425-3843), also operates a basic campground on its property. See "Accommodations" below.

Thousand Lakes RV Park & Campground

Utah 24, 6 miles west of Capitol Reef National Park (P.O. Box 750070), Torrey, UT 84775. ☎ **801/425-3500.** 58 RV sites with hookups, 9 tent sites, 2 cabins. $13.50–$16.50 RV site, $9–$10.50 tent site, $26–$29 cabin. DISC, MC, V. Closed Nov–Mar.

Good views of surrounding rock formations are a plus for this campground, which also has some shady trees. RV sites are gravel, and tent sites are grass. The bath house is particularly attractive, and there is also a convenience store, dump station, heated swimming pool, horseshoes, and barbecues.

6 Accommodations

There are no lodging or dining facilities in the park itself, but the town of Torrey, just west of the park entrance, can take care of most needs. Room tax adds about 9% to lodging bills.

While you're in Torrey, art lovers might want to stop at the **Entrada Institute,** 85 W. Main St. (☎ 801/425-3265), which displays works by Utah artists and sponsors a variety of workshops, lectures, and other programs. Recent projects have included three-day workshops for photographers and watercolorists, with excursions into the national park and surrounding scenic areas. Costs run from $110 to $200 per person.

Best Western Capitol Reef Resort

2600 E. Utah 24 (P.O. Box 750160), Torrey, UT 84775. ☎ **801/425-3761** or 800/528-1234. Fax 801/425-3300. 30 rms. A/C TV TEL. Apr–Oct $59–$95 double; off-season $49–$75 double. AE, CB, DC, DISC, MC, V.

Located a mile west of the national park entrance and built in 1992, this well-maintained Best Western provides an excellent location for park visitors. Try to get a room on the back side of the motel; you'll be rewarded with fantastic views of the area's red rock formations. Standard rooms have two queen-sized beds, white stucco walls, and southwestern-style scenic prints. A restaurant serves three meals daily year-round. A plus is the outdoor heated pool, whirlpool, and sundeck, all out back away from road noise, with glass wind barriers and spectacular views.

Rim Rock Rustic Inn

2523 E. Utah 24 (P.O. Box 750264), Torrey, UT 84775. ☎ **801/425-3843** or 800/354-0786. Fax 801/425-3855. 31 rms. TV TEL. $55–$75 double. AE, CB, DC, DISC, MC, V.

A slow renovation process was in the works when we checked this place out in 1995, as new owners were striving to make the Rim Rock Rustic Inn a little less rustic, while retaining its Old West ambiance. Built in 1961, rooms have one rough wood wall and three white stucco walls, and most offer splendid views. Some rooms have air-conditioning while others have fans. Standard rooms offer a choice of two double beds, one queen, or one king; and three family rooms each have three queen-sized beds. The more recently renovated rooms are nicer, of course, but during our visit all units appeared clean and well kept. There's an indoor heated pool and a whirlpool, and a restaurant serves three meals daily year-round. Pets are welcome.

The Rim Rock also operates a basic campground on the property. It has 35 sites with hookups, 30 tent sites, and an attractive bath house. Camping fee is $15 with hookups and $10 for tenters.

✪ Skyridge Bed & Breakfast Inn

On Utah 24, just east of the intersection of Utah 24 and 12 (P.O. Box 750220), Torrey, UT 84775. ☎ **801/425-3222**. 5 rms. TV. $68–$98 double. Rates include breakfast. MC, V.

This combination bed-and-breakfast and art gallery offers a delightful alternative to the standard motel. The three-story contemporary inn, with territorial-style appearance, has five distinctive rooms, each with private bath, a queen-size bed or two, television, and VCR. Each bedroom is decorated with an eclectic mix of antiques, collectibles, folk sculpture, and contemporary art, including at least one piece by innkeeper/artist Karen Kesler. One room has a private deck with a hot tub, and another has a two-person whirlpool tub. The shared gallery/living room has an impressive fireplace, decorated with over 30 pounds of roofing nails, plus books, games, and a collection of classic and contemporary movies. The inn is located on

75 acres, with its own hiking and biking trails and spectacular views of the national park and Boulder Mountain. Full breakfasts include homemade granola, fresh-baked muffins or scones, and a hot entree such as green chile cheese frittata, or a fresh vegetable or smoked trout omelet. Smoking is not permitted inside.

✪ Wonderland Inn

At the junction of Utah 24 and 12 (P.O. Box 67), Torrey, UT 84775. ☎ **801/425-3775** or 800/ 458-0216. 50 rms, 2 suites. A/C TV TEL. Summer $58–$80 double; winter $40–$60 double. AE, CB, DC, DISC, EU, JCB, MC, V.

This modern motel, built in 1990, is on a hill set back from the highway, making it very quiet and peaceful. Built, owned, and managed by Ray and Diane Potter and family, the property is especially well kept. Standard motel rooms have two queen-sized beds or one king, and typical modern motel decor with some genuine wood touches. It has a combination indoor/outdoor heated swimming pool with a tanning room, whirlpool, and sauna; there is also a beauty salon and a gift shop. A restaurant serves three meals daily year-round, with a popular breakfast buffet in the summer.

7 Dining

Brink's Burgers Drive-In

165 E. Main St., Torrey. ☎ **801/425-3710.** Most items $1–$4.50. No credit cards. Daily 11am–8pm. Closed in the winter. BURGERS/SANDWICHES.

This nonfranchise fast-food restaurant serves great burgers and English-style chips in a cafe-like decor, or you can take your food outside to picnic tables. Like most fast-food restaurants, you order at the counter and pick up your food when your number's called. But in addition to much-better-than-average burgers, including a pizza burger, other possibilities are chicken and fish selections, cheese sticks, onion rings, zucchini sticks, and spicy potato wedges. Milk shakes and ice cream cones are also available; no alcohol is served.

Cafe Diablo

599 S. Main St., Torrey. ☎ **801/425-3070.** Main courses $10.95–$14.95. MC, V. Apr 15–Oct, open for lunch and dinner; call for hours. Closed Nov–mid-Apr. SOUTHWESTERN.

Looks are deceiving. What appears to be a simple small-town cafe in a converted home is actually a very fine restaurant, offering innovative beef, pork, chicken, and seafood selections, many created with a southwestern flair. The menu varies, but could include pumpkinseed-crusted local trout, served with cilantro-lime sauce and rice pancakes; eggplant enchiladas, slices of eggplant rolled in vegetables and jack cheese and baked with a spicy salsa; or a basic charbroiled skirt steak, served with oven-roasted potatoes, onions, and carrots. Pastries, all made on the premises, are spectacular, and beer is available.

15

Lake Powell & Glen Canyon National Recreation Area

This huge canyon is a spectacular wonderland of stark contrasts—parched desert, deep blue water, startling red rocks, rich green hanging gardens. A joint effort by man and Nature, Lake Powell and Glen Canyon National Recreation Area is a huge water park, with more shoreline than the West Coast of the continental United States. It's also a place of almost unbelievable beauty, where millions of visitors each year take to the water to explore, fish, water-ski, swim, or simply lounge in the sun.

Named for Major John Wesley Powell, a one-armed Civil War veteran who led a group of nine explorers on a scientific expedition down the Green and Colorado rivers in 1869, the lake is 186 miles long and has almost 100 major side canyons that give it 1,960 miles of shoreline. And with more than 160,000 surface acres of water, it's the second largest manmade lake in the United States (after Lake Mead).

Glen Canyon National Recreation Area, with Lake Powell as its heart, is three parks in one: A major destination for boaters and fishermen, a treasury of scenic wonders, and an important historic archive. Lake Powell is, in fact, best enjoyed by boat, gliding through the numerous side canyons among delicately sculpted sandstone forms—intricate, sensuous, and sometimes bizarre—formed by millions of years of erosion. One rock formation that's considered a must-see for every Lake Powell visitor is Rainbow Bridge, a huge natural stone bridge sacred to the Navajo people. But there's much more to see: the 1870s stone fort and trading post at Lees Ferry, the ancient Anasazi ruins of Defiance House, and the dam itself, which supplies water and electric power to much of the West.

1 Just the Facts

ACCESS POINTS: THE MARINAS

Located in southern Utah and northern Arizona, Lake Powell and Glen Canyon National Recreation Area has four major access points: **Wahweap Lodge & Marina** (☎ 520/645-2433) on the lake's south end, is the most developed, with the largest number of facilities, plus lodging, dining, and services in nearby Page, Arizona; **Bullfrog Marina** (☎ 801/684-3000) and **Halls Crossing Marina** (☎ 801/684-7000) are mid-lake, and are also fairly well developed. **Hite**

Marina (☎ 801/684-2278) the lake's northernmost access point, is the smallest and least developed.

All four marinas, operated by Lake Powell Resorts and Marinas, are accessible by car, operate year-round, and provide boat rentals, docks, fuel, service, fishing and other supplies, and accommodations. A fifth marina, **Dangling Rope,** is accessible by boat only, and offers fuel, repairs, fresh water, ice, and limited supplies. **Lees Ferry,** about 15 miles downriver from Glen Canyon Dam, is a historic river crossing popular with hikers and campers, but does not offer direct access to Lake Powell.

GETTING THERE

Wahweap Lodge and Marina and **Glen Canyon Dam** are just off U.S. 89, about 6 miles north of Page, Arizona. Wahweap is 150 miles southeast of Bryce Canyon National Park; 130 miles northeast of the north rim of Grand Canyon National Park; about 65 miles east of Kanab; 267 miles east of Las Vegas, Nevada; and 381 miles south of Salt Lake City. **Halls Crossing** is 280 miles northeast of Wahweap, and **Bullfrog** is 283 miles northeast; both are reachable via Utah 276. **Hite,** about 40 miles uplake from Halls Crossing and Bullfrog, is off Utah 95,

By Plane   **Delta/Skywest Airlines** (☎ 800/453-9417) flies into Page Airport (☎ 520/645-2494). Kanab Municipal Airport (☎ 801/644-2904) is served by **Pacific Air West Airlines** (☎ 800/729-7229).

Rental cars are available at the Page Airport from **Budget** (☎ 520/645-3977 or 800/527-0700). In Kanab, car rentals, including four-wheel-drives, minivans, and RVs, are available from **Hunt's Rentals** (☎ 801/644-2370).

By Car   Motorists can reach the dam and **Wahweap Marina** via U.S. 89 from Kanab or Grand Canyon National Park; and via Ariz. 98 from the the east.

To get to the **Lees Ferry** section of the recreation area, south of Wahweap, drive south on U.S. 89 and then north on U.S. 89A to Marble Canyon, where you pick up the Lees Ferry access road.

Bullfrog and **Halls Crossing** marinas, which are connected by a toll ferry mid-lake, are accessible via Utah 276, which loops southwest from Utah 95. The cost for the 20-minute, 3.1-mile crossing is $10 for cars and trucks less than 20 feet long, with increasing rates for longer vehicles and vehicles with trailers. Bicyclists and adult foot passengers are charged $2 (children $1), and motorcyclists $3. Ferries run six times daily each direction in the summer, less often at other times. The service is often shut down for several weeks in December for maintenance. **Hite Marina,** the northernmost section of the national recreation area, is just south of Utah 95.

INFORMATION & VISITOR CENTERS

For advance information, contact Superintendent, **Glen Canyon National Recreation Area,** P.O. Box 1507, Page, AZ 86040, or call the **Carl Hayden Visitor Center** (☎ 520/608-6404). For lodging, tour, and boat rental information, contact the licensed park concessionaire, **Lake Powell Resorts and Marinas,** Box 56909, Phoenix, AZ 85079 (☎ 602/278-8888 or 800/528-6154; fax 602/331-5258), which also makes available books and videos on the lake and the national recreation area.

Numerous services, including lodging and dining, are available in nearby Page, Arizona. For information, contact the **Page/Lake Powell Chamber of Commerce,** P.O. Box 727, Page, AZ 86040 (☎ 520/645-2741). The **John Wesley Powell Memorial Museum** in Page (☎ 520/645-9496; fax 520/945-3412) also provides area lodging, dining, and attraction information.

Glen Canyon National Recreation Area

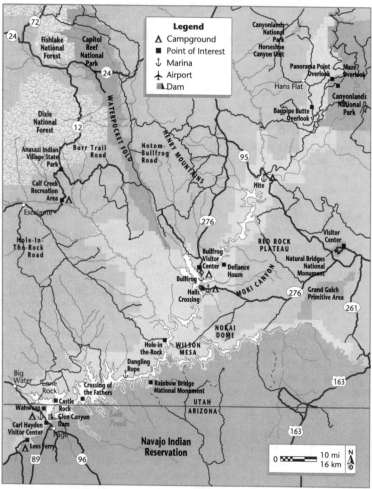

The **Carl Hayden Visitor Center** at Glen Canyon Dam, 2 miles north of Page, Arizona, via U.S. 89, has exhibits on the construction of the dam and is the starting point for year-round self-guided and summer-only guided tours of the dam, which usually take from 30 to 45 minutes. Audio-visual programs, free brochures, and books, maps, and videos are available.

At the **Bullfrog Visitor Center,** at mid-lake off Utah 276, you'll find a variety of exhibits and information. Ranger stations at Lees Ferry, Dangling Rope, Halls Crossing, and Hite also have park information, but these stations are only open when rangers aren't busy doing something else.

FEES, BACKCOUNTRY PERMITS & REGULATIONS

Entry into the park is free. Backcountry permits, which are also free, are required for overnight trips into the Escalante Canyon section of the national recreation area.

The standard National Park Service regulations apply, such as not damaging anything and driving only on established roadways. Additional regulations here are aimed at protecting water quality of the lake by prohibiting dumping garbage or sewage into the water; and to protect boaters' safety by requiring life jackets to be worn by children 12 and younger, as well as other safe-boating requirements. Keep in mind that boating regulations are slightly different in Utah and Arizona. Brochures listing regulations are available at recreation area marinas.

Pets must be leashed at all times, except on houseboats, and are prohibited in public buildings. Dogs are permitted on standard, but not carpeted, houseboats.

SEASONS & AVOIDING THE CROWDS

The park is open year-round, and is busiest in the summer, when it's also the hottest, with temperatures sometimes reaching over 100°F. Spring is pleasant, but can be a bit windy. Our choice is October, when the water's still warm enough for swimming but most of the crowds have gone home. Winter can also be beautiful, with snow only rarely dusting the rock, and daytime temperatures usually in the 40s and 50s. Another advantage to visiting in the off-season is that there are discounts on lodgings and tours from November through March, and on boat rentals between October and May.

RANGER PROGRAMS

Amphitheater programs take place several evenings each week in the summer at Wahweap and Bullfrog Basin campgrounds. Topics vary, but may include such subjects as the animals or plants of the park, geology, or the canyon's human history.

Free guided tours of the dam leave from the Carl Hayden Visitor Center daily, and rangers give periodic talks at Rainbow Bridge.

Kids 12 and younger can become **Junior Rangers,** and receive badges by completing projects in an activity book available free at the Carl Hayden or Bullfrog visitor centers.

A BIRD'S-EYE VIEW OF LAKE POWELL

The quickest way to see the sights here is by air. **Scenic Airlines,** P.O. Box 1385, Page, Arizona 86040 (☎ 520/645-2494 or 800/245-8668), provides half-hour flights over the dam, Rainbow Bridge, and other scenic attractions, at about $65 per person; and 1-hour flights over the lake to the Escalante River and Hole-in-the-Rock, a favorite hide-out of outlaw Butch Cassidy, for about $115 per person.

2 Exploring Lake Powell by Boat

The best way to see Lake Powell and Glen Canyon National Recreation Area is by boat, either your own or a rental, or on a boat tour. Our favorite way to explore is to rent a houseboat for at least a week, and wander among the numerous side canyons.

However, if your time is limited, try to spend a few hours touring the dam and seeing the exhibits in the Carl Hayden Visitor Center, particularly the excellent relief map that helps you see the big picture. Then take one of the boat tours, such as the half-day trip to Rainbow Bridge. An option for the more adventurous is to rent a boat for the day, buy some good maps, and explore the canyons on your own. But whatever you do, try to get to Rainbow Bridge.

BRINGING YOUR OWN BOAT

If you happened to bring your own boat with you, whether it's a one-person kayak or family-size cabin cruiser, you'll have a wonderful time. Boat launching ramps are at Wahweap, Lees Ferry, Bullfrog, Halls Crossing, and Hite; and fuel, supplies, sewage pump-out stations, drinking water, and boat repairs are available at all of these except Lees Ferry, plus Dangling Rope Marina, about 40 miles up-lake from Wahweap Marina and accessible only by boat. Pick up maps and charts at one of the marinas (see above).

BOAT RENTALS

Lake Powell Resorts and Marinas, Box 56909, Phoenix, AZ 85079 (☎ 602/278-8888 or 800/528-6154; fax 602/331-5258) rents powerboats of all sizes, from two-passenger personal watercraft to luxurious 50-foot houseboats for 10 or more.

Generally, anybody who can drive a car can pilot a boat. The only tricks are learning to compensate for wind and currents; and be sure to spend a few minutes practicing turning and stopping. No lessons or licenses are required, and the marinas supply all the equipment you'll need.

Summer is the most expensive time to rent a boat, spring and fall are 25% less, and winter rates are the lowest—40% less than summer. Summer rates for houseboats that sleep from 6 to 12 people range from $700 to $2,000 for three days, and $1,275 to $3,750 for seven days. Rates for smaller runabouts, ski boats, and personal watercraft range from $70 to $250 per day, or $300 to $1,200 per week in summer. Damage deposits are also required. Most types of boats, although not necessarily all sizes, are available at Wahweap, Bullfrog, Halls Crossing, and Hite marinas. Reservations well in advance are strongly recommended.

BOAT TOURS

Year-round boat tours will take you to those hidden areas of the lake that you might never find on your own. Tours range from a 1-hour trip aboard the paddle wheeler "Canyon King," for $10 per person, to the all-day tour to Rainbow Bridge that's about $75 per person, including lunch. Rates for children from 3 to 11 years old are slightly over half adults' prices. There are also sunset cruises, dinner cruises, half-day trips to Rainbow Bridge, Colorado River float trips, and numerous packages for tours with lodging and/or RV spaces. For information and reservations, contact **Lake Powell Resorts and Marinas,** Box 56909, Phoenix, AZ 85079 (☎ 602/278-8888 or 800/528-6154; fax 602/331-5258).

3 Seeing the Sights

Among the many scenic and historic attractions here, several deserve special mention as must-sees. They're arranged here geographically, from the south end of the lake to the north.

LEES FERRY

Downriver from Glen Canyon Dam, Lees Ferry is an historic river crossing and the site of a stone fort built by Mormon pioneers in 1874 for protection from the Navajo, and used later as a trading post. You can see remains of the fort and a post office, built in 1913. Nearby, at Lonely Dell, are 19th- and early 20th-century ranch buildings, an orchard, and a cemetery containing graves dating from 1874 to 1928. Upriver, during low water, you can spot the remains of a steamboat, the *Charles H. Spencer,* a 92-foot-long paddle wheeler that was used briefly in the early part of this century to haul coal for a gold-dredging operation.

Lees Ferry is also the starting point for white-water river trips through the Grand Canyon.

Lake Powell: Natural Wonder or Manmade Curse?

If preservationists had had their way in 1937, Lake Powell would not exist. There would be no dam, no electric generators—only the free-flowing Colorado River. If their proposal had been adopted, that which is Glen Canyon National Recreation Area and Canyonlands National Park would instead be one 6,000-square-mile protected area called Escalante National Park.

The story actually goes back to the early part of the 20th century, when a major flood of the Colorado River brought to everyone's attention the need for agreement among western states on flood control and water rights. A federal commission created the Colorado Compact in 1922 to allocate water, and in 1935 Hoover Dam was built to help control water supplies in the lower part of the Colorado River Basin. States in the upper basin couldn't agree on what to do. Everyone became distracted by World War II, and the issue was put aside for a few years.

Finally, in 1953, the U.S. Bureau of Reclamation proposed a series of dams. These would be on the Colorado River in Glen Canyon, on the San Juan River in northwestern New Mexico, on the Green River in northwestern Colorado through Dinosaur National Monument, and on the Gunnison River in western Colorado.

The inevitable war between development and preservation factions began, with the needs for water storage and electric power pitted against the value of preserving the unspoiled wilderness. There was a loud cry that building Glen Canyon Dam would drown a magnificent system of canyons, but this battle was overshadowed by an even louder battle to save Dinosaur National Monument. Eventually a compromise was reached: The Dinosaur National Monument project was dropped, and a dam over the Green River in northeastern Utah, at Flaming Gorge, was added. Glen Canyon Dam would also be built. Some say that Glen Canyon was ultimately sacrificed for the principle of keeping development out of a unit of the National Park Service.

Today, close to four million people visit Glen Canyon National Recreation Area each year, and the boats that canvass Lake Powel allow almost all of them to see spectacular Rainbow Bridge and the wondrous canyons and formations that would be practically inaccessible without the dam. And although most people wouldn't deny the beauty of Lake Powell and the Glen Canyon Recreation Area today, many conservationists remain bitter, saying that the dam flooded what could have been one of our country's most magnificent national parks.

GLEN CANYON DAM

Construction began on this U.S. Bureau of Reclamation project in October, 1956; by the time the $155-million dam was completed in September of 1963, almost 10-million tons of concrete had been poured, creating a wall 587 feet high and 3,700 feet long. It took until 1980 for the lake to reach its "full pool," covering much of the area that had been explored over 100 years earlier by Major John Wesley Powell. Today the dam provides water storage, mostly for agriculture and hydroelectric power. Its eight generators, which cost an additional $70 million, produce more than one million kilowatts of electrical energy per day.

So we have a curious ensemble of wonderful features—carved walls, royal arches, glens, alcove gulches, mounds, and monuments. From which of these features shall we select a name? We decide to call it Glen Canyon.
—Explorer Major John Wesley Powell, August 3, 1869

RAINBOW BRIDGE NATIONAL MONUMENT

This huge natural bridge is held to be sacred by the Navajo, who called it a "rainbow turned to stone"; in the summer of 1995, they briefly blocked the route to the bridge to conduct a blessing ceremony, and in protest of what they considered the bridge's commercialization. Located about 50 miles by boat from Wahweap, Bullfrog, or Halls Crossing marinas, the bridge is so spectacular that it was named a national monument in 1910, long before the lake was created by the construction of Glen Canyon dam. Believed to be the largest natural bridge in the world, Rainbow Bridge is almost perfectly symmetrical, measuring 275 feet wide and 290 feet tall. The top is 42 feet thick and 33 feet wide. Get here if you can manage it—you won't be disappointed.

DEFIANCE HOUSE

This archaeological site 3 miles up the middle fork of Forgotten Canyon, up-lake from Halls Crossing, is believed to have been occupied by a small clan of Anasazi between A.D. 1250 and 1275. The cliffside site includes ruins of several impressive stone rooms, food storage areas, and a kiva where religious ceremonies would have taken place. There's a rock art panel high along a cliff wall that includes a pictograph for which the ruin is named—it's an image of three warriors carrying clubs and shields. The panel also includes paintings of sheep and men.

4 Sports & Activities

FISHING

Although March through November is the most popular season, the fishing is good year-round, especially for the huge rainbow trout sometimes caught in the Colorado River between the dam and Lees Ferry. Lake fishermen also catch largemouth, smallmouth, and striped bass; catfish; crappie; and walleye. Because Glen Canyon National Recreation Area lies within two states, you'll need Utah and/or Arizona fishing licenses, depending on where you want to fish. The marinas sell licenses as well as fishing supplies.

HIKING, MOUNTAINBIKING & FOUR-WHEELING

Although boating and related water sports are the main activities here, most of this recreation area is solid ground—actually hard rock. Hikers and other land-based recreationists will find plenty to do. The only problem is that there are few marked trails, and changing water levels create a constantly changing shoreline.

Hiking   You can get panoramic vistas of Lake Powell via several short hikes. For a view of the lake, Wahweap Bay, the Colorado River channel, and the sandstone cliffs of Antelope Island, drive 0.6 mile east from the Carl Hayden Visitor Center, crossing a bridge, and turn left onto an unmarked gravel road; follow it for about a mile to its end and a parking lot in an area locally known as **The Chains.** Heading north from the parking lot, follow the unmarked but obvious trail across sand, up slickrock, and across a level gravel section to an overlook that provides a magnificent view of the lake. This is usually a 10-minute walk one way. To extend the hike, you can find a way down to the water's edge, but be aware that the steep sandstone can be slick. The Chains is a day-use area only.

Several hikes start in the Lees Ferry area, including a moderate 2-mile round-trip hike through narrow **Cathedral Canyon** to the Colorado River. The trailhead is at the second turnout from U.S. 89A along Lees Ferry Road. This hike isn't along a marked trail, but rather down a wash, past intriguing rock formations. During wet weather, be alert for flash floods and deep pools. Allow one to 1 1/2 hours.

Another relatively easy hike, the **River Trail,** starts just upriver from the Lees Ferry fort, and follows an old wagon road to a ferry-crossing site, passing the historic but submerged steamboat, the *Charles H. Spencer.* Allow about an hour for this 2-mile round-trip walk. A self-guiding booklet is available at Lees Ferry.

A heavy-duty 34-mile hike through **the Paria Canyon Primitive Area,** leaving from Lonely Dell Ranch at Lees Ferry, takes you through beautiful but narrow canyons. Beware: flash flooding can be hazardous. It requires a permit from the Bureau of Land Management office in Kanab (☎ 801/644-2672).

Although most visitors take an easy half- or full-day boat trip to see beautiful Rainbow Bridge National Monument, it is possible to hike to it, although the 14-mile one-way trail is difficult and not maintained. It crosses the Navajo Reservation and permits are required. Contact the Navajo Nation, Recreational Resources Dept., P.O. Box 308, Window Rock, AZ 86515 (☎ 520/871-6647).

Serious backcountry hikers should obtain current maps of the area and discuss their plans with rangers before setting out. It's recommended that hikers carry at least a gallon of water per person, per day.

Mountainbiking & Four-Wheeling Mountainbikers and four-wheel-drive enthusiasts must stay on established roadways within the recreation area, but there are actually quite a few challenging dirt roads, both in the recreation area and on adjacent federal land. Get information from the national recreation area office (see above), and Canyonlands National Park office (☎ 801/259-4351).

In the Hite area, the **Orange Cliffs** are particularly popular among mountainbikers. The 53-mile one-way **Flint Trail** connects Hite with Hans Flat in the far-northern section of the national recreation area. It's rocky, with some sandy stretches and steep grades. For a shorter ride, the **Panorama Point/Cleopatra's Chair Trail** follows recreation area routes 744, 774, and 775 for 10 miles (one way) from Hans Flat to Cleopatra's Chair, providing a spectacular view into Canyonlands National Park. Camping in the Orange Cliffs area requires a permit, and strict regulations apply; contact the Hans Flat Ranger Station (☎ 801/259-2652).

The Escalante River canyons of the national recreation area are accessible by four-wheel-drive vehicle via the 57-mile one-way **Hole-in-the-Rock Road,** which leaves Utah 12 five miles east of Escalante. Managed by the Bureau of Land Management (☎ 801/826-5499), the dirt and sometimes rocky road passes through **Devil's Rock Garden,** an area of unique rock formations, and offers a spectacular overlook of Lake Powell. Although four-wheel-drive is not always needed, the last 5 miles of the road require a high clearance vehicle. Regardless of what you're driving you'll want to avoid the road in wet weather. Allow about 6 hours round trip.

5 Camping

National recreation area concessionaire **Lake Powell Resorts and Marinas** (☎ 602/278-8888 or 800/528-6154; fax 602/331-5258), operates year-round full-service RV parks at Wahweap, Bullfrog, and Halls Crossing, with complete RV hookups, showers, modern restrooms, coin-operated laundries, RV dump stations, drinking water, and groceries. Rates are about $22 per site in the summer and $14 in the winter. Package deals that include RV sites and boat tours are also offered.

The concessionaire operates several campgrounds without hookups, but with showers and flush toilets, that cost $9 to $16 per night, with no reservations. These campgrounds are open year-round at Bullfrog and Halls Crossing, but in the summer only at Wahweap.

The National Park Service operates a campground year-round at Lees Ferry, with 51 sites, flush toilets, and drinking water, but no showers or RV hookups. Reservations are not accepted; rates are $8 per site.

The only camping at Hite is a primitive campground, with no showers. It's open year-round and camping is free.

There are also several free primitive campgrounds in the recreation area's backcountry. Free dispersed camping is permitted throughout the recreation area, except within 1 mile of marinas and Lees Ferry, and at Rainbow Bridge National Monument.

6 Accommodations & Dining

Lake Powell Resorts and Marinas (☎ 602/278-8888 or 800/528-6154; fax 602/331-5258) operates all of the recreation areas lodging and dining facilities, as well as the houseboat rentals; call them to make your reservations.

Although there are plenty of hotels, motels, and condominium-type units available, our choice for lodging is that wonderful floating vacation home, the **houseboat**. Powered by two outboard motors and complete with full kitchens, bathrooms with hot showers, and sleeping for up to 12, houseboats serve not only as your home-away-from-home, but also your means to explore the fascinating red rock canyons that make Lake Powell the unique paradise that it is. Hungry? There's the refrigerator, and in addition to the kitchen stove with oven there's also a gas barbecue grill. For prices and additional information, see the "Exploring Lake Powell by Boat," above.

Additional facilities are available in Page, Arizona. For information, contact the **Page/Lake Powell Chamber of Commerce,** P.O. Box 727, Page, AZ 86040 (☎ 520/645-2741).

Where to Stay & Eat at Wahweap   If you prefer a bedroom that can't float away in the night, consider the **Wahweap Lodge,** the largest (350 units) and fanciest hotel in the area. Right at the Wahweap Marina, it offers good access for boat tours and rentals, has two swimming pools and a whirlpool, and provides shuttle service into Page. Rooms on the west side have spectacular views of Lake Powell. Rates for two range from $115 to $199 from the spring through fall, with discounts of about 35% in the winter. Nearby, the **Lake Powell Motel** offers 24 standard motel rooms, with two queen-sized beds and views of the lake. Rates for two are $70 to $80 in the spring, summer, and fall. There are also family suites ranging from $135 to $150. The motel is closed from November through March.

Restaurants at Wahweap Marina include the **Rainbow Room** at Wahweap Lodge (☎ 520/645-2433), serving very good American and southwestern dishes, along with a panoramic view of Lake Powell. Breakfast, lunch, and dinner are served daily, with dinner main course prices in the $13 to $20 range. There is also a fast-food restaurant at the marina, open from April through mid-September.

Where to Stay & Dine at Bullfrog & the Other Marinas   The concessionaire also operates **Defiance House Lodge** at Bullfrog Marina, an attractive lodge with beautiful views of the lake, and prices for two ranging from $105 to $119 in the spring, summer, and fall, and $75 to $85 in the winter. There is also a fine-dining restaurant open year-round and a fast-food restaurant open in the summer only.

Condominium-style housekeeping units are available at Bullfrog, Halls Crossing, and Hite marinas. Prices for two in the summer are in the $119 to $129 range, in fall and spring from $89 to $99, and in the winter from $75 to $85.

7 In Memory of John Wesley Powell: A Nearby Museum

John Wesley Powell Memorial Museum

6 N. Lake Powell Blvd., Page, AZ 86040. ☎ **520/645-9496.** Fax 520/945-3412. Free admission, donations welcome. May–Sept Mon–Sat 8am–6pm, Sun 10am–6pm; slightly shorter hours and closed Sundays mid-Feb–Apr and Oct–mid-Dec. Closed mid-Dec–mid-Feb.

The boat on the front lawn immediately tells you that this small museum has something to do with water. Actually, it's dedicated to the memory of Major John Wesley Powell, who in 1869 led a small group of men on a courageous—some said foolhardy—expedition down the Green and Colorado rivers, traveling almost 1,000 miles through largely uncharted territory. The museum documents Powell's expedition with photographs, etchings, and artifacts. It also contains exhibits of Native American arts and crafts, from ancient Anasazi pottery to modern Navajo and Hopi weavings, pottery, and jewelry. A highlight of the museum is the collection of fluorescent minerals. Changing exhibits of works by local artists are also featured.

16 From Moab to Arches & Canyonlands National Parks

Canyonlands country they call this—a seemingly infinite high desert of rock, with spectacular formations and rugged gorges that have been carved out over the centuries by the force of the Colorado and Green Rivers. Massive sandstone spires and arches that seem to defy gravity define the national parks of southeastern Utah. This is a land that begs to be explored outdoors—if you've come to Utah for mountainbiking, hiking, four-wheeling, or rafting, this is the place. And the region holds a few surprises, too, from ancient Anasazi dwellings and rock art in Canyonlands to Arches Vineyards, Utah's only legal commercial winery.

1 Moab: Gateway to the National Parks

Named for a biblical kingdom at the edge of Zion, the promised land, Moab has evolved into a popular base camp for mountainbikers, four-wheel-drive enthusiasts, hikers, and rafters eager to explore the red rock canyon country that dominates southeastern Utah. A drive down Main Street confirms that yes, this is a tourist town, with scores of businesses catering to visitors.

Close to the Colorado River, Moab sits in a green valley among striking red sandstone cliffs, with scenic beauty that has lured Hollywood filmmakers for hits that include John Wayne's *The Comancheros,* the biblical epic *The Greatest Story Ever Told,* and *Indiana Jones and the Last Crusade.* It's also become a favorite location for Madison Avenue. Remember those great Chevy commercials where the car sits perched on top of a huge red tower of stone? That's Castle Rock, one of the Moab area's landmarks—and the only way to get to the top is by helicopter. According to Bette Stanton, director of the Moab to Monument Valley Film Commission, when the first commercial in the series was being made in 1963, Chevrolet successfully hauled a car and a negligee-clad model to the top of the 1,000-foot tower, but by the time filming was done for the day, gusty winds made it impossible for the helicopter to land to pick up the model. However, a crew member, carrying extra clothes, was dropped to keep her company, and after a chilly night they were both airlifted down the next morning.

Like most Utah towns, Moab was established by Mormon pioneers sent by church leader Brigham Young. But Moab was actually founded twice. The first time, in 1855, missionaries set up

Elk Mountain Mission, to see to the spiritual needs of the local Utes. Apparently unimpressed with the idea of abandoning their own religion for the ways of the LDS church, the Utes killed several missionaries, sending the rest back to Salt Lake City in a hurry. It wasn't until 20 years later that the settlers tried again, this time bringing cattle and sheep, and successfully established a small farming and ranching community.

Today Moab remains a relatively small town, with only 4,000 or so permanent residents, but that still makes it the the biggest town in southeastern Utah, offering the best services for the traveler. Practically within walking distance of Arches National Park, Moab is also close to Canyonlands National Park, and surrounded by the Manti-La Sal National Forest and vast open spaces under the jurisdiction of the Bureau of Land Management.

ESSENTIALS
GETTING THERE
By Plane **Alpine Air** (☎ 801/373-1508) provides daily commuter service between Salt Lake City and Moab's Canyonlands Field Airport (☎ 801/259-7421).

The closest major airport is Walker Field in Grand Junction, Colorado (☎ 970/244-9100), which has direct flights or connections from most major cities on **America West Express** (☎ 800/235-9292); **Delta/Skywest** (☎ 800/453-9417); **Mesa Airlines** (☎ 800/637-2247); and **United Express** (☎ 800/241-6522). From Grand Junction it's easy to rent a car and drive the 125 miles to Moab.

By Car Situated on U.S. 191, Moab is about 30 miles south of I-70 (take Exit 180 at Crescent Junction) and 53 miles north of Monticello. Moab is 238 miles southeast of Salt Lake City and 399 miles northeast of the north rim of Grand Canyon National Park. From Salt Lake City, follow I-15 south to Spanish Fork; then take U.S. 6 southeast to I-70; follow it east to Crescent Junction, where you'll pick up U.S. 191 south to Moab.

By Train The closest train transportation is via **Amtrak**'s (☎ 800/872-7245) *Desert Wind,* which makes flag stops in Thompson, about 32 miles north, as well as providing service to Salt Lake City and Grand Junction, Colorado, several times weekly. If you plan to go from Thompson to Moab, you'll need to make arrangements, in advance, with **West Tracks Taxi and Shuttle** (☎ 801/259-2294).

VISITOR INFORMATION
For advance information, contact the **Grand County Travel Council,** P.O. Box 550, Moab, UT 84532 (☎ 801/259-8825 or 800/635-6622; fax 801/259-1376).

Once you've arrived, the **Moab Information Center,** located in the middle of town at the corner of Main and Center Streets (☎ 801/259-3911), is open 8am to 9pm in the summer, with slightly shorter winter hours. This multi-agency visitor center is staffed by the Park Service, Bureau of Land Management, U.S. Forest Service, and local tourism officials, who are very knowledgeable about the area. In addition, you can request free showings of a number of videos on Southwest attractions, pick up brochures describing numerous local motels, restaurants, and outfitters, and purchase books, videos, and other materials. A board displays current weather and campground conditions.

GETTING AROUND
Rentals, either standard passenger cars, vans, or four-wheel-drive jeeps, are available from **Thrifty** (☎ 801/259-7317 or 800/367-2277), which offers a shuttle service to get you to their office from the airport. Other local companies specializing in

four-wheel-drive rentals include **Canyonlands 4X4 Rentals and Guided Tours** (☎ 801/259-4567), **Farabee 4X4 Rentals** (☎ 801/259-7494), and **Slickrock 4X4 Rentals** (☎ 801/259-5678), which also rents cellular phones in case you're afraid of getting lost or stuck.

Local taxi service is provided by **West Tracks Taxi** (☎ 801/259-2294).

FAST FACTS: MOAB

Allen Memorial Hospital, 719 W. 400 North (☎ 801/259-7191), is a full-service hospital offering 24-hour emergency care. The **post office** is at 50 E. 100 North (☎ 801/259-7427).

The best grocery store in town is **City Market,** 425 S. Main St. (☎ 801/ 259-5181), open 24 hours a day, seven days a week. Hikers, mountainbikers, and four-wheelers can pick up sandwiches from the deli, assemble their own salads at the salad bar, or choose fresh-baked items from the bakery before hitting the trail. The store also sells hunting and fishing licenses, money orders and stamps, offers photo finishing and Western Union services, and has a pharmacy.

SPECIAL EVENTS

The **Moab Rodeo** takes place each Thursday evening, from May through October, starting at 7:30pm at the Spanish Trail Arena (☎ 801/259-6226), 5 miles south of Moab on U.S. 191. There's bull riding, barrel racing, team roping, and bareback riding, and kids are invited to join in the sheep riding. Another popular event is the Women's Cowboy Roping, which is just exactly what it sounds like (though they don't get to keep the cowboys). Admission costs $8 for adults, $4 for children 4 to 11, and kids under four are admitted free. The arena also hosts the PRCA Canyonlands Rodeo each June, as well as horse racing, team roping, the county fair in August, occasional concerts, and other events. Call to find out what's happening when you're in town.

GETTING OUTSIDE: MOUNTAINBIKING & MORE

The Moab area is one of Utah's main outdoor playgrounds, an ideal spot for hiking, boating, camping, or just plain horsing around (with or without the horse). In addition to the nearby national parks, Arches and Canyonlands, which are covered in full later in this chapter, there's plenty of room to roam on land administered by the **Bureau of Land Management's Grand Resource Area** office, 885 S. Sand Flats Rd., Moab, UT 84532 (☎ 801/259-8193), and the **Manti-La Sal National Forest's Moab Ranger District,** 2290 S. West Resource Blvd. (P.O. Box 386), Moab, UT 84532 (☎ 801/259-7155).

The **Moab Information Center,** at Main and Center Streets (☎ 801/259-3911), is staffed by Park Service, Bureau of Land Management, U.S. Forest Service, and local tourism officials, who are very knowledgeable about the area.

Much of the best of the federal land surrounding Moab is isolated and remote— not somewhere you'd want to get lost. So stock up on detailed topographic and trail maps of the specific areas you plan to explore. These, along with guidebooks, compasses, knives, and other supplies are available, either in person or mail order, at **T.I. Maps, Etc.,** 29 E. Center St., across from the Moab Information Center (☎ 801/259-5529; fax 801/259-7741).

Because of the extreme desert heat in the summer, the best time for most outdoor activities is spring or fall—and even the relatively mild winters are inviting. But if you

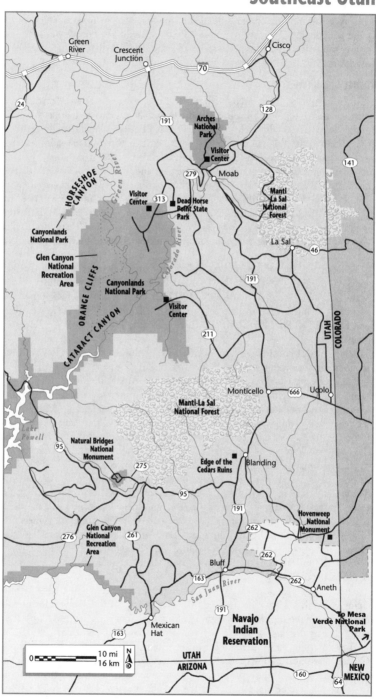

Green River

Crescent Junction

Cisco

70

24

128

191

Arches National Park

141

Visitor Center

279

Moab

Manti La Sal National Forest

Visitor Center

313

HORSESHOE CANYON

Dead Horse Point State Park

Green River

Canyonlands National Park

La Sal

46

Glen Canyon National Recreation Area

Colorado River

ORANGE CLIFFS

Canyonlands National Park

191

CATARACT CANYON

Visitor Center

211

Monticello

666

Ucolo

Manti-La Sal National Forest

UTAH

COLORADO

Lake Powell

Natural Bridges National Monument

95

275

Edge of the Cedars Ruins

Blanding

95

191

Hovenweep National Monument

262

Glen Canyon National Recreation Area

276

261

262

Bluff

163

San Juan River

262

Aneth

To Mesa Verde National Park

191

Navajo Indian Reservation

163

Mexican Hat

0   10 mi
     16 km

N

UTAH

ARIZONA

NEW MEXICO

160

64

end up vacationing in the middle of the summer, plan your serious hiking and mountainbiking early in the day, take a siesta along the river or a swimming pool during the heat of the afternoon, and take a short hike in the evening, just before sundown.

MOUNTAINBIKING

With hundreds and hundreds of miles of trails, a wide variety of terrain, and spectacular scenery, Moab is easily the mountainbike capital of Utah, and possibly of the United States (although the folks in Crested Butte, Colorado, might disagree). In addition to the mountainbiking possibilities on four-wheel-drive roads (described in this chapter's sections on Arches and Canyonlands National Parks), there are abundant trails on Bureau of Land Management and National Forest lands that are much less trafficked than national park trails. Your first stop when you get into town should be the Moab Information Center (see above) to pick up free copies of the pamphlets *Moab Area Mountain Bike Trails* and *Moab Slickrock Bike Trail*. Be sure to discuss your plans with the rangers there; they're very knowledgeable and will be able to help you find the trails that are most suitable to your interests, ability, and equipment.

You can also get information, as well as rent or repair bikes, at **Rim Cyclery,** 94 W. 100 North (☎ 801/259-5333), and **Poison Spider Bicycle Shop,** 497 N. Main St. (☎ 801/259-7882 or 800/635-1792). Rentals cost about $30 per day, including helmet. Bike shuttle services are available from **West Tracks Taxi and Shuttle** (☎ 801/259-2294) and **Coyote Shuttle** (☎ 801/259-9687), among others.

Several local companies (see "Outfitters," below) offer four-to-seven day mountainbike/camping tours, with prices starting at about $550.

The area's most famous trail is undoubtedly the **Moab Slickrock Bike Trail,** a scenic but challenging 9.6-mile loop that crosses a mesa of heavily eroded pale orange Navajo sandstone just a few minutes from downtown Moab. Along the way it offers views far and wide that take in the towering La Sal Mountains, the red rock formations of Arches National Park, a panorama of Canyonlands National Park, and the Colorado River. The trail, open to both mountainbikes and motorcycles, is physically demanding and technically difficult, and not recommended for children, novices, or anyone who is out-of-shape or has some medical problem. Allow 4 to 5 hours, and expect to have to walk your bike in some areas. If you're not sure you're ready for the Slickrock Trail, there's a 1.7-mile practice loop to give you an idea of what lies ahead. To get to the trailhead from the visitor information center, take Center Street east to 400 East. Turn south (right) and follow 400 East to Mill Creek Drive. Turn east (left) onto Mill Creek Drive and follow it to Sand Flats Road, which you take 2.3 miles east to the Bureau of Land Management's Sand Flats Recreation Area and the trailhead.

Those looking for a somewhat less challenging experience might try the **Gemini Bridges Trail,** a 13.5-mile one-way trip that shows off the area's colorful rock formations, including the trails' namesakes, two natural rock bridges. Considered relatively easy, this trail follows a dirt road mostly downhill, ending at U.S. 191, so it's best to arrange a shuttle. To get to the trailhead from the Moab Information Center, drive north along U.S. 191 to Utah 313, turn west (left) and go about 13 miles to the trailhead. Allow a full day for this ride, including getting to and from the trail, and be sure to watch for the magnificent view of Arches National Park from a hilltop as you approach U.S. 191 near the end of the ride. The trail ends at U.S. 191 just under 10 miles from the center of Moab.

Although there are dozens of fabulous trails to explore in the immediate area, mountainbikers who really want to go somewhere—perhaps all the way to Colorado to get some full-strength beer—will want to check out Kokopelli's Trail and the San Juan Hut System.

Winding for 128 miles across sandstone and shale canyons, deserts, and mountains, **Kokopelli's Trail** connects Moab and Grand Junction, Colorado. It combines all types of mountainbiking, from demanding single track to well-maintained dirt roads, and there are primitive campsites along the way. The west end of the trail is near Sand Flats Road in Moab and the east end is at the Loma Boat Launch, 15 miles west of Grand Junction. The project was organized by the Colorado Plateau Mountain-Bike Trail Association, P.O. Box 4602, Grand Junction, CO 81502 (send a self-addressed stamped envelope for a free trail map).

The **San Juan Hut System** links Moab with Telluride, Colorado, via a 206-mile-long network of backcountry dirt roads. Every 35 miles are primitive cabins, each with bunks, a wood stove, a propane cooking stove, and cooking gear. The route is appropriate for intermediate level mountainbike riders in good physical condition; an advanced technical single track is found near the huts for more experienced cyclists. The cost for riders who plan to make the whole trip is about $450, which includes use of the six huts, three meals daily, sleeping bags at each hut, and maps and trail descriptions. Shorter trips, guide services, and vehicle shuttles are also available. **Trail system offices** are in Telluride at 117 N. Willow St. (☎ 970/728-6935). For a brochure write to P.O. Box 1663, Telluride, CO 81435.

FOUR-WHEELING

There are thousands of miles of four-wheel-drive roads in the Moab area, most left over from mining days, that offer a popular way to explore this scenic country without exerting too much personal energy.

A number of local companies (see "Outfitters," below) provide guided trips, starting at about $50 per person for a half-day trip and $80 for a full day. Photographers especially enjoy the Lin Ottinger tours, designed especially for catching the right light and the right angles. You can also rent a 4X4 of your own, usually from about $80 per day, and fill it up with your kids and even the family dog (see "Getting Around," above).

Those who want to hit the trail themselves, either with a rental or their personal 4X4, will find a number of possibilities, from fairly easy dirt roads to "You-don't-really-expect-me-to-take-this-$30,000-truck-up-there-do-you?" piles of rocks. Several four-wheel-drive trips are described in the Canyonlands section of this chapter, and a free brochure, available at the Moab Information Center, (see above) describes several others.

Our favorite is ✪ **Poison Spider Mesa Trail,** which covers 16 miles of 4X4 road, providing stupendous views down to the Colorado River and Moab Valley. It's considered moderately difficult; a short-wheelbase high-clearance vehicle is best. Allow at least 4 hours. To reach the trail from the Moab Information Center, drive north on U.S. 191, for about 6 miles and turn west (left) onto Utah 279. Continue another 6 miles to the "Dinosaur Tracks" sign, where the trail leaves the pavement to the right, passing through a cattle guard. From here you'll simply follow the main trail, which is usually obvious, up switchbacks, through a sandy canyon, and over some steep, rocky stretches. From a slickrock parking area on top you can take a short walk to Little Arch, which really isn't so little.

One easy 4X4 road is the **Gemini Bridges,** which four-wheelers share with mountainbikers, and is described above in the mountainbiking section. Those with

4X4s often drive the route in the opposite direction than mountainbikers do, though, starting at a dirt road departing the west side of U.S. 191, about 10 miles north of the Moab Information Center. This involves more uphill driving, which is safer for motor vehicles—mountainbikers usually prefer going downhill, for some reason.

The self-guiding **Mill Canyon Dinosaur Trail** gives you a close-up view of dinosaur bones and fossils from the Jurassic period, 150 million years ago, that include a sauropod leg bone, vertebrae, ribs, and toe bones. You'll also see the fossil remains of a large tree trunk. To reach the trailhead, drive about 15 miles north of Moab on U.S. 191, then turn left at an intersection just north of highway mile marker 141. Cross the railroad tracks and follow a dirt road for about 2 miles to the trailhead. Allow about 1 hour. On the south side of the canyon you'll see the remnants of an old copper mill that operated in the late 1800s. Also nearby are the ruins of the Halfway Stage Station, a lunch stop in the late 1800s for stagecoach travelers making the 35-mile trip between Moab and Thompson, the nearest train station. From the dinosaur trailhead go north as though you were returning to U.S. 191, but at the first intersection turn right and drive to a dry wash, where you turn right again onto a jeep road that takes you a short distance to the stage station. The trail is managed by the **Bureau of Land Management's Grand Resource** Area office, 885 S. Sand Flats Road, Moab, UT 84532 (☎ 801/259-8193).

Hiking

There are hundreds of hiking possibilities in the Moab area, many of them just a few miles from town. Talk to the BLM and national forest rangers at the Moab Information Center (see above), and pick up their free brochure that describes seven local trails. Hikes in nearby Arches and Canyonlands National Parks are described in those parks' sections of this book. Especially in the summer, carry at least a gallon of water per person; wearing a broad-brimmed hat is also a good idea.

A favorite locals' hike is the **Negro Bill Canyon Trail,** named for William Granstaff, who lived in the area in the late 1800s. Allow about 4 hours for this hike, which is 4 miles round-trip and is easy to moderate. Be prepared to get your feet wet, depending on the level of the stream you follow up the canyon. To get to the trailhead, go north from Moab on U.S. 191 to Utah 128, turn east (right), and go about 3 miles to a dirt parking area. About 2 miles up the trail, in a side canyon to the right, you'll find Morning Glory Bridge, a natural rock span of 243 feet. Avoid touching the poison ivy that grows by a pool under the bridge (in case you don't remember from your scouting manual, poison ivy has shiny leaves, growing in clusters of three, with serrated edges).

✪ **The Hidden Valley Trail** is a bit more challenging, taking you up a series of steep switchbacks to views of rock formations and a panorama of the Moab Valley. Allow about 3 hours for the 4-mile round-trip hike. To get to the trailhead, drive about 3 miles south of the Moab Information Center on U.S. 191, turn west (right) onto Angel Rock Road and go two blocks to Rimrock Road. Turn north (right), and follow it to the parking area. The trail is named for a broad shelf, about halfway up the Moab Rim. Many hikers turn around and head back down after reaching a low pass with great views of huge sandstone fins (the 2-mile point), but you can extend the hike by continuing all the way to the Colorado River on a four-wheel-drive road.

The highly recommended ✪ **Corona Arch Trail** offers views of three impressive arches, a colorful slickrock canyon, and the Colorado River. Allow 2 hours for this 3-mile round-trip hike, which involves a lot of fairly easy walking plus some rather steep spots with handrails and a short ladder. From Moab, go north on U.S. 191 to

Utah 279, turn west (left), and go about 10 miles to a parking area on the north side of the road. You'll find a registration box and trailhead near the railroad; after crossing the tracks, follow an old road bed onto the trail, which is marked with cairns (piles of stones).

WATER SPORTS: BOATING, CANOEING, RAFTING & MORE

After spending hours in the blazing sun looking at mile-upon-mile of huge red sandstone rock formations, it's easy to get the idea that the Moab area is a baking, dry, rock-hard desert. Well, it is. But Moab is also the only town in Utah that sits along the Colorado River, and it's rapidly becoming a major boating center.

You can travel down the river in a canoe, kayak, large or small rubber raft (with or without motor), or speedy, solid jet-boats (see "Outfitters," below). Do-it-your-selfers can rent kayaks or canoes for $25 to $40 for a half day and $30 to $50 for a full day, or rafts from $50 to $60 per half day and $65 to $90 for a full day. Half-day guided river trips cost from $25 to $35 per person, and full-day trips are usually in the $35 to $60 range. Multiday rafting expeditions, which include meals and camping equipment, start at about $300 per person. Jet-boat trips, which can cover a lot more river in a given amount of time, start at about $30 for a 1^1/2-hour trip, with full-day trips about $75 per person. Children's rates are usually about 20% less. Some companies also offer sunset or dinner trips. Sheri Griffith Expeditions even offers a 4-day, three-night "Expedition in Luxury," at about $900 per person, offering gourmet food served with white tablecloths, wineglasses, and candles; and your every need anticipated. See "Outfitters," below.

Public boat launching ramps are opposite Lion's Park, near the intersection of U.S. 191 and Utah 128; at Take-Out Beach, along Utah 128 about 10 miles east of its intersection with U.S. 191; and at Hittle Bottom, also along Utah 128, about 23.5 miles east of its intersection with U.S. 191. Recorded information on river flows and reservoir conditions statewide can be obtained from the Colorado Basin River Forecast Center (☎ 801/539-1311).

GOLF

It might be hard to keep your eye on the ball at the 18-hole, par-72 Moab Golf Club course, 2750 S. East Bench Rd. (☎ 801/259-6488). Located 5 miles south of downtown Moab in Spanish Valley (take Spanish Trail Road off U.S. 191), the challenging course, nestled among red sandstone cliffs, has spectacular views in every direction. Open daily year-round (weather permitting), the course has a driving range, pro shop and lessons, cart rentals, and a snack bar serving breakfast and lunch.

HORSEBACK RIDING

Those who want to see the canyons and rock formations from on top of a horse can choose from several companies that lead guided rides (see "Outfitters," below). Prices start at about $15 for a 1-hour ride; about $90 for all day. Sunset and dinner rides are also available.

WINTER SPORTS

Although the immediate Moab area does get some snow in the winter, for the best winter sports conditions you'll want to head into the mountains of the Manti-La Sal National Forest to the southeast. Snow turns many forest roads into perfect snowmobile and cross-country ski trails, and you'll also find good telemarking terrain. However, the mountains are also subject to avalanches, so it's a good idea to check on conditions first with the rangers at the **Manti-La Sal National Forest's Moab Ranger District office,** 2290 S. West Resource Blvd. (P.O. Box 386), Moab,

UT 84532 (☎ 801/259-7155). The Forest Service also maintains a recorded **avalanche and winter weather–condition hotline,** updated daily (☎ 801/259-SNOW).

OUTFITTERS

Although Moab offers plenty for the do-it-your-selfer, some 50 local outfitters offer excursions of all kinds, from lazy canoe rides to hair-raising jet-boat and four-wheel-drive adventures. The chart below lists some of the major companies that want to help you fully enjoy this beautiful country. They are all located right in Moab, and the zip code is 84532. Advance reservations are often required for outings, and it's best to check with several outfitters before deciding on one. In addition to asking about what you'll see and do and what it will cost, it doesn't hurt to make sure the company is insured and has the proper permits with the various federal agencies. Also ask about its cancellation policy, just in case.

Outfitter	4X4	Bike	Boat	Horse	Rent	Shuttle
Adrift Adventures 378 Main, Box 577 ☎ 801/259-8594, 800/874-4483	●		●	●		●
Canyon Voyages River Trips 352 N. Main, Box 416 ☎ 801/259-6007, 800/733-6007			●		●	
Kaibab Mountain Bike Tours 391 S. Main ☎ 801/259-7423, 800/451-1133		●			●	
Lin Ottinger Tours 600 N. Main ☎ 801/259-7312	●					
Moab Rafting Co. 4725 S. Zimmerman Lane Box 801 ☎ 801/259-RAFT, 800/RIO-MOAB			●			
Navtec Expeditions 321 N. Main, Box 1267 ☎ 801/259-7983, 800/833-1278	●	●	●			●
Nichols Expeditions 497 N. Main ☎ 801/259-7882, 800/648-8488	●	●	●	●		
North American River Expeditions 543 N. Main ☎ 801/259-5865, 800/342-5938			●			
Old West Trail Rides US 191, S of Moab Box 302 ☎ 801/259-7410				●		

Outfitter	4X4	Bike	Boat	Horse	Rent	Shuttle
Pack Creek Ranch US 191, S of Moab P.O. Box 1270 ☎ 801/259-5505				●		
Red River Canoe Co. 497 N. Main ☎ 801/259-7722			●		●	●
Rim Tours 1233 S U.S. 191 ☎ 801/259-5223, 800/626-7335		●			●	●
River Runner Sports 401 N. Main ☎ 801/259-4121			●		●	
Sheri Griffith Expeditions 2231 S. U.S. 191 Box 1324 ☎ 801/259-8229, 800/332-2439			●			
Tag-A-Long Expeditions 452 N. Main ☎ 801/259-8946, 800/453-3292	●		●		●	●
Tex's Riverways 691 N. 500 West Box 67 ☎ 801/259-5101			●		●	●
Western River Expeditions 1371 N U.S. 191 ☎ 801/259-7019			●		●	
Western Spirit Cycling 38 S. 100 West Box 411 ☎ 801/259-8732, 800/845-BIKE		●			●	

SEEING THE SIGHTS

Arches Vineyards

420 Kane Creek Blvd. ☎ **801/259-5397** or 800/797-6702. Fax 801/259-3332. Free admission. Mon–Thurs 11am–7pm; Fri–Sat 11am–9pm; slightly shorter hours in the winter. Closed legal holidays by state law. From U.S. 191 on the south side of town, turn west at McDonald's; the winery is about a half mile ahead on the right.

Utah's only legal commercial winery offers free personalized tours, lasting from 15 to 30 minutes, during which you can learn how wine is made and see much of the process for yourself, from the pressing equipment to the French oak barrels to bottling. Free tastings of the winery's dozen or so varieties are offered, and wine can be purchased at the winery or state-run liquor stores. Bottles cost $5 to $20. Arches Vineyards' wines are also served at several local restaurants. The wine bottle labels, depicting scenes of Arches National Park, were designed by a Salt Lake City artist.

The Dan O'Laurie Museum

118 E. Center St. (two blocks east of Main Street). ☎ **801/259-7985.** Free admission, donations welcome. Summer Mon–Sat 1–5pm and 7–9pm; winter Mon–Thurs 3–5pm and 7–9pm, Fri–Sat 1–5pm and 7–9pm.

This small museum has numerous displays depicting the history of Moab from prehistoric times to the present. We start with exhibits on the geology of the area, and the resultant uranium and radium mining. Early home medical remedies are on display, as is the first incubator, which used only a 25-watt bulb and was invented by a local doctor. You'll see primers from the early 1900s and a 1920 high school annual called "The Whizzer"; and the expected ranching and farming exhibits—even a handmade quilt depicting brands. Upstairs is a gallery with changing art exhibits from local artists. There is also a small gift shop.

Hole 'n the Rock

La Sal Route. ☎ **801/686-2250.** Admission $2.50 adults, $1.50 children 6–12. Daily 9am–5pm; open until 6pm in the summer. Take U.S. 191 15 miles south of Moab.

This 5,000-square-foot cave-home was excavated from solid stone by Albert and Gladys Christensen, who removed some 50,000 cubic feet of sandstone over a 12-year period to create their living space. Today, tours of the 14 rooms are given every 10 minutes. Visitors can see the fireplace—with a 65-foot chimney drilled through solid rock—and other rock-solid furnishings, and browse through the gift shop.

Moab to Monument Valley Film Commission Museum & Gift Shop

50 E. Center no. 1 (half a block east of Main Street). ☎ **801/259-6388.** Free admission. Call for hours.

Southeastern Utah has been in so many Hollywood movies that some directors, actors, and crew members are starting to call it home. From 1925, when *The Vanishing American* was filmed in Monument Valley, numerous films have been shot here, including countless westerns—John Wayne was a regular. Plenty of non-westerns used this area as a backdrop, too, such as *Thelma and Louise* and *Indiana Jones and the Last Crusade.* Various movie leftovers, photos, posters, and related memorabilia have been collected, and can be seen at the film commission office, located behind the Moab Visitor Center. However, at this writing, commission director Bette Stanton was hoping to find larger quarters to properly display the collection, so check with the visitor center before searching for the museum.

WHEN YOU NEED TO COOL OFF

A good way to beat the summer heat is with a day or even a few hours at **Butch Cassidy's King World Waterpark,** 1500 N. U.S. 191 (☎ 801/259-2837). Hidden on 17 acres back from the highway on the north side of town, this family-oriented water park has three large water slides, two kiddie slides, three pools, sand volleyball, a refreshment stand, and picnic areas. There are paddle boats in a pond once used by outlaw Butch Cassidy as a watering hole for stolen horses and cattle. The water park is open mid-April to mid-September, weather permitting, usually daily 10am to 10pm, although Sunday hours may be slightly shorter. An all-day pass costs $7.50 for adults, $6.50 for children 12 and under, and those over 65 or under 3 are admitted free. Lower fees are charged for shorter periods of time.

Those looking for a regular swimming pool, open year-round, can head to the **Moab Swim Center,** 181 W. 400 North (☎ 801/259-8226), which has open swimming most afternoons and evenings. Admission costs $3 for adults, $1.50 for youth under 18, and is free for children three and under.

SHOPPING

Moab may not be a shopper's mecca, but you'll find enough interesting stores to keep you busy for an afternoon, and possibly some unique items to take home.

For hand-crafted Navajo, Hopi, and Zuni jewelry, as well as pottery, weavings, and carvings, try **Lema Indian Trading Company,** 60 N. Main (☎ 801/259-5055), or **Hogan Trading Company,** 100 S. Main (☎ 801/259-8118). If it's Native American music you're after, **Music of Moab** at 82 S. Main (☎ 801/259-4405), is the place to go, with a huge selection on tape and compact disc.

The **Moab Rock Shop,** 600 N. Main (☎ 801/259-7312), has all sorts of rocks, minerals, gems, dinosaur bones, and fossils. **The Western Image,** 79 N. Main (☎ 801/259-3006), has western art and collectibles, cowboy boots, and genuine Stetson hats; while the **One-Shot Gallery,** 40 N. 100 West (☎ 801/259-2700), sells local art, crafts, and gifts. In the beverage category, there's the local wine, **Arches Vineyards** (see above) and the local beer, Eddie McStiff's (see "Where to Dine" below). The **Utah State Liquor Store** is at 260 S. Main (☎ 801/259-5314).

WHERE TO STAY

The highest room rates in Moab are generally charged from mid-March through October, and sometimes drop by up to half in the winter. Rates may also be higher during special events. Room tax of about 11^{1}/2% is added to all bills. Pets are not accepted unless otherwise noted.

Most visitors are here for the outdoors, and since they don't plan to spend much time in their room, they book into one of the very adequate but cookie-cutter chain and franchise motels. The town's largest lodging property is the **Super 8 Motel,** on the north edge of town at 889 N. Main St. (☎ 801/259-8868 or 800/800-8000; fax 801/259-8968), with 146 rooms, charging $46 to $76 double during the high season. The **Days Inn,** 426 N. Main St. (☎ 801/259-4468 or 800/DAYS-INN; fax 801/259-4018), charges $45 to $85 double in the high season. Moab has two Best Westerns: The **Best Western Canyonlands Inn,** 16 S. Main St. (☎ 801/259-2300 or 800/528-1234; fax 801/259-2301), charges $89 to $106 double, including breakfast, in the high season; and the **Best Western Green Well,** 105 S. Main St. (☎ 801/259-6151 or 800/528-1234; fax 801/259-4397), has rates of $45 to $110 double in the high season.

✪ Bowen Motel

169 N. Main St., Moab, UT 84532. ☎ **801/259-7132** or 800/874-5439. 40 rms. A/C TV TEL. $62–$70 double. Off-season 40% less. AE, DC, DISC, MC, V.

This family-owned and -operated motel offers fairly large, comfortable, clean, basic rooms with one or two queen-sized beds and shower/tub combos. Most rooms have attractive wall murals that add interest to the plain white walls, and two family rooms sleep up to six each. The original structure was built in the 1940s, with additions made in the 1980s, and a major renovation was completed in 1993–94. There's an outdoor heated swimming pool and locked bike storage ($2 per night extra). Several restaurants are within easy walking distance.

The Lazy Lizard International Hostel

1213 S. U.S. 191, Moab, UT 84532. ☎ **801/259-6057.** 30 dorm beds, 5 private rms, 4 cabins, 1 teepee; total capacity 55 persons. $7 dorm bed; $20 private rm; $25 cabin; $10 teepee. Hostel membership not necessary. No credit cards.

On the south side of town, behind a bowling alley and self-storage units, this hostel offers exceptionally clean, comfortable lodging at bargain rates for those willing to share. The main house, which is air-conditioned, has basic dorm rooms plus one private room. A separate building contains four additional private rooms, which look much like older motel units (with fans but no air-conditioning). The best facilities are the four cabins, constructed of real logs and with beds for up to six. The teepee is, well, a teepee. Everyone shares the bath houses, and there's a telephone in the main house. Guests also have use of a fully equipped kitchen; a living room with television, VCR, and a collection of movies; a gas barbecue grill; and picnic tables. Groups should inquire about the two nearby houses that can be rented by the night ($120 for the one that sleeps 20; $90 for the one that sleeps 10).

Red Stone Inn

535 S. Main St., Moab, UT 84532. ☎ **801/259-3500** or 800/772-1972. Fax 801/259-2717. 50 rms. A/C TV TEL. Winter $29.95–$34.95 double; summer $49.95–$54.95 double; slightly higher during special events. AE, DISC, MC, V.

This centrally located motel, built in 1993, is among Moab's best deals for travelers who want a clean, quiet place to sleep at a bargain rate. Although the exterior gives the impression that these are cabins, inside you'll find basic modern motel rooms, somewhat small, with either one queen-sized bed or two doubles. Roll-away beds are available at $5 extra. Three handicapped-accessible rooms have shower/tub combos, while the rest have showers only. Rooms are decorated with posters and maps showing off the area's attractions. There is no swimming pool, but a picnic area has gas barbecue grills for guests' use. Pets are permitted at an extra charge of $5.

✪ Sunflower Hill Bed & Breakfast Inn

185 N. 300 East, Moab, UT 84532. ☎ **801/259-2974.** 11 units. A/C TV. Mar–mid-Nov and holidays $75–$150 double; mid-Nov–Feb $45–$120 double. Rates include breakfast. MC, V.

This country-style B&B is located three blocks off Main Street on a quiet dead end road, and offers quiet rooms and lovely outdoor areas for relaxing. The grounds are grassy and shady, with fruit trees and flowers in abundance. There's an outdoor hot tub (usable year-round), a swing, a picnic table, and a barbecue for guests' use. In a small pantry area is a stocked refrigerator, plus space to put your own food.

Each guest room has a different motif, but all have handmade quilts with matching sham pillows and coordinated sheets on the beds, and combination tub/showers. The Rose Room has roses stenciled on the walls, an old picture of a mother and daughter with roses in the lower left corner, and a rose-design wallpaper. The Sun Porch has a flowered rock-wall mural in the bedroom, and sunflowers stenciled along the bottom of the walls in a separate sitting area, which overlooks the shady side yard. The Garret, an upstairs suite, is decorated in an apple motif, and its bath has a wonderful old claw-foot tub, painted red outside, with a surround shower curtain.

Breakfasts are substantial, with a buffet offering homemade breads and granola, fruit juices, fresh fruits—often from the Sunflower Hill's own garden and trees—fresh ground Colombian coffee, and yogurt, plus a hot entree, which might be Belgian waffles, baked French toast, or individual casseroles.

CAMPING

✪ Canyonlands Campark

555 S. Main St., Moab, UT 84532. ☎ **801/259-6848** or 800/522-6848 outside Utah. Total sites 140 (108 pull-throughs, 32 tent), 70 with full hookups, 38 with water and electric only. $19 full hookup, $17 with water/electric, $14 tent. AE, DISC, MC, V.

A good choice for those with RVs—or for anyone who wants a hot shower after hiking or mountainbiking all day—this campground is surprisingly shady and quiet given its in-town Main Street location. It's open year-round. There's a dump station, a self-service laundry, a playground, and an outdoor unheated swimming pool. A convenience store has food and some RV supplies, and a City Market grocery store is just a block away.

WHERE TO DINE

Center Cafe

92 E. Center St. ☎ **801/259-4295.** Reservations recommended. Main courses $8.95–$19.95. DISC, MC, V. Daily 5:30–10pm; Sun brunch 9am–1pm. Closed Dec–Feb. About one block east of Main Street. CONTEMPORARY AMERICAN.

Not really a cafe at all, this fine small restaurant, with white tablecloths, black chairs, and a bright, contemporary look, is the place to come for innovative game, vegetarian, and pasta selections. The menu changes seasonally, but might include Cajun shrimp fettuccine, tossed in a spicy cream sauce with vegetables; a roasted vegetable salad with grains, wilted greens, and sun-dried tomato dressing; or grilled rabbit sausage with a shiitake mushroom sauce. The Sunday brunch offers basic eggs, fancy omelets, and some exotic creations such as French toast made with walnut-fig bread; and the Egg in a Hole (an egg, cooked in brioche with smoked trout sauce, in case you were wondering). The restaurant has full liquor service.

Eddie McStiff's

57 S. Main St. (in Western Plaza, just south of the information center). ☎ **801/259-2337.** Reservations not accepted. Main courses $5.50–$16.50; pizza $5–$20. MC, V. Daily 3–10pm. Closed Dec–Jan. ECLECTIC.

This bustling, somewhat noisy brew pub is half family restaurant and half tavern. In the restaurant dining room, you'll find Southwest decor and paintings by local artists, while the tavern looks just like a tavern should, with a long bar, low light, and lots of wood. The menu, which changes seasonally, usually has Italian dishes and specialty pizzas, but you'll also find southwestern items, at least one charbroiled steak, fresh fish, and several creative salads. The popular spinach lasagna is usually available; it's prepared in-house with four cheeses and a homemade tomato sauce. House specials include veal piccata—medallions of veal sautéed in white wine, lemon juice, capers, tomato, shallots, and mushrooms, and served with pasta. From the southwestern side of the menu we recommend the black bean burrito, a flour tortilla stuffed with beans and jack cheese, topped with green and red chile sauce, and served with guacamole, salsa, and sour cream. At least a dozen fresh-brewed beers are on tap at any time, and can also be purchased to go in 22-ounce bottles and half-gallon refillable growlers. Mixed drinks, wine, and beer are sold in the dining room with food only, and beer can be purchased with or without food in the tavern. (You must be at least 21 to eat in the tavern.)

✪ Fat City Smokehouse

36 S. 100 West (one block west of Main Street just south of Center Street). ☎ **801/259-4302.** Main courses $4.75–$15.95. AE, MC, V. Daily 11:30am–10pm. Closed Sun in the winter. BARBECUE/VEGETARIAN.

Genuine Texas-style pit barbecue has made this a favorite of locals, who pile into the plain, cafe-style dining room for pork or beef ribs, brisket, chicken, and homemade sausage, all rubbed with a variety of seasonings, slow-cooked from 12 to 14 hours, and served with the restaurant's own sauce. Flame-grilled dinners, cooked over apple and cherry hardwoods, include fresh catfish with sweet pepper seasoning; a popular summer special is the 24-ounce T-bone. For the non-barbecue-lover, there are several vegetarian sandwiches, such as the veggie club, with grilled eggplant, zucchini, onion, and green pepper on three layers of toasted nut bread, with fresh tomato pesto and a choice of cheese. Service at this casual restaurant is fast and friendly, and beer is available with meals.

Honest Ozzie's Cafe & Desert Oasis

60 N. 100 West (one block west of Main Street and just north of Center Street). ☎ **801/ 259-8442.** Breakfast items $2–$5.50; main dinner courses $4–$9.75. No credit cards. Daily 7am–noon and 6–10pm. Closed Nov–Feb. HEALTH FOOD.

This cheery little cafe, decorated with plants and local artwork, offers very personal service. In fact, you may have to wait a bit at dinner if it's busy, but it's usually worth your time. Try the Ozzie Oriental, fresh vegetables and sprouts stir-fried in your choice of glaze and served with steamed brown rice; or the huge Burrito Mondo, with beans, steamed vegetables, and cheese wrapped in a whole wheat tortilla, smothered with more cheese, sour cream, and your choice of sauces. There's also a fresh seafood special daily, lots of salads, and one or two chicken dishes. Breakfasts include gigantic pancakes, blintzes, omelets, and granola, and all baked goods come from Honest Ozzie's in-house bakery. During the summer you can eat in the garden patio while watching the resident hummingbirds. The restaurant has full liquor service.

✪ Moab Diner

189 S. Main St. (two blocks south of Center Street). ☎ **801/259-4006.** Breakfast items $2.99–$4.75; lunch items $3.75–$5.50; main dinner courses $4.75–$15.95. MC, V. Daily 6am–10:30pm. Closes earlier in the winter. AMERICAN/SOUTHWESTERN.

Late risers can get breakfast—among the best in town—all day here, with all the usual egg dishes, biscuits and gravy, six kinds of omelets, and a spicy breakfast burrito. The decor tells you that this is definitely a diner, but it does have lots of green plants (real, not plastic). Hamburgers, sandwiches, and salads are the offerings at lunch, of course, and for dinner there's steak, shrimp, and chicken platters, plus liver and onions. Dinners include roll, potato, and soup or salad. In addition to ice cream, you can get sherbet, frozen yogurt, malts, and shakes, plus sundaes with seven different toppings. No alcoholic beverages are served.

Poplar Place Pub & Eatery

11 E. 100 North (just east of Main Street, one block north of Center Street). ☎ **801/259-6018.** Pizza $7–$16.75; main courses $4.95–$6.95. MC, V. Daily 11:30am–11pm. Shorter hours in the winter. MEXICAN/ITALIAN.

This two-story corner pub has been a busy lunch stop for locals since it opened in 1972, serving several microbrewed beers plus lots of pizzas, pasta, and Mexican dishes. The pizzas are probably the most popular items on the menu. Crust and sauces are homemade, and they come with either a tomato or Alfredo sauce and your choice of toppings. For the indecisive, several specialty pizzas are also listed. Mexican selections include crab or vegetable enchiladas, chicken burrito with green chile sauce, and what the Poplar Place calls a "faco," a cross between a fajita and taco. There is full liquor service.

MOAB AFTER DARK

For a small town in conservative, nondrinking Utah, this is a pretty wild place. After a day on the river or in the back of a jeep, don't be surprised to see your outfitter letting his or her hair down at the **Rio Colorado Restaurant and Bar,** one block west of Main on Center Street (☎ 801/259-6666). Locals just call it The Rio. There's live regional music—usually rock, reggae, or jazz—most weekend evenings in the summer.

Another local hangout is the **Sportsman's Lounge,** 1991 S. U.S. 191 (☎ 801/ 259-9972), which claims to have the biggest dance floor in town. There's live country music on summer weekends, and dart tournaments and other fun activities during the week.

Popular with beer drinkers is **Eddie McStiff's,** 57 S. Main St. (☎ 801/259-2337), a microbrewery that's part family restaurant (see "Where to Dine" above) and a busy tavern, with several TVs plus a game room with pool tables, foosball, and shuffle- board. There are a dozen fresh-brewed beers on tap, and for those who order food of some kind, a full bar.

Those looking for a foot-stompin' good time and a western-style dinner (but no alcohol) will want to make their way to the **Bar M Chuckwagon Live Western Show and Cowboy Supper,** 541 S. Mulberry Lane (☎ 801/259-2276), which is similar to chuckwagon suppers in other parts of the West. You're outdoors if skies are clear, under a tarp if it rains. Diners go through a supper line to pick up barbe- cued beef or chicken, potato, beans, applesauce, biscuits, dessert, and beverages. After dinner there's a stage show of western-style music, jokes, and down-home silliness from the Bar M Wranglers. The grounds, which include a small western village and gift shop, open at 6pm, with dinner at 7:30pm and the show at 8:30pm. The Bar M is open Fridays and Saturdays in April and May, and Monday through Saturday from June through September. Supper and show cost $14 for adults, $6 for children 4 to 10, and free for children under four.

Canyonlands by Night (☎ 801/259-5261) is an evening river trip, operating May through mid-October, that combines a sunset boat ride, with stories of outlaws and rock formations, with a show of colored lights on the canyon walls. The office and dock are just north of Moab at the Colorado River Bridge. Cost is $20 for adults, $10 for children 6 to 12, and free for children under six. Reservations are recommended.

The **Fallen Arches Square Dance Club** (☎ 801/259-5637) invites visitors to join them Thursday evenings year-round at the Moab Community Civic Center, at 100 N. 400 East. Line dancing lessons start at 6:30pm and square dance lessons begin at 7pm; square dancing starts at 8pm. Admission costs $5 per couple.

HEADING NORTH FROM MOAB VIA GREEN RIVER

Travelers heading north to Salt Lake City or west toward Nevada will undoubtedly go through the village of Green River, which sits along the banks of the Green River about 109 miles northwest of Moab, and offers an interesting break.

The **John Wesley Powell River History Museum,** 885 E. Main St., Green River (☎ 801/564-3427), details the phenomenal river expedition of explorer John Wesley Powell, a one-armed Civil War veteran who explored the Green and Colorado Rivers in the late 1800s. Museum exhibits also detail the geology of the region and the history of river running, from a replica of Powell's heavy wooden boat, the Emma Dean, to examples of boats and rafts used on the river since then. A 20-minute multimedia program on Powell's adventures is shown throughout the day. Admission to the museum is free, although donations are welcome. It's open daily from 8am to 8pm in the summer; daily 9am to 5pm in the winter.

✪ **Green River State Park,** on Green River Road (☎ 801/564-3633) is a lush green oasis, with big old Russian olive and cottonwood trees. Located right on the river, the park has a boat ramp for launching your raft or canoe, but be aware that once you start heading downstream you'll need a motor or mighty powerful arms to fight the current back to the park. A 9-hole championship golf course is scheduled to open in the summer of 1996. Day-use admission costs $3 per vehicle or $1 for walk-ins, bicyclists, and motorcyclists; and camping costs $9 per night Sunday through Thursday, $10 per night Fridays, Saturdays, and holidays. Camping reservations are accepted from mid-March through mid-October, using MasterCard or Visa, with a $5 nonrefundable fee (☎ 800/322-3770). The shady 42-site campground, open year-round, has modern restrooms and hot showers, but no RV hookups.

Several river-running companies offer one- and multi-day trips on the Green. These include **Holiday River Expeditions** (☎ 801/564-3273 in Green River or 801/266-2087 in Salt Lake City). Cost, including lunch, is about $60 per adult and $45 for youths.

For additional information on Green River, stop at the **Green River Information Center** in the John Wesley Powell River History Museum (see above), or contact the **Grand County Travel Council,** P.O. Box 550, Moab, UT 84532 (☎ 801/259-8825 or 800/635-6622; fax 801/259-1376).

2 Arches National Park

Natural stone arches and fantastic rock formations, sculpted as if by an artist's hand, are the defining feature of this park, and they exist in remarkable numbers and variety. Just as soon as you've seen the most beautiful, most colorful, most gigantic stone arch you can imagine, walk around the next bend and there's another—bigger, better, and more brilliant than the last. It would take forever to see them all, with some 1,700 officially listed and more being discovered or "born" every day.

Sitting next to Canyonlands National Park in eastern Utah, Arches is much more visitor-friendly, with relatively short, well-maintained trails leading to most of the park's major attractions. It's also a place to let your imagination run wild. Is Delicate Arch really so delicate? Or would its other monikers (Old Maid's Bloomers or Cowboy Chaps) really be more appropriate? And what about those tall spires? Your kids can imagine they're castles, giant stone sailing ships, or perhaps petrified skyscrapers of some ancient city.

Exploring the park is a great family adventure. The arches seem more accessible and less forbidding than the spires and pinnacles at Canyonlands and other southern Utah parks. Your kids can think of arches as bridges, and imagine the power of water that literally cuts a hole through a solid rock. (Actually, to geologists there's a big difference between arches and bridges. Bridges are formed when a river cuts a channel, while the often bizarre and beautiful contours of arches result from the erosive force of rain and snow, freezing and thawing, as it dissolves the "glue" that holds sand grains together, and chips away at the stone.)

Although arches usually grow slowly—*very* slowly—something dramatic happens every once in a while. Like that quiet day in 1940 when a sudden crash instantly doubled the size of the opening of Skyline Arch, leaving a huge boulder lying at its feet. Luckily, no one (at least no one we know of) was standing underneath at the time. The same thing happened to the magnificently delicate Landscape Arch in 1971, when a slab of rock about 60 feet long, 11 feet wide, and 4.5 feet thick fell from the underside of the arch. Now there's such a thin ribbon of stone that it's hard to believe it can continue hanging on at all.

Spend a day or a week here, exploring the terrain, watching the rainbow of colors deepen and explode with the long rays of the setting sun, or the moonlight glistening on ribbons of desert varnish on tall sandstone cliffs. Watch for mule deer, cottontail rabbits, and the bright green collared lizard as they go about the difficult task of desert life. And let your own imagination run wild among the Three Gossips,

Arches National Park

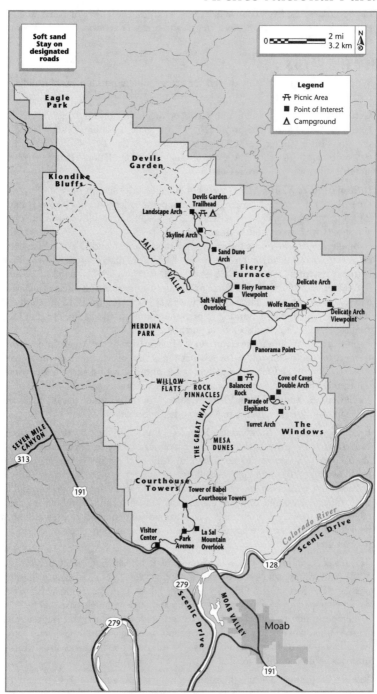

Soft sand
Stay on
designated
roads

0   2 mi
3.2 km

N

Legend
⚎ Picnic Area
■ Point of Interest
△ Campground

Eagle
Park

Klondike
Bluffs

Devils
Garden

Devils Garden
Trailhead
Landscape Arch ■ ⚎ △

Skyline Arch ■

Sand Dune
■ Arch

Fiery
Furnace

Delicate Arch ■

■ Fiery Furnace
Viewpoint

Salt Valley
Overlook

Wolfe Ranch ■

Delicate Arch
Viewpoint

SALT VALLEY

HERDINA
PARK

■ Panorama Point

WILLOW
FLATS

ROCK
PINNACLES

⚎
■
Balanced
Rock

Cove of Caves
Double Arch

Parade of
Elephants

Turret Arch ■

The
Windows

THE GREAT WALL

MESA
DUNES

SEVEN MILE
CANYON

313

191

Courthouse
Towers

Tower of Babel
Courthouse Towers ■

Visitor
Center ■

Park
Avenue

La Sal
Mountain
Overlook

Colorado River

Scenic Drive

128

279

Scenic Drive

MOAB VALLEY

Moab

279

191

the Spectacles, the Eye of the Whale, the Penguins, the Tower of Babel, and the thousands of other statues, towers, arches, and bridges that await your discovery in this magical playground.

JUST THE FACTS

See the Moab section of this chapter for other camping possibilities, plus lodging, restaurants, and services.

Getting There   To get there from Moab, drive 5 miles north on U.S. 191. Arches National Park is located 27 miles east of Canyonlands National Park's Island in the Sky Visitor Center, and 233 miles southeast of Salt Lake City. The park is 404 miles northeast of the north rim of Grand Canyon National Park in Arizona, and 371 miles west of Denver, Colorado.

Information & Visitors Centers   For advance information on what to see in the park, plus hiking and camping, contact Superintendent, **Arches National Park,** P.O. Box 907, Moab, UT 84532-0907 (☎ 801/259-8161). It's best to write early, and specify what type of information you need.

Books, maps, and videos on Arches as well as Canyonlands National Park and other southern Utah attractions can be purchased from the nonprofit **Canyonlands Natural History Association,** 30 South 100 East, Moab, UT 84532 (☎ 801/259-6003; fax 801/259-8263). Some publications are available in foreign languages, and several videos can be purchased in either VHS or PAL formats. MasterCard and Visa are accepted. Those wanting to help the nonprofit association can join ($20 annually) and get a 20% discount on purchases.

Once you arrive in the area, you can get information at the **Moab Information Center,** located in the middle of town at the corner of Main and Center Streets (☎ 801/259-3911). Open 8am to 9pm in the summer, with slightly shorter winter hours, the center is staffed by Park Service representatives.

The **Arches National Park Visitor Center,** located just inside the entrance gate, has maps, brochures on hiking trails, and other information.

Fees, Regulations & Backcountry Permits   Entry into the park (for up to seven days) costs $4 per private vehicle or $2 per motorcycle, bicycle, or pedestrian. A $10 annual pass is also available. Free permits, available at the visitor center, are required for all overnight trips into the backcountry.

Backcountry hikers should practice minimum-impact techniques, packing out all trash. Of course, feeding or molesting wildlife, vandalism, and disturbing any natural feature of the park is prohibited. Wood fires are not permitted. Dogs, which must be leashed at all times, are prohibited in public buildings, on all trails, and in the backcountry.

Seasons & Avoiding the Crowds   Summer days here are hot, sometimes reaching 100°F, and winters can be cool or cold, dropping below freezing at night, with snow possible. The best time to visit, especially for hikers, is in the spring or fall, when daytime temperatures are usually between 60 and 80°F and nights are cool.

The peak months follow the temperatures, with June, July, and August being busiest, when you're likely to experience parking problems, and the quietest times being December, January, and February. As with most popular parks, avoid visiting during school vacations if possible.

Ranger Programs   During the summer, rangers lead guided hikes on the Fiery Furnace Trail twice daily (see "Sports and Outdoor Activities" section below), as well as daily nature walks from various park locations. Evening campfire programs, also in the summer only, are on topics such as rock art, geological processes, and wildlife. A schedule of events is posted at the visitor center.

EXPLORING THE PARK'S HIGHLIGHTS BY CAR

Arches is the easiest of Utah's national parks to see in a day if that's all you can spare. An 18-mile (one-way) **scenic drive** offers splendid views of countless natural rock arches and other formations, and several easy hikes open up additional scenery. Allow 1^1/$_2$ hours for the 36-mile round-trip drive, adding time for the optional hikes.

You can see many of the park's most famous rock formations without even getting out of your car—although we strongly urge you to get out and explore on foot. You have the option of walking short distances to a number of viewpoints, or stretching your legs on a variety of longer hikes along the way (see "Sports and Outdoor Activities" below). The main road is easy to navigate, even for RVs, but parking at some viewpoints is very limited. Please be considerate and leave trailers at the visitor center parking lot.

Start out by viewing the short slide show at the **visitor center** to get a feel for what lies ahead. Then drive north along the Moab Fault to the overlook parking for **Park Avenue,** a solid rock "fin" that reminded early visitors of the New York skyline.

From here, your next stop is **La Sal Mountain Overlook,** where you look southeast to the La Sal Mountains, named by early Spanish explorers who thought the snow-covered mountains looked like huge piles of salt. In the overlook area is a "desert scrub" ecosystem, composed of sagebrush, saltbush, blackbrush, yucca, and prickly pear cactus, all plants that can survive in sandy soil with little moisture. Animals that inhabit the area include the kangaroo rat, blacktail jackrabbit, squirrel, several species of lizards, and the coyote.

Continuing on the scenic drive, you begin to see some of the park's major formations at **Courthouse Towers,** where large monoliths such as Sheep Rock, the Organ, and the Three Gossips dominate the landscape. Leaving Courthouse Towers, watch for the **Tower of Babel** on the east (right) side of the road, then proceed past the petrified sand dunes of **Dune Mesa** to **Balanced Rock,** a huge boulder weighing about 3,600 tons, perched on a slowly eroding pedestal.

Continuing, you'll soon take a side road to the east (right) to **The Windows.** Formed when erosion penetrated a sandstone fin, they can be seen via a short walk from the parking area. Also in this area you'll see **Turret Arch** and the **Cove of Caves,** believed to have been used for shelter by early Native Americans. As erosion continues in the back of the largest cave it will probably become an arch. A short walk from the parking lot takes you to **Double Arch,** which looks exactly like what the name implies. From the end of this trail you can also see the delightful **Parade of Elephants.**

Return to the main park road, turn north (right), and drive to **Panorama Point,** with an expansive view of Salt Valley and the Fiery Furnace, which can really live up to its name at sunset.

Next, turn east (right) off the main road onto the Wolfe Ranch Road and drive to the **Wolfe Ranch** parking area. A very short walk leads to what's left of this ranch. John Wesley Wolfe and his son Fred moved here from Ohio in 1888, and in 1907 were joined by John's daughter Flora, her husband, and their two children. The cabin seen here was built for Flora's family (John's cabin was later destroyed by a flash flood). In 1910 the family decided this was not the greatest location for a ranch, and they packed up and returned to Ohio. If you follow the trail a bit further, you'll see some Ute petroglyphs. More ambitious hikers can continue for a moderately

Impressions

Ten thousand strangely carved forms in every direction, and beyond them mountains blending with clouds.

—Major John Wesley Powell, 1869

difficult 3-mile round-trip excursion to **Delicate Arch,** with a spectacular view at trail's end. If you don't want to take this hike, you'll be able to see Delicate Arch from a 1-mile round-trip viewpoint at the driving tour's next stop, the **Delicate Arch Viewpoint,** where you'll get at least a distant view of this arch, probably the park's most famous landmark.

Returning to the park's main road, turn north (right), and go to the next stop, the **Salt Valley Overlook.** The various shades and colors in this collapsed salt dome have been caused by varying amounts of iron in the rock, as well as the amount of air present at the time of oxidation.

Continue now to the viewpoint for **Fiery Furnace,** which offers a dramatic view of colorful sandstone fins. This is also the starting point for 2-hour ranger-guided hikes in the summer.

From here, drive to a pull-out for **Sand Dune Arch,** located down a short path from the road, where you'll find shade and sand, a good place for kids to play, along with the arch. The trail also leads across a meadow to Broken Arch (which isn't broken at all—it just looks that way from a distance).

Back on the road, continue to **Skyline Arch,** which doubled in size in 1940 when a huge boulder tumbled out of it. The next and final stop is the often crowded parking area for the **Devil's Garden Trailhead.** From here you can hike to some of the most unique arches in the park, including **Landscape Arch,** among the longest natural rock spans in the world. It's a pretty easy 1.6-mile round-trip hike.

From the trailhead parking lot, it's 18 miles back to the visitor center.

SPORTS & OUTDOOR ACTIVITIES

Four-Wheeling   Although there aren't nearly as many four-wheel-drive opportunities here as in nearby Canyonlands National Park, there are a few—but check first with rangers on possible road closures or conditions that make the routes impassable. One possibility, which is also a moderately strenuous mountainbike excursion, is the 19-mile round-trip Willow Flat to Klondike Bluffs Road. From Balanced Rock parking area this scenic trip climbs to high desert terrain, allowing panoramic hilltop views of surrounding mountains and red rock formations. The route also passes Eye of the Needle Arch, views of Elephant Butte (the highest point in the park at 5,653 feet), and the imposing Courthouse Towers. Also seen along the route are drifting sand dunes and the red rock Marching Men formation.

Four-wheel-drive vehicles are available for rent, or you can travel in a jeep tour, with several companies based in Moab. See the "Moab" section earlier in this chapter.

Biking   Bikes are prohibited on all trails, as well as forbidden to travel cross-country within the national park boundaries. This leaves the park's established scenic drive, which is open to cyclists, although you need to be aware that the 18-mile dead end road is narrow and winding in spots, and can be a bit crowded with motor vehicles during the summer.

Mountainbikers also have the option of tackling one of several four-wheel-drive roads (see the "Four-Wheeling" section above). For guided mountainbike trips, as well as rentals, repairs, and supplies, see the earlier section of this chapter on Moab.

Hiking   Most trails here are short and relatively easy, although because of the hot summer sun and lack of shade, it's wise to carry a good amount of water on any jaunt expected to last more than 1 hour.

One easy walk, and a good place to take kids who want to play in the sand, is to **Sand Dune Arch.** It's only 0.3 mile long (round-trip), but you can add an extra 1.2 miles by continuing on to Broken Arch. Sand Dune Arch is hidden among and shaded by rock walls, with a naturally created giant sandbox below the arch. By the way, please resist the temptation to climb onto the arch and jump down into the sand. Not only is it dangerous, but it can damage the arch. Those who continue to Broken Arch should watch for mule deer and kit foxes, which inhabit the meadow you'll be crossing. Allow about 30 minutes to Sand Dune Arch and back; 1 hour to Broken Arch.

From the **Devil's Garden Trail** you can see about 60 arches, on a fairly long, strenuous and difficult hike, or view some exciting scenery by following only part of the route. We suggest taking at least the easy-to-moderate 1.6-mile round-trip hike to ✪ **Landscape Arch,** a long, thin ribbon of stone that is one of the most beautiful arches in the park. Allow about an hour. Past Landscape Arch the trail becomes more challenging, but offers numerous additional views, including the curious Double O Arch, and on to a large, dark tower known as Dark Angel. You are now 2.5 miles from the trailhead. Allow about 3 hours round-trip.

Considered by many as the park's best and most scenic hike, the 3-mile round-trip ✪ **Delicate Arch Trail** is a moderate-to-difficult hike, with slippery slickrock and some steep drop-offs along a narrow cliff, but it rewards hikers with a dramatic and spectacular view of Delicate Arch. Along the way, you'll see the John Wesley Wolfe ranch and have an opportunity to take a side trip to a Ute petroglyph panel that includes images of horses, and drawings that may represent a bighorn sheep hunt. When you get back on the main trail, watch for collared lizards. Arches' largest lizard, up to a foot long, they are usually bright green with stripes of yellow or rust, and a black collar. Feeding mostly in the daytime, they particularly enjoy insects and other lizards, and can stand and run on their large hind feet in pursuit of prey. (Didn't we see this in *Jurassic Park*?) Continuing along the trail, watch for Frame Arch, off to the right. Its main claim-to-fame is that numerous photographers have used it to "frame" a photo of Delicate Arch in the distance. Just past Frame Arch, the trail gets a little weird, having been blasted out from the cliff. Allow 2 to 3 hours. Those who opt not to take this hike should consider the 1-mile round-trip Delicate Arch Viewpoint Trail, which provides an ideal location for a photo, preferably with the arch highlighted by a clear blue sky. Allow about 30 minutes for this moderately easy walk.

The ✪ **Fiery Furnace Guided Hike** is a difficult 2-mile round-trip naturalist-led hike to some of the most colorful formations in the park. Guided hikes are given into this restricted area twice daily, by reservation only, and last from 2 to 3 hours. Permits to enter the Fiery Furnace on your own may also be available.

Horseback Riding   Commercial outfitters offering guided trail rides into Arches National Park are listed in the first section of this chapter, on Moab.

CAMPING IN THE PARK

Located at the north end of the scenic drive through the park, **Devil's Garden Campground** is Arches' only developed campground. The 51 well-spaced sites are nestled among rocks, with plenty of piñon and juniper trees. There are no showers or RV hookups. Camping costs $7 per night, with no reservations. There's water and flush toilets in the summer; chemical toilets and no water from November through mid-March.

3 Canyonlands National Park

Utah's largest national park is not for the sightseer out on a Sunday afternoon drive. It rewards those willing to spend time and energy—*lots* of energy—to explore the rugged backcountry. Sliced into districts by the Colorado and Green Rivers, the park's primary architects, this is a land of extremes: vast panoramas, dizzyingly deep canyons, dramatically steep cliffs, broad mesas, and towering red spires.

The most accessible part of Canyonlands is the Island of the Sky District, in the northern section of the park, where a paved road leads to viewpoints such as Grand View Point, overlooking some 10,000 square miles of rugged wilderness. Island in the Sky also has several easy-to-moderate trails, offering sweeping vistas of the park. A short walk offers views of Upheaval Dome, which resembles a large volcanic crater but may actually be a meteorite crater. For the more adventurous, the 100-mile White Rim Trail takes experienced mountainbikers and those with high-clearance four-wheel-drive vehicles on a winding loop tour through a vast array of scenery.

The Needles District, in the park's southeast corner, offers only a few viewpoints along the paved road, but numerous possibilities for hikers, backpackers, and those with high-clearance 4X4s. Named for its tall, red-and-white striped rock pinnacles, it is a diverse area of arches, including the 150-foot-tall Angel Arch, as well as grassy meadows and the confluence of the Green and Colorado Rivers. Backcountry visitors to the Needles District will also find ruins and rock art left by the ancient Anasazi some 800 years ago.

Most park visitors don't get a close-up view of the Maze District, but instead see it off in the distance from Grand View Point at Island in the Sky, or Confluence Overlook in the Needles District. That's because it's inhospitable and practically inaccessible. You'll need a lot of endurance and at least several days to see even a few of its sites, such as the appropriately named Lizard Rock and Beehive Arch. Hardy hikers can visit Horseshoe Canyon in one day, where they can see the Great Gallery, an 80-foot-long rock art panel.

The park is also accessible by boat, and that's just the way explorer Major John Wesley Powell first saw the canyons in 1869, when he made his first trip down the Green to its confluence with the Colorado, and then downstream, eventually reaching the Grand Canyon. River access is from the towns of Moab and Green River, and several local companies offer boat trips of various duration.

Among the cottonwoods and willows along the rivers you'll find Canyonlands' greatest variety of wildlife. Watch for deer, beaver, an occasional bobcat, and various migratory birds. Elsewhere in the park, you're apt to see red-tailed hawks in search of a tasty rodent, bighorn sheep, coyote, Colorado chipmunks, and white-tailed antelope squirrels.

Impressions

We glide along through a strange, weird, grand region. The landscape everywhere, away from the river, is of rock.
>   —Major John Wesley Powell, during his 1869 boat trip
>   down the Green and Colorado Rivers.

Canyonlands National Park

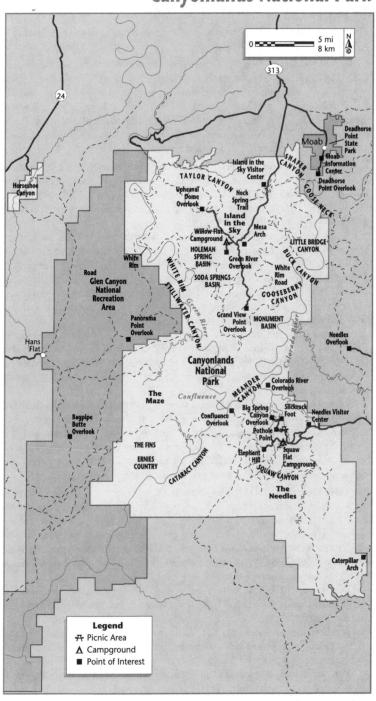

0 — 5 mi
8 km

N

313

Horseshoe Canyon

24

Moab

Deadhorse Point State Park

Island in the Sky Visitor Center

SHAFER CANYON

Moab Information Center

Deadhorse Point Overlook

TAYLOR CANYON

GOOSENECK

Upheaval Dome Overlook

Neck Spring Trail

Island in the Sky

Mesa Arch

Willow Flat Campground

LITTLE BRIDGE CANYON

HOLEMAN SPRING BASIN

Green River Overlook

White Rim

WHITE RIM

White Rim Road

BUCK CANYON

SODA SPRINGS BASIN

GOOSEBERRY CANYON

STILLWATER CANYON

Road Glen Canyon National Recreation Area

Green River

Grand View Point Overlook

MONUMENT BASIN

Panorama Point Overlook

Needles Overlook

Hans Flat

Colorado River

Canyonlands National Park

MEANDER CANYON

Confluence

Colorado River Overlook

The Maze

Bagpipe Butte Overlook

Confluence Overlook

Big Spring Canyon Overlook

Slickrock Foot

Needles Visitor Center

Pothole Point

THE FINS

Elephant Hill

Squaw Flat Campground

ERNIES COUNTRY

CATARACT CANYON

SQUAW CANYON

The Needles

Caterpillar Arch

Legend

⚴ Picnic Area
△ Campground
■ Point of Interest

295

JUST THE FACTS

There are no lodging facilities, restaurants, or even stores inside the national park. Most visitors use Moab as a base camp.

Getting There/Access Points To reach the Island in the Sky Visitor Center, take U.S. 191 (which runs north–south through eastern Utah from Wyoming to Arizona) to Utah 313, which you follow south into the park. It's 34 miles west of Moab. To reach the Needles Visitor Center, leave U.S. 191 at Utah 211, which you follow west into the park. It's 75 miles southwest of Moab. Getting to the Maze District is a bit more interesting. From I-70 east of Green River, take Utah 24 south. Watch for signs and follow two- and four-wheel drive dirt roads east into the park.

Information & Visitor Centers For advance information on what to see in the park, plus hiking and four-wheel-drive trails and camping, contact Superintendent, **Canyonlands National Park,** 2282 SW Resource Blvd., Moab, UT 84532-8000 (☎ 801/259-7164). It's best to write at least a month before your planned visit, and specify what type of information you need.

If you want even more details to help plan your trip, you can order books, some very useful maps, and videos from the nonprofit **Canyonlands Natural History Association,** 30 South 100 East, Moab, UT 84532 (☎ 801/259-6003 or fax 801/259-8263). Some publications are available in foreign languages, and several videos can be purchased in either VHS or PAL formats. MasterCard and Visa are accepted. Those wanting to help the nonprofit association can join ($20 annually) and get a 20% discount on purchases.

Once you arrive in the area, you can get information at the **Moab Information Center,** located in the middle of town at the corner of Main and Center Streets (☎ 801/259-3911), and open 8am to 9pm in the summer, with slightly shorter winter hours. This multi-agency visitor center is staffed by representatives from the park service.

Canyonlands National Park operates two visitor centers—**Island in the Sky Visitor Center,** in the northern part of the park, and **Needles Visitor Center,** in the southern section—where you can get maps, free brochures on hiking trails, and most importantly, talk with rangers about your plans. We can't stress too strongly that the terrain at Canyonlands can be brutal, and it's important that you not only know your own limitations, but also the limitations of your vehicle and other equipment.

Fees, Regulations & Backcountry Permits Entry into the park (for up to seven days) costs $4 per private vehicle or $2 per motorcycle, bicycle, or pedestrian. A $10 annual pass is also available.

Permits, available at either visitor center, are required for all overnight stays in the park except at the two established campgrounds. Permit reservations can be made in advance (☎ 801/259-4351). The fee for overnight four-wheel-drive trips is $25, and for overnight mountainbike trips is $10.

There is also a $5 day-use fee for those visitors bringing motor vehicles, horses, or mountainbikes on roads into Salt Creek/Horse Canyon and Lavender Canyon in the Needles District.

Backcountry hikers should practice minimum-impact techniques, packing out all trash. Feeding or molesting wildlife, vandalism, and disturbing any natural feature of the park are all prohibited. Also prohibited are wood fires.

Dogs, which must be leashed at all times, are prohibited in public buildings, on all trails, and in the backcountry. This includes four-wheel-drive roads—they are not permitted even inside your vehicle.

Seasons & Avoiding the Crowds   Summers here are hot, and that's an understatement, since the temperature sometimes reaches 100°F. Winters can be cool or cold, dropping well-below freezing at night, with light snow possible. The best time to visit, especially for hikers, is in the spring or fall, when daytime temperatures are usually from 60 to 80°F, with cool nights. Late summer and early fall visitors should be prepared for afternoon thunderstorms.

Although Canyonlands does not get nearly as crowded as most other national parks in Utah, the summer is still the busiest time, and reservations for backcountry permits are recommended from spring through fall. As with most parks, if you want to avoid human contact, pick the longest and most difficult trail you can handle.

Safety Concerns   Due to the terrain's extreme conditions, the main safety problem at Canyonlands is that people underestimate the hazards. Rangers warn hikers to carry at least one gallon of water per person per day, to be especially careful near cliff edges, avoid overexposure to the intense sun, and carry maps when going off into the backcountry. During lightning storms, avoid lone trees, high ridges, and cliff edges. Four-wheel-drive vehicle operators should be aware of their vehicles' limitations and carry extra food and emergency equipment. Also, everyone going into the backcountry should let someone know where they're going and when they plan to return. It's best to not travel alone.

Ranger Programs   Both of the main campgrounds have campfire programs on various aspects of the park on summer evenings, and short morning talks are also presented during the summer at the Island in the Sky Visitor Center and other locations.

SEEING THE HIGHLIGHTS

Canyonlands is not an easy place to see on your own in a short period of time. In fact, if your schedule permits only a day or less, we suggest skipping the Needles and Maze Districts entirely, and driving directly to the **Island in the Sky Visitor Center.** After looking at the exhibits, drive to several of the overlooks, stopping along the way for a short hike or two. Make sure you stop at the **Grand View Point Overlook,** at the south end of the paved road. Among the trails we recommend for this quick trip are the **Grand View Trail,** especially scenic in late afternoon, when you literally get the "Grand View" of the park. Allow about 1¹/₂ hours for this easy 2-mile walk. We also recommend the **Upheaval Dome Overlook Trail,** which should take about a half hour and lets you see a mile-wide crater and ponder its origins.

Perhaps a better choice for a quick visit to the park, especially for those with a bit of extra cash, is to take a guided tours—by four-wheel-drive vehicle, plane, or raft. See the "Moab" section of this chapter for a list of operators.

EXPLORING CANYONLANDS BY CAR

There is no driving tour, per se, that we can recommend for Canyonlands. There are about 20 miles of paved highway in the Island in the Sky District, some gravel roads accessible in two-wheel-drive vehicles, and several viewpoints. The Needles District has fewer viewpoints and only 8 miles of paved roads. Although pavement does reach some of the Needles' viewpoints and trailheads, there are many more that require high-clearance four-wheel-drive vehicles, mountainbikes, or plain old foot-power. The Maze District has no paved roads. Essentially, both of the park's roads lead to trailheads, and unless you plan to leave your car and hike for at least a half hour or so, it would be better to skip Canyonlands and spend your time instead at nearby Arches National Park, which is much more accessible by car.

Canyonlands' Creatures Great & Small

You'll find a fascinating mixture of mountain and desert animals in Canyonlands, depending on the time of year and particular location within the park. The best times to see most wildlife are early and late in the day, especially in the summer when the midday sun drives all Canyonlands residents in search of shade. Throughout the park you'll probably hear—if not see—coyote, and it's likely you'll spot white-tailed antelope squirrels and other rodents scampering among the rocks as well. Watch for the elusive and rather antisocial bighorn sheep along isolated cliffs, where you might also see a golden eagle or turkey vulture soaring above the rocks in search of food. In the little pools of water in slickrock that appear after rainstorms, you're likely to see tadpole shrimp—1-inch-long crustaceans that look as though they would be more at home in an ocean. The best chances of seeing deer, beaver, and other mammals are along riverbanks and the few natural springs in the park.

Of course, if your "car" happens to be a serious 4X4, and you're equally serious about doing some hard-core four-wheeling, this is the park for you. See the "Sports & Activities" section below. Due to changing conditions of dirt roads, we strongly suggest that you discuss your plans with rangers before setting out.

A BIRD'S-EYE VIEW OF CANYONLANDS

Canyonlands is beautiful, but many of its most spectacular sections are difficult to get to, to say the least. One solution is the bird's way. **Redtail Aviation,** P.O. Box 515, Moab, UT 84532 (☎ 801/259-7421 or 800/842-9251), based at Moab's Canyonlands Field Airport, has been flying sightseeing tours over southeastern Utah since 1978, and offers several easy ways to see the most of Canyonlands and surrounding areas. A 1-hour flight covers all three of the park's districts plus Dead Horse Point State Park, at about $60 per person. A 2-hour flight explores the same areas plus Capitol Reef National Park, Lake Powell, and Robber's Roost, where outlaw Butch Cassidy is said to have hidden out; cost is about $130 per person.

SPORTS & OUTDOOR ACTIVITIES

Four-Wheeling Unlike most national parks, where all motor vehicles and mountainbikes must stay on paved roads, Canyonlands has miles of rough four-wheel-drive roads where mechanized transport is king, and jacked-up jeeps with oversized tires rule the day. Four-wheelers must stay on designated 4X4 roads, but keep in mind that the term "road" can mean anything from a graded, well-marked two-lane gravel byway to a pile of loose rocks with a sign that says "that-a-way." Many of the park's jeep roads are impassable during heavy rains and for a day or two after.

The best four-wheel-drive adventure in Canyonland's Island in the Sky District is the ✪ **White Rim Road,** which runs some 100 miles, winding through the district and affording spectacular and ever-changing views, from broad panoramas of rock and canyon to close-ups of red and orange towers and buttes. A high-clearance 4X4 is necessary. Expect the journey to be slow, taking two to three days, although with the appropriate vehicle it isn't really difficult. There are primitive campgrounds along the way, but reservations and backcountry permits are needed. Mountainbikers also enjoy this trail, especially when accompanying a four-wheel-drive vehicle that can carry supplies and equipment.

Four-wheeling in the Needles District can be an end in itself, with a variety of exciting routes, or simply a means to get to some of the more interesting and remote hiking trails and camping spots. Four-wheel-drive fans will find one of their ultimate challenges on the **Elephant Hill Jeep Road,** which begins at a well-marked turnoff near Squaw Flat Campground. Although most of the 10-mile trail is only moderately difficult, the stretch over Elephant Hill itself near the beginning can be a nightmare, with steep, rough slickrock, drifting sand, loose rock, and treacherous ledges. Coming down the hill there is one switchback that requires you to back to the edge of a steep cliff. This is also a favorite of mountainbikers, although bikes will have to be walked on some stretches because of an abundance of sand and rocks. The route offers views of numerous rock formations, from striped needles to balanced rocks, plus steep cliffs and rock "stairs," and side trips can add another 30 miles. Allow from 8 hours to three days. Backcountry permits are needed for overnight trips.

For a spectacular view of the Colorado River, the ✪ **Colorado River Overlook Road** can't be beat. This 14-mile round-trip is popular with four-wheelers, backpackers, and mountainbikers. Considered among the park's easiest 4X4 roads, the first part is very easy indeed, accessible by high-clearance two-wheel-drives, but the second half has a few rough and rocky sections that require four-wheel-drive. Starting at the Needles Visitor Center parking lot, the trail takes you by numerous panoramic vistas to a spectacular 360° view of the park and the Colorado River some 1,000 feet below.

Biking Bikes of any kind are prohibited on hiking trails or in the backcountry, except on designated two-and four-wheel-drive roads. Road bikes are of little use in Canyonlands, except for getting to and from trailheads, viewpoints, visitor centers, and campgrounds in the Island in the Sky and Needles Districts. See "Mountainbiking," below.

Hiking With little shade, no reliable water sources, and temperatures soaring to 100°F in the summer, rangers strongly advise that hikers carry at least one gallon of water per person per day, along with sunscreen, a hat, and all the usual hiking and emergency equipment. Actually, if you expect to do some serious hiking, try to plan your trip for the spring or fall, when conditions are much more pleasant. Because some of the trails may be confusing, hikers attempting the longer ones should also carry good topographic maps, available at park visitor centers and at stores in Moab. While there are dozens of hiking possibilities throughout the park, we have chosen a few of various ability requirements, listed by district.

Island in the Sky: The **Mesa Arch Trail** provides the casual visitor with an easy half-mile round-trip self-guided nature walk through a woods of piñon and juniper trees, mountain mahogany, cactus, and a plant called Mormon Tea, from which Mormon pioneers made a tea-like beverage. The loop trail's main scenic attraction is an arch, made of Navajo sandstone, that hangs precariously on the edge of a cliff, framing a spectacular view of nearby mountains. Allow about a half hour.

Another 30-minute hike, although a bit steeper and moderately strenuous, leads to the **Upheaval Dome Overlook.** Upheaval Dome doesn't fit with the rest of the Canyonlands' terrain—it's obviously not the result of gradual erosion like the rest of the park, but rather a dramatic deformity in which rocks have been pushed into a domelike structure. At one time it was theorized that the dome was formed by a hidden volcano, but a more recent theory places the cause on a meteorite that may have struck the earth some 60 million years ago. This hike is about 1 mile round-trip; a second overlook adds about a half mile, and 15 minutes.

An easy 2-mile hike, especially scenic at sunset, is the ✪ **Grand View Trail.** Allow about 1¹/₂ hours. The trail follows the canyon rim from Grand View Point, showing off numerous canyons and rock formations, the Colorado River, and distant mountains.

A bit more strenuous is the 5-mile **Neck Spring Trail,** which starts about a half mile south of the Island in the Sky Visitor Center. Allow 3 to 4 hours for this hike, which follows the paths that animals and early ranchers created to reach water at two springs. You'll see water troughs, hitching posts, rusty cans, and the ruins of an old cabin. Plus, because of the water source, there are types of vegetation not usually seen in the park, such as maidenhair ferns and gamble oak. The water also draws wildlife, including mule deer, bighorn sheep, ground squirrels, and hummingbirds. Climbing to the top of the rim, you get a beautiful view of the canyons and even the Henry Mountains, some 60 miles away.

Those looking for more of a challenge can explore the **Lathrop Trail,** which meanders some 5 miles down into the canyon to the White Rim Jeep Road, affording beautiful views as you descend. Allow 5 to 7 hours for this strenuous hike over steep terrain and loose rock, remembering that it's another 5 miles back. It is possible to continue down to the Colorado River from here (another 4 miles each way), but check with rangers about the feasibility of this overnight trip before attempting it.

Needles: Hiking trails here are generally not too tough, but keep in mind that slickrock can live up to its name, and there is little shade along most of these trails. One relatively easy hike is the 0.3 mile **Roadside Ruin Trail,** a short, self-guided nature walk that takes about a half hour round-trip and leads to a prehistoric granary, probably used by the Anasazi some 700 to 1,000 years ago to store corn, nuts, and other foods. Although easy, this trail can be muddy when wet.

For a bit more of a challenge, try the **Slickrock Foot Trail,** a 2.4-mile loop that leads to several viewpoints and takes 2 or 3 hours. Slickrock, a general term for any bare rock surface, can be slippery, especially when wet. Viewpoints show off the stairstep topography of the area, from its colorful canyons and cliffs to its flat mesas and striped needles.

From **Elephant Hill Trailhead** you can follow several interconnecting trails into the backcountry. The road to the trailhead is gravel, but is graded and driveable in most two-wheel-drive passenger cars, although those in large vehicles such as motorhomes will want to avoid it. The 10.5-mile round-trip Elephant Hill–Druid Arch hike can be accomplished in 4 to 6 hours and is moderately difficult, with some steep drop-offs and quite a bit of slickrock. But it's well worth it, taking you through narrow rock canyons, past colorful spires and pinnacles, and on to the huge Druid Arch, its dark rock somewhat resembling the stone structures at Stonehenge, England.

Another worthwhile jaunt is on the ✪ **Confluence Overlook Trail,** a 10.5-mile round-trip day or overnight hike that leads to a spectacular view overlooking the confluence of the Green and Colorado Rivers and the 1,000-foot-deep gorges they've carved. The hike is moderately difficult, with steep drop-offs and little shade, but shows off splendidly the many colors of the Needles District, as well as views into the Maze District of the park. Allow 4 to 6 hours.

For those staying at Squaw Flat Campground, the **Big Spring–Squaw Canyon Loop** is a convenient, moderately difficult 7.5-mile loop over steep slickrock that can be hiked in 3 to 4 hours. The trail winds through woodlands of piñon and juniper, offering views of the needles for which the district is named, plus nearby cliffs and mesas as well as distant mountains. Watch for wildflowers from late spring through summer.

Horseshoe Canyon: This detached section of the park was added to Canyonlands in 1971 mainly because of its Great Gallery, an 80-foot-long rock art panel with larger-than-life figures, believed to be at least several thousand years old. There's only one road into the Horseshoe Canyon Unit, and you'll have to drive some 120 miles (one-way) from Moab and then hike 6.5 miles (round-trip) to see the rock art. To get to the area by two-wheel-drive vehicle, take I-70 west from Green River about 11 miles to U.S. 24, go south about 24 miles to the Horseshoe Canyon turnoff (near the "Watch for Sand Drifts" sign), turn left, and follow this maintained dirt road for about 30 miles to the canyon's west rim, where you can park. From here it's a 1.5-mile hike down an 800-foot slope to the canyon floor, where you turn right and go 1.75 miles to the Great Gallery. There is no camping in Horseshoe Canyon, but primitive camping is available on Bureau of Land Management property just outside the park boundary.

Mountainbiking   Because bikes are not permitted on hiking trails, mountainbikers find themselves sharing four-wheel-drive roads with motor vehicles of every size, plus occasional hikers and horseback riders. Since some of the four-wheel-drive roads have deep sand in spots—which can turn into quicksand when wet—mountainbiking may not be as much fun as you'd expect, although it certainly is a challenge. It's wise to talk with rangers about conditions on specific roads before setting out. Among rides that are popular with mountainbikers are the Elephant Hill and Colorado River Overlook jeep roads, both in the Needles District. The 100-mile White Rim Trail, in the Island in the Sky District, also makes a great mountainbike trip, especially for bikers who can arrange for an accompanying 4X4 vehicle to carry water, food, and camping gear. See the "Four-Wheeling" section above.

CAMPING

There are two developed campgrounds in the park. In the Island in the Sky District, **Willow Flat Campground,** at an elevation of 6,200 feet, has 12 sites, virtually no facilities, and no fee is charged. In the Needles District, **Squaw Flat Campground,** at an elevation of 5,100 feet, has 26 sites, pit toilets, and trucked-in water in the summer; Squaw Flat charges $6 per night. Neither campground accepts reservations. Primitive campsites are also available throughout the park for four-wheelers and backpackers (see the "Fees, Regulations & Backcountry Permits," above).

Near Island in the Sky, the campground at **Dead Horse Point State Park** has electric hookups (see "Nearby Places of Interest" below). Additional camping facilities are available on nearby public lands administered by the Bureau of Land Management and U.S. Forest Service, and there are commercial campgrounds in Moab and Monticello. See the "Moab" section earlier in this chapter.

NEARBY PLACES OF INTEREST
DEAD HORSE POINT STATE PARK

One of Utah's most scenic state parks, this might be considered a junior Canyonlands. From the Dead Horse Point Overlook you have a splendid view across the nearby national park, as well as down past seven distinctive and colorful layers of rock to the Colorado River. A strip of land only 30 yards wide connects the point with the rest of the mesa, and in the late 1800s this natural corral was used by cowboys, who herded wild horses in, roped the ones they wanted, and left the rest to find their way out. According to one story, a herd of rejected horses couldn't find their way off the point and died of thirst within sight of the Colorado River, 2,000 feet below.

Just the Facts

From Canyonlands' Island in the Sky Visitor Center, drive north out of the park for $3^{1}/_{2}$ miles to the intersection with Utah 313, and turn right. The state park's visitor center is about $7^{1}/_{2}$ miles down the road. From Moab, head north on U.S. 191 for $16^{1}/_{2}$ miles, and turn south on Utah 313 for about 20 miles to the park (passing the access road for Canyonlands National Park).

To receive a brochure on the park and/or answers to specific questions, contact **Dead Horse Point State Park,** P.O. Box 609, Moab, UT 84532-0609 (☎ 801/259-2614).

The visitor center/museum is located near the entrance to the park, with exhibits on the park's geology, history, plants, and animals. Rangers are on hand to assign campsites and answer questions; and books, posters, maps, and souvenirs are sold. A video presentation on the human and geologic history of the area is shown by request in the visitor center; and during the summer, nightly campfire programs and short guided walks are scheduled.

Day-use fee is $3 per vehicle (up to 8 people), or $1 per person who enters the park on foot, by bike, or by motorcycle. In addition to the usual regulations requiring vehicles and bikes to be kept on roads, pets to be leashed, etc., visitors are asked to conserve water (it has to be trucked in) and to avoid stepping on cyanobacterial crusts—the fragile, bumpy, black mats composed of bacteria, algae, lichen, moss, and fungi that you'll often see along trails and roads.

Exploring the Park

Dead Horse Point Overlook is about 2 miles from the visitor center via a paved road. A short, wheelchair-accessible paved walkway leads from the parking area to a platform overlook that provides a magnificent panoramic view of the deep red canyons, Colorado River, and distant mountains. The lighting's best either early or late in the day, but this is a worthwhile stop anytime.

Although you can easily drive to Dead Horse Point Overlook, it's a fun hike if you have the time. The main trail starts at the visitor center, follows the east rim of the mesa to the overlook, and returns on the west side. The loop is 4 miles long and fairly easy, and you can add another 3 miles in side trips out to overlook points. Along the way you'll see a variety of rock formations while scrambling over the slickrock.

Another 3.5-mile loop leads from the visitor center to a series of potholes (holes in the rock that catch rainwater and may contain tadpole shrimp and other aquatic life) and a canyon overlook.

Although it would seem at first that no animals would endure this barren, rocky terrain, you're likely to see ground squirrels, rabbits, lizards, and raptors. There are desert bighorn sheep in the area, but they're rarely seen in the park.

Camping

The park's very attractive campground has 21 sites, all with electric hookups and covered picnic tables, plus flush toilets and an RV dump station. However, because water must be trucked in, there are no showers and campers are asked to conserve the small amount of water available. Because the electric outlets are hidden on the underside of picnic tables, which may be 50 or 60 feet from the site parking area, those with recreational vehicles will likely need long extension cords. Camping costs $7 weeknights and $8 Fridays, Saturdays, and holidays. Reservations are accepted (☎ 800/322-3770), with a $5 processing fee, from mid-March through mid-October. Those without reservations will find that the campground usually fills by mid-afternoon during the summer.

NEWSPAPER ROCK

This former state park, now administered by the Bureau of Land Management's **San Juan Resource Area office** (☎ 801/587-2141), is famous for a large sandstone panel covered with petroglyphs that date from 1,500 to 200 years ago, from the Fremont people to the Anasazi, and finally the Utes and Navajo. The panel also includes initials and names left by early white settlers, including one J.P. Gonzales of Monticello, who herded sheep in the canyon in the early part of the 20th century. The site is located in Indian Creek Canyon, along the road to Canyonlands' Needles District, Utah 211, about 12 miles west of U.S. 191. There's a primitive campground nearby, with eight sites but no drinking water.

The Four Corners Area

The major archaeological center of the United States, the Four Corners area—where Colorado, New Mexico, Arizona, and Utah's borders meet—is surrounded by a vast complex of ancient villages that 1,000 years ago dominated this entire region. Here among the reddish brown rocks, abandoned canyons, and flat mesas you'll discover another world, once ruled by the Anasazi, and today largely the domain of the Navajo.

Wander among the scenic splendor of Monument Valley, where the Navajo still tend their sheep and weave their rugs, and then step back in time to discover a civilization that vanished more than seven centuries ago, leaving behind more questions than answers. Those particularly interested in the ancient and modern Native American tribes of the Four Corners region will want to continue their travels into Arizona, New Mexico, and Colorado. Frommer's Travel Guides to those states can provide additional information.

The southeast corner of Utah is sparsely populated—downright desolate and deserted, some might say—and you're not going to find your favorite chain motel, fast-food restaurant, or brand of gasoline right around every corner. That's assuming you can even *find* a corner. So, many travelers find a place they like, rent a room or campsite for a few days, and take day trips. We've laid out this chapter with a base in the town of Bluff, and from there, we'll take you on a series of excursions that ring the town. Each can easily be a day trip from Bluff. First we'll head southwest to Monument Valley, then north to Natural Bridges National Monument, then east to Edge of the Cedars State Historical Monument. (If you're driving to Bluff from the north on U.S. 191, you'll actually pass Edge of the Cedars on your way here, just north of Blanding.) Then we'll head east, to Hovenweep National Monument and Four Corners Monument. Finally, we'll venture beyond Utah's borders into Colorado, where we'll visit Mesa Verde National Park, site of the most impressive cliff dwellings in the United States.

1 A Base Camp in Bluff

We particularly enjoy the tiny village of Bluff, sitting near the intersection of U.S. 191 and U.S. 163, with roads leading off toward all the attractions of the Four Corners. With a population of 250, Bluff is one of those comfortable little places with most basic services, but not a lot else. Founded by Mormon pioneers in 1880, the townsite had already been home to both Anasazi and Navajo peoples. Local businesses distribute a free historic walking and biking tour guide that shows where ancient rock art and archaeological sites are located, as well as some of Bluff's handsome stone homes from the late 19th century.

WHITE-WATER RAFTING TRIPS & OTHER ORGANIZED TOURS OF THE AREA

Along the San Juan River, Bluff is a center for river rafting. ✪ **Wild Rivers Expeditions** (☎ 801/672-2244 or 800/422-7654; fax 801/672-2365) offers river trips on the San Juan that are not only fun, but let you learn something, too. Led by archaeology and geology professionals, boaters see dozens of Native American sites along the river plus spectacular rock formations. Trips, ranging from one full day to several weeks in length, are offered from March through October, starting at $75 for the full day trip, which includes lunch.

Guided tours into Monument Valley Navajo Tribal Park and other scenic areas and archaeological sites surrounding the town are offered by **Tours of the Big Country** (☎ 801/672-2281; fax 801/672-2284), starting at $75 per person for a full-day Monument Valley tour in a four-wheel-drive vehicle, including lunch. Naturalist-led walking expeditions to Bluff-area canyons and archaeological sites are also available, at about $50 per person.

WHERE TO STAY, CAMP & DINE

Facilities in this part of the state are few and far between, but you will find lodging, restaurants, vehicle fuel, and supplies in Bluff, Blanding, Monticello, and Monument Valley. For information, contact the **San Juan County Travel Council**, P.O. Box 490, Monticello, UT 84535 (☎ 801/587-3235 or 800/574-4386; fax 801/ 587-2425).

You'll find quiet, clean, and inexpensive rooms at ✪ **Recapture Lodge,** P.O. Box 309, Bluff, UT 84512 (☎ 801/672-2281 or fax 801/672-2284). This older, well-kept motel on the main street near the center of Bluff has an attractive western decor. A nature trail follows the San Juan River along the back of the motel property. Most of the 35 rooms have two double beds or one queen, with shower/tub combos; and several budget rooms are available with shower only and one double bed. The motel has air-conditioning and televisions, but no room telephones. Rates for two range from $32 to $46. Pets are welcome.

Campgrounds include **Cadillac Ranch RV Park,** U.S. 191 on the east side of town (☎ 801/672-2262 or 800/538-6195), a down-home sort of place with sites around a small fishing lake, where there's no license needed and no extra charge. There are 20 RV sites (17 with full hookups and 3 with water and electric only) and 15 tent sites, and modern restrooms with showers. The campground is open year-round, although water is turned off in the winter. Cost per site is $14.

As expected, food in this part of the state has been influenced by the Navajo. If you'd like to try a Navajo taco—fry bread topped with green chile, beans, ground beef, cheese, lettuce, and tomatoes—stop at the Sunbonnet Cafe, on the historic Bluff Loop (☎ 801/672-2201). Open Monday through Saturday from 7am to 9pm, the Sunbonnet is a comfortable small-town cafe, with tables, booths, and a counter. In addition to the Navajo specials, there's a good selection of burgers, sandwiches, and dinners such as country-fried steak, fried chicken, and pork chops. Dinner prices range from $7 to $10; sandwiches from $2.50 to $5.50. No alcoholic beverages are served.

2 Monument Valley Navajo Tribal Park

You've been here before. You've seen Monument Valley's majestic stone towers, delicately carved arches, lonely windswept buttes, forbidding cliffs, and mesas covered in sand and sagebrush. You may have seen the proud Navajo gazing out across his land, herding sheep, or weaving a beautiful rug. Perhaps you didn't know you were in Monument Valley, instead believing this to be Tombstone, Arizona, or Dodge City, Kansas, or New Mexico, or Colorado. And possibly you couldn't fully appreciate the deep reddish brown colors of the rocks or incredible blue of the sky, which lost a bit of their brilliance in black and white.

For most of us, Monument Valley *is* the Old West. We've seen it dozens of times in movie theaters, on television, and in magazine and billboard advertisements. This all started in 1938, when Harry Goulding, who had been operating a trading post for local Navajo for about 15 years, convinced Hollywood director John Ford that Ford's current project, *Stagecoach,* should be shot in Monument Valley. Released the following the year, *Stagecoach* not only put Monument Valley on the map but it also launched the career of a little-known actor by the name of John Wayne.

Ford and other Hollywood directors were attracted to Monument Valley then by the same elements that draw visitors today. This is the genuine, untamed American West, with a simple, unspoiled beauty of carved stone, blowing sand, and rich colors, all compliments of Mother Nature. The same erosional forces of wind and water carved the surrounding scenic wonders of the Grand Canyon, Glen Canyon, and the rest of the spectacular red rock country of southern Utah and northern Arizona. But here the result is different: colors seem deeper, natural rock bridges are almost perfect circles, and the vast emptiness of the land around them gives the towering stone monoliths an unequaled sense of drama.

JUST THE FACTS

Operated as a tribal park by the Navajo Nation (the country's largest tribe), Monument Valley straddles the border of southeast Utah and northeast Arizona. U.S. 163 goes through the valley from north–south, and a tribal park access road runs east–west.

Getting There   Monument Valley is 50 miles southwest of Bluff; 150 miles south of Moab; 160 miles west of Cortez, Colo.; and 395 miles south of Salt Lake City.

From Moab, Monticello, and most points in eastern Utah, take U.S. 191 south to the village of Bluff, turn west (right), and follow U.S. 163 to Monument Valley. An alternative is to turn off Utah 95 south onto Utah 261 just east of Natural Bridges National Monument, follow Utah 261 to U.S. 163, turn southwest, and follow U.S. 163 to Monument Valley. This latter route is quite scenic, but because of switchbacks and steep grades is not recommended for motorhomes or vehicles pulling trailers. Those coming from Arizona can take east–west U.S. 160 to U.S. 163, turn north, and follow it into Monument Valley.

Information & Visitor Centers   For a brochure on Monument Valley and answers to questions, contact **Monument Valley Navajo Tribal Park,** P.O. Box 360289, Monument Valley, UT 84536 (☎ 801/727-3353 or 801/727-3287); or the **Navajo Parks and Recreation Department,** P.O. Box 308, Window Rock, AZ 86515 (☎ 520/871-4941, ext. 6647).

The **visitor center/museum** is located about 4 miles east of U.S. 163 on the Monument Valley access road. It has a viewing deck, exhibits on the geology and human history of the valley, a gift shop, and a refreshment stand.

Hours, Fees & Regulations   The tribal park is open daily from 7am to 7pm from May through September, and from 8am to 5pm from October through April. It is closed Christmas and New Year's Day plus the afternoon of Thanksgiving Day.

Admission costs $2.50 for those from 8 to 59 years old, $1 for those 60 and older, and is free for children under 8. National Park passes are not accepted.

Since this is part of the Navajo Nation, laws here are somewhat different than those in Utah, Arizona, or on public lands. All alcoholic beverages are prohibited within the boundaries of the Navajo reservation. Visitors must stay on the self-guided Valley Drive unless with an approved guide, and rock climbing and cross-country hiking are prohibited. Although photography for personal use is permitted, permission is required to photograph Navajo residents and their property, and you will usually need to pay them. All commercial photography requires a permit from the tribal government.

Both Utah and Arizona are on mountain time, and although the state of Arizona does not recognize daylight saving time, the Navajo Nation does.

A BIRD'S-EYE VIEW OF MONUMENT VALLEY

Slickrock Air Guides of Moab (☎ 801/259-6216 or 800/332-2439; fax 801/259-2226) offer a 2-hour scenic flight from Moab that includes Monument Valley, Canyonlands National Park, and Natural Bridges National Monument. Cost is about $140 per person.

EXPLORING MONUMENT VALLEY BY CAR

Driving the 17-mile self-guided loop lets you see most of the major scenic attractions of Monument Valley at your own pace, and at the lowest cost. The dirt road is a bit rough—not recommended for low-slung sports cars or vehicles longer than 24 feet, although it is passable for smaller motorhomes. The road's first half mile is the worst, and you have to drive it both at the beginning and end of the loop. There are no restrooms, drinking water, or other facilities along the route. Allow about 2 hours.

A free brochure and a more detailed booklet ($1) provide rough maps and information on 11 numbered sites, such as The Mittens, rock formations that resemble (you guessed it) a pair of mittens, plus the aptly named Elephant and Camel Buttes, Totem Pole, and The Thumb. You'll also see Yei-Bi-Chei, a rock formation that resembles a Navajo holy man; and John Ford Point, a favorite filming location of famed Hollywood director John Ford, where he shot scenes from *Stagecoach, The Searchers,* and *Cheyenne Autumn,* among others. It's still popular with producers—watch for crews working on feature films, television shows, or commercials as you drive the loop.

GUIDED TOURS

Guided tours are the best way to see Monument Valley—without a guide, visitors are restricted to the 17-mile scenic drive, but Navajo guides can take you into lesser-visited areas of the tribal park, give you their personal perspectives on the landscape, and often arrange weaving demonstrations and other activities.

You'll find numerous guides waiting in the visitor center parking lot, offering trips in vehicles ranging from little four-passenger Jeeps to 10- and 12-passenger four-wheel-drive trucks. The fee is usually about $15 per person for a 1¹/₂-hour tour, which essentially covers the same route you can drive for yourself, and about $25 per person for a 2¹/₂-hour tour, which includes that, plus excursions into restricted areas. Some guides also offer longer tours. From mid-March through October, **Goulding's** (see "Where to Stay & Dine," below) offers a 2¹/₂-hour tour for $25, a highly recommended 3½-hour sunset tour for $30, and an all-day tour, with lunch, for $60. Children are charged about one-third less. Also, refer earlier in this chapter for tour operators based in Bluff.

Horseback tours of Monument Valley are available from **Ed Black Stables** (☎ 801/739-4285 or 800/551-4039; fax 801/739-4210), with rates from $25 for a 90-minute ride, plus very popular sunrise and sunset tours from $25 to $50 per person.

HISTORIC SITES

Goulding's Trading Post Museum at Goulding's Lodge (see "Where to Stay & Dine," below) is the original Monument Valley trading post opened by Harry and Leona (Mike) Goulding in 1924; it served as their home as well as a trading post for many years. It's furnished much as it was in the 1920s and 1930s; exhibits include Goulding family memorabilia, historic photos of the area, Navajo and Anasazi artifacts and crafts, and posters and other items from movies filmed at the trading post and in Monument Valley. The museum is open daily from April through October; call the lodge for hours. Admission costs $1. Nearby, a more modern trading post sells souvenirs, books, videos, and top-quality Native American arts and crafts.

CAMPING

Mittenview Campground (☎ 801/727-3287), operated by the tribal park administration, is across the access road from the visitor center/museum, and offers good views of Monument Valley's rock formations. It has about 100 sites with picnic tables and grills. There is an RV dump station but no hookups. From the spring through early fall there are modern restrooms with hot showers, and campsites cost $10 per night. During the rest of the year primitive camping is available at a reduced rate.

Goulding's Monument Valley Campground, on the Monument Valley access road about 3 miles west of its intersection with U.S. 163 (☎ 801/727-3231 or 801/727-3235; fax 801/727-3344), also offers splendid views of Monument Valley's scenery, plus full RV hookups including cable television, an indoor swimming pool, modern restrooms with showers, a playground, and a large convenience store. The campground is open from mid-March through October. Tent sites cost $14–$17; and RV sites are $22–$25.

WHERE TO STAY & DINE

Goulding's Lodge, P.O. Box 1, Monument Valley, UT 84536 (☎ 801/727-3231 or 800/874-0902; fax 801/727-3344), on the Monument Valley access road about 2 miles west of its intersection with U.S. 163, has 62 modern motel rooms, each with southwestern decor, VCR, and private patio or balcony. There's a small indoor heated swimming pool and a restaurant serving three meals daily, with dinner prices in the $7 to $22 range. Room rates for two are $95 to $115 from mid-April through mid-October, and $65 to $85 the rest of the year. County room tax adds about 9%. Pets are welcome.

3 Natural Bridges National Monument

Utah's first National Park Service area, Natural Bridges was designated primarily to show off and protect its three outstanding natural rock bridges, carved by streams and other forms of erosion over millions of years. You can see the bridges from roadside viewpoints, take individual hikes to each bridge, or hike a loop trail that connects all three.

JUST THE FACTS

Natural Bridges National Monument is about 45 miles west of Blanding, 40 miles north of Mexican Hat, about 50 miles east of Glen Canyon National Recreation Area's Hite or Halls Crossing marinas, and about 360 miles south of Salt Lake City.

Getting There   The national monument is located in southeast Utah, off scenic Utah 95, via Utah 275. You can get there from Monument Valley, follow U.S. 163 north to Utah 261 (just past Mexican Hat); at Utah 95, go west to Utah 275 and the Monument. Beware, though—This route has numerous steep switchbacks; it's not recommended for motorhomes, those towing trailers, or anyone with acrophobia. The less adventurous and RV-bound should stick to approaching from the west, via 95.

Make sure you have enough fuel for the trip to Natural Bridges; the closest gas stations are at least 40 miles away in Mexican Hat or Blanding. In fact, there are no services of any kind within 40 miles of the Monument.

Information & Visitor Centers   For a color brochure and other information, contact the Superintendent, **Natural Bridges National Monument,** Box 1, Lake Powell, UT 84533 (☎ 801/692-1234).

A **visitor center** at the park entrance has exhibits and a slide show on bridge formation, the human history of the area, and the monument's plants and wildlife. Rangers are available to advise you about hiking trails and scheduled activities. The visitor center is also the only place in the monument where you can get drinking water.

Fees & Regulations   Admission to the monument is $4 per vehicle or $2 per person on foot, bicycle, or motorcycle. Regulations are similar to those in most areas administered by the National Park Service, which emphasize protecting the area. Be especially careful to not damage any of the fragile archaeological sites in the monument; climbing on the natural bridges is prohibited. Overnight backpacking is not permitted within the monument, and vehicles may not be left unattended overnight. Because parking at the overlooks and trailheads is limited, those towing trailers or extra vehicles are asked to leave them at the visitor center parking lot. Pets must be leashed and are not allowed on trails or in any buildings.

Seasons & Avoiding the Crowds   Although the monument is open year-round, winters can be a bit harsh at its 6,500-foot elevation; the weather here is best between late April and October. Because trailhead parking is limited and most people visit during school vacations in June, July, and August, the best months to see the park, if your schedule permits, are May, September, and October.

Ranger Programs   A series of programs on geology, history, and other subjects are presented. Schedules are posted at the visitor center.

SEEING THE HIGHLIGHTS

Giant Sipapu Bridge is considered a mature bridge. It's 220 feet high with a span of 268 feet, and is thought to be the second largest natural bridge in the world, after Rainbow Bridge in nearby Glen Canyon National Recreation Area (See Chapter 15). **Owachomo Bridge,** thought to be very elderly and possibly on the brink of collapse (then again, it could stand for centuries), is the smallest of the three at 106 feet high, with a span of 180 feet. And the youngest, **Kachina Bridge,** is 210 feet high with a span of 204 feet. At 93 feet wide, it's also the thickest of the monument's bridges. All three bridges were given Hopi names: Sipapu means the "gateway to the spirit world" in Hopi legend; Owachomo is Hopi for "mound of rocks," so called because of a pile of rocks on one side of the bridge; and Kachina Bridge was named as such because rock art on it resembles decorations found on traditional Hopi kachina dolls.

Natural Bridges National Monument will not be your major vacation destination, but you can easily spend a half day or full day, even two days, here. For those who want to take a quick look and get on to the other, larger national park lands in southern Utah, stop at the visitor center for a brief introduction, and then take the 9-mile (one-way) loop drive to the various natural bridge overlooks. Those with time and inclination might also take an easy hike down to Owachomo Bridge; it's a half-hour walk.

GENERATING ELECTRICITY IN THE MIDDLE OF NOWHERE: MORE TO SEE AT THE MONUMENT

Isolated, virtually in the middle of nowhere, Natural Bridges National Monument has been forced to become self-sufficient. To provide power for the visitor center, offices, and employee housing, photovoltaic cells convert the sun's energy to electricity. Only about 10% of the sun's energy striking the cells is converted, but the small field of photovoltaic cells is able to produce about 50 kilowatts of power, sufficient for the daily needs of the monument and enough extra to store in batteries for use at night and during cloudy periods. You can see the photovoltaic cells, located across the main monument road from the visitor center, and read explanations of how they operate.

SPORTS & ACTIVITIES

Hiking is the number-one activity here. From the trailheads, you can hike separately to each of the bridges, or start at one and do a loop hike to all three. Hikers should be prepared for summer afternoon thunderstorms that can cause flash flooding; watch out for rattlesnakes as well. Also, summers are hot, and all hikers should wear hats and other protective clothing, use sunscreen, and carry a gallon of water per person for all but the shortest walks.

The easiest hike—more of a walk—is the four-tenths of a mile trail (round-trip) to **Owachomo Bridge.** Look toward the eastern horizon to see the twin buttes named "Bear's Ears." Allow a half hour.

The Sipapu and Kachina Bridge trails are both considered moderately strenuous, and one hour should be allocated for each. To **Sipapu Bridge,** you'll have a 500-foot elevation change, climbing two flights of stairs with three ladders and handrails on a 1.2-mile round-trip trail. This is the steepest trail in the park, but you'll have a splendid view of the bridge about halfway down.

The 1.5-mile round-trip hike to massive **Kachina Bridge** has a 400-foot elevation change, descending steep slickrock with handrails. Under the bridge you'll notice a pile of rocks that fell in June 1992, slightly enlarging the bridge opening.

Those planning to hike the **loop to all three bridges** can start at any of the trailheads, although rangers recommend starting at Sipapu. Round trip, including your walk back across the mesa, is 8.6 miles. Although the trails from the rim to the canyon bottom can be steep, the walk along the bottom is easy.

CAMPING

A primitive **13-site campground** has pit toilets, tables, tent pads, and grills, but no drinking water, showers, or other facilities. It's limited to vehicles no more than 21 feet long, and only one vehicle is allowed per site. Cost is $5 per night, and sites are allotted on a first-come, first-served basis.

There's also an overflow campground—essentially a parking lot—where you can stay at no charge. It's about 7 miles from the visitor center, just off Utah 261 near its intersection with Utah 95.

4 Edge of the Cedars State Historical Monument

The site of an ancient Anasazi ruin, occupied from about A.D. 750 to 1220, the monument includes six complexes lying in a generally north–south alignment on top of a ridge. Only one of the complexes has been excavated and is open for viewing. The other five sites are still underground, and they give the visitor an idea of what to watch for when hiking in the Southwest.

There's also a modern **museum** here, which functions as the regional repository for the long-term care and storage of archaeological collections excavated from public lands in southeastern Utah. There is a very fine collection of pottery on display, and a gift shop with the usual tourist fare.

The state historical monument is located at 660 West and 400 North, on the north side of Blanding, just off U.S. 191 (☎ 801/678-2238). It's open daily from 9am to 6pm in the summer; 9am to 5pm the rest of the year. Closed Thanksgiving, Christmas, and New Year's Day. Admission costs $1.50 for adults, $1 for ages 6 to 15, free for children under six, and a maximum charge of $6 per family.

5 Hovenweep National Monument

Located along the Colorado-Utah border, Hovenweep (the Ute word for "deserted valley") contains some of the most striking and most isolated archaeological sites in the Four Corners area.

JUST THE FACTS

No lodging, food, gasoline, supplies, or even phones are available in the national monument. The closest motels and restaurants are in Bluff (see earlier this chapter).

Getting There/Access Points Hovenweep National Monument is 35 miles northeast of Bluff; 47 miles west of Cortez, Colorado; 122 miles south of Moab; and 366 miles southeast of Salt Lake City.

Access is by graded dirt roads that become muddy—sometimes impassably so—during and immediately after rainstorms. You can get to Hovenweep from either Colorado or Utah. From Utah, follow U.S. 191, southeastern Utah's major north–south route, to Utah 262, between the towns of Blanding and Bluff. Head east on Utah 262 to Hatch Trading Post, then, watching for signs, follow gravel roads to the monument. An option is to take Utah 163 east from Bluff toward the village of Aneth, turn north (left) onto an unnamed road and follow signs to the monument.

From Cortez, Colorado, follow U.S. 666 north to the community of Pleasant View and turn west (left) onto gravel roads, following signs to the monument.

Visitor Information For advance information or questions about current road conditions, contact **Hovenweep National Monument,** P.O. Box 8, Mesa Verde National Park, CO 81330 (☎ 970/529-4461).

Fees, Regulations & Safety Concerns Admission to the national monument is free. Regulations are much the same here as at most National Park Service properties, with an emphasis on being careful not to damage archaeological sites. Summer temperatures can reach over 100°F and water supplies here are limited; take your own

Kokopelli: Casanova or Traveling Salesman?

Of the many subjects of rock art that you can find in the West, there's one that claims a name and a gender: He's Kokopelli, and he's been found in ruins dating as early as A.D. 200 and as late as the 16th century. The consistency of the depictions of him over a wide geographic area indicates Kokopelli was a well-traveled and universally recognized deity of considerable importance. The figure is generally hunchbacked, playing a flute, and often extremely well endowed. His image is still used by potters, weavers, and painters, as well as for decoration on jewelry and clothing. Kokopelli has never been an evil character, although he's frequently been a comic one.

Until quite recent times, legends of Kokopelli were still current in the Pueblo peoples of the Four Corners area. Although the many stories differ in detail, almost all are faithful to the fertility theme. Sometimes he was a wandering minstrel with a sack of songs on his back; other times he was greeted as a god of the harvest.

The Hopi of First Mesa seem to identify him with an unethical guide of Spanish friars searching for the Seven Cities of Cibola in 1539. This guide was more interested in making passes at Hopi maidens than in searching for the fabled cities, according to the legend, and Hopi men consequently shot him with arrows and buried him under a pile of rocks. Another Hopi village holds Kokopelli to be sort of a traveling salesman, with deerskin shirts and moccasins he traded for brides. Yet another Hopi legend has him seducing the daughters of a household and sewing shirts, while his wife, incidentally, chased the men.

The Hopi also make kachina dolls of Kokopelli, and one of his wife, Kokopellimana, which are sold to tourists. As with most kachina dolls, there was also a real-life kachina dancer, who used to make explicit gestures to female tourists and missionaries, until the visitors found out what the gestures meant. Many early peoples welcomed Kokopelli around corn-planting time, and married women, hoping to conceive, sought his blessing. Single maidens, however, fled from him in panic.

and carry a canteen, even on short walks. During late spring and early fall, gnats can be a nuisance. Dogs must be leashed, but are permitted on trails.

EXPLORING THE MONUMENT

Hovenweep is noted for its mysterious and impressive 20-foot-tall sandstone towers, some of them square, others oval, circular, or D-shaped. Built by the Anasazi (or ancestral Pueblo people, as they're also known), the solid towers have small windows up and down their masonry sides. Archaeologists have suggested a myriad of possible uses for these structures, their guesses ranging from guard towers to celestial observatories, ceremonial structures to water towers to granaries.

In addition to the towers, you'll see the remains of cliff dwellings and a kiva, petroglyphs, stone rooms, walls, and a reconstructed dam. One of the first ruins you'll see is stately **Hovenweep Castle,** probably built around A.D. 1,200, about the same time Europeans were constructing their much larger castles. Home for several families, this site contains two D-shaped towers plus additional rooms.

During your walk among the 700-year-old buildings you'll see yucca, cactus, saltbush, juniper, and even some cottonwood trees. Watch for lizards and snakes, rabbits, hawks and ravens, and an occasional deer or fox.

A **ranger station,** with exhibits, restrooms, and bottled drinking water, is located at the Square Tower Site. This should be your first stop. The other five sites are difficult to find, and you'll need to obtain detailed driving directions and check on current road conditions before setting out. The ranger station is open daily from 8am to 5pm year-round, but may be closed for short periods while the ranger is on patrol.

At the Square Tower Site, near the ranger station, the 2-mile **Square Tower self-guiding trail** includes three loops, which can be hiked individually or together. They wind past the remains of ancient Pueblo buildings, such as the appropriately named Hovenweep Castle, both square and round towers, cliff dwellings, and rock art. A trail guide, available at the ranger station, discusses the ruins and identifies desert plants used for food, clothing, and medicine. The three loops are not difficult, but can be rough in spots; allow about 2 hours for the entire trail.

This is but one of the six groups of archaeological sites in the monument; information on the others can be obtained at the ranger station.

CAMPING

The **Hovenweep Campground,** with 31 sites, is open year-round. It has restrooms, drinking water, picnic tables, and fire pits, but no showers or RV hookups. Most sites will accommodate trailers. Cost is $6 per night and reservations are not accepted, although the campground rarely fills, even during the peak summer season.

6 Four Corners Monument

This is the only place in the United States where you can stand (or sit, if you prefer) in four states at once. Operated as a Navajo Tribal Park, there's a flat monument marking the spot that Utah, Colorado, New Mexico, and Arizona meet, on which visitors perch for photos. Official seals of the four states are displayed, along with the motto, "Four states here meet in freedom under God." Surrounding the monument are the states' flags, flags of the Navajo Nation and Ute tribe, and the U.S. flag.

There are rows of booths where vendors sell traditional Navajo food, such as fry bread, along with plenty of traditional American junk food. There are often crafts demonstrations, and there's an abundance of jewelry, pottery, sand paintings, and other crafts, plus your basic T-shirts, postcards, and souvenirs for sale.

Located one-half mile northwest of U.S. 160, the monument is open year-round, daily from 7am to 8pm in the summer, with shorter hours in the winter; admission costs $1.50 per person.

7 Farther Afield in Colorado: Mesa Verde National Park

Mesa Verde is the largest archaeological preserve in the United States, with some 4,000 known sites dating from A.D. 600 to 1300, including the most impressive cliff dwellings in the Southwest.

The area was unknown until ranchers Charles and Richard Wetherill chanced upon it in 1888. More-or-less uncontrolled looting of artifacts followed the discovery until a Denver newspaper reporter's stories aroused national interest in protecting the site. The 52,000-acre site was declared a national park in 1906—it's the only U.S. national park devoted entirely to the works of man.

The earliest-known inhabitants of Mesa Verde (Spanish for "green plateau") built subterranean pit houses on the mesa tops. During the 13th century they moved into shallow caves and constructed complex cliff dwellings. These homes were obviously a massive construction project, yet the residents occupied them for only about a century, leaving in about 1300 for reasons as yet undetermined.

Some of the archaeological sites at Mesa Verde can be seen up-close only on ranger-led tours (see below).

JUST THE FACTS

Getting There/Access Points   Mesa Verde National Park is about 30 miles east of Cortez, Colorado; 76 miles east of Hovenweep National Monument; 125 miles east of Bluff; and 390 miles southeast of Salt Lake City.

The park entrance is off U.S. 160, midway between Cortez and Mancos, Colorado. Daily air service and rental cars are available in Cortez (see "Information" below).

Morefield Village, site of Mesa Verde's 477-site campground (see below), is 4 miles in from U.S. 160.

Information & Visitor Centers   For a park brochure, contact Superintendent, P.O. Box 8, **Mesa Verde National Park,** CO 81330 (☎ 970/529-4461 or 970/529-4475). For information on camping, lodging, and dining, call park concessionaire **ARA** (☎ 970/533-7731). Additional area information is available from the **Mesa Verde-Cortez Visitor Information Bureau,** P.O. Drawer HH, Cortez, CO 81321 (☎ 800/253-1616).

Far View Visitor Center, 15 miles south of the park entrance, is open in the summer only, providing exhibits and general visitor information.

Fees, Open Hours & Regulations   Admission is $5 per vehicle. The park is open 24 hours a day year-round; the cliff dwellings are open daily 9am to 5pm; the Chapin Mesa Museum is open daily 8am to 6:30pm in the summer, daily 8am to 5pm the rest of the year. Full interpretive services are available from mid-June to Labor Day. Dogs, which must be leashed at all times, are prohibited on all trails, in the backcountry, and in public buildings.

Seasons & Avoiding the Crowds   Summer is the best time to visit, mainly because that's when you'll get to see the most. Because of the elevation here—from 6,954 feet to 8,572 feet—winters can be quite cold and snowy, and although the park is open in the winter, activities are curtailed and even the Ruins Road drive may be temporarily closed by snow. However, a blanket of white snow can be beautiful, and the park won't be crowded.

Ranger Programs & Tours   The only way to get a close-up view of several of the well-preserved Native American sites here is on a ranger-led tour. A free tour of the Long House on Wetherill Mesa is offered in the summer only, and tours of Cliff Palace and Balcony House are also offered in the summer, at a charge of $1.25 each. In the winter, a free tour of Spruce Tree House is available. Check at the Chapin Mesa Museum or Far View Visitor Center for schedules and reservation information. Also in the summer, rangers give nightly campfire programs at the campground.

Park concessionaire ARA offers guided park tours, which cost about $15 for a half day and $20 for a full day.

SEEING THE HIGHLIGHTS

Open year-round, the **Chapin Mesa Museum,** 21 miles south of the park entrance, provides visitor information, and houses artifacts and specimens related to the history of the area, including other nearby archaeological sites. It's open daily 8am to 6:30pm in the summer, daily 8am to 5pm the rest of the year.

The **Cliff Palace,** Mesa Verde's largest and most famous site, is a four-story apartment complex with stepped-back roofs forming porches for the dwellings above. Its towers, walls, and kivas (large circular rooms used for spiritual ceremonies) are all set back beneath the rim of a cliff.

For those who want to avoid hiking and climbing, the two loops of the 12-mile **Ruins Road** provide easy access to overlooks of more than three dozen cliff dwellings and other archaeological sites. Snow may close the road in the winter. During the summer, you can drive to **Wetherill Mesa,** where rangers conduct tours of several cliff dwellings and villages.

But if you want to get out and walk (and we encourage you to do so) you'll find yourself hiking and climbing to get to the various sites. Several longer hikes into scenic **Spruce Canyon** let you stretch your legs and get away from the crowds. Hikers must register at the ranger's office before setting out.

If you'll be visiting in the winter, consider taking your cross-country skis or snowshoes; they will provide an excellent means of exploring the Ruins Road when it's closed by snow.

CAMPING

Open from early May through mid-October, **Morefield Campground** (☎ 970/533-7731), 4 miles south of the park entrance, has almost 500 sites, including 15 with full RV hookups. There are modern restrooms, showers, picnic tables, grills, and an RV dump station. Reservations are not accepted. Cost is about $10 for sites without hookups and about $17 for sites with hookups.

ACCOMMODATIONS & DINING

Contact the **Mesa Verde-Cortez Visitor Information Bureau,** P.O. Drawer HH, Cortez, CO 81321 (☎ 800/253-1616), or consult *Frommer's Colorado* for lodging and dining choices in the Cortez area.

For additional information on local camping, lodging, and dining, call park concessionaire **ARA** (☎ 970/533-7731).

Open from mid-April through mid-October, **Far View Lodge,** P.O. Box 277, Mancos, CO 81328 (☎ 970/529-4421; fax 970/533-7831), offers 150 rooms in 17 separate buildings right in the park, with spectacular views in all directions. Rates are in the range of $75 to $90 for two people. A lodge restaurant serves dinner nightly, specializing in steak, seafood, and game, with prices ranging from $7.95 to $16.95. Nearby, another lodge-operated restaurant serves three meals daily.

Index

FROMMER'S COMPLETE TRAVEL GUIDES

(Comprehensive guides to sightseeing, dining, and accommodations, with selections in all price ranges from deluxe to budget)

Acapulco/Ixtapa/Taxco, 2nd Ed.
Alaska, 4th Ed.
Arizona '96
Australia, 4th Ed.
Austria, 6th Ed.
Bahamas '96
Belgium/Holland/Luxembourg, 4th Ed.
Bermuda '96
Budapest & the Best of Hungary, 1st Ed.
California '96
Canada, 9th Ed.
Caribbean '96
Carolinas/Georgia, 3rd Ed.
Colorado, 3rd Ed.
Costa Rica, 1st Ed.
Cruises '95-'96
Delaware/Maryland, 2nd Ed.
England '96
Florida '96
France '96
Germany '96
Greece, 1st Ed.
Honolulu/Waikiki/Oahu, 4th Ed.
Ireland, 1st Ed.
Italy '96
Jamaica/Barbados, 2nd Ed.
Japan, 3rd Ed.

Maui, 1st Ed.
Mexico '96
Montana/Wyoming, 1st Ed.
Nepal, 3rd Ed.
New England '96
New Mexico, 3rd Ed.
New York State '94-'95
Nova Scotia/New Brunswick/Prince
    Edward Island, 1st Ed.
Portugal, 14th Ed.
Prague & the Best of the Czech Republic,
    1st Ed.
Puerto Rico '95-'96
Puerto Vallarta/Manzanillo/Guadalajara,
    3rd Ed.
Scandinavia, 16th Ed.
Scotland, 3rd Ed.
South Pacific, 5th Ed.
Spain, 16th Ed.
Switzerland, 7th Ed.
Thailand, 2nd Ed.
U.S.A., 4th Ed.
Utah, 1st Ed.
Virgin Islands, 3rd Ed.
Virginia, 3rd Ed.
Washington/Oregon, 6th Ed.
Yucatan '95-'96

FROMMER'S FRUGAL TRAVELER'S GUIDES

(Dream vacations at down-to-earth prices)

Australia on $45 '95-'96
Berlin from $50, 3rd Ed.
Caribbean from $60, 1st Ed.
Costa Rica/Guatemala/Belize on $35, 3rd Ed.
Eastern Europe on $30, 5th Ed.
England from $50, 21st Ed.
Europe from $50 '96
Greece from $45, 6th Ed.
Hawaii from $60, 30th Ed.

Ireland from $45, 16th Ed.
Israel from $45, 16th Ed.
London from $60 '96
Mexico from $35 '96
New York on $70 '94-'95
New Zealand from $45, 6th Ed.
Paris from $65 '96
South America on $40, 16th Ed.
Washington, D.C. from $50 '96

FROMMER'S COMPLETE CITY GUIDES

(Comprehensive guides to sightseeing, dining, and accommodations in all price ranges)

Amsterdam, 8th Ed.
Athens, 10th Ed.
Atlanta & the Summer Olympic Games '96

Bangkok, 2nd Ed.
Berlin, 3rd Ed.
Boston '96

Chicago '96
Denver/Boulder/Colorado Springs, 2nd Ed.
Disney World/Orlando '96
Dublin, 2nd Ed.
Hong Kong, 4th Ed.
Las Vegas '96
London '96
Los Angeles '96
Madrid/Costa del Sol, 2nd Ed.
Mexico City, 1st Ed.
Miami '95-'96
Minneapolis/St. Paul, 4th Ed.
Montreal/Quebec City, 8th Ed.
Nashville/Memphis, 2nd Ed.
New Orleans '96
New York City '96

Paris '96
Philadelphia, 8th Ed.
Rome, 10th Ed.
St. Louis/Kansas City, 2nd Ed.
San Antonio/Austin, 1st Ed.
San Diego, 4th Ed.
San Francisco '96
Santa Fe/Taos/Albuquerque '96
Seattle/Portland, 4th Ed.
Sydney, 4th Ed.
Tampa/St. Petersburg, 3rd Ed.
Tokyo, 4th Ed.
Toronto, 3rd Ed.
Vancouver/Victoria, 3rd Ed.
Washington, D.C. '96

FROMMER'S FAMILY GUIDES

(Guides to family-friendly hotels, restaurants, activities, and attractions)

California with Kids
Los Angeles with Kids
New York City with Kids

San Francisco with Kids
Washington, D.C. with Kids

FROMMER'S WALKING TOURS

(Memorable strolls through colorful and historic neighborhoods, accompanied by detailed directions and maps)

Berlin
Chicago
England's Favorite Cities
London, 2nd Ed.
Montreal/Quebec City
New York, 2nd Ed.

Paris, 2nd Ed.
San Francisco, 2nd Ed.
Spain's Favorite Cities
Tokyo
Venice
Washington, D.C., 2nd Ed.

FROMMER'S AMERICA ON WHEELS

(Guides for travelers who are exploring the USA by car, featuring a brand-new rating system for accommodations and full-color road maps)

Arizona and New Mexico
California and Nevada

Florida
Mid-Atlantic

FROMMER'S SPECIAL-INTEREST TITLES

Arthur Frommer's Branson!
Arthur Frommer's New World of Travel,
  5th Ed.
Frommer's America's 100 Best-Loved
  State Parks
Frommer's Caribbean Hideaways, 7th Ed.
Frommer's Complete Hostel Vacation Guide
  to England, Scotland & Wales

Frommer's National Park Guide, 29th Ed.
USA Sports Traveler's and TV Viewer's
  Golf Tournament Guide
USA Sports Minor League Baseball Book
USA Today Golf Atlas

FROMMER'S BEST BEACH VACATIONS

(The top places to sun, stroll, shop, stay, play, party, and swim, with each beach rated for beauty, swimming, sand, and amenities)

California
Carolinas/Georgia
Florida
Hawaii

Mid-Atlantic from New York to
Washington, D.C.
New England

FROMMER'S BED & BREAKFAST GUIDES

(Selective guides with four-color photos and full description of the best inns in each region)

California
Caribbean
Great American Cities
Hawaii
Mid-Atlantic

New England
Pacific Northwest
Rockies
Southeast States
Southwest

FROMMER'S IRREVERENT GUIDES

(Wickedly honest guides for sophisticated travelers and those who want to be)

Amsterdam
Chicago
London

Manhattan
New Orleans
San Francisco

FROMMER'S DRIVING TOURS

(Four-color photos and detailed maps outlining spectacular scenic driving routes)

Australia
Austria
Britain
Florida
France
Germany
Ireland

Italy
Scandinavia
Scotland
Spain
Switzerland
U.S.A.

FROMMER'S BORN TO SHOP

(The ultimate travel guides for discriminating shoppers from cut-rate to couture)

Great Britain
Hong Kong

London
New York

FROMMER'S FOOD LOVER'S COMPANIONS

(Lavishly illustrated guides to regional specialties, restaurants, gourmet shops, markets, local wines, and more)

France
Italy